CW01238974

ALSO BY MIRANDA KAUFMANN

Black Tudors

HEIRESSES

Marriage, Inheritance and Caribbean Slavery

MIRANDA KAUFMANN

A Oneworld Book

First published in the United Kingdom, Republic of Ireland
and Australia by Oneworld Publications Ltd, 2025

Copyright © Miranda Kaufmann, 2025

The moral right of Miranda Kaufmann to be identified as the Author of this work has been asserted by her in accordance with the Copyright, Designs, and Patents Act 1988

All rights reserved
Copyright under Berne Convention
A CIP record for this title is available from the British Library

ISBN 978-0-86154-801-9
eISBN 978-0-86154-802-6

Typeset by Tetragon, London
Printed and bound in Great Britain by Clays Ltd, Elcograf S.p.A.

Every reasonable effort has been made to trace the copyright holders of material reproduced in this book, but if any have been inadvertently overlooked the publishers would be glad to hear from them.

No part of this publication may be reproduced, stored in a retrieval system, or transmitted, in any form or by any means, electronic, mechanical, photocopying, recording or otherwise, or used in any manner for the purpose of training artificial intelligence technologies or systems, without the prior permission of the publishers.

The authorised representative in the EEA is eucomply OÜ,
Pärnu mnt 139b–14, 11317 Tallinn, Estonia
(email: hello@eucompliancepartner.com / phone: +33757690241)

Oneworld Publications Ltd
10 Bloomsbury Street
London WC1B 3SR
England

Stay up to date with the latest books, special offers, and exclusive content from Oneworld with our newsletter

Sign up on our website
oneworld-publications.com

MIX
Paper | Supporting
responsible forestry
FSC® C018072

*For Sophie and Juliette,
my favourite people to share stories with.*

'Are you quite sure you want to hear it?' he asked. 'Sometimes Maria, a story that one hears starts one off doing things that one would not have had to do if one had not heard it.'

—ELIZABETH GOUDGE,
The Little White Horse (1946)

Contents

A Note on Language   ix
A Note on Currency   xi
Preface   xiii

Introduction   1

1 Sarah Newton (1723–1794)   13
2 Frances Dalzell (1729–1778)   55
3 Mary Ramsay (1717–1794)   97
4 Jane Cholmeley (c.1744–1836)   135
5 Martha Baker (1747–1809)   171
6 Jane Jarvis (1772–1796)   215
7 Elizabeth Vassall (1771–1845)   251
8 Isabella Bell Franks (1768–1855)   311
9 Anna Susanna Taylor (1781–1853)   349

Conclusion   393
My Family and Enslavement   407
Intellectual Debts   411
Acknowledgements   413
Illustration List   417
Bibliography   421
Notes on the Text   431
Index   505

A Note on Language

A new vocabulary is emerging to talk about enslavement, challenging problematic assumptions embedded in existing terminology. Words and phrases like 'slave', 'slave owner', 'slave master', 'slave trade' and 'slavery' have been rightly castigated for dehumanising men, women and children, reproducing enslavers' prejudices by characterising African people as cargo or property. Instead, words like 'enslaver', 'enslaved' and 'enslavement' reflect a status imposed on individuals, rather than their central identity. I talk about 'trafficking Africans' or 'slaving' instead of 'the slave trade'. I write Black with a capital letter as it conveys a shared cultural identity, but white in lower case. Terms like 'planter', 'mistress', 'slave wife', 'housekeeper' and 'lover' obscure realities – 'planter' sounds bucolic, while the latter terms romanticise unequal and predominantly coercive and abusive sexual relations. When I talk about sex between white men and Black or mixed-ancestry women – so commonplace in this story – I try to correctly identify rape, and use the word 'relationship' when describing long-term sexual relations, resulting in multiple children, advisedly; this is not intended to convey a completely consensual or remotely equal partnership. I use 'mixed ancestry' or 'mixed heritage', because 'mixed race' suggests the existence of pure biological races. Such neologisms may at first seem inelegant or strange; I believe they are preferable to continuing to dehumanise enslaved people and obscure the violence they endured. Apart from when quoting directly from a source (many of which inevitably use terms that are offensive today), I will be using this language. As Wittgenstein said: 'The limits of my language mean the limits of my world.' If we want to make our world better, we could do worse than begin by changing our vocabulary.

A Note on Currency

During the period covered by this book, currency in the British Caribbean was worth less than British pounds sterling – £1 8s currency was approximately equal to £1 sterling. All figures in the text are converted to sterling, except where I have specified 'currency'. Occasionally currency is not specified in the original document, and I have made an educated guess. This is indicated in the notes at the end of the book.

Preface

'*Le secret des grandes fortunes sans cause apparente est un crime oublié, parce qu'il a été proprement fait.*'

'The secret of large fortunes without an apparent source is a forgotten crime, forgotten because it was done properly.'

HONORÉ DE BALZAC,
Le Père Goriot (1835)

UNTIL RECENTLY, the extent to which Britain profited from enslavement, from the founding of its first Caribbean colonies in the seventeenth century to emancipation in 1834, has successfully been obscured. Now, the perpetrators are emerging from the woodwork: merchants, plantation owners, insurance brokers, colonial officials. But one category still largely escapes our notice. Women.

Men always aspired to pass down property from father to son. Real life, though, proved messier. The male line often failed: then wives, daughters, sisters and nieces became enslavers and plantation owners in their own right. For almost two centuries, generations of these heiresses brought huge fortunes back to Britain under cover of matrimony.

Heiresses tells the stories of nine such women. Using surviving family papers, letters, diaries and portraits, we will trace the source of their wealth, sometimes reaching back to the very beginning of English colonisation. We will follow their experiences from childhood through a series of dramatic twists and turns, the plot thickened by dastardly stepfathers, ardent suitors and lovers, disapproving parents and disappointing children, war and revolution, bigamy, adultery and divorce, bankruptcy, suicide and insanity. One woman found herself on trial for theft, facing transportation to Australia or the death penalty. Another faked her daughter's death. In a truly incredible case, the daughter of a woman born enslaved wed the son of a Scottish Earl.

These predominantly white women forged personal connections between Caribbean enslavement and sites of British identity, from the Battle of Hastings to Aston Villa Football Club. In the following pages, we will encounter people and places we thought we knew: naval hero Horatio Nelson; novelists Jane Austen and Tobias Smollett; dramatist David Garrick; poets Robert Burns and Lord Byron; portrait painters Thomas Gainsborough, Joshua Reynolds and Johan Zoffany; London's exclusive Sloane Square; the British Museum; and Britain's stately homes – even royal residence Windsor Castle.

Heiresses is a story with global reach. We will journey from Jamaica to Sierra Leone, Charleston, South Carolina and Germany; from Antigua to India, China and Australia; from St Kitts and St Vincent to France and Italy. Along the way, we will meet American Founding Fathers, European rulers – notably Marie Antoinette and Napoleon – and a future Governor of New South Wales.

We will also encounter several individuals the heiresses enslaved. As in my first book, *Black Tudors*, which told the stories of Africans living free in early modern England, I have endeavoured to tease out every last inch of meaning from the slight documentary records of their lives. Again, extraordinary stories emerge. Of a Jamaican carpenter collecting caricatures of his enslavers. Of an Antiguan heiress's former nurse writing to her in India requesting her freedom. Of a woman who travelled all the way from Barbados to London to confront her enslavers.

This is not a story of the distant past. Rather, legacies of enslavement can be traced in many aspects of our lives today. Many British public institutions, buildings and infrastructure were funded by these ill-gotten gains. Most pressingly, the racism and racial inequality that still poison our world are ongoing consequences of this dehumanising system.

British enslavers were compensated to the tune of £20 million for the loss of human 'property' in the 1830s, incurring a government debt fully paid off only in 2015. Which means British taxpayers – including those of Black Caribbean descent – helped pay that money back. Some 3,000 families resident in Britain received compensation; far more had profited from enslavement over the previous two centuries. How many descendants must be alive today?

This isn't merely a thought experiment for me. I have discovered some of *my own* maternal ancestors engaged in trafficking Africans and enslaving people in Jamaica. Two were Liverpool merchants who invested in multiple slaving voyages in the latter part of the eighteenth century. Another was a solicitor and enslaver in Jamaica, acquainted with some of the characters in this book. It was a jolt when his name jumped out from the documents several times during my research. My family history is British History in microcosm; we are all living in the ruins of empire.[*]

I hope sharing the stories in this book will provoke much-needed conversations and lead to educational, creative and reparative work in partnership with descendants of enslaved people *and* enslavers on both sides of the Atlantic. Together, I hope we can start to make sense of our shared history, and use that understanding to work towards a fairer future.

---

[*] Phrase borrowed from Akala, author of *Natives: Race and Class in the Ruins of Empire* (2019). See 'My Family and Enslavement' at the end of the book for more details.

A MASTER-KEY
TO THE
RICH LADIES TREASURY.
OR,
The WIDOWER and BATCHELOR's DIRECTORY.
CONTAINING
An exact ALPHABETICAL LIST of the

Duchefs Marchionefs Countefs } Dowagers. Vifcountefs Baronefs	Ladies by Curtefie, Daughters of Peers. Baronets Widows. Widows, *and* Spinfters in *Great-Britain*.

WITH

An ACCOUNT of their PLACES of ABODE, Reputed FORTUNES, and FORTUNES they poffefs in the STOCKS.

By *a* YOUNGER BROTHER.

——— *He took his Stand* ———
Upon a Widow's Jointure Land.
HUDIBRAS.

LONDON:
Printed for J. ROBERTS in *Warwick-Lane*,
M.DCC.XLIII.
[Price 1 s.]

The 1742 fortune hunter's *Directory of Heiresses*, listing 'Rich Ladies' with their 'Reputed Fortunes', Bank of England, East India and South Sea Company stocks.

Introduction

It is a truth universally acknowledged that a single *woman* in possession of a good fortune, must be in want of a *husband*. Inheriting Langley's estate in St Mary, Jamaica, from her uncle in January 1791 transformed fourteen-year-old Clementina Clarke from insignificant schoolgirl to wealthy heiress – and enslaver of some 150 men, women and children – overnight. Unable to contain his excitement, her guardian, Bristol merchant William Gordon, was 'so highly imprudent as to state the particulars by reading them in a public coffee house, surrounded by a variety of gentlemen of all descriptions'.

Richard Vining Perry, a 'dissipated but handsome' apothecary, wasted little time, initiating an exchange of clandestine notes with the underage girl. Then, one Wednesday in March, a message arrived at Clementina's school, purportedly from her guardian, inviting her to tea. Shortly afterwards, a carriage bearing Mr Gordon's livery appeared at the door. Clementina stepped into the chaise and was promptly whisked away to Gretna Green and a new life as Mrs Perry.

Her schoolmistress gave chase, following the couple as far as Ghent, but to no avail. Newspapers and caricaturists salivated at every detail of the scandal. Following reports Perry had brandished a pistol, *The Times* salaciously riposted: 'A PISTOL in the hands of CLEMENTINA PERRY would be absolutely a very dreadful weapon – were that same PISTOL at all like the lady in its readiness to GO OFF!'

Forced to return to England by the French invasion of the Netherlands in 1793, Perry was imprisoned and charged with 'forcible abduction, or stealing an heiress ... for lucre'. But he regained his freedom after Clementina, now pregnant with their second child, testified she had *intended* to elope with him. As one shrewd observer put it, it was folly 'to dream of a Woman's bastardizing her own Babies and hanging the

Father ... for the patriotic Desire of saving future Heiresses!' Clementina may have later regretted her loyalty. At his trial, Perry had described the providential way 'their eyes met in attraction, and with a kind of electrical fire shook them to their souls.' But, before long, her husband abandoned her in Bath, to die in poverty aged just thirty-eight, while he squandered her fortune.[1]

This picaresque adventure sounds like it belongs in a sensational romance novel, farcical play or period drama. As will many elements of the equally dramatic stories you'll find in this book. Marriages brokered against a backdrop of fancy London townhouses and sweeping country estates; characters desperate to climb the social ladder; fortunes won, only to be lost by prodigal husbands or children; adultery, divorce, insanity. But there is one key difference from the stories we're used to. The *source* of Clementina's and the other heiresses' wealth.

Heiresses had always been an attractive commodity in the marriage market. They could restore – or transform – a family's fortunes. For example, the prodigious wealth of the Dukes of Westminster (currently estimated at around £10 billion) can be traced back to Sir Thomas Grosvenor's 1677 marriage to the twelve-year-old Mary Davies, heiress to the 500-acre Ebury Manor estate – today's Mayfair and West End.[2] Such windfalls were akin to winning the lottery, catapulting a lucky few into an entirely different social league.

Though they would vow 'for richer, for poorer', bachelors of a certain class were looking for wealth just as much as they were looking for love. A contemporary advice book for young men commented:

> Nothing can be more sordid, than to bargain for a wife as you would for a horse ... But do not fly to one who has nothing but beauty, or, if you please, affection to recommend her. A fair Wife with empty pockets is like a noble house without Furniture, Showy, but Useless: As an odious one with abundance, resembles fat land in the midst of fens, rich, but uninhabitable.[3]

Of course, we are not immune to such considerations today; tabloids, soap operas and romcoms still delight in the classic tale of rich girl, poor boy. But such was the barefaced avarice of some Georgian suitors that in 1742 a directory of eligible women, listed by social status and size of fortune, was published anonymously by 'a younger brother'. Browsing its pages, widowers and bachelors could find 'an exact alphabetical list' of ladies 'with an account of their places of abode, reputed fortunes, and fortunes they possess in the stocks'. The author shamelessly dedicated his publication to the woman he was courting, a Miss Fetherston of Southampton Row, listing her £30,000, alongside significant investments in the South Sea Company, the East India Company and the Bank of England.[4]

From the late seventeenth century, a new kind of heiress was on offer: women whose wealth came from Britain's thriving new Caribbean colonies.[5] Within thirty years of establishing their first foothold in the Americas at Jamestown, Virginia, in 1607, the English had arrived in St Kitts, Barbados, Nevis and Antigua. In 1655, they seized Jamaica from the Spanish. The island would become Britain's most profitable American colony. So profitable that in the middle of the American Revolution, when Jamaica was at risk of French invasion, the British Commander in Chief, Henry Clinton, willingly diverted 4,000 troops under Lord Cornwallis to its aid.[6]*

Over the next century and a half, as the European powers struggled for ascendancy in the region, several other islands and territories would be ceded to Britain by the French and the Dutch. These colonies, and the huge profits from the sugar – 'white gold' – they produced, were founded on the displacement and attempted eradication of indigenous peoples, and the back-breaking labour of millions of Africans trafficked across the Atlantic.

Lady Maria Nugent, wife of Jamaican Governor Sir George Nugent, came face-to-face with the harsh reality when visiting a sugar plantation in 1802. She found enslaved men hard at work in the boiling house, stirring cauldrons and filling barrels. When the overseer told her the men worked twelve-hour shifts, she exclaimed:

> how dreadful to think of their standing 12 hours over a boiling cauldron, and doing the same thing; and he owned to me that sometimes they did fall asleep and get their poor fingers into the mill; and he shewed me the hatchet that was always ready to sever the whole limb, as the only means of saving the poor sufferer's life! I would not have a sugar estate for the world![7]

---

* The order was countermanded a week later after the threat passed.

This is just one detail of a transatlantic economic system predicated on treating human beings like livestock, or worse. Legally, they were considered chattel – not people but property. Exhausting work, horrific punishments, disease and malnutrition meant about one-third of Africans died within three years of arriving in the Caribbean; the rest would be lucky to survive more than seven.

British people and institutions profited from enslavement in numerous ways. They invested in slaving voyages, either through direct ownership or by becoming shareholders. Some insured the ships; others provided copper manillas – horseshoe-shaped armlets or bracelets used as currency in West Africa – iron manacles or guns. British merchants imported sugar, rum, coffee and tobacco produced by enslaved workers, sending plantation supplies back to the colonies. Those appointed as governors or to other colonial posts had lucrative salaries. Finally, there were the plantation owners, each an enslaver of hundreds of people. Marrying an heiress, however, is often overlooked as a route to acquiring this wealth.

When we picture an enslaver, we usually imagine a man, but the lottery of human reproduction and mortality led to many women inheriting human 'property'. This was especially true in the Caribbean, where death rates were so high that 'once in seven years' there was 'a revolution of lives', which 'would soon leave the place a desert, did not daily recruits come over from Great Britain'.[8] Women were usually the last resort, after the supply of sons, nephews, male cousins and godsons had been exhausted. Nonetheless, over forty per cent of individuals awarded compensation when enslavement ended were women.[9]

Soon, rich enslaving families began to return to Britain, hoping to buy a place in society. Over two centuries, more than 150 Caribbean heiresses and their money were grafted into British society. They proved as attractive to aristocrats and gentlemen as to chancers like Richard Vining Perry. At least one Duke, several Earls, Lords and Knights all wed Caribbean heiresses. Fifteen MPs augmented their fortunes by such marriages, queuing up alongside merchants, naval officers, soldiers, writers, scientists, even clergymen.[10]

Various famous figures joined the queue. While stationed at Nevis a youthful Horatio Nelson married Fanny Nisbet, niece of John Richardson Herbert, President of the island's council.[11] Elizabeth Langley Rose of

Jamaica took as her second husband Sir Hans Sloane, whose collections form the basis of the British Museum, the British Library, the Natural History Museum and the Chelsea Physic Garden. Ann Lascelles, who had 'the expectation of a fortune of three thousand pounds in West Indian property', married the novelist Tobias Smollett, then serving in Jamaica as a Royal Navy surgeon.[12] Sir Humphry Davy, inventor of the Davy mining lamp and possible inspiration for Mary Shelley's Dr Frankenstein, married Jane Apreece, née Kerr, of Antigua: her wealth allowed him to quit employment and focus solely on research.[13]

The gargantuan scale of Caribbean fortunes became legendary; one fictional Jamaican character arrived in London 'with rum and sugar enough belonging to him to make all the water in the Thames into punch'.[14] Heiress Elizabeth Knight, who married Lord Onslow in 1708, was so fabulously wealthy – with a fortune of £70,000 – she was known as the 'Indian Queen'.[15] Most heiresses had dowries closer to the £5,000 considered necessary to merit a mention in the *Directory of Heiresses*. As this figure exceeded the vast majority of people's annual income, it made them very attractive, especially if the dowry were just a harbinger of the inheritance to come.[16] Sixteen-year-old Maria Glenn, who, it was anticipated, would inherit her grandfather's St Vincent property when she turned twenty-one, was described in the *Taunton Courier* in 1817 as 'like a deposit in our savings Bank, to be reserved until a few more years have improved the amount of her fortune, and the value of her affections.'[17]

All this wealth was injected with abandon into the British economy. In Tobias Smollett's novel *The Expedition of Humphry Clinker*, he rather hypocritically has gouty Welsh squire Matthew Bramble complain that:

> Every upstart of fortune, harnessed in the trappings of the mode, presents himself at Bath ... Clerks and factors [traders] from the East Indies, loaded with the spoil of plundered provinces; planters, negro-drivers, and hucksters from our American [including Caribbean] plantations ... knowing no other criterion of greatness, but the ostentation of wealth, they discharge their affluence without taste or conduct, through every channel of the most absurd extravagance.[18]

His disdain is a ripe example of the perennial prejudice against 'new money' or the *nouveau riche* amongst the upper classes. 'Old' families prided themselves on their aristocratic ancestry, and genteel wealth based on landownership, ideally tracing both the family line and grant of land back to the Norman Conquest. Though, as John Stuart Mill pointed out, there is nothing very noble about acquiring property through 'conquest and violence' rather than 'just partition, or acquisition by industry', however many centuries ago it happened.[19] They sneered – with a touch of jealousy – at 'nabobs' and 'negro-drivers', who had amassed their wealth 'in trade', and were now eager to buy their way into high society. But as Shakespeare's Timon put it, enough 'glittering precious gold':

> ... will make
> Black white, foul fair, wrong right,
> Base noble, old young, coward valiant.[20]

Caribbean heiresses and their husbands did their best to establish genteel credentials but had to tread the fine line between 'good' taste and tasteless extravagance.[21] They had portraits painted by leading artists. Townhouses, country houses and estates were bought, built or renovated with their new fortunes.[22] Hosting lavish entertainments in these splendid homes for guests including famous writers, politicians and royalty projected families further up the social ladder. Some inheritances funded extensive travels to fashionable destinations across Europe. Others bankrolled the military careers of husbands and sons fighting Britain's colonial wars or were invested in the East India Company or new colonies like Australia. Very few funded philanthropic endeavours, beyond customary bequests to the Church and poor parishioners.[23]

Though Caribbean heiresses' wealth usually outweighed all other considerations, suitors and their families still harboured anxieties about them. As 'new money', these women were unlikely to sport much of a pedigree. They might even have criminal ancestry, given transportation to the Americas had been a common punishment in the early years of colonisation, well before Australia became an option. In one popular play, 'Miss Patty Plumb of Jamaica' faced gossip that 'her grandfather was transported for robbing a hen-roost'.[24] Good breeding and preserving the family line from any vulgar taint remains an obsession amongst the British upper classes. As Lady Bracknell put it in Oscar Wilde's *The Importance of Being Earnest*, on learning that Jack had been found as a baby in a handbag at Victoria Station, and has no idea who his parents are:

> You can hardly imagine that I and Lord Bracknell would dream of allowing our only daughter – a girl brought up with the utmost care – to marry into a cloak-room, and form an alliance with a parcel?[25]

Heiresses who grew up in the Caribbean faced another nagging suspicion: would they prove as temperamental as their home climate? Mrs Bertha Rochester, née Mason, in Charlotte Bronte's *Jane Eyre* – in stark contrast to the meek and mild heroine – embodies this prejudice. Mr Rochester, a younger son, sets out for Jamaica to seize Bertha and her £30,000. After marriage, however, he finds her 'intemperate and unchaste'. Her 'violent and unreasonable temper' matches the 'fiery West Indian' nights. Eventually, he hides away the 'wild beast' he has married; she became the archetypal 'madwoman in the attic'.[26]*

British men also feared unknowingly marrying a woman with African ancestry. In reality, such heiresses were rare, though several appear in literature, most famously Miss Lambe in Austen's *Sanditon* and Miss Swartz in Thackeray's *Vanity Fair*.[27]† Only twenty per cent of mixed-heritage children in Jamaica were given their freedom, let alone an inheritance. Of the 150 women I surveyed, eighteen had African ancestry.[28] They were born, at best, from extremely unequal relationships between white men and Black women, or, at worst, as a consequence of an environment where repeated rape was not only commonplace and committed with impunity but considered a shrewd financial move: begetting more human 'property'.[29]

Some heiresses were in line to inherit people and plantations from a very young age; others had a more remote chance or waited for decades for an elderly relative to die. Some fabled fortunes proved a mirage.

---

* Anna Eliza, Duchess of Chandos, who inherited a Jamaican estate from her first husband, became a real-life Mrs Rochester, certified insane by a Commission of Lunacy in 1791 after his untimely death. 'Duchess of Chandos Anna Eliza Brydges formerly Elletson (née Gamon)', LBS: http://www.ucl.ac.uk/lbs/person/view/2146640763; Sturtz, '"Dimduke"'; Young, 'Negotiating', pp. 581–602.

† Although Bertha Mason is never explicitly described as of African descent, references to her 'thick dark' hair and 'discoloured', 'black' face, and her 'swelled and dark lips' plus the fact that her parents wanted her to marry Rochester because he was 'of a good race' have led some scholars to this conclusion.

Volatile Caribbean investments meant marrying an heiress was high-risk, as likely to lead to litigation and bankruptcy as the high life. Much of their property was in human beings; their plantation land worth little without enslaved labour; their funds advanced against the putative profits of next year's crop. Unlike traditional fortunes founded on British landownership, with a steady rent roll, incomes based on sugar and rum proceeds faced numerous hazards; which is why so many colonial families bought land in Britain. Lady Maria Nugent complained conversation in Jamaica revolved around 'death, debt and disease'. One might add 'war, weather and resistance', and later 'abolition and emancipation', to the list of threats to Caribbean wealth. In a society as sensitive to events as today's capital markets, where goods and services were bought 'on credit', reputations and fortunes rose or plummeted in tandem.

Men on the make, like Richard Vining Perry, sought to benefit from the legal principle of *femme couverte*; until 1882, a woman's worldly goods became her husband's upon marriage. Feminist Mary Astell complained in 1700 that a man might, when courting a woman, call himself her '*slave* a few days, but it is only in order to make her his all the rest of his life' (emphasis added). She urged women to think very carefully before they subjected themselves to the 'inconstant, uncertain, arbitrary will' of a husband.[30]

However, husbands did not always have full control over their wives' Caribbean assets. While we might assume prenuptial agreements are a modern phenomenon, historically, heiresses usually had the protection of a marriage settlement. These contracts sought to safeguard their inheritance, specifying funds were 'for her own sole use independent of any husband'. In aid of this, fortunes were placed in trust (that ancient innovation of English law, so often aimed at preserving wealth), overseen by two or more trustees, legally obliged to manage the property for the heiresses' benefit.

Similar provisions appeared in family wills. Besides trustees, executors were nominated to carry out the deceased's wishes. Executors must apply for probate (the legal right to deal with someone's property, money and possessions after they die) before they can distribute assets. Apart from rare cases where they took on the executorship themselves, heiresses had to grapple with executors, trustees and lawyers – who did not always have their best interests at heart – to take possession of their property.

Heiresses took an active role in managing their Caribbean estates from afar, particularly before marriage, or during widowhood. They engaged with every aspect of the business, from implementing the latest agricultural and industrial innovations, to choosing trustworthy attorneys to represent their interests in the colonies and negotiating with metropolitan merchants to sell their sugar and rum. As wives, they did not simply retreat into domesticity but continued to influence their husbands with their often superior knowledge and connections.

None of the heiresses in this book appear to have questioned the morality of their actions. However, enslavement did not find universal acceptance in their society. Some white people recognised enslavement was wrong long before the abolition campaign gathered strength. Prominent Quakers spoke out against slaving from the 1670s; in 1761, they expelled anyone who engaged in this 'repugnant', 'Unchristian traffick' from their Society. In 1774, the founder of the Methodist Church, Reverend John Wesley, declared enslavement a 'violation of justice, mercy and truth'. A far more establishment figure, Dr Samuel Johnson, once proposed a toast in Oxford to the 'next rebellion of the negroes in the West Indies'.[31] Sir George Ellison, eponymous hero of Sarah Scott's 1766 novel, visits Jamaica after marrying an heiress. He deplores 'the cruelty exercised on one part of mankind by another: as if the difference of complexion excluded them from the human race, or indeed as if their not being human could be an excuse for making them wretched'.[32] Though even his seemingly sympathetic lament allowed for the possibility Africans were not human. Being an abolitionist did not make a person immune from being racist.

Most new arrivals quickly became inured to the brutality. Those heiresses who grew up on the islands accepted it as the natural order of things; those who had never visited or left as young children hardly interrogated it either. Anna Eliza, Duchess of Chandos, who never met the people she held in bondage, wrote in 1776: "Tis true they are born to labour in a manner peculiar to their colour; but we who reap the fruits of that labour, ought to soften it to them, as much as possible, by every proper indulgence'.[33]

The telling phrase is 'as much as possible'. Ultimately her concern, echoed in the letters of many an absentee enslaver, rings hollow when contrasted with archaeological and documentary evidence of injuries and illnesses, low life expectancy and records of vicious punishments meted out to those who resisted. Women were certainly not more naturally empathetic. Financial considerations always came first, even when couched in general platitudes about improving conditions. There are a few examples of enslavers overall, mostly Quakers, who decided to set the people they inherited free.[34] And a couple who expressed the sentiment, but didn't follow through.[35] Ultimately, enslaved people were too valuable, too large a percentage of their assets, for most enslavers even to consider emancipating them.

By the time calls for abolition and emancipation intensified in the late eighteenth century, enslavers, including several heiresses' husbands, had infiltrated the political class. They were able to delay, oppose and obstruct any change in the law. When it became clear they had lost the moral and legal argument, heiresses' husbands were prominent amongst the enslavers pressing the government for compensation when enslavement was finally abolished in 1834. The £20 million payout represented forty per cent of government spending that year. Some female enslavers received astronomical sums; the ten women with the largest pay-outs netted £301,587 between them – at the most conservative estimate more than £34 million today.[36]

We cannot understand these women without understanding the people they enslaved, several of whom shared their surnames, or even first names. In some cases, they were intimately connected. Though most heiresses were white, some were children of enslaved women, meaning they might eventually 'own' their own mothers.[37] Some heiresses were suckled by Black wet nurses, remaining in contact years later. Those who grew up in Britain were often waited on by Black people their families had brought home from the Caribbean. Heiresses enquired after specific individuals or sent gifts of clothes or money to people they hadn't seen for decades.

The heiresses' family papers reveal personal stories like these – often lost in the grand narrative of the millions trafficked across the Atlantic or the hundreds 'owned' by a particular family – including occasional letters written *by* an enslaved person. Many resisted enslavement, whether through everyday acts of defiance or risking their lives in uprisings. Some freedom seekers escaped temporarily, others permanently, even crossing oceans. Just to survive each day on a plantation, building families and making lives for themselves in the most difficult of circumstances, required extraordinary bravery and resilience.

Inevitably, many people are recorded only by name (and that imposed) and estimated 'value', their experiences forever lost to us. Nonetheless, we must recognise the human struggle of each and every individual whose labour supported the heiresses' extravagant lifestyles, and whose fates depended on their whims or inaction.

The stories that follow are of nine women – Sarah, Frances, Mary, Jenny, Martha, Jane, Elizabeth, Isabella and Anna Susanna – whose lives are bursting with drama and intrigue, but also help paint a picture of the wider story of Britain's colonial past, and collide spectacularly with the history we thought we knew. On first-name terms, we will follow both their personal trials and tribulations and their efforts to obtain, maintain and retain their inheritances. Re-tracing their steps will lead us to surprising places, deep into the tangled web of enslavement that stretched into every corner of British society. Let's begin, though, not with Sarah Newton, but with a woman she enslaved, Betsy Newton, and her quest to claim freedom for herself and her children.

Lady Sarah Holte, née Newton, painted *c.*1763 a few years before the artist, Tilly Kettle, departed for India. After her husband's death, she fought with her sister-in-law over who should keep the pearl necklace.

I

Sarah Newton (1723–1794)

*Tracing Sarah Newton's inheritance takes us from
the earliest years of English settlement of Barbados,
the crucible of British Caribbean sugar production, to
people and places at the heart of life in Britain today.*

IN JANUARY 1795, an enslaved woman named Betsy Newton made a desperate journey from Barbados to London. The overseer at Newton plantation had executed her brother. She had been clapped in irons and sent to work in the field. Without her care, her newborn baby boy had died. She had appealed for help from the plantation attorney, but his wife turned her away from their home, taunting: 'Your mistress will give you all away to Strangers.' Loath to leave her other four young children behind, Betsy nevertheless decided she must appeal directly to her enslaver, for all their sakes. If she returned home, the overseer would 'certainly kill her'. Come hell or high water, she must sail for England.

She knew that Lady Sarah Holte (née Newton), one of two sisters who had enslaved her and her family for the last decade, had recently died; the other, Elizabeth Newton, lay seriously ill. As neither sister had any children, no one knew who was going to inherit Betsy and her family. She must reach England before the will was finalised. The only way she could be reunited with her children would be to return to Barbados carrying a certificate of her freedom and an order for her children to be released. Surely this was only right? Twenty-seven years earlier, an English court of law had ruled that her grandmother, Mary Hylas (née Revill), was a free woman. But the Newton family had defied the judge's order to return Mary to England. Betsy, however, refused to be ignored.[1] She would confront her enslaver face-to-face.

To understand how Sarah came to jointly inherit Betsy, her family, over 400 other people and almost 800 acres of prime Barbados real estate, we need to begin at the beginning. Or, more precisely, with her great-grandfather Samuel Newton and his older brother Robert. Extensive family records allow us to trace the Newtons' ascent and Sarah's own trials and tribulations, as well as revealing the dramatic stories of Mary Hylas and Betsy Newton. Uniquely, hundreds of skeletons found at Newton plantation reveal incontrovertible truths about enslavement's physical impact.

When Robert set out for Barbados as a young man in the early 1640s, the Newtons were a fairly lowly yeoman family, with a small estate at Northedge Hall near Ashover in Derbyshire.[2] Robert had high hopes, joining a wave of ambitious men flocking to Barbados, seeking to make a fortune from planting sugar.

Sugar could catapult a man from obscurity to greatness. James Drax, second son of a Warwickshire vicar, arrived in Barbados in 1627 with £300. He pioneered sugar cultivation using enslaved labour. By the

Richard Ligon's 1657 map of Barbados, showing colonists driving camels and shooting runaways.

time of his death, he enjoyed an annual income of over £1,000 from Barbados, held extensive estates in England and had been knighted by Oliver Cromwell. The Drax family are major landholders in England and Barbados to this day.[3]

Armed with £170 from his father and a loan from London merchant John Kirkham, by 1647 Robert had 'by God's providence ... begun a plantation'. There, 'amongst others', he employed two men 'which I have bought, commonly called Negroes, commonly called by the names of Dick and Tymme [Tim]'.[4]

The English had first arrived on Barbados, a small island of just 166 square miles, in 1627. By the time Robert arrived, the white population was growing fast; numbers more than doubled from 14,000 in 1640 to 30,000 in 1650. Although we often think of North America as the 'New World', between 1640 and 1660, two-thirds of transatlantic emigrants headed for the Caribbean, mostly to Barbados.[5]

As in Virginia and New England, religious intolerance in Britain prompted Puritans, Quakers, Catholics, Jews and other non-conformists to make new lives for themselves on the island. Similarly, many people arrived as indentured servants; Robert Newton employed a number on his plantation. Not all came willingly. To be 'Barbadosed' was to be kidnapped; many were 'deceived or enticed away'. Long before Australia was 'discovered', criminals were sentenced to transportation to Virginia or Barbados. In 1655, one visitor condemned Barbados as 'the Dunghill whereon England doth cast forth its rubbish: rogues, whores and such like people.'[6]

The British Civil Wars, waged between 1642 and 1653, also had a major impact. Many Royalists were compelled to leave their homes after their property was destroyed or confiscated. Richard Ligon, who headed to Barbados in 1647, recounted how he had 'lost (by a Barbarous Riot) all that I had gotten by the painful travails of my youth, by which means I was stripped and rifled of all I had, left destitute of a subsistence, and brought to such an Exigent, as I must famish or fly'.[7] Cromwell sold captured Royalists as indentured servants in Barbados. Thousands of Scottish and English prisoners of war arrived on the island after his victories at Dunbar and Worcester; tens of thousands of Irish during his reconquest of Ireland. Reflecting on their fate, Cromwell was 'persuaded that this is a righteous judgement of God upon these barbarous wretches, who have imbrued their hands in so much innocent blood.'[8]

Africans 'bred up amongst the Portugals', who had been producing sugar in Pernambuco and Bahia in Brazil for years, helped the English unlock the 'secrets of that mystery'; London financiers were persuaded to invest capital in this 'sweet business'.[9] The first large shipment of sugar – '70 full chests' – had left Barbados in 1643 and by 1645 cane covered forty per cent of the island's less than 1,000 acres of arable land. Within twenty years, this figure would double.[10] Barbados's annual crop was worth over £3 million by the early 1650s – £1 million more than the annual cost of supporting the entire English army and navy – making it 'one of the richest spots of earth under the sun'.[11]

As production skyrocketed, prices in London plummeted, transforming sugar from a luxury of the rich – witness Elizabeth I's blackened teeth – to a necessity for all. British demand for sugar became insatiable; to sweeten newly fashionable coffee, chocolate and tea; to make jam and a whole host of puddings; even added to everyday items like bread and porridge.[12]*

Robert Newton may have purchased a plot of land 'ready furnished and stocked with Servants, slaves, horses, cattle, assinigoes [donkeys, a word borrowed from the Portuguese], cane, &c. with a sugar work and an ingenio [mill]'. However, given his modest means, he more likely had to start from scratch, and 'endure all hardships, and a tedious expectation, of what profit or pleasure may arise, in many year's [sic] patience'.[13]

Robert knew he had taken a huge gamble. He made a will just before returning to Barbados from England in June 1647, acknowledging the 'uncertainty of life'. It proved to be a prescient act – he died less than four months later. Whilst he left Africans Dick and Tim to a Barbados friend and neighbour, the plantation went to his 'loving brother Samuel Newton' (Sarah's great-grandfather) and London merchant John Kirkham.[14] Samuel initially promised to give Kirkham the plantation to pay off his brother's debts. But in 1654 he had a change of heart – possibly influenced by his wife Barbara, who was a Quaker – and went out to Barbados to claim it for himself.

---

* British consumers remain addicted to sugar to this day, consuming over three times the amount recommended by NHS guidelines. Diabetes Research and Wellness Foundation, 'Most People': https://www.drwf.org.uk/news-and-events/news/report-on-diet-finds-most-people-in-the-uk-are-consuming-almost-3-times-the-recommended-daily-sugar-intake/.

Samuel continued to struggle with Kirkham over who owned the plantation until 1659, when the merchant finally relinquished it before the Lord Mayor's Court in London, for a payment of 276,000 lbs of muscovado sugar.'[15] By this time, Samuel's plantation consisted of 174 acres, '15 Christian servants, 76 negroes young and old, 32 cattle young and old and ten horses, 5 coppers, 3 stills and utensils.'[16] Casual listing of people alongside livestock and even equipment typifies enslavers' attitudes towards their human 'property'.

The word 'plantation' evokes a pastoral scene – acres of lush vegetation overlooked from shady verandas – but the industrial nature of sugar production, with specialised equipment, machinery and buildings needed for each stage of the process, makes the phrase 'factory in the field' more apt.[17] 'Forced labour camp' better reflects enslaved people's experiences; producing sugar was back-breaking, even fatal, work.

After sprouting from an old cutting planted lengthways, it took fourteen to eighteen months for sugar cane to reach its full height of eight feet: a period of constant weeding, manuring and pest control. Once cut, cane had to be processed within two days or the juice began to sour. Labourers rushed it to the mill, feeding it back and forth through rollers, squeezing juice into a tray below.

The juice then travelled down a pipe to the boiling house, 'where there are six or seven large coppers or furnaces kept perpetually boiling; and from which with heavy ladles and skimmers they skim off the excrementitious parts of the cane'. As skilled men and women gradually transferred the liquid from the biggest to the smallest copper vat, it reduced and purified, becoming darker and thicker. When the head boiler judged the liquid was about to crystallise, it was transferred to a cooling cistern. Once cool, workers poured the juice into clay pots headed for the curing house. There, another group drained the molasses, taking it to the still house to be distilled into rum. The remaining liquid took about a month to dry out fully, becoming brown muscovado.

Every stage of this process was dangerous, even life-threatening. One enslaver listed possible 'mischances' in 1689: 'If a Stiller slip into a Rum-Cistern, it is sudden death: for it stifles in a moment. If a Mill-feeder be catch't by the finger, his whole body is drawn in, and he is squeez'd to

---

* This unrefined brown sugar was used for sixty per cent of transactions in Barbados by 1648. Menard, *Sweet Negotiations*, p. 17.

An ox-driven sugar mill in Brazil. From Willem Piso's
Historia Naturalis Brasiliae, published 1648.

pieces. If a Boyler get any part into the scalding Sugar, it sticks like Glew, or Birdlime, and 'tis hard to save either Limb or Life.'[18] This was why, as Lady Nugent observed in Jamaica, an axe was always on hand to sever the limb before the whole body followed.

To make more valuable white sugar, muscovado was placed in a mould, then smeared with wet clay. Water then percolated through the clay for four months, draining off all impurities.[19] An Italian Jesuit priest in Brazil marvelled how dirty mud could turn sugar white, 'just as the memory of our sins mixed with tears of repentance purifies and whitens our souls'.[20]

Despite modern technology, the urgency of getting sugar cane from field to mill remained. Trinidadian historian and cricket writer C.L.R. James captured the drama in *Beyond a Boundary*, relating how factories worked round the clock, grinding cane as fast as it could be cut. If something went wrong with the engines, 'the tension was immediately acute'. Cutters for miles around downed tools, while the engineers 'worked frantically like men on a wrecked ship'. When the engines were repaired, an 'enthusiastic crowd' celebrated the 'miracle'.[21]

Although Samuel continued to employ a dozen or so 'Christian servants' throughout his lifetime, he and his contemporaries soon became dependent on African labour.[22] The earliest Black people in Barbados had been captured from Iberian vessels by privateers. In 1641 the *Star* of London became the first English slaving ship to arrive directly from West Africa. By the 1650s, 3,000 Africans were trafficked to Barbados each year. The Black population grew rapidly from around 1,000 in 1640 to 20,000 in 1655, outnumbering the white population by 1660. By 1700 seventy-five per cent of the island's inhabitants were of African descent. George Downing – who later built Downing Street – remarked while visiting Barbados as a chaplain fresh out of Harvard that Africans were 'the life of this place … and the more they buy, the better able they are to buy, for in a year and a half they will earn (with God's blessing) as much as they cost'.[23]

The key features of chattel enslavement, specifically service for life and enslaved status being hereditary through the mother, soon appeared. In 1635, the oldest surviving Barbados plantation inventory listed white servants with the date their indentureship expired, alongside a 'negro' with no end to his service. In 1654, one visitor observed 'miserabell Negors borne to perpetual slavery they and their seed', whose owners 'sell them from one to another as we do sheep'. Three years later, when 'Mary a negro', recently manumitted (set free)* by Colonel John Higginbotham, claimed her three children should now also be free, the Council ruled that, as she was enslaved when they were born, they remained Higginbotham's property.[24] And, as we know, in 1647, Robert Newton was able to bequeath Dick and Tim to his friend.

However, it was not set in stone that all Africans were automatically someone's property. In 1636, the Governor and Council ruled: 'Negroes that came here to be sold, should serve for life, *unless a contract was before made to the contrary*' (emphasis added). In 1654, a Black man named Anthony Iland was released from William Leachy's control after explaining he had arrived on the island as a free man. Baptism was also seen as a potential path to freedom, as it had long been thought immoral to enslave fellow Christians. For this reason, colonists increasingly avoided converting Africans.[25]

Any remaining grey areas were eliminated in 1661, when the Council issued 'An Act for the better ordering and governing of Negroes', whom they characterised as 'heathenish, brutish and an uncertain, dangerous kind of people'. Enslaved Africans became ineligible for trial by jury. There was no punishment if they were injured or even killed by their enslavers. Conversely, if they so much as hit a 'Christian' (a term by now

---

* The word manumit comes from the Latin *manus* (hand) and *mittere* (to send), literally to send out of the hands of; similarly emancipate comes from 'e'- out of, *manus* and *capere* – to take.

nearly synonymous with 'white'), they would be 'severely whipped'. If it happened again, they would be branded in the face and have their noses slit. The Barbados Act was the first comprehensive English colonial 'slave code'; it would influence lawmakers across the British Americas.[26]

African enslavement was not the inevitable consequence of the encounter between Black and white. Holding Africans in bondage was still unfamiliar enough in England when Robert wrote his will in 1647 for him to have to spell out Dick and Tim's status in Barbados. Over 300 Africans had lived free lives, many as baptised Christians, in Tudor and early Stuart England. They were paid wages, allowed to testify in court and to marry white English people. There was, however, one rule at home and another abroad. The labour demands of Caribbean plantations; the precedent set by the Spanish and Portuguese; the increasingly ready supply of enslaved labourers; and the fact that more work could be brutally extracted from them than from indentured servants: all conspired to cement African enslavement as the keystone of the English colonial economy.[27]

Though Robert Newton laid the foundations of the family's fortune in Barbados, it was his brother Samuel, Sarah's great-grandfather, who made his ambition a reality. Once in Barbados he put all his energies into developing and expanding the modest plantation he had inherited. He pursued an aggressive programme of land accumulation, growing his holdings in Christ Church parish to 581 acres by 1679.

Deeds held in the Barbados archives reveal how Samuel leveraged his connections with prominent men, collected debts in kind and preyed on others' misfortunes to acquire parcel after parcel of land and property. Sometimes he simply purchased twenty acres or so from a neighbour, using island currency – '£100 current' was roughly equal to £70 sterling – or just 'good merchandable muscovado sugar'. But other acquisitions suggest friends in high places, from Council members to Chancery Court judges.[28]

Samuel went into business with sugar merchant John Searle – probably a relation of Daniel Searle, late Parliamentarian Governor of Barbados – operating from a counting house in Oistins Bay. Embracing the latest technology, he acquired new ironware for his sugar furnaces on a trip to Derbyshire with Searle in 1664, and replaced his cattle-driven mills with windmills, which turned faster and more forcefully, extracting more juice.[29]

As his operation expanded, the number of people Samuel Newton enslaved grew in tandem, from seventy-six individuals in 1659 to 260 twenty years later. Although they left no written records, their skeletons, unearthed by archaeologists in the twentieth century, testify loud and clear to both the harrowing conditions endured, and the ways they retained elements of West African culture, while adopting new habits such as smoking tobacco.

Becoming one of the island's wealthiest men, Samuel accrued increasing social and political status. He rose from Captain in the Barbados Militia in 1659 to Colonel, leading a 434-strong 'regiment of horse', in 1680.* He served on the Barbados Council from 1672.[30] In 1676, his children's tutor – a white indentured Scotsman – praised Samuel as the best master in the island: 'in nature meek, gentle and kind and noblie generous, exceeding rich' and 'most in favour with our Governor than any'.[31]

Though considered 'a quiet man', Samuel was very particular about his position. In 1683, he complained Sir Martin Bentley had insulted him at the funeral of Lady Ann Willoughby of Parham, the widow of a former Governor. Bentley 'confessed that, owing to the crowd of coaches, his coach was before Colonel Newton's. He had, however, punished his coachman for taking place of Colonel Newton's and intended no disrespect to the Colonel or to the Council'. Samuel and his fellow councillors were satisfied but stressed: 'Sir Martin and his lady should henceforth not only know, but observe their places in the island.'[32] This preoccupation with hierarchy was common amongst Samuel's contemporaries, 'new money' keen to ape the English upper classes, but anxious about how they were viewed from the motherland. The concern was not unfounded; one observer remarked in 1655: 'A rogue in England will hardly make a cheater here. A bawd brought over puts on a demure comportment, a whore if handsome makes a wife for some rich planter.' Island hospitality was rumoured to be so 'debauched' that guests were too drunk to return home after dinner; one clergyman complained the 'inhabitants had pissed £15,000 against the wall ... by their excessive drinking'.[33]

Samuel Newton now bought his family a place in British society. He had sold his modest childhood home, Northedge Hall in Derbyshire, to his associate John Searle in the 1660s. When another Barbados enslaver,

---

* These were more honorary than active positions; the militia would be deployed only in the event of an invasion or uprising.

Newton Family Tree

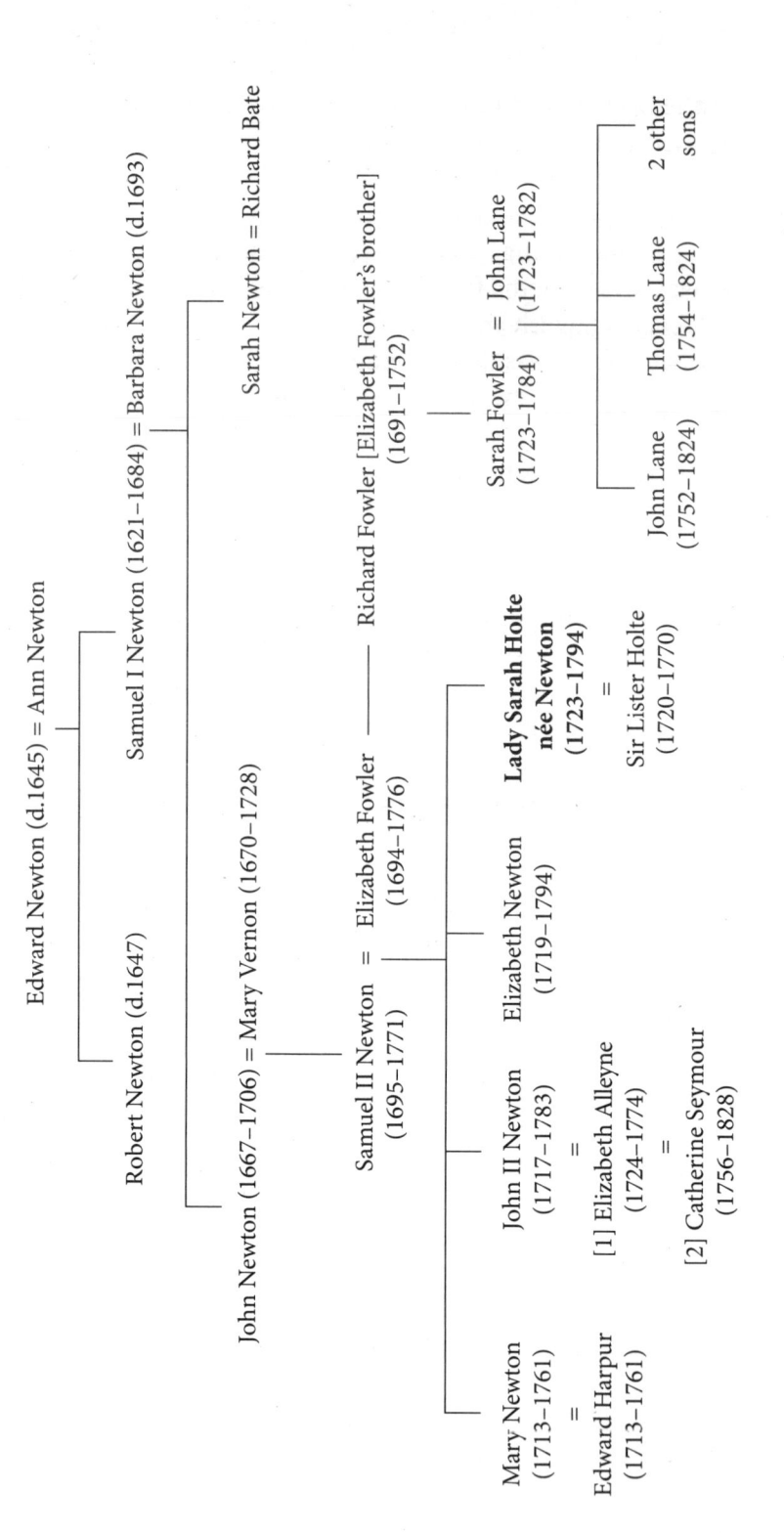

Edward Newton (d.1645) = Ann Newton

Robert Newton (d.1647)   Samuel I Newton (1621–1684) = Barbara Newton (d.1693)

Sarah Newton = Richard Bate

John Newton (1667–1706) = Mary Vernon (1670–1728)

Samuel II Newton (1695–1771) = Elizabeth Fowler (1694–1776) —— Richard Fowler [Elizabeth Fowler's brother] (1691–1752)

Elizabeth Newton (1719–1794)

Lady Sarah Holte née Newton (1723–1794) = Sir Lister Holte (1720–1770)

Sarah Fowler (1723–1784) = John Lane (1723–1782)

John Lane (1752–1824)   Thomas Lane (1754–1824)   2 other sons

Mary Newton (1713–1761) = Edward Harpur (1713–1761)

John II Newton (1717–1783) = [1] Elizabeth Alleyne (1724–1774) = [2] Catherine Seymour (1756–1828)

Charles Agard, died in 1679 owing him over £3,000, Samuel took land as payment from his executors. He acquired Kings Bromley estate near Lichfield in Staffordshire for himself, and nearby Foston in Derbyshire for his daughter Sarah and her new husband, Richard Bate.[34] Samuel died in 1684, leaving half his assets to his wife Barbara and half to their teenage son John; the family left Barbados soon after. When John died in 1706, his English and Barbados estates passed to his eleven-year-old son, Samuel.[35] It was this second Samuel Newton who was the father of our heiress Sarah, the future Lady Holte.

When Sarah Newton was born in December 1723 her chance of inheriting the family fortune seemed remote. She was the youngest of four, with two older sisters, Elizabeth and Mary, and an older brother, John. They grew up at Kings Bromley Hall, a grand neoclassical mansion her father had built to crown the Staffordshire estate, which had swelled from 130 to over 2,000 acres during the family's tenure. The 'handsome house' was considered 'a fit habitation for a gentleman'; Sarah's father Samuel's appointment as High Sheriff of Staffordshire in 1728 confirmed his place in society.[36]

However, between building such a grand home and 'the expense he has been at for some years upon his Barbados estate', Samuel had amassed debts of £4,000 by the time Sarah was a teenager, almost five times his annual income.[37] Some of his problems in Barbados were inherited; his grandmother Barbara and his father John had spent decades unsuccessfully chasing their Newton tenants for unpaid rent and compensation for the loss of several enslaved people.[38] Besides the immediate pressure on the family finances, Samuel worried about his children's futures. How would he fund dowries for three daughters?

The answer was to send his son John to Barbados to marry an heiress. Sixteen-year-old Elizabeth Alleyne was 'of respectable descent' – at least by colonial standards – from 'one of the most ancient families' on the island, known for their 'humanity and good sense'. More importantly, the Alleynes were wealthy, with extensive landholdings worked by several hundred enslaved people.[39] Samuel did not know the family personally, but his lawyer helped him strike a deal with Elizabeth's father Reynold Alleyne through a mutual friend. Not only would Elizabeth bring £6,000 to the marriage, but Reynold undertook to pay off all Samuel's debts. In return, Samuel would settle Newton plantation on John, amply supporting the young couple and their future children.

Sarah and the rest of her family found it hard to part with John, 'a young gentleman whose good qualities and natural disposition' prompted a 'tender regard' from 'all who knew him'.[40] They did not know when, or if, they would see him again. Around a third of Europeans who arrived in the Caribbean died within three years, predominantly succumbing to yellow fever or malaria.[41] But the deal had been done; John left for Barbados in the autumn of 1739.

The £6,000 Samuel received from Reynold Alleyne would provide £2,000 dowries for Sarah and each of her two sisters. Mary, who was ten years older than Sarah, made a good match in 1743, marrying Edward, third son of Sir John Harpur of Calke Abbey, Derbyshire. But neither Sarah nor Elizabeth attracted a suitor. Left at home together for the next decade, they developed a strong bond.

Sarah was thirty-two, ten years older than the average well-to-do bride, when she finally married on 30 June 1755.[42] The groom was thirty-five-year-old Sir Lister Holte of Aston Hall near Birmingham. The Holtes had been Warwickshire landowners since the fourteenth century. Sir Thomas Holte – rumoured to have killed his cook with a meat cleaver – purchased the baronetcy in 1611 from James I, who had

Portrait of Sir Lister Holte by Tilly Kettle, *c.*1763.

created the noble title of 'baronet' as a money-making scheme to offset the huge debts inherited from Elizabeth I's long-running war with Spain.

Sir Lister had attended Eton, then Magdalen College, Oxford, where the Holtes enjoyed privileged status as 'founder's kin'. 'Very good natured', he had 'a handsome face and good person'. On first meeting, he could be 'sadly awkward', but 'he mends upon knowing'. Sarah had known Sir Lister for years, probably ever since the Newtons supported his successful campaign to become Tory MP for Lichfield in 1741.

When they first met, Sir Lister was already a 'sorrowful widower', wearing a diamond ring containing a lock of his late wife's hair. Anne Legge, the Earl of Dartmouth's daughter, had come with a dowry of £12,000. Sir Lister had been 'most violently fond' of her, but she succumbed to smallpox in 1740, after just eight months of marriage.*

Sir Lister did not marry again until 1748. His second wife was Mary Harpur, sister to Sarah's brother-in-law Edward. Mary 'possessed ... all the valuable accomplishments that adorn her sex', with a dowry of £10,000 to boot. However, the second Lady Holte died of a brain haemorrhage three years later.[43]

With no children, it is surprising Sir Lister did not seek a younger woman on his third attempt at marital bliss. Sarah's £2,000 dowry paled in comparison to what his first two wives had brought to the table. However, her brother John Newton had been married fifteen years without producing any legitimate children, increasing the possibility she and her sisters might inherit the family's growing fortune.[44] John and his wife had inherited half of Mount Alleyne in St James, Barbados, from her father; her grandmother Elizabeth Hannay would soon leave her Seawells, five miles east of Newton.[45]

The Newton family wealth, accrued in Barbados and invested in the trappings of gentility in Staffordshire, had enabled Sarah to marry a baronet and become Lady Holte. Her new home, Aston Hall, set in over 300 acres of parkland, was considered 'the most superb in that neighbourhood, fit to grace the leading title of nobility'. The pleasure gardens featured a bowling green and a cottage 'tearoom' furnished with Chinese

---

* Before Edward Jenner discovered cowpox vaccination gave immunity to smallpox in 1796, the disease killed some 400,000 Europeans a year, including monarchs Mary II, Louis XV and Emperor Joseph II. It had also proved one of the Europeans' most potent weapons in colonising the Americas: alongside other common viruses such as measles and flu, smallpox killed ninety per cent of indigenous people.

chairs and a mahogany table.[46] Like so much furniture found in Britain's most affluent homes, Sarah's table was probably made from Jamaican trees felled by enslaved people – the word mahogany may derive from the Taíno word *maga* or the West African Yoruba word *oganwo*. Today, the Hall stands in the shadow of Aston Villa Football Club, built in 1897 on top of gardens Sarah would have strolled through. Her marital home will be a familiar sight to Villa fans, who stream past it on match days; her married name equally so to anyone who has ever stood in the Holte End stand.

Many heiresses were served by Black people their families brought to Britain from the Caribbean. We usually know very little about these individuals. But as John Newton ended up in court over his treatment of two people he brought to Kings Bromley from Barbados, we learn rather more. The unsavoury episode would have long-reaching repercussions for both the Newton family and the people they enslaved.

In 1754, the year before Sarah married Sir Lister Holte, John Newton returned from Barbados after an absence of fourteen years, with his wife Elizabeth and her sister Judith Alleyne. Elizabeth and Judith each brought a favourite enslaved attendant with them. John Hylas,* a young man in his early twenties, was Judith's choice. Elizabeth had chosen Betsy Newton's grandmother, Mary Revill, probably in her late thirties.[47]

This was the first and only time Sarah met anyone her family enslaved. We do not know what she made of John and Mary, but her brother later told their neighbour, poet Anna Seward, the 'Swan of Lichfield', that Africans 'were of a nature so sordid and insensible, as to render necessary a considerable degree of severity, and to make much lenity alike injurious to the indulger and the indulged'.[48] Perhaps John's wife Elizabeth also believed Mary Revill was 'insensible' to emotional pain. By insisting Mary travel with her to England, Elizabeth forcibly separated her from her teenage daughter Doll and her three younger children, fathered by a white man named Nat Saer: Mary Ann, around ten, John, who was disabled, and George, still an infant.[49]

Bringing Africans to England raised the question of whether their legal status changed on leaving colonial jurisdiction for the metropole,

---

* In classical mythology, Hylas was a favourite companion of Hercules, kidnapped by nymphs during the voyage of the *Argo*.

where English Common Law took precedence. During the Tudor period, Africans previously enslaved by the Spanish or Portuguese had become free on arrival in England. However, once the English began to enslave people in their own colonies, the concept of 'free soil' began to clash with the strongly held principle of an Englishman's right to property. There had been numerous conflicting legal decisions, but if the Newtons' right to enslave John and Mary in England was challenged, they could quote the Yorke–Talbot opinion of 1729. Attorney General Philip Yorke, 1st Earl of Hardwicke, and Solicitor General Charles Talbot had made this statement to an eager crowd of enslavers after a dinner at Lincoln's Inn. They held that an enslaved person's status *did not* change upon arrival in England; baptism *did not* confer freedom; and they *could* legally be compelled to return to the plantations.[50] Though uttered by the country's most senior lawyers, it was not an official judgment, far less statute law, as John Newton would learn to his cost.

Mary Revill and John Hylas got married on 30 December 1758 at St Chad's Church in Lichfield.[51]* Sometime after Judith Alleyne died in 1763, Hylas (presumably with Mary), 'left the Family with the consent of Mrs [Elizabeth Alleyne] Newton'. Hylas then 'lived more than a Year and a day in a free state without being claimed'; but then the Newtons demanded he return. When Hylas refused, John Newton 'found he had no power to compel him' in England but nevertheless considered legal action against his new employer, a Mr Hone, probably the painter and Royal Academy co-founder Nathaniel Hone. Hylas was baptised 'Thomas John Hylas' on 31 January 1766 at St James's, Piccadilly, Nathaniel Hone's parish church, perhaps in a renewed effort to assert his free status.[52]

Later that year, the Newtons 'forcibly carried away and transported' Mary back to Barbados without her husband's consent. Hylas did nothing for two years, fearful he might 'likewise be trepanned [trapped] and transported'. Enslavers regularly sent Africans back to the Caribbean, often for sale, when they no longer had use for them in England. In 1773, an African confined on a ship on the Thames shot himself rather than return to the Caribbean. Abolitionist poets Thomas Day and John Bicknell imagined his final thoughts in *The Dying Negro*:

---

* Marriage between two Africans in Britain was not particularly unusual in the period. The earliest known examples come from St Dunstan's and All Saints, Stepney in 1608–10. Chater, *Untold Histories*, pp. 204–5; Kaufmann, *Black Tudors*, p. 124.

... better in th'untimely grave to rot,
The world and all its cruelties forgot,
Than, dragg'd once more beyond the Western main,
To groan beneath some dastard planter's chain ...[53*]

In December 1768, John Hylas brought a case – probably of *habeas corpus*, a law protecting the individual from arbitrary imprisonment – against John Newton for damages for the loss of his wife. The ensuing legal struggle, presided over by Chief Justice Sir John Eardley Wilmot (who, ominously, counted Yorke and Talbot amongst his mentors) in the Court of Common Pleas, was about whether a husband's rights over his wife trumped an enslaver's rights over his human property, and whether the latter, legislated for in the colonies but not the mother country, remained in force in England.

Abolitionist Granville Sharp took a great interest in the case. He attended court, hoping the proceedings would help his struggle to obtain a definitive legal decision that Africans became free on arrival in England and could not be sent back to the colonies. Sharp had begun his campaign in 1765, shocked at the treatment of Jonathan Strong, an African from Barbados, whom he met outside his brother's surgery. Strong had been badly beaten by his enslaver, David Lisle, and left for dead. Sharp helped Strong get hospital treatment and a new job. When Lisle tried to sell Strong to Jamaica, Sharp successfully defended him in court – the first of a string of such victories.

John Newton's defence was mounted by his friend Sir Fletcher Norton, MP, a duplicitous character, nicknamed 'Sir Bull-Face Double-Face'.[54] He seized on the fact Hylas had asked for damages, but not Mary's return, suggesting he did not miss his wife, so did not deserve much compensation. Although the Habeas Corpus Act fixed damages at £500, 'besides treble costs', Judge Wilmot awarded Hylas only one shilling. He did, however, decree 'the defendant was bound, under a penalty, to bring back the woman, either by the first ship, or at farthest within six months'.

---

* Ironically, Day had no problem depriving orphaned English girls of their liberty; he acquired two, aged twelve and eleven in turn, from London's Foundling Hospital, and unsuccessfully tried to train them to become his perfect wife. His relationship with his eventual bride, Esther Milnes, appears to have been a classic case of coercive control. Moore, *How to Create the Perfect Wife*.

Despite this, Mary remained in what Sharp called 'unlawful confinement beyond the seas'. Did the Newtons simply refuse to allow Mary to return to England, or did she prefer to stay with her children and grandchildren in Barbados, where the family had a relatively privileged position on the plantation? Or had she heard John had a new wife? There are records of two sons born to a John and Frances Hylas in London in 1769 and 1771, one baptised at St James's, Piccadilly, where Hylas himself had been baptised.[55]

The Hylas case did not set a clear precedent – just what enslavers wanted. Lord Chief Justice Mansfield remarked in 1771: 'I don't know what the consequences may be, if masters were to lose their property by accidentally bringing their slaves to England. I hope it will never finally be discussed; for I would have all masters think them free, and all Negroes think they were not, because then they would both behave better.'[56] But Granville Sharp would not give up, and in 1772, in *Somerset v Stewart*, Lord Mansfield ruled deportation illegal. Though he tried to make his judgment only narrowly applicable, it was widely misinterpreted as freeing all Africans in England.

It was whispered that Sarah called the shots in her marriage. According to a later family chronicler, 'though not an old man', Sir Lister 'yielded himself more and more to the influence and management of his wife'. A concrete sign of her ascendancy came in 1768, when *she* chose a neighbour and friend from Staffordshire, Ralph Pickstock, as the new steward for Sir Lister's estates; the faithful retainer remained in her service until her death.

Sir Lister and his younger brother, Charles, had been inseparable when they were younger. But Charles blamed Sarah for the rift that now developed between them. Lamenting 'the many instances I have lately received of the loss of your affection', he even questioned whether Sir Lister cared 'where I lived or if I lived at all'. Soon Charles 'was in the habit of entering the dining room when Lady Holte withdrew'.

Taking Charles and his wife Anne's side, the later family chronicler – descended from their side of the family – called Sarah 'haughty, cold and selfish', while Anne's 'high spirits and keen wit ... could ill brook the assumption of superiority indulged in by Lady Holte.' Even at the time, a family friend contrasted 'the complacency of the temper of one and the violence of the other'.[57] Anne was from an old Warwickshire family.[58]

It seems possible that Sarah, insecure about her family background, jealously guarded and asserted her newfound status as a baronet's wife as strongly as her great-grandfather had insisted on his carriage going ahead in a funeral procession.

The birth of a daughter, Mary Elizabeth, to Charles and Anne in 1757 seems only to have heightened the tension. Sarah and Sir Lister had no children. In an era where many married women were almost constantly pregnant, this may indicate Sarah suffered from infertility or endured a series of miscarriages. Though, as neither of Sir Lister's previous wives had provided an heir, *he* may have been the infertile one. Nonetheless, women were usually blamed; perhaps Sarah envied her sister-in-law's 'success'.

The crisis came in May 1758, when Sir Lister disinherited his infant niece in favour of his first wife's nephew, Heneage Legge. If Legge had no sons, another nephew, Lewis Bagot, would inherit, and if his line failed, Wriothesley Digby, the son of an old family friend, would become the residuary heir. Heneage Legge had apparently overtaken Lewis Bagot in the running 'owing to him being a married man', and having 'married the woman Lister liked'.

Charles and Anne were sure Sir Lister had 'been induced to make this unjust disposition' by Sarah. The will certainly accorded significant power to her and her family. Sarah and her brother John were both named as executors, alongside their relative, lawyer Fettisplace Nott.[59]

In 1769, Sarah and Sir Lister travelled to Bath in hopes of a cure for his failing health, probably staying at 9, the Circus, her brother John Newton's prestigious new address. But by the time they returned to Aston in early March 1770, Sir Lister was 'far advanced in a dropsy, his legs, thighs and every surface of his body greatly swelled and distended with water'. His doctors had 'slight punctures' made in his legs to drain the liquid. For three weeks after he returned home, this treatment seemed to be working; the swellings subsided, and his strength and appetite returned. But then 'every prospect of relief almost suddenly and entirely vanished, the discharge of water became immense, his strength entirely exhausted, and every effort of constitution to assist him failed'. Sir Lister died on Sunday 8 April. Sarah's brother John and sister Elizabeth were by her side, but she hardly saw anyone else. Her friend John Ash reported: 'Poor Lady Holte although she continues much indisposed, is better than she was the first three days; as her late husband might be said to be absolutely dying for four or five days ... the shock was the less alarming'.[60]

Even as he lay on his deathbed, Sir Lister refused to see his brother. They had not spoken since Sir Lister refused Charles financial support in a 'cruel manner' two years before. Anne had desperately tried to reopen communications, but concluded she had 'offended past forgiveness, and that an intercourse of even distant civilities cannot be restored.' By this time, Sir Lister's silence may not have been entirely voluntary. His ill health and residence in John Newton's house both gave Sarah more sway; one acquaintance questioned whether his doctor was 'one of his bodyguards'.[61]

Sarah did very well from Sir Lister's will. She was to have an annuity of £1,500 a year, Aston Hall and its park, with five adjoining meadows, their furniture, wines, spirits, horses and carriages, most of the jewellery and £1,000 cash. She spent little time at Aston, preferring Kings Bromley Hall, now home to her widowed mother and her sister Elizabeth. She became such a frequent visitor that a room there was still known as 'Lady Holte's Bedchamber' in 1869.[62]

At forty-seven, Sarah was now independent, powerful and wealthy in her own right. But on New Year's Day 1773 she was horrified to learn Heneage Legge, Lewis Bagot and Wriothesley Digby had applied to Chancery to render Sir Lister's will null and void.[63] As executors, she and her brother John would have to defend their position in court.

It soon became clear Charles and Anne, now Sir Charles and Lady Anne, were behind the suit. Sir Charles had inherited the baronetcy, 8,000 acres around Aston Hall, his brother's library, and a £10,000 dowry for his daughter Mary Elizabeth. But it was a terrible blow that, after Sir Charles's death, Mary Elizabeth's future children would be passed over in favour of Legge, Bagot and Digby. Local antiquary William Hutton, in his 1783 *History of Birmingham*, decried the disinheritance as 'one of the most unaccountable assignments that ever resulted from human weakness.' He imagined the ghost of Sir Lister visiting Aston Hall, meeting 'repeated buffetings' from generations of 'shades' of his 'venerable ancestors', for, 'in one fatal moment' 'barring, unprovoked, an infant heiress of £7,000 a year, and giving it, unsolicited, to a stranger, having failed to produce his own issue', through his 'own imbecility'. These sentiments, according to Hutton, 'exactly coincide with those of the world'.[64]

Adding insult to injury, Lady Anne found it 'mortifying' only £200 had been added to her existing jointure – the annual allowance she was set to receive after her husband's death – whereas any future wife might have £700. She and Sir Charles resented Sarah not allowing them to live at Aston Hall, while leaving the grounds 'in such a condition one would imagine it a common.' They also found it suspect the will left nothing to Sir Lister's other relations, but a codicil added just two days before his death left a legacy of £200 to Sarah's sister Elizabeth. They persuaded Legge, Bagot and Digby to object to this provision, as well as demanding Sarah pay off Sir Lister's substantial debts and her annuity be reduced.[65] These measures would not directly benefit the couple; this was vengeance.

Sarah sought assistance from her second cousin, John Lane, a barrister at Lincoln's Inn, who insisted, 'for God's sake my Dear Lady H: Despise them and make their malice the object of your laughter, for believe me your affairs are too well sure to be affected by their rancorous baseness of heart'. Despite her friends' and family's efforts to comfort her, Sarah fretted about the case for over two years, increasingly preoccupied by petty details. John Lane advised against trying to reclaim a favourite pearl necklace.

Eventually, in March 1775, Sarah received the good news that 'every particular wherein your Ladyship is at all interested or concerned is fully settled in your favour and nothing remains from which any future disputes can arise.'[66] However, there would soon be a new family conflict, leading to a most distressing scandal. It would also make Sarah and Elizabeth more likely to inherit the Barbados estates. Following Elizabeth Hannay and Judith Alleyne's deaths, these now comprised Newton, Seawells and all of Mount Alleyne.

In February 1774, John's wife, Elizabeth Alleyne Newton, died of gangrene, after refusing an amputation.[67] The couple had no living children.[68] John was fifty-seven, 'an elderly man' according to one servant. If he died without an heir, his assets would go to Sarah and her sister Elizabeth (their elder sister Mary Harpur had died in 1761). However, John soon 'formed a great affection' for Catherine Seymour, the nineteen-year-old daughter of Lord Francis Seymour, Dean of Wells, and married her in June 1776. He was forty years her senior, 'a quiet sober sort'; she a lively, 'free and flighty' teenager.[69] Besides the mismatch in age and temperament, John Newton was punching above his weight socially. Catherine was the Duke of Somerset's granddaughter and could trace her ancestors back to the brothers of Henry VIII's third wife, Jane Seymour. This was the most illustrious connection the Newtons had bought with their Barbados profits yet, but it would cause far more trouble than it was worth.[70]

Unlike her Holte relations, Catherine seemed to warm to Sarah immediately. When the newlyweds visited Aston Hall, the two women spent several evenings chatting by the fire in Sarah's dressing room. Sarah showed Catherine 'many marks of friendship and civility'. On their departure, she produced 'most excellent cider' and some 'inimitable poultry' for the journey; Catherine declared, 'I never anatomised a chicken with so good a glee in my life.' Sarah insisted they keep in touch. Catherine's letters professed 'the truest Affec[tion] & most unfeign'd Friendship'; pouring out 'effusions of regard with which my bosom is fill'd.' She even wrote an ode to Sarah ending: 'How much O Holte you all your sex excel!'[71]

Catherine was keen for Sarah to visit her at Spettisbury House in Dorset, 'an elegant Mansion House … fit for a Nobleman's family' John Newton had owned since 1761.[72] She tried to entice her with the prospect of visiting the Glastonbury Abbey ruins, and the opportunity to have her portrait painted by miniaturist Thomas Redmond. Sarah had visited Spettisbury in the past, but she did not make the journey to see Catherine. At the end of 1776, John put the house up for sale. He had decided to move to Kings Bromley Hall following his mother's death earlier that year. On Christmas Day, Catherine wrote to Sarah that they were leaving Dorset, but 'the prospect of scenes as delightful in Staffordshire … particularly augmented by the enjoyment of your society & that of the worthy Eliza's' provided consolation.

But before that happy reunion could take place, John and Catherine decided to spend the first few months of 1777 in Bath. Catherine continued to beg her 'beloved sister' Sarah to visit, exclaiming: 'were I with you I would kneel to solicit you, & never rise till you had granted my request. – Indeed, my dear sister (I think I hear you say) you might walk upon your knees all your life time if that was the case.'

As Catherine had anticipated, her invitation was not accepted and by the end of January, she had 'given up the hope, tho with reluctance of seeing you anywhere but at Aston.' Her efforts to persuade her other sister-in-law Elizabeth to visit were equally unsuccessful. One reason for Sarah's reluctance may have been a bout of ill health. Catherine was 'extremely Anxious' when she heard about this 'feverish complaint'. She feared Sarah was 'a little like your dear Brother – Too inattentive to yourself. – I hope you have proper advice – & remember you do not live merely for yourself.'[73]

Why was Catherine so keen to have her much older sisters-in-law to stay? It certainly seems odd given how other evidence suggests she was spending her time. According to John Newton, at Spettisbury, Catherine:

> showed by her conduct and behaviour that she was a woman of loose and vicious disposition who took and allowed liberties with other men and she became improperly and intimately connected with several gentlemen in the neighbourhood.

When they moved to Bath, she 'became even more open in her vicious indiscreet and improper behaviour such as walking arm in arm and singing with people of lower station.' Gossips feasted on her overfamiliarity with Mr Brett, a singer, and Mr Dash, a riding master.

Such behaviour was extremely concerning; as Dr Samuel Johnson put it, 'the chastity of women' was 'of the utmost importance, as all property depends upon it'. Besides the blow to his heart, a cuckold must live with the nagging doubt that his heir might be another man's son. When the Bastard's legitimacy in Shakespeare's *King John* is questioned, he exclaims: 'Heaven guard my mother's honour – and my land!'[74]

Sarah enquired whether Catherine had any 'marvellous' news, trying to pin down exactly what her sister-in-law was doing. But Catherine's letters revealed nothing untoward. She mentioned Mr Brett only once – she was 'much pleas'd' with his 'sweet harmonious voice' – but emphasised her husband's Barbados friend, John Charnock, had introduced them, giving the connection an air of respectability. Catherine insisted she was 'obliged' to go out for the sake of politeness, only seeing company and returning visits 'Heaven knows thro' necessity!' She protested she was: 'a very unfashionable Creature ... for I never dance, never play cards, never saunter about the Town of a morning, never go to the Pump room, never sit & abuse my neighbours, never do anything to make people talk of me'. Catherine wrote tenderly of John, 'my dear N.', and 'all his excellencies'. It was 'my duty as well as inclination to accommodate myself to his pleasure', and to look after his health, partly 'for the sake of his dear and valuable sisters'.[75] Nevertheless, her father Lord Seymour told John he was 'very uneasy at her behaviour' and encouraged him to restrain her.

After Catherine and John moved to Kings Bromley Hall in April 1777, Sarah could observe the young woman's behaviour for herself. She continued to stay there regularly; the Newtons visited Aston at least once. That summer, Catherine was observed in compromising situations with her footman Isaac Hatheway; Thomas Cope, the new coachman; and Isham Baggs, a young gentleman studying at Merton College, Oxford, whom John Newton had 'brought up and educated at his own expense, from his infancy'. Baggs's room had an interconnecting door with Catherine's; the housekeeper often saw them lying on Baggs's bed 'toying and playing together'. She was convinced 'the connection and intercourse between them was of a criminal nature'.

By early October, Sarah was also sure Catherine had been unfaithful. It was one thing to cede the family fortune to her own nephew or niece; quite another to risk it going to a child fathered by Baggs, or even worse, a servant. After Sarah broke the news to her brother in a letter, he immediately sacked Thomas Cope, sent Baggs back to Oxford and arranged for Catherine to be placed in a French convent, with a quarterly allowance of £100.[76]

The Newtons were doing everything in their power to avoid a public scandal. But Catherine forced John's hand by returning from France and persuading her father to apply for a legal restoration of conjugal rights. The appeal accused John of cruelty and improper behaviour. John retaliated with the help of his second cousins, John Lane and his brother Thomas Lane, also a

Catherine Newton with Isham Baggs as depicted in *The Trial of the Hon. Mrs Catherine Newton.*

lawyer. He accused Catherine of adultery, lining up a handful of servants as witnesses.

Scandal was now unavoidable. Such proceedings were still relatively rare, and the press loved reporting every titillating detail.[77] A scurrilous pamphlet, *The Trial of the Hon. Mrs Catherine Newton*, covered the story at such length it came in two parts. The *Ramblers' Magazine* imagined Catherine insatiably switching between multiple lovers, explaining: 'I chose to have more than one in my suite, for the same reason I kept a larder, that I might not be disappointed in always having something that pleased me.'

The writer then slipped into the realms of pornographic fantasy. He imagined Catherine leaning out of her bedroom window in Bath one day, catching the eye of Thomas Cope and Isaac Hatheway below. Isaac encouraged his friend:

> Tom, now is your time, if you have a mind to make a bold push – she has been this hour impatiently waiting for the actor, and I am positive you can supply his place entirely to my Lady's satisfaction – for, poor gentleman, she has made him rehearse so often that his pipe is almost sore.

Cope hurried to her room and 'boldly made an attempt – *a la levrette* [from the French for female greyhound; from behind]', as she was still leaning out the window. Catherine, 'not insensible or displeased at this unexpected attack', cried:

> 'Heavens! who is that?' 'Only your man, Thomas' replied the coachman. 'Oh, very well,' resumed Mrs N_n, 'drive on, coachman.'[78]

When Catherine gave birth to a son on 22 November 1780 John brought another case to ensure the boy could not inherit. Over thirty witnesses, including Catherine's sister, agreed she and John had not seen each other since separating in 1777. Furthermore, John's two doctors, his butler and his housekeeper confirmed he had been in such a 'debilitated state of body' since the winter of 1779 that he could hardly climb the stairs, let alone father a child. The Newtons were sure the father was John Acland, a captain in the militia quartered at Wells.[*][79] Sarah was doubtless of one

---

* Acland would later reject Catherine to marry Jamaican heiress Elizabeth Fuller.

mind with her sister Elizabeth, who later vowed: 'not a farthing shall go to that nasty little Bastard ... as he was no more my Brother's child than he was mine.'[80]

The Court granted separation from 'bed and board', but John did not obtain a full divorce by Act of Parliament until May 1782. However, Catherine's son was not officially disinherited. Though the Lord Chancellor, Lord Thurlow, denounced her conduct, he thought it unfair that a 'guiltless infant', 'born in wedlock', should be left with nothing.

John Newton died eighteen months after the divorce. In his will, he repeated that Catherine's son 'was and is a Bastard', enjoining Sarah and Elizabeth to 'withstand to the utmost all attempts which may be made to set up the said child'.[81] The sisters had it inscribed in stone that John 'died without issue' on his memorial in Kings Bromley church. The statement was of the utmost importance to them. For Sarah and Elizabeth now became their brother's heiresses, jointly inheriting Newton and Seawells plantations in Barbados.*

Sarah and Elizabeth now 'owned' 430 men, women and children. Their brother John had always insisted 'the purchase, employment, and strict discipline of the negroes were absolutely necessary to maintain our empire, and our commerce in the indies'. By the 1780s, however, abolitionist ideas were gathering momentum. John, and quite possibly his sisters, had found it necessary to assure their friends 'accounts of the cruelties practised upon the slaves by their masters was [sic] false, or at least infinitely exaggerated.' Rather, 'the high price and value of the subjugated, inevitably preserves them from the dire consequences of this imputed barbarity'. If anything, enslavers always insisted *they* had more to fear. Sarah and Elizabeth knew the cautionary tale of their Lichfield neighbour Charles Ashwell. A 'hapless wreck of negro cruelty', he had lost an arm and two fingers aged fourteen when his uncle was murdered by the people he enslaved in Grenada, despite his 'compassionate temper'.[82]

However, the skeletons unearthed by archaeologists at Newton tell a different story. Human remains were first discovered at Newton in the mid-twentieth century, by workers planting casuarina trees. Local people had long known where the 'old people' were buried. A team of

---

* Mount Alleyne in St James was returned to the Alleyne family.

archaeologists arrived to investigate in 1972; they uncovered bones barely two centimetres deep on their very first day.[83] They also found coffin handles, brass buttons, tobacco pipes, jewellery and other artefacts. Newton Burial Ground appears today to the uninitiated eye to be just a gently sloping field, the crest of the hill dotted with trees. However, beneath lies the largest undisturbed plantation cemetery ever found. Many burial sites have been destroyed by modern farming methods, but Newton was never ploughed due to shallow soil and limestone lying just below the surface. An estimated 570 people were buried at Newton. In 1972 and 1973, 104 skeletons were disinterred; remains of forty-six further individuals were exhumed and analysed in 1997 and 1998.

The archaeologists' conclusions are made all the more chilling by their precise scientific language. The evidence 'does not support Newton as a healthy population', even in comparison to other African diaspora examples. Rather 'extreme stress, particularly for Newton females, is evidenced by the lowest relative mean age at death of any diaspora skeletal sample': just 19.97 years, in comparison to estimates of 34.3 in Europe and 26.4 in Africa (a figure thought to have been higher before European contact).[84]

Written records dating mostly from the late eighteenth to early nineteenth century confirm enslaved people at Newton rarely died of old age. Instead, they predominantly succumbed to tuberculosis, dropsy, dysentery, leprosy and measles.[85] Of course, these diseases were also common amongst white populations in the Caribbean and Europe – Sir Lister had died of dropsy. However, enslaved Africans died younger, and in far greater numbers, due to overwork, hunger and poor living conditions. Or, as one plantation doctor commented, 'It is not an unusual thing to lose in one year ... ten, twelve, nay, as far as twenty' out of 180 labourers, 'by fevers, fluxes, dropsies, the effect of too much work, and too little food and care.'[86]

The hospital at Newton was 'a horrid unhealthy hole most ill-contrived', where 'men & women are most indecently mixed together, with other detestable circumstances.' However, as one Newton overseer observed, it was 'impossible to tell when a person is sick or not except he be really ill' and so 'for fear of accident, they are confined [in the hospital] till they profess themselves ready to work again'.[87] Spending time in a plantation hospital often made patients worse; others were subjected to medical experiments using methods that would not have been countenanced in Britain.[88]

Many skeletons had lower limb and other traumatic injuries. Three-quarters had evidence of pulling and tearing of muscle attachments; twenty-five per cent had hernias. Whereas sugar cane harvesters today wear metal shin guards, people at Newton sustained 'skin lacerations ... easily caused by sharp and rusty tools', while 'leg abrasions and lesions, including those from yaws,* could become further infected as workers kneeled in the dirt to dig and plant young cane'.[89] It was hard for exhausted, overworked and underfed labourers to focus on the task in hand for hours on end, day and night. At Newton in 1693, one man 'in the night walking over the worm tubs [so named for the coiled tubes used to distil rum] happened to slip in & scald himself', which 'affected his bowels'. Although 'all care was taken', he died two weeks later.[90]

Dental evidence shows enslaved people were chronically malnourished and suffered episodic starvation. Many had lost teeth; most showed signs of advanced gum disease and tooth decay, likely caused by chewing cane and drinking black strap molasses.

Unusually, Newton had no provision grounds – allotments for food crops – so people could only grow small amounts of things to eat by their houses. The workforce subsisted largely on a diet of lentils, pigeon peas, some fish and seafood and salted meat. The lack of major rivers and scattered springs on the island meant that, while white Barbadians used cisterns and wells, enslaved people were compelled to drink from ponds, sometimes sharing this stagnant, probably contaminated, water with livestock.[91]

Some were so hungry they resorted to eating dirt. Formally known as geophagy, this practice – recorded by Hippocrates and still around today – was common amongst enslaved people in the Americas. Several individuals at Newton, like Sue in 1791, were labelled: 'dirt eater'.[92] Geophagy is associated with extreme hunger – giving the feeling of a full stomach – and an effort to obtain sufficient iron and minerals, especially during pregnancy. However, soil might be contaminated with lead, bacteria, hookworm or other parasites, causing digestive problems and stomach disorders.[93]

With a crude birth rate of just 0.037, there was no natural increase in the enslaved population. This low fertility resulted from poor nutrition, 'high pathogen load' (evidence of infection), environmental toxins (lead,

---

* Yaws is an infectious disease that affects the skin, bones and cartilage, causing disfiguring raspberry- or cauliflower-shaped lesions and swellings.

from contaminated rum) and 'devastating physical and psychosocial stresses'.[94] These dire outcomes are the logical consequence of a system made profitable by literally working people to death. As enslaved people observed, 'Buckra* make whip do every ting, but make life, and that it no able to do, but it make plenty dead.'[95]

Nevertheless, the people of Newton made lives for themselves despite the appalling conditions. Their remains, and objects found alongside them, reveal glimpses of their cultural and daily experiences, including practices surviving from West Africa. Smoking was ubiquitous; archaeologists found many pipe fragments and twenty-one whole pipes, plus pipe wear on forty per cent of teeth. Wearing beads was popular; 900 were found at Newton. As one Welsh clergyman and naturalist observed in 1750: 'our slaves, in their mirth and diversions, differ according to the several customs of so many nations intermixed. However, all agree in this one universal custom of adorning their bodies, by wearing strings of beads of various colours ... twined round their arms, necks, and legs.'

Thirty per cent of the skeletons were African-born, originating from at least three different areas in modern-day Ghana, Senegal and the Gambia. Five individuals had filed or intentionally chipped teeth – modifications traditionally practised in many parts of Africa for decorative and or group identity purposes, sometimes as a rite of passage. One young woman had been buried face down in a large mound of earth, far from the others; treatment meted out in West Africa to those ostracised for witchcraft or suicide. By contrast, a Ghanaian style pipe, a knife, bracelets, rings and a necklace were found alongside the skeleton of a fifty-year-old man, suggesting he was a highly respected healer and diviner. His necklace, of a style traditionally worn by Asante priests, was made of twenty-one drilled dogs' teeth, fourteen European glass beads, seven cowrie shells and five drilled fish vertebrae. The central carnelian bead would have come all the way from Khambhat in southern India. Both carnelian and cowrie shells had deep sacred significance, imbuing the wearer with spiritual powers.[96]

On 7 June 1784, Sarah and Elizabeth's attorney Sir John Gay Alleyne (Elizabeth Alleyne Newton's second cousin) appraised Newton and Seawells for them.[97] The valuation, four pages of neat italic writing sent

---

* 'Buckra' meant master/white man, derived from the Ibibio-Efik (languages spoken in modern-day Nigeria) word *'mbakara'*, originally meaning demon.

back to England, now in a London archive, is dominated by the listed names and purported values of men, women and children, the total amounts writ large with a flourish by the team of three local appraisers. They concluded Newton's 454 acres, 'with the ruined buildings thereon', were worth £13,620; the 242 people enslaved there: £7,448 10s. With the addition of fifty-seven cattle, twenty-four calves and eleven sheep, the whole estate was valued at £21,716. Similar calculations were made to assess Seawells, where 188 people worked 342 acres. The grand total came to £37,495.[98]

Recent natural and man-made disasters had severely affected the properties' value. The buildings had been ruined by a devastating hurricane in 1780, which 'destroyed every vestige of a house, garden, trees and every other pleasurable object'.[99] The American Revolution had disrupted trade, causing not only shortages of food and supplies, but also of new labour. The numbers of captive Africans arriving in Barbados dropped dramatically from 879 in 1775 to a mere seven individuals in 1778. These factors combined had a serious impact on the bottom line. The estates sustained losses of £1,362 in 1783 and £3,657 the following year.[100]

Sarah and Elizabeth could have gleaned some fragmentary information from the valuations about the individuals who toiled on their behalf. At Newton, Old Toby and his son Little Toby were smiths; Tomboy and Mingo were watchmen; the cook was called Monday; a man named Ned worked alongside him in the house; Julias and Peter were stable hands. Tom Rogers was a carter; Jack Tom minded cattle, while another Ned cared for calves. The drivers of the three gangs* were Saboy, Robin and Dicky; another Old Toby made baskets. Skilled men specialised in each stage of sugar production: mill-feeder Billy; Peter the boilerman; Pauly the distiller; clarifiers Reynold and James; and Old Sambo the clayer. One man named Minimas was 'absent', perhaps having escaped permanently as he was listed without a value.

At Seawells, Jeffry was the ranger (head officer); Quan a boiler, Joe a carpenter; Peter, William and Dick Mingo were coopers; Dick, Frank, Nick and another Jeffry were masons; Will was a joiner, Mingo the cook and Jack the butler. Betty and Grace worked in the house, Rose cooked for the children, Judy cared for the calves. Ben, Cudjoe, Nick and Obbo

---

* Labourers were divided into three groups who worked on various tasks depending on their age and strength.

were watchmen, Bacchus a carter and Sandy, Ayon and a woman named Matty were drivers. Matty was probably too old for field labour and so oversaw the third gang, made up of children aged roughly between six and fourteen, who did lighter work such as weeding or collecting fodder for animals.[101]

Though they did not have access to the forensic analysis of modern archaeologists, Sarah and Elizabeth could see several people were unwell or injured. At Newton, Peter, who worked in the stable, was 'unhealthy', as was Dublin. Bristol had a lame hand, Saboy was 'infirm', Jack, Addo, Rittah and Merindah had leprosy. Molly G was a 'cripple', and several others were so old they were described as 'superannuated', and listed with a market value of £0. At Seawells, Phebe and Nanny were sick nurses, Prince, Natt and a boy named Frank were lepers, Bessey consumptive and James, Gallipah and Sary 'superannuated'.

Did Sarah and Elizabeth notice the absence of Mary Hylas, whom they had known in England for the better part of a decade? Mary had been 'infirm' in 1783 and so probably died shortly before the valuation was made, quite likely of tuberculosis, which ran in her family. Reunited with her four children, Doll, Mary Ann, John and George, in 1766, she had become the matriarch of a relatively privileged extended family, many of mixed heritage, 'better used than the generality of Slaves'. They even, one overseer remarked, had 'a kind of right to be idle'.[102] Was this preferential treatment linked to residual guilt about failing to return Mary to England?

Mary's eldest daughter, Doll was now in her late fifties, with five grown-up children, including Betsy, who would later flee to England. Betsy had been named after Elizabeth Alleyne Newton, who 'before her death' sent her 'a present of a ring'. Doll worked in the kitchen and had recently become plantation midwife, initially receiving 6s 3d for each delivery. But from 1784 the payment was two gallons of rum per birth; a pragmatic move as the island had a huge excess since exports had been curtailed during the war.

Like Doll, the rest of Mary Hylas's daughters and granddaughters officially had domestic roles. As they had 'not learnt to do anything', however, they remained 'at leisure'. Records from the 1770s show them receiving items such as shoes, hats and special cloth. This was particularly significant given – despite the sanitised images in many artworks of the period, including this book's cover image – many enslaved people wore minimal clothing and most went barefoot.

Hylas Family Tree

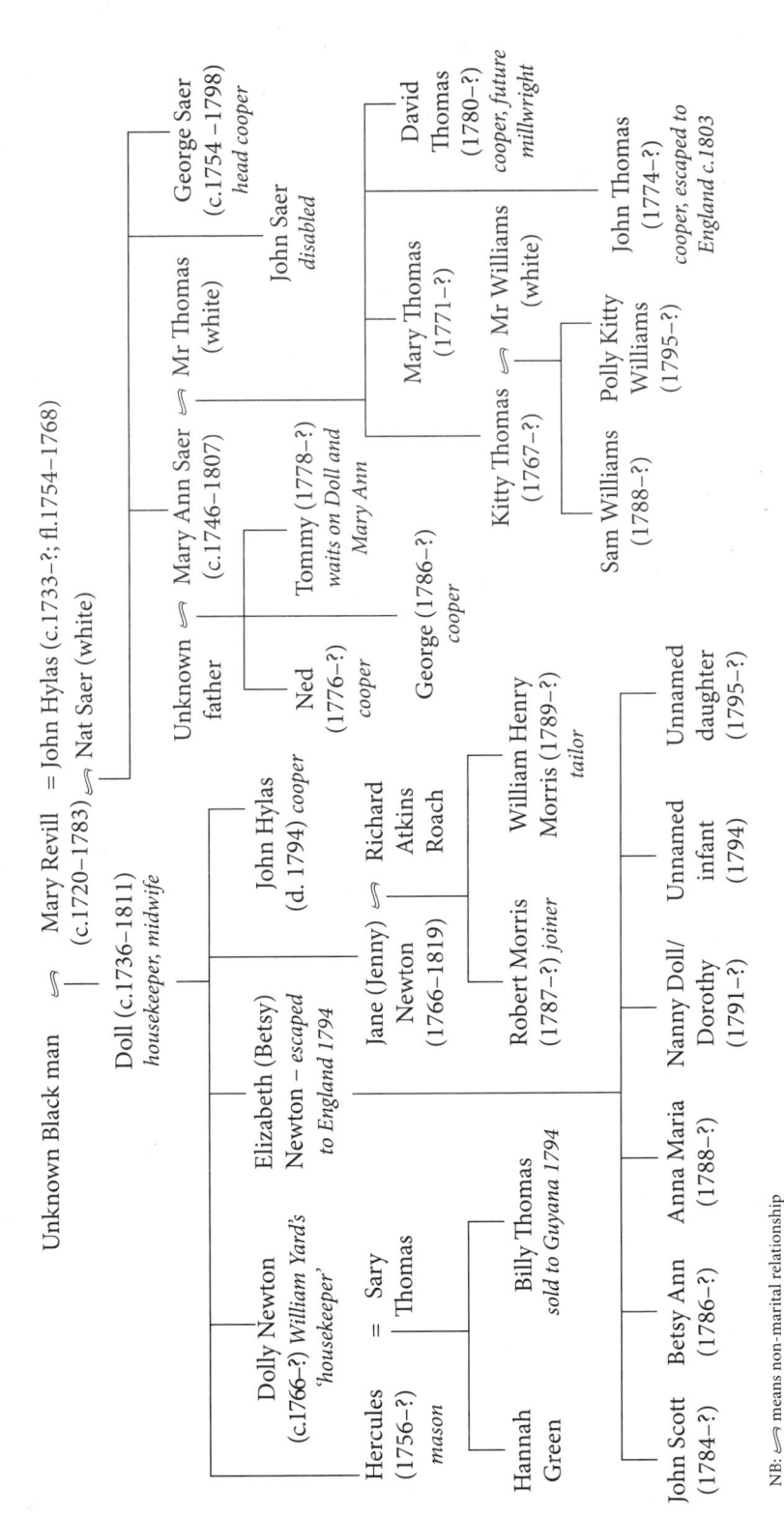

Unknown Black man ↶ Mary Revill (c.1720–1783) = John Hylas (c.1733–?; fl.1754–1768) ↶ Nat Saer (white)

- Doll (c.1736–1811) *housekeeper, midwife*
  - (with Unknown father)
    - Ned (1776–?) *cooper*
    - Tommy (1778–?) *waits on Doll and Mary Ann*
  - Mary Ann Saer (c.1746–1807) ↶ Mr Thomas (white)
    - George (1786–?) *cooper*
    - Mary Thomas (1771–?)
      - David Thomas (1780–?) *cooper, future millwright*
      - Kitty Thomas (1767–?) ↶ Mr Williams (white)
        - Sam Williams (1788–?)
        - Polly Kitty Williams (1795–?)
      - John Thomas (1774–?) *cooper, escaped to England c.1803*
  - George Saer (c.1754–1798) *head cooper*
  - John Saer *disabled*

- Elizabeth (Betsy) Newton – *escaped to England 1794*
  - Dolly Newton (c.1766–?) *William Yard's 'housekeeper'*
    - Hercules (1756–?) *mason* = Sary Thomas
      - Billy Thomas *sold to Guyana 1794*
      - Hannah Green
        - John Scott (1784–?)
        - Betsy Ann (1786–?)
        - Anna Maria (1788–?)
        - Nanny Doll/ Dorothy (1791–?)
        - Unnamed infant (1794)
        - Unnamed daughter (1795–?)
  - John Hylas (d. 1794) *cooper*
  - Jane (Jenny) Newton (1766–1819) ↶ Richard Atkins Roach
    - Robert Morris (1787–?) *joiner*
    - William Henry Morris (1789–?) *tailor*

NB: ↶ means non-marital relationship

Doll and her younger half-sister Mary Ann Saer even 'had the privilege of a slave to wait upon them': Mary Ann's son Tommy. They claimed his services because when Mary Ann's white father Nat Saer died, he bequeathed a woman named Esther to care for their disabled brother John Saer. Despite opposition from his heir-at-law, 'Esther became the property of Mary Ann and her family, and consequently of their owners', as, in time, did her twelve children and grandchildren.

The men of the family were skilled craftsmen, with better working conditions and greater freedom of movement than field labourers. Mary Hylas and Nat Saer's other son, cooper George Saer, was 'an excellent workman in his own trade – a good carpenter – almost a good anything – always at work, always willing, and always ready and good humoured – strictly honest and sober.'

Some of Mary Hylas's descendants, listed in the 1784 valuation made when Sarah and her sister inherited Newton plantation.

During most of Sarah and Elizabeth's ownership, the Hylas clan retained their relatively privileged status. After William Yard became overseer at Newton in 1782, he began a sexual relationship with Betsy's sister Dolly.[103] He also grew fond of Betsy's nephew Billy Thomas, who became his personal attendant. Billy was 'in great confidence with his Master & trusted with everything, even lay in his chamber' – perhaps suggesting a sexual element to Yard's favouritism. This physical proximity to Yard allowed the family access to plantation storehouses. They took 'dry goods, rum, sugar, and other commodities' both for their own use, and to sell at Sunday markets, probably through Betsy's husband, a huckster. Reportedly 'all the family except George Saer, were concerned in these Rogueries'. Yard, a 'large heavy fat man', who enjoyed his drink, was either oblivious or simply didn't care.

Appalled, a later manager exclaimed: 'Good God! What supine indolence it must have been that this pilfering work could be carried on and Mr Yard not find it out for so long a time.' Conversely, enslaved people applauded the widespread habit of appropriating goods. He who could 'rob the most without being detected was the best fellow … for a thief to steal from a thief makes God laugh.'[104]

Beyond the requisitioning of rum and provisions, 'dances, cockfights, gaming tables were plenty in the Estate … and Every relaxation and debauchery.' This included sexual exploitation of enslaved women, extending far beyond Yard's relationship with Dolly. Most women in the Hylas family, according to one overseer, 'either have or have had white husbands, that is men who keep them'. The broader phenomenon is confirmed by archaeologists finding five to ten per cent European admixture in the Newton population's genetic makeup. Three young skeletons had dental stigmata indicating congenital syphilis; an estimated ten per cent of children were born with venereal disease.[105]

The Newton overseer's likening of these arrangements to marriage – using the word 'husband' – should not lull us into romanticising the coercive reality. Jamaican enslaver Thomas Thistlewood recorded drunken parties where a man got 'beastly drunk and wanted to force Rose', while another, being 'in Liquor', 'went to the Negroe house and had Little Lydde in Jenny's house'.[106]

Yard's negligence went beyond his 'relaxed discipline'. What his successor blamed him for the '<u>most</u>' – a word he underlined – was the estate's bad 'condition and repair'. His 'method of planting was wrong', exposing young canes to extreme heat in the dry season. He had allowed soil erosion and let buildings and equipment deteriorate. He left the boiling house 'in a very poor predicament', with ill-maintained coppers. Equally, the blacksmith's shop had not been maintained properly; the tubs for distilling rum were in terrible condition.[107]

Yard also neglected workers' houses. Poorly maintained accommodation had devastating consequences for their health. Samuel Smith grew up in housing formerly inhabited by enslaved people in Antigua. He recalled the roof had so many holes they could only 'cork the big ones and leave the smaller holes to whistle when the wind would blow … we would generally get wet when it rain'. The floors rotted, leaving only earth beneath. That earth was 'full of jiggers' (mite larva), which burrowed 'into the feet of the person and keep them from walking properly'. The houses were so rat-infested 'you would have to wrap up your feet at night', and 'babies could not be left alone'. Scorpions lurked in clothes, their sting sometimes deadly, and lice were so prevalent that 'at every stroke of the comb the lice would ... drop like falling rain'. There was no privacy, and so 'good or bad was practiced openly. Picknee could not escape the open vice ... so a young gal usually start to have children at age thirteen'. Smith reflected: 'we used to live together like a flock of cattle ... there was no difference to speak of between the life of animals and ours'. Though 'we got used to it. Only now, I can say it was hell, living hell and more than that.'[108]

An ocean away, Sarah and Elizabeth blithely continued their genteel lives in the palatial surroundings of Aston Hall and Kings Bromley Hall. From the perspective of profit, all seemed in order. A couple of years after the American Revolutionary War, their income from Barbados began to recover. Average profits of over £3,000 a year compared very favourably as a return on investment with those reaped both in Barbados and across the British Caribbean.[109]

Although Sir John Gay Alleyne maintained he had 'studied' to fulfil his responsibilities to Sarah and Elizabeth to the best of his 'ability & faithfulness', he rarely visited their estates. His home, St Nicholas Abbey, lay in the distant northerly parish of St Peter, so he could not oversee how 'the sugars are sent on board, so perfectly and constantly as I might.' Furthermore, besides being Speaker of the House of Assembly, his hands were 'full of business' as attorney for several other absentees. According to Betsy Newton, by the late 1780s, he had 'grown old and leaves everything to Yard', who had 'it all his own way'.[110]

Sir John later claimed 'he never had observed any of the deficiencies or want whenever I had come to Newton'. Perhaps this was because 'he was always treated plentifully and sumptuously, nay elegantly and luxuriously', drinking 'the best Claret and Noyau'.[111]*

Jane, Sir John's young, constantly pregnant, second wife (and cousin) discouraged him from taking any trouble over the estates for two reasons: the effect on his worsening health and to keep him away from the

---

* A liqueur, named for an old French word meaning 'kernel', made of brandy flavoured with peach or other fruit kernels, giving an almond-like flavour.

'debauchery'. It has been suggested the 'luxurious' hospitality Sir John received from Yard included sex with enslaved women.

The underlying tensions came to a head one day in 1794 when 'some of the female part of' Sir John's family caught Yard with Dolly. They 'either surprized the two Lovers in the fact itself – or heard such indisputable proofs of it from the next chamber as put it out of doubt.' Sir John – clearly under marching orders from his unforgiving female relations – gave Yard 'a severe reprimand on the impropriety of such behaviour' and 'the detriment it might be to the Estate'.[112]

Yard now turned vindictively on the family he had favoured for years. He sent the women out of the house into the fields, even though they were likely 'to do nothing, a mockery of punishment'. Doll, though deemed too old for fieldwork, was replaced as plantation midwife. Betsy's son John Scott lost the opportunity of becoming an apprentice carpenter.

The fall from grace meant the family lost access to the plantation stores. Undeterred, Billy Thomas and a white bookkeeper, Patrick Paine, encouraged Betsy's brother Hylas to steal Yard's key. When Yard found out, Hylas was hanged. Though Yard's successor claimed Hylas had been 'upon the fullest evidence condemned', Betsy's version, that there was no trial, and Yard ordered the execution 'under a pretence that Sir John had desired it', is more convincing. It was not a decision taken lightly. Hylas was 'a cooper, a valuable man', worth as much as £100 to Sarah and Elizabeth; they would receive only £25 compensation from the Barbados government following his execution.

Yard may have hanged Hylas to protect Billy, who had not been 'detected amongst the Stealers of the sugar' and could have been convicted only on Hylas's testimony. He now sold his favourite to Dutch Demerara for £60, placing him beyond British jurisdiction. There was some relief amongst the family, according to a later manager, because Billy could easily have incriminated the rest, but more likely due to their love for their 'near relation'. Still, they were 'all up in arms against Mr Yard for his severity against Hylas' – none more so than Betsy – putting Yard 'in fear of his Life'.

Doll and Betsy appealed to Sir John to intervene, but his plea 'not to ill use the women' only incensed Yard further. Betsy was clapped in irons and separated from her young son. Without his mother's milk, he died. Distraught, Betsy went again to Sir John to complain, but this time Lady Alleyne refused her admittance.

This was the last straw for Betsy. She fled the plantation, leaving her four young children behind, just as her grandmother Mary Hylas had been forced to do over forty years earlier. Betsy was at large in Barbados for several months, perhaps sheltered by friends or relations on other plantations, or lost in Bridgetown's crowds. Yard threatened 'if he could catch her to put her in Irons and many other severities'.

The conflict seriously curtailed Sarah and Elizabeth's profits; Newton made under £500 in 1794, less than a quarter of the usual income. Later managers at Newton were adamant this was down to the Hylas family, who were 'absolutely a nuisance in the field and set the worse example to the rest of the Negroes.' They had 'great influence with the slaves and if I compel them to labour tis unknown how far they may carry their resentment ... they have it in their power to injure the property many thousands without us knowing the principals'.

Lady Sarah Holte died suddenly on 1 April 1794, aged seventy. Elizabeth, who had been by Sarah's side at Aston Hall when the end came, 'seemed very much distressed by her sister's death'.[113] She erected a monument to her and Sir Lister, sculpted by Richard Westmacott the elder, at St Peter and St Paul church, a stone's throw from Aston Hall, 'as a memorial of his virtues, and in compliance with the wishes of his Widow.'

When the news reached Barbados that summer, Sir John Gay Alleyne expressed his 'grief and surprise at the melancholy and unexpected ... mournful' event; 'from the cheerful style in which she concluded the last epistle I was favoured with at her hands, I could not draw the least presages'. He sent his 'tenderest condolence to her afflicted sister on her loss, which considering the infirm state of her own health, must be an irreparable one.'[114]

Sarah had left her half of Newton and Seawells and the people living there to Elizabeth. The fate of Betsy and her family now hung in the balance. Betsy knew the seventy-five-year-old Elizabeth Newton was ill, so unlikely to live long, and had no children. Lady Alleyne had taunted her: 'Your mistress will give you all away to Strangers, and what should Sir John trouble himself about it for – If I was to be your mistress I should know what to do with you.' With these words ringing in her ears, she decided to risk a journey to England 'in hopes of procuring an order from Mrs Newton' – she meant Elizabeth, it was common for unmarried women of a certain age and rank to be called Mrs, pronounced mistress – 'to release her children', before she died.[115]

Betsy left the island in January 1795, heading for the closest British-occupied island, St Vincent, a hundred miles to the west and long a destination for people fleeing Barbados.[116] The usual dangers of such a journey were heightened by the fact Britain was at war with Revolutionary France, a conflict also playing out in the Caribbean. War broke out in St Vincent in March; Betsy 'took shelter' on a ship headed for England. She may have convinced the captain she was free, purchasing her passage with money saved by the family from their market trading; or paid a bribe, while admitting her true situation.[117]

When she arrived in London, Betsy was received warmly by 'the great Barbados planters', who, the Newtons' second cousin, John Lane, snidely remarked, 'are taken in by [her] and have been taking care of her to let her laugh at them. They have been giving her flannel and the Lord knows what.'[118] Lane did not say *who* had harboured Betsy. Amongst the most prominent Barbadian families at the time were the Lascelles, Earls of Harewood; the Estwicks – Samuel Estwick was an MP and agent for Barbados from 1778; and the Brathwaites – John Brathwaite succeeded Estwick as agent in 1792. It is possible Betsy contacted the Blackman or Daniel families who had sold Newton sugar for decades; or the Bromes, who owned Hannay's in St Lucy (Elizabeth Alleyne Newton's grandmother, who had owned Seawells, was a Hannay).[119]

After Sarah's death John Lane volunteered to help Elizabeth with her affairs and wrote to Sir John Gay Alleyne, who 'readily accepting a continuance of the trust which I was honoured with by the two worthy ladies', agreed to continue as the family's attorney on the island.[120] Elizabeth 'hardly had spirits to undertake' the task of making a will. She rallied only when reminded that 'if she should die intestate the whole of the real estate would be claimed by Mrs [Catherine] Newton's son' – 'that nasty little bastard'.

Elizabeth knew who Sarah thought should inherit the Derbyshire estate and accordingly left it to Reverend John Arden, their first cousin once removed. She also followed Sarah's advice to compensate Sir John Gay Alleyne's nephew, Edward Bouverie, who had lost a chance of a Barbados inheritance on his uncle's second marriage; he received £2,000. She was less sure who should inherit the Staffordshire and Barbados estates, but eventually decided they would go to John Lane and his brother Thomas. Nearer relatives were unhappy the Lane brothers inherited so much, but after helping with the Chancery Court case over Sir Lister's will and John Newton's divorce, John Lane in particular was 'the friend and relation in whom both Lady Holte and Mrs N had ever put the greatest confidence'. Elizabeth died less than nine months after Sarah, on 24 December 1794, leaving monetary legacies totalling £23,500 to friends and family.[121]

The Lane brothers decided to divide the property, with John taking Seawells and Thomas taking Newton.[122] It was therefore to Thomas Lane that Betsy made her appeal. By this time, she had a new baby girl.[123] She didn't know how her four children in Barbados were faring, and desperately wanted to return to them. They were, she avowed, 'all free born and living at Newtons', but were 'seized as slaves during the life of Mrs Newton by her agent Mr Yard.' She 'pleaded strongly for her liberty, with her little girl in her arms'. She dared not return to Barbados without a certificate of freedom, 'for Yard would certainly kill her'. Thomas Lane conceded Betsy was free 'by setting foot on English ground'. He offered to send her back to Barbados, but ignored her plea for formal manumission.

So, Betsy's children remained enslaved. By 1796, her twelve-year-old son John Scott was apprenticed to a mason; Betsey Ann and Maria, ten and eight, were employed in picking grass and Nanny Doll, aged five, as yet did 'nothing'. Betsy stayed in England, marrying a Mr Miler and continuing to write to her family in Barbados. In 1801, having heard her children had been 'very severely treated', she tried again, asking Thomas Lane for 'a certificate of her own freedom and an order upon his agent for the release of her children', to no avail. In 1819, her daughter Betsey Ann wrote to Betsy, by now married to a Mr Betts, asking her to intercede with Lane again to obtain freedom 'for all their family', but Betsy could not afford to pay the required manumission fees.[124]

When the Lanes heard about the Hylas clan saga, they replaced Yard immediately, and wanted the whole family sold off the island. Instead, new overseer Sampson Wood attempted to make peace. He brought the women back into the house, appointing Dolly's sister Jenny as his housekeeper. But when Doll asked Wood to send Jenny's sons, Robert and William Henry, to school, he refused, fearing that 'to bestow on them the powers of reading and writing, it is of little good, and very frequently produces of mischief.'

Nonetheless, the Hylas clan continued to be granted unusual privileges, receiving specialist medical treatment and 'handsome' funerals.[125] Several female family members gained their freedom well before enslavement ended, usually with the help of white men they were in sexual relationships with.[126] Mary Ann Saer's son, carpenter John Thomas, 'a very good looking and apparently well informed man', managed to escape to England like his cousin Betsy, this time via Grenada. Sampson Wood characterised the family as 'a set of disaffected people and conceive they should have been long ago manumitted' – a feeling perhaps based on that 1768 judgment in an English court that their ancestor, Mary Hylas, was a free woman.[127]

Newton and Seawells remained in the Lane family into the twentieth century. They sold Newton for £40,000 in 1921; sugar cultivation continued there until at least 1982. The burial ground now belongs to the Barbados Museum and Historical Society. When Barbados became a republic in 2021, plans were announced to build an African-inspired memorial on the site, featuring 570 timber columns – one for each person buried there – accompanied by a museum and research institute. The government commissioned the design from David Adjaye, the prominent Ghanaian-British architect behind the Smithsonian's National Museum of African American History and Culture in Washington DC. Seawells, purchased by the Barbadian government in 1937, now forms part of Grantley Adams International Airport.[128*] A ruined industrial building with a tall chimney is still visible from the runway. Sarah's home, Aston Hall, is now a museum, dwarfed by the adjacent Aston Villa football stadium. Her dressing room has been reinterpreted in collaboration with local young people of colour as a Black teenage girl's room, featuring Kente cloth, a bottle of cocoa butter and a hot comb. A recorded poem plays when visitors enter:

> Hello Sarah Newton
> Aka Lady Holte
> But you are no lady, just a lady at fault …
> I am here to confront your participation in the Atlantic Slave trade
> Let you hear about the privilege you have gained from Black people's pain
> Here I am a Black woman taking up space in your own place
> I may have not been alive to put you in your place
> But I am here now on behalf of my race …[129]

---

* Named after the Barbadian National Hero, Labour Party founder and first Prime Minister of Barbados.

Over a million tourists fly into Barbados each year, often oblivious to the history beneath their feet.[130] Likewise, the 40,000 fans who attend most Aston Villa home matches, some sitting in the Holte End stand, have no conception of the link to Barbados. One of Villa's most famous fans was the locally born poet Benjamin Zephaniah, son of Barbadian post office manager Oswald Springer and Jamaican nurse Lenive Faleta (Valerie) Honeyghan. For him, going to Villa Park was 'like going to Church … it's the place where I worship … nothing beats standing in the Holte End singing our hearts out'. Zephaniah married his second wife, Qian Zheng, at Aston Hall in 2017. After he died in December 2023, his *Ode to Villa* was played on the stadium's big screens ahead of an FA Cup match against Arsenal.[131] Yet, just as the first bones were found a mere two centimetres beneath the soil at Newton, we need only scratch the surface of seemingly English places like Aston Hall museum and Aston Villa Football Club to find connections not only to Barbados but to the transatlantic, intertwined lives of women like Sarah Newton, Mary Hylas and Betsy Newton.

We often think of enslavement in binary terms: Black or white; enslaved or free. Yet the lives of Mary Hylas and her descendants on Newton plantation show it was not that simple. Leveraging their intimacies with their enslavers, they were able to obtain certain privileges, and even grasp freedom. With a white father and grandfather, four of Mary Ann Saer's children were described by a later manager as being 'as white as himself'. The white men in their story, however, were bookkeepers or overseers. What became of children fathered by plantation *owners*? Could their daughters, despite their skin colour, become heiresses?

Frances Duff, née Dalzell, probably painted in the 1750s. Sadly, she is not wearing the gold chain her mother sent her from Jamaica.

2

Frances Dalzell (1729–1778)

*Frances Dalzell, daughter of a woman born
enslaved in Jamaica, became legally 'white' in 1738
and married into the Scottish aristocracy. Despite
her African ancestry, Frances could not afford
to show mercy to the people she enslaved.*

LORD BRACO AND HIS WIFE were most unhappy when they learnt in 1757 that their beloved youngest son, George, wanted to marry a girl from Jamaica. Their other children had already made dismal choices of partners – as far as enhancing the family's status was concerned. George's eldest brother had seduced his mother's maid. His sister had leapt from a window to elope with an ageing Jacobite, soon finding herself a destitute widow living in exile with three young children.[1]

True, the Jamaican girl in question, Frances Dalzell, boasted a famous General for a grandfather. The military hero had retired aged eighty-seven, the oldest serving officer in Britain, having weathered 'eighteen campaigns under the greatest commanders in Europe', many with the Duke of Marlborough during the War of the Spanish Succession. And the Dalzells *claimed* descent from the Earls of Carnwath.

But Frances' more immediate relations were quite another matter. Her father Gibson was merely a colonial merchant and enslaver, now being sued by the South Sea Company for embezzlement. Her mother Susanna, still living in Jamaica, was not married to her father. What's more, Susanna had been born enslaved. Would Frances's illegitimate birth and African ancestry prove a deal-breaker? Or would her prospects of inheriting half the riches her parents had amassed, besides a legacy from her grandfather – who could not be long for this world – conquer all?

How did Frances, a woman of mixed heritage, become an heiress? As we saw with the Hylas family, relationships between white men and Black or mixed-heritage women were commonplace in the Caribbean, existing on a spectrum from brutal rape to long-term cohabitation, resulting in multiple children; but always involving a coercive element or at best an extreme imbalance of power. The agent for Jamaica told the Board of Trade in June 1763 that the scarcity of white women (white men outnumbered white women on the island two to one) 'has introduced, to a most scandalous degree, an unlawful commerce with Negro Slaves; which habit reconciles, and numbers sanctify'. Newly arrived Governor's wife Lady Maria Nugent observed in 1802: 'white men of all descriptions, married or single, live in a state of licentiousness with their female slaves.'[2]

Satirists regularly lampooned the habit in salacious caricatures. Even Prince William Henry (later King William IV), did not escape their scrutiny. In *Wouski* – a print later suppressed – Gillray depicts him lying in a hammock aboard his ship, the *Pegasus*, embracing an attractive Black woman.[*] The Prince admitted contracting gonorrhoea 'in my pursuit of the *Dames de Couleurs*' while serving in the Caribbean as a young naval officer; it was even rumoured he brought a Black woman home with him. He certainly trashed Rachel Pringle Polgreen's Bridgetown brothel – Bullingdon Club style – during his time in Barbados.

More pertinent to Frances Dalzell's family story is an etching published anonymously in London in 1808 entitled *Johnny Newcome in Love in the West Indies*, which goes from him 'being smitten with the charms of Mimbo Wampo a sable Venus' on arrival, to leaving behind nine 'hopeful young Newcomes' when he departs from 'Frying Pan island', including 'Lucretia Diana Newcome, a delicate girl much like her Mother; only that she has a great antipathy to a pipe, and cannot bear the smell of Rum'.[3] Like Newcome, Frances's grandfather, French Huguenot merchant John Augier, had at least eight daughters and three sons, all described as 'mulattoes' – a now offensive term derived from the Portuguese word for mule, used to denote someone with one white and one Black parent. We do not know who their mother was, or even whether they all had the same mother. Judith, Nelly and Sarah, 'three old Negro slaves', later manumitted and given pensions in Augier's business

---

[*] Wouski was the name of Yarico's Black maid in George Colman's popular comic opera *Inkle and Yarico* (1787).

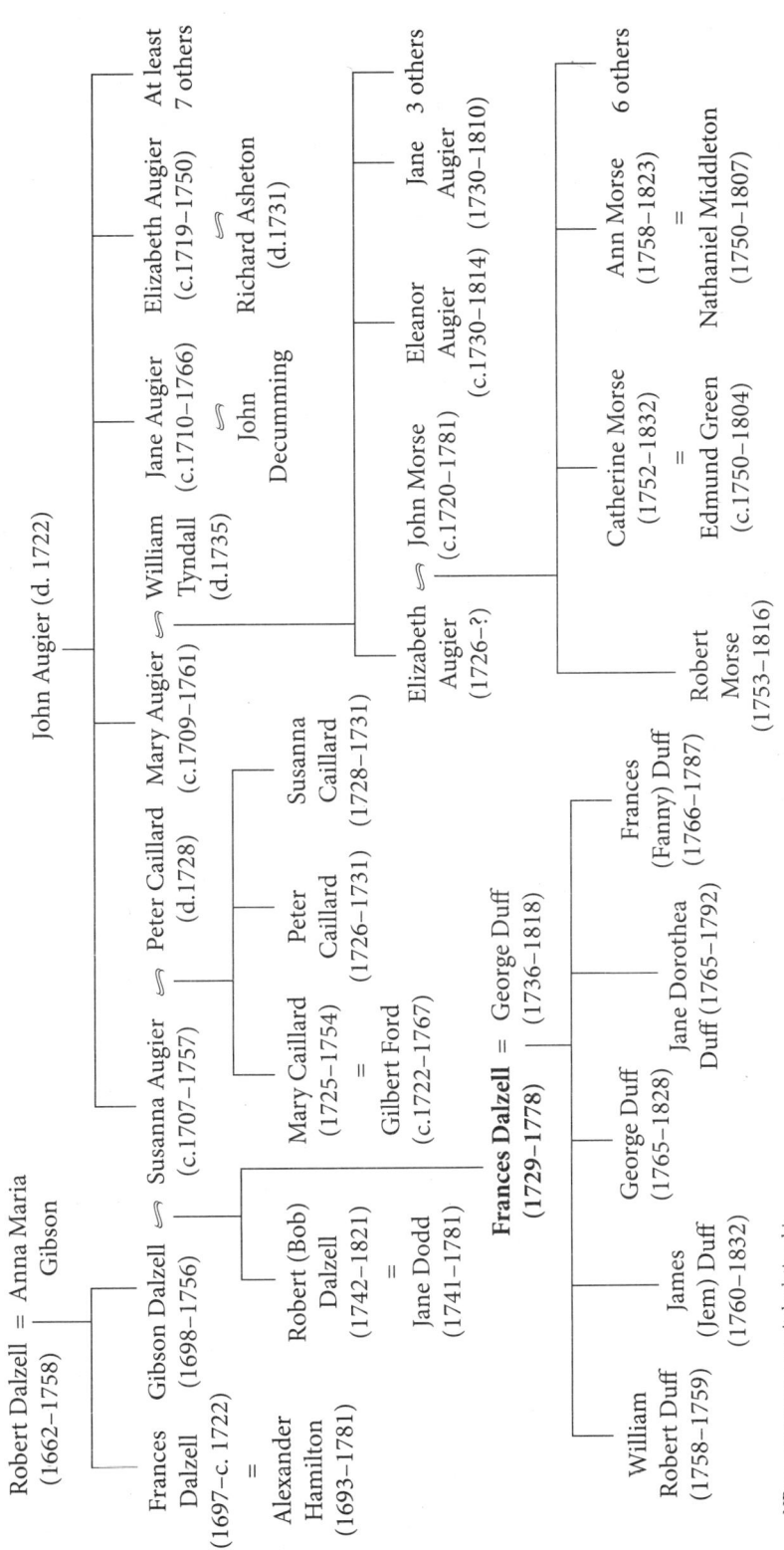

Augier and Dalzell Family Tree

Robert Dalzell = Anna Maria Gibson
(1662–1758)

John Augier (d. 1722)

Frances Dalzell (1697–c. 1722) = Alexander Hamilton (1693–1781)

Gibson Dalzell (1698–1756) ∽ Susanna Augier (c.1707–1757) ∽ Peter Caillard (d.1728)

Mary Augier (c.1709–1761) ∽ William Tyndall (d.1735)

Jane Augier (c.1710–1766) ∽ John Decumming

Elizabeth Augier (c.1719–1750) ∽ Richard Asheton (d.1731)

At least 7 others

Robert (Bob) Dalzell (1742–1821) = Jane Dodd (1741–1781)

Mary Caillard (1725–1754) = Gilbert Ford (c.1722–1767)

Peter Caillard (1726–1731)

Susanna Caillard (1728–1731)

Elizabeth Augier (1726–?) ∽ John Morse (c.1720–1781)

Eleanor Augier (c.1730–1814)

Jane Augier (1730–1810)

3 others

Frances Dalzell = George Duff
(1729–1778)   (1736–1818)

Catherine Morse (1752–1832) = Edmund Green (c.1750–1804)

Robert Morse (1753–1816)

Ann Morse (1758–1823) = Nathaniel Middleton (1750–1807)

6 others

William Robert Duff (1758–1759)

James (Jem) Duff (1760–1832)

George Duff (1765–1828)

Jane Dorothea Duff (1765–1792)

Frances (Fanny) Duff (1766–1787)

NB: ∽ means non-marital relationship

partner Peter Caillard's will, are possible candidates. Six of the Augier sisters – including Frances's mother Susanna – would go on to have long-term sexual relationships with white men.[4]

While such families proliferated, the children rarely inherited a fortune. In fact, eighty per cent of mixed-heritage people in Jamaica were *never even manumitted* by their fathers. Fewer still were left any sort of legacy.[5] The Augier family were fortunate in this respect. When John Augier died in 1722 his will freed and left legacies to several children.

However, he left nothing to Frances's mother Susanna. There was no need to emancipate her; she was already free.[6] And no need to provide for her because she had another source of support: his business partner, fellow Huguenot Peter Caillard. At seventeen Susanna conceived her first child by Caillard, a daughter named Mary. He was then nearing sixty and had known Susanna from birth. Mary was born in January 1725, Peter followed in March 1726, and Susanna in May 1728. The sexual abuse may have started several years earlier; Caillard may even have purchased her freedom.[7]

The English had invaded Jamaica in 1655, after their abject failure to capture the larger and richer neighbouring island of Hispaniola (now shared by Haiti and the Dominican Republic) from the Spanish. Oliver Cromwell's 'Western Design' had aspired to challenge Spanish dominance; Jamaica was a consolation prize.

Unlike Barbados, Jamaica had been inhabited before European contact by indigenous Taíno, who gave the island its name, Xaymaca, meaning 'land of wood and water'. In 1494, Christopher Columbus claimed the island for Spain, enslaving the Taíno and forcing them to dig for gold. After many died from this back-breaking toil or European diseases, the Spaniards began to import Africans, mostly from the Kingdom of Kongo and the Portuguese colony of Angola. But, finding no treasure, the Spanish neglected the island. When the English invaded in 1655, many Africans fled to join the remaining Taíno in the mountains, forming Jamaica's earliest Maroon communities. The remaining Spaniards and Africans didn't put up much of a fight.

In the first forty years of English occupation, Jamaica was primarily a base for piracy against the Spaniards. Port Royal, frequented by the likes of Captains Henry Morgan and Blackbeard (Edward Teach), became known as the 'wickedest city on earth'. New colonisers had also begun planting ginger, indigo, pimento trees (bearing berries that make allspice), cotton and coffee. Cacao (to make cocoa and chocolate) initially proved the most popular crop. But, by the early eighteenth century, Jamaica increasingly attracted men wishing to emulate Barbados's success by cultivating sugar.[8]

Caillard and Augier were in business together by 1693, making them amongst the first residents of the new town of Kingston.[9] The settlement had been founded after a devastating earthquake hit nearby Port Royal in 1692, killing 2,000 people and causing two-thirds of the place to collapse into the sea. One mile long by half a mile wide, Kingston was laid out in a regular grid pattern of streets surviving downtown to this day, with wide thoroughfares making it easy to transport goods between the port and the plantations now proliferating throughout the island. Kingston grew rapidly and, by 1716, was the largest settlement in Jamaica, though Spanish Town, some twelve miles to the west, remained the official capital and administrative centre. Kingston's boom was fuelled by its role as a major entrepôt for the transatlantic trafficking of Africans. Some 4,000 out of 6,000 captives arriving each year were re-exported; a quarter heading to New York, one-tenth to Virginia, but the majority to Spanish colonial ports: Cartagena, Havana, Portobello and Veracruz, after Britain was granted the right or *asiento* to do so in the 1713 Treaty of Utrecht.[10] In the eye of the storm, Caillard and Augier did well for themselves; Caillard became a Member of the Assembly in 1716; and by 1718 the two men had established a plantation in St Andrew, near the source of Wagwater River.

Peter Caillard died in May 1728, the same month Susanna gave birth to their youngest child. He left Susanna one of the most substantial legacies ever bequeathed to a mixed-heritage person in colonial Jamaica. Caillard's personal property was valued at almost £20,000. This included 170 enslaved people.[*] As well as their Kingston home on Water Lane, Susanna inherited storehouses on Mathews Lane, two Kingston public houses, the New York Arms and the White Cross, and several properties on the high street in Spanish Town. She also became proprietor of the Wagwater plantation in St Andrew, and two cattle pens and two plots of land in St Catherine.[11]

---

[*] We know the names of twenty-six people Caillard enslaved in Kingston. These were men named Quashee, Isaac, Fulham, Weston, Cajo, Primus, Robin, Pereau, Old Jack, Little Jack; women Marea, Belinda, Pendall, Pheba (and her baby Caesar), Quasheba, Quasheba Corm, Quasheba Wawy, Cuba, Lady (and her two young children Jasmon and Countess); boys Philip, Quashee, Quao and a girl, Betty.

Despite Susanna's newly inherited wealth, having the protection of a white man still brought significant advantages, whatever the personal cost. Within months of Caillard's death, Susanna met Frances's father, Gibson Dalzell.

Gibson Dalzell was born in Portsmouth in 1698. He had been conceived out of wedlock, after his mother Anna Maria Gibson became 'enamoured' with his father, Robert, a 'giddy and extravagant' Captain in her father's Regiment of Foot. When the Colonel found out, he initially tried to have Robert court martialled, before agreeing to promote him if he married Anna Maria.[12] Robert Dalzell rose through the ranks, obtaining Gibson an income from fraudulent army commissions while he was still a child, then sending him to Christ Church, Oxford.[13] After he graduated, Robert, now a South Sea Company director, found Gibson a lucrative job as an agent.* Aged twenty-two, Gibson set out for Cartagena, moving on to Cuba two months later.

During his five years working as a factor in Cuba, Gibson received 'several cargoes of Negroes for the use of the company'. Though today it is remembered primarily for the bursting of its economic bubble in 1720, the South Sea Company had trafficked over 30,000 captive Africans to the Spanish colonies by 1739. This was a small fraction of the dehumanising annual quota of 4,800 *piezas de india* – a Spanish measure whereby a healthy grown man counted as one unit, while older men, women and children were 'worth' less – agreed in the 1713 Treaty of Utrecht.[14] However, Gibson and his fellow agents actually made more profit from selling contraband goods such as flour and woollen clothing. Some even disguised sailors as Africans on arrival in Spanish ports to conceal their main cargo.[15]

Gibson's South Sea Company career came to a dramatic end when war broke out between Britain and Spain in 1727. In June of that year Spanish officials raided his premises, seizing several Africans, over 20,000 lbs of snuff (powdered tobacco for export to Europe), and all his paperwork. Two months later Gibson was arrested and imprisoned. He managed to escape to a Franciscan convent, but was driven off the island in April 1728 by the 'vigorous prosecution of the Governor'. He made it home to London via Kingston, Jamaica, but the Company directors refused to compensate him for losses of over £5,000.[16] So

---

* The salary was 1,000 pieces of eight (about £300), plus five per cent commission on sales.

Gibson returned to Kingston, hoping his main contact there, South Sea Company agent Edward Manning – a politically powerful Member of the Assembly and amongst the wealthiest men in Jamaica – would help him get back on his feet.[17] Within months of arriving, he obtained a royal patent for 500 acres in Portland.[18]

It may have been Edward Manning who introduced Gibson to Susanna, as Manning was in business with William Tyndall, long-term partner of Susanna's sister Mary. Although Gibson was far closer to Susanna in age than Caillard, and showed her affection, we do not know what she felt for him. Whether she cared for him or not, it was an intrinsically unequal relationship; Gibson held most of the cards. They conceived Frances almost immediately; she was born in Kingston on 16 June 1729.[19]

Frances spent her early years living in the well-furnished townhouse in Water Lane that Susanna had inherited from Caillard, just two blocks north of the bustling harbour. When she was nine, her mother lodged a surprising petition with the Jamaica Assembly. Susanna asked that she, her two surviving children – Frances and her thirteen-year-old half-sister Mary Caillard – and any future children she might have be granted the 'rights, privileges, immunities and advantages whatsoever *as if they ... were born of and descended from White Ancestors.*'

Five years earlier, the Jamaica Assembly had taken the unprecedented step (in a British jurisdiction) of legally defining whiteness. They wished to deny the growing numbers of propertied people with mixed ancestry the vote, but to do so they had first to 'ascertan who should be deemed mulattoes, and how far their corruption of blood should extend'. Following the Iberian example, Jamaicans ruled anyone four generations removed from a black ancestor (i.e. with only one Black great-great-grandparent) was legally white.

Many members of Jamaica's small mixed-heritage elite – including Frances and her family – did not qualify, so began to petition for exemption from the 'pains and penalties' now legally inflicted on 'other free negroes and mulattos'. Besides the right to vote, they wanted to be tried for any crimes they might be accused of as 'free and natural born subjects of the Crown of Great Britain', and allowed to give evidence in court. Over the following century, over 700 people would be legally recognised as 'white' by the Jamaica Assembly, their status confirmed by the British government. As lodging a petition cost £90, roughly the price of three enslaved people, the process marked a stark division between rich and poor Jamaicans with African ancestry.

Susanna became the second recorded individual, and the first woman, to submit such a petition. She was careful to emphasise her daughters' Church of England education and that she had 'established and acquired a very considerable fortune and estate'. Though she did not explicitly mention her white father John Augier, or her relationship with Gibson, these were common knowledge. It did not hurt that Gibson had by now been appointed to two official posts, becoming a Provost Marshal, and Serjeant at Mace of the Jamaican High Court of Admiralty. The Assembly passed the bill on 19 July 1738, adding that Susanna was 'posses'd of Several Slaves'. This underlined that she, like other elite people of colour, had a stake in upholding the system and so could be trusted.[20]

The very existence of the 1733 legislation and subsequent privilege petitions shows racial categories were more fluid than one might expect. By this time close to 100,000 Africans lived in Jamaica, outnumbering their enslavers ten to one.[21] This imbalance was a constant source of concern for the Jamaican authorities. They had issued legislation to control the enslaved population in 1664, closely modelled on the Barbados code, and several 'deficiency laws' imposing fines on enslavers who did not employ enough white men. French Huguenot refugees like Augier and Caillard had received financial incentives to emigrate to Jamaica to bolster the white elite.

This fear of the Black majority led officials to consider free mixed-heritage people as potential allies. In 1746, Governor Trelawny believed 'having a due Proportion of Freemen (of one Colour or another, white, black, or yellow, since white Men enough cannot, at least immediately be got)' was vital to the island's security. Ideas about race were not fully dictated by skin colour, but were also influenced by class, religion, language, education, dress, gender and ideas of 'civility' – elements highlighted by Susanna and other petitioners. 'Rights of whites' were also granted to four of Susanna's siblings and their children in 1747.[22] Frances and her family were being co-opted to bolster white supremacy on the island.

Shortly after being granted the 'rights of whites', Frances was dispatched to boarding school in England; her imminent departure may have motivated the timing of the petition. It was commonplace for children to be sent to Britain from the Caribbean for a 'polite and generous' education, unobtainable in the colonies. A visitor to Jamaica in 1739 observed, 'Learning is here at the lowest Ebb'. Men preferred 'Gaming to *Belles Lettres*'; while some 'Ladies read, they all dance a great deal, coquet much.' Parents also feared their children acquiring the 'drawling dissonant gibberish ... awkward carriage and vulgar manners' of enslaved people.

Thousands of young people of colour like Frances left the Caribbean for Britain; more than 360 coming from Jamaica alone. While Jamaicans were attuned to every gradation of skin colour, in England, according to Jamaican enslaver and historian Edward Long:

> the many Mulatto, Quateron, and other illegitimate children ... are often sent to the most expensive public schools, where the history of their parentage is entirely unknown; they pass under the general name of West Indians; and the bronze of their complexion is ignorantly ascribed to the fervour of the sun in the torrid zone.[23]

If her portrait depicts her accurately, most people would have assumed Frances was white. She had dark hair and eyes, and perhaps a slight curl to her hair, but very fair skin (though one wonders whether the artist purposefully exaggerated this) and a slim, straight nose. She was fortunate to arrive in Britain in the 1730s, before attitudes towards people of mixed heritage became more rigid. In one 1798 novel, no 'child of colour' was admitted to a school 'however exalted her fortune, or future rank in life might be', because they 'would be slighted by the creole [i.e. Caribbean-born white] young ladies and it would prove a certain source of trouble'. More famously, in Thackeray's *Vanity Fair*, Amelia and Becky's schoolfellow Miss Swartz, the 'rich, woolly-haired mulatto from St Kitts', had to pay double to attend Miss Pinkerton's academy. Though 'generous and affectionate', she was also negatively stereotyped as 'impetuous', 'woolly-headed' (in both senses), and overly emotional, making 'hysterical YOOPS' when parted from Amelia.[24]

Frances now met her grandfather, the formidable Colonel Robert Dalzell, for the first time. As long-standing Treasurer of the Sun Fire Office, the first London insurance house to undertake fire risks (now RSA Insurance Group), he lived at the business's premises at Craig's Court, Charing Cross. Still a serving officer at the age of seventy-seven, he had just replaced the 3rd Duke of Marlborough as Commander of the 38th Foot. Unfortunately, no record remains of the encounter between the old soldier and his young, illegitimate, mixed-heritage granddaughter. It is perhaps telling that it was Frances's wealthy grand-aunt Susanna Gibson who paid her school fees.[25]

In summer 1743, Gibson received a letter written on his father's orders from his brother-in-law, Alexander Hamilton, urging him to return to London immediately. His 'way of life' in Jamaica was giving Colonel Dalzell 'the most sensible concern & uneasyness'. Hamilton, who also acted as the family lawyer, warned him this might 'induce him so to settle his estate ... in such a way as will not be to your satisfaction'.[26] The General prayed daily for Gibson's safe arrival; he would reward his prodigal son. Though he did not 'care for the trouble' of keeping a coach, when Gibson returned 'he shall have that and every thing he likes'.

As a further enticement for his son to come home, the Colonel intimated his largesse would be extended to Frances. Gibson's aunt wrote: 'Miss Fanny is very well, your Father was saying, if one heard of a good match for her, he would give her a fortune.' She thought Frances too young to marry, and insisted no decisions should be taken before Gibson's return.[27]

Gibson had many reasons to stay in Jamaica. He and Susanna had just had a little boy, named Robert after his grandfather, but affectionately known as Bob. Thanks to the 1738 privilege grant, by now ratified by the Privy Council in London, he was legally 'white'. Gibson had also recently been promoted to Deputy Provost Marshal General, and bought a new house in a smarter part of town, further from the harbour and close to Parade, Kingston's main square.[28]

Then there were the plantations to manage. Though Susanna's 950-acre Wagwater estate, worked by eighty enslaved people, was too mountainous and wooded to cultivate sugar cane, it produced a good export crop of coffee and ginger. These sold well, except when London was hit by a long frost in winter 1740, leaving that year's cargo languishing in a warehouse, rendering the coffee 'middling', and the ginger 'much worm eaten'.[29]

Gibson and Susanna also had the beginnings of a sugar plantation, which they optimistically named Lucky Hill. Susanna had obtained a royal patent for 300 acres at Bagnall's Thickets in St Mary – a mountainous northeasterly parish, prone to flooding – in January 1739; she sold this to Gibson for five shillings in June 1741. A week later, Gibson bought another 1,000 acres in St Mary, east of White River.[30]

Sugar was booming as Jamaican production strove to meet burgeoning demand in Britain and North America, outstripping Barbados's exports by the 1720s. The number of Jamaican sugar estates rose from 70 in 1670 to 492 in 1739. The value of sugar, molasses and rum exports increased by 196 per cent between 1719 and 1744. By the eve of the American Revolution, the average white Jamaican was more than thirty-five times as wealthy as his counterpart in Britain's North American colonies, and more than fifty times as wealthy as the average man in England and Wales.[31]

Susanna also needed Gibson's help claiming the full inheritance due to her and her daughter Mary from Peter Caillard. Instead of transferring his assets, account books, mortgage documents and other loan agreements to Susanna, Caillard's executors and their successors, most of whom were in relationships with other Augier sisters, began receiving most of his rents, profits and debt repayments themselves. Without access to Caillard's paperwork it was nigh impossible for Susanna to collect what she was due. Although she authorised Gibson to act on her behalf to recover her money, and he complained to the Council about how she was being treated, by 1742, only *one* out of the over fifty men who owed Caillard money had paid her in full.[32]

When Edward Manning and John Decumming (another Kingston merchant, who fathered four children with Susanna's sister Jane) became executors, they claimed *she* owed *them* money. In November 1743 she filed a complaint in Chancery against their 'unlawful Combination and Confederacy'. Having been granted the 'rights of whites', Susanna was now permitted to testify against a white person in court. However, she was powerless compared to her adversaries, who described Susanna's complaint as full of 'Manifold Errors untruths Imperfections & inefficiencys'.[33]

It may have been as a bargaining chip that Gibson now sold half of his 500 acres in Portland, with a half-interest in the fifteen people enslaved there, to Edward Manning. The move was also pragmatic. They agreed Manning would 'manage the estate for their mutual interest' during Gibson's absence from the island. Heeding his brother-in-law's warning, Gibson had decided to return to London, to his father, and to Frances.[34]

Before his departure, Gibson made generous provision for Susanna and Bob, giving careful instructions to his attorneys regarding their welfare. Susanna was welcome to live at Lucky Hill; she would be supplied with sheep, hogs and fowls to eat, and horses and mules for travel. He made the smart Kingston house over to her for life; eight 'house negroes under her command': Lucy, Nurse Cuba, Rose, Chloe, old Sarah, Essex, Titus and Deborah were to 'serve her as long as she pleases'. Gibson issued Susanna a bond (essentially an IOU) for £1,479 7s 6d; if she needed more money, his attorneys should take it out of plantation produce. If 'any accident should happen' to Susanna they must take good care of Bob, and if Gibson died, they should 'send him to England at the age of three years to be well educated'.[35]

Frances was a young woman of fifteen when she was reunited with her father after a six-year separation. But she did not know how long her father would stay. Alarmed by reports Lucky Hill was 'in a miserable condition', Gibson was soon itching to return to Jamaica. In December 1746, he went so far as to make formal provision for Frances in his absence, arranging a quarterly allowance of £120, as well as assigning her the proceeds of twenty gallons of rum from the next ship.[36] But Gibson's father, recently promoted to General, was determined to keep him in London. He spent £4,450 buying his son a twenty-one-year lease of a City of London coal meter's place. These officials had monitored the volume of coal imported into London since the time of Edward III. By the eighteenth century the role was largely honorific, with attractive 'fees, profits and commodities'. The General also had Gibson enrolled in the Fletchers' Company, granted the freedom of the City of London, and made a director of the Sun Fire insurance company. Gibson had to admit his father 'behaves very well'.[37]

A clear indication Gibson had accepted his fate, and would remain in London, was the arrival of Frances's little brother Bob from Jamaica. Now aged seven, he was sent to Westminster School.[38] While Gibson saw fit to bring his children to England for an exclusive education, their mother Susanna, like most women in her situation, would stay in Jamaica. There was no guarantee they would ever see her again.*

The Dalzells lived in fashionable Mayfair, also leasing a country house in Hertfordshire.[39] Frances's clothing bills in the late 1740s and early

---

* There were some exceptions, for example Charlotte Sproule, née Taylor, whom we will meet in Chapter 9, or my fifth great-grandmother, Priscilla Kelly, whom Robert Cooper Lee brought to England from Jamaica along with their five children, marrying her in 1771. (See 'My Family and Enslavement' at the end of the book.)

1750s show Gibson was happy to deck her out in gowns, mantuas, negligees and nightgowns all trimmed and lined in the latest style.[40] He also subscribed – presumably for Frances's benefit – to *The Lives of Cleopatra and Octavia* by Sarah Fielding, sister to Henry Fielding, author of *Tom Jones*. One wonders what young Frances thought of being instructed to emulate the sacrifices of Mark Antony's 'amiable and gentle' Roman wife; shunning the 'abandoned consequences, and the fatal catastrophe' of his 'haughty and intriguing' African mistress.[41]

Prevented by his father from returning to Jamaica, Gibson relied on attorneys to oversee his interests on the island, especially the management of Lucky Hill. It was a worrisome business, not knowing what news the next letter might hold. With his father too old, and his son too young, he increasingly confided in Frances, even entrusting her with a copy of his will when she was seventeen.[42] Frances began to get a sense of how plantations were run, and their many challenges, as she observed Gibson's concerns and dilemmas.

Gibson's agents consistently predicted huge returns for the following year, then made excuses for poor performance.[43] Lucky Hill suffered from heavy rains and negligent overseers. Sugar was pilfered while being shipped to Kingston via the north coast port of Oracabessa.

Several workers were executed or transported for seeking their freedom.[44] In 1751, five men joined fugitives led by Quaco Venter, or Venture, who had 'infested' the neighbourhood for 'a great many years', and 'committed many Murders of late'. They were captured, imprisoned and found guilty at a trial in Spanish Town. Four were hanged and one burnt alive.[45]

Soon afterwards, Venture was shot dead by George Currie, a Maroon from Accompong, who also captured his wife, Beauty. The Maroons, originally escaped Africans and some Taíno, now had well-established communities in the mountainous interior, occasionally augmented by new recruits fleeing plantations. Led by Captain Cudjoe in the west and Nanny of the Maroons in the east, they had regularly raided English settlements. In 1728 the conflict escalated into the First Maroon War. In the 1739 peace treaty, the Maroons had agreed to help track down fugitives. Currie received a bounty of £100 for bringing in Venture.[46]

Gibson was also increasingly worried about Susanna's financial situation. There had been no progress in her Chancery case against Edward Manning and John Decumming. However, Susanna lived in fine style.

Her home was adorned with mahogany furniture; she dined at a marble-topped table, laid with silver and ivory cutlery, and silver plate crested with the Dalzell coat of arms.[47]

By 1749, Susanna owed a considerable amount of money to her son-in-law Gilbert Ford, an English lawyer recently married to her daughter Mary Caillard. But Ford was in turn indebted to John Morse, a wealthy Member of the Assembly in a long-term relationship with Susanna's niece Elizabeth Augier.[48] To get his money back, Morse persuaded Susanna to sign over Gibson's bond to Ford. By this time, the bond with interest was worth over £2,000. When Morse demanded payment, Gibson and his attorneys were left scrambling to find the funds.[49]

Susanna went to see Dr William Aikenhead, one of Gibson's attorneys. She blamed Morse for everything and told Aikenhead she was 'now Convinced of her folly in delivering up ye Bond to Ford'. Susanna agreed with Aikenhead that she would buy Gibson's Kingston house for £500. Aikenhead worried Gibson would think this 'far too small a sum', but advised him Susanna's money was safer 'vested in a realty' than a bond. More importantly, he had 'taken the liberty of advising' Susanna to make a will, leaving everything to Frances and Bob.[50] The following year, Gibson wrote: 'I am very glad to hear Mrs Augier behaves so well, but had she behaved so before, I should not have been so distressed & reflected upon as I have been.'

Nonetheless, Gibson continued to express affection for Susanna. He wrote her several letters; also sending her his love via his business correspondents: 'tell her I sincerely wish her health & happiness'. He added that Frances and Bob also 'desire their duty to her'. Maintaining personal relationships from afar was difficult. Frances wrote to her mother, but both mother and daughter suffered long waits while letters voyaged between London and Jamaica. In July 1751, Frances had still not received a reply to a letter she had sent the previous November, although she was happy to wear a gold chain Susanna had sent her.[51]

Despite talk of finding a match for Frances in her early teens, she was almost twenty-seven by the time she found a suitor. She met the Honourable George Duff, a twenty-year-old cornet in the 10th Regiment of Dragoons, in Bath – that famous marriage-mart so familiar from the pages of Jane Austen. George was captivated, declaring that such was 'the power you have over me you can use me ill or well as you please'.[52]

Educated at Edinburgh and St Andrews, George was set to inherit estates in Banffshire and Moray yielding over £1,000 a year.[53] He was the fourth son of William Duff, Lord Braco of Kilbryde, and his second wife Jean, daughter of MP and baronet Sir James Grant. The family lived at Rothiemay Castle, a large medieval house in Banffshire. To ensure the perfect view from their new formal gardens and extensive landscaped parkland, they thought nothing of demolishing an entire village, even the kirk (church).[54]

Lord Braco could have afforded an even grander home. He commissioned leading Scottish architect William Adam to build the imposing Duff House in 1730. However, when costs exceeded £70,000, he took 'that villain Adam' to court and refused to live there. He could not even bear to look at the place; whenever he was obliged to drive past, he drew down the blinds of his coach.[55]

In March 1756 Frances introduced George to her father. The following day George confessed:

I have loved your Daughter ever since I had the happiness to know her, and it is in your power and hers to make me happy or miserable for ever. I never can be happy without her, but rather than you should be displeased with her, I'll suffer all the torments the world affords.[56]

Frances was fond of George, whom she addressed as 'my dear Duff', but was perhaps not quite as smitten as he.[57] He reproached her for not returning his devotion 'with that tenderness which such a behaviour merits'. While they were apart, he insisted: 'I could not be said to live.' He swore: 'I would be a sincere friend and careful servant to you in any situation of life. I could work for your smile at poverty and say it was happiness above expression while I had my Fanny.'[58] An easy compliment for a gentleman to make to an heiress.

Before things could progress further, Gibson died, aged fifty-eight, in May 1756. After the funeral at St Martin-in-the-Fields, Westminster, Frances wrote to Susanna to inform her of 'our irreparable loss'. She assured her mother: 'It will always give me great pleasure to hear of your happiness, and to serve you in everything in my power, whatever you want, please to command me.' She even promised: 'next year if there is peace I shall come to Jamaica to pay my duty to you.'[59] But the Seven Years' War still had six and a half years left to run.

Gibson's will placed his assets in trust, the income to be shared equally between his two children. The Jamaican estates consisted of 250 acres in Portland (half the plantation Gibson had shared with Manning, now named Friendship) and 1,700 acres in St Mary (Lucky Hill). Gibson's total personal property in Jamaica was worth £5,798. As was the case across the Caribbean, human beings represented almost seventy-five per cent of this figure. This was one reason why enslavers would later fight tooth and nail against emancipation.

Frances and Bob now owned 133 people: sixty-four men and thirty-nine women, sixteen boys and fourteen girls, in Kingston, Portland and St Mary. Amongst the 111 at Lucky Hill were three drivers, Tom, Cato and Oxford; three coopers, Prince, Marsh and Horace; a doctor named Kent; two head boilers, Coomy and Colraine; Lincoln, a distiller; George, head mule man and Coventry, head cattle man. Six men and five women: Boatswain, Hector, Sam, Barkly, Caesar, Sampson, Dellia, Sue, Venus, Mimba and Kell, were all labelled as 'sickly'.

Additionally, Gibson left Frances the income from fifty shares in the Sun Fire Office; ten shares in a Scottish mining company, worth £1,000; and the remaining ten-year lease of the City of London coal meter's place. Unusually, Bob would benefit from these assets only in the event of Frances's death without children, reflecting the close father–daughter bond.[60]

Frances faced several obstacles in taking control of her inheritance. Gibson had told her his friend Charles Price, a major Jamaican landowner and enslaver with an estate near Lucky Hill, would be his executor.[61] Normally, testators nominate at least two executors to carry out their wishes. But Gibson's final will did not name Price, or anyone else. Frances was certain her uncle Alexander Hamilton had drafted the document 'with a bad design, for he has named himself trustee and has given me much trouble since my father's death'.[62] As a trustee and a lawyer, Hamilton was in a position of considerable power. With Frances a young woman and fourteen-year-old Bob still a minor, ample opportunities might arise for him to profit illicitly from the situation.

However, Frances refused to allow Hamilton to take advantage of her. In cases where there is no executor, a beneficiary may apply for probate. Having successfully opposed Hamilton and the other trustees, Frances was granted administration on 2 July 1756, taking possession of her father's assets.[63] However, to secure Gibson's property in Jamaica, she needed a grant from the Governor. Within days, Frances wrote assertively to Charles Price and Samuel Howatt – the surgeon at Lucky Hill, nominated in the will as an additional trustee – to inform them of Gibson's death and ask for help. She asked Howatt to keep her informed of developments, keeping careful accounts to ensure her brother (or rather, the trustees, on his behalf) 'may give us no trouble'.

Frances put her faith in Thomas Bontein, a lawyer and enslaver of over 200 men and women in St Catherine, who had 'given himself much trouble to advise me and to prevent my affairs from being ruined'.[64] Frances was not Bontein's only client; he was also attorney to the novelist Tobias Smollett and his wife, Jamaican heiress Ann Lascelles.[65]

Bontein set out for Jamaica with copies of Gibson's will, Frances's letters of administration and a new Power of Attorney naming him and Charles Price as her agents on the island. Frances had chosen Price without his consent, but now demanded his protection, applying to him 'as a father', and reminding him of his longstanding friendship with Gibson, and that he was Bob's godfather. Frances also asked Bontein to confirm Bob's date of birth, so they could identify exactly when he would come of age, and to send her chocolate, Madeira wine and a hogshead (a hogshead cask held about sixty gallons or 300 litres) of rum.[66]

Frances had gone through all her father's papers, partly to find some note of Price being named executor. She took up business where Gibson left off, asking Samuel Howatt to 'let me know about ye bill of exchange you mention in your last letter to my father'. Eight months earlier Howatt had promised to send Gibson the paperwork for 450 acres he had sold in St Mary, to the east of White River, as soon as the title deeds were signed.

Wary of one of the men who had cheated her mother, Frances also urged Howatt to 'be cautious about the affairs of Manning'. Howatt's final letter to Gibson had warned that Edward Manning and his relation George Paplay were intentionally running Friendship into the ground to force Gibson to sell his share. They had even commissioned a valuation behind his back. Paplay (who also acted as one of Gibson's attorneys) had urged him to sell up. Friendship was haemorrhaging more money every year, he warned. Perhaps hoping to encourage Gibson to settle for a low price, he emphasised it would be hard to find a purchaser, as 'the Badness of the Roads & the Continual Rains there deters every body'. Though he suspected Paplay's motives, Howatt had also advised Gibson to sell. Frances now asked Howatt to 'let Mr Bontein who understands accounts transact with Manning in an amicable manner if possible'. She also wanted Bontein to find out 'what remainder Mr Paplay has in his hands belonging to my Father'.[67]

Frances had a clear grasp of exactly what was involved in the management of a sugar plantation. She wanted a clean slate, asking Bontein to 'value all things belonging to the Estate, Negroes, Mules, Cattle, mills, Utensils &c.'; and 'to take away all the Books of the Plantation & place new Books'. She had opinions on crops and technology, ordering him 'Not to plant Cotton nor any thing else' and to look into installing a watermill.

Frances dictated that all the produce should be shipped to Mure and Campbell in England, and plantation expenses be charged to her account with them.[68] Hutchison Mure – esteemed by David Hume as 'a gentleman of a very mechanical Head' – and Duncan Campbell (who would later become contractor for the first convict voyage to Australia) were Scottish colonial merchants based in London. Besides importing sugar and rum on 2.5 per cent commission, and exporting plantation supplies, they helped recruit overseers and bookkeepers and provided banking services.[69] Mure was probably recommended by his nephew William, who was in a relationship with Susanna's sister, Frances Augier.

Frances knew how important it was for 'sundry necessaries' to be sent out from England 'to save the Exorbitant Expence' of buying them in Jamaica.[70] Mercantilist economics dictated:

> the inhabitants of the West India islands and the southern continental colonies wear not a rag of their own manufacturing; drive not a nail of their own forging; eat not out of a platter or cup of their own making ... so entirely do these colonies depend upon the mother-country for all manufactures![71]

Frances sent Mure and Campbell a shopping list, asking them to 'please send these things to Jamaica as soon as you can':

12 Barrels of Beef
20 Barrels of Herrings*
2 Boxes of Soap
2 Ditto of Candles

---

* During Gibson's tenure, enslaved people at Lucky Hill had an allowance of three herrings a week. AUL, MS 3175, Z/259/1(i) (Gibson Dalzell to trustees in Jamaica, c.1745).

3 Firkins [a small barrel holding 56 lbs or 25kg] of Butter
A Barrel of Rape Oil
A Keg of Tallow [animal fat]
2 Grindstones
A Cask half Crown Nails
500 Iron Hoops for Puncheons [a puncheon barrel held 102 gallons or 465 litres] & Rivets per Ditto
1000 Wooden Hoops
8 pieces of Oznabrigs [osnaberg, a coarse fabric used to make enslaved people's clothing] & thread for Ditto.
6 pieces of Kendall Cottons for Blankets for Negroes
A Ream of writing paper
2 pair of Brass Candlesticks
A Brass kettle for Washing Clothes
As much stuff [material] as will make two mosquito nets for the great house Beds.[72]

Frances directed Bontein to 'purchase new Negroes in the name of my Brother & me & to have our mark'.[73] She meant they were to be branded to show they were the Dalzells' property. It was commonplace for owner's initials, or letters signifying their plantation, to be burned with hot irons onto people's shoulders or chest. The Royal African Company used the brand DY for 'Duke of York' while the future James II was Governor.* People 'owned' by the Church of England's Society for the Propagation of the Gospel at Codrington plantation in Barbados were branded 'SOCIETY'. As abolitionist Thomas Clarkson observed, 'some of these brand marks, consisting, as they often do, of several letters, must have tortured no inconsiderable portion of flesh'.[74] Following Frances's instructions, Thomas Bontein bought twenty people for Lucky Hill from prominent Kingston firm Richards, Gordon and Kennion for £719 12s 10d in summer 1759. If Frances hoped her brand would deter freedom seekers, she was mistaken. A man named Portland escaped in September 1757.[75]

Despite the ongoing war, Frances considered travelling to Jamaica to take charge and to see her mother. She found the prospect daunting,

---

* In 2020 artist Rachel Reid placed a branding iron in the hands of a statue of James II in Trafalgar Square. Reid, 'Why I Put Branding Irons into Royal Hands': https://rachel-c-reid.medium.com/why-i-put-branding-irons-into-royal-hands-7859f71638e9.

writing to Charles Price: 'if my courage was equal to my inclination of seeing you I certainly should be at Jamaica in three months' time'. However, she mastered her fears, writing to Howatt that she intended to live at Lucky Hill during her stay, asking him to 'let me know if there is anything necessary for the house that I may bring them with me.'[76] But, despite these careful preparations, changing circumstances would prevent Frances from making the trip.

Frances probably pursued her inheritance so urgently because she needed to have a clear source of income to marry George. After George told his parents they were engaged in late 1756, he received an angry letter from his mother; his father threatened to disown him. The Duffs never explicitly stated *why* they objected to the match. Was the problem Frances's African ancestry, her illegitimate birth, her status as a merchant's daughter, or all of the above? Despite their landed wealth, political influence and titles, the family were still self-conscious about their social position. Lord Braco was the son of a merchant, and had held his title only since 1735. Frances's background would do nothing to assuage their fears that the elite looked down on them as 'a new family, mere upstarts from the Dunghill'.

However, Frances's light skin, good education and wealth spoke in her favour, and by February 1757 George's parents had relented. Jean wrote that Lord Braco had 'softened a little', and George would find him 'not only reconciled to you, but likeways to your proposal'. She, however, still reserved judgement: 'my Lord will consent to your marriage, and you must take your chance of me'. One of George's uncles described Frances as 'a Grand Child of General Dalziel's, by whom he [George] got a good Fortune'.[77] It is telling he glossed over her parentage, instead emphasising her wealth and the more palatable connection to the famous General.

Novelists exploited the tension between pursuing great riches and fear of marrying someone with African ancestry for dramatic effect, though the most famous examples date to the nineteenth century. In Austen's unfinished novel *Sanditon* (1817), Lady Denham sees Miss Lambe, the wealthy heiress 'about seventeen, half mulatto, chilly and tender, [with] a maid of her own', as a good prospect for her nephew. As in Frances's case, her 'immense fortune' trumped considerations of race and class. Wealthy Miss Swartz in Thackeray's *Vanity Fair* is seen as a tempting prospect for George Osborne by his father, but he refuses:

'Marry that mulatto woman? ... I don't like the colour, sir. Ask the black that sweeps opposite Fleet Market, sir. I'm not going to marry a Hottentot Venus'.[78]*

Lord Braco proposed to pay George a yearly allowance of £200 once he was married. He asked one of his sons and Jean's brother Sir Ludovick Grant to visit General Dalzell 'to know his mind with regard to the intended marriage', and whether he would agree to leave Frances any money. The answer was satisfactory enough for a marriage settlement to be drawn up. Dr John Maule, apothecary of Piccadilly – an 'intimate friend' of George's – and London merchant Francis Wilson – a neighbour and possible associate of the General's in Charing Cross – were appointed trustees. Like many heiresses' settlements, Frances's emphasised she was to retain control of her inheritance after marriage, and continue to receive her income from Jamaica free from her husband's control. She also had the right to bequeath her assets as she saw fit.[79]

With her financial interests seemingly secure, Frances married George Duff on 7 April 1757 at St Martin-in-the-Fields. The union was kept secret for some months after the fact. One of George's older brothers, Alexander, wrote to their father: 'I suppose he has wrote you of his marriage, he has not made it publick as yet for reasons which are known to himself and his wife is still called Miss Dalzell.'[80]† This mysterious silence may have been linked to Frances's efforts to take control of her Jamaican assets. The Power of Attorney she sent to Jamaica had been made out in her maiden name. Changing her surname and status might invalidate the document, giving Howatt, Manning and Paplay an excuse not to cooperate.

Susanna did not live to hear of her daughter's happiness. She had died

---

* Sarah Baartman, a Khoikhoi woman from the Eastern Cape of South Africa, was exhibited as 'the Hottentot Venus' in London in 1810 before touring England and France, where she died aged just twenty-six. She was subjected to prurient scientific racism because of her steatopygian figure (characterised by large buttocks and thighs). French anatomists dissected her corpse; her skeleton and a cast of her body remained on display at the Musée de l'Homme in Paris until the 1970s; her remains were finally returned to South Africa for burial in 2002. Qureshi, *Peoples on Parade*, pp. 130–1, 144–7, 219, 282; McGreal, C., 'Coming Home', *Guardian*, 21 February 2022: https://www.theguardian.com/education/2002/feb/21/internationaleducationnews.highereducation.

† Former Prime Minister David Cameron is a direct descendant of George's brother Alexander Duff, making Frances and George Cameron's fifth great-grand-aunt and uncle.

quite suddenly in February 1757, buried according to her own wishes in a plain mahogany coffin in the courtyard of her Kingston townhouse. By May, the news had reached London: Frances had lost both her parents in the space of a year.[81]

Once they were married, Lord Braco invited the newlyweds to Scotland. If Frances liked it there, he would give George an estate near Elgin in Moray, which he had intended to leave him only at his death, so they could live there and 'improve' it. He was advocating George join the growing number of 'improving' landowners embracing the Enlightenment principles of the agricultural revolution – doing something useful with his life. Jean was also in favour, reminding George that Moray was a very 'pretty country' and of Elgin's convenient weekly markets. She anticipated meeting them at Edinburgh, then progressing north together, meeting friends who would 'rejoice at our happiness and make us very welcome'. George's sister Anne and her husband also sent their sincere congratulations; she looked forward to 'being made acquainted with' Frances and the 'enjoyment of her society'.[82]

But in the event, George made the trip north without Frances. His brother Alexander commented to Lord Braco: 'English ladies have unreasonable prejudices against our northern region, which they with difficulty ever get over'.[83] Somewhat curiously, he saw Frances as an 'English' lady, with no reference to her Jamaican birth, or her African ancestry. We do not have any clearer indication of whether the Duffs fully embraced Frances after the wedding. Her reluctance to visit them suggests otherwise. Nonetheless, the education her parents had chosen for her, sending her away from Jamaica aged nine, had delivered the desired effect.

In reality, Frances had little choice but to stay in London. She had urgent business to attend to as Gibson's administratrix. He owed £2,300, and his creditors were beginning to circle. But most of his assets – including his human 'property' – were in Jamaica. Frances was still waiting for news from Bontein on that front. There were Gibson's stocks and shares, and the coal meter's place, but in terms of ready money he had left only £380.[84] Furthermore, the long-running, expensive dispute with the South Sea Company, which accused Gibson of purloining over £8,000, remained unresolved.[85] Frances was 'distressed for want of money, which made me a little peevish'. Bob was concerned he would be unable to continue at Westminster School if the debts were not cleared.[86]

Frances and Bob might have expected to inherit the majority of Susanna's wealth. Their only surviving half-sibling, Mary Ford (née Caillard), had died childless 'after a lingering illness' in Clifton, Bristol, in December 1754.[87] But Bontein warned Frances that Susanna had died 'before she had time to make one intended alteration of her will in you & your brother's favour', or make Bontein executor as Frances had hoped. Instead, Susanna left substantial assets to her Augier relations in Jamaica; favouring Frances's cousins Jane and Eleanor, the daughters of Mary Augier and William Tyndall, in particular.[88]

Even if Susanna had left them everything, the inheritance would not have been as substantial as might have been expected. There was of course the Kingston house, Wagwater (her coffee and ginger plantation in St Andrew), her cattle pen in St Catherine, and an untenanted house in Spanish Town. But the cash situation was much more precarious. Susanna had owed her son-in-law Gilbert Ford over £2,000 in 1749; it is unclear how much of that sum she had been able to pay off by the time she died. She had never been able to retrieve Caillard's paperwork from the succession of executors. Even if she had, the documents would hardly have been worth the paper they were written on. It was notoriously difficult to get debtors to pay up, so much so that in 1732 Parliament had passed an Act for the More Easy Recovery of Debts in His Majesty's Plantations and Colonies in America, giving creditors priority over the deceased's heirs, and mandating that real estate and enslaved people be auctioned off to service debts. But the debts owed to Caillard dated back to the 1720s and many of his debtors had died. In the end, Susanna's total personal property in St Andrew – including only eight enslaved people, possibly the same group of domestics Gibson had left under her command when he left Jamaica – was valued at just £783.57, a fraction of the £18,679 Caillard had left thirty years before.[89]

The obvious solution was to sell some of Gibson's investments. The fifty Sun Fire Office shares were worth some £4,000; the Scotch Mine shares around £450. It was harder to estimate the value of the coal meter's place, but her lawyer Thomas Goostrey warned creditors might make an attempt on it anyway. However, although Frances was entitled to the income these assets produced, she did not have the right to sell them. The trustees, Alexander Hamilton in particular, objected to selling anything. In July 1757 Frances and George sued Hamilton and the other trustees she suspected of 'bad designs' in Chancery. In August, they renounced their trusteeship, and in December, the Court approved

Frances and George's choice of Dr John Maule and Francis Wilson, the trustees of their marriage settlement, as replacements. They probably helped Frances sell most of her fifty shares in the Sun Fire Office, as by 1776 she only owned fifteen.[90]

Meanwhile, Bontein's biggest challenge in furthering Frances's interests in Jamaica was that Samuel Howatt refused to accept him and Charles Price as her attorneys. Howatt's insistence he should continue to manage Lucky Hill proved particularly problematic because he lived there; possession being nine-tenths of the law. Incensed, Frances threatened to fire Howatt as surgeon and force him to 'pay rent for the house, & pay for the use of every thing which he may use belonging to my Brother & me.'[91]

Following the death of Gibson's partner Edward Manning in December 1756, George Paplay took on the management of Friendship. Frances complained: 'Mr Paplay is very entertaining in his news of the French Fleet, I had rather he had sent me a clear account of the estate'. Bontein suspected Howatt of coveting a cut of Friendship's proceeds and apologised to Frances for 'the negligence of people who pretend to be so thorough with other affairs, I mean Howatt, Paplay & Furnell'.[92]*

Bontein eventually succeeded in obtaining Letters of Administration in Jamaica in September 1757 and Gibson's probate inventory in June 1758. Frances was grateful to receive the valuation, telling Bontein: 'I can easily see the estate was nothing when you was so friendly to take it on hand' (Bontein's influence at Lucky Hill even extended to a boy there being named 'Bontein').[93] With the official paperwork complete, and following Howatt's death in 1759, Frances, George and Bob could finally look forward to receiving an income from Lucky Hill.

General Robert Dalzell died on 14 October 1758, at the impressive age of ninety-six. He had harboured grandiose plans to be buried at Westminster Abbey, 'desiring the dean and chapter to attend his funeral' and a marble plaque to be erected to 'the oldest General in His Majesty's Dominions', boasting of his 'eighteen campaigns under the greatest commander in Europe'. However, he changed his mind six weeks before he died, perhaps because the cost would exceed his £300 funeral budget.[94]

---

* Peter Furnell, one of Kingston's most prominent importers of captive Africans, was one of Susanna's executors. Affronted when Gibson replaced him as his sugar broker in 1753, he had reason to be hostile to Frances. AUL, MS 3175, Z/61/1 (Peter Furnell to Gibson Dalzell, 31 January 1753); 'Peter Furnell', LBS: https://www.ucl.ac.uk/lbs/person/view/2146655477.

While the average gentry funeral cost £32, being buried in the same Abbey as most monarchs dating back to Edward the Confessor, aristocrats, and luminaries including Chaucer, Handel and Sir Isaac Newton was rather more expensive. Newton's 1727 funeral cost £1,036; half spent on erecting a large marble monument.[95]

As always, grief at a death in the family intermingled with financial considerations. George's eldest brother James ran from one to the other in his condolences on 'the loss of your Dear Grandpapa he was a very intimate easy friend to you both, & therefore I doubt not but you sensibly feel the loss of his merry conversation, however to be serious, pray acquaint me how he has left his affairs, as I am always most anxious after all your concerns'.[96]

Frances and George's relationship with her grandfather had not perhaps been as rosy as James Duff imagined. In January 1758, Frances had sent a letter to the General via a friend asking him to help George get ahead. His answer was 'a frown of resentment', followed by angry words: 'I patronize him? Not I! Let her trounce him as much as she can; he cannot be humbled too much, he treats me as nothing'.[97] Perhaps the General was unimpressed George left the army soon after marrying Frances; or was refusing to seek promotion for him because he failed to show the necessary obsequiousness. The son of a Lord might not feel the need to pay homage to an army officer, of whatever rank. This may be why, when the General left £1,500 in trust for Frances in his will, he reserved it for her 'separate use ... independent of the said George Duff her husband', enjoining trustee John Maule to pay it to her directly.[98]

The General left Bob considerable landholdings in Berkshire and Hampshire, subject to an annuity to his grand-aunt Susanna Gibson. Although Frances would inherit only if Bob died without any children, Frances and George believed they might have a claim on the rental income, and again ended up in Chancery, arguing the case with Bob and his guardians for several years.[99] Frances's relationship with Bob became strained. She told Bontein she seldom saw her brother, but he was fond of Reverend Richard Dixon, whom the General had named as his guardian. 'I know nothing how he goes on, he is always uneasy if I mention or interfere about his affairs, that I have entirely given up having any more to do with him.'[100]

Between selling Gibson's shares, and her legacy from the General, Frances was now finally able to settle her father's most pressing debts. It was not a moment too soon. One of Gibson's creditors, Jamaican enslaver William Beckford, Lord Mayor of London, was on the verge of filing a lawsuit to recover his £500. Another angry creditor, Captain Nicholas Harman, whose ship the *Sea Nymph* had regularly carried Gibson and Susanna's produce to London, had been haunting Frances's lawyer Thomas Goostrey's chambers. When Francis Wilson finally paid Harman in November 1758, it 'brightened up the muscles of his countenance and nobody is more your well wisher'.[101] The case with the South Sea Company was finally settled in February 1759; the vast majority of the reputed debt was written off.[102] Frances also paid Bontein's bills, 'sensible of the obligation' she owed him. Convinced of his honour and honesty, she had 'not the least uneasiness as long as my affairs are in your hands'.[103]

Bontein had not been able to provide for every eventuality, however. In December 1758, Frances and George received 'melancholy accounts' of the *Oracabessa* 'having foundered at sea' carrying thirty hogsheads of sugar from Lucky Hill. The misfortune was magnified threefold by Bontein having failed to insure the voyage, owing Hutchison Mure £400; and the last sugar shipment having been of such low quality that it fetched less than half the normal price.[104] Even with a trusted attorney in place, the Duffs could not rely on a steady income from Jamaica.

Tacky's War would change everything for people with mixed ancestry. The conflict started on Easter Sunday 1760 (uprisings were often planned for the rare days enslaved people had holidays). Nearly one hundred freedom fighters from St Mary stormed Fort Haldane, near Port Maria. There, they seized arms and provisions before commencing a series of attacks on the parish's plantations. Lucky Hill, separated by mountains, rivers and woods from the freedom fighters' path, went unscathed. Tacky, Jamaica and other leaders, it soon emerged, were recently arrived 'Coromantees' (Akan people from modern-day Ghana), their military experience ironically gained in wars fomented by Britain.

It took the combined efforts of the island militia, the Maroons, and a British army regiment with naval support to quash Tacky's army. On 14 April, in a battle at Rocky Valley, 200 men were captured; Tacky, Jamaica and twenty others killed. But the uprising was not the isolated incident in St Mary the enslavers hoped. Several other conspiracies were uncovered across the island, including on one of Charles Price's plantations in St John, where 'Coromantees' had 'agreed to rise, ravage the estates, and murder the white men'.

In May, a major uprising led by Apongo (named Wager by the British) broke out in Westmoreland. From there, freedom seekers trekked through the mountains into St Elizabeth and eventually Clarendon, attacking several plantations on the way. The conflict continued well into 1761, leaving more than £100,000 of property in ruins. Five hundred enslaved people, sixty free mixed-heritage people and sixty white colonists had died in the struggle. Many freedom fighters were executed in horrific ways, to set an example to others.

With the island's white population vastly outnumbered, the threat of rebellion had always lain just under the surface. During the eighteenth century, the British Caribbean experienced more than seventy aborted or actual uprisings. White people voiced naked fear in hysterical reports of 'desperate wretches, who in their fury spared neither age nor sex', and 'cut and mangled … bodies after a most shocking manner.' Lurid accounts emerged of rebels drinking murdered white men's blood mixed with rum. In one case, they allegedly sawed their enslaver's 'skull asunder, and made use of it as a punch bowl'.

Freedom fighters Fortune and Kingston, captured during Tacky's War, gibbeted alive on the outskirts of Kingston, Jamaica. They survived for seven and nine days respectively before being dissected, sewn back up and placed back on display as a warning to others. Drawing by Pierre Eugène du Simitière, Kingston, 10 May 1760. Library Company of Philadelphia.

Although free people with African ancestry who enslaved Africans themselves had as much to lose as white enslavers, they had lost the trust of Jamaica's ruling elite. The ruling class increasingly believed the very existence of mixed-heritage individuals threatened white power on the island by blurring the lines between white and Black; enslaved and free.

Enslavers suspected mixed-heritage people had leveraged their lighter skin to pose as free, travelling between plantations, spreading news of planned uprisings. To avoid this in future, they passed a law that freed people must carry their certificates of freedom and wear special badges denoting their status. In an era long before widespread use of passports or other identification papers, this constituted an extreme discriminatory measure.

Another piece of legislation was more significant for elite people with African ancestry like Frances. In 1761, the Jamaica Assembly passed a law limiting inheritances for mixed-heritage people to £2,000 Jamaica currency (£1,200 sterling) – a tiny fraction of Frances, Bob and their mother Susanna's legacies. They objected to larger bequests because they:

> tend greatly to destroy the distinction requisite, and absolutely necessary, to be kept up in this island, between white persons and negroes, their issue and offspring, and may in progress of time be the means of decreasing the number of white inhabitants.

The fewer white people, the higher the risk they would be unable to quash resistance. From this perspective, unions such as Gibson and Susanna's could be fatal. Rumours circulated that the uprising in St Mary had been triggered when 'a white overseer' took 'the wife of one of this [Coromantee] people to his bed'.[105]

The inheritance cap challenged Englishmen's treasured rights to leave their property freely. When asked to justify the measure to the Board of Trade in London, the Assembly launched an enquiry into 'what exorbitant grants and devises have been made to negroes and mulattoes, or the illegitimate issue of the negroes or mulattoes within the fourth degree'. When the committee reported back in November 1762, it listed thirteen notorious cases by name. The very first examples given were Peter Caillard's will in favour of Susanna and her children, and Gibson Dalzell's legacy to Frances and Bob.

Jamaican enslavers were deeply troubled by these bequests; their feelings are on full display in the petition submitted to the Board of Trade by Lovell Stanhope, agent for Jamaica (and future MP for Winchester), in June 1763. Asking for assent to the inheritance cap law, he outlined how the measures taken in 1733 had aimed to uphold the vital 'distinction of colour' by limiting the political and civic power of people with mixed ancestry. However, no laws had been made regarding inheritances as the Jamaican ruling class had 'little imagined that their successors would ever degenerate so as to devise their Estates to a spurious Progeny'.

Stanhope highlighted 'the ascendency which the Mulattoes, especially the Females, have already in that Country over dissolute Minds, and of the necessity which there is of restraining them'. If action was not taken 'a great part of the property of the Island will be in the hands of Mulattoes' and 'as Power ever follows property ... the Power will then be in their hands, and the Island become a Colony of Negroes and Mulattoes ... a People without Spirit, religion or Morality ... degenerate and dastardly'.

Stanhope's diatribe did not immediately convince the Board of Trade, which also sought the opinion of several prominent absentee Jamaican enslavers, including Gibson's debtor William Beckford, and Florentius Vassall (who we will meet in Chapter 7). Unsurprisingly these absentees were unanimous in their support for the law; nonetheless the Board took five years to endorse it.[106]

There was a growing fear in Britain that mixed marriages would 'pollute' the gene pool. The hero of one 1766 novel felt a 'union between those of different complexions' was 'indelicate and almost unnatural'. In 1774, Henry Laurens, a major importer of Africans to Charleston, South Carolina (who we will meet in the next chapter), feared that within six years 'there will be at least 20,000 mulatties [sic] in London'. The following year, Samuel Martin, an absentee enslaver from Antigua, insisted migrants be banned to 'save the natural beauty of Britons from the Morisco tint'.

Despite this hyperbole, the majority of discussion around the dangers of relationships between white and Black people focused on the working poor. Even Jamaican enslaver Edward Long, who likened such unions to bestiality with phrases like 'goatish embraces', made an exception for men like Gibson Dalzell. If a man had no legitimate heir, 'his illegitimate child may be, by the polish of a good education, and moral principles', be found 'well deserving to possess' his fortune. He even mentioned in passing that 'this yellow brood' might be well received in England, though 'a well-educated Mulatta must lead a very unpleasant kind of life here'.

At the same time, just as Stanhope feared a threat to white political power in Jamaica, Long warned: 'the alloy may spread so extensively as even to reach the middle, and then the higher order of the people' in Britain. A man with African ancestry might win the lottery and so buy himself a seat in Parliament. Joshua Steele of Barbados declared in 1789: 'descendants of Negroes ... may now, perhaps, be seated among the Nobles and Commons in Parliament; (for without doubt, there had crept a little Negroe Blood among them...)'. [107]

In two known cases, he was right. Enslaver and West India merchant Richard Beckford, MP for Bridport, Arundel and Leominster in succession between 1780 and his death in 1796, was the son of Gibson's debtor William Beckford and an enslaved Jamaican woman.[108] James Townsend served as MP for the notoriously rotten boroughs of West Looe in Cornwall from 1767 to 1774, then Calne in Wiltshire between 1782 and 1787. His grandfather James Phipps, Governor of Cape Coast Castle in modern-day Ghana, had married the daughter of an African woman and a Dutch soldier. In other words, only three generations removed from his African ancestor, Townsend, like Beckford, would have been subject to the Jamaican inheritance cap.[109]

Despite the cap, some women of mixed heritage continued to be bequeathed far more than £1,200 by their fathers. In 1806, Alexander Fullerton left £10,000 in trust for his 'reputed natural' daughter Elizabeth Fullerton, born in Jamaica, then at school in Hackney. The four daughters of James Hay of Grenada and Elizabeth Junor, 'a free coloured woman', each inherited £10,000 from their father in 1819. Helen Bogle, daughter of St Domingue-born Adelaide Lamoinary, inherited £25,000 from her father, Jamaican merchant and enslaver (and business partner of Hutchison Mure) George Bogle, in 1813.[110]

Frances was lucky she had inherited from Gibson in 1756, five years before the inheritance cap law was passed in Jamaica. Otherwise some distant Dalzell relatives might have come knocking, claiming the money was rightfully theirs. Other family members were not so fortunate. When John Morse died in 1781, the vultures descended. Morse had left his five children with Frances's first cousin Elizabeth Augier almost £20,000 each. Their white relatives contested the will, claiming that they should be subject to the inheritance cap. This came as quite a shock to Nathaniel Middleton, husband to Morse's daughter Ann; until this moment he had been 'an entire Stranger' to her African ancestry. Though the Morse siblings were eventually victorious, their legal struggle dragged on until 1806.[111]

By the early 1760s, managing Lucky Hill from London was proving too difficult. In 1762, Frances, George and Bob granted a twenty-one-year lease to Hutchison Mure, formerly of Mure and Campbell, for £840 a year. According to the lease, if Mure was six weeks late with the rent, the Dalzells had the right to repossess the plantation. In stilted legal language, the document allowed for every disaster. Provision was made for the possibility that some of the 139 labourers – valued at £6,406 13s 9d – might be killed in an invasion or a rebellion or put to death for a crime; or buildings damaged by earthquakes, hurricanes or invasions.

Mure was to keep the place in good repair. But the valuation attached to the lease made it clear significant expenditure would be required. Though the boiling house and still house had recently been reroofed, the curing house roof was 'entirely out of repair, in want of a new coat of shingles'. The mortar of the plantation house walls was 'cracked and defaced in many places'; the boiling house walls 'greatly out of repair', and those of the curing house in a 'ruinate condition, cracked and broke down'. New stills, vats and tanks had recently been purchased, but the coppers were 'old and wore'.[112]

As Mure was based in London and approaching fifty, hoping to shortly retire to Suffolk, Lucky Hill was probably run on a day-to-day basis by his attorney James Kerr. Kerr owned Jamaican plantations in Westmoreland, Hanover and St James. He would soon play a cameo role in the story of Granville Sharp's legal struggle. For it was he who purchased Jonathan Strong from David Lisle in 1765 to be transported to Jamaica in one of Hutchison Mure and his partner Richard Atkinson's ships. Even after Sharp secured Strong's freedom with a writ of *habeas corpus* from the Lord Mayor of London, Kerr persisted with his claim, until he was forced to pay treble costs for wasting the court's time.

Hutchison Mure turned out to be a very bad tenant, who didn't pay the rent, or, it turned out, many other bills. By 1766, despite profiting from owning three other Jamaican estates and several slaving ships, he had run up private debts of £30,000. Although he managed to conceal this 'alarming and disgraceful secret' until 1781, the stress of keeping it was so overwhelming that 'he had sometimes feared for his reason'. After his firm was pronounced bankrupt in 1794, Hutchison died 'of a broken heart, in consequence of the ruined state of his affairs.'[113]

By 1770, Lucky Hill had been leased to Robert Graham. Graham was 'a near kinsman' of Thomas Bontein's, whom Frances, George and Bob had appointed alongside him as their attorney in 1768. He had arrived in Jamaica aged seventeen in 1752, quickly rising, with Bontein's help, to a position of power and influence, marrying into the wealthy Taylor family chronicled in Chapter 9. Like so many contemporaries – including Bontein – he had children with enslaved women, writing in 1760:

> I was not remarkable for that cold Virtue, Chastity ... and gave rather too great a latitude to a dissipated train of whoring, the consequence of which I now dayly see before me in a motely variegated race of different complexions.[114]*

But in December 1770, Robert Graham sent word to George that he and his wife Ann were ill, and with their daughter growing up, were 'very solicitous to leave the Island'. Might he end his lease before the term expired? In exchange, he would be willing to sell the 'very considerable additional stock of negroes and cattle' he had brought to Lucky Hill. It seems the Duffs did not take him up on the offer, as in 1784 Graham still held fifty-one people there.[115]

Meanwhile, Frances, George and Bob lost Friendship to the Paplay family. Following Gibson and Edward Manning's deaths, there remained 'numerous accounts open between them', and their attorneys, George Paplay and Thomas Bontein, went to arbitration to decide who owed what. In 1763, it was determined Gibson Dalzell's estate owed Manning's over £2,600. To pay this debt, Bob and Frances were ordered to convey their half of Friendship to George Paplay.

At the time of transfer, this included ownership of eighteen men and twenty-eight women. Their names, the only sense we have of these otherwise anonymous individuals, are the usual odd mixture of classical (Caesar, Jupiter, Venus); British place names (London, Malbrough, Gloster, Bristol, Middlesex, Portland); and (sometimes jumbled) African names. Those giving some indication of where they might have been

---

* In the same year, he sent Mary, one of the women he abused, to be sold in Belize, complaining she was too talkative. Brown, *Tacky's Revolt*, p. 211.

from, or which weekday they were born (based on Akan day-names), include Angola Will; Acra (perhaps from Accra in modern-day Ghana); Cudjoe (Kojo) and Juba (Adwoa), both born on a Monday; Quaco (Kwaku), born on a Wednesday; Yabba, born on a Thursday; Cuffy (Kofi) and Phibba (Afua), both born on a Friday; and Quasheba (Akosua), born on a Sunday. As 'Blind Rose' could not see, the valuers considered her worth nothing. By this time, George Paplay had died, and so this all passed to his son, Edward Manning Paplay. Manning and Paplay's scheming against the Dalzells had finally paid off.[116] Between the loss of Friendship and unsatisfactory tenants at Lucky Hill, there was little profit coming to Frances from Jamaica.

Despite his parents' continuing entreaties, Frances and George refused to live in Scotland. Both preferred the high life in London.[117] George's father became Earl Fife in April 1759; their own status advanced accordingly. The couple attended Court on 4 June 1760 to celebrate the birthday of Prince George, who would shortly be crowned George III. Jean disapproved of such 'passing time away idly, gazing upon fine people with whom … [one] had no connection'. She warned him: 'these sorts of amusements are a dream that will soon vanish, and leave nothing behind, but regret for loss of time.'[118] George's older brother James, a longstanding MP, encouraged George to run for Parliament, but he – having never shown much interest in a useful occupation – refused.[119]

The family blamed Frances for the couple's reluctance to live north of the Tweed. George's father formally excluded Frances from the income from George's estates near Elgin in June 1760. He claimed this was 'due to sufficient provision by her father', but it feels more like pique.[120]

George continued to dote on Frances, writing to her in May 1761: 'Don't be surprised at a love letter to a wife'. In 1767, prompted by 'love and affection', but also 'good and onerous causes and considerations' – probably a fear his family would not support her properly – he made a 'bond of provision' for her. On his death, she was to receive £100 a year, and inherit his Elgin and Milton estates as well as his furniture, plate, china, chaises and horses, and other household items.[121]

The advent of grandchildren improved relations with George's mother at least. Frances and George's eldest son, William Robert, was born in July 1758, and baptised the following month at St James's, Piccadilly. Jean, 'in perfect friendship', sent the christening suit that had served all fourteen of her children, wishing 'all the happiness that your heart can desire'.[122] Sadly the baby died the following April, just shy of nine months old.

A year later, in March 1760, Frances gave birth to their next son, James, affectionately referred to as 'Jem'. Frances wrote tongue-in-cheek to George: 'Jem is universally admired. I wish some old batchelor would take a fancy to him, & leave him a good estate; it would not perhaps be unexceptable if he left it first to his father' – a hint that, with the uncertainties of Jamaican property, their finances were still unstable.[123] Jean wrote to congratulate Frances, offering her help. But in the same breath she asked again whether they intended to visit Scotland that year, and complained George owed her several letters.[124] Frances joked:

> Mr. Duff observing that I am at a loss for subject to write to your Ladyship ... desires me to apologise for his not being a better correspondent, I answer that he has so often practised that part of epistolary writing, that he can do it infinitely better than I can.[125]

Frances's relationship with Bob had thawed too. In 1761 Bob, now nineteen, had recently started at Gibson's old college, Christ Church, Oxford. He sent his infant nephew Jem 'a great curiosity ... a map of England in a handkerchief', and invited Frances to visit him, insisting it would be 'extremely pleasant' to see her.[126] The following year he made an advantageous marriage to Jane, daughter of John Dodd, a wealthy Berkshire landowner and MP for Reading. Jane was described as 'an agreeable young lady of large fortune, and with every other accomplishment necessary to adorn the marriage state'. They lived at Tidmarsh Manor House in Berkshire and had three children.[127] As with Frances, Bob's African ancestry had not impeded his prospects in Britain. The next generation of mixed-heritage people would not be so fortunate.

Twins George and Jane Dorothea joined little Jem in the Duff nursery in March 1765, closely followed by their youngest daughter, Frances. She soon became the family pet, known affectionately as Little Fan, or Fanny. Frances told her mother-in-law: 'the children ... give us many agreeable hours, indeed ... their company makes us very happy.'

The family moved to a country house in Putney after George had an accident and broke his leg; then on to Hanwell Heath in Ealing. Though this was considered a more salubrious locale for George's health, Frances found herself 'at a loss for want of amusements' besides her children. George's brother Arthur complained they lived too far from town for a morning call, and griped at the 15s coach fare. All his brothers complained of George's 'want of friendliness and sociability'.

Unfortunately, Jem was, as one nineteenth-century family historian put it, 'insane from early life'. It is hard to know what his modern diagnosis would be, or how his symptoms first manifested. In a letter to Jean, Frances exclaimed: 'Jem just now read to me, good gods! how he does read. He is a riddle, I hope some sensible man will expound him.' Jem was still well enough in 1769 for George to make the nine-year-old his heir in a will drafted that year. However, some time afterwards he suffered 'a severe fit of illness and the visitation of God totally deprived him of his understanding'. When he was thirteen, Frances and George sent him to a small private asylum called Beaufort House on North End Road in Fulham, where he was cared for by their old friend and trustee Dr John Maule. He became known as 'James Thompson' as 'a matter of delicacy and family feeling'.[128]

Young George attended Norland House Academy in today's Holland Park. In April 1776 Frances reprimanded him: 'My Dear be obedient … & attend to your learning', likening his education to any other investment by remarking: 'it is the only return that you can make to us, for our love and affection for you'.[129] Meanwhile, by the age of eight, Fanny was progressing more slowly than her talented ten-year-old sister Jane Dorothea, 'who reads English and French extremely well, speaks both languages very easily, writes and counts to admiration, and is I am told very good at her needle, and as to her carriage it is quite elegant.'

Jean, widowed since 1763, increasingly extended her hospitality to her grandchildren at Rothiemay, though this was tiring; during one visit in 1775 she was 'so plagued and hurried that I can scarce turn me' – a feeling most grandparents can relate to! She also looked after the children when they were ill.[130] However, some signs of tension persisted. In 1768 Jean complained to George when her grandchildren didn't visit: 'they are not more welcome in your house than they ever were in mine.' She did not blame Frances, 'since I never found her but kind and affectionate to me', but could not guess 'what occasioned this strangeness in you to me … only I am conscious that I never deserved it'.

Frances herself still only rarely appeared in Scotland. In March 1777, Jean was disappointed Frances and George did not intend to visit Rothiemay that summer, saying of Frances: 'were she as happy in being with me as I would be to have her, she would not be so great a stranger'.[131] Strained relationships between daughters-in-law and mothers-in-law are hardly unusual. Yet the family papers refuse to satisfy our curiosity about the precise fault lines in this one. Did Frances still resent Jean's initial opposition to the marriage? Or her judgemental attitude to their London lifestyle? Did racial prejudice play a role? Perhaps all of the above.

Frances died in London in July 1778, aged only forty-nine. She was buried at St Martin-in-the-Fields, like her father and grandfather.[132] Her will was short and straightforward, naming her husband (who outlived her by forty years) as trustee and executor. She left Jem £100, and £200 each to Jane Dorothea and Fanny. With Jem in an asylum, the 'remainder of all the real and personal estates of whatever nature or kind soever in the Island of Jamaica' was to go to her younger son George. He also received twelve shares in the Sun Fire Office; the other children had one share each. Hoping her husband and children would not suffer the same trials she had endured, Frances exhorted her will 'may be understood in the plain sense without quibbling or any lawyers perverting my meaning'.[133]

It was probably for the best Frances did not live to see how her children's lives turned out. Neither daughter married, perhaps in part because they had no great fortune. This was apparent in Fanny's case when, aged eighteen, she was courted by one James Urquhart. His father forbade the match, as 'any marriage which does not bring money along with it, must end in his Destruction, and put an End to our Family with Regard to its Station among the landed Gentry of this Country'. Suffering smallpox, jaundice and consumption, Fanny died two years later. Jane Dorothea ended up keeping house for her father, dying in 1792 aged twenty-eight. After losing her, George finally moved to Elgin.

Young George joined the army, his uncle James Duff, now 2nd Earl Fife, obtaining a commission as ensign for him in the 1st Regiment of Foot Guards (now the Grenadier Guards) in 1781. Lord Fife hoped the 'young chap will do very well' under the command of young George's illegitimate cousin, Sir James Duff.* Instead, he metamorphosed into an

---

* General Sir James Duff, Lord Fife's son with his mother's maid, Margaret Adam, later acquired a Jamaican plantation through marrying heiress Basilia Dawes in 1785. He is former Prime Minister David Cameron's first cousin six times removed. Tayler and Tayler, *Book of the Duffs*, vol. 1, p. 169; 'General Sir James Duff', LBS: https://www.ucl.ac.uk/lbs/person/view/19162; 'How Do We Know David Cameron Has Slave Owners in Family Background?', *Guardian*, 29 September 2015: https://www.theguardian.com/world/2015/sep/29/how-do-we-know-david-cameron-has-slave-owning-ancestor.

'extremely giddy and thoughtless' gambler, spendthrift and philanderer, eloping to Europe with a married woman, Elizabeth Herbert. There, he developed 'a paralytic complaint which deprived him of the use of his limbs and his faithful partner carried him up and down stairs on her back to the tune of *All for love or the world well lost*.' Her aggrieved husband successfully sued George for 'criminal conversation';* the court decreed George must pay an eye-watering £15,000 damages.[134] This probably contributed to his decision to sell his half of Lucky Hill in 1800 to Kingstonians James Laing, Humphrey Ewing and John Jacques (an ancestor of Marcus Garvey's wife, Amy Euphemia Jacques)[135] for £3,214 5s 8 d. Bob sold his half to the same men for the same price.[136]

Jem outlived all his siblings but spent his entire life in Beaufort House asylum. In 1828, Dr John Maule's son William, who after his father's death 'executed the same office of friendship by watching over the well-doing and proper treatment of the said James Duff, otherwise Thompson', reported 'that I saw him a few days ago, when he was still in the same hopeless state of fatuity in which I have seen him for the last forty years upwards, that his infirmity is irremediable, and that he is in every way incapable of managing the most ordinary affairs.' Jem died in the asylum in March 1832, aged seventy-four, having lived there for over sixty years.[137]

Frances's African ancestry didn't prevent her from joining the British aristocracy, but she was, as far as we know, the *only* heiress of such heritage to do so. Others wed, variously, surgeons, soldiers, merchants, a wool broker, a lawyer, and an old Etonian MP who was also a poet, besides men whose careers were not prominent enough to make a mark on the historical record.[138]

Of the eighteen heiresses with African ancestry known to have married in Britain in the eighteenth or early nineteenth century, one who stands out is Jane Harry. A talented young artist who befriended Dr Johnson, she inherited £1,200 sterling – the exact figure specified by the inheritance cap law – from her father, Jamaican enslaver and merchant George Hibbert, in 1780. She married Worcester surgeon Joseph

---

* 'Conversation' in this sense meant sexual intercourse. Until 1857, under English common law, husbands could sue a man who committed adultery with his wife, regardless of whether she consented. Criminal conversation is still on the statute books in the US states of Hawaii, Kansas, Maine and North Carolina.

Thresher two years later. It was not so much her heritage that occasioned this relatively lowly match – although one of her husband's associates referred to her disparagingly as 'that West Indian girl' – but the fact that she was shunned by London society after converting to Quakerism in 1778. Her faith led her to an unusually abolitionist stance. After her father's death she 'formed a design of going to Jamaica ... with a view to procure the freedom of her mother's Negroes, and to instruct them in the principles of the Christian religion'. Like Frances's mother Susanna, Jane's mother, Charity Harry, was a free mixed-heritage woman who had inherited wealth and enslaved people. Just as the Seven Years' War impeded Frances's efforts, Jane was thwarted by the danger of travelling during the American Revolutionary War. She died aged just twenty-eight in 1784.[139] Jane was rare amongst women of similar birth in thinking of emancipation. Others, like Frances, had no qualms in keeping their enslaved property, which often made up a large proportion of the value of their inheritance, even when they became the owners of their own mothers.[140]

The most famous child of an enslaved woman in Georgian Britain, Dido Elizabeth Belle, was not the great heiress she is sometimes portrayed as (most recently in Amma Asante's film *Belle*).[141] Though she grew up living a genteel life at Kenwood House in Hampstead, her father, naval captain Sir John Lindsay, did not mention her in his 1788 will, and she inherited only £500 plus a £100 annuity from her grand-uncle, Lord Mansfield, in 1793. This may explain why her husband, Frenchman John Davinier, whom she married at the relatively advanced age of thirty-two, was merely a gentleman's steward or valet.[142]

Frances was lucky to inherit when she did, when factors such as education, Protestant faith, wealth and having white relations could somewhat mitigate prejudice against skin colour. The prejudices that began to crystallise in the wake of Tacky's War became even more entrenched following the outbreak of the Haitian Revolution in 1791. The British preferred to believe unrest in the French colony of St Domingue had been triggered by the actions of a free man with mixed ancestry named Vincent Ogé, rather than by the horrors of enslavement itself. Like Frances and Bob, Ogé had been educated in Europe. Having witnessed the early months of the French Revolution in Paris, he attempted a military coup, seeking equality for all free men in St Domingue. Although he was defeated and executed, this heightened tensions between the *gens de couleur* and white planters. Even abolitionists such as William

Wilberforce and Thomas Clarkson (who had met Ogé in Paris) believed it was 'seeing their Lords and Masters ... at daggers drawn' that decided people to 'take advantage of the divisions ... to assert their violated rights by force of arms'. The British didn't just fear the prospect of educated young people with mixed ancestry returning to the colonies and spreading revolt. In the more lurid tales of Haitian violence, mixed-heritage sons murdered their white fathers in cold blood. Rebellious at best, patricidal at worst, these people could no longer be trusted.[143]

We can see this shift in attitudes in the stories told about mixed-heritage women. In a 1743 novel, *The Dramatic History of ... Mrs. Llwhuddwhydd* – amongst the first to have a mixed-heritage protagonist – young Chloe, who is described as a 'quadroon',* rises from undercook to respectable and wealthy woman by marrying her Welsh landlord, David Llwhuddwhydd. However, her subsequent adultery is presented to the reader as proof positive that her true, immoral, nature cannot be changed. But significantly, this stems just as much from her father's criminality – he was a lawyer transported to America for fraud – as her mother's African ancestry.[144]

By the 1790s, when heiresses with African ancestry began to appear more frequently in literature, the prejudice that characters express against skin colour grows far more pronounced. In *The Woman of Colour* (1808), when Augustus first sees Olivia Fairfield, heiress to £60,000, he – echoing George Osborne's later revulsion at the thought of marrying a 'Hottentot Venus' – 'started back with a momentary feeling nearly allied to disgust; for I beheld a skin approaching to the hue of a negro's, in the woman whom my father introduced to me as my intended wife!' Augustus's sister-in-law is even worse. When the family sit down to a meal, Olivia is served a huge plate of steaming rice. Her hostess explains: 'I understood people of your – I thought that you almost *lived* upon rice'. Olivia exclaims: 'that *she* considers *me* as but *one* remove from the brute creation is very evident'.[145]

Frances Dalzell may have been long forgotten by the novel-reading public by 1848, yet there are striking parallels between her and Miss Swartz in Thackeray's *Vanity Fair*. Both are mixed-heritage women sent to boarding school in England from the Caribbean as children; both

---

* A now offensive term from the Latin word *quartus*, used to describe people with one Black grandparent, who were therefore a quarter African.

face challenges on the marriage market, but ultimately succeed. Just as Frances married the Honourable George Duff, son of Lord Braco, Miss Swartz is eventually wed 'to a young sprig of Scotch nobility', the Honourable James McMull, son and heir of one Lord Castletoddy. The McMulls, like the Duffs, take their place in society amongst the 'nobs of the West End', and the last we hear of Miss Swartz is: 'Rhoda McMull will disengage the whole of the Castletoddy property as soon as poor dear Lord Castletoddy dies, who is quite epileptic; and little Mac*duff* [emphasis added] McMull will be Viscount Castletoddy.'[146]

Yet the true story of Frances Dalzell is more gripping than fictional Miss Swartz's. It's the rags-to-riches tale of how a descendant of enslaved Africans became an heiress. How her mother and grandmother endured sexual violence and made impossible choices to survive so that she could thrive. Unlike many literary heroines, Frances displayed keen business acumen. Like her mother, she had to fight to gain and retain control of her inheritance.

By the criteria of her time, Frances's was a success story. She traded her wealth for a place in the British aristocracy, climbing higher than any other known mixed-heritage heiress before or since. But her position was dependent on the very system that had oppressed her maternal ancestors. If we expected Frances or Susanna to show sympathy for the people they enslaved, we'd be wrong. The stain of human exploitation permeated their 'success' as deeply as Frances's initials were branded on the people of Lucky Hill.[147]

Portrait of Mary Oswald, née Ramsay, by Johan Zoffany, c.1763–4. The painting was acquired by the National Gallery, London, in 1938.

3

Mary Ramsay (1717–1794)

Mary Ramsay's story weaves threads across the Atlantic from Scotland to Jamaica, London to Sierra Leone, Germany to East Florida, as she goes from Kingston merchant's daughter to grand dame of an Ayrshire estate, attracting a savage epitaph from Rabbie Burns.

RICHARD OSWALD knew how profitable selling Africans to British colonies could be. As a young man he had seen the scramble to acquire them each time a new ship docked in Kingston, Jamaica, or the James River, Virginia. He had once invested in a voyage trafficking Africans to Virginia from Jamaica. His current business imported valuable colonial products – tobacco, sugar, rum – to London, while supplying plantations with everything from linen to nails. He even dabbled with exporting wigs.

Now an irresistible opportunity arose: to buy a slaving fort with his associates. Bance Island, in the mouth of the Sierra Leone River, was ideally situated to attract slavers who sought to fill their ships in one swoop, rather than make several troublesome stops along the coast. But the fort lay in disrepair. Twenty years previously, it had been attacked by an Afro-Portuguese trader and a cohort of Africans, who had blown up the underground powder magazine (storehouse) and burned down the buildings; damage not completely rectified by the last owner. Richard needed a quick injection of cash to pay for his share of the renovations. That money would come not from the profits of colonial trade, nor from the privateering he had sponsored in the last war, but from his new wife, an heiress from Jamaica.

The North-west Prospect of Benselandon the River Sierra-Leone

Bance Island, in the Sierra Leone River, c.1727.

Following Mary Ramsay's footsteps will lead us on a global journey, from the streets of a small Scottish town, through the wharves and counting houses of Kingston, Jamaica, and the City of London, to war-torn Germany during the Seven Years' War, and finally to a grand country estate in Ayrshire. Following her capital, invested in her husband's business, will take us even further, to a small island off the coast of Sierra Leone with archaeological remains as revealing as those at Newton Burial Ground, to the ships that plied the Atlantic from there to Charleston, South Carolina, packed with captive Africans, and to a 20,000-acre parcel of land in East Florida, laboured on by hundreds of enslaved people. A hard-nosed businesswoman, Mary played a key supporting role in her husband's extensive slaving and colonial enterprises. But, as Robert Burns asked in his vituperative ode to Mary:

> Can thy keen inspection trace
> Aught of Humanity's sweet, melting grace?[1]

The daughter of Alexander Ramsay and his wife Jean (née Ferguson), Mary was born in her mother's native town, Alloa, near Stirling in Scotland on 9 September 1717. The Ramsay family hailed from the Catholic strongholds of Laithers, Aberdeenshire, and Melrose, Banffshire, in north-east Scotland. Scotland had only recently been united into one kingdom with England by the Act of Union of 1707, and there were many, especially in the Highlands – known as Jacobites – who favoured the return of a Catholic Stuart King over the rule of the Protestant imported from Hanover by the English. The Ramsays probably sympathised with the Jacobite cause.

Following the failure of the uprising of 1715, intended to put James Francis Edward Stuart, the 'Old Pretender', on the throne, Mary's father had moved south to the busy port of Bo'ness, around seventeen miles north-west of Edinburgh.[2] Daniel Defoe described Bo'ness as 'a long town, of one street, and no more, extended along the shore, close to the water', peopled by 'the best seamen in the Firth; and particularly they are not sailors only, but even pilots for the coast of Holland, they are so acquainted with it, and so with the Baltick, and the coast of Norway also'.[3] It was here Alexander Ramsay began his mercantile career, probably exporting coal. Like many of his countrymen, who left Scotland for the colonies in droves, he was 'a Convert to the Scots maxim of seeking, as the last resort, in a more distant region or scene of business that fortune which shall be denied [him] at home'.[4]

Taking ship with a toddler for a voyage lasting five to seven weeks, the Ramsays endured cramped quarters, seasickness, meagre rations and unrelenting heat as they sailed south, but would also have been 'diverted with many new and surprising sights in the watery world'. Their route took them south, across the Bay of Biscay, past Portugal; in sight of Madeira, they picked up the prevailing trade winds that swept them across the Atlantic.

Nothing they saw at sea would assault their senses like the experience of arriving in Jamaica. As they approached land, they saw the soaring Blue Mountains, lush vegetation, and the ports of Port Royal and Kingston crowded with sails. Another Scot recalled: 'gazing on what was now to be our Country and our Home ... I could not help a crowd of thoughts that pressed upon me. I remember the happy Climates, and the dear Acquaintance I had left behind ... while I was now to settle in a place not half inhabited, cursed with intestine Broils [internal strife]'.

A popular ditty amongst the Kingston market women warned: 'Newcome buckra, He get sick, he take fever, He be die; He be die.'[5] However, for Alexander Ramsay, the high-stakes gamble of emigrating to Jamaica paid off. Joining a close-knit circle of Scottish expats, he established himself as a merchant in Kingston, operating from a counting house between Princess Street and Mathews Lane, a couple of blocks north from the waterfront, where his wharf – co-owned with another Scottish merchant, William Gordon, and his brother-in-law James Ferguson – lay between Harbour Street and Port Royal Street. He acquired a sloop, or one-masted sailing ship, rather narcissistically named *Alexander*, and a wherry, or light rowing boat, used for ferrying cargo and passengers between the sloop and the wharf. He exported sugar to Britain on behalf of the island's oldest and wealthiest enslaving families, while importing wine and beer for the Jamaican market. He also imported indigo – which, when fermented in urine, made blue dye for clothing – from other European colonies, probably for re-export to England.[6] A canny operator, Ramsay thrived despite the disruption of the First Maroon War, and a concurrent dip in London sugar prices.

By 1726, like his near contemporary Gibson Dalzell, Ramsay was looking to establish his own plantation. That April he obtained permission from the Governor, Henry, Duke of Portland, to settle 300 acres in Westmoreland. At the island's westernmost extremity, Westmoreland was still largely unoccupied by enslavers, who feared Maroon attacks. Ramsay sold his land to his friend Robert Rutherford for a token £10, bought seventy-five labourers and lent Rutherford over £5,000, expecting they would share the plantation, named Spring Garden, as equal partners. But Rutherford died in 1734, before he could legally transfer half the ownership to Ramsay. Rutherford had been 'greatly distressed' financially after buying more land, and the plantation was by now mortgaged to three other men. In the end, Ramsay settled for a financial claim on the estate's proceeds.[7] By 1735, Spring Garden was producing eighty-five hogsheads of sugar, nineteen puncheons of rum, and eighty planks of mahogany annually, which Ramsay exported on commission.[8]

In less than twenty years on the island, Alexander Ramsay became extremely rich, signalling his status by carrying a gold-tipped cane and living in one of the grandest houses in Kingston. Mary grew up next door to Sir Nicholas Lawes, who served as Governor of Jamaica from 1717 to 1722, on the south side of Parade, Kingston's most elegant square, also home to the parish church, the main town well and the military magazine. Inside their home a marble table, mahogany furniture, Delft china and silver plate spoke to the family's genteel aspirations. They even kept their tea strainer in a sharkskin leather case. Mary got a sense of both of her parents' homeland and her family's colonial context from the pictures on the walls: nine prints of gentlemen's country seats and palaces, alongside maps of Scotland, England, the Caribbean and North America. Although they lived next door to the Protestant church, they hung a large painting of the Virgin Mary on their wall.[9]

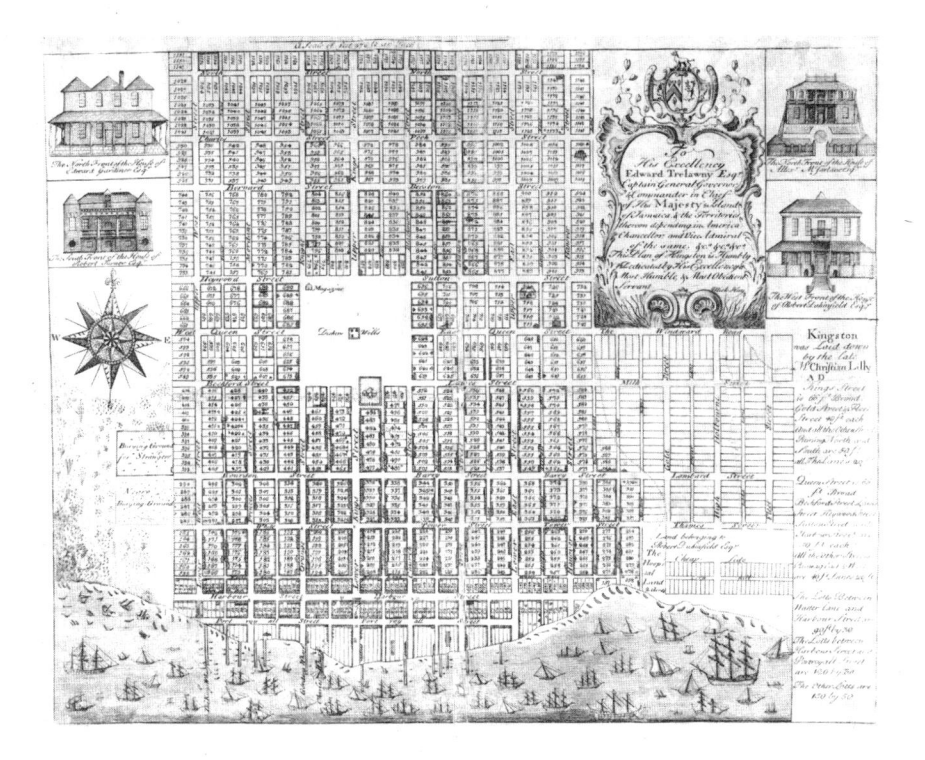

Michael Hay's Map of Kingston, c.1740. Mary's childhood home may have resembled the house in the top right corner, which belonged to her 'good friend' Alexander MacFarlane, who she appointed as her 'attorney, factor and agent' in 1740.

Unlike Frances Dalzell, Mary was not sent to school in Britain. It may be that her father preferred to keep his only child and heir close, valuing mercantile over academic skills. Whatever the nature of her formal education, living in close proximity to her father's counting house and wharf allowed Mary to pick up an understanding of his business – it would serve her well.

Despite the elite's efforts to create a refined society, young Mary encountered Kingston's brutal realities daily. Enslaved people judged guilty of crimes were gibbeted (hung alive in chains) until they died – sometimes days later – right outside her house on Parade.[10] She would have seen slaving ships coming and going whenever she visited her father at work. It was said you could smell these ships coming from miles away, packed as they were with men, women and children lying in their own excrement and vomit.

On arrival in Kingston, Africans were inspected like horses by enslavers looking to replace those they had worked to death, or purchase them for re-export. Newly oiled to give their skin a healthy-looking sheen, some had their anuses plugged to disguise the tell-tale signs of dysentery. A number were sold on deck, the rest herded into 'slave yards'. The standard method for selling these men, women and children was known as the 'scramble':

> As soon as the hour agreed on arrived, the doors of the yard were suddenly thrown open, and in rushed a considerable number of purchasers, with all the ferocity of brutes. Some instantly seized such of the negroes as they could conveniently lay hold of with their hands. Others, being prepared with several handkerchiefs or a rope tied together, encircled with these as many as they were able. It is scarcely possible to describe the confusion ... The poor astonished negroes were so much terrified by these proceedings, that several of them, through fear, climbed over the walls ... but were soon hunted down and retaken.

Some Africans believed 'they were seized on by a herd of cannibals ... to be speedily devoured'.[11] Their screams of terror would have been audible from Ramsay's nearby wharf and counting house, perhaps even from his townhouse six blocks north.

While the majority of trafficked people were destined for the sugar plantations, a sizeable number remained in Kingston – the town developed the largest Black population of all Britain's colonial settlements.[12] Alexander Ramsay himself kept four men to row his wherry, Will, George, Weir and London, plus two wharfingers, Bamff and Mingo, to oversee daily activity at the docks. Nine others worked directly for his shipping operation: four smiths, Elford, Scipio, Dick and Boston; four sailors, Shrewsbury, Adam, Sambo and Cosh; and Peter, a sailmaker. The Ramsays' smart townhouse on Parade would not have functioned without the requisite number of staff. Seven men: Dick, Titas, Henry, Cato, Tom, Jack and Adam; and four women: Katty, Mimba (who had a young child), Pheba and Eve worked as domestics.[13]

So, Mary grew up surrounded by enslaved Africans: on the streets, working in her father's counting house and wharf, and waiting on her at home. Again, their classical (Scipio, Cato, Titas) and British place names (Bamff, Boston, Shrewsbury) tell us more about their enslavers than themselves. Pheba (Afua – born on a Friday) and Mimba (Amba – born on a Saturday), however, retained Akan day names; Mingo's name meant chief in Wolof, Sambo's signified uncle in Fula and second son in Hausa.

Urban and domestic workers were at as much risk of brutality as field labourers. Bermuda-born Mary Prince recalled that her mistress, besides 'all sorts of household work … taught me (how can I ever forget it!) … to know the exact differences between the smart of the rope, the cart-whip, and the cow skin, when applied to my naked body by her own cruel hand.'[14] Mary Ramsay was probably initiated into disciplining domestics – who would form part of her inheritance from her father – from an early age.[15] One woman, Flora, was so unhappy working for the family that she took the risky decision to run away.[16]

At twenty, Mary was still legally a minor when her father died in late 1737. Unusually, she chose her own guardians, nominating her uncle James Ferguson and Kingston merchant Mathias Phelp. It seems Jean was in Britain when Alexander died. This explains why Mary, like Frances Dalzell, 'took on herself alone the burden' of acting as her father's sole executrix, proving his will in January 1738. She inherited the bulk of his fortune and began to receive his 'rents, issues and profits'.[17]

Mary inherited 104 people, itemised in Alexander Ramsay's probate inventory with monetary values, just like his mahogany table or china plates. Seventy-five were simply listed as being employed at Spring Garden plantation. We know only one of their names; in 1737, Caesar received ten shillings 'for shooting a runaway negro'.

The skilled men at the wharf in Kingston were the most 'valuable'. While appraisers rated labourers at Spring Garden at about £22 on average, the wharfingers were listed at £27 each, the wherry men and smiths at £29; Shrewsbury the sailor at £43; and Peter the sailmaker at £71. Mary also inherited her father's half of two men, August and Cuffee, both valued at £18, who had been co-owned with her uncle James Ferguson.[18]

Like Peter Caillard, Alexander Ramsay was owed money by a long list of people when he died. Mary and Jean (who had now returned to Jamaica) initiated a case in the Jamaican Chancery Court against Robert Rutherford's executors to get back the money Alexander had loaned him.[19] As Susanna Augier knew well, many debtors would do anything to avoid paying up.

Mary and Jean saw no reason to stay in Kingston. They had inherited more than enough money to escape the ongoing threats of disease, extreme weather, uprisings and foreign invasion, and buy themselves a comfortable existence back in Britain. In late May 1738, the two women signed a Power of Attorney, electing Mary's guardians – James Ferguson and Mathias Phelp – as their representatives on the island.[20] Knowing Scotland only from her parents' pictures and maps, and their friends' conversations, Mary would finally see her birthplace as a grown woman. Naturally impatient – by her own admission – she no doubt found the lengthy voyage keeping her from her new life tedious. Over twenty years later she pondered:

> I sometimes think I am Like one at Sea on a long voyage, that when there's a long Cross Wind they begin to say they will never get to Land, but when a little breeze of fair wind blows up they say we are so much nearer the end of our voyage than we was yesterday. I Remember that was our way.[21]

Less than a year after they arrived in Glasgow, news arrived from Jamaica that Mary's uncle James Ferguson had died. As Mary put it: '(after Sundry Legacies bequeath[ed] to Sundrys)' – including a £50 annuity for her mother Jean – he 'Devised the Whole of his Remaining Estate Real and personal to me'. Though he had not named her as executrix, James's will authorised Mary to transact on his estates' behalf, displaying a high level of trust in the young woman. In reality, she had to find someone else to supervise her business in Kingston, and in March 1740 signed a new Power of Attorney, naming her 'good friends', Kingston merchants Alexander MacFarlane* and Patrick Kerr, and William Lindsay of Spanish Town, clerk to the Grand Court, as her new agents. We get a sense of a self-possessed woman, as she asserts 'now and for some time past' – in reality only nineteen months – she had 'arrived at the full years of Majority and of Age to act by and for myself'.[22]

Her new attorneys were tasked to bring her former agent, Mathias Phelp, and James Graham (another Kingston merchant) to account for their 'Intrumissions' – criminal interference – with her inheritance

---

* Alexander MacFarlane was also a gifted mathematician and astronomer who observed the stars from his house in Kingston and left his instruments to the University of Glasgow. Bryden, 'Jamaican Observatories', pp. 261–72.

from her father. In Scots law, vicious intromission is defined as illegally taking over the deceased's moveable property, punishable by becoming liable for all the dead person's debts.[23] Phelp probably coveted Mary's money due to his own indebtedness; he died owing £33,000.[24] Was this the first time Mary experienced what she later called 'the falseness ... of the generosity of Mankind'? She concluded: 'Most people is [sic] for themselves, and that you find to your cost and embarrassment.'[25]

By the late 1740s, Mary had moved from Glasgow to the heart of the City of London, living in the parish of St Stephen's, Coleman Street, between the Guildhall and the recently erected Bank of England. Her mother died sometime between 1747 and 1751.[26] Unlike leafy Mayfair, with its newly laid out squares lined with the homes of aristocrats and gentlemen, where young Frances Dalzell was living at this time, the City was a busy port, crowded with merchants and tradesmen, counting houses and coffee houses, a 'confused Babel ... a Hotch-Potch of half-moon and serpentine Streets, close, dismal, long Lanes, stinking Allies, dark, gloomy Courts, and suffocating Yards'.[27]

Despite being an heiress, Mary evaded wedlock for over a decade after she returned from Jamaica. There is a hint she had options in a comment she made more than ten years later: 'I have ... never had any reason to regret not being married to a title, as they say in London.'[28] Perhaps, not needing a husband for financial support, she chose to lead an independent life, rather than marry an impoverished nobleman. Or perhaps her heart had already been captured, and she was waiting patiently for a man she had met as a teenager in Jamaica.

Mary had first encountered Glasgow merchant Richard Oswald, then in his early thirties, at the Kingston home of her family doctor, Alexander Grant. The son of a Presbyterian minister from Dunnet, Caithness, Richard was a 'man of great knowledge and ready conversation'. Ambitious and astute, with an eye for detail and a love of logistics, he wore glasses, having seriously weakened his eyes with avid reading. When Mary met him he was in a relationship with a Glasgow woman named Agnes Barr, who bore him two sons, Richard and George, during the 1730s.

Though mostly based in Norfolk, Virginia, Richard visited Jamaica regularly, representing his cousins' firm. Richard and Alexander Oswald were the fifth-largest importers of Virginian tobacco in Glasgow, also importing Madeira, Canary wine and Caribbean sugar. They were known as 'kindly, hospitable, and generous old bachelors, with a special warm side to any one from Caithness'; but when it came to business, their motto was 'show no mercy'.[29] As their agent, or supercargo, Richard was responsible for overseeing the enslaved people loading their ships, negotiating sales and collecting debts. In 1734, Richard made his first foray into trading in human beings, investing in his cousins' ship, the *Amity*, when it transported twenty-three Africans from Jamaica to Virginia.[30]

Mary met Richard again in London sometime after he moved to the city in early 1746. They were thrown together both socially – as in Jamaica, the network of Scots was close-knit – and geographically; Mary's home lay just half a mile from Richard's new counting house at no. 17 Philpot Lane. It is also possible Mary sought Richard's advice on how to manage her Jamaican assets from afar. Popular memory in Glasgow a century later had it that Richard had travelled to London to help a young 'West India' heiress and 'in the course of his communications regarding the improvement of this lady's estate, he captivated herself and married her.'[31]

Since they had last met, Richard had made an eye-watering £15,000 from sponsoring privateering voyages with his cousins during the War of the Austrian Succession, giving him the capital necessary to move from Glasgow to London, where he soon became the city's ninth-largest tobacco trader. As his business grew, like other colonial merchants such as Hutchison Mure, he acted on commission as a factor, insurance broker, stockbroker, banker, executor, trustee and guardian. He even bought some clients lottery tickets. He also continued to supply Virginia with captive Africans, transporting twenty from Antigua to Hampton on his ships the *Johnson* and the *Richard* in 1750–1.[32]

Mary married Richard on 17 November 1750 at St Martin-in-the-Fields. A mutual friend reported, sounding somewhat surprised: 'R. Oswald has lately got a wife!'[33] Certainly, both Mary and Richard were far older than average to be getting married. At thirty-three, Mary, like Sarah Newton, wed a decade later than most women from wealthy backgrounds. Forty-five-year-old Richard was almost twenty years older at marriage than most mercantile men.[34] Nonetheless, in their portraits painted around this time by William Denune, they look well-matched, both with rather serious expressions, firm set mouths and a steady gaze. Mary is modestly dressed, a string of dark beads her only adornment.[35]

Only love could have induced Mary to marry. She called Richard 'my Dearest Life'. In her opinion, it was 'a Wife's duty to be as much with

Twin portraits of Mary and Richard Oswald by
William Denune before their marriage.

her husband as possible while Love and Harmony subsists. When that is over, the greater distance the better.'[36] Given their continuing closeness, we can conclude love and harmony survived throughout their thirty-four-year marriage. Like Sarah, Mary remained childless. Without the cares of motherhood Mary was able to channel her considerable energies, common sense and experience into supporting her husband and his colonial enterprises.

Mary was now plunged straight into the heart of Richard's business operation, living cheek-by-jowl with his associates, clerks and servants at 17 Philpot Lane. The house lay halfway between the quays and wharfs around London Bridge and the Lombard Street banks, a stone's throw from the maze of City coffee houses clustered round the Bank of England. Richard visited establishments like the Carolina Coffee House daily, garnering the latest colonial news and conducting business with fellow merchants. From their private office, Richard and his partner John Mill, a Scottish merchant who mostly traded between Aberdeen and Newcastle, kept a close eye on the clerks in the next room, satisfying Richard's obsession for detail. It was less ideal as a marital home as the Oswalds' bedroom abutted Mill's, while clerks slept in the attic above. Mary's relationship with Mill was not entirely cordial: as she later remarked, they rarely agreed on politics; 'partnerships is [sic] disagreeable, & many unforeseen inconveniences may arise'.[37]

Mary's money and social network helped elevate Richard from prosperous tobacco merchant to a leading figure in the transatlantic economy. Her £20,000 fortune comprised £8,285 of personal assets – including enslaved Africans and debts owed – and £11,372 in real estate: the Kingston properties and her interest in Spring Garden.[38] Mary had sold her father's counting house in Princess Street in 1747 or 1748, but still received an average net rent of £90 a year from properties on Port Royal and Harbour Streets in the 1750s.[39] The Jamaican Chancery Court had ruled in Mary's favour in 1744, ordering Robert Rutherford's executors to repay her father's initial loan plus interest – just over £5,820. They received about half that year, but instalments then slowed to an irregular trickle.[40]

Richard also leveraged Mary's family connections with plantation and mercantile communities in Jamaica and Scotland. Her relative Thomas Melville, Governor of Cape Coast Castle, a major slaving fort in Ghana, would later secure a job for Richard's son, and prove useful as his involvement in trafficking captive Africans increased.

Richard wasted no time in assigning the remaining debt owed Mary by Robert Rutherford's executors to Robert Scott, a wine merchant, in exchange for £5,000 needed to pay for his share of refurbishing Bance Island,* the slaving fort in the mouth of the Sierra Leone River he had purchased with his business partners in 1748. His partners in the venture were John Mill; Alexander Grant (the doctor from Jamaica); father and son Augustus and John Boyd (St Kitts enslavers and East India Company investors); and linen merchant John Sargent, who later became a director of the Bank of England.[41]

Bance Island, established by the Royal African Company in the 1670s, was one of around forty such fortified slaving stations operating along the West African coast between Mauritania and Benin. Bance had a chequered history, raided by the French in 1695 and 1704, and by pirates in 1719 and 1720. The Royal African Company used it less after they lost their monopoly in 1712, and abandoned it entirely in 1728 after

---

* The island was originally named Bence Island after Captain John Bence, a Royal African Company official. In the 1730s and 40s, during George Fryer's ownership, it was known as George's Island. Richard Oswald knew it as Bance Island, but today it is most frequently referred to as Bunce Island.

Afro-Portuguese trader José Lopez da Moura's attack. George Fryer, the slaver who sold the island to Richard and his associates, had found it useful to store his goods and as a 'defence against the French in wartime', but failed to turn a profit.

To operate from the fort, Richard and his partners had to pay an annual rent, plus customs duties on all exports, to the local ruler, the Bai Sama of the Bullom Shore, who collected payment in person, sometimes dressed in a tartan kilt. African traders, usually Mandigo, Fula or Susu, brought young men (and some women) downriver to Bance Island. Captives had usually travelled long distances; many were prisoners of war. These conflicts were often provoked by European demand for captives and fuelled by European weapons. The traders headed to the island's 'palaver house' to exchange human beings for weaponry, cloth, alcohol and tobacco. These transactions were cruel and calculating. One slaving ship's captain refused to buy a young mother in Bimbia in modern-day Cameroon, because he did not wish to be 'plagued with a child on board'. African traders brought the sorrowful woman back next day without her child. It 'had been killed in the night to accommodate us in the sale'.[42]

Once purchased, men and women were separated into two adjacent holding yards to await the next ship. Though Richard hired translators to tell them where they were going, to quell fears white men would eat them, some still became catatonic. Slavers anticipated resistance, designing forts to withstand attack from within. Large quantities of cannon, shackles, handcuffs, forelocks (fastening devices) and chains were imported annually, fashioned in Birmingham and Black Country factories from iron forged around Telford, Wrexham and Merthyr Tydfil.* After Richard and his associates rebuilt the crumbling fort, the yard where Africans were imprisoned had a double door entrance and a strong wall so that 'in the event of an insurrection 10 men are better able to quell it now than 30 could formerly'.[43]

The ruins of another building in the complex reveal another violent reality of captives' daily lives. Jutting out from the western wall in the women's holding yard is a stone structure containing a basic sort of bathroom and another chamber. As there was no similar structure in the men's holding yard, it has been identified as the 'rape house', where the

---

* The official Black Country flag, designed by an eleven-year-old schoolgirl in 2012, is controversially dominated by a chain motif.

white men would routinely violate female captives.[44] Mary's inheritance helped pay to erect or restore these buildings.

At first fewer than a dozen white, predominantly Scottish, factors – characterised as 'the dregs of society' – resided on the island, but between 1756 and 1776, this number tripled. They lived in a large house in the centre of the fort, operating from a counting house not unlike Richard's in Philpot Lane. They were dependent on a much larger skilled workforce of *gremetes*: free, waged, local African men, who grew in number from 48 in 1756 to 142 in 1776, living in their own village at the island's southern end. Supplying all these men with wages and provisions cost at least £2,000 a year.[45]

Cruel treatment of captives was starkly juxtaposed with their captors' attempts at refinement. Immediately behind the 'rape house' was an orchard planted with orange trees. When the writer Anna Maria Falconbridge visited in the 1790s, she 'strolled ... involuntarily' to the window before dinner:

> without the smallest suspicion of what I was to see; – judge then what my astonishment and feelings were at the sight of between two and three hundred wretched victims, chained and parceled out in circles, just satisfying the cravings of nature from a trough of rice.[46]

Anna Maria's hosts mostly became inured to it all, with the help of copious drinking, and regular games of golf. The Bance Island golf course consisted of two holes, each the size of a man's head, a quarter of a mile apart. African caddies, wearing tartan loincloths made in Oswald's Kilmarnock wool factory, carried the tennis-ball-sized balls and clubs made from rare Central American woods. This was the first golf course recorded in Africa, all the more remarkable as only a handful existed in Europe. The first in America was only established (in Charleston, also staffed by enslaved caddies) in 1786.

Not everyone found golf and drinking sufficiently diverting. One young clerk, desperate to leave the island, complained 'the way of life here and my disposition will not coincide.' He died soon afterwards. Richard and the other Bance Island proprietors found their employees' 'frequent mortality' – half died every year – unsurprising. Their deaths owed as much to their 'irregular way of life as to any bad effects of the climate'.[47]

From 1755 onwards, as some 1,000 Africans departed from Bance Island each year, the profits began rolling in. Amongst the English slavers supplied by Grant, Oswald and Co. was John Newton, the later abolitionist and composer of the hymn *Amazing Grace*.[48] Bance Island shipped more Africans to mainland North America than any other fort, attracting slavers from Newport, Rhode Island, New York, New London, Connecticut and Salem, Massachusetts. The owners of South Carolina and Georgia rice plantations were keen to acquire people from the so-called 'Rice Coast' – stretching from Senegal to Sierra Leone – to exploit their expertise in cultivating the crop. People shipped to Charleston from Bance Island were sold by local merchant Henry Laurens. In turn, Richard sold Laurens's rice and indigo in London. Laurens also shipped oars, planks, masts, pine tar, pitch and turpentine produced in South Carolina to Bance Island.

Besides his shares in the slaving fort, Richard also owned, or part-owned, at least sixteen ships – including one named the *Mary* – that embarked over 7,000 Africans over more than three decades, mostly from Bance Island or the broader Sierra Leone estuary, to be transported across the Atlantic, primarily to Charleston, but also to Antigua, St Kitts and Grenada. Around 1,000 of these individuals did not survive the crossing.[49] This was just under the general estimated average of fifteen per cent mortality; it was said sharks followed in the slaving ships' wake, waiting for bodies to be thrown overboard.

There is a glimpse of the fatal impact of transatlantic voyages in Laurens's assessment of one consignment he received from Richard in 1756. Five captives had just died and 'another lies so very ill there is very little hopes of her and eight more so meagre & sickly that ... they can't appear in the yard. Several have very bad sore eyes, others have the yaws. Upon the whole they were not a fine cargo.'[50]

Over the thirty-six years Richard was involved, nearly 13,000 Africans left Bance Island for the Americas. The company made over £30,000 profit. Richard initially owned a third, but after he bought Sargent's share in 1770, and inherited Mill's the following year, when he died of a 'Paralytick Stroke', this rose to 5/9ths, so he gained more than £12,500 overall.[51] Much of this colossal profit had been made possible by leveraging Mary's interest in Spring Garden plantation.

Four years after Mary and Richard married, they were thrust into what she called a 'labyrinth of troubles' by the outbreak of hostilities known as the 'French and Indian War' in North America.[52] Richard was amongst the enslavers, plantation owners, people traffickers and colonial merchants who petitioned the British government to protect their interests from the 'Incursions of the Enemy & the Indians'. Two years later, the rival powers began the European territorial struggle now known as the Seven Years' War. Fearing the conflict would spread to the Caribbean, the Oswalds sold Mary's remaining property in Kingston.[53] Henry Laurens warned in April 1756: 'People bought Slaves with great spirit all the last Summer', but now 'the scene is so much altered for the worse', that 'it cannot amend before a peace shall be established'. However, sales soon revived.[54] South Carolina continued to import nearly 2,000 Africans every year; Bance Island continued to thrive.

Mary's life, however, was about to be thrown dramatically off course. In summer 1758, her beloved husband won a contract to supply British and Prussian forces in Germany with bread, forage for horses, wagons and other necessities. He was also to provision the Navy – deploying some 70,000 soldiers and sailors – with turpentine and tar from North Carolina. Richard soon set out for Kassel, in northern Hesse, leaving Mary behind, to oversee the gargantuan operation of feeding the army in person. He established an extensive network of bread magazines, bake houses and grinding mills, scattered across the 66,000 square miles where troops were encamped.[55]

After two years' separation, Mary could bear it no longer and insisted on joining her husband in Germany. She could not often be by his side, but found lodgings in towns a safe distance from the front. One friend was 'persuaded you are happier being near Mr Oswald', although he was concerned she would suffer as much as the soldiers, for: 'You who wishes happiness to every living Creature, must ever feel the miseries of war, which so many individuals groan under.'[56] Mary was indignant with what she found, commenting Richard had 'a very shocking life at present'. She even went so far as to exclaim, in a stunningly unreflective statement: 'I have always looked upon Government Service as a sort of Slavery, and now I know it by experience!'[57]

Richard's operation suffered from, in Mary's eyes, 'continual plague and harassments'.[58] Bad weather and poor roads combined put 'a Barr to all enterprises'. On one occasion, after heavy rain, bakers and horses drowned attempting to cross the River Nethe, leaving bread to rot on one bank, while troops grew hungry on the other.[59] Mary considered Richard's employees 'rogues' and 'worthless creatures', who 'do not study your peace or interest.' She was exasperated when one man gave her several reasons why the latest batch of bread was not up to scratch, 'not one of them that might not have been prevented had he told me sooner.'[60] Furthermore, although the roads were strongly guarded by patrols, there was always the danger the French would seize wagons, take a magazine or block deliveries by besieging a town. Mary sighed: 'business cannot be right speedily done while subject to constant alarums.'[61]

For the next two years Mary wrote Richard copious letters as she followed in his wake around north-west Germany, taking lodgings in various towns including Paderborn, Höxter and Hamelin. Although she begged Richard to burn them 'else I couldn't write you freely', he kept them all.[62] From these 400 or so pages of dense scrawl, we get a sense of Mary as a strong, forthright character, who loved her husband and was prepared to live in a war zone to support him. It was a severe test: 'everybody here Seems to be quite out of patience. I appear to have the most, but that I Suppose You'll Scarce Credit knowing how Small my Stock Is'. She was always ready with an opinion, be it on hiring servants, the war's progress, or advising Richard not to get involved with a court martial proceeding: 'everyone in the army is touched by it, yet you may make enemies if you appear in it'.[63]

Her business acumen and administrative abilities, first learnt in Kingston, were evident. As she modestly put it: 'I know my presence here is of some little service.' Because she was further away from the front line, letters often reached her first. She would then forward these to Richard, along with administrative papers, such as bread receipts, and rumours about the whereabouts and activities of the French. She helped oversee the supply of bread to the troops, made purchases, paid wages and collected money on Richard's behalf, keeping careful records 'for fear of mistakes' and guarding his paper chest day and night. She well knew 'the importance of business and the necessary as well as unnecessary delays to be put off.'[64] She often took the initiative, occasionally going against Richard's wishes – paying an 'old waggoner', and for postage rather than entrusting her letter to private hands – while still avoiding expenses she knew he would disapprove of.[65]

Despite her frequent complaints, Mary led a fairly merry life during the war, wearing silk dresses, sleeping in late, taking tea or coffee or dining with officers, prominent locals and other British figures abroad. One Colonel declared her claret 'the best he had drunk in Germany.' Mary wrote to Richard: 'I wish You don't think me extravagant … I believe it does no hurt.'[66] One day in June 1761, she confessed: 'Today I have had a vast inclination to begin snuffing again. I believe above 20 times today without thinking I have had my hand in my pocket for my snuff box.' She knew Richard would chastise her – snuffing was generally condemned in women, supposedly ruining their complexions and rendering them unkissable – and promised to stop when he returned. But then, likening her snuffing to his foul language, she threatened to 'take a snuff for every Oath you Swear.'[67]

The war took its toll on Mary. Her main source of anxiety was Richard. Requests for 'just a few lines' to let her know he is well pepper her correspondence. Alongside the very real threat of Richard's capture or death, she imagined him being robbed while travelling at night or drowning in a storm on a voyage to London. Equally concerned for his health, she admonished him to 'put on dry clothes immediately' if he got caught in the rain, and not to 'stand out in the cold looking at the horses'.[68] She regularly sent him comforts and provisions: clothing, newspapers, 'your own bed', little cheeses ('things I know you like'), tea, English mustard, kippers, rum, champagne, Madeira from Hamburg, Rhenish wine and the ubiquitous claret.[69]

Richard's silences caused Mary's spirits to sink, and, she believed, exacerbated her own health problems. These ranged from colds, coughs and fevers to gripes (acute intestinal pain), inflamed eyes, a crick in the neck and a sore back. She took various medicines, including barley water, rhubarb, sulphur powder and even laudanum, which 'had the desired effect' though her doctor disapproved.[70] But a letter from Richard, or even better a visit, would truly 'set me all to Rights'; 'now was you with me I think I would be happy though I never saw another face.'[71] Though Richard begged her to return home to convalesce, Mary refused, insisting 'we shall never have the sea betwixt us again.' Being parted would be 'like leaving the flesh from the bones. If it please God to recover my health He can do it as well here as in any other place.'[72]

With a very personal interest in the war coming to a speedy conclusion, Mary monitored its progress in minute detail. A keen and knowledgeable observer, she coolly analysed the situation with confidence and accuracy. In May 1761 she knew the British navy was targeting Belle Île, a strategically important island off the Brittany coast, but predicted that even if its capture led to peace, the troops would not leave Germany before the winter. The British took the island the following month, but the war dragged on. On 19 March 1762, in Hamelin, she made the only reference in her entire wartime correspondence to the struggle beyond Europe, exclaiming, 'God grant they [the papers from Holland] may bring us good news of the West Indies.'[73] They may well have done, as Admiral George Rodney had successfully captured the French island of Martinique the month before. Her Jamaican assets and friends were safe for now.

Mary was cool in her assessments, giving little credit to overexcited talk of a 'cessation of arms' in April 1761, or that 'we have beat and routed the French' towards the end of that year.[74] Victory seemed in sight after Tsar Peter III, a fervent admirer of Frederick the Great, came to the throne in January 1762, withdrawing his army from Prussia and sending troops to fight under Frederick's command. However, Spain and Portugal were drawn into the struggle on opposing sides; the war would drag on for another year. The combatants eventually ran out of money (Empress Maria Theresa of Austria had even pawned her jewels); the peace treaty was signed in Paris on 10 February 1763. Over four and a half years, Richard, with Mary's able support, had provided more than five million loaves of bread to over 100,000 soldiers.[75]

The Oswalds' mood was buoyant when they returned from Germany in early summer 1763. They had survived – and made £125,000 profit from – the war, and might now 'be happy hereafter'.[76] Though Robert Burns lambasted Richard as a 'plunderer of armies', most counted him amongst the more honest army contractors.[77] Mary was proud to hear her husband's work being praised by friends, superiors and even the commander of the Hanoverian troops, Prince Ferdinand of Brunswick. As she told Richard during the war: 'though peace of conscience is the principal thing to be valued, Yet I ever thought the good opinion of the World (Bad as it is), is not to be despised.'[78]

Mary quickly regained her health, but fretted lest Richard overindulge at the turtle feasts laid on when the fleet returned from the Caribbean. She begged him to 'be upon your guard as you have been little used to that way of living lately & you know you are easily hurt when you exceed but a very little'.[79] She was right to be worried; these fashionable banquets were notorious for gluttony. The poet Robert Browning (whose grandmother was an heiress from St Kitts, rumoured to have African ancestry, and whose wife Elizabeth Barrett came from a Jamaican family) evoked the dish in *The Pied Piper of Hamelin*, where the mayor's 'paunch grew mutinous / For a plate of turtle, green and glutinous'.[80] Eating too much turtle was thought to infect the blood and turn skin yellow. Turtles, imported live from the Caribbean, were so large (one weighing 500 lbs, or 226 kg, arrived in 1758) that some were said to feed 100 men at one sitting. Every part was consumed, from calipash (dark back meat) and calipee (white belly meat), to the fins (served in a clear Madeira broth), making for a meal of several courses. The green fat, with a butter-like consistency, was considered the greatest delicacy. To attend such feasts, jested one satirist, required special 'turtle-clothes' – loose when beginning the meal, tight as a drum by the end.[81]

In November 1763 Richard was elected to the Society for the Encouragement of Arts, Manufactures and Commerce (now the Royal Society of Arts), both a sign of social recognition and an unrivalled networking opportunity. The Society had been founded at Rawthmell's Coffee House, just off Fleet Street, nine years earlier, and already boasted over 2,000 members, including Dr Samuel Johnson, James Boswell, Adam Smith (whom Richard had known as a young man in Glasgow), Edmund Burke, Josiah Wedgwood, Horace Walpole and Benjamin Franklin. As wives were permitted to accompany husbands to meetings, Mary also benefited from this honour and its social cachet.[82]

Richard splashed out on a full-length portrait of Mary by Johan Zoffany, wearing a fashionable blue taffeta dress – the fabric dyed with indigo produced by enslaved people. The grand scale had a price to match, inflated still further by costly blue pigments used to render the cascading taffeta; and the ornate gilt rococo frame. The finished portrait projects wealth and status rather than beauty, while the girlish frippery of the fashionable straw hat on her lap (probably a prop) seems ill-suited to Mary's serious demeanour.

It is said Zoffany also portrayed Richard in the background, but was obliged to paint him out after he suffered from a fit of 'bashfulness'. Another story goes that Mary made the painter cover her husband's image with a cloud, though a recent X-ray revealed nothing. Possibly any discussion took place before Zoffany put brush to canvas. Or perhaps these rumours surfaced to explain why Mary was painted without her husband, unusually for Zoffany, who specialised in family groups.[83] Richard's absence accentuates her position as a woman of substance in her own right.

Back at Philpot Lane, Richard had invited a former colleague from Glasgow, Michael Herries, to replace John Mill. Herries was an animal lover, and soon Mary was living alongside two parrots (one named Gallant Piquero, who suffered from a runny nose, and one with 'a fine Pipe', who spoke Portuguese); a monkey, who often broke loose of his chain and smashed the neighbours' furniture; a dog, Mrs Juno, who produced five puppies in September 1764; and a gazelle. A screaming baby was added to the mix when Herries's wife Anne gave birth to a son in 1765.

The conditions at Philpot Lane, which Herries found 'most intolerably dirty & nasty, not having had any sort of cleaning for many years', can have only fuelled the couple's desire to live somewhere more appropriate for their rising place in society. Mary began to examine the map between Dover and Portsmouth as it was 'the nearest sea-coast to London'. She deferred to Richard's opinion, 'for the place my dearest likes is the only one that will be agreeable to me.' They found a villa near Brighton, with a 'pleasant situation' and 'a fine view' of all the passing ships, naming it Oswald Villa. They later acquired a second place much nearer to London, Oswald House in Kent, not far from Eltham Palace, the childhood home of Henry VIII. In 1772, they upgraded their London address by leasing no. 14 Great George Street in fashionable Westminster.[84]

The Oswalds were amongst the many enslavers who had Black people in their London households. In August 1764, an African named Caesar ran away from Philpot Lane, and 'as no account could be got of him' Herries was on the verge of placing an advertisement offering a reward for his return when he received a letter from the gardener at Oswald House 'advising his safe arrival there' five days earlier. Over 1,000 such advertisements for freedom-seeking Africans were placed in British newspapers between 1655 and 1780.[85] Detailed physical descriptions show the majority were young men or boys, many with signs of physical abuse, some wearing metal collars – a very visible symbol of enslavement.

Mary would have known at least two Black people from her friends' households who had successfully found freedom. Robert Scipio Laurens, who had travelled to England with Henry Laurens in 1771, was imprisoned in Shropshire in 1774, charged with bigamy and stealing 'a gammon of ham'. This forced Laurens to return to America without him. After serving a year in gaol he changed his name to John Moreton and found employment in London. In 1777, George was ejected from the house of merchant William Manning (who we will meet again in Chapter 5), and promptly got himself baptised at St Andrew's Undershaft as 'William Wells' – the name of his former enslaver in St Kitts.[86] They would join the growing numbers of people of African descent, like John Hylas and Betsy Newton, living free lives in Britain, marrying British people, being paid wages, or working independently in a range of professions: soldier, sailor, priest, actress, weaver, cabinet-maker, even parish constable.[87]

Richard now looked to further diversify his and Mary's assets. He got involved with the East India trade and invested heavily in the stock market – which in the eighteenth century traded not equities but government debt. By the end of 1764, his portfolio was worth £100,000.[88] He also looked to acquire land in the colonies. Mary, with her Jamaican experience, may well have influenced his decision to reject the Caribbean, not wanting to 'risk his life and fortune to purchase in a sickly island when there is a great choice of valuable land at North America to be had for a small consideration.' In July 1764, he obtained a grant of 20,000 acres in East Florida, newly ceded to Britain by the Spanish. He became a leading light of the East Florida Society, established to encourage settlement there, securing land for friends and acquaintances through the new Governor, James Grant, kinsman of his Bance Island partner, Dr Alexander Grant.[89]

When Richard acquired his land in East Florida, near the conjunction of the Tomoka and Halifax Rivers, it was a 'wilderness', 'covered in cabbage trees' – native palmettos, now the official 'state tree' adorning the flags of both Florida and South Carolina ('the Palmetto State'). Richard divided his property into five settlements, starting by producing indigo at 'Mount Oswald'. Ferry and Adia settlements grew provision corn, some indigo and rice; Cowpens, as its name suggests, was a grazing and breeding ground for cattle. But Richard placed his greatest hopes in 'Swamp' plantation. Here, he was to plant sugar.

Richard paid lip service to the government stipulation to employ white Protestants, but quickly concluded 'money must be laid out on negroes before any financial advantage can be hoped for.' By 1780, some 230 people had arrived at Mount Oswald alone, most sent to Henry Laurens from Bance Island (including a group of 100 *gremetes*). Refusing to accept their fate, some escaped, and when Samuel Hewie, their drunken and abusive first overseer, drowned in 1766 during a fishing trip, Laurens was sure it had not been an accident.[90]

Mary continued as Richard's confidante, forthright with her opinions on his business affairs, just as in Germany. As her husband grew older, she helped him recall key details and transactions. A passing comment in a letter from Henry Laurens regarding the duplicitous behaviour of his junior partner John Hopton gives us a glimpse of her role. Hopton had falsely informed all their London clients Laurens was retiring and had 'resigned all business in his favour'. Laurens was horrified, as he had 'always endeavoured to inculcate quite different Principles in his Mind' and 'advised him over and over again, not to make Haste to grow rich, not to grasp too eagerly at Business'. Mary was at her husband's side when Hopton made his overtures, trying to take over all consignments from Bance Island. Richard, 'not very well pleased with such Importunity ... declined or refused it.' Laurens reported: 'that is what Mr. Oswald has informed me of, after taking time to recollect what had pass'd, with the Assistance of Mr. Herries his partner, and Mrs Oswald, who were present.'[91] One can imagine the Oswalds' animated discussion of young Hopton's betrayal and their self-congratulatory tone as they recalled seeing through his subterfuge.

Not content with their villas near London, Mary and Richard purchased a place in the landed gentry by acquiring the 7,000-acre Auchincruive estate in Ayrshire, sixty miles south of his family and friends in Glasgow, in 1764. Around the same time, they acquired the equally large Cavens estate in Kirkcudbrightshire and Dumfriesshire. This was just the beginning of acquiring huge swathes of countryside south of Glasgow; by 1782 they owned 102,679 acres.[92]

Auchincruive was a far cry from the 'Retirement ... in a Comfortable Cottage' where they might 'enjoy ourselves quietly at our own fireside' Mary had dreamed of during the war.[93] She wrote to Richard: 'I'm afraid I shall think you have been too extravagant', though she clearly liked the idea of 'our being Lord & Lady of a place you seem to have so great a liking for'. With her usual shrewdness, she recognised they had got a good deal because the previous owner had not finished building the house.[94] He had, however, commissioned a design from the up-and-coming Adam brothers (sons of William Adam who built Duff House), and Richard took up where he left off. Mary opined, 'Bye & bye I hope we shall get ourselves in a comfortable situation, Rome was not builded in one day is the old saying.' The couple made regular visits to Scotland to supervise construction over the next seven years.[95]

Though less ostentatious than many other Ayrshire seats, Auchincruive was carefully calculated to project gentility and good taste. Decorative motifs throughout the house of laurels, olives and grapevines signalled peace, victory, fame, regeneration and abundance.

Mary proudly described their extensive art collection, including works by Canaletto, Carracci and Rubens, as 'a specimen of my husband's good Taste in art as well as in all others in which he had an opportunity to show it'. Her portrait by Zoffany hung in pride of place in the entrance hall.[96]

The house was surrounded by the usual beautiful landscaped gardens and park. More remarkable was an ornate tea house inspired by the sixth-century mausoleum of Theodoric, king of the Ostrogoths, at Ravenna. Richard's hot houses were the first to be built in Scotland. He grew pineapples and experimented with sugar cane, sending the resulting seedlings to his plantation in East Florida. With the estate, the Oswalds also took on patronage of the local church, St Quivox. Renovations included adding a new aisle; building the 'Auchincruive gallery' to have the best seats in the house; and designing a family burial vault.[97]

Robert Burns, who had humble beginnings in Alloway, less than six miles from Auchincruive, accused Mary of pride and avarice, remarking, 'among her servants and tenants I know that she was detested with the most heartfelt cordiality'.[98] It's hard to gauge the truth of this aspersion. Mary paid average wages.[99] However, having spent her formative years being waited on by enslaved domestics, she may well have treated her Scottish servants with disdain. She certainly ascribed the moral turpitude of an adulterous woman she met in Germany to her having been 'a serving maid in a lady's house ... worthless enough you may believe'.[100] As for her tenants, one who had been forgiven his rental arrears thanked 'Good Mrs Oswald ... by whom I ought forever to be forgot, as I have behaved so ill.'[101] But in his position, who would not try to curry favour? On balance, Burns's judgement was probably correct.

Through the Oswalds, money from enslavement and colonial trade boosted Scotland's infrastructure and economy. Richard's 'improvements' in Ayrshire – which in turn swelled their profits by increasing land rental values – included building over a hundred miles of better roads, quarrying lime to fertilise fields and establishing the Maryburgh Salt Works in Prestwick. Further afield, he built a factory in Pittenweem, Fife, to make carpets from Kilmarnock wool and helped finance the Aberdeen Whaling Company and the Forth–Clyde Canal.[102]

Richard and Mary often lent or gave away money to help friends in financial distress. As she put it, 'we have substantial joys in being able to assist with ease some of our worthy friends and acquaintances that want it.' From 1764, Richard was also a subscriber to the charitable Scots Corporation, allowing him both to help poor Scots in London, and to associate with many eminent and well-connected Scottish donors.[103]

Some loans were ploughed back into colonial endeavours. Alexander Grant borrowed over £13,000 because he was struggling to manage his Jamaican plantations; John Boyd used a loan of £5,000 to finance the purchase of seven plantations in Grenada and Dominica. Though he had initially chosen to invest in East Florida over the Caribbean, in the early 1770s Richard gained a financial interest in John Mill and his cousin David Mill's Carriacou cotton plantation, as well as estates in Grenada and St Kitts through foreclosing on mortgages. He also tried, unsuccessfully, to buy the 1,100-acre Rhine plantation in Jamaica in 1778.[104]

Although Mary and Richard had no children together, she shared his solicitude for his two sons with Agnes Barr – a source of more pain than joy. The elder, Richard, was a ne'er-do-well. He failed to prosper as a clerk at Cape Coast Castle in Ghana (the job obtained through Mary's relative, Governor Thomas Melville), embezzled magazine funds while working for Richard in Germany, then contracted a 'violent fever' after foolishly enlisting in a regiment stationed in Jamaica. Richard extricated him and set him up in a house in Camberwell. He was sincerely grateful that despite having 'so often deceived you in my promises of a better behaviour', his father still showed him great 'tenderness'. The prodigal son died young, on a Grand Tour of Europe bankrolled by his father.

His younger brother George developed tuberculosis in his early twenties, and died in Toulouse in the arms of his friend Laurence Sterne, author of *Tristram Shandy*, in 1763. When the news reached Germany, Mary showed no sign of resenting Richard's children by another woman. Instead, she sadly opined 'while the life is in, there is always hope, but now no more'. Thinking immediately of Agnes, whom 'I pity from my heart', she suggested Richard write to her, 'But you're best judge if that would be proper.'[105]

Mary and Richard also took a close interest in Henry Laurens's sons when he brought them to England in 1771 after their mother's untimely death. Laurens wrote to his brother commending his 'worthy and valuable friend Richard Oswald Esq. who interests himself in the Welfare of your nephews as if they were his own, and Mrs Oswald is equally good!' They showed particular affection for the eldest, fifteen-year-old John, who has recently become known to a new generation through *Hamilton! The Musical*. Richard introduced John into the 'circle of his friends in the Law'. However, John abhorred the 'horrible prospect' of 'get[ting] my bread by the quarrels and disputes of others.' He left London in 1777 to join his country's fight for independence, leaving behind a pregnant young wife he would never see again.[106]

In March 1773 Henry Laurens wrote to his son John: 'American affairs wear a bad aspect. A Cloud is gathering in New England which if not dispelled by foresight & wisdom will distress this Kingdom more than anything that has happened since the [Glorious] Revolution' – when Catholic James II had been ousted by Protestant Dutch ruler William of Orange in 1688. Laurens's own home in Charleston had been invaded at the height of the Stamp Act crisis in October 1765, by a mob crying 'no taxation without representation'. The storm broke on 19 April 1775, when the first shots of the American Revolution were fired at Lexington and Concord in Massachusetts. The following year, Richard's nephew John Anderson, newly returned from Maryland, warned him of a certain General named George Washington: 'a man of prudence and courage, whose prudence is to be feared more than his courage'.[107]

With his years of experience in America and extensive colonial connections, Richard became a sought-after government adviser.* He knew Georgia, the Carolinas and Virginia, with their economic reliance on enslaved labour, aristocratic aspirations and close trading relationship with the Caribbean, were of a different character to their northern allies. He believed that with the help of key trading concessions, such as allowing South Carolina to export rice (its primary crop) to the Caribbean, Britain might tempt 'these prodigals' to abandon the 'Mob of Northern Yeomen ... that despicable Rabble of Rioters' in New England and renew their allegiance to George III.

Once France entered the war in 1778, Richard advised the British to focus on North America, rather than be diverted by fighting their imperial rivals at sea. He maintained this position despite the fact it left Bance Island without naval protection. In March 1779, the French seized all British ships in the fort's vicinity. They commandeered two;

---

* Not all his advice was sound; in 1782 he entrusted Mary with a secret memorandum suggesting Russia launch an attack from Siberia against Spanish California and Mexico. Morris, *Peacemakers*, pp. 293–4.

sent those laden with captive Africans to St Domingue (modern Haiti); one with a cargo of ivory back to France; and burnt the rest. Then, they ransacked the fort for six days, leaving nothing but 'a heap of Ruins'. Trafficking from Bance Island came to a standstill, not resuming until peace was restored.

The conflict would also sound the death knell for Richard's efforts in East Florida, where he had invested £18,000. Scarcely any grantees turned a profit in the twelve short years between the Seven Years' War and the American Revolution. Richard lamented: 'the description published of the province induced many to set about planting ... and made little doubt of soon acquiring great fortunes; all they met with was disappointment on disappointment.'[108]

In September 1780, Mary and Richard were appalled to hear Henry Laurens had been captured at sea on his way to negotiate an alliance with the Dutch, and thrown into the Tower of London, charged with high treason. The government wanted Richard to extract a confession, but instead he campaigned for his friend's release, eventually raising £4,000 bail. Although Mary did not visit Laurens during this 'long ... expensive & painful farce', he called on her after he got out. Alarmed by his 'weak condition', she continued to demand regular reports on his health.[109]

Following the American victory at Yorktown in October 1781, the British government appointed Richard to negotiate the peace in Paris with Benjamin Franklin, John Jay and John Adams. George III himself agreed Richard was the 'fittest Instrument for the renewal of ... friendly intercourse' with the thirteen states. Franklin, who had previously met Richard at East Florida Society meetings, praised his 'Candour, Probity, good Understanding, and good Will to both Countries'; his time in America and business experience would facilitate the 'framing of such a Peace that may be firm and long-lasting'. John Adams was struck by his sincerity and John Jay his 'candid and proper manner'; though Richard found Jay 'uncommonly Stiff and particular'.[110]

Some saw the septuagenarian Richard – described by John Quincy Adams as 'an ugly looking man, blind of one eye', with his ear horn and walking stick – as a symbol of Britain's spent force, by contrast to the vigorous, newborn United States.[111]

Just as Mary had supplied Richard during their years in Germany, she regularly sent tea to her husband in Paris. He appreciated its 'great and good effect', helping him weather the 'fatigues and frustrations' of the negotiations.[112]

On 28 November, just two days before the preliminary articles were due to be signed, the still frail Henry Laurens arrived in Paris with a burning issue on his mind. He wanted to ensure the tens of thousands of Africans who had escaped enslavement by joining the British during the war – known as Black Loyalists – would be returned to the Patriots.

Throughout the war, Britain had promised people freedom in exchange for military service, not due to any anti-slavery sentiment, but to swell their numbers, whilst at the same time undermining the enemy's plantation economy. The colonists were appalled. One wrote: 'Hell itself could not have vomited anything more black than this design of emancipating our slaves.' The true character of British policy was revealed when they expelled some 2,000 Black Loyalists to face enemy fire, recapture or starvation during the siege of Yorktown.

The escapees formed their own units: the Ethiopian Regiment and the Black Pioneers wore badges with the radical slogan 'Liberty to Slaves'; the Black Brigade were skilled in guerrilla warfare. By the war's end, 50,000 had joined the British. Amongst them were those formerly 'belonging' to George Washington, James Madison, Thomas Jefferson and Patrick Henry – 'Founding Fathers' who opined that 'all men are created equal' in their Declaration of Independence.

Laurens 'spoke forcibly' on the importance of ensuring Black Loyalists were returned to their former enslavers, citing several examples of friends who had lost human 'property'. Several freedom seekers had escaped his Mepkin plantation in South Carolina, ransacked by British troops in June 1780.*

He may have had an even more personal motivation. His son John Laurens – ironically an ardent abolitionist and advocate of Black battalions – had been killed in August 1782 near Beaufort, South Carolina. Might John have been shot by one of the Black Loyalists involved in the skirmish? Given the large numbers of Africans imported into South Carolina from Bance Island, it is not beyond the realms of possibility that John's killer had been exported from Richard's slaving fort and sold in Charleston by his own father.

Laurens's eleventh-hour intervention – so last-minute the additional clause had to be inserted into the preliminary treaty with a caret – met

---

* Laurens owned over 200 people working on four South Carolina plantations (Mepkin, Wambaw, Wrights Savannah and Mount Tacitus), and two in Georgia (Broughton Island and New Hope), totalling over 20,000 acres.

with no opposition from a group of men, who, with the exception of John Adams, were all enslavers. As Adams recounted to his wife Abigail: 'We all agreed. Mr Oswald consented. Then the Treaties were signed, sealed and delivered, and We all went out to Passy* to dine with Dr Franklin.' The prohibition against 'carrying away any Negroes or other Property of the American Inhabitants' became Article VII of the final peace treaty, signed on 3 September 1783.[113] It had the potential to re-enslave tens of thousands of African Americans.

Laurens reported to Mary after the business was concluded: 'to tell Mrs Oswald that he is one of the best Men in the World would be to give no Information, but to say that everybody thinks him so & everybody loves & Respects him must afford some pleasure.'[114] The feeling was mutual. Richard brought two portraits of Franklin back from Paris, and he and Mary entertained the Americans when they passed through London on their way home. But while the Americans loved him, Richard's deal was roundly condemned in Parliament as overly generous; Lord Shelburne and his Cabinet were forced to resign.

It was one thing for five men to solve the 'problem' of Black Loyalists in a comfortable hotel in Paris, and quite another for their solution to be enforced on the other side of the Atlantic. George Washington was furious when Sir Guy Carleton informed him in May 1783 that 'a large number of Negroes' had already left New York for Nova Scotia. When Washington argued he was violating the treaty, Carleton coolly insisted the condition could only apply to people who escaped *after* the preliminary articles were signed.[115]

Twenty thousand Black Loyalists were evacuated, mostly from Charleston and New York. The majority sailed for Nova Scotia, where the newly founded Birchtown became for a short time the largest free Black settlement in the Americas. From there, some moved on to Jamaica, the Bahamas and St Lucia. Hundreds travelled to London. Unable to find work, they were reliant on handouts from the newly established Committee for the Relief of the Black Poor, who then decided to found a free settlement for them in Sierra Leone, just twenty miles from Bance Island. This scheme was hatched by the unscrupulous botanist, entomologist and traveller Henry Smeathman, who sent a copy of his plan to Richard's office in Philpot Lane in July 1784. Richard soon had the

---

* Passy was a village to the west of Paris, now in the sixteenth *arrondissement*, where Franklin had been provided with a smart townhouse.

'papers under consideration.' Known as 'Mr Termite' for his squirming efforts to ingratiate himself, Smeathman obsessively sought sponsorship for the plan – which he must have known from his time in Sierra Leone was unworkable – approaching prominent Quakers, Benjamin Franklin, Granville Sharp, even the King of Sweden.

In January 1787, over 400 men, women and children sailed for Sierra Leone, after a four-month wait in terrible conditions aboard ships anchored on the Thames near Deptford.* By this time, Smeathman was dead, and both Granville Sharp and Olaudah Equiano (author of an acclaimed autobiography charting his own journey to freedom) had become embroiled in the project.

The hostile climate in Sierra Leone made it impossible to establish crops or maintain adequate shelter. By September 1788 two-thirds of the settlers had succumbed to disease and starvation. Some survivors resorted to stealing provisions from Bance Island, only to be enslaved. In December, their settlement was burnt to the ground by the local Temne ruler, King Jimmy, after the hostile agent at Bance Island provoked him by persuading a British ship to fire on his town. The survivors fled; some to Bance Island, where they joined the *gremetes*, helping to traffic yet more Africans across the Atlantic.[116] For the descendants of people who had been shipped to America from Bance Island, this was a strange kind of homecoming.

Could Richard's well-informed advice, which Smeathman never received, have averted this devastating outcome? The owner of Bance Island, like his agent, would surely have been instinctively against the idea of a neighbouring colony of liberated Africans.

The people enslaved on Richard's East Florida plantation were also displaced by the war. In 1781 they set sail for Georgia under the supervision of Richard's nephew James Anderson, but American privateers attacked the ship, killing some, and abducting seventy others. The survivors travelled with Anderson to an abandoned estate near Savannah, belonging to John Graham, the Loyalist Lieutenant Governor of Georgia, a relative of one of Richard's army contacts. But when the British evacuated Georgia in July 1782, they fled back to East Florida, alongside 'thousands of refugees and negroes'. 'Greatly reduced in number', their fate hung in the

---

* The majority were Black men, but also aboard were Black women 'married to white men', 'white women married to black men', and even a few 'white women wanting to be married'.

balance again, after the treaty Richard himself had negotiated dictated the colony be returned to the Spanish.[117]

On 9 August 1783, Richard asked Henry Laurens to sell the remaining 170 or so people. However, within a week, he had a change of heart. Looking to avoid the 'violent separations of Man & Wife, Parents & Children' resulting from a sale on the open market, he now sought a new home for them. Laurens offered one of his abandoned plantations in Georgia, reassuring Richard his 'pious intentions will be gratified'. Laurens urgently instructed his attorney in Savannah to ensure 'there may be houses standing for their reception & where they may be immediately put to labour,' and to 'follow Mr Oswald's directions & consult his best Interest.' Already, the discussion had turned back to concern for the bottom line. Laurens counselled moving the people to the Ninety-Six District in South Carolina in two or three years' time. Not only would this location be 'more healthy and more agreeable to the Negroes', 'the profits arising from their labour … will not be less to you'.

Mary seems to have been behind this sudden, rather surprising, concern for the feelings of families enslaved in East Florida. In 1786, she wanted to know what had become of 'Bob & his Wife', a couple who had first arrived in East Florida, probably via Bance Island, in 1771. Laurens wrote: 'My dear friend Mrs Oswald may rest assured her pious wishes respecting those people shall not be frustrated from a want of my interposition.' Laurens's emphasis on Mary's piety, echoing so closely his words to Richard three years before, suggests she had influenced her husband's earlier volte-face.

Laurens found out Bob and his wife had left Georgia, and 'followed those Negroes purchased by the late Mr Ferguson.' Thomas Ferguson, a wealthy politician and sawmill operator in South Carolina, had owned over 2,000 acres of rice and indigo plantations in St Paul's, Colleton County. Laurens reported Bob and his wife had been living upon one of Ferguson's plantations 'in a state of Freedom, that is to say inoffensively to act as they pleased', suggesting they were too old for fieldwork, so were allowed a kind of retirement.[118]

'Superannuated' people did not usually receive such care. In his 1737 will, John Alleyne, Elizabeth Alleyne Newton's uncle, instructed his heirs to 'ship off and dispose of such Negroes as shall from time to time become useless to my plantation'.[119] In the 1780s, Jamaican enslaver George Bedward – who had acquired Spring Garden in Westmoreland through marrying Susannah Rutherford, the daughter of Alexander

Ramsay's old business partner – habitually threw men and women he deemed no longer worth supporting into a remote ravine, inspiring this song:

> Take him to the Gulley! Take him to the Gulley!
> But bringee back the frock and board.
> Oh! Massa, massa! Me no deadee yet!
> Take him to the Gulley! Take him to the Gulley!
> Carry him along![120]

It is unclear whether Thomas Ferguson bought *all* the survivors, allowing families to stay together, but at least Bob and his wife were not separated. However, his recent death in Charleston would 'render a Farther enquiry necessary' as to their ultimate fate, especially as he had married five times and left multiple heirs.[121] It is unclear what was behind Mary's concern for the couple, or even why she knew their names. No enslaver's interest in the wellbeing of enslaved people could be purely altruistic. After all, as John Laurens had observed to his father, whenever he challenged 'a native of the southern provinces or the West Indies' on the institution's morality, their 'absurd' pro-slavery arguments ultimately boiled down to the refrain: 'Without Slaves how is it possible for us to be rich?'[122]

By the time he returned from Paris, Richard, now almost eighty, had largely retired from business, leaving most affairs in the capable hands of his nephews John and Alexander Anderson. Richard died on 6 November 1784 in his bedroom at Auchincruive. Henry Laurens wrote to the Andersons: 'The exit of our dear friend was happy, a transit of one short hour from mortality to never ending Life, just as I think I have often heard him wish.'

Mary had lost her 'dearest life', her partner of thirty-four years, described in his *Morning Chronicle* obituary as 'the best of husbands'. Laurens sympathised: 'who can so deeply feel its Effects as his dear surviving Partner? Nothing but the piety of Mrs Oswald and her own good sense can mitigate the anguish of her heart; she will say as Wisdom dictates under such Trials, my friend is gone forward only a little before me & "it is well".'

Laurens himself wept 'for the loss of a faithful, valuable friend', initially 'forgetting that he had passed the common age of Man, almost that he was mortal.' On hearing of Richard's death, Benjamin Franklin remarked, 'it is unlucky I think in the affairs of this world, that the wise and good be as mortal as common people, and that they often die before others are found fit to supply their places.'[123]

The Times noted Richard had 'appropriated in his Will' (spanning sixty pages) 'half a million at least ... which renders his family estate one of the most opulent in the United Kingdom.' Mary inherited the sum of £5,000 outright, plus an annuity of £1,000. She would also receive the income from his property in the Caribbean, North America and Africa, becoming an enslaver in her own right once again.

Substantial legacies and annuities were left to family and friends in Scotland, Germany, India, Jamaica and Georgia. Richard placed his remaining fortune in trust to buy land in Scotland. Mary would receive the proceeds during her life; then they would go to Richard's nephew, the Glasgow tobacco merchant George Oswald of Scotstoun. Just as she had been her father's executrix almost fifty years earlier, Mary now became Richard's, alongside his nephews, John and Alexander Anderson, his partner Michael Herries and his lawyer, Charlton Palmer.[124]

After Richard's death, Mary moved back to Westminster, residing at 32 Great George Street, across the road from her former home at no. 14. A particular friend in these years was Charles Mason, 'much beloved and esteemed for his integrity and upright conduct', who 'constantly attended' her, and 'assisted her in all her affairs.' Charles had worked for Richard in Germany; they became so close Charles named his eldest son 'Richard Oswald Mason'.[125]

Mary's 'affairs' during her widowhood included applying for government compensation for the loss of Richard's property in East Florida. She lodged her claim in November 1786, eventually receiving £1,568 – a fraction of his investment in the ill-fated colony.[126] More seriously, she brought a Chancery case against Richard's other executors in April 1787. She argued against the residue of Richard's estate being used to buy land in Scotland and demanded her marriage portion be returned to her. The case wore on until June 1788, when the court ruled *it* would manage the estate while Mary lived.[127] The feud meant the Andersons no longer shared Henry Laurens's business letters with her; it took over a year before he realised he must write to her directly regarding 'the affairs of our late dear friend Mr. Oswald'.[128] Meanwhile, from 1784, the *Mary* resumed trafficking some 150 Africans from Bance Island to Charleston and St Kitts each year.

*

Mary died at home in Westminster on 6 December 1788. Charles Mason had come 'by express to attend her at the time of her death from his house in the Country'.[129] In due course, an 'immense retinue' took Mary's body north 'in great funeral pomp' for burial beside Richard at St Quivox. Just a day's journey from their destination, the cortège was caught up in a terrible January storm and sought shelter at the Queensberry Arms in Sanquhar. To accommodate them, the innkeeper, Edward Whigham, was forced to eject a regular, who had already begun 'a friendly bowl' of tobacco – and no doubt several rounds of drinks – with his hosts.

Robert Burns – for it was he – was furious to be turned out of 'so comfortable a place of rest', and 'forced to brave all the horrors of the tempestuous night'. Weary 'in body and soul', he was 'obliged, amid the shades of night, bitter frost, howling hills and icy cataracts, to goad his jaded steed twelve miles farther on', to the next inn at New Cumnock.

While this twelve-mile journey does not sound very far to us today – it is less than twenty minutes' drive along the A76 – in 1789 it was quite another matter. In perfect weather, with a fresh horse, on a good, flat road, trotting at a speed of 8–10 mph, Burns might have arrived at New Cumnock within an hour and a half. But his horse Pegasus was, like Burns, 'much fatigued with the labours of the day'. The route took him uphill 'through the wildest moors and hills of Ayrshire,' on a dark, windy, freezing night. And, though Pegasus was his favourite horse, he was not necessarily the ideal mount. In his poetry, Burns admitted: 'Poor slipshod giddy Pegasus / Was but a sorry walker.' Worse, 'O'er Pegasus' side ye ne'er laid a stride, / Ye but smelt, man, the place where he sh–t.'

As he forced his reluctant steed through the storm, Burns composed vituperative verses in his head. In a later ode to the virtues of 'Scotch Drink', Burns called it 'an liquor guid to fire his bluid' and so it was on this occasion. After a good fire at New Cumnock had thawed his 'frozen sinews' he wrote his 'Ode, Sacred to the Memory of Mrs Oswald of Auchicruive'. He began by addressing the Devil, announcing Mary's arrival in Hell, 'unpitied and unblest', in 'widow weeds', her face withered with age. She deserved, he said, to be there, a miserly inhumane woman, with 'hands that took, but never gave'.

The next verse addressed Richard, the 'plunderer of armies', letting him know his 'trusty mate' was coming to join him, 'Doom'd to share thy fiery fate'. Burns finished by contrasting Mary, whose 'Ten thousand glittering pounds a year' could not help her now, with a ragged Beggar, who would go to Heaven with a clear conscience. He didn't object to how Mary got her wealth – before he found success as a poet in 1786, he had been ready to become a 'poor negro driver' in Jamaica himself – but he heartily resented her refusal to spend it.

Burns's friend Frances Dunlop called the ode an 'infusion of gall, wormwood and aquafortis', asking: 'Are you not a sad, wicked creature to send the poor old wife straight to the devil because she gave you a ride in a cold night?' Burns admitted he'd been a little extreme and changed the title to 'Mrs A– of O' to 'soften the matter a little'. Nevertheless, the *Edinburgh Courant* rejected the poem, later published by the less scrupulous *London Star* under a pseudonym.[130]

Was there any truth in Burns's characterisation of Mary? She was generous perhaps to a small number of relatives, friends and acquaintances, but her hands certainly took more than they gave, not only in Burns's Scotland, but in Jamaica, Sierra Leone and East Florida.

No expense was spared on Mary's lavish funeral. Copious food and drink were laid on for the guests, who consumed amongst other things 9 st 2 lbs of beef, twenty gallons of brandy, and seventy-two bottles of Mary's trademark claret. Her gravestone was carved by a local mason with stone hewn from Ayr quarry. However, the greatest outlay was on providing new mourning clothes for the entire household. Not simply black clothing, but silk gowns, shoe buckles, stockings, ribbons, bonnets and hair pins. It was a good day at the office for local mantua-maker (or ladies' dressmaker) Nelly Donaldson.[131]

As decreed in Richard's will, the Scottish estate passed to his nephew, George Oswald of Scotstoun. John and Alexander Anderson took over at Philpot Lane, making renewed investment in the trade with Africa, buying out Alexander Grant's and John Boyd's shares in Bance Island and spending £20,000 rebuilding the fort. They petitioned Parliament against abolition in May 1798. After trafficking Africans became illegal in 1807, they tried in vain to entice the government to buy Bance Island, reluctantly abandoning it after an uprising of *gremetes* two years later.[132]

Back in Germany, Mary had described her life ambitions to Richard: 'the esteem of the worthy; an easy fortune and contentment is in my opinion the great and substantial parts of greatness in the world'. Apart from the judgement of Burns, whom Mary is unlikely to have considered 'worthy', she achieved these goals. The only indication she had qualms about her 'easy fortune' was her 'pious' concern for the fate of one couple enslaved on Richard's East Florida plantations. But, like many enslavers, Mary never considered ending the system her wealth both depended on and sustained. She saw no irony in complaining that from her 'earliest days' she had 'so much access to know the falseness ... of the generosity of Mankind ... I am now most weary of it'.[133] The 104 people she inherited in Jamaica from her father; the 13,000 or so souls shipped to the Americas from her husband's slaving fort; and the hundreds of people under his whip in East Florida had far more reason to be weary – their sentiments went unrecorded.

Mary's £20,000 inheritance helped Richard to expand his transatlantic trading empire, win lucrative contracts and gain the status required to be a peace commissioner. The Oswalds rose from relatively humble origins to become a power couple at the centre of the Atlantic world. They purchased gentility in the form of imposing portraits, landed estates and homes designed by leading architects.

The Oswalds' physical and human legacies are scattered across the globe. The counting house on Philpot Lane has long gone; the street is now dominated by the 525-ft-tall skyscraper known as the 'Walkie Talkie'. Bance Island, christened the 'Pompeii of the Atlantic Slave Trade', has become a site of pilgrimage for Gullah Geechee people from the coastal areas and sea islands stretching from Jacksonville, North Carolina, to Jacksonville, Florida, seeking traces of their ancestors. Michelle Obama's Gullah roots mean *her* ancestors may have passed through Bance Island, whilst George W. Bush's great-great-great-great-grandfather, Thomas 'Beau' Walker, trafficked from the fort regularly until his crew threw him overboard in 1797.[134]

In East Florida there remain places named Oswald Bluff, Mount Oswald, Ramsay Bay and Oswald Key. The remains of Richard's Swamp Plantation sugar factory are featured on the Ormond Beach Historical Society's 'Scenic Bus Tour'.[135] In Scotland, Auchincruive is home to an agricultural college, headquarters for biotech and agricultural consultancy firms, a croquet club and a drug addicts' rehabilitation village. Copies of Richard and Mary's youthful portraits hang in the entrance hall of their former home, largely anonymous to corporate visitors. Cavens has become a luxury hotel, where you can spend the night in the Oswald room, gazing at a copy of Zoffany's portrait of Mary. Those attending services at St Quivox still use the Communion cups presented by the Oswalds in 1765. The tea house at Auchincruive, however, with its bricked-up entrances, broken windows and encroaching vegetation, has been placed on the Buildings at Risk register.

Mary's portrait by Zoffany now hangs in London's National Gallery alongside an equally large one of Queen Charlotte. She is high on the wall, so one is forced to look up to her; the brief label obscures more than it reveals. In 2007, the Gallery marked the 200th anniversary of abolition with an art installation by British Nigerian artist Yinka Shonibare. Mary's portrait and one of army officer and anti-abolitionist MP Sir Banastre Tarleton – who came from a family of Liverpool slavers – were replaced by two headless figures shooting at pheasants, dressed in Shonibare's trademark 'African' wax print fabrics.* Visitors could not fail to respond to this provocative intervention. But the exhibit was only temporary. No trace of it remains in the Gallery today.[136]

---

* Shonibare sees the fabric as a metaphor for colonialism, as it was first mass-produced for the West African market by the Dutch, inspired by batik designs in Indonesia, where they also had an imperial presence.

Portrait of Jane 'Jenny' Leigh Perrot, née Cholmeley, as she appeared while on trial for shoplifting, by G.G. and J. Robinson, *The Lady's Magazine*, 1 May 1800.

4

Jane Cholmeley (*c.*1744–1836)

Jane Austen's stingy aunt – a Barbados heiress – grew immensely wealthy despite the machinations of her stepfather. Some see echoes of her character quirks in no fewer than three of Austen's characters.

WHEN SIR THOMAS BERTRAM returned from his estate in Antigua, his usually timid niece Fanny Price avidly inquired 'about the slave-trade'. She exclaimed to her cousin Edmund: 'I love to hear my uncle talk of the West Indies. I could listen to him for an hour together. It entertains me more than many other things have done.' Unfortunately for Fanny, as the rest of the family did not share her interest, the conversation soon ended in a 'dead silence'.[1]

Fanny is the fictional heroine of Jane Austen's *Mansfield Park*, but several *real* people in Austen's social circle and extended family would have been well qualified to answer questions about enslavement. Austen's nearest relation with personal experience of the Caribbean was her aunt Mrs Jane Leigh Perrot (née Cholmeley). Unlike Fanny, who so enjoyed her uncle's conversation, Jane Austen actively disliked her Barbados-born aunt. Not because of the *source* of her wealth, but because she was so disinclined to share it. Had Austen asked her aunt about Barbados, she could have heard a story as dramatic as any novel – a tale of avarice, deceit, and fortunes won and lost. The truth, as they say, is stranger than fiction.

Jane Cholmeley, whom we will call by her nickname, Jenny, to distinguish her from her famous niece, was born in Barbados in the mid-1740s to Robert Cholmeley and Ann (née Willoughby). Jenny was the youngest of three surviving children, following siblings Katherine and James.[2]

They lived in Bridgetown, in a house Ann's father had given her. Robert, educated at St John's, Cambridge, and Lincoln's Inn, had practised law since arriving in 1732. It was a lucrative profession; colonists constantly needed wills, marriage settlements, Powers of Attorney and business contracts drawn up – the kind of lengthy legal documents I became only too familiar with researching this book – and then representation in court when the inevitable disagreements arose.

Like Samuel and Barbara Newton a century before, Robert and Ann keenly asserted their social status. When they married, Robert proudly presented his wife with a gold watch imported from England, engraved with the Cholmeley and Willoughby arms. Both could claim relatively exalted pedigrees. Robert was a younger son of the long-established Cholmeley family of Easton Hall in Lincolnshire; Ann distantly related to the Lord Willoughbys of Parham, seventeenth-century Governors of Barbados. The couple were well embedded in the island's ruling class. Robert had been friends with Lord Howe, another former Governor. Young Jenny and her family attended services in Bridgetown's St Michael's Cathedral, sitting in the pew immediately behind Governor Henry Grenville.[3]

Like Frances Dalzell, Jenny was packed off to boarding school in England at an early age. She found a surrogate family in the Lincolnshire Cholmeleys, growing particularly close to her cousins, Mountague and Penelope. Jenny lived for the holidays at Easton, impatiently counting 'the intervening days between my imprisonment and my return to the Comforts of a home'. Despite detesting school, Jenny was an avid reader, later admired for her 'great mental accomplishment'.[4]

Jenny's father Robert died soon after she left Barbados. Imprudently, especially for a lawyer, he had failed to write a will, so Ann had to apply to be his administratrix. After she paid his debts, just over £10,000 of assets remained. As his widow, Ann took a third, splitting the rest equally between her three children.[5] Since she was a minor at school in England, Jenny's share remained with her mother.

Ann would not prove a safe pair of hands. Soon after Robert died, Ann loaned the majority of her wealth to Reverend Edward Brace and his wife Ann, perhaps attracted by the agreed eight per cent return.[6] The Braces had only recently arrived in Barbados, but already faced serious financial problems. The Reverend's theological education at St John's, Cambridge, hardly prepared him for managing the 213-acre plantation in St George, home to around sixty enslaved people, that he had inherited eight years before. His uncle had intended the estate to be 'delivered to him free and clear of all manner of encumbrances', and 'kept up and supplied with Negroes, stock and all other things that may be wanting and improved to the best advantage'.[7] But the prosperous impression conveyed in these legal phrases had proved misleading. As Ann's finances depended on his success, Brace's shortcomings and travails would have a longstanding impact on Jenny's prospects of an inheritance from her mother.

After three years of widowhood, Ann remarried. Her new husband, Thomas Workman, was at least ten years younger. His first wife had recently died following childbirth, leaving him with two sons, Francis and Hamlet, aged seven and four.[8] An up-and-coming government administrator, Workman became Receiver General of His Majesty's Casual Revenue (the Crown's chief tax-collector for the colony) and Registrar of the Court of Vice Admiralty (clerk to the court judging maritime disputes) in 1759.[9]

He was not an honest man, as Jenny would later learn to her cost. In 1761, the Auditor General complained about Workman's 'fraudulent behaviour' to the House of Lords, accusing him of embezzling funds. He was allegedly aided and abetted by Hamlet Fairchild, husband to Jenny's older sister Katherine. In 1765, the government removed Fairchild from his office of Treasurer for 'mismanagement', confiscating then auctioning off virtually all his property. He had 'lost all hope of ever receiving any fortune from his father' – who had died some years before – and had 'been prevailed upon to apply the whole of his wife's fortune' to settle inherited debts. Nothing remained to fund the £214 he had settled on Katherine.[10] Thomas Workman evaded such consequences, however, and continued to rise in the island's administration.

Workman was equally unscrupulous in his personal life. His exploitative behaviour towards Ann later earned him a reputation as a 'villainous' man of 'rapacity and dishonorable principles', but again he was able to act with impunity for many years. Ann had been somewhat hasty entering her second marriage. Shortly after the wedding she 'became greatly distressed in her mind; and lamented' not having a marriage settlement, eventually persuading Workman to draw one up.

The resulting post-nuptial settlement of 1758 was not at all in Ann or her children's favour. Rather, Workman did his best to take full advantage of her assets. He insisted her house in Bridgetown be made over to him; promptly selling it and pocketing the cash. He also took over her interest payments from Reverend Edward Brace. Nine people – a man named Quash; three women: Affey, Katey and Cubah; four boys: Venter, Samson, Cudjoe and Charles; and a girl named Hester – were placed in trust for him, meaning he could charge for their labour.

Provision was also made for the future. If Ann died before her significantly younger husband, he would receive a lump sum of £1,071. Katherine and her heirs would inherit £1,071; Jenny and hers, £714. If both Jenny and Katherine died without children, Workman would inherit the whole £2,856 owed by the Braces. Strangely there was no provision for their brother James or his future children. Perhaps there had been some sort of estrangement, or it was deemed necessary to provide only for female relatives. After Katherine had a son, John Cholmeley Fairchild, in August 1758, the deed was altered to allocate him a third of the £1,071 previously assigned to Katherine. However, the remaining terms continued to unduly favour Workman.[11]

The Workmans travelled to England at some point in the late 1750s or early 1760s, for an extended stay. Jenny left boarding school to live with her mother and stepfather. She noticed her mother's 'displeasure against her husband' and would soon have reason to hate him herself. Jenny's most prized possession was a book of her father's poetry and drawings, bound in 'most splendid Morocco … richly gilt' by his appreciative friends. Unfortunately, Sir Thomas Robinson, an 'obnoxious' former Governor of Barbados, learnt of this 'sacred deposit'. Afraid it might contain 'sarcastic humour' against him, he promised Jenny his Opera box for a whole season if she would lend it to him. Insisting her father 'had never disgraced his book with anything of the kind', Jenny refused. But one day, while Ann and Jenny were out, Workman gave Robinson the book. Jenny was 'almost broken-hearted' to lose this memento of 'the very best of fathers', but, not wanting to increase the acrimony between her mother and her stepfather, she repressed her anger.[12]

Jenny was still a teenager when she received a proposal from twenty-nine-year-old James Leigh Perrot. James was the eldest child of Reverend Thomas Leigh, rector of Harpsden near Henley in Oxfordshire, and his wife Jane (née Walker). Educated at St John's, Oxford, James had 'abilities which might have stood him in good stead in any profession, had he adopted one.' However, he had no need to do so. Aged sixteen, he had inherited the substantial Northleigh estate in Oxfordshire from Thomas

Perrot, his grand-uncle on his mother's side, on condition he adopted the Perrot name and arms.

Besides a reputed income of £3,000 a year, James possessed 'what is superior to all fortune, a liberal and benevolent mind, with the greatest urbanity of manners that endear him to all that have the pleasure of his acquaintance'. His 'kind and affectionate disposition' combined 'an easy temper with ready wit, and much resolution of character'.[13] He enjoyed writing 'clever epigrams and riddles', even publishing some anonymously. On the marriage of a Captain Foote to a Miss Patten, he wrote:

> Through the rough paths of life, with a patten your guard,
> May you safely and pleasantly jog;
> May the knot never slip, nor the ring press too hard,
> Nor the *Foot* find the *Patten* a clog.[14]

To grasp James's joke today we need to know 'pattens' were thick wooden soles mounted on iron rings, strapped on to raise shoes out of the mud. Jane Austen wore them in country lanes; in *Persuasion*, the 'ceaseless clink of pattens' echoed on the streets of Bath on a wet afternoon.[15]

After hearing James was to marry Jenny, a relation of his, Mrs Wentworth declared at a party that: 'he was going to throw himself away upon a girl from one of the Islands, to which she supposed her Father & Mother had been transported'. A Cholmeley relative 'caught fire, & said, loud enough to be heard by the company, she wondered how Mrs W. could suppose such a falsehood could gain credit as it was well known that Mr Leigh Perrot's choice was not one which could ever disgrace him'. Far from being criminals, she added, the Cholmeleys were a junior branch of the Cheshire Cholmondeleys, who could trace their ancestry back to the Norman Conquest. Jenny's defender 'had the pleasure of seeing Mrs Wentworth completely humbled'. Her mother Ann, perhaps anticipating the prejudices her daughter might face, adopted Robert's old tactic; her wedding present to Jenny was a gold watch engraved with the Cholmeley and Leigh arms.[16]

Jenny married James on 9 October 1764 at St Martin-in-the-Fields – the same church chosen by Mary Ramsay and Frances Dalzell.[17] The day after the wedding, Thomas Workman drew up from memory an 'Account of the legacies of Robert Cholmeley who died intestate in 1754, and the state of Miss Cholmeley's fortune once the debts have been taken care of'. By his calculation, Jenny's inheritance had, with eight per cent interest, grown to £3,988 3s ¼d in the intervening decade.

However, Workman then deducted almost a third of this figure, claiming he had spent as much supporting her since he married Ann. The newlyweds were not even to receive the remaining money as a lump sum. Rather, Workman, in a bizarre arrangement very much in his own favour, agreed to pay them the:

> interest on the balances that shall be found due to Miss Cholmeley on a settlement once every year after my arrival in England, from the time the sum or sums exceed £100 sterling at the rate of three per cent, the rate at which I could securely have placed it out in the public funds.

His financial contortions may have been necessitated by Jenny's money being held not in cash or investments but against debts owed from the estates of two deceased Barbados enslavers.[18] Whatever the cause, Jenny's unscrupulous stepfather retained full control of the family finances.

In the same year Jenny married James, his sister Cassandra married Reverend George Austen. They made their family home at Steventon parsonage in Hampshire, where George augmented his modest income by taking in boarding pupils. George and Cassandra went on to have six sons and two daughters. Their second daughter, and youngest child, born in 1775, would become the novelist, Jane Austen.

The year after they were married, James (who had by now sold Northleigh to the 4th Duke of Marlborough) bought an estate once owned by his mother's family: Scarlets, near Wargrave in Berkshire. Jenny and James enlarged and improved the house, filling it with beautiful furniture and ceramics. Jenny particularly cherished an Indian cabinet James had given her – not for its intrinsic beauty, but because it was the finest in the neighbourhood.

As 'a number of gentlemen's places of moderate size were congregated within easy reach of each other', they were able to enjoy an active social life and entertained lavishly. Jenny later recalled: 'we lived much more for company than for ourselves, by choice … dining with thirty families, & frequently with our house filled'. On one occasion, the Leigh Perrots attended a fancy-dress masked ball, complete with firework display, hosted by the young Earl of Barrymore. James disguised himself as a 'Counsellor', Jenny was a 'strikingly elegant Pilgrim, in an Irish stuff [material] bound with ermine, and a rich diamond cross in her high-crowned hat.' Barrymore, nicknamed 'Hellgate' by the Prince of Wales, had spent £60,000 building a private theatre to host such festivities. The county's social mood was considerably dampened when he accidentally shot himself, aged just twenty-three, and the theatre was demolished to pay his debts.[19]

Jenny and James were considered 'the most affectionate pair in the neighbourhood'. James was so devoted that some gossips called him a 'Jerry Sneak', after a character in Samuel Foote's play *The Mayor of Garret* (1764) – by this time slang for a henpecked husband. Aged seventy, James wrote to his wife after a two-day absence: 'If I was able to say to you how much I love you and how much I long to be with you, perhaps you would not believe me.' In January 1800, he gave her a small pearl necklace, with this accompanying verse:

> My dearest Wife
> With thee no Days can Winter seem,
> Not Frost nor Blast can Chill;
> Thou the soft Breeze, the Chearing Beam,
> That keeps it Summer Still.[20]

Despite their mutual affection, like the Holtes and Oswalds, the couple never had any children. Jenny recalled in her widowhood: 'we were too happy in each other ... whilst I had him, He was the whole World to me.'[21] On another occasion, discussing their finances, she exclaimed: 'What a comfort that we have no children!', suggesting it would be a 'frightful expense'.[22]

Meanwhile, the Workmans had returned to Barbados. Jenny's sister Katherine had been widowed in 1767.[23] Four years after her disgraced husband died she made a more illustrious match, marrying Governor William Spry. They moved into the newly refurbished Government House at Pilgrim – today the President's official residence – living there in high style on his £3,000 salary. But, as a later chronicler put it, Spry 'had not long enjoyed the delights of this union before he was removed to another, and more perfect state of felicity'.[24] Katherine gave birth to their daughter Wilhelmina two months after his death; then took ship for England. Reunited with Katherine in 1773, Jenny was 'most

Cholmeley–Austen Family Tree

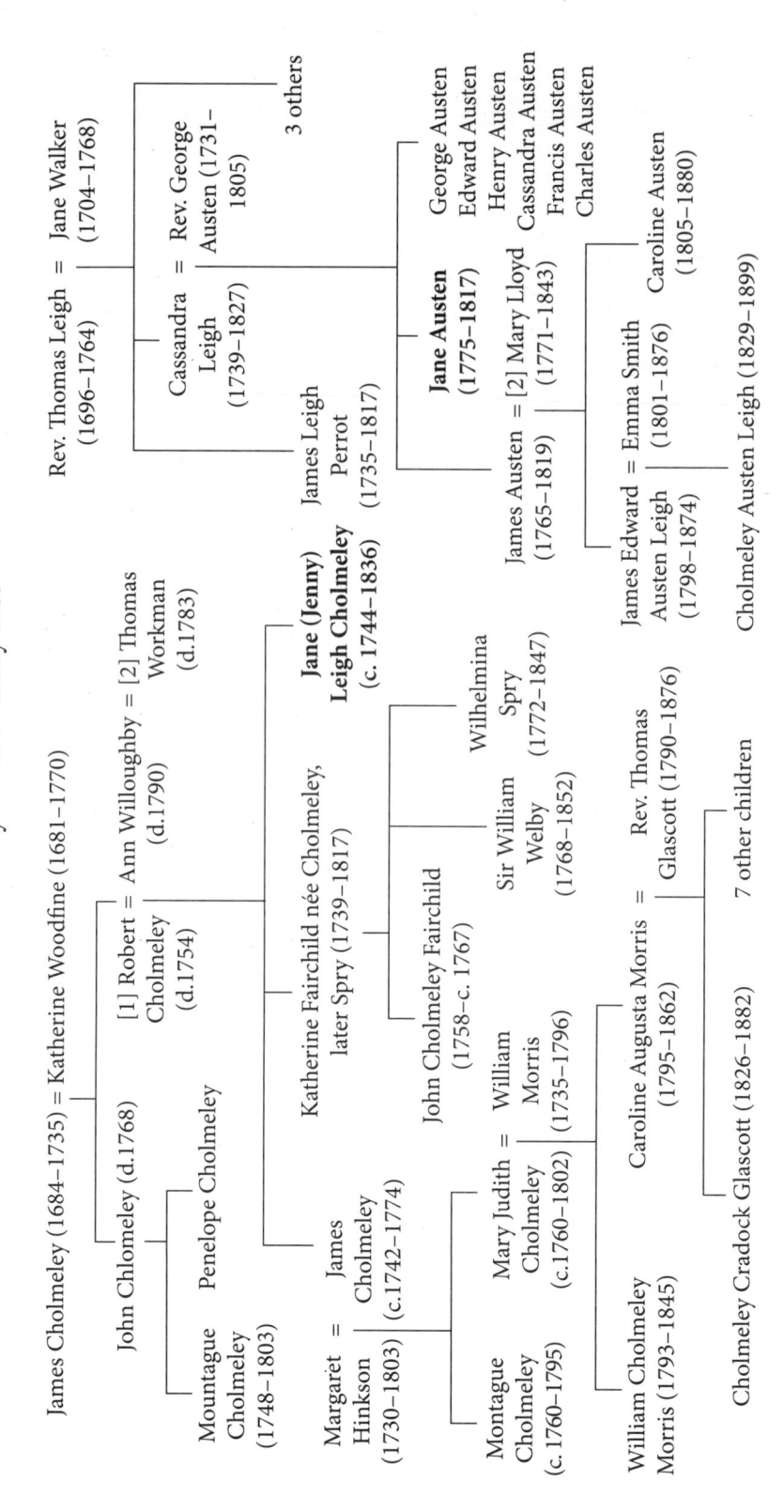

James Cholmeley (1684–1735) = Katherine Woodfine (1681–1770)

- John Chlomeley (d.1768)
  - Mountague Cholmeley (1748–1803)
  - Penelope Cholmeley
- [1] Robert Cholmeley (d.1754) = Ann Willoughby (d.1790) = [2] Thomas Workman (d.1783)
  - Katherine Fairchild née Cholmeley, later Spry (1739–1817)
    - John Cholmeley Fairchild (1758–c. 1767)
    - Sir William Welby (1768–1852) = Wilhelmina Spry (1772–1847)
  - Margaret Hinkson (1730–1803) = James Cholmeley (c.1742–1774)
    - Montague Cholmeley (c. 1760–1795)
    - Mary Judith Cholmeley (c.1760–1802) = William Morris (1735–1796)
      - William Cholmeley Morris (1793–1845)
      - Caroline Augusta Morris (1795–1862) = Rev. Thomas Glascott (1790–1876)
        - Cholmeley Cradock Glascott (1826–1882)
        - 7 other children
- Rev. Thomas Leigh (1696–1764) = Jane Walker (1704–1768)
  - Cassandra Leigh (1739–1827) = Rev. George Austen (1731–1805)
    - George Austen
    - Edward Austen
    - Henry Austen
    - Cassandra Austen
    - Francis Austen
    - Charles Austen
    - **Jane Austen** (1775–1817)
    - James Austen (1765–1819) = [2] Mary Lloyd (1771–1843)
      - Caroline Austen (1805–1880)
      - James Edward Austen Leigh (1798–1874) = Emma Smith (1801–1876)
        - Cholmeley Austen Leigh (1829–1899)
  - James Leigh Perrot (1735–1817) = **Jane (Jenny) Leigh Cholmeley** (c. 1744–1836)
  - 3 others

affectionately interested' in her baby niece, a 'little pale Creature, of 3 months old', who had come to meet 'her dearest & nearest connections'.[25]

Although, as a relative later remarked, Jenny and Katherine's 'distinguished merits, and superior accomplishments' had placed them both 'in a state of affluence', they were both still set upon receiving their due inheritance from Barbados. Jenny was expecting £1,428 on their mother's death; Katherine had been 'repeatedly assured … she might consider the whole of Brace's Plantation as her own'. However, their prospects hinged on the fortunes of Brace's estate and the unreliable character of their stepfather, Thomas Workman.

Reverend Brace had never been able to turn a profit from his plantation. He managed to service the debt to the Workmans for twelve years, drawing on other assets, but thereafter ran into difficulties. In 1766, with his debts mounting, Brace sold the plantation, along with forty-five people, for £7,500 (subject to the £2,857 debt to the Workmans) to one Thomas Payne, of Christ Church, who styled himself a 'gentleman'. He sold Payne his other estate, Martin's Castle in St George, the following year. But by 1774, Payne was 'much involved in debts and his creditors becoming clamorous'.

Workman took advantage of Payne's predicament to take control of Brace's. He 'prevailed on Payne and his Creditors, to appoint Him their sole Trustee', for two years. By the time the trust expired, Payne was dead; Workman refused to surrender Brace's to Payne's executors.

His intention was to make the estate so unprofitable it could not pay the £229 annual interest owed him; 'he should soon have the whole property, for the Arrears'. He appointed his elder son Francis as overseer on 'a most exorbitant salary', though he was 'totally incapable of such an employment', also exacting 'large and unjustifiable Emoluments' – salaries or fees – from the property.

After three or four years, the arrears amounted to over £700. This gave Workman an excuse to sell off parcels of land and several of the most 'valuable' people – tearing families apart – to service the debts. He sold the land most distant from the buildings to neighbours and contrived 'in a clandestine manner' to buy some twelve or thirteen of the 'best' workers at a heavily discounted price. Then, he hired their labour back to the plantation, at exorbitant rates.[26]

As Workman's star continued to rise in the island's administration, he seemed untouchable. In addition to his roles with the Revenue and the Vice Admiralty Court, he was now Deputy Secretary and Master of the Chancery Court. He used his influence to obtain similarly influential roles for his son Francis.[27] Father and son were now so embedded in the system that it would be hard for anyone to take legal action against them for the way they were behaving at Brace's.

Thomas Workman would almost certainly have achieved his aim of taking over Brace's were it not for an Act of God. On 10 October 1780, a hurricane – the same that ravaged buildings at Newton and Seawells just before Sarah and Elizabeth inherited them – hit the island, destroying everything in its path. With estimated wind speeds of 200 mph, it would today be classified as Category Five, the strongest on the scale. Not a tree was left standing on the whole island. Heavy cannons were blown a hundred feet from where they stood. All the ships in the harbour lost their moorings, some sank, others were driven out to sea; the *Albemarle* was swept all the way to Antigua. When Admiral George Rodney arrived in December from New York, he reported: 'the whole country appears one entire ruin and the most beautiful island in the world has the appearance of a country laid waste by fire and sword.'

Still the deadliest Atlantic hurricane on record, it took the lives of over 22,000 people as it raged through the Lesser Antilles. In Barbados, at least 4,000 died; 'whole families were buried in the ruins of their habitations; and many, in attempting to escape, were maimed and disabled ... the strongest colours could not paint the miseries of the inhabitants' who found 'the ground covered with mangled bodies of their friends and relations.' Jenny's mother Ann almost died, but her life was saved by her granddaughter Mary Judith (the daughter of Jenny's brother James). Thomas Workman's health was also 'much impaired'.

At Brace's, two enslaved people were killed. All the buildings were flattened; crops were destroyed; cattle and livestock died. Perhaps massaging the figures to obtain the maximum compensation, Workman estimated his losses at over £2,000. This was well above average for even the thirty worst-hit 'sufferers' in St George; most registered less than £100. Overall, Barbados enslavers submitted compensation claims for almost £950,000 worth of damage – including the loss of 2,033 enslaved people.[28]

This unforeseen event 'deranged' Workman's plans. He had by this time sold off fifty of the 'most inconvenient' acres at Brace's and 'pocketed the money'. He would need the remaining land, labourers and what was left of the buildings and cattle, as collateral to finance rebuilding the sugar works. His health had been so badly affected by the hurricane that he began to fear he would not live long enough to 'accomplish his Design in the gradual, but sure, mode, that he had projected.' So, he tried to pressurise Ann to assign the whole £2,857 debt to his son Francis, who would pay her an annuity for life. As family friend and Barbados government official William Morris recounted to Jenny:

> This proposal was, for some time, continually pressed upon Her in the most urgent manner. She, at first, rejected it, very resolutely; but, at last, began to give way to incessant importunity: fortunately, however, before she had expressly consented, she disclosed the matter to Miss [Mary Judith] Cholmeley; and desired her advice in it. Miss Cholmeley assured her, that, if she was in her place, no ill treatment whatever, nor any extremity to which she would be reduced, should ever make her submit to so base an attempt, and, accordingly, that very night, she gave Him a firm and decided Denial, and made a solemn Vow, that she never would comply with his Request. Ever after this, they lived at constant variance.

Morris lauded Mary Judith's 'sensible and spirited advice'. She had defeated Workman's plan 'almost in an instant'. Nonetheless Workman continued to squeeze every ounce of profit he could out of Brace's, flogging off 'all the Coppers, stills, leaden pipes, and every material of the Buildings, that could be sold for anything'.[29] With each sale, Workman grew richer, and Jenny and Katherine's inheritances shrank.

Workman's health did not improve; in November 1783, he left for England in hope of recovery. But he died five days after setting sail. He was buried in St John's, Antigua, the next port of call. His *Barbados Mercury* obituary claimed he had 'at all times acted with the strictest impartiality, integrity and conscientiousness'.[30] However, the will he wrote the week before his departure more accurately reflects his character.

Workman bequeathed all his assets 'share and share alike' to his two sons, Francis and Hamlet. He left no annuity or cash to Ann at all. She merely had the use of his furniture, plate, china, and his horse and chaise, for life. Workman also granted her the right to purchase ten people (possibly her domestics) – Joanna, Rittah, George, Jubbah Bess, Judy, Celia, Trinculo's Judy, Joe, Little Trinculo and Polly-Judy – for a 'reasonable' price from his sons. If she chose not to, she and her heirs – including Jenny – still had a right to their labour.[31]

The only money Ann received, 'directly or indirectly out of her Husband's property after his Death', was £50, which Francis and Hamlet paid her to surrender her legal rights over the ten people. Both 'were exceedingly dissatisfied that she had even this trifle' and bemoaned their father's lack of foresight in buying them in his own name and not theirs. They insisted it was now up to Jenny and Katherine to take financial responsibility for their mother.

Brace's was left so asset-stripped it could not raise a sum anywhere near the interest due to Francis and Hamlet. Ann was forced to borrow money to meet their demand for immediate payment. It took a Chancery judgment for her to gain possession of the struggling estate.[32]

By the late 1780s, Ann Workman was an invalid, 'totally unable to help Herself, in any manner'. Her granddaughter Mary Judith became her 'constant Companion; and her Supporter and Cherisher, through the most afflicted, infirm and helpless part of all her time'. Despite her illness, Ann felt well enough to 'form a resolution to go to England ... to see her beloved Children once again'. However, it was not to be. She died on 21 August 1790.

In her condolences to Jenny, Mary Judith alluded to Ann's will with some awkwardness:

> I have not as yet sufficient strength nor Spirit, to write as much as I wish to do, concerning the property of my dear Grandmamma, and her disposal of it ... I shall only observe, that her Estate has been appraised, by five Freeholders, at £5,600 current money of this Island [£4,000 sterling]. How it is left you will see by the authentic copies of the Will and Appraisement, which the executors intend to send you.

Finding her niece's reticence extremely frustrating, Jenny wrote immediately to William Morris, demanding to know when she and her sister might expect their legacies. However, she did not hear back from him and the other executors until April 1791. The 'state of Mrs Workman's affairs' was not as she had hoped.

Ann had left Jenny £714, half the sum she had expected. Katherine felt equally hard done by. Although she was bequeathed Brace's it had shrunk from 213 to 158 acres since 1766. With the sugar works still not rebuilt, Ann had borrowed over £400, and sold several people 'to make up the deficiency of her crop'. When the estate was appraised 'it was found that … several of the Slaves were afflicted with incurable disorders, and others nearly worn out with age and labor; and that … two or three Slaves have actually died'. Ann recognised the hard work of Jubber, who nursed 'the sick slaves on the plantation', dictating that she 'be supported and maintained' at Brace's and receive £2 a year, but only 'provided she shall duly discharge her duty … as long as she shall be able'.

Both sisters felt slighted in favour of Ann's two grandchildren in Barbados. Mary Judith's brother Montague Cholmeley, whom Ann did not even like, inherited £286, a mason named Cuffey and a boy named Joe. The favoured Mary Judith was to receive £714; 'all my plate and household furniture and my horse and chaise'; her prized gold watch engraved with the Cholmeley and Willoughby arms; two women, Joanna and Minna; three girls, Ritta, Jubbah Bess and Philly Ann; and two boys, George and Will Thomas.

Jenny no doubt shared Katherine's suspicion that 'some enemy had been undermining the promise' their mother had made of 'leaving her the principal part of her Fortune'. In a nineteen-page-long *apologia*, William Morris took pains to quell their misgivings. Far from anyone having undue influence over Ann's decisions, the will had been drawn up by 'an entire stranger'. He expressed surprise that Katherine, who, like Jenny, lived in 'opulent circumstances':

> seems not to entertain sentiments quite So kind and generous towards her Nephew and Niece, as I had always thought she did. Next to her own Daughter and yourself, they are the nearest Relations she has in the World; and therefore, it might have been reasonably supposed (able as she is to provide amply for Miss Spry [her daughter Wilhelmina]) that she would have approved and been glad of, rather that resented, their Grandmother's intended kindness towards them.

By his reckoning, the sisters had actually had a lucky escape. He estimated:

> if Mr Workman had lived till the end of the year 1789, he must inevitably, have had the whole Plantation for his interest money, [leaving] Mrs Workman … so far from having anything to leave either to her children or Grandchildren that she must, actually, have depended on her Daughters.

Far from begrudging Mary Judith's good fortune, they should be grateful to her for stopping Ann from assigning the debt on Brace's to Francis Workman after the hurricane. They were fortunate she had supplied 'the *want of a filial assiduity and humane attention* which she would, doubtless, have experienced from her Daughters had they been on the spot' (emphasis added).

There was one beneficiary whom William Morris believed Ann Workman had been overly generous to: an enslaved man named Gusman. He was to be set free – incurring a £36 manumission fee – and given three acres of land on Brigg's Hill (where the Gun Hill Signal Station is now located) plus £3 11s to build a house. Morris regretted that with Gusman 'valued' at £57 – clearly a skilled worker at the height of his powers – Ann's bequest cost the estate £96 11s, plus three acres.[33]

Gusman is an uncommon name, possibly indicating an Iberian or Jewish connection. The surname *Guzman* is a toponymic from a village near Burgos in Spain; in Yiddish it means metalworker. He had lived at Brace's for over twenty-four years, as there had been a man and a boy of that name there – probably this Gusman and his father – when Thomas Payne bought it in 1766. Gusman was freed and received the land; he died in Bridgetown in 1801. In 1817 and 1820 a Gusman Workman, probably his son – it was common for people to adopt their former master's surname – registered 'a Slave his own Property', a sixty-three-year-old Barbados-born field hand named Robin. Gusman Workman also appears on a list of 'Free Black and Coloured Persons' receiving a parish pension in St George of £2 17s a year between 1821 and 1825.[34]

It became clear where William Morris's loyalties lay when he married Mary Judith in 1792. Jenny does seem to have accepted his version of events, later acknowledging Mary Judith had been 'her grandmother's affectionate attendant at her death', and staying in touch with the Morris family when they moved to Devon.[35] It probably helped that Jenny and Katherine's legacies were paid following the sale of Brace's to Thomas Applethwaite in 1791.[36*] Nonetheless, Jenny's aggressive pursuit of her Barbados inheritance and lack of generosity to her niece and nephew would prove typical.

*

* He consolidated it into his neighbouring plantation, Walker's; a local village still bears the name Workmans. 'Walkers [previously Willoughby's; incorporating Brace's later Workman's]', LBS: https://www.ucl.ac.uk/lbs/estate/view/534.

Jane Austen kept a 'sharp look-out' for a legacy
from her aunt Jenny Leigh Perrot.

As he got older, Jenny's husband James began to suffer from gout and 'Bath was judged necessary.' Sometimes confined to a wheelchair, he occasionally stayed at home in his pyjamas.*[37] Jenny and James had visited the fashionable spa town occasionally since at least the early 1770s, when James helped to fund the new Upper Assembly Rooms. In the 1790s they began spending half of each year there, renting a smart townhouse at no. 1 The Paragon. Jenny and James enjoyed the Bath social scene, entertaining as extravagantly as they did at Scarlets. In April 1799 they gave a party for ninety guests.[38] More often, they hosted smaller evening gatherings, where they drank tea and played cribbage or whist.[39]

---

* In early June 1799, Jane Austen wrote: 'My Uncle overwalked himself at first and can now only travel in a Chair but is otherwise very well.' Two and a half weeks later, he was 'still in his flannels, but is getting better again.'

Jane Austen, with her mother and sister Cassandra, came to stay with Jenny and James for about a month from 23 November 1797. She visited again by herself from 17 May to 26 June 1799. As one nephew perceived, these visits gave Jane 'good opportunities for studying the Bath varieties of human nature'. Shortly after her first stay she began writing *Susan*, later published as *Northanger Abbey*.

Two of the books Jane references in the novel – Hume's six-volume *The History of England* and Thomson's *The Seasons* – were gifts from James. They were not necessarily both gratefully received. Though her heroine Catherine Morland 'can read poetry and plays', she is aghast Hume took 'so much trouble filling great volumes, which ... nobody would willingly ever look into ... labouring only for the torment of little boys and girls'.[40]

In December 1800, Rev. and Mrs Austen suddenly announced they were moving to Bath, causing Jane 'such a shock that she fainted away'. It was time to pass Steventon on to James Austen and his young family. The ageing couple were attracted by the spa's much-vaunted health benefits, and the chance to see more of Mrs Austen's brother. Jenny was delighted with the prospect. Jane wrote to Cassandra: 'it is an event which will attach her to the place more than anything else could do, &c. &c. – She is moreover very urgent with my mother not to delay her visit to Paragon if she should continue unwell.' According to Fanny Caroline Lefroy (James Austen's granddaughter), Jenny and James thought the move had been made to remove Jane from continuing an unsuitable attachment to William Digweed, who lived at nearby Steventon Manor. Fanny did not believe Jane was interested, though 'it might have been so on the gentleman's side'.[41]

By late January 1801 the Austens were house hunting, attempting to exercise their preferences against the force of Jenny's domineering personality. They eventually settled at no. 4 Sydney Terrace, and afterwards lived in Green Park Buildings, until George Austen's death in 1805. Jane Austen saw quite a lot of her aunt and uncle over these four years, during which she found little time or space for writing. Jane disliked attending card-playing evenings at The Paragon, exclaiming: 'I hate tiny parties – they force one into constant exertion.' This was characteristic of Jane's sentiments about the town and the Leigh Perrots' hospitality. As she wrote to Cassandra, 'Tis really very kind in my Aunt to ask us to Bath again, a kindness that deserves a better return than to profit by it'. Nonetheless, 'it was of the first consequence to avoid anything that might seem a slight to them.[42] After all, she was only a poor relation.

Jane resented Jenny for failing to provide for the Austen family and being somehow dissatisfied with her lot. She often wrote archly to Cassandra of Jenny's exaggerated complaints, be it their house being so dirty and damp on their arrival in Bath that they had to spend a week in an inn; inferior servants; disagreeable neighbours; poor health – 'they are tolerably well – but not more than tolerable'; or her unassuageable fear that The Paragon might be broken into in their absence. In May 1801, Jane warned Cassandra that Jenny was 'deafer than ever' and had a 'violent cough' – 'do not forget to have heard about that when you come'. In April 1805 she remarked: 'My Aunt is in a great hurry to pay me for my Cap, but cannot find it in her heart to give me good money.' Rather than much-needed cash, Jenny offered Jane tickets for a party in Sydney Gardens. 'Such an offer I shall of course decline; & all the service she will render me therefore, is to put it out of my power to go at all, whatever may occur to make it desirable'.[43]

Jenny *did* provide for her niece on one occasion. In November 1800 Jane Austen wore her aunt's gown and handkerchief to a dance at Hurstbourne Park, the Hampshire home of John Wallop, 3rd Earl of Portsmouth.[44] Jane reported that her sister-in-law, Mary Austen, thought she looked 'very well' in it; her brother Charles liked the dress too.

That night, Jane drank too much wine and danced with not one but two enslavers. The first, John Hooper Holder, was from an absentee Barbados family. His uncle James, who lived at nearby Ashe Park, owned Holder's (or Black Rock) plantation in St James. Jane had met his mother and sister amongst Jenny's social circle in Bath. The second, Antigua-born Brownlow Mathew, brother of James Austen's first wife Anne, had been bequeathed £1,000 by a 'West India merchant', and would inherit estates in Dominica from his father, late Governor of Grenada and Commander in Chief of the Windward Isles.[45]

These connections were far from unusual in Jane Austen's family circle. Her grandmother Rebecca's family, the Hampsons, were enslavers and attorneys in Jamaica. Jane knew the 7th Baronet, Sir Thomas, and mentions him several times in her letters. Two of Rebecca's grandchildren from her first marriage – Jane's half-cousins William and George Walter – went out to Jamaica. George died there in 1779; William bought a Jamaican estate in 1786, but died the following year aged thirty-seven. Mrs Austen complained to their sister Phila Walter 'you might as well be in Jamaica keeping your brother's house, for anything that we see of you'.[46]

James Austen's godfather, James Langford Nibbs, owned two Antigua plantations, Popeshead, and Haddons or Week's. Jane knew his son George, who was educated at Steventon, where his father's portrait hung on the wall. George Austen was a trustee of Nibbs's 1760 marriage settlement, making him legally responsible for his Antiguan property, including enslaved people, even if his co-trustee, a lawyer, did most of the work.[47]

Jane's youngest brother, naval officer Charles Austen, married in succession a pair of sisters from Bermuda, Frances and Harriet, daughters of Attorney General John Grove Palmer. Her sister Cassandra's fiancé Thomas Fowle, whom both sisters knew from childhood, died in modern-day Haiti of yellow fever in 1797, having travelled there as personal chaplain to his cousin Lord Craven, sent to try to capture and re-enslave the island following the Haitian Revolution. He left Cassandra £1,000.[48]

One of Jane's possible suitors, the Reverend Samuel Blackall, went on to marry Susannah Lewis, who inherited £4,000 from her father, owner of Lewisburg plantation in St Mary, Jamaica. Jane remarked: 'I should very much like to know what sort of a Woman she is!'[49] In 1793 William Chute of The Vyne, one of the Austens' friends and neighbours in Hampshire, married Eliza Smith, granddaughter of Antiguan slaver Nathaniel Gilbert.[50] In other words, *Mansfield Park*'s absentee enslaver Sir Thomas Bertram had many real-life prototypes amongst Jane Austen's friends and acquaintances, besides her aunt Jenny. Given the myriad connections to enslavement in genteel society, it is hardly a surprise to find them in Austen's world; it's more remarkable that they appear so infrequently in her novels.

While some of these links may seem peripheral, Jane also profited from enslavement directly thanks to a woman she met through Jenny in Bath: Mrs Willielma Johanna Lillingston (née Dottin). Mrs Lillingston had inherited £4,000 from her father Abel Dottin of Grenada Hall, Barbados, in 1760. When she died in 1806, estranged from her own daughter, she left £50 each to Jane and Cassandra. This sum covered all Jane's expenses for 1807 and allowed her the luxury of renting a piano. As acting executor, it was James Leigh Perrot who transferred the money to Jane and Cassandra.* Mrs Lillingston may also have bequeathed a

---

* Jenny and James also received legacies. Jenny had five guineas to buy a mourning ring; James, who acted as executor, netted over £300.

literary legacy: it has been suggested Austen had her in mind when creating Lady Anne Russell in *Persuasion*. Both women lived on Rivers Street in Bath and had treasured libraries, though there is no mention of Anne Elliot's godmother having any connection to Barbados.[51]

Jenny and James's comfortable life, split between Bath and Berkshire, was rudely interrupted in 1799. On 8 August they were accosted in Bath Street by one Elizabeth Gregory, who managed Smith's millinery and haberdashery shop. Jenny had bought some black lace there just half an hour before; now the shopkeeper demanded: 'Pray, Madam, have you not a card of white lace as well as of black?' Jenny said she did not, and proffered up the parcel for inspection, insisting: 'If I have, your young man must have put it in in mistake'. By Jenny's account, on finding a card of white lace, Gregory chirped 'Oh here it is', and returned to the shop. Gregory, on the other hand, claimed she had cried: ''Tis no such thing, you stole it! You are guilty!'[52]

Jenny was, by now, according to Gregory, trembling with fright and 'coloured as red as scarlet', as well she might after being accused of theft in a busy street. Jenny, however, recalled being unconcerned, believing the confusion must have arisen 'from shop hurry or negligence'. It was only when Charles Filby (who had wrapped up her purchase) accosted the couple

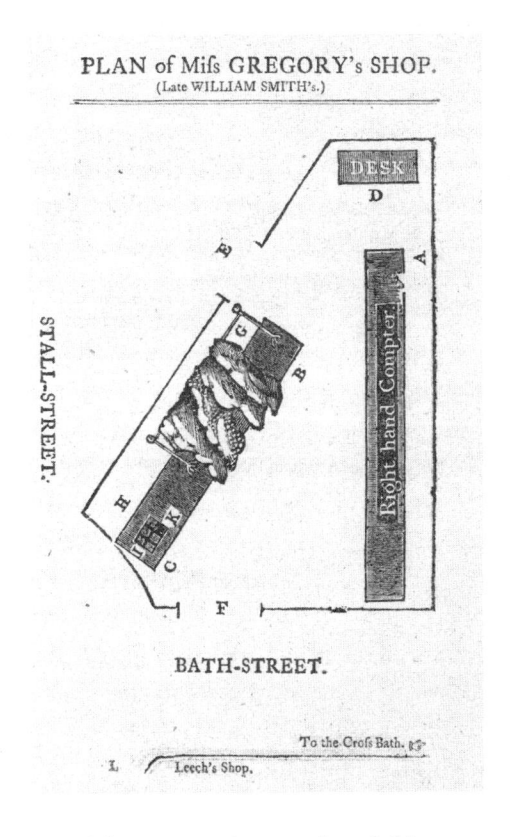

The prosecution produced this 'Plan of Miss Gregory's shop' to help make the case that Jenny was a shoplifter; a crime punishable by death or transportation.

soon afterwards asking for Jenny's name and address, that she became alarmed. But after hearing nothing more for several days, her fears subsided.

Arriving home after dinner on 12 August, Jenny found an anonymous letter addressed to 'Mrs Leigh Perrot, Lace dealer':

> Your many visiting Acquaintances, before they again admit you into their houses, will think it right to know how you came by the piece of Lace stolen from Bath St. a few days ago. Your Husband is said to be privy to it!

A blackmail plot was afoot.[53] The Leigh Perrots were ideal targets. Besides their wealth, James's well-known devotion to Jenny made him especially likely to pay up rather than see his wife's character dragged through the mud. Who were the culprits? The shopman Charles Filby had twice been declared bankrupt, giving him ample motive. Jenny enquired about lace in the shop the day before the alleged theft. Knowing she would return, Filby and Gregory conspired to set her up by wrapping some white lace up with the black in her parcel.

Two days later a constable arrived at no. 1 The Paragon, with a warrant for Jenny's arrest. James immediately leapt up from his sickbed 'forgetting everything but my danger', to accompany her to the Town Hall. Having received no response to their blackmail note, Filby and Gregory had upped the stakes by reporting the theft to the local Magistrate. As the white lace was valued at twenty shillings, the charge was 'Grand Larceny': a crime punishable by death – as were all thefts of property worth more than one shilling. This was often commuted to transportation, leaving the possibility that Jenny – once disparaged as the child of criminals deported to Barbados – might spend the rest of her life in Australia. (Family tradition had it that 'in case of an adverse verdict, followed by transportation, he [James] would sell his property and accompany his wife across the seas'.)[54] The Mayor and Magistrates of Bath, who Jenny and James knew socially, 'lamented their being obliged' to send her to prison to await trial. Unfortunately, she had just missed the summer assizes so would have to wait for the High Court judges to return in the spring.*

---

* Since the time of Edward III, England and Wales had been divided into six circuits, which senior judges toured twice or three times a year.

Jane Cholmeley (c.1744–1836) · 155

James adamantly refused to let Jenny suffer this ordeal alone, joining her in the Somerset county gaol in Ilchester. As Jenny wrote to her cousin: 'my dearest affectionate Husband, ill as he was, never left me – his tenderness has been beyond description. After above seventeen weeks' confinement, with his large Shoe [due to gout], and unable to move but with two sticks he has never seemed to have a thought but for me'.

Conditions at Ilchester gaol were grim. Over sixty prisoners – half of whom were debtors – crowded the building. It was liable to flooding and outbreaks of gaol fever (epidemic typhus, transferred by body lice). In 1730, prisoners from Ilchester had brought the infection with them to the Lent Assizes at Taunton, killing the judge, sergeant, sheriff and many townsfolk. Two decades after Jenny's stay, an MP testified to 'the badness of the bread, and the impurity of the water – to the absence of air and sunshine, and to the presence of instruments of torture unparalleled but by those brought over in the Spanish Armada'.[55]

For a price, Jenny was exempted from wearing the coarse brown-and-yellow striped prison uniform; and the couple were provided with accommodation in gaoler Edward Scadding's house. Jenny was amused that Scadding was styled 'Governor' of the prison, remarking to her cousin Mountague, 'what would my poor Sister say to this?' – Governor Scadding's standing being rather less exalted than her sister's late husband, Governor of Barbados.[56]

Jenny found the ordeal a fate worse than death. She enumerated to her cousin the 'many evils we must unavoidably endure in this House of Misery', full of 'Vulgarity, Dirt, Noise from Morning till Night'. Though 'we were bearing a thousand disgusting matters as to our accommodations, food &c.' she refused to send for her servants as 'I should not have their murmurs added to my other troubles.' Jenny insisted she was most distressed by her husband's discomfort:

> Cleanliness has ever been his greatest delight and yet he sees the greasy toast laid by the dirty Children [Scadding and his wife Martha had twelve] on his Knees, and feels the small Beer trickle down his sleeves on its way across the table unmoved … Mrs. Scadding's Knife well licked to clean it from fried onions helps me now and then – you may believe how the Mess I am helped to is disposed of – here are two dogs and three Cats always full as hungry as myself.

Jenny's health also suffered. She lost weight, partly due to stress-induced diarrhoea – 'anxiety of mind is not good for bowels naturally tender'. Her frequent headaches were, she claimed, mild compared to the heartache she was suffering. She resorted to taking a dubious but extremely popular quack medicine, Dr James's Fever Powder.*

While at Ilchester, the Leigh Perrots received many sympathetic letters from their friends and relatives, including Jenny's Cholmeley cousins and her sister Katherine, who 'seems to suffer much on our accounts'. Few visited, though Mrs Austen, Jenny's 'dear affectionate sister', tho' in a state of health not equal to trials of any kind, has been with the greatest difficulty kept from me.' Mrs Austen also offered to send Jane and Cassandra to look after Jenny, but she refused. There was no space for them to live in the house and she could not 'let those Elegant young Women be ... Inmates in a Prison nor be subject to the Inconveniences which you are obliged to put up with'.

Jenny knew she was the subject of much gossip and speculation. By September her initials had been leaked to the papers; it was only a matter of time before her name was printed in full. She could hardly bear being the 'wanton sport of malice and villainy in every shape'. Jenny heard from Katherine in January 1800 that 'a Mr. Casamajor chose to tell my strange story'. He had learnt it from his relation Sir William East, who had it 'from Payne of Maidenhead'.[57] Jenny's nephew John Cholmeley passionately intervened. She asked his father, cousin Mountague, to thank him and 'tell him I trust I shall never make him blush at having taken up my defence'. She also countered the gossip with an aspersion of her own: 'Miss Molly Casamajor may love Scandal as well as other creatures of his description', i.e. gay men.†[58]

While in gaol, James received two letters from anonymous informants confirming the couple's fear of a blackmail plot. By this time, William Gye, a local printer and fraudulent charity fundraiser, who owned a share of Smith's shop, had joined Filby and Gregory in bringing the prosecution. He threatened to publish a 'ludicrous print': the Leigh Perrots' crest 'with a card of lace, & other articles in the parrot's

---

* Although used by figures as illustrious as George III and Horace Walpole, its efficacy was dubious. The main ingredient, antimony, is toxic; the powder's overuse is thought to have contributed to the death of playwright Oliver Goldsmith.
† The 1785 *Dictionary of the Vulgar Tongue* defined 'Molly' as: 'a miss Molly, an effeminate fellow, a sodomite'.

bill'.[59] Jenny was aghast at this 'combination of deep laid schemes' and could only 'think with additional horror of what Art may do against Innocence.' She would rather die than pay them off; she would prove her innocence in court.

Jenny's trial was held on 29 March 1800 at Taunton Assizes. She had hoped several relatives would attend in support. Her nephew James Austen (Jane's eldest brother), 'a perfect son to me in affection', and his wife Mary, 'a relation of Lord Craven's well-bred and sensible', had shown 'firm friendship all through this trying business'.[60] However, they were prevented from coming after James fell from his horse and broke his leg. Mrs Austen once more offered to send her daughters but Jenny could not 'accept the offer of my nieces – to have two young creatures gazed at in a public court would cut one to the very heart'. Her Cholmeley cousins actually turned up, taking Jenny and James from Ilchester to Taunton in their 'chariot', ensuring 'it will be seen to what Family you belong, and that that family are proud to acknowledge you.'

The proceedings were delayed by half an hour by the 'the throng tumult and confusion, occasioned by the sudden irruption of a vast promiscuous multitude' of 2,000 curious spectators. Many 'could not possibly hear a word', but were willing to endure being 'almost pressed to death, and suffocated with the heat, merely for the satisfaction of *seeing*' the spectacle. Jenny 'appeared perfectly calm and collected, talking with her counsel and friends'. She had retained a crack legal team of four distinguished barristers to the prosecution's two.[61]

The witnesses for the prosecution, Elizabeth Gregory, Charles Filby and Sarah Raines (an apprentice they had inveigled to corroborate their concocted story), all gave evidence in minute, but unconvincing, detail. Filby testified Jenny had been holding the black lace in her right hand, and when he went to change her £5 note, took the white lace with her left, concealing it beneath her cloak. But how then could she pick up four coins, as he said she did, with her right hand while still holding the black lace? How could he have seen her do it while his back was turned? And, if he saw her take the white lace, why had he allowed her to leave the shop? Jenny later insisted that she hadn't even been wearing a cloak.

A series of high-status character witnesses appeared. Longstanding friends from Berkshire and Bath (including Lord Braybrooke, Provost-Marshal of Jamaica, and MP George Vansittart, 'a man polluted by residence in India'),[62] vicars from their local churches, and Jenny's cousin

Penelope Cholmeley all took the stand. She was, they testified, 'incapable of any act of dishonesty'; 'free from levity, vanity and extravagance'; an example for her fellow parishioners in 'moral and religious duties'. Bath shopkeepers praised her as the perfect customer, 'just in her dealings and punctual in her payments'. Besides casting doubt on the accusation, these protestations of good character were intended to mitigate Jenny's sentence should she be found guilty.

Though neither Jenny nor James were legally allowed to give evidence on oath, she was entitled to make an unsworn statement. But 'after speaking a few sentences she became so much agitated that her voice failed her'. The judge asked her lawyer, Joseph Jekyll, to sit by her and repeat loudly what she wished to say. His speeches at the bar usually mixed 'quaintness with jesting', but he read Jenny's prepared statement with a straight face. She began by asking why on earth a woman as wealthy as herself would be so 'depraved' as to commit this crime. Her 'noble and highly respectable friends' had attested to her good character. 'Is it possible', she asked, that 'at this time of life my disposition should so suddenly change and that I should foolishly hazard the well-earned reputation of a whole life by such conduct, or endanger the peace of mind of a husband for whom I would willingly lay down that life?' She made no comment on the evidence, trusting the jury would act 'with justice and mercy', and, calling on God to judge her, asserted her innocence. While Jekyll read this address, 'the prisoner and her husband were frequently excessively affected and distressed.'

The jury did not deliberate more than half an hour. They were unconvinced by Filby and Gregory, and probably agreed with the judge when he particularly noted: 'it did not carry the appearance of guilt' to return to Bath Street, walking straight past Gregory's shop within thirty minutes, without first going home to hide the stolen property. The verdict was Not Guilty. Jenny and James embraced in the dock, rejoicing in their triumph.

Freedom regained, the couple returned to Bath, before a restorative stay with Rev. George and Mrs Austen at Steventon. Jenny wrote to cousin Mountague: 'Once more I address you unprison'd, but oh! how I have been wrung! – to the very quick I believe. You will rejoice to hear that I was most honorably acquitted – but you will grieve with me that we cannot punish my vile antagonists'.

With the cost of prison accommodation, lawyers and renting a house for the witnesses at Taunton, the episode had not come cheap. However,

Jenny's complaint the expense was 'ruinous' hardly rings true; they remained extremely wealthy. Nonetheless, she insisted they would feel poorer for a long time, while protesting 'we are not expensive people and believe me, lace is not necessary to my happiness.'

In the weeks following the trial, Jenny received many visits and letters from well-wishers, even one from Martha Scadding the gaoler's wife, whom Jenny rewarded with an unusually generous gift of £25. She also received another anonymous letter, threatening the satirical parrot print again; this time she must donate 100 guineas* to Bath General Hospital (one of William Gye's 'charitable' causes) to prevent publication.

Even though the parrot never appeared in print, Jenny still feared she might be 'killed by popularity'. The case certainly drew much unwanted press attention; three pamphlets were devoted solely to relating the proceedings.[63] Jenny became the number one story in *The Lady's Magazine* for April 1800; the text 'embellished with an elegant portrait'. This cheap and popular publication was sure their lady readers would want a detailed description of Jenny's appearance. She:

> appeared very pale and emaciated, between fifty and sixty years of age, and rather thin. She was dressed in a very light lead-colour pelisse, a muslin handkerchief on her neck, with a cambric cravat. Her hair of a dark-brown, curled on her forehead; a small black bonnet, round which was a purple ribband, and over it a black lace veil which was thrown up over her head.[64]

Amidst her notoriety, Jenny had managed to become a fashion plate.

Despite the Not Guilty verdict, Jenny's character had not been completely redeemed in the court of public opinion, and rumours about her – including a colourful account of being caught trying to steal a plant by picking it up in her handkerchief – continued to circulate for years.† Several Austen scholars have assumed her guilt; her case is cited in modern studies of shoplifting.[65]

---

* The guinea coin was so named because it was originally made from West African gold.

† On a visit to Worthing in 1805, Jane Austen heard her aunt had been 'universally shunned' after 'cheapening' for plants. This seemingly idle gossip came from Penelope Hind of Findon, who had it from a Berkshire friend, Matilda Rich, who lived in Sonning near Scarlets. Pugsley, D., 'Dr Harington's Epigram', Jane Austen Centre Blog, 7 June 2024: https://janeausten.co.uk/blogs/extended-reading/dr-harington-s-epigram.

*

Jenny and James were catapulted to another level of wealth when his distant relation Mary Leigh died on 2 July 1806. James became one of three possible heirs due to the imprecise wording of her brother's 1786 will, vaguely bequeathing his fortune after Mary's death to 'the first and nearest of his kindred, being male and of his blood and name, that should be alive at the time'. There ensued a 'palpable scramble for Stoneleigh' in Warwickshire, considered by Jane Austen 'one of the finest estates in England'; possibly her model for Pemberley in *Pride and Prejudice*. Mrs Austen joked the vast mansion house, with its sprawling corridors, would benefit from signposts.

James travelled to London for the reading of the will, along with a horde of other Leigh relations. The exception was his cousin, Reverend Thomas Leigh, who headed straight for Stoneleigh in the spirit that possession was nine-tenths of the law. Aggravated by the delay caused by his absence, James wrote to Jenny that when he 'thinks proper to make his appearance, some proposals and steps must be made and taken towards an accommodation; I hope and flatter myself they will be satisfactory to you and me'.

Jenny and James were tough negotiators, eventually squeezing £24,000 plus an annuity of £2,000 – not forgetting an annual gift of venison from Stoneleigh Park – out of Reverend Leigh in exchange for relinquishing James's claim on the estate. Resisting the Reverend's suggestion that they distribute £8,000 of this windfall amongst their Austen and Cooper nephews and nieces 'who are so very numerous', they decided to postpone any such bequests until after Jenny's death. The lawyers observed Jenny's 'influence' had 'great weight with his [James's] determination'.[66]

This was quite a blow for the Austens, who had hoped for some share in the spoils. Jane wrote to Cassandra, 'I do not know where we are to get our Legacy – but we will keep a sharp look-out.' The siblings might have had £1,000 each; a life-changing sum for Jane Austen. Since George Austen's death in 1805, the three Austen women got by on £460 a year. Jane could not even afford £10 to buy back the copyright of *Susan* (later *Northanger Abbey*) in 1809, after the publisher had failed to print it for six years.*

---

* The only Austen to see any money from Jenny was James Austen, gifted an allowance of £100 a year. Jane Austen was unimpressed. Though 'Nothing can be more affectionate than my Aunt's Language in making the present … My expectations for My mother do not rise with this Event.'

When Jenny finally wrote to Mrs Austen regarding the 'Stoneleigh business', her letter contained 'as little as may be on the subject by way of information and nothing at all by way of satisfaction'. Rather, Jane remarked, her aunt looked 'with great diligence and success for Inconvenience and Evil'. Jane's disgust is clear: 'In spite of all my Mother's long & intimate knowledge of the Writer, she was not up to the expectation of such a Letter as this; the discontentedness of it shocked & surprised her – but *I* see nothing in it out of Nature – tho' a sad nature.'[67]

Jenny's failure to appreciate her good fortune is evident in how she recollected the event:

> When the Stoneleigh settlement increased our income, horses and a new chariot were purchased – but alas! Ill-health was then making the considerable addition of Fortune of less use to us – we could not keep the company we had always been used to.

Nonetheless – perhaps still scarred from her time in Ilchester prison – she felt 'I ought to be made some amends for late deprivations'. They could now afford to abandon the lease on no. 1 The Paragon, and buy 49 Great Pulteney Street, moving in just after Christmas 1810.[68]

Never quite satisfied, Jenny seems to have sometimes regretted sacrificing Stoneleigh, which by the mid-nineteenth century generated an income of £30,000 a year. When Reverend Thomas Leigh died in July 1813, his nephew James Henry Leigh inherited the estate. Jane Austen wrote to her brother Frank:

> There is another female sufferer on the occasion to be pitied. Poor Mrs L. P. [Leigh Perrot] would now have been mistress of Stoneleigh had there been none of the vile compromise, which in good truth has never been allowed to be of much use to them. It will be a hard trial.[69]

When Jane Austen's first novels were published (anonymously) to great acclaim – *Sense and Sensibility* in October 1811, followed by *Pride and Prejudice* in January 1813 – Jenny and James, like most of her circle, had no idea she was the author. The secret was out by summer 1813, as Jane Austen's brother Henry could not resist boasting about his sister's success. Jenny probably shared her great-nephew James Edward's reaction, expressed in amateurish verse:

> No words can express, my dear Aunt, my surprise ...
> When I heard for the first time in my life
> That I had the honour to have a relation
> Whose works were dispersed through the whole of the nation.[70]

We do not know whether Jenny enjoyed *Sense and Sensibility* – the theme of poor relations may have given her pause – but she delighted in *Pride and Prejudice*. After *Emma* was published in 1815, Jane Austen noted:

> Mr & Mrs Leigh Perrot – saw many beauties in it, but cd not think it equal to P. & P. – Darcy & Eliz had spoilt them for anything else. – Mr K. however, an excellent Character; Emma better luck than a Matchmaker often has. – Pitied Jane Fairfax – thought Frank Churchill better treated than he deserved.

Jenny felt much the same when she read *Emma* a second time years later:

> I still cannot like it so well as poor Jane's other novels. Excepting Mr Knightly & Jane Fairfax, I do not think anyone of the characters *good*. Frank Churchill is quite insufferable. I believe *I* should not have married him, had I been Jane. Emma is a vain meddling woman. I'm sick of Miss Bates. *Pride & Prejudice* is the novel for me.[71]

We do not know what Jenny made of two of the Austen characters critics have identified with her: Mrs Allen in *Northanger Abbey* and Aunt Norris in *Mansfield Park*. Mr and Mrs Allen are a wealthy, childless couple who introduce Catherine Morland to Bath society in *Northanger Abbey*, as Jenny and James did Jane Austen. Mrs Allen is vain and self-centred, with an aversion to dirt and an appreciation of fine clothing. Both Mrs Allen and Mrs Norris criticise the fashion for white dresses; Jenny thought her Barbados friends, widow Philippa-Elliot Holder and her daughter Margaret-Dehany Holder's white gowns in Bath 'an absurd pretension in this place'.[72] There is perhaps also something of Jenny's experience in Mrs Allen's reaction when her old schoolfriend, Mrs Thorpe, recounts her six children's achievements at length. Mrs Allen 'had no similar information to give, no similar triumphs to press upon the unwilling and unbelieving ear of her friend, and was forced to sit and appear to listen to all these maternal effusions'. Mrs Allen consoled herself 'with the discovery, which her keen eye soon made, that the lace on Mrs Thorpe's pelisse was not half so handsome as that on her own' – could this be an allusion to Jenny's fraught experience with lace?

Jane Austen's characterisation of Aunt Norris in *Mansfield Park* is more malicious. Her tendency towards 'sponging', pocketing curtain material, cheese and eggs from her sister's home, and even acquiring 'a beautiful little heath, which that nice old gardener would make me take', might well have been inspired by Jenny's alleged shoplifting, first the lace and later the plant. Mrs Norris is also childless, stingy and condescending; 'Aunt Norris lives too far off, to think of such little people as you'.[73]

Austen may have named her character after Robert Norris, the Liverpool slaver who had betrayed abolitionist Thomas Clarkson by initially cooperating with him, but then changing sides and testifying to Parliament that 'the voyage from Africa to the West Indies was one of the happiest periods of a negro's life'. Jane Austen was 'in love' with Clarkson as an author; the story of Norris's treachery appeared in his 1808 *History of the Abolition of the Slave Trade*. Austen's deployment of names like Mansfield (Judge Mansfield had presided over the Somerset case, declaring Africans could not be deported from England) and Hawkins (after Sir John Hawkins, the first English slaver) as the maiden name of the objectionable Bristol-born Mrs Elton in *Emma* has been interpreted as a subtle critique of enslavement.[74] Perhaps 'Norris' was also intended as a suggestive jibe at her aunt Jenny and her ties to Barbados.

James Leigh Perrot died at Scarlets on 28 March 1817, aged eighty-two. On hearing her uncle was at death's door, Jane Austen wrote: 'Indeed I shall be very glad when the Event at Scarlets is over, the expectation of it keeps us in a worry'. Her mother sat 'brooding over Evils which cannot be remedied & Conduct impossible to be understood' – presumably James's failure to share his windfall from the Stoneleigh affair.

Jenny felt the loss deeply. Jane Austen wrote: 'poor Woman! so miserable at present ... that we feel more regard for her than we ever did before.'[75] Without James, Jenny lived 'in a world that has lost its charms'. Her sense of isolation can only have increased with the loss of her sister Katherine just six weeks after she became a widow.[76] Jenny now thought of death as 'a change which may re-unite me to the husband I never shall cease to reflect on without grateful affection.'[77] His portrait was a comfort and she also wore a pearl bracelet with his picture set in diamonds.[78]

James's will sprung another nasty surprise on the Austens, who continued to 'keep a sharp look-out' for a legacy, especially following the devastating collapse of Henry Austen's bank the year before.'[79] James left Jenny £10,000, the houses at Scarlets and Great Pulteney Street in Bath, and all their other possessions. Although James Austen was named residual heir as expected, and legacies of £1,000 each made out to Jane, Cassandra and their other brothers, *none* of this was to be paid out until after his 'very dear wife's' death. It could be a long wait. Jane predicted 'the Property may not be theirs these ten years. My Aunt is very stout'. Interestingly, James's granddaughter Fanny Caroline Lefroy later remarked: 'It has always struck me that in leaving so much power in her hands he wished to mark in the strongest way possible his confidence in her probity & rectitude for that rectitude had been greatly doubted by many.'

The bad news physically rocked Jane. Some biographers believe it exacerbated her ongoing illness and even brought on her own death. It is the natural conclusion to draw from the letter she wrote to her brother Charles on 6 April:

> the shock of my Uncle's Will brought on a relapse, & I was so ill on Friday & thought myself so likely to be worse that I could not but press for Cassandra's returning with Frank after the funeral last night … I am the only one of the Legatees who has been so silly, but a weak body must excuse weak nerves. My Mother has borne the forgetfulness of <u>her</u> extremely well; – her expectations for herself were never beyond the extreme of moderation, & she thinks with you that my Uncle always looked forward to surviving her.[80]

'Poor Jane', as Jenny called her, died three months later, on 17 July 1817, aged just forty-one.

Jane Austen's prediction Jenny might outlive James by at least ten years proved perspicacious. She survived almost another twenty! Jenny stopped visiting Bath, preferring Scarlets and its happy memories of 'true domestic enjoyment'. While she waited to be reunited with James,

---

* James lost £10,000 when the bank collapsed. Jenny berated Henry's 'imprudence'; ruminating that without the Stoneleigh settlement, 'Where would my pretty Scarlets have gone then?' *Austen Papers*, ed. Austen-Leigh, p. 263.

she passed the time reading – including rereading her niece's novels – sewing, gardening, pampering her three 'handsome' pet dairy cows and investing in the stock market – by 1832, her portfolio was worth £81,250.[81]

By the 1820s she was too unwell to travel, and so deaf it was impossible to 'enjoy society'. There appears to have been one last hurrah on 13 October 1824 with 'a large dinner party at Scarlets'.[82] In August 1835, she wished Cassandra Austen (by now in her early sixties) could visit her but joked her own deafness and Cassandra's loss of teeth would make communication impossible. Instead, she preferred to stay by her 'dear comfortable fireside', and do as she pleased, for 'old women are licenced to do whatever makes them most comfortable'. Her whims certainly varied; in February 1834, she wished 'there were female MPs, and I were one'. Parliament had finally voted to end enslavement the previous summer; one can imagine her contributions to that debate!

Jenny enjoyed passing judgement on and interfering in her younger relatives' lives, hurling grenades from her armchair. From what she heard of her great-niece Anna's husband Benjamin Lefroy, she (rightly as it turned out) concluded he would not make old bones. Three years before his death, she made plans to buy his living as rector of Ashe in Hampshire for her great-nephew James Edward. When another great-nephew, Edward Knight, eloped with Mary Dorothea Knatchbull, his sister's stepdaughter, in May 1826, she wrote to Mary Austen, 'full of the news', which left her 'very much agitated'. In May 1834, she remarked the memorial to James Austen's first wife Anne Mathew was 'far too pompous for the little Steventon church'.

A host of ailments provided cause for lengthy complaint: a cough, short-term memory loss, aching sides, irritable bowels and a leg wound the size of a new half-crown. She disliked her doctors (whom she was too deaf to hear), and the inadequate, expensive and sometimes painful remedies they inflicted on her. She adamantly rejected the suggestion of a waterbed. In May 1833 she had a fall in her room and hurt her head and hip.[83] By 1834, she was confined to a wheelchair. She wondered whether travel in warmer climes would improve her health, like a neighbour whose consumption was cured by a stay in Madeira, but could not bear to leave her dear Scarlets. On reflection, she was grateful for her 'good sight, memory and an even spirit'.

*

Jenny's major preoccupation was deciding who would inherit the huge fortune she had preserved through her 'very unexpensive manner of living.' She was so penny-pinching that she asked her great-nephew James Edward if he knew a cheaper way to post letters.

For years, she would keep her family guessing, using the promise of great wealth to continue exerting her influence and guarantee regular visits to enliven her solitary existence. James Austen seemed the favourite to begin with, but they fell out over his sole trusteeship of her husband's estate; she withdrew his £100 annual allowance, on grounds of 'her own poverty'; he died not long afterwards.[84] Jenny next 'turned her thoughts towards' another Austen nephew, her godson, Captain Frank Austen, but 'never concealed from him that such intention was by no means fix't.' Though he named a short-lived son Cholmeley in 1823, Jenny eventually ruled Frank out. His naval career might cause him to neglect her beloved Scarlets.* She also disapproved of his second marriage, to Martha Lloyd, in July 1828, finding the news 'hard of digestion'.

Her great-nephew, James Edward Austen, increasingly seemed the most suitable heir, especially after he announced his engagement to Emma Smith in September 1828. 'So amiable a character', from a rich family, would make a very suitable future mistress of Scarlets.† When Emma met Jenny, she remarked, 'Mrs L Perrot is not at all a stupid [meaning dull] person; she is a ladylike little old woman & though for years she has been quite out of the world, yet she once lived in it & talks agreeably of past times.'[85]

James Edward and Emma invited Jenny to be godmother to their first son – inevitably named Cholmeley. Jenny doted on the 'dear fair-faced black frocked' child. The greatest sign of favour came at Christmas 1834 when she gave Cholmeley the gold timepiece her mother had given her as a wedding present, hoping he was 'pleased to find that his watch has wheels'.

---

* Frank's naval exploits had included blockading the Mysore coast in 1791, escorting troops to the Caribbean in 1795, fighting in the Battle of San Domingo in 1806, escorting East Indiamen home from St Helena in 1808 and eventually being promoted to Commander in Chief of the North America and West Indies station in 1844, spending time in Bermuda and Nova Scotia.
† Emma was the niece of Eliza Chute (née Smith), like her connected to Antiguan wealth through her grandfather Joshua's marriage into the Gilbert family. James Edward had met Emma at the Chutes' Hampshire home, The Vyne. *Jane Austen's Letters*, ed. Le Faye, pp. 572–3; 'Joshua Smith', LBS: https://www.ucl.ac.uk/lbs/person/view/2146650997.

Full of opinions on his upbringing, Jenny suggested her godson read bestselling educational children's book, *Sandford and Merton*, penned by her neighbour, the abolitionist and abusive husband, Thomas Day. The eponymous rich boy Tommy Merton, whose moral character is reformed by spending time with farmer's son Harry Sandford, was the son of a Jamaican enslaver. He had been 'spoiled by too much indulgence' as a child, waited on by enslaved Africans 'forbidden upon any account to contradict him'.[86]

We do not know whether Jenny read the manuscript of Jane's unfinished novel, *Sanditon*. If she had, the unflattering portrait of Lady Denham, a 'thoroughly mean' wealthy widow, surrounded by younger relatives vying for her fortune, who 'talked & talked only of her own concerns', and 'takes alarm at a trifling … expence', might have struck a sour note. Strikingly Lady Denham is also very proud of her 'milch asses' and her great generosity in giving her nephew a gold watch.[87]

Now in her eighties, Jenny was pressed by all to make her final decision known. Not before 'repeatedly representing the possibility of altering my intention' – perhaps in favour of her Cholmeley relations – in October 1828 she announced she would write a new will favouring James Edward Austen. In compensation, she paid Frank £10,000, allowing him to buy himself a house in Portsmouth. As a bird in the hand, he might have found this preferable to remaining subject to her whims. Nonetheless, Frank dispatched a letter so long, unpleasant and querulous that Jenny burnt it.[88]

Jenny died on the morning of Sunday 13 November 1836, having passed her ninetieth birthday. For much of the previous year she had been bedridden, sometimes too weak to read or speak. By her deathbed stood Cassandra, James's widow Mary Austen, and her two children, James Edward and Caroline. Jenny was buried at her local church, St Mary's, Wargrave, in a vault beside her 'dear & ever lamented husband'. The rest of the Austen brothers, her niece Wilhelmina with her husband Sir William Welby, and representatives of the Cholmeley family attended the funeral.

Jenny's will, last amended only a month before, was read on 17 November, finally ending almost twenty years' suspense. James Edward Austen was to inherit the bulk of her estate. She also made significant provision for several Cholmeley relatives, leaving £5,000 of investments to her niece Wilhelmina and the same to her great-niece Caroline Augusta Glascott (the youngest daughter of Mary Judith and William

Morris), and *her* son Cholmeley Glascott. James Edward lost no time seizing his inheritance. He moved into Scarlets with his family on 3 January 1837, adding the name Leigh by deed poll, as stipulated in Jenny's will, the following day.[89]

In 1913, James Edward Austen Leigh's son and grandson summarised Jenny's character in their *Life and Letters of Jane Austen: A Family Record*. Though 'hardly formed for popularity … she was highly respected. She was not exactly open-handed, but she had a great idea of the claims of family ties, and a keen sense of justice as between herself and others'.[90] Living to such an old age inevitably leads to being primarily remembered as a deaf, stingy, disgruntled old woman, rather than the girl sent away from her family aged six, the young bride suspected of having criminal ancestors or the hostess of lavish parties. Her reputation as both tight-fisted with money, yet always covetous for the finer things in life – be it an Indian cabinet or expensive lace – persisted throughout her long life. Her aggressive pursuit of her Barbados inheritance showed a rapacious desire to amass ever more wealth, despite already living a life of luxury.

Certainly, Jenny could have done so much more for her talented niece, especially in the years between Jane leaving Steventon in 1800 and moving to Chawton Cottage on her brother Edward's Hampshire estate in 1809, when she was unable to focus on her writing. It would have taken a fraction of Jenny's immense fortune to give Jane Austen the space and financial security aspiring women writers often lack – as Virginia Woolf put it, to write, a woman needed £500 a year and 'a room of one's own'. Worse, disappointment at the 'vile compromise' over the Stoneleigh inheritance, then the shock of James Leigh Perrot's will, may have hastened Jane's death aged just forty-one.

When Jenny makes a cameo appearance amongst the ever-increasing plethora of Austen scholarship, it is as Jane's wealthy yet stingy aunt, the alleged lace thief. Yet few delve into Jenny's origins in Barbados, even when Jane Austen's other and much more indirect links to colonialism and enslavement are placed under a magnifying glass. When stories such as her father's link to the Nibbs family of Antigua, or the simple fact she drank tea sweetened with Caribbean sugar, hit the media, they cause a furore. Recent headlines in the *Telegraph* – 'Jane Austen's tea drinking will face "historical interrogation" over slavery links' – and the *Daily Mail* – 'Jane Austen museum launches BLM-inspired "interrogation" of author's love for drinking tea and wearing cotton due to slave trade links' – reduce the debate to absurdity; a storm in a teacup if you will. There are some who cannot bear to have their cosy, TV period drama vision of Austen's world disrupted by the realities of how several of her acquaintances funded their genteel lifestyles. They may find it distressing to learn Jane herself accepted a legacy from a Barbados heiress, Jenny's friend Mrs Lillingston – the largest sum she ever inherited, for all her sharp look-outs. It should not, however, come as a shock that Jane's aunt Jenny was from Barbados, or that several real-life Sir Thomas Bertrams (and probably more still to be discovered) appear amongst her social circle. To truly understand Jane Austen and her novels, we must accept that her world was unavoidably peopled with the beneficiaries – and exploiters – of empire.

Portrait of Martha Swinburne, née Baker, wearing the croix étoilée given to her by Empress Maria Theresa of Austria, by Richard Cosway, engraved by Mariano Bovi.

5

Martha Baker (1747–1809)

Martha's story takes us beyond Barbados and Jamaica to St. Kitts, St. Croix and, most importantly, St. Vincent – an island fought over by the French and British. Here, her efforts to claim land clashed with the interests of the indigenous Garifuna, fighting for their independence.

MARIE ANTOINETTE, famously frivolous and fashionable, appeared 'much altered' when she granted Martha Swinburne a private audience on 8 May 1789. The Queen had 'lost all her brilliancy of look', and was 'very low spirited'. 'You arrive at a bad moment, dear Mrs Swinburne. You won't find me happy at all; I have much weighing on my heart.'[1]

Marie Antoinette's heart ached because her eldest son lay dying; Martha's mind, on the other hand, was burdened with business. She had come back to Versailles to ask for her friend's help. Her St Vincent estate had been destroyed during the French invasion of 1779, and she had been seeking compensation from both the French and British governments ever since. Her efforts in London had been rebuffed; she now hoped that Marie Antoinette could persuade King Louis XVI to support her cause.

But the Queen's power was waning fast, as the storm clouds of Revolution gathered. She sorrowfully apologised to Martha; 'I fear that at this moment I can't be of any use to you, but if things improve, you know that I never forget my friends.'[2]

A melancholy encounter; Martha burst into tears the moment she left the room. But did she weep for Marie Antoinette? Or did Martha's grief stem from the bitter realisation her old friend was now in no position to help her, and she might never be able to regain her family fortune?

Martha was born in St Kitts on 31 March 1747, the daughter of John Baker and his wife Mary (née Ryan). John already had a five-year-old son, John Proculus, from a previous marriage, and Martha would have three surviving younger brothers: Thomas, Robert and Joseph.[3]

Martha's father John was, like Jenny Cholmeley's father, a lawyer; but of more lowly birth, the second son of a grocer from Chichester. Since his arrival in St Kitts's capital, Basseterre, in 1740, he had enjoyed a lucrative career. In 1749 he was appointed Deputy Solicitor General of the Leeward Islands – St Kitts, Antigua, Montserrat and Nevis – and promoted to Solicitor General the following year.[4] To supplement his official annual salary of £50, John offered litigious colonists legal representation and assistance with their reams of wills, deeds and contracts. He was also a prolific diarist – his brief entries, often merely jottings in note form, scattered with unreliably spelt phrases in Latin, French, Italian and, occasionally, German, allow us to build a detailed impression of his world – and by extension, Martha's.

In 1753, John gained some celebrity as prosecutor in a sensational murder trial. Matthew Mills, a prominent member of Kittian society, had been shot dead by newly arrived Huguenot lawyer John Barbot following a dispute over an estate sale. The island's elite, outraged by the murder of one of their own – John invoked the 'many hearts that are yet bleeding, for his death' – demanded retribution. However, the only eyewitnesses were two enslaved Africans, unable to testify in court. John was forced to rely on hearsay evidence from two white men (who reported what the Black men had said). The *London Magazine*, reporting on the trial at length, called this 'a dangerous sort of proof'. Nonetheless John's 'strength and perspicuity' secured a guilty verdict.[5]

Making regular trips between islands, John built up a valuable network of clients and connections with all the Leewards' leading families. In 1754, his place among the island's ruling class was cemented when he became one of twenty-four Members of the St Kitts Assembly.[6] His swift ascent was aided by an advantageous marriage: Martha's mother Mary Ryan came from a family of wealthy Irish Catholic enslavers, who had lived on Montserrat since the seventeenth century.[7] Due to religious persecution in Britain, Catholics were much more likely to make the Caribbean their permanent home than Protestants. Many flocked to Montserrat. Now known as the 'Emerald Isle of the Caribbean', it is the only country outside Ireland where St Patrick's Day is a national holiday.

In his role as Solicitor General, John regularly prosecuted enslaved Africans. Outnumbered eight to one by a population of over 20,000 Black people, enslavers attempted to keep control through a punitive judicial regime.[8] John personally sentenced at least seven men to death between 1752 and 1755, laconically noting their crimes and punishments in his diary. Tom (enslaved by Christopher Hodge) had raped a girl named Moll, belonging to Daniel Mathew (son of Governor William Mathew and uncle to James Austen's first wife Anne). Will was accused of stealing the huge sum of £43; Cabenus and Mingo (both enslaved by John Mills, brother of the murdered Matthew) of taking a schooner. These three were probably making plans to escape. Two men protested violently against their oppressors: another Mingo instigated 'a riot', wounding thirteen-year-old Francis Warren Rossington; Devonshire was hanged for strangling Mr Wharton's overseer, Mr Runnells.

Young Martha would probably have known Chocolate, 'hanged and thrown in the sea' for theft. The Bakers were intimate enough with his enslavers, the Gallwey family, that Martha slept at their Pond estate overnight aged four. Three of the other condemned men – Will, Cabenus and Rossington's adversary Mingo – belonged to family friend Ralph Payne, Chief Justice of St Kitts.[9] Living in Basseterre, Martha, like young Mary Ramsay and Frances Dalzell in Kingston, or Jenny Cholmeley in Bridgetown, would have seen their rotting bodies hanging from gibbets long after their executions.

The Spanish had made pit stops on the Leewards in the sixteenth century, stocking them with swine but otherwise 'never had leisure to think of these inconsiderable islands'. The English first arrived in St Kitts in 1624, led by Sir Thomas Warner, who became the island's first Governor. This was three years before they began settling Barbados; making St Kitts the oldest English colony in the Caribbean. The French landed a year later, sharing the island until 1713. All the Leewards were tiny compared to Barbados or Jamaica. Their mountainous interiors – Montserrat even had a dormant volcano – left an even smaller area of cultivatable land. However, fertile Kittian soil produced abundant yields of very high-quality sugar. By the mid-eighteenth century, St Kitts had outpaced Barbados's exports and become, per acre, the most profitable of all Britain's American colonies.[10]

As with the other islands in the Lesser Antilles, St Kitts was at first home to large numbers of indigenous Kalinago, who named it Liamuiga,

Baker Family Tree

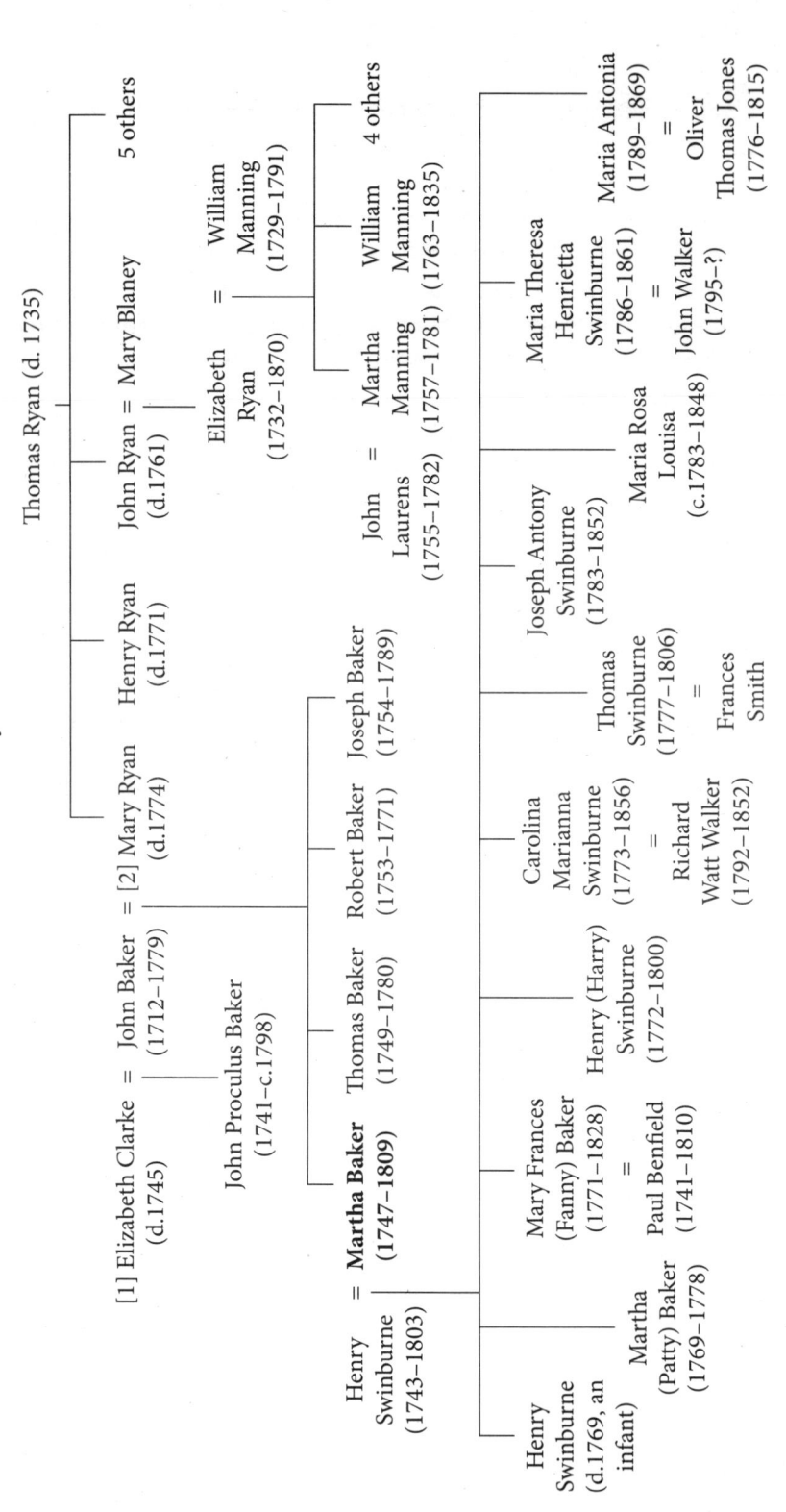

Thomas Ryan (d. 1735)

- [1] Elizabeth Clarke (d.1745) = John Baker (1712–1779) = [2] Mary Ryan (d.1774)
- John Ryan (d.1761) = Mary Blaney
- Henry Ryan (d.1771)
- 5 others

Elizabeth Ryan (1732–1870) = William Manning (1729–1791)

John Laurens (1755–1782) = Martha Manning (1757–1781) | William Manning (1763–1835) | 4 others

John Proculus Baker (1741–c.1798)

Henry Swinburne (1743–1803) = **Martha Baker (1747–1809)** | Thomas Baker (1749–1780) | Robert Baker (1753–1771) | Joseph Baker (1754–1789)

Mary Frances (Fanny) Baker (1771–1828) = Paul Benfield (1741–1810)

Henry (Harry) Swinburne (1772–1800)

Carolina Marianna Swinburne (1773–1856) = Richard Watt Walker (1792–1852)

Thomas Swinburne (1777–1806) = Frances Smith

Joseph Antony Swinburne (1783–1852)

Maria Rosa Louisa (c.1783–1848)

Maria Theresa Henrietta Swinburne (1786–1861) = John Walker (1795–?)

Maria Antonia (1789–1869) = Oliver Thomas Jones (1776–1815)

Henry Swinburne (d.1769, an infant)

Martha (Patty) Baker (1769–1778)

meaning 'fertile land'.* Skilled seafarers, the Kalinago hunted, fished and traded from Anguilla in the north to Grenada in the south in their large canoes (a Kalinago word). But European policy towards them was nothing short of genocidal. In 1626, English and French forces massacred 2,000 Kalinago at a Kittian headland still known as Bloody Point; some survivors were captured and enslaved, others fled to the mountains. Not only were the Kalinago a military threat – they almost wiped out the English settlers on Antigua in 1640 – but they were occupying land wanted for sugar production.[11]

In 1675, Sir Thomas Warner's son Philip carried out a pre-emptive raid on the Kalinago of Dominica, killing some eighty people; a town on the site is now named Massacre. Amongst those murdered was his own half-brother, Thomas 'Indian' Warner, whose mother was Kalinago. 'Indian' Warner had been enslaved by his English stepmother after his father's death, and fled to Dominica. There, he became such a powerful figure that he was courted by the French and the English, and appointed Governor of Dominica after visiting Charles II's court. Philip Warner was imprisoned for fratricide in the Tower of London, but later sent for trial in Barbados where he was judged not guilty.[12]

Not long afterwards, Charles II authorised 'war on the Carib Indians', after the Governor of the Leewards made the 'necessity for destroying' them clear.[13] By the time of Martha's birth, the majority of Kalinago in the region lived in Dominica and St Vincent, where the English and French had agreed to leave them unmolested, a promise they would later break.

Martha was 'exceeding[ly] dear' to her parents. When just four, her father proudly boasted she had 'acquired a manner of curtseying and such a carriage and behaviour as, I will assure you, you seldom meet with in a girl of her age in England.' Great care was taken over her education; she had dancing lessons from the age of five, learnt to play the harpsichord and became a voracious reader.[14] Her father had a theatrical bent, acting in *King Lear*, *Othello* and Henry Fielding's farce *The Mock Doctor* with his friends. Martha's first recorded trip to the theatre was on 7 October 1755, aged eight, when she saw Joseph Addison's *Cato* and

---

* The Europeans called the people they found in the Antilles 'Caribs' – hence Caribbean. Kalinago is closer to what they called themselves, and the term adopted by their descendants in Dominica today. Murphy, *Creole Archipelago*, pp. 23–4.

David Garrick's *Lying Valet* with her mother. The following February she 'went to Master Warner's to act King and she Queen', playing at royalty with a descendant of the island's founding Governor.[15]

Martha also travelled and socialised within her parents' close-knit circle from an early age. Aged five, she attended a turtle feast hosted by the powerful Phipps family, who sent their own chaise to collect her and her mother. The grandest homes on the island were young Martha's playgrounds, and like any child she occasionally misbehaved. She 'wounded her eye with scissors' during a stay with her grandparents in Montserrat when she was seven and her parents had to miss a dinner engagement to look after 'poor dear Patty's eye' – still 'all red and yellow' more than a fortnight later. Two years later, Martha was horse-whipped by her mother for her 'behaviour around midnight'.[16]

Martha regularly witnessed her father's brutal policing of enslaved people in their home. On 3 August 1755, John 'gave Othello a severe whipping for lying out [staying a night away], and Tycho a good smart one for concealing it.' Though many enslaved men were called Othello, John naming a man after Shakespeare's most famous Black character is particularly ironic given he had played the role himself. Harsh treatment also led to tragedy for Fatima, who was 'brought to bed of a dead son' in December 1757. She had been on an errand 'coming from the River', but was forced to stop on the way home to give birth – like other enslaved women, she was made to work throughout her pregnancy.

John's control was far from complete; in May 1756, he 'found negroes gaming in the kitchen' at two in the morning. The same month, a newly arrived African boy, whom Baker called 'Sunday', successfully escaped, but died at Halfway Tree in St Thomas Middle Island two months later.[17]

One man enslaved by the Bakers had a freedom of movement that challenges our assumptions about enslaved peoples' lives. Jack Beef was trusted to run errands on horseback, even travelling to other islands on his master's business, fetching bottles of beer from Nevis, and letters from Montserrat. In May 1754, he sailed to Nevis 'bringing back James Gardner's Nerode'.[18] John trusted Beef would not seek freedom for himself or help Nerode escape.

In 1750, when Martha was three, John Baker was invited to join a syndicate he called the 'quadripartite concern', consisting of his brother-in-law, Henry Ryan, and two of the Ryans' prominent Monserrat neighbours, Laurence Bodkin and Nicholas Tuite. Tuite, the instigator, whom John admired for his indefatigability and 'clear and penetrating foresight,' recruited John for his legal expertise. The plan was to buy land on the nearby Danish island of St Croix ahead of King Frederick V of Denmark's anticipated takeover from the Danish West India Company. Under royal protection the island would, Tuite believed, become a free port and boom, the price of land rising accordingly. In the wake of new discriminatory legislation against Catholics in Montserrat, Tuite also hoped St Croix would become a new haven, later petitioning Frederick V for liberty of conscience.[19]

Tuite offered John the chance to buy land on 'very favourable terms'. John exclaimed to his brother: 'you will hardly believe the terms of the purchase, when I tell you how easy and advantageous they are, it looks like a dream!' The four men bought over 1,000 acres at £10 an acre. St Croix was only a day's sail from St Kitts and John made frequent trips there during Martha's childhood. However, he relied on Ryan and Bodkin's on-the-ground supervision; 'were they dead or to quit it, I would at once renounce it and sell out.'[20] Before long, John was invested in two estates, Concordia and Plessens.[21]

The partners purchased fifty people with Concordia, adding a further 150 people by January 1751, but still required much more labour.[22] The island was too small to attract many transatlantic traders, so John took on the task of acquiring captives, both from ships arriving in St Kitts, and from local enslavers. In April 1753, he bought three women from Archibald Thompson for £70 and sent them to St Croix in George Robinson's sloop; that June, he sent 'Mr Liliot's Jack', Peter and Old Nanny with Captain Hart. In February 1754, followed 'Rose's Cato', Daphne and her newborn son, and a man named Fortune, recently bought from James Hazell. When the *Fanny*, a Liverpool ship captained by William Jenkinson, arrived in June 1755, with '69 Pappah slaves from Guinea' – 'Pappah' referred to people from the area between West Nigeria and Togo – he went straight aboard and bought fifty individuals to send to Tuite on St Croix in one of Ryan's sloops, plus a further six for himself.

John knew the market well. Attending a sale held by William Wells in January 1754, he exclaimed: 'some Ibbo negroes sold at £32 sterling – what madness! Better-looking seasoned negroes at the same time sold for £50 currency, etc [a similar price].'[23] He had learned 'seasoned' Africans – who had already lived a few years in the Caribbean – were more likely to survive. One of the 'Pappah' men he purchased from the *Fanny*, and named Friday, died less than nine months later.'[24]

However, John grew increasingly frustrated with this piecemeal approach, exclaiming: 'I see no prospect of stocking the plantations out of Guinea ships or any other probable way in the world then sending out a vessel to Guinea … we want a sweep of 60 or 70 fine ones at once.' His wish was soon granted as his partner Laurence Bodkin became a leading trafficker of Africans to St Croix during the Seven Years' War, importing 470 people directly from Africa in 1760 alone.[25]

The rapidly expanding Black population of St Croix – a 1758 census counted 11,807 Africans and 1,690 Europeans – planned to seize their liberty at Christmas 1759. After killing their oppressors, setting fire to plantations and seizing the West End fort, they would control the island. Suspicions were raised when a man named Cudjo threatened some white men at Bagge's plantation, 'You look out that some of your heads won't lie at your feet pretty soon.' He was arrested, then betrayed by his own brother, Quamina, who gained his freedom and fifty rixdollars (£2 10s sterling) by being the first to confess to the authorities. After torturing several captives, Judge Engelbrecht Hesselberg identified seventy-nine male and ten female suspects, including a man enslaved by Tuite named Jupiter. Jupiter was amongst the forty-nine men acquitted. Five men managed to escape capture, and all the women were released, but those found guilty suffered terrible punishments. Cudjo was 'burned alive on a pyre, lived in the fire 4 ½ minutes'. French and Prince Quakoe (Kwaku) were 'broken on the wheel with an iron crowbar'; their heads later impaled on stakes. William Davis, a free man identified as the uprising's leader, had sworn whilst in custody: 'if they cut him up piece by piece, and roasted him on the fire he would nevertheless confess nothing'. Though he took his own life before he could be executed, his 'dead body was dragged through the streets by a horse, by one leg; thereafter hanged on a gallows by a leg, and finally taken down and burned at the stake'.[26]

Such was John's commitment to his investments in St Croix that in 1760, having learnt a little Danish, he accompanied Tuite on a trip to Copenhagen. King Frederick V acknowledged Tuite as 'the founder of the colony, the sole source of its greatness'. John was tasked with copying

---

* Baker took the remaining five: Monday, Tuesday, Wednesday, Thursday and 'Old Man', to Soufrière Hills, Montserrat, in March 1756.

'propositions of commerce of Danish islands', putting the legal skills Tuite recruited him for to good use. In the middle of doing so, he was interrupted by a letter from his wife reporting young Martha had fallen from a swing.[27]

Martha was nine years old when the Seven Years' War broke out. Proximity to Martinique and Guadeloupe left the Leewards especially vulnerable to French attack. War also threatened delivery of vital supplies. John was nevertheless reluctant to leave St Kitts and tried to continue business as usual. But, as the situation deteriorated, he and Mary fought about money and, cryptically, what he 'told her of myself'. On 23 May 1757, Governor Gilbert Fleming reported St Kitts had only two more weeks' worth of bread and flour. The Bakers set sail for England three weeks later. They arrived in London at the end of July, to a warm welcome from John's family and friends. They rented a house in Red Lion Square, Holborn, for a year, before moving to Teddington. In June 1761, the family settled at Grove Place in Nursling, near Southampton.[28]

Accompanying the family was Jack Beef. As in St Kitts, he was trusted with important errands and business. He was well dressed, had his own horse, accompanied John on his travels, and took the Baker boys to and from school at Eton and Winchester. He was much in demand among John's friends for cooking turtles and bottling wines. He visited the theatre with other household members and attended at least one 'Ball of Blacks' in London. The Bakers also employed a Black coachman named Ellis and an African American cook named Eudosia.[29]

Martha's education progressed rapidly. She grew fond of Joseph Kelway, the organist of St Martin-in-the-Fields, who taught her the organ, harpsichord and spinet. More unusually for a young woman she also learnt Greek, Latin and several modern languages. She developed a passion for the arts and history, influenced by her father, who boasted dramatist David Garrick and painter William Hogarth as friends.[30]

At first, Martha attended Church of England services, but by August 1757, aged ten, she was investigating alternatives, attending Catholic Mass at the Sardinian embassy with her mother one week, the Quaker meeting at Chichester with her paternal grandmother the next. On 17 June 1759, John recorded in his diary *'petit brouiller* [sic] *circa figlia andante con madre a la missa'* (a small quarrel about daughter going with her mother to Mass). John may have been worried becoming Catholic would limit Martha's prospects, at a time when British hostility to 'Papists' extended to curtailing their civic rights. Royals lost the right to inherit the throne if they married a Catholic (a prohibition lifted only in 2013); few of their subjects would find the idea of a Catholic bride appealing.

Nevertheless, Martha adopted her mother's Catholic faith and was sent to an Ursuline convent in Lille. Known for championing women's education, the order, named for St Ursula, had been founded in Brescia in 1535, and by the eighteenth century boasted 350 convents across Europe and North America. Martha was one of over 300 students, overseen by thirty-two nuns and thirteen sisters. The abbess was Bridget Skerrett, 'a tall handsome English lady ... whom they called St Edward' – one can only guess what characteristics she might have shared with King Edward the Confessor. Her establishment was probably recommended by Nicholas Tuite, whose wife was a Skerrett from Antigua.

In May 1763, when Martha was sixteen, John arrived in Lille to move her to the Ursuline convent in Paris's Rue Saint-Jacques. She bade her friends farewell with parting gifts and tea at La Nouvelle Adventure, 'a sort of cake house and garden'. After arriving in Paris, John took Martha sightseeing. They visited the famous Sèvres porcelain factory and Versailles, where they saw the Queen, Dauphin and Dauphine dining, from a distance.

Though John would later protest the thought had never crossed his mind, the move to Paris was partly about finding Martha a suitable husband. The Bakers were soon introduced to Lady Helen Webbe, a Jacobite dowager who played matchmaker for English Catholics. Her credentials included having made a lucrative match herself eighteen years before, marrying the eighty-year-old Sir John Webbe three months before he died. Lady Webbe took Martha under her wing, and – in the time-honoured fashion of matchmakers from Cinderella's fairy godmother to Hollywood rom-coms – helped her acquire a new wardrobe.

A potential suitor soon appeared: Charles Howard, a relation of Catholic grandee the Duke of Norfolk. The day they met, John underlined the eligible young man's name in his diary. However, although 'intelligence was marked in his features, which were likewise expressive of frankness and sincerity', 'Nature had cast him in her coarsest mould'. Not long after John left Paris, Martha rejected Howard's proposal.[31]

Another contender was Charles Carroll, scion of a hugely wealthy enslaving family in Maryland. He would go on to be the only Catholic signatory of the American Declaration of Independence. Martha was suggested to Carroll as a potential bride in autumn 1763 by his tutor, a Jesuit priest named Alexander Crookshanks. He believed her to be 'the only daughter & sole heiress of a West India gentleman', assuming Martha's father was hugely wealthy from 'the unlimited credit he allows his daughter'. After only the briefest acquaintance, allowing him to judge merely her figure 'agreeable' and she 'good natured', Carroll was keen to begin a formal courtship. He was confident Martha's 'youth and inexperience' would 'smooth the path of victory', and 'favour' his 'design'. He claimed he had not *entirely* lost sight of the importance of mutual affection, unconvincingly assuring his father: 'her fortune however great shall not tempt me to sacrifice mine or her happiness to ambition or avarice'.

The young fortune-hunter lost no time in applying to John, who 'was far from being altogether a stranger to the name' Carroll, but expressed surprise, claiming, rather disingenuously, that at sixteen Martha was still too young 'to engage in the married state'. He had 'great reason to believe that her own affections' were 'as utterly disengaged as they were ten years ago'. John warned Carroll Martha was not set to inherit as much as he had been told. She was not his only child, and he was 'somewhat embarrassed' by a debt of £10,000 borrowed to 'clear, settle and plant his sugar lands' in St Croix. Undeterred, Carroll assembled a prestigious legal team, led by Queen Charlotte's Attorney General, to draft a marriage settlement, and asked Nicholas Tuite to give a detailed summary of John's assets.

Tuite confirmed John's 480-acre Concordia plantation, worked by about 150 Africans, was producing 300 hogsheads of sugar and 150 of rum each year. He was also entitled to half the profits of Plessens, now over 900 acres, where 300 to 350 labourers extracted 500 hogsheads of sugar and 250 of rum annually. After paying for insurance, commissions, 'overseers' wages, taxes, doctors' fees, mortality of negroes & cattle, feeding the negroes, boards, staves & hoops & all other charges', John made an annual profit of £3,775. Conspicuously absent from the calculations, by comparison with a modern business, was *a figure for workers' wages*.

Tuite optimistically forecasted that as the plantations were 'yearly improving', with rising prices for sugar and rum, 'the net produce of the whole may be justly rated at £4,500 p.a. for the next twenty years to come and may be much more'. However, all this paled in comparison to the Carroll family's American assets, comprising several town and country houses, an iron works, over 70,000 acres and over 400 enslaved people. John admitted Carroll's fortune was 'far more considerable than my daughter might be (what the world calls) intitled to'.

Ultimately the match foundered not on finances but because Charles Carroll insisted Martha move to Maryland with him. Her mother Mary refused to countenance losing her only daughter and made her views clear when Carroll visited the Bakers at Grove Place in January 1764. 'Had I known the mother before I opened the affair to Mr Baker', Carroll repented, 'I should have entirely dropped the thought of that marriage.'[32]

In 1766, Lady Webbe introduced Martha to twenty-three-year-old Henry Swinburne, newly arrived in Paris following a tour of Italy. She found his good looks, vitality, and interest in art and culture – he had studied antiquities and paintings at the Royal Academy in Turin – extremely attractive. The couple were later described as 'two persons united, not only by the tenderest ties of affection, but by the utmost uniformity of taste, studies, and mental endowments'. It was said: 'no desire animates the one, save that of drawing forth and exhibiting in the most favourable light the talents and accomplishments of the other'.

Henry wrote to John – now back in St Kitts – asking for Martha's hand. John had no objection. Henry hailed from an old Catholic family, the third surviving son of Sir John Swinburne, 3rd Baronet of Capheaton, Northumberland, and had inherited an annuity and a small estate, Hamsterley near Durham, in 1763. Henry and John agreed Martha should have a marriage portion of £4,000, by 'letters that passed between [them] then at great distance and at different parts of the world'. On marriage this sum, alongside a further £4,000 put forward by Henry, was to be 'put out at interest', at a rate of five per cent, the income paid to the couple half-yearly. Martha married Henry at Aix-la-Chapelle on 24 March 1767; they honeymooned at the fashionable resort of Spa in Belgium.[33]

By the time Martha married, the nature of John Baker's Caribbean investments, and so the source of her dowry, had changed. St Croix had lost its status as a thriving entrepôt following the end of the Seven Years' War in 1763, when the Danish acted to regulate trade and replaced its corrupt Governor. John had sold his share of Concordia by 1766 and his interest in Plessens by 1770.[34] He took on the management of a Kittian estate belonging to his friend John Estridge.[35] But his major new venture was purchasing land in St Vincent.

Alongside Grenada, Dominica and Tobago, France had ceded St Vincent to Britain in the 1763 Treaty of Paris, directly contravening earlier promises made to the Kalinago. St Vincent, or Youloumain – named for Youlouca, the rainbow spirit – was a heavily wooded and mountainous island in the eastern Caribbean, some twenty-two miles long and fourteen to sixteen miles wide. At the northern end lay an active volcano, La Soufrière, which had last erupted in 1718. Large swathes of the north and eastern or 'windward' side were inhabited by the Garifuna, whom the English described as 'Black Caribs', and a much smaller number of Kalinago.[36] The Garifuna had both Kalinago and African ancestry. Various, difficult-to-corroborate, early accounts survive of Africans arriving on the island aboard a shipwrecked slaving vessel, others were certainly captured in Kalinago raids on French plantations, and many probably escaped from enslavement on other islands. As Betsy Newton knew, the current naturally swept ships from Barbados to St Vincent, 100 miles downwind.[37]

Large tracts of St Vincent – about a third of the island – were sold off in the decade following 1765 by a team of Crown commissioners led by Sir William Young. An Antiguan enslaver and friend of the Bakers, Young would soon acquire extensive property in the ceded islands and become Governor of Dominica.[38]* Together with Dr John Collins of St Kitts, John bought 228 acres in St George, the most southerly parish, near the eastern branch of the Warrawarrou (now Greathead) River.[39] John probably didn't visit St Vincent himself; instead Collins undertook to establish the plantation on the ground. By 1771, 110 Africans worked on Baker's estate.[40]

While the French – many of whom remained on the island – had contented themselves with cultivating less intensive crops, particularly coffee and tobacco, on the 'leeward' (western) coast, the British were intent on cultivating sugar. However, the land they thought most promising and fertile was on the windward side: Garifuna territory. The Garifuna had no intention of recognising British sovereignty or giving up their homeland. '*Quel roi?*' – 'What King?' – asked their most prominent leader, Chief Joseph Chatoyer (now a Vincentian National Hero), when George III's name was mentioned. When the British attempted to build a road through the windward side in 1768 – a clear precursor to occupation – they were ambushed by some 200 armed Garifuna and forced to abandon the project.

---

* When Martha's mother saw him on 24 July 1770, Young boasted he had kissed the King's hand that day as Governor. *Diary of John Baker*, ed. Yorke, p. 199.

Alarmed by the Garifuna's military strength and expertise in guerrilla warfare, Sir William Young warned: 'suffering the Charaibs [Caribs] to remain in their present state, will be very dangerous, and may at some period prove fatal to the inhabitants of the country'. He feared the Garifuna might harbour Africans who sought their freedom and ally with the French. Worse, he knew he was powerless to punish them for any 'outrages' they committed. In August 1769, the British sunk four Garifuna canoes, suspected of importing supplies from French St Lucia, leaving eighty men to drown. Ignoring their indigenous heritage, St Vincent enslavers proposed the Garifuna be 'removed to the part of the world from whence their ancestors came', suggesting some 'unoccupied tract of 10,000 acres of woodland' with a river, 'upon any part of the coast of Africa'.

Engraving of Garifuna leader Chief Joseph Chatoyer (*right*) with several women, purportedly his wives. Charles Grignion, 1796, after a 1775 original by Agostino Brunias.

Responding to such appeals, the British government deployed two regiments from North America to 'reduce' the Garifuna in autumn 1772. Though hugely welcome to Vincentian enslavers, some British voices called out the immorality of this action. The *Scots Magazine* decried the 'murderous commission' sent out to 'extirpate' the island's rightful owners, just to 'gratify avaricious merchants, land holders and venal commissioners' like John Baker and Sir William Young. In Parliament, when a spokesman for St Vincent maligned the Garifuna as 'a faithless people … abandoned to every species of vice', particularly polygamy and drinking, he was met with the rejoinder 'if they love women and wine, liberty and property, where is the difference, except in colour, between them and Englishmen?'

British soldiers were no match for the Garifuna's guerrilla tactics on land, but by sea they succeeded in cutting off arms and ammunition supplied by the French, and made it impossible to fish. Eventually Chief Joseph Chatoyer and twenty-eight other leaders signed a treaty in February 1773: the southern boundary of their land was moved north from the Yambou to the Byera River, a substantial territorial gain for Britain. Like the Maroons in Jamaica – the British even used a copy of the 1739 treaty for reference – the Garifuna were expected to return any freedom seekers who fled to their territory, and – ominously – were promised help if they wanted to leave the island.[41]

After Martha and Henry married, they went to live at Hamsterley Hall near Durham; 'a handsome mansion house, in a warm sheltered valley on the Pontburn, surrounded by rich woodlands disposed with more than usual taste and felicity'.[42] They added a two-storey east wing to the house, with Gothic windows, castellations and interiors. They put their joint initials 'HMS' in several places as a decorative motif. The garden combined 'the classic precision of the Italian style with the more wild and sylvan boldness of English park scenery.'[43]

Martha's first child, named Henry after his father, died while still an infant, in 1769. More children quickly followed. By 1772, the couple had four-year-old Martha, nicknamed Patty, one-year-old Mary Frances, known as Fanny, and a second baby Henry, known as Harry.[44]

Country life with the county set did not suit the Swinburnes. While they 'almost exclusively devoted themselves to literature and the arts', their 'provincial acquaintance' thought of 'little else than of corn or turnips … [or] the pursuit of foxes'. The women of Martha's circle were completely:

absorbed in the performance of their maternal and domestic duties ... as little able to comprehend or estimate her talents, as she was to appreciate the skill with which they executed those pickle and preserve accomplishments that constituted the glory of a north country housewife.[45]

Thanks to her Kittian roots, Martha was nonetheless able to make citronelle – a rum liqueur also known as *eau de Barbades*, flavoured with lemon and orange peel, cloves, coriander and, of course, sugar – so delicious that on one occasion her husband and his friends happily polished off a whole bottle while she was out.[46]

Soon Martha and Henry fled south with their young family, using her parents' new home, Horsham Park, in West Sussex, as a base to visit London and Brighton. Martha and Patty had their portraits painted by Nathaniel Hone, the painter who probably employed John Hylas, but John did not like the result.[47]

In March 1770, Martha gave Jack Beef and her parents' maids theatre tickets in the gallery to see *Zenobia* – a tragedy by Arthur Murphy about the third-century Syrian Queen who defied the Roman Empire – and *Peep Behind the Curtain* – a farce by Garrick – at Drury Lane. But Martha and Henry were not in town when Jack Beef died on 6 January 1771, only four days after leaving John's service. He had intended to return to St Kitts a free man, but instead died in his sleep, after a good dinner, at lodgings in London. The funeral at St George's, Bloomsbury, arranged by John, was attended by a number of the family's servants and their Black former coachman, Ellis.[48]

Keen to travel, the Swinburnes left for the Continent in February 1774. Patty would start school in Paris, Harry was too young to leave his mother, but three-year-old Fanny was left behind with her grandparents. This decision was not easily made. John and Mary had a '*grand brouillée*' (big quarrel) in front of the Swinburnes about something Mary said to Martha about Fanny.[49] Unfortunately we do not know what they disagreed about. Perhaps Mary didn't want to be saddled with a toddler!

She would not suffer for long. Mary died on 19 March 'in all respects as if going to sleep without the least rattling, hiccoughs, groan or aught else usually attending it'. John 'kissed her several times – Good God! How terrible and racking it was!' Knowing how upset Martha would be, he went to great lengths to ensure Henry could break the news gently. He sent a letter to Henry enclosed inside one addressed to one

Pompeo Batoni's portrait of Henry Swinburne, Rome, 1779.

of the Swinburnes' friends in Paris, with strict instructions to deliver it directly into his hands without Martha's knowledge. He even avoided adding his seal to the letter in case Martha recognised it and suspected something was wrong. Instead he used a 'strange seal ... the white one with a head once Jack Beef's'.* However, all John's precautions were in vain, as Martha had already learnt of her mother's death with 'surprise and shock' from an indiscreet family friend before her father's missive arrived.[50] Now a widower, John gave up his establishment at Horsham, and little Fanny was sent to join her family.

The Swinburnes spent most of the next decade travelling around Europe. They particularly enjoyed their time in Italy, where Henry

---

* It is not clear whether the seal bore a depiction of Jack Beef's head, or whether it was white with a head on it, and used to belong to Beef; the latter raising the fascinating possibility Beef was literate and carried out his own correspondence.

wrote: 'my wife has the same propensities as myself for antiquities and our mode of life is so pleasant in this delicious climate, where no impediment of weather prevents our daily journeys of discovery.'[51] In Rome, like many other British travellers, they had their portraits painted by Pompeo Batoni, and Christopher Hewetson sculpted busts of them cast in bronze.

Henry became something of a travel writer, publishing *Travels through Spain in the Years 1775 and 1776*, followed by *Travels in the Two Sicilies, 1777–1780*. Both were illustrated with his own sketches, and went into second editions, abridgements and translations. In a strong measure of his readability, a recent survey of library users shows his most popular work, *Sicilies*, had been borrowed 140 times by eighty-four users of eighteen different collections by 1800, making his work far more sought-after than, for example, Adam Smith's *Theory of Moral Sentiments*, borrowed only twenty-eight times in the same period.[52]

Martha made a significant contribution to Henry's writing. He was 'accustomed not only to consult her opinions, previous to commencing his literary labours, but submitted his manuscript to her inspection during the process of composition, and unhesitatingly followed her suggestions and corrections.' Her father John also read drafts and helped Henry negotiate with London booksellers.[53]

Henry was thrilled to find himself admired by Georgiana, Duchess of Devonshire, cited by historian Edward Gibbon and recommended by the British Ambassador to Naples, Sir William Hamilton, to Sir Joseph Banks. However, while the *Critical Review* praised *Travels through Spain* as 'the greatest and most distinct account of Spain that has hitherto been published', a Spanish critic remarked: 'This Englishman ... is endowed with such penetrating insight that in a stay of two or three days in Spain he was able to observe that all the roads are bad, the inns and taverns all detestable, that the country appears to be a hellish place where stupidity reigns &c.'[54]

'Extremely loath that he should let slip the favourable opportunity of visiting a country so badly described by previous travellers', Martha had stayed behind in Tarbes – a 'dull town' on the French side of the Pyrenees – with the children, while Henry toured Spain with his friend Sir Thomas Gascoigne. She might not have been so in favour had she known of Gascoigne's reputation for being 'addicted to Venery ... scattering your seed all over the face of the earth, and throwing your money after it'. His last tour had ended abruptly after he and his friends wounded four men during a 'drunken riot' in Rome, one of whom later died.[55]

The Swinburnes had a happy knack of making friends wherever they went, with other English travellers, local literati and nobles, even kings and queens. Ten years earlier, Martha had been a tourist at Versailles; now she and Henry became habitués of the premier courts of Europe. In Paris, Henry was the last person to be introduced to Louis XV before he died. In Rome, the family were presented to Pope Pius VI, who gifted Martha an agate necklace. Ministers Henry met in Spain sent 'letters of recommendation to all the principal people at the Neapolitan court'. Maria Carolina, Queen of Naples, developed 'such a sincere regard' for Martha that 'she should have looked upon it as the greatest happiness of her life to have made her her constant companion', and gave her 'a pair of diamond bracelets, with her picture and ciphers, and two fine medals'.

The Swinburnes' children helped endear them to the Queen; Maria Carolina admired the 'estimable qualities' of 'so dignified and good a mother' with a 'charming family'. Martha gave birth to her second surviving son, Thomas, in Naples in 1777. He and the other Swinburne children played with the young royals, and the Queen gave them silver filigree baskets filled with bonbons, covering diamond necklaces and bracelets (one wonders whether they were more excited by the sweets or the jewels!).[56]

Once they had befriended Maria Carolina, she introduced them to her mother, Empress Maria Theresa of Austria, and her sister, Marie Antoinette. In Vienna, Maria Theresa took 'a great fancy' to Martha, frequently spending her evenings with her and the Archduchess Marianne. Emperor Joseph took the trouble to translate a play verse by verse for Martha during a trip to the theatre and stood as godfather to her son Joseph Antony. She was honoured with the order of *'la croix étoilée'*, meant only for Austrian noblewomen.[57] Just as they had named their third son Joseph after the Emperor, the Swinburnes did homage to their royal friends by naming their younger daughters Carolina Marianna, Maria Theresa Henrietta, Maria Rosa Louisa and Maria Antonia.

Henry teased Martha for her 'Jacobitical adoration' – perhaps fostered by Lady Helen Webbe, an old friend of Bonnie Prince Charlie – but this was considerably weakened when they met some *actual* Stuarts on their travels. Martha left a church service in Frescati prematurely after

Cardinal York – son of the Old Pretender – insisted she took off her hat. As it was fastened on with long pins, the operation would have required a hairdresser. Henry concluded the 'foolish-looking' York was, like his grandfather James II, 'full of pride, and just such another obstinate bigot.' In Florence, they saw York's brother, the Young Pretender (Bonnie Prince Charlie), being carried home from the theatre 'half asleep and completely intoxicated' – apparently a nightly habit. Nevertheless when his wife, the Countess of Albany, visited England, it was rumoured the 'pinchbeck [sham] Queen Dowager of England' was 'going to see Mrs Swinburne in Yorkshire, who, it seems is a friend of all sorts of queens.'[58]

Tragedy hit when their adored eldest daughter, Patty, died aged nine in September 1778 while the family was in Rome. Henry had been such a proud father that when he saw Murillo's painting of St Anne teaching the Virgin to read at La Granja palace in Spain in June 1776, he thought: 'the girl is the very picture of my little Patty'. He also wrote in his copy of Shakespeare: 'my beloved child at the age of nine fully appreciated and understood the beauties of this book.'

The lengthy inscription on the expensive marble monument Martha and Henry erected in the English College in Rome shocked local clergy, for it had 'not a word of religion'. Instead it extravagantly extolled Patty's virtues. Besides an impeccable character and an impressive list of academic achievements, she had played the harpsichord, danced 'with strength and elegance' and 'sang the most difficult music at sight with one of the finest voices in the world'. It also noted that:

> [her] docility and alacrity in doing everything to make her parents happy could only be equalled by her sense and aptitude with so many perfections amidst the praises of all persons from the sovereign down to the beggar.

'Think then', exhorts the monument, 'what the pangs of her wretched parents must be on so cruel a separation ... the torments they endure at the loss of a beloved child'.

Martha plunged into a 'lethargy of grief' for over four months, taking consolation in her faith, going to the English College to hear Mass every Sunday and feast-day until after Christmas. She mustered the strength to write a letter of condolence to Maria Carolina, Queen of Naples, when her three-year-old son Charles died in December. Maria Carolina wrote to Martha that Charles – her favourite – 'was a child in perfect health, growing in beauty and capacity, and perfectly robust. In less than 60 hours I lost him. This is the kind of pain that can destroy you.' The shared grief of losing a beloved child 'in whom they had placed all their hopes, consolations and complaisances', as the Queen put it, brought the two women closer.[59] But the friendship of Maria Carolina's sister, Marie Antoinette, would prove more significant to Martha's life and fortunes.

While the Swinburnes toured the courts of Europe, John Baker's health was deteriorating. Approaching his sixty-sixth birthday, he began to dwell on the fact he was approaching the age *his* father had been when he died. A 'dead weight on all and a useless burthen on earth', he believed it would be better for everyone if his life ended sooner rather than later. Even a rise in the price of sugar failed to raise his spirits; he 'could not think of buying' three or four Africans he was offered by a Kittian acquaintance.

Much of John's melancholy stemmed from his 'late losses and heavy strokes in matter of fortune'. Martha expected to inherit an equal share of her father's wealth alongside her brothers, but that share was fast diminishing. In March 1776, his agent, Kittian merchant William Manning, calculated John would owe £6,600 by Christmas.[60*]

John's investment in St Vincent – Martha later claimed he'd spent over £30,000 establishing Baker's plantation – had not proved profitable. After he bought Collins's half of the estate in 1776, Collins continued to live on the plantation and act as John's attorney on the island, besides buying another estate for himself. A mutual acquaintance told John that Collins was an 'ingenious man but too great a speculatist', and not a 'good planter'. The challenges facing Collins included the 'dreadful ravage of the borer' larvae[†] and lack of rain. However, John was exasperated when Collins reported the water mills had ground to a halt in dry weather. Why had he not used the several mules John knew were on the estate to drive the mills? He vented in his diary: 'fine doings this indeed!'[61]

---

* Manning had married Mrs Baker's niece Elizabeth Ryan. An associate of Henry Laurens and acquaintance of Richard Oswald's, he was also heavily involved in trade with South Carolina. It was Manning's daughter Martha whom John Laurens had impregnated, married, then swiftly deserted to fight in the American Revolutionary War. *Diary of John Baker*, ed. Yorke, pp. 16–17, 271; Flavell, *When London Was Capital*, p. 22.

† *Diatraea saccharalis*; the larvae bore into sugar cane stalks, causing the tops of mature plants to weaken or die, and killing shoots in younger plants.

The St Croix syndicate had outstanding debts; Bodkin had died insolvent, so the remaining partners were left to pick up the pieces. On 4 March 1778 John had a '*dio negro*' (black day). Bad news proverbially comes in threes: first, he received a demand for 400 lbs of St Croix sugar, then he learnt a fall in the price of sugar meant he could not sell twenty hogsheads just arrived from St Vincent; and finally, James Pepper, the Horsham stage-coachman who owed him £50, sent word he was ill and could not pay.[62]

The American Revolution placed all John's business interests, and thus Martha's prospects, at risk. He could no longer add to his workforce in St Vincent, as no slaving ships arrived there during the war.[63] In March 1778, the word on the street was 'we should not keep our W India islands long, that the French and Americans were going against Jamaica'. In July, he heard Valentine Morris, Governor of St Vincent, was 'at odds with all the council and officers and vast disorder about it.' In November, he learnt the French had taken Dominica, and a friend told him (incorrectly) that St Vincent and Grenada had also been captured. John exclaimed '*Quam celerrime mea mala!*' ('How quickly my woes come upon me!').[64]

The biggest personal and financial blow – also hitting Martha – came in August 1778 when her brother Tom Baker was arrested for a debt of £5,889 and flung into the King's Bench prison. It was only four years since he had been promoted from Solicitor General to Attorney General for Grenada, the Grenadines, St Vincent and Tobago, offices he had gained in his early twenties thanks to John's aggressive lobbying. But, like his father, Tom had not been able to resist the lure of greater riches than those offered by the legal profession. Borrowing thousands of pounds to buy plantations and people in Tobago and Grenada, he boasted to William Manning that though he had borrowed at sixteen per cent interest, he would soon obtain profits of fifty per cent.[65]

A significant amount of Tom's capital had come from a £3,000 legacy Martha's uncle, Henry Ryan, had left her on his death in 1771. In July 1773, John loaned Tom £2,000 of the money held in Martha's name. He authorised William Manning to perform this transaction after spending the afternoon with Martha and his grandchildren, 'walking in meadow, making hay, etc.' While Henry was aware of the decision, it is not clear whether Martha was privy to it. By 1776, John had lent Tom the remaining £1,000.[66]

Far from disowning his disgraced son – the arrest was reported in the *Morning Chronicle*, the *Morning Post* and *Publick* – John pored over Tom's affairs with Manning; even offering to sell his St Vincent estate for less than it was worth to repay Tom's debts. But the situation was unsalvageable; Tom died in prison bankrupt, aged only thirty-one.[67]

It was some small mercy John did not live to see the day. After a painful decline, with episodes of paralysis in his left side (at times leaving him unable to walk), memory loss and deteriorating eyesight, John died in March 1779. He had outlived his father by just over fourteen months.

When writing his will, John had lamented: 'my fortune and circumstances in life are so greatly impaired … there will be little or no residue to divide among my children'. Martha was entitled to one-quarter of John's assets, besides Tom's creditors and her two surviving brothers: John Proculus, now a wealthy lawyer in Jamaica, and Joseph, an East India Company merchant.* Although John's will confirmed Martha was still owed her £3,000 legacy from Henry Ryan and her £4,000 marriage portion, the consequences of John and Tom's overweening ambitions meant these sums would only ever be hers on paper.[68]

The French attacked St Vincent in the middle of June 1779. Victory was assured by the participation of over 1,000 Garifuna, who canoed to St Lucia – a five-hour journey – wearing French colours, to acquire weapons. When the British surrendered, Chief Joseph Chatoyer 'set forth exactly his complaints against' them 'for infractions of the 1773 treaty'. During the French occupation of the island, the Garifuna retaliated against their British oppressors, killing some, and driving others off their plantations and burning their houses.[69]

Baker's lay directly to the east of the strategically important Dorsetshire Hill fort. Once the French seized the fort, they occupied the estate, using its buildings as barracks and 'the negroes and cattle in military labour to the great detriment of the plantation'. Sugar production 'was for several years greatly injured', but the people enslaved there bore the brunt of this martial regime.[70]

Martha and Henry soon 'received accounts that the whole of their property in the West Indies had been devastated and utterly laid waste

---

* Martha's brother Robert had died aged seventeen on his way to Bombay; his ship, the *Aurora*, was wrecked passing Madagascar, 'a channel dangerous at all seasons'. *Gentleman's Magazine*, 41, April 1771, p. 237.

by the French and Caribs'.[71] With the help of Marie Antoinette, they immediately applied to Louis XVI for compensation. In summer 1782, Martha was granted 1,000 carreaux[*] of 'good' land '*dans la partie de vent*' – on the island's windward side, to the north of General Robert Monckton's lands.[†]

Martha's grant looked good on paper, but on the ground it was completely unfeasible. Though the assigned land was part of the territory officially ceded to Britain by the Garifuna in 1773, they had taken it back during French occupation. The Marquis de Bouillé, Governor of Martinique, wrote to Paris explaining: 'on account of various encroachments 1,000 carreaux of good land could not be had in the quarter without trouble and litigation'.[72]

In November 1782 Martha obtained a second 'sweeping' grant from Louis XVI. In language that would be disputed for years, it accorded her 'all the lands, uncultivated, undefined, and unceded of the island of St Vincent, which do not belong to the Caribs or anyone in particular'.[73]

When the American Revolutionary War came to an end, Louis XVI at first intended to keep St Vincent. However, as peace negotiations progressed, it became clear France would lose the island. Nonetheless, Marie Antoinette personally ensured Martha's 'sweeping' grant was sealed before the peace was signed. The grant was not specifically mentioned in the Treaty of Versailles (1783). The British ambassador to France, George Montagu, 4th Duke of Manchester, explained to Henry: 'it would be improper to introduce the name or business of a private individual into the Negotiation between two Great Nations'. However, he reassured him he had agreed with the Comte de Vergennes that the King's grant to the Swinburnes was 'fully covered ... good, valid and ratified to its full extent'.[74]

The existence of this odd grant, gained as a favour by Martha, the accomplished courtier, was deeply unpopular both in St Vincent and with the government in London. Martha's attorney on the island, her father's old business partner John Collins, warned her that, though he

---

[*] Approximately 3,180 acres – though Martha rounded it up considerably to 3,500 in her correspondence with the British government.

[†] Monckton had captured St Vincent, along with Grenada, St Lucia and Martinique, in 1762. He had been granted 4,000 acres north of the Yambou River, reaching from the coast to the mountains, between modern-day Stubbs and Biabou villages. He sold the land in 1775 for £31,750: 'Hon. Robert Monckton', LBS: https://www.ucl.ac.uk/lbs/person/view/2146665465.

would do his best for her, 'here your Grant is considered an invidious right and every opposition that is possible will be given to it'. Though this opposition 'cannot invalidate your title', she should expect 'infinite vexation and expense' – a warning that would prove prophetic.[75]

Demand for land on St Vincent was fierce, especially from Loyalists fleeing the American South and East Florida. The St Vincent Assembly soon declared a tax on all uncultivated land, making the Swinburnes liable for £1,000 to £1,200 a year. When added to the levy due to the Crown, they faced an annual tax bill of £1,500.[76] With their expensive Continental lifestyle, multiple children to support, and Martha's inherited debts from her father far outweighing Henry's income from Hamsterley, they could ill afford such a sum.

The Swinburnes decided to sell. At first there was quite a lot of interest. The keenest potential purchaser was Sir William Young, erstwhile Commissioner for land sales, now in great debt, particularly to the government. He suggested exchanging his own St Vincent estate, Pembroke, valued at £36,000, for the Swinburnes' grant.[77] However, when William Pitt the Younger replaced the Duke of Portland as Prime Minister in December 1783, 'that negotiation fell to the ground'. Aggravated by the irregularity, Pitt decided the Crown should buy the Swinburnes out. He initially asked Sir William Young and Robert Wynne, another of the Commissioners, to value the land grant; they produced a figure of £30,000. Baulking at this huge sum, Pitt asked St Vincent's new Governor, Edmund Lincoln, to make his own estimate.

Unlike the men in Paris and London, Lincoln tried to enumerate exactly what land the 'sweeping' grant covered. He sent the Lords of the Treasury a map identifying 26,377 'unappropriated' acres. Less than ten per cent seemed cultivable, 'the remainder being deemed absolutely impracticable'. Lincoln commissioned six men 'who from their character and long residence were most likely to be competent judges' to assess the remaining 710 acres of 'good woodland' – which required clearing – and 1,535 acres of 'inferior' land. Figures varied wildly, but on average came to £7,830 for the land, plus £3,808 for 'three chains' – an area of approximately sixty metres into the sea – attached to each plot of coastal land.[78]

Although John Collins condemned these estimates as the 'wildest conjectures', concocted by men hostile to the grant, Pitt 'declared that he did not feel himself justified in paying more than the lowest valuation', and offered £6,500. After all, the government was at this time processing hundreds of compensation claims from those who, like Mary

Oswald, had lost estates in East Florida and other American colonies. Though far from happy with Pitt's offer, the Swinburnes needed cash and Collins urged them to accept for the preservation of peace on the island. The Commons approved the payment of £6,500 on 26 May 1786; the Swinburnes conveyed their right to all 'unappropriated' lands, as outlined in the 'sweeping' grant, on 6 August. Martha was 'solely and separately examined consenting thereto' by Lord Loughborough, Lord Chief Justice of the Court of Common Pleas. She reluctantly agreed, 'reserving to herself the resource of appealing in happier times to [the King's] well-known clemency and sense of justice'.[79]

Soon after the deal was done, Martha and Henry obtained new information. It seemed that before the French conquest Governor Valentine Morris had illegally granted himself and others the same land identified in the Swinburnes' first 1,000 carreaux grant. As the deal with Pitt in 1786 had related only to the second 'sweeping' grant, they now believed they had a claim on the British government for further compensation.[80] In summer 1788 Martha returned to Paris to seek French support, taking Harry and Fanny with her. Specifically, she wanted the French to confirm the second 'sweeping' grant did not supersede the first. In hindsight, it was not a brilliant moment to travel to France, but at the time Martha had no intimation of the drama to come. Just that May, Henry had declared, 'I do not think there is steadiness, spirit, or union requisite for a revolution to be found in the French nation'.[81]

However, Martha's attempts to secure an audience with Marie Antoinette were repeatedly thwarted. In July, she found 'The Queen's mind is torn to pieces'; in August 'it would be madness to ask an interview at the present moment for everything is in the most dreadful confusion'. By October, fearing Marie Antoinette might do her cause more harm than good, she sought out Finance Minister Jacques Necker, who left her 'perfectly satisfied'. The Queen finally summoned her to a tête-à-tête on 5 November 1788, assuring her she could 'reckon upon the continuance of her protection'. However, considering the tumultuous state of French politics, processing the paperwork Martha required was going to take some time.

After a few months back in England, Martha returned to Paris in March 1789, this time partly to secure a free education for her eldest son, Harry. With their finances increasingly strained, the Swinburnes were delighted when Marie Antoinette offered to enrol him as a royal page. This was a great honour, never before bestowed on an Englishman; Harry hardly qualified as having the required 200 years of '*noblesse directe*'. The royal pages received excellent tuition, though Martha worried: 'the elder pages have too much power over the younger ones, who are treated like fags at Eton' – the school her brother Tom had attended.

Martha renewed her efforts to see Necker and the Queen, with increasing urgency from April when she heard the British Attorney General and Solicitor General had ruled against her latest claim. But the situation in France was deteriorating rapidly. Martha told Henry his old prophecy that the Queen would end her days in prison might well come to pass; Louis XVI would 'soon have the straight waistcoat on'. She did, however, grow more sympathetic towards the Queen after their interview on 8 May, when she saw how miserable she was about her dying son – Martha well knew the pain of losing a child.

As for Necker, Martha believed he would no longer be minister by the end of June. Her guess was close enough: he lost his job on 11 July. Unmoved by his predicament, she crowed: 'If I get my decree, I shall be satisfied to see dust return to dust, or dirt' – a hypocritical dig at the fact Necker (like Martha, a lawyer's child) had no noble title. But she remained blind to the true significance of the political crises unfolding before her eyes.

On 1 July, Martha had written to Henry that though 'the fermentation seems to be strangely increased … I am assured there can be no danger for us, and that the unpopularity of the court will not affect private individuals'. But within a fortnight she was 'a prisoner' in her Parisian house, 'for everybody says it is not safe to stir from home'. Nevertheless, on the morning of 14 July – the day the Paris crowd would storm the Bastille – she heard a *gard bourgeoise* had been established to restore order and decided to take her coach to visit friends. Though both her coachman and footman wore the new Revolutionary cockades of blue and red in their hats – the white was added only on the 27th – she was stopped twice, searched and examined, bravely insisting she wasn't in the least bit scared. Though scolded for her 'impudence' in going out, she was glad to have 'had a sight of the proceedings'. Hearing 'The Queen's head … cried about Paris streets', she declared 'the Civil War is begun'.

Martha was relieved when the King visited Paris a few days later to recognise the people's sovereignty, and she was able to travel to Versailles and be reunited with Harry. She still feared the royal palace would come under attack but insisted on staying there to collect her certificate.[82] The dreaded event came to pass on 5 October, when thousands of

Parisians, led by the *poissardes* (fishwives, or market-women), marched on Versailles. Martha wrote to Henry: 'We have had dreadful doings … at night, a set of wretches forced themselves into the château, screaming, "*La tête de la reine! À bas la reine! Louis ne sera pas plus roi – il nous faut le Duc d'Orleans – il nous donnera du pain celui-la!*"'* Two royal guards were 'butchered like sheep'; mixing her tears with 'an unfortunate father' who had lost his only child, Martha prayed Harry would not meet a similar fate.[83] The royal family was marched back to Paris by a crowd of over 60,000. On arriving at the Tuileries, the King began to read Hume's history of Charles I; Martha told Henry that Louis made 'a point of acting quite contrary' to the unfortunate British King, executed by his subjects in 1649.[84]

Martha feared she had risked her life in vain, lamenting, 'the unfortunate Louis XVI, had lost all the influence he once had at home, and therefore could not have enough in a foreign court to obtain redress for me'. Although Necker, Finance Minister once more, wrote a letter to Pitt on her behalf, the Attorney General and Solicitor General stuck to their conclusion there was no case to answer.[85]

Martha took her final leave of Marie Antoinette in November 1789, 'a great favour, as she receives no one'. The Queen expressed envy Martha was returning to her 'happy family in a peaceful country where calumny and cruelty could not follow her'. Martha 'ventured a few words of consolation', that 'times were improving, and that her popularity and happiness would be restored'. But when the Queen shook her head, Martha dropped all pretence. She proposed that Marie Antoinette escape with her to England, disguised as her maid. The Queen thanked her and smiled faintly, but protested she would not desert her family, and anyway, the plan was sure to be discovered by spies. Martha said goodbye 'with regret and affection'.[86]

In the event, it was lucky the Queen did not attempt to escape with Martha, because, when she reached Boulogne, her carriage was 'assailed by a hoard of *poissardes*', now 'the true sovereigns of France', who had 'proved themselves to be more bloody-minded than their vile countrymen'. The women accused her of being the Duke of Orleans' mistress – he had been captured trying to escape and imprisoned in

---

* 'The head of the Queen! Down with the Queen! Louis won't be King anymore, we need the Duke of Orleans [the King's cousin Louis Phillipe, who supported the Revolution at first, but was later guillotined], he will give us bread!'

Boulogne – and declared she should not leave France. Martha's response, at least as she told it, showed both courage and wit under fire:

> Imagine my terror. I put my head out of the window to address them, '*Ecoutez, ecoutez*' [Listen! Listen!] said one or two of them. '*Mesdames*', said I, as politely as my fear would let me, '*ayez la bonte de me regarder. Je ne suis ni jeune ni jolie; Monsieur le Duc d'Orleans, aurait-il si mauvais gout?*' [Have the kindness to look at me. I am neither young nor beautiful. Does the Duke of Orleans have such bad taste?] This made the creatures laugh, and some said, '*Pas si mal – pas si mal.*' [Not so bad, not so bad.] Never did beauty long to be admired more than I desired to be thought ugly.

Martha was rescued when a local innkeeper, Mrs Knowles, a rotund Englishwoman who heartily disliked the French, intervened and vouched for her. She endured a stormy crossing, but 'the elements alarmed me less than the torrent of human violence which I had just escaped.' When Martha got home, Queen Charlotte summoned her to court to recount her colourful story.[87]

Harry meanwhile had stayed in France; Martha refused to 'ensure his safety at the expense of his honour', though her friends promised to send him home 'on the first appearance of danger'. However, after sustaining a head injury during an assault on the royal retinue as they left a Parisian theatre, he too fled. In June 1791, the royal family were imprisoned – as Henry had predicted – in the Tuileries, following their unsuccessful flight to Varennes.[88] The French monarchy was abolished the following year, and Louis XVI and Marie Antoinette lost their heads in 1793. Soon France was at war with the rest of Europe.

Just as Haitians had taken advantage of the crisis to fight for freedom, the Garifuna in St Vincent seized the opportunity to reassert their dominion over the island. Once again obtaining arms from the French, the Garifuna launched attacks on British plantations in March 1795. Alongside several French residents, they captured Dorsetshire Hill fort on 12 March, raising the tricolour flag. The same day, Chief Joseph Chatoyer issued a revolutionary letter, demanding all French residents unite with him against the British in the name of liberty. He threatened those who did not would be seen as traitors, to be punished with 'iron and fire'; their estates burned; their wives and children murdered 'in order to annihilate their race'. Chatoyer was killed when the British retook the fort on the night of 14 March; by one account, with 'five bayonets being dashed into the sanguinary monster's breast at the same moment'.[89] But the Garifuna fought on.

As Baker's lay so close to the fort, the people Martha enslaved there inevitably got caught up in the struggle. The plantation played a cameo role on 26 September when Brigadier General Sir William Myers, freshly arrived from Martinique, marched a large detachment there from Dorsetshire Hill. This feint distracted the enemy just long enough to allow the British to evacuate their besieged military post at Vigie. Britain only regained control of the island after 4,000 troops led by Sir Ralph Abercromby arrived in June 1796. Though the French surrendered immediately, it took months before the Garifuna capitulated.[90]

With little hope of any income from St Vincent, Henry was forced to borrow £1,600 from his nephew Sir John Edward Swinburne in 1791.[91] Martha and Henry retreated to Hamsterley, where it was possible to live a little more cheaply. They were increasingly worried about how they were going to support their large family, especially their five daughters, who would struggle to marry without dowries. Salvation of a sort came when twenty-two-year-old Fanny married Paul Benfield, a stupendously wealthy East India Company 'nabob' and MP, in September 1793. Aside from illicitly amassing £400,000 during his time in India, he had profited from co-ownership of a Jamaican plantation and enslaved over 1,500 people on ten estates – totalling 6,555 acres – in Berbice.*

Fanny's diamond engagement ring alone was worth 3,000 guineas. Benfield promised her a jointure of £3,000, plus £500 'pin money' a year; their future children would inherit £10,000 each. Benfield had also 'taken two of her sisters to bring up under his immediate care and protection'. Given the disparity in age – Benfield was thirty years older than Fanny – and the groom's unappealing character – Edmund Burke denounced him as an 'execrable tyrant ... insulter, oppressor, betrayer and scourge of a country [India] ... a criminal who long since ought to have fattened the region [sic] kites with his offal' – Fanny's happiness was effectively sacrificed for the sake of her family.

But Benfield was not the solution to their problems for long. After a disastrous foray into banking, he was declared bankrupt in 1800. Having sought to recover some debts in France during the Peace of Amiens in

---

* Berbice was a Dutch colony west of Suriname, now part of Guyana.

1802, he was interned there when the war resumed the following year, leaving Fanny and their three children living in poverty in cramped London lodgings. Henry had also invested in Benfield's schemes; his son-in-law's collapse only added to his financial woes.[92] The creditors were circling closer. In Hamsterley, while some chased Martha for small debts owed because they were 'frightened for themselves' and needed the money, others simply wished to 'fish in troubled waters', even if it 'drove Mrs. Swinburne away'.[93]

The Swinburnes' French royal connections were now more a liability than an asset. When Henry travelled to France – he called it 'Tigerland' due to the ferocity of the Terror – to negotiate an exchange of prisoners in 1796, he found one of the five Directors* 'violently against me', on account of Martha's 'friendship with queens, and Harry's having been a page'. He was appalled to hear Harry's former tutor, Octavien d'Alvimart, had been guillotined for having a letter from Harry amongst his papers – gossip that turned out to be untrue.[94†] Overestimating his sway with the new regime, Martha sent Henry letters in code – dangerous if intercepted – begging him to help some émigré friends return to France. Wandering around Fontainebleau, Henry told Martha, reminded him of a verse from her favourite Psalm: 'I myself have seen them in great power, and flourishing like a green bay-tree; I went by, and lo! They were gone, and their place could nowhere be found'. As Martha well knew, the biblical text condemned the powerful as 'wicked' or 'ungodly', an implicit criticism Henry probably considered unwise to state openly.[95]

Though Harry survived the French Revolution, he would not survive the French Revolutionary Wars. Left in need of employment by the family's financial problems, he gained a commission in the 82nd Foot, acting as aide to General John Knox, the new Governor of Jamaica. The regiment sailed for the Caribbean aboard the *Babet* in autumn 1800. When they had not heard of his safe arrival in Kingston by January 1801, Martha and Henry became uneasy. In February, Henry wrote to Martha: 'every day sinks so much of my hopes that I feel myself unmanned by every desponding expression or look of other people'. His 'thoughts'

---

* The Directory was a five-person committee that ruled France from 1795 to 1799.
† D'Alvimart may really have been executed for calling the uniform of the National Guard a 'monkey suit'. Selin, S., 'Gaëtan-Octavien d'Alvimart: Soldier, Adventurer, Artist', January 2020: https://shannonselin.com/2020/01/gaetan-octavien-dalvimart/.

were 'on the rack' about Martha's 'health, and the improbability your shattered nerves should be able to resist a blow as this may prove'. However, Martha was more 'resigned to the will of the Almighty' than her husband, and showed 'fortitude under this severest of trials'. By April, all hope was gone. Martha sent Henry a 'gentle soothing letter'. Henry hoped 'time will teach me to be patient and devout like you.' The fate of the *Babet*, and her 170-strong crew, last seen departing Martinique on 25 October 1800, was never determined.[96]

A year after losing Harry, Martha had to face seeing Henry embark on an equally risky journey, taking their youngest son Joseph Antony with him. Desperate for employment to repay his debts, Henry had obtained the post of vendue master – supervising auctions, including sales of human beings – in Trinidad. He was also entrusted with supervising the return of St Croix, St John and St Thomas to the Danes. He left Portsmouth on 31 December 1801, hoping to return soon and spend the rest of his life 'at home and in content at Hamsterley'.

Stopping at Martinique and St Pierre, Henry saw Dominica, Guadeloupe and Martha's childhood home, St Kitts, from the ship, later visiting Tortola and Montserrat. He received hospitality from many enslavers and officials, though he was disappointed not to have been served a 'single West Indian dish, or pepper-pot, &c., except "floating island"'.[97]*

Conversation in St Croix in March 1802 was dominated by talk of Haitian military leader Toussaint L'Ouverture, who had published a constitution, confirming the abolition of enslavement and declaring himself Governor General for life the previous summer. Henry reported to Martha that General Leclerc, whom Napoleon had dispatched with 20,000 men to take back control, 'had published a proclamation of Buonaparte to the inhabitants, full of equality and fraternity. Toussaint has retired into the Grandbois mountains, and probably much bloodshed will ensue'. The enslavers feared what peace with France would mean for Haiti, and the wider Caribbean: 'if pacific measures are adopted, there

---

* This might be the dish now known as *îles flottantes* (meringues floating in a sea of custard), first recorded as *œufs à la neige* in François-Pierre de la Varenne's 1651 cookbook *Le Cuisinier François*. This suggests it was a French delicacy, without a particular link to the Caribbean, despite the apt name. Nineteenth-century celebrity chef Auguste Escoffier's *îles flottantes* dish was different again, with Savoy biscuits replacing the meringue.

will scarcely be a probability of keeping the blacks in the other islands quiet. Here the planters perceive a growing spirit, and restless talk about liberty, in the young slaves.'[98]

Henry arrived in Trinidad in June 1802 and took a house in St Juan, four miles east of Port of Spain. He was indignant to find no places named after Sir Walter Ralegh, who had attacked the island in 1595, and advised Martha to 'get some general collection of voyages and read the original narrative of the conquest'. While his letters home tended to keep a cheerful tone, with long descriptions of magnificent scenery and reports on the progress of his *Flora of Trinidad*, Henry had arrived at a tumultuous time.

Trinidad had been captured from Spain by the British in 1797 and had been governed by a Welsh soldier named Thomas Picton ever since – 'a rough foul-mouthed devil as ever lived', according to the Duke of Wellington. Henry had told Martha before leaving home that 'the commission given to the governor makes him almost despotic', and after meeting him, wrote to his nephew: 'the present military Governor is rather too harsh for Britons'. Nevertheless, he dined regularly at Picton's home, where he had 'a general invitation'. Though he never mentioned her to Martha, his hostess would have been Rosetta Smith, a mixed-heritage woman with whom the Governor had four children.[99]

Martha also learnt nothing from Henry about Picton's violent regime. Keen to accelerate the island's sugar production, Picton sought to increase the workforce. In the first decade of British rule, 22,887 Africans arrived, despite Parliament's resolution in 1792 to 'gradually' abolish the traffic. Sugar exports duly rose from 8.4 million lbs in 1799 to 14.2 million in 1802. Henry observed: 'the expense of new negroes is very great, for numbers die in bringing the new lands into tillage'; he knew twenty-five people enslaved by Picton had died in the rainy season – roughly June to December – of 1802 alone.[100]

Picton imposed his own brutal 'slave code'. After a spike in unexplained deaths on one plantation, he instituted a 'poisoning commission' to investigate. Large numbers of enslaved people accused of 'sorcery and poison by means of charms' were interrogated and tortured. Sixteen suffered public execution and mutilation: some were burned alive, some decapitated.[101] However, Picton's most infamous crime would be the 'picketing' of Louisa Calderon, a free mixed-heritage teenage girl, viewed more sympathetically by the British public due to her free status, gender and lighter skin. The torture involved suspending one wrist by a rope, then tying the other wrist to one foot, leaving the victim forced to balance their entire bodyweight with the other foot on a narrow wooden peg known as a picket. Picketing became so closely associated with Picton it was sometimes called Picton-ing.[102] Many of Picton's brutalities were carried out at the St Joseph gaol, close to where Henry was living, but all he told Martha was that his proximity to the 'grand' army barracks 'enlivened' the view from his house 'as some scarlet coat or other is always galloping' past.[103]

Henry knew full well what had been going on. When the British government ended military rule, appointing Picton as one of three civilian rulers, alongside William Fullarton and Samuel Hood, Henry urged him to resign:

> were I Alexander, I would write to his Majesty, that I was bred a soldier, had accepted the command of a conquered country, which I had governed *à la militaire* for five years; that I knew nothing of civil affairs, therefore was a very improper man to act a secondary part.

Frontispiece to *The Trial of Governor T. Picton* depicting the torture of Louisa Calderon.

This would 'satisfy his enemies, and forever lay all quarrels to sleep, and he would have a ribbon or a regiment.' Henry told Martha that Picton 'acknowledged that I was right but he had private reasons for seeing them out, as they call it. I wish he may not say, O Cassandra!'

Henry was soon able to say 'I told you so'. On 25 March 1803 he wrote to Martha:

> The quarrel between our governors is come to such a pitch, that yesterday Colonel Fullarton moved in the council an accusation against General Picton for various illegal acts, condemnations, and executions, during his government, before the commissions came out, which must be sent home; and ministry have no choice; they must order Picton home for trial.

Henry added unsympathetically: 'if this brings an old house upon Picton's head, it is his own doing, and he may repent not following my advice.'[104]

Unlike other British men who visited Trinidad at the time and were shocked by what they found there, Henry's approach was politique, remaining 'perfectly well with all parties'; 'these fracas and quarrels are very unpleasant', he mused, 'although one has nothing to do with them'. More interested in the main chance, Henry even considered purchasing land in Trinidad, viewing some properties for sale, though concluding 'there is danger in acquiring estates here for many years to come'; deriding those 'fools' that 'flock here, as to Eldorado, without any previous enquiry'.[105]

Martha and Henry knew the dangers of Caribbean investments only too well and brooded on their losses in St Vincent often. Yet rather than blaming the French for their misfortunes, they found some easier-to-vilify scapegoats: the Garifuna. The depth of their bitterness is made clear in a letter Henry wrote to Martha after a visit to the Catholic mission of Santa Rosa de Arima in January 1803. There, he encountered 'the widows, wives, and daughters of the black Charibs of St Vincent's, who destroyed your estates there, and whose bones lie blanching on the rocks of Becuya, where they were carried, or on the sands of Rattan.'[106]

Henry was vindictively alluding to the inhuman way the Garifuna had been treated after the Second Carib War ended in 1796. The British had forcibly removed 4,776 Garifuna to the tiny, rocky Grenadine island of Baliceaux (which Henry confused with Becuya or Bequia, another of the Grenadines), ten miles to the south; a place with no running water and so inhospitable that it is entirely uninhabited to this day.[107] This had the desired effect, and by March 1797, when a British fleet arrived there to transport them to Roatan (Henry's 'Rattan'), a Spanish-held island off the Honduran coast, only 2,248 people had survived. Such genocidal treatment was the logical outcome of the attitudes Europeans displayed towards indigenous people from the beginning. As early as 1681, the Governor of the Leeward Islands had insisted on the 'necessity of destroying these Carib Indians ... if their destruction cannot be total, they must be driven to the main'.[108] Despite this policy coming to fruition, the Garifuna, with their language, dance, music and culture, survived on 'the main', soon spreading from Honduras, into Belize, Guatemala and Nicaragua.

The women and children Henry saw were amongst a number of Garifuna who had escaped this mass deportation, but they continued to be targeted by the authorities. Thirteen women and twelve children had been imprisoned in St Vincent's Fort Charlotte (named for George III's wife) from early 1799 until August 1801, by which time another four or five children had been born. Drewry Ottley, President of the Council and Chief Justice of St Vincent (whose family had been part of the Bakers' social circle in Martha's youth), sent this group to Trinidad, to be placed in the mission's 'care'. He had refused to give the Garifuna women the £300 allowed for their maintenance, claiming their 'extreme ignorance' meant they would lose the money to fraudsters, 'or at best lay it out in trifles not necessary for their support'.[109]

In summer 1805, the St Vincent Council congratulated themselves on having established these women and children 'in comfort and security' under the 'guidance and instruction' of a missionary who appeared well qualified to 'secure their allegiance to the British Government and so reclaim them from their wild and savage manners'.[110] In reality, they had undergone multiple traumas – losing their husbands, fathers and homeland – and were now forced to live within the exploitative confines of the Arima mission. Although the Spanish had ostensibly established the mission to allot land to indigenous people while converting them to Catholicism, the place was closer to a labour camp. Many became so miserable they turned to the bottle; the Church profited not only from the cocoa cultivated by indigenous people, but also from selling them rum.[111]

Henry observed the Garifuna women and children living 'in a street by themselves', suggesting social isolation. He had no sympathy for them, only remarking they spoke English and French, were 'well behaved' and 'very much like negroes'. In this last observation, he aligned himself with the many who had weaponised the Garifuna's partial African ancestry to undermine their claim to the land of their birth and justify transporting them between colonies at whim.

As Henry and his party passed their street, one woman spotted Dr Archibald Gloster, the former Attorney General of St Vincent (where he had made a 'rapid fortune'), now fulfilling the same role in Trinidad. She called out, 'Dere Liar Gloster!'[112] Her words ring clear through the centuries; she and her people had been betrayed.

Back in England, Martha still insisted the British government owed her money. Henry had begged her to give up before he left for Trinidad, asking her 'a thousand times' to 'think of your health and leave such questions to time and the chapter of accidents'. However, following the peace with France in March 1802, Martha knew better than most that 'arrangements [were] shortly to be made in St Vincent and Trinidad'. Why shouldn't one of those arrangements be to her advantage?

Martha asked John Collins to write to the new Home Secretary, her friend Lord Pelham, on her behalf. At first, he tried to redirect her to Lord Hobart, Secretary of State for War and the Colonies, but she persevered. On Pelham's advice, Martha prepared a petition to George III, with independent testimony from William John Struth (who would later serve as Mayor of Bristol and Governor of St Vincent) that the lands she had sold for £6,500 were actually worth £40,000. She also enlisted the support of William Manning, the son of her father's old London agent. Now an MP and a Director of the Bank of England, as well as an agent for St Vincent, he vouched for Struth and Collins as 'gentlemen of the strictest veracity'.

Appealing to the King's 'well-known clemency and sense of justice', Martha petitioned him to grant her 3,000 acres in St Vincent or Trinidad in compensation. She further pleaded that:

> as any fresh lands will require a large expenditure in cultivation and will afford no immediate provision to your petitioner and her numerous family (chiefly females) she trusts that your Majesty's generosity and benevolence will be induced to bestow a pension on her and her daughters for their present maintenance.

An annual payment, she calculated, might be easier to obtain in the short term.

The need to support her children was uppermost in Martha's mind as her financial situation continued to deteriorate. As she wrote to Lord Pelham in December:

> This tedious affair has been attended with heavy expenses which have greatly impaired my fortune, and submitted me to many unaccustomed privations, hard to bear in the decline of life; and doubly hard with a numerous family.[113]

Henry's nephew had to prevent 'the violent measures of a silly blockhead' named Wright who attempted to bring a suit against the Swinburnes for debt. Martha was forced to sell Henry's library with his collection featuring 'elegant Persian manuscripts, pictures, prints, coins, cabinets, and other curiosities'. It took seven days to auction off the 1,586 lots.[114]

More significantly, in May 1803, Martha, along with her brothers, their heirs and debtors, mortgaged Baker's in St Vincent to one George Maitland for £16,000. However, Maitland only paid them £2,537 before his death in 1809. Martha viewed Baker's simply as an asset she might squeeze to alleviate her 'poverty'. But for the 205 people listed as property in the mortgage deeds – amongst them her namesakes 'Old Martha' and 'Young Martha' – poverty was very much a relative concept.[115]

Martha missed Henry terribly and wrote to ask whether she and the children could join him in Trinidad. 'Were I a man to consult my own pleasure', he replied, 'I should undoubtedly be delighted to have you all here; but many reasons militate against the voyage. The expense is great; the dangers of the passage something; of the climate more.' Henry wished he could return to his wife and family:

> If you feel the want of my society, think how I must feel the want of yours. Nothing interests me, nothing but the thoughts of distant home occupies my mind! I shall soon be like what we read of the Indians and Africans who think when they die they shall be transported back to their native groves. I wish I could think so.[116]

Enslavers had long observed that Africans, especially new arrivals, believed they would return to their ancestral home after death. Blaming this belief for the high suicide rate, they sought to undermine the idea by beheading or otherwise mutilating the bodies of those who took their own lives. Nevertheless, the belief did not die. Royalist Richard Ligon encountered it in Barbados in the 1640s; Henry in Trinidad over a century and a half later.[117]

Henry died suddenly from sunstroke on 1 April 1803, ironically, a day after boasting to Martha that he could ride in the 'delightful' Trinidad sun 'with the same unconcern that I did near dear Ischia and Capri.' He had succumbed just like the 'young adventurers, just come out, who drink, wench, and get soaked with rain – officers that live hard and ride out hunting and shooting in the midday sun' that he had derided for their foolish behaviour.[118]

A friend of Henry's, Sir Ralph Woodford, raised a monument to his memory in St Juan Church. The epitaph read: 'An accomplished gentleman, a polite scholar, a warm friend, an affectionate husband and a tender parent. More excellencies never met in one man. *Heu! Quando ullum inveniemus parem*' ('Alas! When will we look upon his like again?').*

Alongside the pain of losing Henry, the circumstances surrounding his death made Martha's financial situation even worse. As her daughter, Maria Antonia, recalled, Henry's secretary, 'a villain named Hayes', 'carried off money, papers and every valuable thing he could lay his hands upon, and ran off the Island'. This caused much confusion, leaving the administration unable to account for £60,000 of public money. While Henry's conduct in office was under investigation, 'not a farthing of his private property could be touched by his family'. Though Martha and her children placed all the blame on Charles Augustus Hayes, a young lawyer whom Henry had described as 'a clever, fidgeting, company-seeking man', Henry certainly had motive to embezzle public funds.[119]

It may be Hayes had seized Henry's papers as potential evidence against Picton; he acted as barrister for the prosecution in the Trinidadian Sessions Court mandated by the British Court of King's Bench to collect information on the Calderon case in 1804. The 'blood-stained Governor of Trinidad' was found guilty of torturing Louisa Calderon in London in 1806, but managed to return to the army, finding lasting fame after his 'heroic' death leading a successful bayonet charge at Waterloo. He is the only Welshman with a monument at St Paul's Cathedral. Hayes, meanwhile, was gaoled then expelled from Trinidad in September 1805, as someone 'dangerous to the peace and tranquillity of the colony'.[120]

---

* A quote from Horace's *Odes*, Book 1, Poem 24 – popular on gravestones.

As the Picton scandal broke, Martha doubtless feared Henry's name would be tainted by association. Nonetheless, she secured his post of vendue master, with its salary of between £300 and £400 a year, for their son Joseph Antony. But the role was cursed. On a voyage to the Caribbean, Joseph Antony fell from the ship's mast and 'his intellect became disordered'. Beyond a 'silly childish expression', the signs of insanity later observed included not understanding the stock market, and preferring to play billiards alone. At times, 'he would laugh immoderately without any assignable cause, rush across the room to the door, and hastily open and shut it again, and frequently dance and laugh to himself without any reason for so doing'.* In a bizarre twist of fate, he became a resident of a private asylum at Grove Place, in Nursling, near Southampton – the very house his grandparents had occupied in the 1760s.[121]

Martha also made further attempts to reopen the St Vincent compensation case with the government, once again pulling all the strings she could, but to no avail. She petitioned the Lords of the Treasury in May 1806, and sent them a further memorial in August, but they merely referred her back to the Attorney General and Solicitor General's 1789 opinion.[122] She did, however, manage to secure a payment of £2,000 from Christian VII of Denmark, upon whom Henry's diplomacy in St Croix – where, he had joked to Martha, he had reigned as King for a moment between the hauling down of the British flag and the raising of the Danish one – had made a good impression.[123]

One day in 1807, a woman calling herself Frances Swinburne arrived at Hamsterley with devastating news. Martha's eldest surviving son, Thomas, by now a Lieutenant in the Royal Navy, had drowned when his ship the *Athenienne* was wrecked on a voyage from Gibraltar to Malta on 20 November 1806. Before leaving Portsmouth he had married this Frances in Lambeth. A will written while his ship lay off Cádiz left her all his worldly goods, and she intended to sell up. Martha and her children would have to leave immediately. Years later, her younger daughters still recalled 'the tragic scene of their departure from their old home'; they left 'weeping with some of their favourite books and treasures gathered up and hidden in their aprons'.[124]

---

* His affliction was possibly exaggerated by family members who wished to profit from his assets. Once he was declared insane in 1843, his cousin Edward Swinburne took control of his affairs.

Martha now moved to Arundel in Sussex, not far from her father's family in Chichester. She reignited her friendship with her former suitor Charles Howard, now, thanks to the deaths of three unmarried Dukes in quick succession, the 11th Duke of Norfolk. Mourning the premature deaths of three children and her husband, she sought spiritual consolation. Her close friend, Sarah Wesley, niece of John Wesley, the founder of Methodism, praised her 'constant study of the scriptures' and considered her 'a most edifying Christian', who bore her misfortunes with 'resignation and piety'. Martha seems to have strayed from her Catholic faith, as Sarah also observed, she 'neither believed in the Pope, nor held the worship of images, nor ... the notion that Protestants could not be saved'. She also corresponded with the painter Philip de Loutherbourg and his wife Lucy, whom she may have originally met in the early 1770s, when Loutherbourg designed scenery for her father's friend David Garrick at Drury Lane Theatre. The Loutherbourgs were at this time exploring kabbalah and faith healing. Martha is said to have shared their interest in 'mystical subjects', perhaps seeking solace beyond Christianity in the supernatural and occult.

The government investigation into Henry's official papers dragged on for six years. Eventually, according to Maria Antonia:

> such was the high opinion entertained of Mr Swinburne's honour and integrity that after much investigation ... the Auditors for Public Accounts passed Mr Swinburne's account. But alas! This quietus which Mrs Swinburne had labored so long to obtain did not occur until a fortnight after her death!

Martha died on 30 January 1809, aged sixty-two, and was buried at St Nicholas, Arundel. She had wished her friend Sarah Wesley to close her eyes, but Sarah arrived only in time to comfort her daughters; their mother's death 'left a deep impression of seriousness on their young minds'.[125]*

*

---

* In a further Swinburne family connection to the profits of enslavement, Martha's daughters Carolina and Maria Theresa Henrietta married into the Liverpool Watt Walker family, who both trafficked Africans and owned people and plantations in Jamaica. My family is also related to the Walkers by marriage. 'Richard Watt Walker', LBS: https://www.ucl.ac.uk/lbs/person/view/43237; 'John Walker', LBS: https://www.ucl.ac.uk/lbs/person/view/45948.

While we may sympathise with Martha's losing two brothers, three children and her husband prematurely, it is easier to do so because we can read her sorrowful letters, see the marble monument she erected to her daughter in Rome and look at her portrait. By contrast, there is hardly any tangible record of the suffering endured by the people her family enslaved, besides the laconic entries in John Baker's diary. Martha spent her first nine years in St Kitts witnessing such cruelty daily and continued to think of Black people as property to exploit throughout her life.

Like her father, Martha leveraged her connections to smooth her family's way, admitting herself that she 'obtained justice in France through favors: it is the only mode every where'.[126] So dogged was her pursuit of compensation that she was willing to risk her life by staying at Versailles to collect her paperwork as the Revolution gathered steam. In Britain, however, her connections failed her. From being a friend of queens she ended her days in relative obscurity. Such was the sense of bathos in the family that her lost riches were later exaggerated. Maria Antonia believed that: 'before the deterioration of the West Indian property [they] were estimated to bring in £100,000 per annum'. Equally erroneously, she remembered her mother as a shrinking violet![127]

While Martha found the government's refusal to consider her appeals hard to swallow, she laid the ultimate blame squarely on the Garifuna. But although she had been driven from her home at Hamsterley, they had been driven from their homeland altogether. Despite Britain's genocidal policy, the Garifuna, and their culture, survived. Today, there are over 600,000 Garifuna people living in Honduras, Belize, Guatemala, Nicaragua, the United States, and even, in small numbers, on the island of St Vincent.

Miniature of Jane Jarvis, wearing an Eastern-inspired turban – then fashionable attire for a ball – by an unknown artist, 1793.

6

Jane Jarvis (1772–1796)

A truly global – but tragic – love story. In Bombay, Antiguan-born Jane meets a dashing Scottish soldier called Lachlan Macquarie – who would go on to become Governor of New South Wales, Australia.

LACHLAN MACQUARIE was in 'the most perplexed, painful, awkward situation that can possibly be conceived'. He was in love. The hitch? Jane Jarvis was a wealthy heiress from Antigua, sister-in-law to East India Company grandee James Morley. As a low-ranking army officer, Lachlan could not hope to 'support her in the style and manner she is entitled to'. His poverty made him a 'coward lover'; he had not yet told her how he felt.

He had assumed no one knew his secret, right up until the moment Morley burst into his lodgings, demanding to know his intentions. If he could not afford to propose, Morley told him he must 'desist from paying his sister [in-law] such assiduous and pointed attentions, as such conduct might in time engage her affections and be the means of preventing her from accepting any other offers.'

Lachlan was so surprised and embarrassed by this unexpected confrontation that he could only answer in an 'incoherent manner'. He confessed his love, admitting he was in no position to make a proposal. He promised Morley he would pause his pursuit until his circumstances improved. Then, Lachlan hoped, not only would Morley support the match, but no one could accuse him of being a gold digger.

Jane Jarvis was born into a wealthy Antiguan dynasty on 16 October 1772. Her father Thomas owned Long Island, Bird Island and 1,000 acres either side of the border between St John and St George, requiring a workforce of some 750 people – placing him in the top twenty landholders and enslavers in Antigua.* Born on the island, he had studied medicine in Edinburgh, Glasgow and Leyden, but gave up his medical practice after inheriting a plantation in Popeshead division from his father in 1747 – originally brought to the family by his mother, heiress Jane Moll. Two years later, Thomas had gained Thibou's and Long Island by marrying Rachel, eldest daughter of the late Jacob Thibou, and Dorothy (née Blizard).

As usual, with wealth came political power and administrative positions. Elected a member of the Antigua Assembly in 1755, Thomas became its President in 1761, a role he would perform on and off for over twenty years. In 1776, when Jane was four, he also became Chief Justice of the Courts of King's Bench and Common Pleas.

At birth Jane had six older brothers (the eldest, Thomas, was twenty-two years older) and five older sisters.[1] Two years later, her parents had their last child, George Ralph Payne, named after their neighbour Sir Ralph Payne (son of the Bakers' friend of the same name), then Governor of the Leeward Islands.[2] Jane was always 'dotingly fond of her worthy and affectionate Mother', and particularly close to her nearest sister Dorothea and her little brother George Ralph Payne, admiring the 'sensibility' and 'goodness' of his heart.[3]

A pretty child, with brown hair and blue eyes, Jane wanted for nothing. She grew up at Thibou's plantation on the north coast, worked by some 300 enslaved people. The family home, Mount Joshua, was later reputed 'one of the most commodious on the island.' Her sister Christiana remembered Antigua as 'that once dear little spot', and it seems Jane likewise had a happy childhood.[4] Like many white children in the Caribbean, young Jane was nursed by an enslaved woman, Dinah, whom she would remember all her life.

The Jarvis family continued to consolidate their position with more advantageous marriages in the next generation. Jane's sister Rachel married Deputy Secretary John Wilkins in 1776. Her brother Thomas married heiress Jane Whitehead in 1782, inheriting Blizard's plantation. In 1785 another sister, Elizabeth, married Dr Archibald Gloster – the

---

* Possession of Long Island brought an unusual advantage. For many years, the 300-acre island exported an improbable 1,000 hogsheads of sugar a year. In reality, ninety per cent had been smuggled in from Martinique and Guadeloupe. Flannigan, *Antigua and the Antiguans*, vol. 1, pp. 159–60.

Garifuna women's 'Liar Gloster'. Jane's brother John Swinton Jarvis acquired 15,000 acres on the half French, half Dutch island of St Martin through marrying Mary Bayley in 1791.[5]

Antigua had been inhabited by Taíno from around the first century CE to about 1100. Kalinago began visiting the island on hunting and fishing trips from the fourteenth century, but did not settle there permanently. The English arrived from St Kitts in 1632, led by Captain Edward Warner, another son of Kittian Governor Sir Thomas Warner. Though only fourteen miles long and eleven miles wide, Antigua was the largest of the four Leeward Islands. By the early eighteenth century, the island had become the fourth largest British producer of sugar after Jamaica, Barbados and St Kitts. According to Tobias Smollett, Antigua was 'more noted for good harbours, than all the English islands in these seas; yet so encompassed with rocks, that it is of dangerous access ... to those who are not well acquainted with the coast'.[6]

The well-sheltered 'English Harbour' was Britain's main naval base in the eastern Caribbean. It is now known as Nelson's Dockyard, as the famous admiral was based there from 1784 to 1787, marrying Frances (Fanny) Nisbet, an attractive young widow, with Prince William Henry (later William IV) as his best man. Frances was the niece of a wealthy enslaver, John Richardson Herbert, President of the Nevis Council. Nelson, then, as he put it, 'poor as Job', excitedly wrote to his uncle that Fanny would inherit £20,000 on Herbert's death, perhaps more if she outlived his daughter. In the end, Fanny received a legacy of £4,000 in 1793, though Nelson was exasperated by the delay in receiving it.*[7]

Some 37,500 Africans were enslaved on the island, outnumbering the 2,500 or so Europeans fifteen to one; a ratio far higher than Jamaica (ten to one), St Kitts (eight to one) and Barbados (four to one). These huge numbers were sustained by regular arrivals of captives; some 30–40,000 Africans were trafficked to Antigua in the two decades preceding Jane's birth in 1772. The island's flat, arid landscape and small size made it hard for Maroon communities to form, though proximity to other islands made it possible to escape by sea. Posing as free, some found work as sailors; others sought to blend into urban populations.[8]

---

* Nelson complained to Fanny, 'As to these West India people I put no confidence in them. I hope we shall get the legacy paid in due time and then I shall not care about them.' Small, 'Montpelier Estate, St John Figtree, Nevis', p. 29.

Jarvis Family Tree

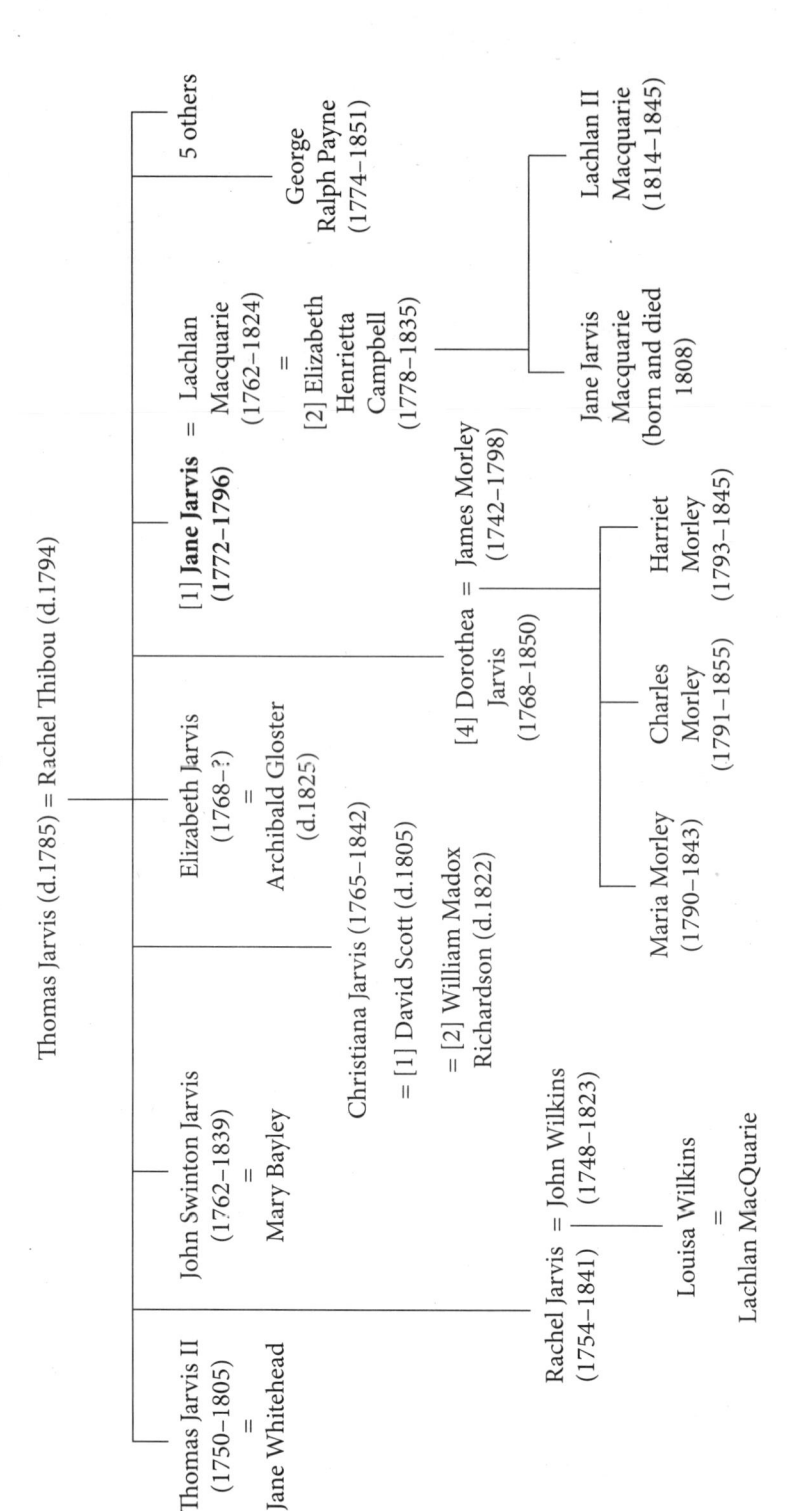

Thomas Jarvis (d.1785) = Rachel Thibou (d.1794)

- Thomas Jarvis II (1750–1805) = Jane Whitehead
  - Rachel Jarvis (1754–1841) = John Wilkins (1748–1823)
    - Louisa Wilkins = Lachlan MacQuarie
- John Swinton Jarvis (1762–1839) = Mary Bayley
- Elizabeth Jarvis (1768–?) = Archibald Gloster (d.1825)
  - Christiana Jarvis (1765–1842)
    = [1] David Scott (d.1805)
    = [2] William Madox Richardson (d.1822)
- [1] **Jane Jarvis** (1772–1796) = Lachlan Macquarie (1762–1824) = [2] Elizabeth Henrietta Campbell (1778–1835)
  - Jane Jarvis Macquarie (born and died 1808)
  - Lachlan II Macquarie (1814–1845)
- [4] Dorothea Jarvis (1768–1850) = James Morley (1742–1798)
  - Maria Morley (1790–1843)
  - Charles Morley (1791–1855)
  - Harriet Morley (1793–1845)
- 5 others
  - George Ralph Payne (1774–1851)

In 1736, Antiguan freedom fighters staged the island's very own Gunpowder Plot. According to information later gleaned through torture, the plan was to eliminate the entire white ruling class by blowing up the Court House during a ball held to celebrate George II's birthday. A carpenter named Tomboy was to play Guy Fawkes, smuggling in ten gallons of gunpowder while erecting seats for the party. The explosion would be the signal for hundreds across the island to kill their enslavers and march on the capital. Prince Klaas (alias Kwaku or Court) – now an Antiguan National Hero, with a statue in St John's – was crowned leader in an Asante ceremony a week before the ball. After the plot was discovered, Prince Klaas and four others were broken on the wheel, six gibbeted, seventy-seven burned and forty-seven banished.[9]

Although Jane did not experience resistance on this scale, violent protest and punishment still played its part in her childhood. On Christmas Eve 1781, when Jane was nine, Giles Blizard, her maternal grandmother's cousin, was shot with a blunderbuss by two enslaved men, one of whom was Geoffry, Blizard's own son. Though they attempted to make it look like suicide, their actions were witnessed by a boy named Diamond. Condemned to death, they were decapitated, their heads dipped in pitch and put on spikes as a warning to others, and their bodies burned in a lime kiln.[10]

Jane was thirteen when her father died on 18 December 1785. The family buried him privately at home. According to local memory 'the planters at Thibou Jarvis estate use to say that massa grave was better than those at Big Church.'[11] Jane's eldest brother Thomas inherited, becoming head of the family. By 1791 he estimated his property on the island was worth £50,000.[12]

Jane would inherit £3,000 on her marriage, 'and the like sum to any future child'. But the will did not only refer to *her* future children. It also stated Jane was entitled to 'the issue of Dinah, Fanny & Jenny'. Dinah had nursed her as a child; Fanny's story remains obscure; Jenny had recently been 'purchased of Thomas Oliver, Esq.'. Oliver, the former Lieutenant Governor of Massachusetts, had fled to Antigua in 1776, acquiring nearby Friar's Hill by marrying Harriet Freeman. Also inheriting his late father-in-law's debts, he sold some land, and probably other people besides Jenny, to the Jarvises.[13]

Thomas thought it a great pity when Jane later decreed that any children she inherited should be taught trades. Field labourers, he complained, were 'the most valuable slaves', whereas 'the island swarms with carpenters, masons and sempstresses, that cannot be hired out, so that they become a dead expence to the owner.'[14]

Jane's mother Rachel now took her youngest three children, Jane, Dorothea and George Ralph Payne, to England, where her jointure of £1,000 a year 'enabled her to support her widowhood in London in a very genteel style'. They moved into 49 Welbeck Street in Marylebone, and the siblings were sent to school.

Like Jane, Dorothea had a £6,000 dowry; she soon attracted a suitor. James Morley was a forty-six-year-old East India Company merchant, who had been married three times before. Born in Bombay (now Mumbai), the son of a prominent Company official, Morley had amassed £25,000 over his thirty-year career, based not only in India, but also at Bushehr in the Persian Gulf.

Dorothea married Morley on 10 March 1789 at St James's, Piccadilly. He proved 'an excellent parent and a fond husband'. Their first child, Maria, arrived in March 1790; Jane delighted in her role as aunt. Soon after, Morley wished to return to Bombay, 'to increase his fortune'.[15] Jane and Dorothea could not bear to be parted, so Jane accompanied the Morleys on the four-month voyage, arriving in Bombay aboard the *Worcester* on 20 September 1790.[16]

Something of a Cinderella by comparison to the wealthier East India Company Presidencies of Bengal and Madras, Bombay was considered unhealthy, poor and dull. The territory's seven islands had been in British hands since Charles II received them as dowry on his marriage to Portuguese Princess Catherine of Braganza in 1661. Strategically, it occupied an awkward position, squeezed between the Marathas in the north, and Tipu Sultan's Kingdom of Mysore in the south. But, blessed with a large natural harbour, and proximity to cotton-producing Gujarat, Bombay became a bustling commercial port and shipbuilding centre with a global reach. One adventurous English milliner remarked in 1784: 'the many fine ships building and repairing with the number of Europeans walking about, almost persuaded me I was at home, till the dress and dark complexion of the workmen destroyed the pleasing illusion.' For Jane, of course, dark-faced workers *were* a familiar part of the scene.

The city had a population of over 100,000 people within the walls and 10,000 without. Tens of thousands of Hindus and Muslims lived

Bombay Harbour as Jane would have seen it when she arrived on an East Indiaman like the *Essex*, shown at anchor here.

alongside thousands of Parsis and 'Portuguese' (Indians converted to Catholicism in the sixteenth century); and smaller numbers of Jews, Malays, Chinese and Armenians; even several enslaved Africans. A naval officer wrote in 1812: 'in twenty minutes' walk through the bazaar of Bombay my ears have been struck by the sounds of every language that I have heard in any other part of the world'.[17]

Europeans were relatively scarce: around 2,000 British soldiers and fewer than 1,000 civilians: merchants, doctors, government officials and their families. The small, close-knit community mostly kept to themselves. Fearing Indian influence, they did their best to replicate life at home, following 'the English fashion in houses, equipage, and dress ... as much as the climate would admit of'. The climate, as Jane's brother Thomas wrote from Antigua, 'being more immediately under the Line, must be much warmer than it is here, and God knows this is hot enough'. Suffering 'languor' and 'lethargy' in Bombay 'no European uses his own legs; but that all ranks and ages must bend to the custom of the place and be carried' in palanquins (litters borne on poles by at least four men). In the hottest months, wealthy families retreated to the surrounding hills.

In another adaptation to their surroundings, 'very few ladies or gentlemen kept European servants'. Instead, they hired Malabaris, 'while the upper servants were usually Mahomedans and Parsees; men of character and family'.[18] The Morleys acquired a full complement of servants, including an enslaved Indian orphan named Marianne, at their Bombay townhouse, The Grove.

Jane was thrust into the centre of Bombay society by her brother-in-law's high status. Morley was now the most senior Company servant in the Presidency, on first-name terms with the Governor and Commander in Chief of the Army in Bombay, Major General Sir Robert Abercromby.*

At nineteen, Jane was 'young and handsome' with 'an excellent figure, rather above the middle size, with a most comely pleasing face and countenance ... but above all a most amiable disposition and temper; with a good understanding', her 'mind well cultivated and instructed by the best and finished education'.[19] Combined with her fortune and family connections this made her extremely alluring.

Soon after her arrival Jane began to receive – and decline – proposals from 'young men and old men, some of them of high rank and large fortunes'. One such admirer was a Mr Stevenson, an 'elderly gentleman'; another Lieutenant Colonel John Nugent, Commandant of the Bombay Battalion of Artillery, who was in his late fifties. A third of 'Miss Jarvis's lovers and great admirers' was the fifty-three-year-old Commodore John Thistleton, superintendent of the Company's marine, described as 'totally unfit for the situation'. Jane came to the same conclusion when assessing him as a suitor. Her refusals reached her brother Thomas in Antigua, who remarked to George Ralph Payne: 'our sister Jane ... appears at present rather difficult to please'. He hoped she would 'in the end accomplish her wishes, by getting a husband suited to her mind'.[20]

On the evening of 7 November 1792, Jane, Dorothea and James Morley paid a visit to the home of banker John Forbes, Morley's agent in Bombay, whom Dorothea thought 'a darling of a man', and Jane considered a 'particular friend'.[21]† There, Colonel James Balfour introduced them to a young Scottish army officer named Lachlan Macquarie.[22]

---

* A veteran of both the Seven Years' and Revolutionary Wars in America, Sir Robert was brother to Ralph Abercromby, who led the troops deployed to fight the Garifuna and the French in St Vincent in 1796.

† Forbes & Company, part of the Shapoorji Pallonji Group since 2002, is one of the oldest companies in India.

Recently returned from besieging Seringapatam during the Third Mysore War against Tipu Sultan, Lachlan was an ambitious career soldier. He had joined the army aged fifteen in 1776, and served in Nova Scotia, New York, Charleston and Jamaica during the American Revolutionary War before arriving in Bombay in 1788. It was while in Jamaica in 1783, visiting friends and relations in St Ann and St Mary, that Lachlan decided 'to go and try my fortune in the East Indies'.[23]

Although he had family connections to the local Macquarie and Maclaine of Lochbuie clans, Lachlan's upbringing, on the isle of Ulva off the west coast of Mull, was humble. His father was a tenant farmer of the Duke of Argyll; his mother illiterate. His mother's brother, Murdoch Maclaine, the 18th chief of Lochbuie, became his patron and protector.[24]

Jane liked the look of Lachlan. Ten years her senior, he was 'a clean-shaved, strong, lusty looking man of about 5ft 10 inches in height, and very broad-shouldered', with sandy hair, brown 'penetrating' eyes and an aquiline nose, his skin tanned after four years in India.[25] Lachlan had already noticed Jane before they were formally introduced, and was immediately 'deeply enamoured'. He found her 'handsome in face and person, elegantly accomplished, a charming disposition, of most agreeable manners', and, last but not least, 'possessing a private fortune of six thousand pounds' sterling'.

Two weeks after their first meeting, Jane danced a reel with Lachlan at a ball given by Governor Abercromby. This was enough to 'rivett his chains and entirely win his affection'. Over the next few months Lachlan dined with the Morleys several times – including on Christmas Day – and always featured on Jane's dance card, even on 'excessively sultry and hot' nights when most ladies 'did not enter much into the humour of Dancing'.

Although Lachlan did not declare himself to Jane, she 'plainly ... had sufficient penetration to see what was going on in his bosom'.[26] His devotion was obvious, not least to her disapproving brother-in-law. A headache prevented Jane from dancing with Lachlan at a farewell ball for Governor Abercromby on 15 July 1793; was the headache feigned at Morley's instruction? At ten o'clock the following morning Morley confronted Lachlan at his lodgings, insisting that he leave Jane alone until his financial circumstances improved. Morley promised not to divulge their conversation to anyone but his wife, but it seems unlikely Dorothea kept it from her sister. Jane would certainly have noticed Lachlan's attempts to distance himself.[27]

Lachlan had always petitioned senior officers for promotion and favours, well aware that who he knew would further his career faster than what he did. Conscious that he must considerably increase his fortune if he wanted to marry Jane, Lachlan now accelerated his efforts to climb the greasy pole and was 'extremely urgent and solicitous to obtain the appointment of Major of Brigade' when it fell vacant.

It did not take long for his campaign to succeed. On 2 August, Lachlan arrived at the Morleys' house for supper with news: Abercromby had appointed him Major of Brigade, significantly increasing his annual income from £500 to £760 a year.[28] The following morning, Jane received a letter from Lachlan, delivered by his Indian servant 'Bappoo',* who had 'strict orders to deliver it into her own hand'. It was a formal proposal of marriage. Jane returned her compliments, but no other answer. She told Dorothea and Morley she wanted to accept the offer immediately, but Morley was still far from convinced Lachlan had the means to 'maintain a wife and family in a genteel way in this country'.

When Morley visited him the next morning, Lachlan *insisted* he 'never thought of Miss Jarvis's fortune', nor was he 'guided or influenced by sordid or mercenary motives'. Anticipating Morley's concerns, he produced 'a Card on which I had noted down my different allowances per month as Capt. Lt., Paymaster. & Major of Brigade to the King's Troops', giving 'as candid and explicit an account of my present circumstances and future prospects as possible.' This 'ingenious and honourable conduct' eventually convinced Morley, especially as Lachlan promised he would not touch Jane's fortune and would settle an additional £1,000 – all his savings – on her. Morley did not pick up on Lachlan's qualification that he would not touch the interest garnered from investing her money, *'unless she herself desired it'* (emphasis added).[29]

When Morley got home, he conferred with Dorothea, then presented Jane with the facts of Lachlan's financial situation, leaving it 'entirely to herself how to act'. Jane wasted no time. Declaring she preferred Lachlan 'to all other men in the world', she sent Morley to deliver this 'most delightful, acceptable and pleasing intelligence'.

The next morning, Lachlan resolved to be a better man, writing a list of resolutions in his diary strikingly familiar to anyone who has ever attempted the exercise. He would rise and go to bed early, do more

---

* This was probably not his real name, but derived from 'bapu', an honorific for a father figure in Hindi, used to address an older man with respect.

exercise, serious reading and study, perform all his duties before midday, be more punctual, drink less and see more of his friends. None lasted the week; Lachlan spent every moment he could with Jane, rejoicing in each new intimacy.

When allowed to go on a carriage ride with Jane and her nephew Charles Morley (who had not yet reached his second birthday, leaving the pair essentially unchaperoned) Lachlan exclaimed: 'Oh! what felicity – I actually thought for some minutes I was in a dream! – blessed adorable Girl! – We had a delightful interesting conversation.' As in Bombay 'a man and a woman in a carriage together were as good as married', the engagement now became common knowledge. One of Jane's many admirers, the elderly Mr Stevenson, spotted them together and appeared 'much discomforted and displeas'd', flashing 'Gorgon looks' at them.

Jane thanked Lachlan with a 'tender note' when he presented her with a copy of Boswell's *Journal of a Tour to the Hebrides*, but the book did not give the best impression of Lachlan's native Ulva. Boswell and Dr Johnson found the weather there cold, dark and stormy; observed superstition and strange feudal customs; and concluded 'there was nothing worthy of observation'. They spent the night with Lauchlan MacQuarrie, the 16th and last clan chief (a cousin of Lachlan's father). His house was 'mean', with broken windows letting in the rain, turning the clay floor to mud. Nonetheless, MacQuarrie was 'intelligent, polite, and much a man of the world'. The tourists were dismayed to learn that though 'his family had possessed Ulva for nine hundred years ... it was soon to be sold for payment of his debts'.

Jane's rather more auspicious engagement present to Lachlan was her mother's 'Dress Watch, Seals &c.', which she insisted he wore 'for her sake'. Lachlan was happy to do so, considering the watch, with its diamond bearings, 'very elegant'. Jane also cut off a lock of her hair for him to wear around his neck as a chain. Captivated, Lachlan exclaimed: 'What a happy fellow I am!'[30]

Morley remained suspicious of Lachlan's motives, and wanted to ensure Jane's fortune was protected from him in their marriage settlement. He took on the trusteeship alongside John Tasker, another senior East India Company figure in Bombay. The document, signed on 2 September, decreed Jane's £6,000, alongside the £1,000 Lachlan had settled on her, be invested in 'the English Funds', through London bankers Francis and William Gosling (whose Fleet Street bank later became part of Barclays). Though the return would probably have been twice as high, Morley and Tasker considered it 'too great a risque to lay out our money' in India.[31]

Jane and Lachlan were married on the Morleys' veranda on 8 September 1793 in the presence of 'a numerous and very respectable company of our mutual friends and acquaintances'. Jane, 'elegantly attired', was beaming as Morley led her out, 'her lovely countenance … full of beneficence, beauty and unaffected modesty', and conducted herself 'with the most correct propriety and fortitude' throughout the ceremony. Once married, Jane was immediately kissed by her ardent Lachlan; then, as was 'usual on these occasions', all the gentlemen present kissed her and all the other ladies.

The wedding was not the only ceremony that evening. In two baptisms, Jane stood as godmother to her four-month-old niece Harriet, while, at Morley's request, Lachlan became godfather to a 'country-born' girl named Sarah or Sally, 'a distant relation of Mr Morley's … the daughter of a Mr Richardson'.[32] 'Country-born' was a euphemism; Sally's mother was Indian. As Lachlan explained in a journal entry soon after his arrival in Bombay, when he danced with 'a Mrs. Capon; – a Country Born lady; – they are sometimes called (Ladies of this description are very numerous here) Blue-Skins, from their dark complexions; being the Offspring of European Fathers, by Moor or Gentoo women.'[33]

Such children were commonplace: as many as one in three British men had relationships with Indian women, known as *bibis*. Even Governor George Dick had an Indian mistress, rumoured to be a spy for the Marathas. James Morley made provision for two 'natural' sons in his will, born to an Indian woman named Marian or Rubra during an earlier sojourn in Bombay. Like Gibson Dalzell and so many other Caribbean colonists, these men considered it normal to send their children to the metropole, separating them from their mothers forever.[34] John Tasker, the other trustee of Jane's marriage settlement, sent a boy named John William Tasker 'who calls me father' home to Upton Castle in Pembrokeshire, informing his steward that his son was 'very dark' but 'of a good disposition'.[35]

At the wedding supper, Jane and Lachlan were flattered when the Morleys placed them at head and foot of the table 'to preside and do the honours of it in their stead'. All was 'mirth and good humour'; several songs were sung; the party did not break up until after midnight.

Then, it was time to go to bed. Dorothea accompanied the happy couple to their new home and helped Jane get ready, perhaps offering some sisterly advice on what was to follow. Hastily ushering Dorothea out, Lachlan:

> undressed as quick as possible and flew on the wings of love to my dearest of Women, to finally crown my measure of happiness and bliss! – My felicity and delight, on this joyous and fortunate night, can only be conceived – but, impossible, to be described! suffice it to say – no Benedict was ever happier, or better pleased with his lot and good fortune, in the choice of a Wife!

For a few days following the wedding, Jane and Lachlan 'staid at home, and saw no Company but Mr and Mrs Morley, and a very few select friends, not wishing to have our own little interesting Society and conversation interrupted'. Though Lachlan gives the impression this was a quiet time, *thirty-eight* people visited the newlyweds in five days. By the end of September, *all* 'the Ladies and Gentlemen of the Settlement' had called to congratulate them. Lachlan rejoiced: 'every one of our acquaintance in this country, thinks it the most suitable, eligible, and happy match that was ever made in Bombay'.[36]

Jane was enraptured with her new husband. She wrote to her sister that she was 'most fortunate and happy in possessing so great a Treasure', and to her new mother-in-law that she was 'supremely happy and contented with the choice I have made of a Husband in your son … no Pair on earth can be happier than we are now'. She also sent handwoven Kashmiri shawls to Lachlan's mother and sister; so coveted in Britain that in Austen's *Mansfield Park* Lady Bertram hopes her nephew William 'may go to the East Indies so I may have my shawl.'[37]

Lachlan's letters to friends and family waxed lyrical about his 'Dulcinea' (after Don Quixote's sweetheart), or 'most agreeable Soncie' (from the Gaelic for good luck). He told Rachel Jarvis that a 'panegyrick of your charming daughter' would not be necessary, as she already knew 'her worth and excellencies'. Instead, Lachlan felt he should recommend himself. 'My fortune is very small … but I believe, I may say without vanity, that my character and connections are unexceptionable and will bear the strictest enquiry'.

Lachlan was keen to extol Jane's pedigree to his uncle Murdoch Maclaine: 'She is a West Indian by birth, *but* [emphasis added] of a very genteel, respectable, and opulent family in that country.' He was clearly concerned Jane's Caribbean birth would leave her open to the prejudices faced by many heiresses in this book. Lachlan emphasised Jane's father had held a pre-eminent position in Antigua as 'Chief Judge and first in Council', wealthy enough to 'handsomely' provide for his widow and their many sons and daughters. He boasted her brother Thomas 'has now an Estate of £2,000 sterling per annum in Antigua'.[38] One wonders how he received this precise financial information. Was it common knowledge in Bombay, whispered whenever Jane entered a ballroom as when Mr Darcy first appears in *Pride and Prejudice*? Or did Morley disclose the figure while discussing finances? Perhaps Jane told him herself.

Life in Bombay, 'where every family of any consequence must live as their neighbours do', was to prove ruinously expensive for the young couple. Jane was very happy with the 'new excellent house' near the Ramparts 'in a clean airy undisturbed part of the town' Morley had found for them. But the rent was £200 a year, three times the cost of Lachlan's previous home; their servants' wages came to £150. Jane found Lachlan's 'little stock of plate, furniture, etc.' inadequate, and so began purchasing all the items *she* considered necessary for their marital home. By the time she was finished, the couple were 'complete in every article of Plate, Furniture, Wines, Liquors and Stores, that is, or will be for some time to come, wanted for House-keeping'.[39]

Then there was the cost of entertaining their large circle of acquaintances. They gave regular dinner parties and attended balls, races and other social events with gusto. Living the high life, it was 'not in their power to save sixpence'. Six weeks after the wedding they were over £500 in debt.[40] Lachlan rued that Bombay society, though 'most undoubtedly desirable', was 'too dearly purchased when people are under the necessity in order to enjoy it of exceeding their income'.[41]

Relief came from an unexpected quarter when John Forbes gave Jane £400 in November 1793, bequeathed by her old admirer, Lieutenant Colonel Nugent, who had recently died. But the impact of this 'Godsend' was short-lived. At the end of January 1794, Lachlan was shocked to learn that he must pay £550 for the company in the 77th Regiment he thought he had been given for free.[42] Soon they had to downsize to a less expensive house near the Dockyard, rented from a Parsi merchant named Dady Nasserwanjee, relinquishing their carriage for a gig drawn by only one horse. Luckily John Tasker lent them his carriage, enabling them to visit their friends in the country, and allowed them the use of his cool townhouse during the hot weather.[43]

The couple 'yearned to quit Eastern luxury for Scotch or English frugality', but felt they must stay in India until Lachlan had made enough money for them to live on back home. Jane in particular was extremely anxious to return to Europe and, Lachlan believed, was doing 'all in her power to save money'. He insisted his 'dearest Girl' was:

> always an excellent Manager and economist, and could make a little go a long way. In all her little arrangements, in Household and Family affairs, she was, without exception, the most frugal and methodical of any Woman I have ever yet known or met with.

Love seems to have made him blind to her lavish spending on their first home, and her order of several 'articles of Perfumery' from London including 'two large down powdering puffs'.[44]

In January 1794, news reached Bombay that Rachel Jarvis was seriously ill. Dorothea decided she and her children should return to London to see her. She would leave her enslaved maid, Marianne, behind with Jane, with whom she would become a 'great favourite'.

On the morning the ship was due to leave, Jane went to her sister's house immediately after breakfast. Both sisters were distraught and had to be physically torn from each other on the dock. Jane, 'quite overcome with Grief', was inconsolable for days.

In Dorothea's absence, Jane and Lachlan's relationship with Morley was initially cordial. In mid-March, Lachlan recorded: 'Mr Morley has dined with us in the friendly way, every Sunday since Mrs Morley's departure for England.'[45] Towards the end of the month, Jane and Lachlan joined Morley on a cruise to Goa in his new ship the *Maria*. But despite their apparent friendship, Morley never really relinquished his suspicion Lachlan was a fortune hunter.[46]

Regardless of the pressure on their finances, Jane and Lachlan kept on spending. Lachlan bestowed largesse on relatives in Scotland; including paying the rent on his mother's farm, funding the education of a nephew and lending a brother £300. They had sent Dorothea to London with a shopping list, commissioning her to buy a carriage for them, an item 'there is no doing without in this country, when there is a lady in the question', and silver plate, to be emblazoned with the Macquarie arms.[47]

As well as her 'articles of Perfumery', Jane specifically wanted William Buchan's *Domestic Medicine* and 'one of the best Cookery Books'. The bill should be sent to Francis and William Gosling, to be paid out of the interest accruing on their investments.[48]

When Morley found out about the Macquaries' spending spree, he flew into a rage. While Jane and Lachlan had assumed they were allowed to use the interest, Morley disagreed. Lachlan's apologies fell on deaf ears; Morley and Tasker relinquished their trusteeship. When his brother-in-law left Bombay, Lachlan snidely remarked he might 'fret himself to death before he reaches England'.[49]

Their disagreement was somewhat academic, as Jane's brother Thomas had not actually transferred her dowry to the Goslings. Jane wrote 'respecting my Marriage, my Fortune, and my Slaves', but 'never received one line from him'. She became so frustrated by her 'sweet and stingy brother' that she soon had 'nothing further to say to him'. She turned instead to Francis and William Gosling requesting, 'by the ships of the next season', 'a stated account of her affairs, made up to the 31st December 1794', followed by regular interest statements.[50] By May 1795, there was still no sign of Thomas producing Jane's dowry and Lachlan threatened to take the matter to court. When pressed by his family to purchase land in Scotland, he had to admit: 'I am now nominally a man of fortune without having the power of making the least use of it.'[51]

Thomas's reluctance was probably fuelled by the uncertainty facing enslavers in the wake of revolutions in France and Haiti, and abolition debates in Parliament. Furthermore, by 1791, Thomas had suffered a series of five bad crops, exacerbated by drought and borer larvae wreaking 'terrible devastations among the cane-fields'.[52] A paucity of fresh running water left Antiguans especially vulnerable to droughts and fires – one Governor likened the island to the 'deserts of Arabia'. Cartographer Emmanuel Bowen, who made a map of the island in 1750, noted: 'in times of drought when all their ponds are dry and their cisterns almost empty, they are obliged to fetch their fresh water from Montserrat in times of War, or in times of Peace from that and Guadeloupe.' Some people even made money from selling water; in 1779 the price was 18d a gallon. The enslaved people, whose needs were considered last, suffered most; an estimated 7,500–9,000 died of dysentery from drinking contaminated water between 1778 and 1780 alone.[53]

Thomas feared another crop failure would 'prove fatal' and place the whole family 'below mediocrity'. Even though he lived with 'great frugality' to 'remit every last shilling' to England, he still owed his brokers, Heywood's of Manchester (later part of Royal Bank of Scotland, now owned by NatWest), over £7,000.[54] Thomas pleaded with his mother to spend only seven or eight hundred of her £1,000 jointure, moving out of London if necessary to economise.[55] He also withheld funds from several other brothers and sisters.[56] Jane was aghast at his 'shameful conduct', particularly his treatment of her sisters Christiana Scott and Rachel Wilkins, both of whom had fallen on hard times since moving to England. Christiana's husband David declared bankruptcy in 1785. John Wilkins's financial situation prompted Christiana to remark 'did you ever know any man so unfortunate?'[57] In her eyes, the many men enslaved by her family did not count as 'men'. Jane berated Thomas fiercely for neglecting his family; how could he 'with any sort of satisfaction enjoy his wealth?'[58]

In mid-June 1794, the 'most melancholly [sic] and afflicting tidings of the death of Mrs Jarvis' arrived in Bombay. She had been suffering 'Saint Anthony's fire on the brain', or ergotism.* A move from London to Southampton 'for the benefit of the Sea air' had proved in vain, and she died on 14 January, two days before Dorothea had left Bombay.

Lachlan 'had not sufficient resolution or command of myself to disclose the afflicting tale to my dearest Jane'. Instead, he left the 'painful task' to her close friends, the 'obliging and sensible' Ellen Stirling, and 'warm hearted' Dorothea Oakes.[59] Though they broke the news to Jane 'with the greatest delicacy, tenderness and friendship', it was still a terrible shock, and Jane 'suffered … the keenest anguish and most poignant grief'.[60] It was November before Jane accepted her loss was 'the will of God, therefore we must yield with humble submission'.[61]

Rachel Jarvis left several Africans to her various children and grandchildren. Jane was bequeathed a boy named Mathias, and two girls named Phibba and Quasheba, 'children of Quick', and any future offspring they might have.[62] Dorothea was to have a boy named Daniel. George Ralph Payne, by now, on Lachlan's recommendation, a Lieutenant in the 36th Regiment, stationed at Pondicherry, was left

---

* Triggered by ergot, a poisonous fungus which grows on rye, ergotism causes convulsions and gangrene. 'St Anthony's fire' was also used to refer to erysipelas, a bacterial infection so called for the red rash that was an early symptom; however, this seems to have been more common in the medieval period, and does not appear to affect the brain.

a 'Mullatto Woman named Sally and her son George,[*] with the future increase of the said Sally'.[63]

In a codicil to her will, Rachel also left Jane and George Ralph Payne a very specific legacy: one-third of the profits made in 1786 from the sale of sugar and rum produced from land the family had purchased from their neighbour Thomas Oliver, former Lieutenant Governor of Massachusetts. She insisted these profits, promised to her in her husband's will, were *still* owed to her by her son Thomas. Jane was surprised the legacy was 'confined to the year 1786'. She tried to recover her share by applying to an Antiguan friend, Samuel Martin, one of her mother's executors, but no money was forthcoming.[64]

In reality, the profits did not exist. As Thomas had informed Rachel in 1791, a later deed of agreement made with Oliver barred her claim; most of the canes had since been cut down. Even if there were any profits, she would also have been liable for 'one third of the expenses of the cultivation, one third of parish and public taxes, one third of the provisions for the support of the Negroes', and several other costs. All these outgoings 'would have amounted to a sum of money far exceeding the trifling produce that was reaped'.[65]

Marrying a soldier, especially while the British East India Company was pursuing an aggressive programme of territorial expansion, meant Jane was always in danger of losing Lachlan to war. Before 1792, the Company had occupied only 9.3 per cent of Indian land, predominantly in the north and east, but in the Treaty of Seringapatam, signed in March of that year, they gained a large portion of Tipu Sultan's territories on the Malabar coast. Meanwhile, the power of the Maratha Confederacy, which controlled large swathes of central and northern India, was increasingly threatened by internecine rivalry; this the British would soon exploit.[66]

News that the French had declared war on Britain and the Netherlands reached Bombay in June 1793; the conflict would have global repercussions. Lachlan was aghast that the revolutionaries had 'put their King to Death with many circumstances of horror and cruelty, after … a mock

---

[*] Though the shared name of George suggests some sort of personal relationship, George Ralph Payne was only twelve when he left Antigua so is unlikely to have fathered Sally's child. Sally wrote to George in 1818, to thank him for his 'benevolent liberality and goodness of heart' when he finally manumitted her. LAO, JARVIS/5/A/4/27 (Sally Jarvis to George Ralph Payne Jarvis, 17 February 1818).

Trial before the infamous execrable National Convention!'[67] Besides her fears for Lachlan, Jane knew war with France placed her family and friends in Antigua in the line of fire; the English Harbour naval base was a sure target. Antiguans had long feared French invasion; Jane's grandfather's 1745 will dictated a legacy of £1,000 should 'be lessened in proportion to my loss … if the French take this island.'[68] Her brothers Jacob Jarvis and John Swinton Jarvis had been taken prisoner fighting against American Revolutionaries in the last war. They were lucky to be returned to Antigua in a prisoner exchange in 1780.[69] Even if the island escaped French attack, war would disrupt commercial shipping, endangering both food imports and profits from exporting sugar to England.

Jane had a scare in July 1794, when Lachlan's regiment was ordered to depart for Madras (now Chennai), but there was a stay of execution when he was then personally directed to remain in Bombay. However, when the 77th were ordered to the Malabar coast in September, Jane and Lachlan faced a quandary. Leaving Bombay would mean relinquishing the role of Major of Brigade, whereas staying would mean he could no longer serve as the regiment's paymaster. Either option would mean a disastrous salary cut. Luckily, a friend named Captain James Dunlop – incidentally the son of Frances Dunlop, who chastised Robert Burns for his harsh poetic treatment of Mary Oswald – offered to deputise in Lachlan's absence for a share of the money.[70]

Just before Christmas 1794, Jane and Lachlan sailed over 500 nautical miles south to Calicut (now Kozhikode, in northern Kerala). The British had operated a trading factory at Calicut since the seventeenth century but had only just wrested the place from Tipu Sultan's control. Though Jane was 'much affected' at leaving her friends, they both hoped it would be easier to live within their means away from the big city.

Lachlan bought a bungalow near Calicut in a 'sweet spot', among 'high airy beautiful hills commanding a charming view and prospect of the country round and of the sea at a distance', from an old comrade, army surgeon Dr Charles Ker. Considering herself 'very comfortably lodged', Jane thanked Dr Ker for the 'good quarters', mature kitchen garden, bullocks, goats and pigeons he had left behind, which she 'meant to take great care of and keep in high order'.[71] After fixing the leaky roof ahead of monsoon season, plastering the hall previously lined with plain bamboo, and some further renovations and improvements, they looked forward to living 'more retired for a while', in a 'recluse corner of the world'. They named their new home 'Staffa Lodge', after a tiny island off the coast of Ulva once owned by the Macquaries, known for its natural beauty.*

Jane was 'charmed with the beauty of the country and the novelty of carrying the knapsack and roughing it as a soldier's wife'. She found a kindred spirit in Anna Shaw, the only other army wife in town, who helped her arrange her furniture, invited her to dinner and lent her a saddle (Jane's had been lost on the voyage from Bombay). Jane enjoyed riding a 'Turkai Breed' horse from Bengal, 'very quiet and gentle, but sufficiently lively for a lady'. Jane was a better rider than Lachlan; 'not the best horseman', he was content with his old grey. On several occasions, she rode while he travelled by palanquin.

Keen to live modestly in Calicut to revive their fortunes, Jane hoped by 1798 they would be in a position to return to England to 'live in some snug Retirement', as near Dorothea as possible. She 'made every retrenchment ... that could possibly be devised; – still keeping up a very genteel appearance'. After six months, the couple had cleared their considerable debts. By the year's end Lachlan had also paid the £550 he owed the army.

Lachlan gave Jane's 'prudent economy and excellent management of our little income' all the credit. However, he also admitted profiting from 'every local and accidental advantage I derived from being Paymaster of the Regiment'.[72] He began to advance loans to himself from the army coffers or borrow from local *shroffs* (bankers) and merchants. In 1795 and 1796, he invested the regiment's pay between three and five months in advance, reaping between three and six per cent interest. By 1799, he had made £9,000 in this fashion.

After Anna Shaw left Calicut in April 1795 to give birth in Bombay, Jane played hostess to the regiment, entertaining officers to a 'sober repast' on Sundays. We should not take the word 'sober' literally. One grocery order from May 1795 included twelve dozen bottles of Madeira and two casks of 'good pale ale'.†

This was a happy time; Lachlan affectionately called Jane 'Lady Mull' or 'Lady of the Isles'. Jane was thinking about having a baby, ordering

---

* Sir Joseph Banks considered Staffa island's sights superior to the Louvre, St Peter's, Rome, or the ancient ruins of Palmyra and Paestum. Watson, J., 'Lure of Staffa goes back to Bronze Age', *The Times*, 10 August 2018: https://www.thetimes.com/uk/scotland/article/lure-of-staffa-goes-back-to-bronze-age-zj66sd9ff.

† It was too hot to make ale in India, but India Pale Ale (IPA) was born when brewers discovered the ship's motion during the six-month voyage to the subcontinent immensely improved the flavour of strong October beer.

(in another lapse from her much-vaunted frugality) a silver rattle from England. She still missed her sister's 'three little dears', and hardly a day passed 'without her naming them with marks of strongest affection'. News of friends having babies, first Anna Shaw, then Dorothea Oakes, who, they heard from Bombay, would 'very soon be in the straw' and 'could hardly walk', can only have intensified her desire to become a mother.

Likewise, Lachlan was keen to have the 'honour of increasing and multiplying the Ancient Shiol Alpin' (seed of Alpin). He was proud Clan Macquarrie could claim descent from Alpin, father of Kenneth MacAlpin, ninth-century King of the Picts. He told his aunt he was 'sorry to say that as yet, there is no appearance of my being made a Papa.'[73]

Two children did arrive at Staffa Lodge, however. In late January, Lieutenant Alexander Gray returned from Dutch Cochin (Kochi), a major port with a thriving market in enslaved people, some 120 miles to the south of Calicut, bringing:

> two very fine, well-looking healthy Black Boys; both seemingly of the same age, and I should suppose from their size and appearance that they must be between six and seven year old. – The stoutest of them Mrs Macquarie has called Hector after my Brother: and the smallest I have called George after her Brother ... The Two Slave Boys cost One Hundred and Seventy Rupees ... We had the Boys immediately well washed, their Hair cut and combed, and well clothed.[74]

There was something paternalistic but intimate about naming the Indian boys,* whom Lachlan found 'so young and helpless', after family members.[75] Lachlan's brother Hector had died from pleurisy as a prisoner in South Carolina in 1778; he fondly kept his Bible as a memento all his life. Jane's adored younger brother George Ralph Payne would actually meet his namesake on a long-awaited visit to Staffa Lodge in July 1795.[76] Both boys took Jarvis as their surname.

Jane no doubt saw enslaved children as another economy; Lachlan noted: 'Gray has executed his Commission much to our satisfaction'.

---

* We know George and Hector were Indian because Lachlan referred to George as a 'native of India' in his will, and during the voyage to New South Wales in 1809 the Macquaries' fellow passenger Judge Advocate Ellis Bent described George as the 'Black Hindoo Servant of Colonel Macquarie's'. TNA, PROB, 11/1692/337 (Will of Lachlan Macquarie, 29 November 1824); NLA, MS 195, f. 40 (Ellis Bent to Mrs Hannah Bent, 15 June 1809).

As Jane was already an enslaver and had grown up with the institution, the acquisition may have been her idea, although British enslavement of Indians, mostly in domestic roles, was common. In 1840, a letter to abolitionist Thomas Fowell Buxton estimated 321,283 people were enslaved in British India.[77] Not all were Indian, as the East India Company had a longstanding history of trafficking East Africans, especially from Mozambique and Madagascar, to India and Indonesia.[78] Occasionally, people of African descent travelled to India from Britain, like Mungo, who accompanied John Peche, a new recruit to the East India Company army, in the early 1770s.[79]

Global events soon brought Jane and Lachlan's time at Staffa Lodge to an end. Inspired by the French Revolutionaries, the Dutch had risen against William of Orange, and, as the Batavian Republic, declared war against Britain in 1795. Ostensibly supporting the Dutch Prince, the British seized Dutch territory in India, with no real intention of returning it. In August 1795, Lachlan set off for Cochin, which his regiment had been ordered to take 'in the name of the Prince of Orange'. If there was any opposition, they would have to 'force the Dutch to a compliance in a hostile way'.

Jane and Lachlan, separated for the first time since marriage, promised to write and 'not a day passed without our having the felicity of hearing from one another.' Lachlan had the siege and his messmates to occupy his time. He marked their second wedding anniversary 'jovially and pleasantly, drinking the health of my dearest Jane in many overflowing bumpers'. But Jane, left behind in Calicut, pined for Lachlan. In mid-September, after the monsoon subsided, she proposed visiting Cochin. Lachlan entreated her to 'drop every idea of this kind', promising to come back the moment the siege was over. It could not take more than a fortnight.

Lachlan had underestimated the tenacity of Dutch Governor Jan van Spall. He did not surrender Cochin until 19 October. Jane 'quite rejoiced' at the news and wrote immediately to congratulate Lachlan and urge his swift return. When he arrived back in Calicut after eleven anxious days, their 'mutual joy and felicity was easier conceived than described'.

Jane's health had deteriorated during Lachlan's absence. She had a severe cold from 'getting wet feet walking in the Garden, which she was in the habit of doing for about an hour every day'. But she had not bothered to see a doctor. Neither did she seem worried by her 'very troublesome Cough', though it made Lachlan uneasy. The couple wasted no time in returning together to Staffa Lodge, though Jane travelled by palanquin, too ill to ride.

Despite her physical complaints, Jane's high spirits 'never forsook her', and 'made her society not only much liked – but also greatly admired'. The new silver plate, emblazoned with the Macquarie arms, had arrived from London; they hosted Jane's brother George Ralph Payne and Colonel Balfour, who had first introduced them, and celebrated the victory at Cochin.[80]

About a fortnight later, Lachlan was called as a witness to a court martial in Bombay. He and Jane arrived there on 23 November, and moved in with their 'kind and hospitable' friends, Major Henry and Dorothea Oakes. Jane's cough returned 'in a light degree' in the middle of December. She slept fitfully, her appetite diminished, and her spirits grew low. Following medical advice, she and Lachlan walked to the Esplanade every morning at sunrise, so she could drink a tumbler of buffalo milk straight from the udder. This she enjoyed; it seemed to do some good.

On 3 December Jane learned Lachlan's regiment was being sent to capture Colombo, capital of modern-day Sri Lanka, from the Dutch. She 'entreated and begged' Lachlan to let her go with him and 'share the toils and hardships of a soldier's life during the campaign'. It was with great difficulty that he persuaded her to abandon the idea. Her next thought was to return to Calicut, closer to Colombo, and wait for him there, but he insisted she was better off in Bombay, surrounded by friends.

Miserable at the thought of Lachlan's imminent departure, Jane now came up with another solution: could he not use his position as Major of Brigade as an excuse to stay behind in Bombay? 'Most earnest in her entreaties and solicitations', she protested she could not survive his absence a second time. She did not believe his reputation would suffer, as he had 'a Public Duty … to perform'. But Lachlan was sure it 'would not satisfy the malicious world, and however wretched' it made him to leave her, 'Honour calls – and I must obey.' Her last stratagem rejected, Jane 'could not be comforted by any mirth', even on New Year's Day, despite her friends' best efforts. When Lachlan left on 3 January 1796, her 'distress was very great'.[81]

Longing for Lachlan, Jane's health deteriorated once more. During this 'painful period' she 'had a full opportunity of distinguishing her real friends from those that were not so'.[82] Amongst the former were Colonel James Kerr and his wife Anne. She moved in with them at their country house, The Mount, near Government House in Parel. Dorothea Oakes and Mrs Coggan, an older widow, close to the Kerrs, were also 'sincere friends' who showed Jane 'great kindness and attention'. Not wanting to worry Lachlan, Jane assured him 'her health was in an improving state'. Their friends' letters never hinted anything was amiss, perhaps at Jane's instruction.[83] When Colonel Kerr finally wrote in March 1796 that Jane had been 'in a very delicate state of health for some time back', Lachlan immediately applied for leave and rushed to her side.

Hoping they would soon return to Staffa Lodge, Lachlan stopped at Calicut to have the house put in order. On his way back to town he encountered a man with letters from Jane and sat down on the road to read them. To his 'inexpressible joy', he read she was pregnant. Such was his delight at the news he was to become a 'happy, happy father' that he read the letters 'over and over at least twenty times – almost, devouring them with kisses!' His housekeeper had to remind him it was getting late and he might miss his ship's departure. He sprang to his feet, 'more anxious than ever to get to Bombay to fold my darling Jane to my heart'.

Jane waited anxiously as the ship bearing Lachlan – coincidentally called the *Jane* – battled difficult weather, taking 'a most tedious, tiresome' three weeks to get to Bombay. When he arrived on 6 May 1796, it was a 'dreadful shock' to find his wife 'almost a perfect Skeleton', 'just in life, and that is all'. He lamented:

> My Angel is in good spirits, and fancies herself pregnant, which gives her great pleasure and contributes to render her insensible to the unhappy and cruel malady with which she is at present afflicted – but alas! – it is only a temporary and pleasing delusion.[84]

Advised sea air might help, Lachlan decided they should sail to China. Growing numbers of British vessels – including Morley's ship, the *Sarah* – were making this voyage from Bombay. Mostly owned by private traders rather than the East India Company, they sought to profit from the insatiable demand for Chinese porcelain, silk and, most of all, tea, back home. The Chinese had little interest in European products, so had to be paid in silver, though there was a growing market for Indian cotton and spices, and more significantly, illicit opium.

Canton (modern Guangzhou), at the mouth of the Pearl River, was the sole Chinese port open to foreign merchants. However, Europeans were only allowed to live there during the trading season from October to January. Foreign women were banned altogether, so merchants with families tended to live in nearby Macao, controlled by Portugal since 1557.[85] The Portuguese were as yet the only European power with a foothold in China; the British would not establish themselves in Hong Kong until 1842, following the First Opium War.

Jane had 'no apprehension of danger' and 'willingly submitted to undertake the voyage'.[86] But they had trouble finding a ship. Finally, Captain Lestock Wilson, a 'very genteel, sensible, pleasant man', who traded regularly to China (and incidentally had Jamaican connections) agreed to give them passage aboard the *Exeter*, insisting they travel free of charge.[87]

They set sail on 18 May 1796. Jane, still seeming blithely unaware of her condition, laughed and chattered and made lists of toys she wanted

Macao *c.*1800. Painting by an anonymous Chinese artist.

to buy in Macao for her godchildren. She was probably thinking of *sing-songs*, the elaborate mechanical and musical toys gifted by British merchants to Chinese officials to grease the wheels of trade. During the six-week voyage Jane's fever disappeared, she took daily exercise walking on the quarter deck, and 'slept tolerably without the assistance of laudanum'.[88] Lachlan began to hope she might recover.

The *Exeter* arrived in Macao on 2 July. Jane rose at daybreak to pack 'all her clothes and trunks with her own hands, ate a hearty breakfast and was in most charming spirits'. She cheerfully endured four hours battling wind and tide to get from ship to shore; remaining 'stout and hearty' enough to enjoy meeting the welcome party. Like Bombay society in miniature, British expatriates in Macao attempted to retain European ways, amusing themselves with regular parties, dinners and balls.[89] Jane and Lachlan were 'pleased and gratified' by their new acquaintance, who offered 'every assistance in their power'.

The house Lachlan had hired was not ready, so he and Jane stayed with local merchant David Reid.[90] Reid, Beale & Co. was the only private British firm in Canton, an antecedent of Hong Kong-based conglomerate Jardine Matheson, which today employs over 400,000 people in China and Southeast Asia, operating everything from hotels to car factories. Reid evaded East India Company oversight under cover of a Danish official post, gaining the moniker of 'Danish Captain'; his partner and fellow Scot, Daniel Beale, meanwhile, was the Prussian Consul.[91] Reid and Beale were increasingly profiting from illegally smuggling opium from Bengal into China.[92] So Jane and Lachlan's host and new friends were essentially drug-dealers, whose activities would in time help to precipitate the First Opium War.

But Jane would hardly have time to enjoy their hospitality. On their second morning in Macao, she woke 'excessively ill and in very great pain, complaining of a great Heat and lightness, and breathing remarkably hard and short'. Her maid Marianne fetched Lachlan. Reid ran to find Dr Alexander Duncan, East India Company surgeon to the factory in Canton. Lachlan feared Jane would 'breathe her last before he would arrive', but Dr Duncan appeared in just a few minutes. Jane was already 'a good deal easier and more composed'. A draught of red wine and spices immediately 'appeared to relieve her pain and shortness of breath'; the doctor prescribed a 'concentrated tincture of yellow bark'.

Despite her illness, or perhaps because of it, Jane was keen to be 'comfortably lodged in a House of our own'. On 5 July they moved to one Jane found 'large, commodious, and pleasantly situated with regard to air and prospect'. Just three days later, Dr Duncan was summoned to Jane's bedside once more. He gravely informed Lachlan: 'there was not the smallest probability of hope remaining of her recovery – her disease was beyond the power of remedy from any medicinal aid; and it was impossible she could live many days longer.'

Though Lachlan did his best to put on a brave face, and remained religiously by Jane's side, he frequently had to yield to his agonies and 'retire to give vent in some adjoining apartment'. He convinced himself his 'beloved Angel never once apprehended that she was in danger', despite the fact that she must have heard him sobbing in the next room. If she did know she was dying, she never mentioned it to Lachlan; 'not a murmur, not a single complaint … ever escaped her lips the whole time, although it was evident she suffered a great deal of pain'. This she bore with 'fortitude, ease, calmness and resignation'. Perhaps it was easier to sustain the delusion her symptoms were caused by the long-wished-for pregnancy. Or could she just not bear discussing the awful truth?

On the night of 13 July, Jane found with surprise 'her feet were no use to her' when she attempted to walk on the terrace with Lachlan as usual whilst her bed was being made. The next morning, she was 'very ill, occasionally much discomposed, and could eat nothing; – but still continued perfectly collected, and sound in all her faculties.' Elizabeth Beale – one of few British wives in Macao, and so, like Anna Shaw in Calicut, a natural ally – came to see her and sat by her bedside until midday 'and though it hurt her to speak, she conversed with this Lady as calmly and rationally as ever she did when in sound good health'.

But at 5 a.m. on 15 July, the 'fatal and cruel Malady with which she was afflicted carried her off', as Lachlan held her in his arms.[93] She was just twenty-three. Bordering on hagiography, Lachlan wrote: 'She died as she has always lived – like an angel and a saint – with perfect ease and tranquillity, resigning her soul to heaven without pain or struggle or even a sigh.' Distraught, he 'clung to her lovely and beloved corpse, bathing it with my tears, and embracing it as if it were still possessed of life for near an hour after she had expired!' Reid and the doctor had to forcibly drag him away from Jane's body, insisting on the 'impropriety of persisting any longer in such conduct'.

Jane's coffin was made in less than ten hours, 'constructed – after the Chinese manner … which preserves the body sweet and incorruptible for many years; and also admits of its being removed from one place to another without injury'.[94] Although mummification usually conjures up images of ancient Egypt, the practice featured in several cultures around the world; the Chinese had mastered the art well before the birth of Christ. The association between China and mummification was so strong Karl Marx used it as a metaphor, writing that the First Opium War had caused China to disintegrate, like 'a mummy carefully preserved in a hermetically sealed coffin ... brought into contact with the open air'. In 1971, the incredibly well-preserved body of Xin Zhui, Lady Dai, who died in 169 BCE, was discovered in Hunan Province. Her body had been wrapped in ten layers of silk, cocooned in four lacquered coffins, made airtight by several feet of clay and charcoal, and submerged in twenty-one litres of acidic liquid found to have traces of mercury.[95] While Jane's corpse is unlikely to have had such elaborate treatment, Lachlan seems to have taken some comfort in knowing his beloved wife's body would remain intact. He was allowed to embrace Jane one more time before the coffin closed forever. Lachlan was sure nothing would ever 'efface from my remembrance the fearful and distracting horrors of these seven eventful sorrowful days'. He donned a black crepe armband, 'the least respect I was bound to pay to her beloved memory', and shut himself away for a month 'to endeavour to compose my spirits'.[96] The armband stayed on for almost four years. Marianne 'bewailed and lamented' Jane's loss in 'the most affecting manner', perhaps mostly out of anxiety about her own fate. She tried to comfort Lachlan, coming to his bedside, holding his hand, and talking to him, endeavouring 'to console and divert my attention', but her attempts had the opposite effect.[97]

During his confinement, Lachlan poured his heart out in lengthy letters to friends and family, detailing Jane's last days in minute detail. The 'mournful and fatal event' had 'not only unhinged and affected my mind most deeply and severely – but has, also, deranged all my present plans and pursuits on life – and rendered me indifferent to all future ones.' Lachlan began to blame himself. If only he had sent Jane back to England in 1795 or 1796, he 'had not a doubt but I should have preserved her precious life'.[98] He resolved never to marry again in India or take a wife there from Britain.

When Lachlan learnt 'the bigoted and superstitious Portuguese' did not allow any 'Protestant or Heretic (as they denominate us) to be buried in their churches or consecrated places', he decided to take Jane's body back to Bombay. This was not straightforward. The Chinese buried their dead as soon as possible; corpses were considered so unlucky no one would want one on their ship. Lachlan spent weeks in Canton, battling many 'vexatious and provoking mortifying impediments from the infamous and litigious Chinese Government'. Eventually, after 'bribing high and paying a good deal of money', permission was granted 'as a very great favor'. He then had to return to Macao where he had left Jane's corpse behind with all his servants and baggage, and charter his own boat to sail eighty miles back towards Canton to meet Morley's ship, the *Sarah*, at Whampoa (modern-day Pazhou) Island. Still fearful of 'farther detention', Lachlan concealed Jane's coffin 'in a very strong wooden case of a square shape; so that no one can know what it contains.'[99]

Lachlan spent Jane's last voyage in 'hourly fear of falling' into the hands of 'the enemy's cruizers'. His apprehension was well justified, as a French fleet captained by Admiral de Sercey was just then setting out from Batavia (modern Jakarta) intent on intercepting British ships from Macao. Luckily for Lachlan, he reached Bombay safely on 13 January 1797. Eighteen days later de Sercey ambushed six East India Company ships headed for China in the Bali Strait.

Lachlan complained vociferously:

> I might have been saved all this expense and trouble, were it not for the foolish obstinacy and superstitious tenacity of the Chinese to old ridiculous customs; to which they are so bigoted that they will not allow the slightest deviation from any of them.

Though he had reason to be frustrated, his extreme language was typical of his countrymen at the turn of the nineteenth century. British admiration of China's civilisation, culture and wealth was being overtaken by resentment of the limitations placed on foreign trade, and lack of reciprocal respect for Britain.

Chinese justice was increasingly perceived as 'barbarous' following the Lady Hughes Affair of 1784. The gunner of the *Lady Hughes*, a Bombay ship docked in Canton harbour, accidentally shot two Chinese sailors while saluting a passing European vessel. The British were outraged when the Chinese subsequently arrested the ship's supercargo, and even more so when the gunner whom they sacrificed in exchange was executed by strangulation, after interrogation, but without trial.[100] The crisis brought all trade to a halt, exposing the fragility of the British foothold in China.

By the time Lachlan and Jane arrived in Macao, Emperor Qianlong's refusal to grant the British a permanent embassy in Beijing, their own trading post, or any easing of trade regulations, was still rankling. Lord Macartney had led an unsuccessful British embassy to China in 1792. The letter the Emperor gave him to deliver to King George III proclaimed 'our Celestial Empire possesses all things in prolific abundance'; the Chinese had 'no need to import the manufactures of outside barbarians'. Granting these inhabitants of a lonely remote island 'cut off from the world by intervening wastes of sea' access to Chinese goods represented an indulgence for which they should be eternally grateful.[101]

Jane was buried in Bombay's European Cemetery, on Queen's Road (now Maharshi Karve Road), on 16 January 1797, six months after her death. At this 'last awful and mournful ceremony', her old friend John Forbes, 'who really lamented her loss as if he had been her Father', walked as chief mourner, and 'six of her most particular and intimate friends' – two major-generals (Balfour and Nicholson), her old admirer, Commodore Thistleton, and three colonels (Kerr, Oakes and Gore) – were her pall-bearers, followed by a 'very numerous and respectable company of friends and acquaintances of the first rank and consequence in this settlement', by whom she was 'universally and sincerely regretted'.[102]

Feeling the need to create a shrine to his personal saint, Lachlan composed a 475-word epitaph. Following an account of her life and death, he extolled Jane as a pattern for other women: 'In her Manners she was mild, affable and polite. In her Disposition sweet and even. In her Opinions liberal. And in her Appearance elegant without extravagance. True Christianity gave a superior lustre to all her virtues.' As her 'fond, affectionate and disconsolate husband', he intended the tombstone to be 'a lasting Monument of their mutual disinterested Love and Affection for One another. For he can safely and without Vanity affirm that never yet lived a happier or a more contented couple in WEDLOCK.'[103]

Lachlan spared no expense. Perhaps inspired by the 'superb' black marble tomb of St Francis Xavier he had seen in Goa, he ordered these words inscribed on one of 'the best and most elegant black marble slabs that can be procured in England'.[104] The cost doubled when the first tombstone was damaged in transit and a second one had to be sent. The monument was finally unveiled on 16 October 1800 – Jane's twenty-eighth birthday. Returning to weep beside her grave, Lachlan recalled their short time together as 'by far the happiest period of my whole life', mourning 'all that constituted that happiness lies mouldering dust'.[105]

Jane's will, made in Calicut in May 1795, was simple, leaving her £6,000, plus interest, to her husband, but also a further £1,000 (presumably the money Lachlan had settled on her when they married) to her poverty-stricken sister, Rachel Wilkins.[106] She also bequeathed a boy named Cassius – perhaps son to Dinah, Fanny or Jenny – to her brother John Swinton Jarvis. Five other children were to have 'their freedom forever'. Jane had inherited Mathias, Phibba and Quasheba from her mother two years earlier. Perhaps the other two, Fanny and Jack, were also Dinah, Fanny or Jenny's children.[107]

But, as neither Jane's will nor her codicil was witnessed, they were declared null and void. Lachlan inherited everything: 'much more money than I shall ever, I hope, live sufficiently long to spend'.[108]

Though not legally obliged to do so, Lachlan did his best to carry out Jane's wishes. With no confidence in Rachel Wilkins's husband, he established a trust for her with Dorothea as a trustee.[109] He also obtained army commissions for Rachel's sons and later tried to help her daughter Louisa find an eligible husband in Bombay. Despite his best efforts – including purchasing for her 'a couple of smart little slave girls … the cheaper the better' – Louisa made an 'impudent union'. The groom was Lachlan's cousin and namesake Lachlan MacQuarie of the 86th Regiment, who had an unfortunate tendency to 'entirely abandon himself to tippling and low drinking all day long'.[110]

Lachlan wrote to his brother-in-law in Antigua regarding the five children: Mathias, Phibba, Quasheba, Fanny and Jack. He was 'extremely anxious' that 'these poor creatures' be freed immediately. He sent a Power of Attorney to enable their emancipation, so they 'will peaceably be allowed to go wherever they please and into whatever service they like best to work honestly for their own future livelihood.' Here, Jane's instruction that the people she enslaved should be taught a trade doubtless proved useful.

Lachlan also insisted on buying freedom for Jane's childhood nurse Dinah at any price, though, given her age, he did not suppose the sum Thomas Jarvis could demand for her would be very high. On his return to Bombay, he had found a letter from Dinah to Jane requesting her liberty. Given 'the great affection she appears to have always had for my Jane', Lachlan considered it only right 'the poor old woman should spend her declining years in ease, freedom and peace', and 'enjoy her liberty and be her own mistress during the remainder of her days'.[111]

Aware how valuable clothing was, especially to enslaved people, Lachlan gifted Dinah £10 'in clothes and money'. He also sent her Jane's shroud and a wrapper (or overgarment) she had specifically requested. When dispatching Jane's clothes (or at least those not 'spoiled and damaged by the white ants and wet weather') to Dorothea, he suggested she send Dinah and her daughters 'a few old things out of them', 'not of use in fashionable England'. He also arranged for all the other people Jane had enslaved – including Cassius, who was not being freed – to have one guinea to buy a suit of clothes.[112]

Lachlan gave Marianne 'a very strong certificate ... of her being <u>perfectly free</u> – and of her never having been even considered for a moment as a slave'. His warning 'to keep this Certificate carefully locked up in her little trunk of clothes' suggests an awareness her freedom might be challenged in the future. Like George and Hector, Lachlan decided Marianne should take the surname of Jarvis 'in honour of her late beloved mistress'. After her christening, he sent her to school in Bombay. When her schoolmistress left India in 1798, Marianne chose to go and work for Mrs Coggan, whom she would have got to know when Jane was staying with the Kerrs, instead of a newly arrived family from England. Mrs Coggan promised Lachlan she would 'take every possible care' of Marianne and continue her education. No further trace of Marianne Jarvis has yet been found.[113]

Jane's money also financed two of her brothers' further colonial adventures. Lachlan sent £300 to George Ralph Payne Jarvis, also offering him a £1,500 loan, and to underwrite a tour of Bengal. He also sent him a 'handsome' hookah pipe set with a silver mouthpiece, 'of the newest fashion', but more significantly, 'the choice and gift of your heavenly angelic sister Jane'.[114] Sorry for his 'many misfortunes and losses during this unfortunate war', Lachlan sent £200 to John Swinton Jarvis in Antigua. He had wanted to have a miniature of Jane belonging to John Swinton copied 'by the very best and most eminent artist in London'. But it had been lost, along with John Swinton's 15,000-acre estate, when the French captured the Dutch half of St Martin in 1795. Lachlan asked John Swinton to offer a reward of fifty guineas for the safe return of this 'precious relic'.[115]

Such threads, stitching together Britain's Caribbean and Indian colonies, were legion. Richard Oswald, his partners the Boyds, Martha Swinburne's brother Joseph Baker and her son-in-law Paul Benfield all straddled the empire in investments and interests (as did the Franks family we will meet in Chapter 8). Women from enslaving families like the Jarvises – for example Frances Dalzell's relations the Morses – married East India Company men or serving soldiers. Mary Gaynor of Antigua, endowed with a fortune of £200,000, married MP and banker Sir George Colebrooke (we will meet him again in Chapter 8) in 1754. He went on to be a director and then chairman of the East India Company.[116] Two of their sons became Company writers; the youngest, Henry Thomas Colebrooke, a Sanskrit scholar, founded the Royal Asiatic Society, and, in a further colonial leap, purchased land in South Africa. George's great-nephew Sir William Macbean George Colebrooke served in uniform in India, Sri Lanka and Java, then became Lieutenant Governor of the Bahamas, Governor of the Leewards, and finally Barbados – overseeing the difficult decades immediately following emancipation.[117] Eliza Kearton Horne, of St Vincent, married George Hamilton Cox, an East India army captain; their firstborn George William Cox went into the Church and wrote a *History of the Establishment of British Rule in India* (1881); another son, Colonel Edmund Henry Cox of the Royal Marine Artillery, fired the first shot against Sevastopol in the Crimean War.[118] Overall, at least 300 Caribbean enslaving families were also present in India during the eighteenth and early nineteenth centuries.[119]

Lachlan used his £6,000 inheritance from Jane towards buying 12,000 acres on the Isle of Mull from his uncle Murdoch Maclaine.[120] The remainder came from regimental funds and army prize money accumulated during his military service in India and Egypt. He fought at Seringapatam in 1799, where Tipu Sultan was killed, sharing the spoils – inlaid boxes, lockets, rings and jewels – with several Jarvis relations.[121] In 1804, Lachlan returned to Scotland with his brother Charles, and his Indian servant George Jarvis, who had accompanied him on all his campaigns (Hector Jarvis had either escaped Lachlan or been kidnapped for resale in Calcutta in October 1799). The conquering hero sat down to a jovial dinner at Mull's Callachally inn with his family and friends, and announced he would name the estate Jarvisfield in honour of his late wife.[122] Lachlan also gave Jane's name to his first child with his second wife, Elizabeth Campbell, whom he married in 1807. Sadly, this Jane Jarvis was even more short-lived than the first, dying before she was three months old, causing her bereft father 'deep distress of mind'.[123]

While he considered it dangerous to take a wife to India, Lachlan saw no problem with Elizabeth accompanying him to Australia when he was appointed Governor of New South Wales, to replace the recently deposed William Bligh, of *Mutiny on the Bounty* fame, in 1809. The Indian George Jarvis also made the journey, later marrying Mary Jelly, a Government House chambermaid who had arrived as a convict. Lachlan became the state's longest-serving Governor, holding the position until 1821. When he died in London in 1824, Elizabeth discovered he had kept to the last a little box containing 'Trinkets, Pocket Books, and different little things of that sort' belonging to Jane.[124]

Lachlan is sometimes called 'the father of Australia'. He oversaw the construction of no fewer than 265 public buildings, roads and other infrastructure, and founded many settlements and schools. He created new public departments, reorganised the police force, issued the colony's first coinage and encouraged the establishment of its first bank (now Westpac). During his 'reign', the population more than tripled, the number of sheep grew tenfold, and cultivated land increased from 7,500 to 32,000 acres. He took a more open-minded view than many on the question of whether former convicts could become reformed characters. As one biographer put it: 'he found a gaol, he left a burgeoning colony'.

However, while Governor of New South Wales, Lachlan commanded punitive, genocidal expeditions against Indigenous Australians. In April 1816, he ordered three military detachments to march 'into the Interior and remote parts of the Colony, for the purpose of Punishing the Hostile Natives, by clearing the Country of them entirely'. He authorised his soldiers 'to fire on them to compel them to surrender; hanging up on Trees the Bodies of such Natives as may be killed ... in order to strike the greater terror into the Survivors'.[125] A week later, in what is now known as the Appin massacre, troops commanded by Captain James Wallis attacked an encampment of Dharawal and Gandangara people by the Cataract River, shooting indiscriminately and chasing them over the 'precipitous banks of a deep rocky creek'. The exact number killed is unknown. The soldiers counted fourteen bodies, including those of old men, women and children. Three men including a warrior named Cannabaygal were decapitated, their bodies hung from trees, their skulls later sent to the Edinburgh Phrenological Society. Lachlan declared his instructions had been 'executed ... to my entire satisfaction'.[126]

Though Lachlan's mausoleum on the Isle of Mull still stands, the 'lasting monument' to Jane he erected in Mumbai was destroyed with the European Cemetery in the 1950s. The space is now a public park, named after twentieth-century Congress Party leader Sadashiv Kanoji Patil. Jane's *name*, however, still survives in Scotland and Australia. There is a Jane Jarvis Way, in Macquarie Fields, on the outskirts of Sydney, near the Macquarie Links golf club. And besides the Scottish Jarvisfield, thanks to the Antill family, there are also two Australian Jarvisfields. Lachlan's friend Major Henry Antill obtained land south-west of Sydney, near a settlement later named Picton after the erstwhile Governor of Trinidad. Antill called his estate Jarvisfield, stamping the name of an Antiguan enslaving family on the Australian landscape, whilst dispossessing Gandangara people who had lived there for thousands of years. Several years later, Major Antill's son Edward Spencer Antill named a sheep station he established in Queensland near the Burdekin River Jarvisfield after his childhood home. Soon afterwards, he and his employees shot fifteen Indigenous Australians – probably Bindal people – dead.[127]

The Jarvis name was also passed on to Indian enslaved people, George, Hector and Marianne – British enslavers didn't stop at the Caribbean. George Jarvis's story is almost as international as Jane's, and resulted in an Indian presence in nineteenth-century Mull. He and his family moved to the island with Lachlan after he left Australia. Lachlan made provision for George in his will, and in 1829 his widow Elizabeth endowed the Macquarie Trust to provide for George's descendants. Now known as the Elizabeth Henrietta Macquarie Trust, it still distributes a few thousand pounds a year to disadvantaged residents of Mull.[128]

Jane's story – spanning the globe from Antigua to England, India and China – and her name, which travelled even further, reveal how Caribbean colonies were intertwined with the global Empire. The Jarvis family wealth supported both Lachlan and George Ralph Payne Jarvis's military careers, and thus the expansion of British rule in India. Inheriting Jane's fortune helped power Lachlan's ascent in the world, culminating in his transformation of Australia, where institutions such as Macquarie Bank and Macquarie University still bear his name. Lachlan was not the only man who had profited from enslaved labour to play a key role in settling Australia. No fewer than 125 individuals, including prominent bankers, politicians, landowners and other establishment figures there, had inherited wealth from the Caribbean, some through marrying heiresses like Jane.[129] Thus, these tainted fortunes exerted influence far beyond metropolitan Britain, into the furthest reaches of her Empire.

Portrait of Lady Elizabeth Webster, née Vassall (later Lady Holland), with her son, later Sir Godfrey Webster, 5th baronet, and her spaniel Pierrot, a gift from her lover, Lord Henry Spencer, by Louis Gauffier, Florence, 1794.

7

Elizabeth Vassall (1771–1845)

Married off to an older man, Elizabeth romps through the salons of Grand Tour Europe, leaving lovers and scandal in her wake. In a bombastic second act, she reinvents herself as society hostess and political mover-and-shaker extraordinaire.

Mrs Phillis felt tired and hungry when she woke on the first Sunday of March 1818. She and many other people enslaved at Friendship and Greenwich in Westmoreland, Jamaica, had arrived at neighbouring Cornwall the previous midnight 'dressed out in their best clothes, and accompanied with drums, rattles, and their whole orchestra'. They woke the owner, Matthew Gregory Lewis – known as 'Monk' Lewis after his 1796 hit Gothic novel *The Monk* – by singing and dancing under his bedroom window. He interpreted this as a 'serenade' showing 'their *enjoyment* on my return'; it's rather more likely they intended to disturb him.

Having spent the night carousing in the village, Mrs Phillis and the others called on Lewis at breakfast. But when everyone else headed home, she stayed behind to ask for news of her enslaver, Elizabeth, Lady Holland. Mrs Phillis's mother had been Elizabeth's nurse, and 'she was very particular in her enquiries as to her health, her children, their ages and names.' Lewis gave her 'plentiful provision of bread, butter, plantains, and cold ham from the breakfast table'. She was so famished she sat down and started eating straight away. She then resolved to 'carry the rest to her piccaninny at home' – probably her twelve-year-old son Richmond – and took her leave.[1]

Half an hour later Mrs Phillis was back. She asked Lewis tentatively for 'a *bit* [7½d coin] to buy tobacco'. When he instead gave her a *macaroni* (a Mexican quarter dollar), she gave 'a great squall of delight'. 'Oh!', she exclaimed, 'now I will not buy tobacco but a fowl!' She promised Lewis she would bring him 'a chicken from it for your dinner' on his next visit, if it wasn't stolen, 'a piece of extraordinary good luck' of which she 'entertain[ed] but slender hopes'.

Mrs Phillis left again, but soon reappeared, exclaiming, 'Well! here me come to massa again!' The food he'd given her had been 'so good, she could not help going on eating and eating, till she had eaten the whole'. Might he possibly give her 'another bit of cold ham to carry home to her child'? Lewis ordered Cubina, a twenty-five-year-old stablehand he favoured, to give her 'a great hunch of it'.[2] Mrs Phillis then departed for good; leaving Lewis to ruminate over the strange fact that she had been suckled at the same breast as his friend Lady Holland.

Lady Holland was born Elizabeth Vassall at Sweet River Pen in Westmoreland, Jamaica, on 25 March 1771.[3] She would be the only child of Richard and Mary Vassall, who had married in New York a year before. Mary was the daughter of Major Thomas Clarke, who had named his home on the Hudson River, now in the heart of fashionable Manhattan, 'Chelsea, as being the retreat of an old war-worn veteran who had seen much service in the British army'.[4]*

The Vassalls, originally Huguenot refugees to England from Caen in Normandy, had been involved in the English colonial project from its inception, amongst the earliest traffickers of Africans, and investors in Virginia and Massachusetts.[5] Elizabeth's great-great-grandfather John Vassall, 'a sober, rational man' and skilled cartographer born in New England, was the first family member to acquire land in Jamaica. In 1669, he was granted 1,000 acres near Black River in St Elizabeth. As the youngest of John's seven sons, Elizabeth's great-grandfather, Florentius, was not set to inherit much. So, he looked to expand into Westmoreland, patenting 160 acres there in 1708.[6] Like so many men in this book, he made a lucrative marriage, into the Herring family, gaining a Beckford brother-in-law. By 1754, *his* son, Elizabeth's grandfather, also named Florentius, owned a vast 8,357 acres across Westmoreland, St Elizabeth and St James, enslaving hundreds of people.[7]

---

* Retired soldiers have lived at the Royal Hospital, Chelsea, since 1692, and are still known as Chelsea pensioners today. Chelsea is also still the name of the New York neighbourhood surrounding the old Clarke estate.

Vassall Family Tree

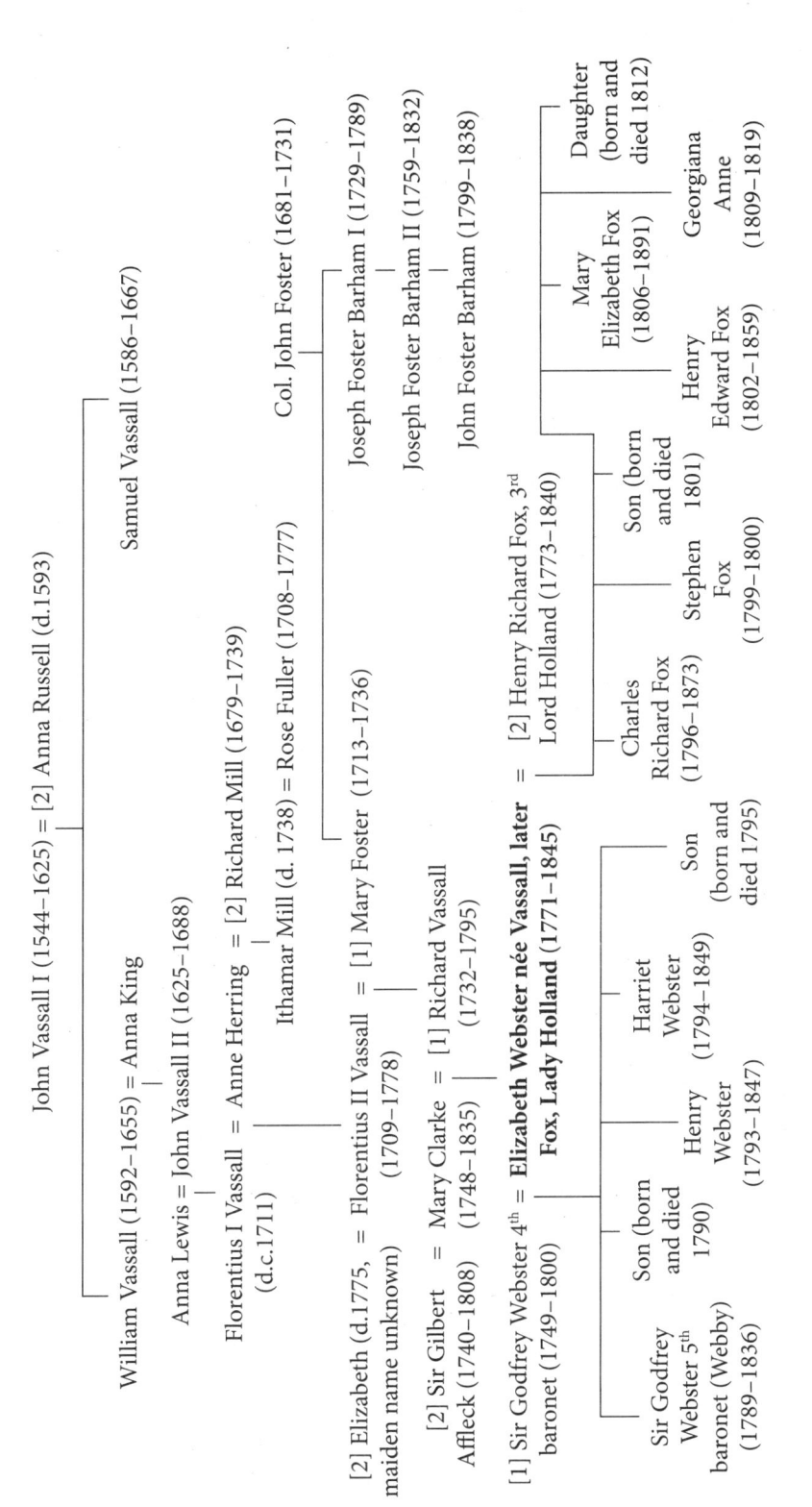

John Vassall I (1544–1625) = [2] Anna Russell (d.1593)

William Vassall (1592–1655) = Anna King

Samuel Vassall (1586–1667)

Anna Lewis = John Vassall II (1625–1688)

Florentius I Vassall = Anne Herring = [2] Richard Mill (1679–1739)
(d.c.1711)

Ithamar Mill (d. 1738) = Rose Fuller (1708–1777)

Col. John Foster (1681–1731)

[2] Elizabeth (d.1775, = Florentius II Vassall = [1] Mary Foster (1713–1736)
maiden name unknown)   (1709–1778)

Joseph Foster Barham I (1729–1789)

Joseph Foster Barham II (1759–1832)

John Foster Barham (1799–1838)

[2] Sir Gilbert = Mary Clarke = [1] Richard Vassall
Affleck (1740–1808)   (1748–1835)   (1732–1795)

[1] Sir Godfrey Webster 4th = **Elizabeth Webster née Vassall, later** = [2] Henry Richard Fox, 3rd
baronet (1749–1800)   **Fox, Lady Holland (1771–1845)**   Lord Holland (1773–1840)

Sir Godfrey   Son (born   Henry   Harriet   Son   Charles   Stephen   Son (born   Mary   Henry   Georgiana   Daughter
Webster 5th   and died   Webster   Webster   (born and   Richard Fox   Fox   and died   Elizabeth Fox Edward Fox   Anne   (born and
baronet (Webby) 1790   (1793–1847) (1794–1849) died 1795)   (1796–1873)   (1799–1800) 1801)   (1806–1891)   (1802–1859)   (1809–1819)   died 1812)
(1789–1836)

Elizabeth spent her earliest years at Sweet River Pen, close to her grandfather Florentius's home, Friendship, which adjoined his other plantation, Greenwich. Like Jane Jarvis, Elizabeth was nursed by an enslaved woman, whose name is unrecorded. The woman's daughter Phillis, born a year later, was perhaps Elizabeth's first playmate.[8]

Elizabeth considered her father Richard 'weak in character, as he idolised my mother and was completely subjected to her dominion.'[9] Her grandfather Florentius was also a dominant figure in the family, firmly cemented into the island's social elite. In 1767 'Mrs Vassall, old Florentius's wife', had been amongst the 'richest dressed of all the gentlemen & ladies at the governor's ball, on the King's birthday'.[10] Inordinately proud of his ancestors, Florentius erected a memorial to them in King's Chapel, Boston, in 1766, celebrating how 'the gallant'

Robert Kirkwood's plan of Friendship and Greenwich in 1784.

John Vassall had fitted out two ships 'at his own expense' to fight the Spanish Armada in 1588, and honoured his son Samuel, who had 'boldly refused to submit' to Charles I's arbitrary taxation.* He also made careful notes on the family history in a memorandum book, 'sometimes to be looked over by myself and by my son & family when I am no more'.

In the same book, Florentius revealed his callous attitude towards the men, women and children he enslaved: 'In June 1757, I had 545 negroes, since I bought above 100 and had above 100 born, and in January 1768 I had not above that number so that I must have lost 200 negroes in ten years.' The cruel treatment Florentius encouraged in his overseers makes this death toll unsurprising. The young Elizabeth probably met one of Florentius's former employees, the sadistic Thomas Thistlewood, by then a family friend, at Sweet River in the 1770s. Thistlewood remains notorious to this day for his incessant infliction of physical and sexual violence, all recorded carefully in his extensive diaries. It was Florentius Vassall who gave Thistlewood his first job on the island, and one of his first lessons in brutality. He hired Thistlewood – a frequenter of Susanna Augier's Kingston pub, the White Cross – as overseer of Vineyard Pen in St Elizabeth in July 1750. Two weeks after Thistlewood arrived, Florentius personally gave Dick, a high-status mixed-heritage driver, 300 lashes 'for his many crimes and negligencies'. Dick was so seriously wounded that it took him nine days to re-emerge from his hut.

A quick learner, Thistlewood soon decided Vineyard was 'a nest of Thieves and Villains', and began his reign of terror. In the space of eleven months he whipped eighteen out of twenty-four men on the estate thirty-one times, and seven of the eighteen women eleven times. Each whipping was at least fifty lashes, some 100 to 150; on one occasion he gave 250 lashes. Though he whipped women less frequently, he repeatedly subjected them to sexual violence. Thistlewood's first rape was committed against Marina, a Congolese woman, on 4 August 1750, just over a month after his arrival. He made her his 'housekeeper', showering her with gifts, clothing and money. He also raped nine other women there on forty-four recorded occasions, in his house, outbuildings, the enslaved people's huts, and the fields.

---

* Florentius grumbled that he had been obstructed from placing it in St Paul's Cathedral by the erection of a plaque to Sir Christopher Wren – the one that famously reads '*si monumentum requiris, circumspice*' ('if you seek his monument, look around').

Thistlewood did not stay long at Vineyard. Less than a year after he began the job he, ironically, complained about the hardships *he* was enduring, and *his* 'ill-usage'. Florentius was furious, exclaiming that if he ever received such a letter again he would 'make the Blood flow about' Thistlewood's face. After quitting Vineyard in May 1751, Thistlewood continued to perpetrate horrific physical punishments and rapes for the rest of his thirty-six years in Jamaica, noting in his diary thousands of whippings and a total of 3,852 acts of sexual violation, with 138 different women. His most infamous punishment was Derby's dose, invented at John Cope and William Dorrill's Egypt plantation in 1756. He ordered Derby, who had been caught eating sugar cane, be flogged, then have 'salt pickle, lime juice & bird pepper' rubbed into his wounds, and, worst of all, have another man defecate in his mouth. He was then gagged, with his mouth full, for four or five hours.

Florentius sold Vineyard soon after Thistlewood's departure, transferring the people there to Westmoreland. Many, including Marina, moved to Elizabeth's childhood home, Sweet River, where their memories of Thistlewood's atrocities would endure. It would be tempting to view Thistlewood as an aberration, an extreme example of what depravity a man can sink to when given complete power over other human beings. However, it may be he was only exceptional in keeping an obsessive record of his daily atrocities. We know Florentius did not hold back with the whip, and it is possible Florentius and Richard Vassall also regularly raped enslaved women. Certainly, Thistlewood records other friends committing rape on more than one occasion.[11] As we saw with Sir John Gay Alleyne's visits to Newton, sexual access to women often formed part of hospitality offered to guests; visitors to Jamaica recalled 'convivial parties', where it was 'not unusual for the female slaves to be collected and shown, that each may choose a companion for the night'.[12]

Florentius died at Sweet River on 9 June 1778, but had wanted to be buried in London beside his wife Elizabeth, who had died three years before. Thomas Thistlewood recorded that his 'bowels, &.c were took out, he was enclosed in a wood coffin & then in lead soldered up'. It took most of the morning following the funeral for the coffin to be carried to the port. After some hours in the heat, 'his smell was very offensive'. The procession 'stopped in the road almost every minute'; the coffin was 'twice, or oftener, thrown down into the road'. Thistlewood found this 'ludicrous', but the enslaved men were probably dropping it on purpose; a death ritual signifying their contempt for the deceased. When burying their own dead, enslaved coffin bearers became mediums, stopping regularly, as if made to do so by the departing spirit, who directed them to significant places or people, especially those who had injured them in life. By contrast, Florentius's friends arranged a seventy-gun salute, one shot for each year he had lived, when the ship bearing his remains set sail.[13]

Florentius's death made Elizabeth, his only son's only child, his heiress. She was just seven years old. While her father Richard became beneficiary of Friendship, Greenwich and Sweet River for his lifetime (subject to several annuities for female relatives), Elizabeth would inherit in full on his death.[14]

Elizabeth now moved to London with her parents. A 'mulatto servant boy', Robert Loftus, accompanied them; he would work for the family throughout Elizabeth's childhood.[15] Richard asked Elizabeth's maternal uncle, New York lawyer Clement Cooke Clarke, to act as his attorney in Jamaica.[16] The Vassalls' sugar and rum would continue to be sold in London by Florentius's stepbrother-in-law Rose Fuller (who, as was common practice at the time, had been given his mother's surname as his first name), and his brother Stephen.[17]

Elizabeth recalled a gloomy existence as an only child, left alone 'in a back room' of her family's house in Golden Square, near Piccadilly.[18] The 'warm, ingenuous affection of youth was never drawn out, but blunted and repressed' by a 'father and mother who did not always agree with each other, and never agreed about me'. With no formal schooling, young Elizabeth was 'entirely left, not from system, but from fondness and inactivity, to follow my own bent'. She devoured books; 'a desire for information' became her 'ruling passion'. Then, 'an old friend of my father's, struck by my looks or my character, to a degree adopted me and became my tutor'.[19] This was their neighbour, Anthony Morris Storer MP, whose family estates lay close to the Vassalls' in Westmoreland. Storer was well qualified as an intellectual mentor. An avid classicist and collector, the 3,000 books and prints he bequeathed to his alma mater, Eton, are now considered the library's 'crowning glory'.[20]

Elizabeth was 'brought up for many years absolutely together' with Charles Rose Ellis, who would become a lifelong friend and a key figure in the struggle against emancipation. Ellis also came from an old Jamaican family, inheriting people and property in St James, Hanover and St Catherine worth over £20,000 at the age of ten, after his parents died in a shipwreck returning to England from Jamaica.[21]

It was only when Elizabeth became a teenager that her family began to pay her any attention 'beyond the necessaries of life'. Not only was she in line to inherit a fortune, but it was becoming clear she would be a great beauty. After spying Elizabeth at a masquerade in February 1786, the playwright and friend of Dr Johnson, Richard Paul Jodrell, composed this ode:

> Imperial nymph, ill-suited is thy name
> To speak the wonders of that radiant frame,
> Where'er thy sovereign form on Earth is seen
> All eyes are *vassals*; thou alone art Queen.[22]

Another admirer sent her his poems, with a dog to protect her till she 'a bolder guardian took'. Elizabeth was not impressed. When he tried to propose with the words 'I love books as much as you do, and we may fairly hope to have a very literary little family', she almost laughed in his face, leaving her mother to send him on his way.[23]

A more serious suitor was thirty-nine-year-old Sir Godfrey Webster, 4th Baronet of Battle Abbey in East Sussex. William the Conqueror had built the Abbey in 1070 to give thanks for his famous victory at Hastings, insisting the high altar be placed in the exact spot King Harold had been killed. After the Reformation, the church was destroyed and the abbot's lodging transformed into a private home, acquired by the Websters in 1721. Though newly elected as Whig MP for Seaford, a constituency near Brighton with a tiny electorate of fewer than 100 voters, Sir Godfrey had little aptitude for politics, remaining silent throughout his first Parliamentary session. He preferred spending his time in the countryside, overseeing his estates, foxhunting, and gambling to excess.

The Webster estates extended beyond Sussex into Surrey, Hampshire, Essex, Hertfordshire and Derbyshire. The family had previously profited from enslavement and trafficking Africans. Sir Godfrey's great-grandfather, also named Godfrey, had been a tobacco merchant, and held £15,000 of South Sea Company stock.

However, by the time Sir Godfrey inherited in 1780, the family finances were under pressure, burdened by numerous annuities.[24] Though he insisted it was 'the elegance of Her person, and Manners, and the Excellence of her Understanding' that attracted him to Elizabeth, he also had good reason to desire her fortune. Mary Vassall did not consider Sir Godfrey a son-in-law she could 'love and admire', but Richard had no problem marrying off his fifteen-year-old daughter to a man more than twenty years her senior.[25] Elizabeth later looked back in disgust at how: 'through caprice and folly, I was thrown into the power of one who was a pompous coxcomb, with youth, beauty, and a good disposition, all to be squandered! The connection was perdition to me in every way.'

Following their marriage on 27 June 1786, Sir Godfrey swiftly removed Elizabeth, now Lady Webster, from the excitements of London society.[26] Sir Godfrey's aunt, the Dowager Lady Martha Webster, still occupied Battle Abbey, so they had to live at Rose Green, a small house nearby. Unimpressed, Elizabeth orchestrated various stunts to persuade Lady Martha to leave the Abbey. On one occasion, she and some friends 'haunted' the house with terrible groans, rattling chains and flying furniture, but the Dowager was unperturbed, exclaiming, 'I won't go'. Another time a crowd disguised as 'panic-stricken country people' arrived at the Abbey, announcing a French invasion. Their hostess merely gave them ample food and drink and told them the French would be made equally welcome. Nonetheless, Elizabeth asked daily 'if the old hag was dead yet'.

Elizabeth gave birth to her first son, Godfrey, known as 'Webby', in 1789, aged eighteen. Another son was born the following year, but died before reaching his first birthday. Elizabeth later described Battle as: 'that detested spot where I had languished in solitude and discontent the best years of my life'. Sir Godfrey increasingly displayed his violent temper; his 'menaces' terrified Elizabeth 'out of my senses'.[27]

Meanwhile the correspondence between her husband and her father grew increasingly acrimonious. Sir Godfrey had hoped marrying an heiress would instantly solve his financial problems. But his debts, exacerbated by his constant gambling, remained unpaid. Like so many absentees, Richard Vassall had not managed his Jamaican estates well from afar. By May 1788, he owed Rose and Stephen Fuller £10,435. The following year, the Fullers considered taking Richard to court, but appear to have dropped the matter after Sir Godfrey negotiated a repayment plan.[28]

Desperate for adventure, Elizabeth pleaded with Sir Godfrey to take her to Europe. In summer 1791, he agreed. After a stay in Paris, they journeyed through Switzerland; to Nice; visiting Turin, Milan, Munich, Dresden, Prague, Vienna and Venice, before reaching Naples in October

1792. On their travels, they encountered Elizabeth's childhood friend Charles Rose Ellis – who had just bought himself a seat in Parliament for £3,500 – and young Harry Swinburne, Martha's son, on his way home from Naples, where 'he was run after by all the ladies'.[29]

For the first time in her life, Elizabeth began to enjoy herself. Young, beautiful, intelligent and titled, she had an entrée into the best society. Her experience in Dresden in July 1792 was typical. Having been received at court, she found 'dinners, fetes, etc., given to me; invitations sent to people on purpose to meet "La charmante Miladi"; my dress copied, my manner studied'. As Lord Sheffield wrote to Edward Gibbon: 'People are apt to spoil her.'[30]

Elizabeth's journey was also an intellectual one; one Nice acquaintance remarked she had 'the strongest memory united with the most comprehensive mind he ever met'. She loved both seeing historic sites and attending scientific lectures; she was particularly fascinated by the 'cruel Experiment' of electrocuting a dead frog 'to prove animal electricity' she witnessed in Turin.[31]*

One night in Salerno in March 1793, while gazing at the sea from her balcony, and listening to 'the lulling sound of the waves' as 'the moon shone bright', Elizabeth 'could not help casting an anxious thought towards my dear father stretched upon a bed of sickness perhaps to rise no more'. She was relieved, though, that she 'had never done anything that could disturb his peace, or render his last moments painful from my misconduct'. More accurately, she hadn't been caught.

In June, Elizabeth received letters from England 'giving me a melancholy account of my poor father's illness', summoning her to his side. Reluctant to leave Italy, she decided to leave her children – Webby and his infant brother Henry – in Florence as 'a pledge for my return'.[32]

The journey home across war-torn Europe was not straightforward. Britain, the Netherlands, Spain and Portugal had recently joined the war being waged against Revolutionary France by Austria and Prussia. Elizabeth's French cook had to pretend to be Swiss to enter Milan. Her progress through Germany was held up by a lack of horses; the French had eaten many during the siege of Mainz. When passing within two miles of French lines near Ypres, Elizabeth felt 'Queer, not to say frightened'. Nonetheless, her natural curiosity outweighed her fear. She

---

* In 1780, Luigi Galvani – whence 'galvanise' – had discovered that an electric spark caused dead frogs' legs to twitch, igniting a major new field of Enlightenment study.

climbed a church steeple to look towards the besieged city of Dunkirk, finding the 'horizon deeply dyed with a mixture of deep red flames and smoke'.

She then passed a 'wretched night' with 'the idea of the bloody tragedy near, the recollection of the haggard countenances of the dying soldiers, and the ... probability that many of my friends were expiring'. Despite not getting a 'wink of sleep', Elizabeth determined to visit Prince Frederick, Duke of York (whose military prowess is satirised in nursery rhyme *The Grand Old Duke of York*). He invited her to dine with him and gave her a tour of his camp. She claimed to feel odd being the only woman there, but one senses that in truth, she revelled in it.

While in the Duke's tent, she heard a pattering noise like rain on the canvas. It was gunshot. The Duke ordered his band to drown out the sound; but she swiftly departed, remarking: 'I should not have dreaded French cruelty to a woman, had I not the melancholy instance of the poor Queen'.*

After dutifully visiting her father at Windsor, Elizabeth spent three months in 'odious' England, filled with 'occupations and vexation'. She spent as little time at Battle as possible, 'half afraid of being detained by some accident'. Visiting Brighton, where she found George, Prince of Wales, building his Pavilion, was more fun. He showed her 'every attention and civility'; she found him 'extremely vain'.[33] In London, George III enjoyed hearing about Elizabeth's intrepid visit to his son's camp at Dunkirk; she described corpses she'd seen on the battlefield 'with as much Rapture as any Vulture'.

Elizabeth now had her first introduction to the Whig party, through Georgiana, Duchess of Devonshire, whom she had met in Nice. The 'fashion was to be in Opposition; the Prince of Wales belonged to it ... all the beauty and wit of London were on that side'. She attended 'delightfully pleasant' parties at Devonshire House, where, she noted with glee, 'I was really very much admired, improved in my manner, and a sort of fashion and novelty by coming from abroad'. She found the Duchess's *bien aimé* Charles Grey (later Prime Minister Earl Grey) 'a fractious and *exigeant* [demanding] lover'; 'a man of violent temper and unbounded ambition' – she would know him for the rest of her life.

---

* At this time, following her husband's execution on 21 January 1793, Marie Antoinette had been separated from her children and placed in solitary confinement in Paris's Conciergerie prison.

Despite her social success in England, and Queen Charlotte herself warning her against travelling through a war zone again, Elizabeth was anxious to return to Italy. In January 1794, the Websters arrived back in Florence, having journeyed through Belgium and Germany to avoid France. Reunited to 'my supreme delight' with her sons, Elizabeth fondly wrote: 'the consciousness of being under the same roof with my dear children gives me a sort of tranquil delight, that my mind and spirits are quite calm: I even feel happy.'[34]

Travel did nothing to improve Elizabeth's relationship with her 'tormentor' Sir Godfrey, who did not share her intellectual passions. Between her 'determined love for being abroad', and his persistent gambling, they were grossly overspending. He blamed her for everything. His 'dreadful derangement' and 'paroxysms' were so terrible that one evening, 'almost choked, suffocated', Elizabeth 'sobbed [herself] sick'. On their wedding anniversary in 1793, Elizabeth contemplated suicide, lamenting: 'This fatal day seven years [ago] gave me, in the bloom and innocence of fifteen, to the power of a being who has made me execrate my life since it has belonged to him.'

Besides overspending, Elizabeth's tendency to attract a flock of admirers wherever she went placed further strain on her marriage. As she remarked, 'a pretty woman is always sure of as many lovers as she chooses', though she found 'more humiliation than glory in such a train'.[35] When one 'tiresome Scotch lover' trailed her carriage from Bex to Lausanne, she was forced to stop and speak 'with cold civility' before he 'embarrassed, took the rebuff and returned back'. When 'that abominable, wicked old fellow', Frederick Augustus Hervey, 4th Earl of Bristol and Bishop of Derry, lay dangerously ill in Naples, his attraction to Elizabeth tipped over into crazed obsession. He created a sort of shrine to her as a comfort, placing her portrait on an easel beside his bed surrounded by candles. In Florence, she was forced to get out of a carriage she was sharing with Sir Gilbert Elliot, to avoid his violent and 'pressing importunities'. His line: '*Pécher en secret, n'est point pécher*' ('to sin in secret is not to sin at all') led her to exclaim, 'Oh! what vile animals men are!'[36]

Elizabeth did not find all her admirers irredeemably vile, however. Soon after their travels commenced, she succumbed to the advances of her husband's political patron, the thirty-five-year-old Sir Thomas Pelham.[37] When he arrived in Lausanne in July 1791, a fellow traveller observed: 'Sir G is more cross than you can imagine; In short, he had just discovered that he is married, and that Mr P has a great regard for his Lady'. Besotted, Pelham always travelled with Elizabeth's portrait and a stock of her favourite books. Though she 'esteemed' him, Elizabeth 'could never return his devotion'. Nonetheless, she poked fun at her detested husband by teaching three-year-old Webby to toast Pelham's name at dinner before his father's; a jest that would come back to haunt her. Her daughter Harriet, born in Florence on 12 June 1794, may have been conceived during a visit to Pelham's house, Stanmer, near Brighton, in September 1793. Pelham certainly believed he was the father, expressing his concern about 'the particular situation you are now in'. Nonetheless, Elizabeth was (unlike some of her friends) careful to time things so Sir Godfrey could still believe the child was his.[38]

The 'first man who had ever produced the slightest emotion' in Elizabeth's heart was the young diplomat Lord Henry Spencer, second son of the 4th Duke of Marlborough. When she met him in Dresden in July 1792, Elizabeth recorded in her journal: 'he became ardently in love with me'. She was painfully embarrassed when Prince Anthony of Saxony mistook them for husband and wife, complimenting Spencer on her beauty, and remarking: 'I see by your admiration and love for her you are worthy to possess her'. Despite Spencer's best efforts, they did not meet again before his untimely death in Berlin in July 1795.[39] Some claim her son Henry – was the name significant? – born in February 1793, was fathered by Spencer, though that would make him ten weeks premature.[40]

These affairs would pale into insignificance, however, when Elizabeth met the love of her life in Florence in February 1794. It was an unpromising start: she found him 'not in the least handsome' with 'many personal defects', though she did take a scientific interest in the 'ossification of the muscles in his left leg'. Henry Richard Fox, 3rd Lord Holland, had just arrived from Spain, and Elizabeth noted: 'his complexion partakes of the Moresco hue'. With his thick black shaggy eyebrows, he bore a strong physical resemblance to his uncle, leading Whig politician Charles James Fox, also known for having skin 'of the dirtiest colour'.[41]

Henry had inherited his title and estates in Wiltshire and Kensington at the age of one. But his father Stephen and uncle Charles James Fox had – with the clichéd profligacy of the third generation – dissipated much of the family fortune founded by their grandfather through gambling and bad management.* This inspired Elizabeth with 'horror and contempt'. Perhaps thinking of Sir Godfrey too, she felt 'gamesters and spendthrifts' were 'a curse to their connections ... bringing ruin and distress'.[42]

As a young man, Charles James Fox had attracted public ridicule when, desperate to pay off his gargantuan gambling debts, he fell victim to notorious con-woman Elizabeth Harriet Grieve. She offered to set him up with one Miss Phipps, a fictional Caribbean heiress with £80,000.† When Fox ardently insisted on meeting his prospective bride, Grieve put him off, first by saying she had smallpox, then that she was pregnant. In the version recounted to Sir Walter Scott, it was only when Grieve told him the girl 'was unfortunately of a mixed colour, somewhat tinged with the blood of Africa' that he desisted. Grieve's other crimes soon caught up with her and she was sentenced to transportation to Virginia. The whole sordid story became common knowledge, inspiring two satirical poems and a play. In *The Cozeners*, Samuel Foote had the imaginary heiress impersonated by Mrs Fleece'em's Black maid from Boston, Marianne, and 'the laugh was universal so soon as the black woman appeared'.[43]

Henry's 'pleasingness of manner and liveliness of conversation' speedily outweighed Elizabeth's objections. At supper, she found him 'quite delightful; his gaiety beyond anything I ever knew; full of good stories.' He was 'eager without rashness, well-bred without ceremony'. He was also 'bent upon politics', like the uncle he idolised 'warm in favour of the Revolution', 'his principles strongly tinctured with democracy' – then considered by many as one step removed from anarchy. Elizabeth put this down to youthful folly. She thought it fortunate he was not able to say such 'foolish, violent things' in Westminster – he could not take his seat in the Lords until he turned twenty-one later that year.[44] More naturally conservative, Elizabeth concluded from 'the example of France', which 'terrifies even the moderate innovators', that 'extremes are dangerous'.[45]

Elizabeth and Henry soon became inseparable. His education at Loughborough, Eton and Christ Church, Oxford, could not have been

---

* Their grandfather Sir Stephen Fox rose from humble origins to become the 'richest commoner in the three kingdoms' thanks to the patronage of Charles II.

† According to Horace Walpole, 'There was such a person coming over, but not with half the fortune, nor known to Mrs. Grieve.' This was perhaps a member of the Kittian Phipps family. 'James Farrel Phipps', LBS: https://www.ucl.ac.uk/lbs/person/view/2146644907.

more different to her own, but, like the Swinburnes, they shared many cultural interests. Henry read aloud to her from his favourite books and wrote her florid poetry. In Florence, they toured the Uffizi Gallery; she attended his coming-of-age ball. By June 1794, Henry admitted to his sister Caroline he liked Elizabeth 'a little more than is wise'. Gossips joked his extended stay in Italy was due to his 'love of sweetmeats'; for Elizabeth it was a time of 'exquisite' happiness.

When Elizabeth's father Richard died on 28 February 1795, she wrote in her journal:

> I lost my poor father; a nobler, better man he has not left behind him. Towards me he was always fond and affectionate. His only failings arose from an excess of goodness ... His death puts me in possession of great wealth, upwards of £10,000 per annum. Detestable gold! What a lure for a villain, and too dearly have I become victim to him.[46]

The villain – Sir Godfrey – wasted no time in taking control of Elizabeth's Jamaican estates. He took on the additional name of Vassall, conforming to the stipulation in Florentius's will that 'every person to whom my plantations shall descend ... shall use the surname ... or lose their interest in my bequests'. He appointed a new attorney: Henry Waite Plummer of St Elizabeth, nephew to Thomas Plummer, a 'West India' merchant in partnership with Joseph Foster Barham (Elizabeth's first cousin once removed).[47] Plummer and Barham would replace the Fullers as consignees of the family's sugar and rum, the firm also taking on the Vassalls' debts. Sir Godfrey invested in the new West India Docks on the Isle of Dogs alongside his new agents; they named a ship plying the route to Jamaica the *Sir Godfrey Webster* in his honour.

Elizabeth's inheritance was not quite as alluring as she believed. Richard Vassall's Jamaican probate inventory recorded no personal property of value, stating only that he owed fellow enslavers James Lawrence and Richard Brissett (who we will meet again in Chapter 9) £5,645. This may be why his will modified the £15,000 Florentius had devised to Elizabeth after his death to an annual payment of £1,000 for fifteen years.[48] Elizabeth did, however, inherit over 3,000 acres Florentius had acquired in Kennebec, Maine – where the town of Vassalboro still bears his name – though neither she nor Sir Godfrey appear to have made any effort to claim it.[49]

*

By spring 1796, Elizabeth was pregnant again, this time certainly by Henry, as she had not seen Sir Godfrey since he left Florence a year before. This made divorce inevitable. While it would be a relief to be parted from her despised husband, 'the certainty of losing all my children was agonising'. Until 1839, the law dictated that fathers gained sole custody of children after a divorce. In desperation, Elizabeth developed a 'visionary scheme' to keep her favourite child. In the village of Paullo on the way to Modena from Bologna, she daubed red spots on her daughter Harriet's arms with her watercolours to convince everyone she had measles. Then she sent the servants away and put together a 'rude coffin', filling her oblong guitar case with stones, a pillow dressed in children's clothes and a wax mask. She sent this strange item to the British Consul in Livorno for burial, then travelled on to Modena to break the news of her daughter's death. Meanwhile she sent Harriet to England via Hamburg, dressed as a boy. It was later rumoured the coffin had also contained a dead baby goat. As Lord Byron put it:

> Have you heard what a lady in Italy did,
> When to spite a *cross husband* she *buried a kid*?

Sir Godfrey, who also 'doted' on Harriet, was 'wretched' on hearing the news and 'wept his lost child for some time'.[50]

Elizabeth arrived back in England in June, moving to Brompton Park, a popular address for those in similar disgrace. One of her neighbours, Lady Seymour Worsley, had scandalously separated from her husband in 1782; though he claimed damages of £20,000 from her lover, he was awarded just one shilling after the prosecution cited his predilection for watching his wife having sex with other men.[51] Elizabeth was now four months pregnant. Henry admitted this 'rendered an *éclat* [spectacle] sooner or later almost certain and any management for her character quite desperate'. Once lost, a woman's reputation was gone forever, with devastating social consequences. As Mary Bennet opines following her sister Lydia's elopement in *Pride and Prejudice*: 'loss of virtue in a female is irretrievable ... one false step involves her in endless ruin ... her reputation is no less brittle than it is beautiful'.[52]

Shortly afterwards, Sir Godfrey embarked on the lengthy legal journey towards divorce, beginning with a case for 'separation from bed and board' on grounds of adultery in the London Consistory Court.[53] His behaviour was volatile. One moment he promised 'that if no dirt was thrown at him he would throw none'; the next he challenged Henry to a duel for asking if he could have a portrait of Elizabeth left languishing in George Romney's studio. Henry found it ridiculous 'that he should risk his life for the copy when he had seemed rather pleased at getting rid of the original'.[54]

After Elizabeth and Henry eloped to France on the advice of Charles Rose Ellis, she was shunned by polite society. Even her mother Mary, though she felt 'no anger or sorrow', refused to speak to her. Henry's uncle Charles James Fox also remained silent, despite his own wife's dubious reputation.* Another uncle, General Richard Fitzpatrick, was more sympathetic, writing: 'that the step you have taken will be condemned by prudent persons must be expected, its ultimate consequences however may prove such as neither you, nor those who love you, will find any reason to lament.'

Although Henry told his sister Caroline: 'as to the rest of the world' Elizabeth had 'not even the smallest wish of endeavoring to mix with it', the social consequences of her actions pained Elizabeth deeply. Having escaped from five years' imprisonment in dull Sussex in 1791, and enjoyed the highest society for the following five, not being received at court, or in any 'respectable' home, was a heavy price to pay for the rest of her life. Over forty years later, when the young Queen Victoria asked Prime Minister Lord Melbourne if Elizabeth was upset she could not come to court, he said 'Perpetually; oh! she feels it very much.'[55]

When their son Charles Richard was born on 6 November, Henry wrote to his sister, 'They are registering the boy by the name of Vassall. It would be unseemly to call him Webster, and this will help his claim to the [Vassall] estate'.

With this irrefutable evidence of adultery, the London Consistory Court granted Sir Godfrey a separation in February 1797. The Parliamentary divorce gained royal assent on 4 July 1797; Elizabeth rejoiced her 'wretched marriage' was over.[56] But, as she feared, Sir Godfrey received custody of their two sons, threatening Elizabeth might never see them again. He had used Elizabeth's teaching Webby to toast Lord Pelham as evidence she had tried to turn their children against him.[57]

The financial settlement was overwhelmingly in Sir Godfrey's favour. Elizabeth fulminated: 'every mean device, every paltry chicane that

---

* Elizabeth Armistead, a former sex worker, had been the mistress of several aristocrats, including the Prince of Wales.

could extort money from us was had recourse to.' Sir Godfrey was awarded £6,000 damages from Henry (though he actually managed to avoid paying up due to being abroad and so beyond the court's jurisdiction). He no longer had to pay Elizabeth's annual £300 allowance and was also entitled to the £1,000 a year assigned to Elizabeth under her father's will. Most significantly, Sir Godfrey was given 'unmolested possession' of Elizabeth's Jamaican estates.[58]

Elizabeth celebrated her Independence Day with the divorce on 4 July, 'signed a deed by which I made over my whole fortune to Sir G W' on the 5th, and married Henry on the 6th. Sir Gilbert Affleck, her mother's new husband, walked her down the aisle; the new Lady Affleck affirmed: 'I am proud in saying I now have a Son to love and admire'. As Lady Webster became Lady Holland, Sir Godfrey discarded the Vassall name. Elizabeth was now 'replete with every blessing human nature is capable of relishing'. Her only regret was being two years and eight months older than her new husband – 'a horrid disparity'! [59]

Unusually for a peer, Henry did not have a country seat. Winterslow, the house that had crowned the family estates in Wiltshire, had burnt down in 1774, not long before his father's death. His mother had rushed to the nursery to rescue him, saving her own life in the process, as all other exit routes were blocked. The lack of a country home was no hardship for Elizabeth, who still shuddered at the memory of rural Sussex. She eagerly embraced the plan of making Holland House in Kensington their main residence, wishing 'to live as near town as possible'.[60]

Ostracised, Elizabeth decided to create her own social salon. The names listed in the dinner books she kept from May 1799 are a who's who of the political and intellectual elite. In the early years, the company mostly consisted of Whig grandees – 'they are all cousins' someone remarked – and Henry's old Eton and Oxford friends. Henry's adored uncle Charles James Fox found Holland House a convenient place to stay on his visits to town; it was there he and his friends decided to secede from Parliament in October 1797. Elizabeth condemned the move, remarking, 'there is bigotry in their adherence to their ineffectual principles that borders upon infatuation'.

Elizabeth thought it important to expand Henry's circle; their guest list became increasingly cosmopolitan. The Prince of Wales appeared on several occasions, as did several former and future Prime Ministers, alongside European figures such as King Louis Phillipe of France and Talleyrand. Writers and poets were also welcome, such as playwright

Richard Brinsley Sheridan – a heavy drinker, who 'lost his dinner' on at least one occasion. Over the next four decades Elizabeth would entertain the likes of Lord Byron, Ugo Foscolo, Charles Dickens and Sir Walter Scott.[61]

Matthew Gregory 'Monk' Lewis made his Holland House debut in 1797. He qualified as a writer, a politician – he served ineffectually as MP for Hindon in Wiltshire from 1796 to 1802 – and a contemporary of Henry's at Christ Church, Oxford. He and Elizabeth may also have been distantly related; certainly, the families were long acquainted as neighbours in Westmoreland where the Lewis's Cornwall estate adjoined Friendship and Greenwich. Though Elizabeth at first found him 'rather ugly and short-sighted', 'not *seduisant* in person or manner', she soon became fond of 'little Lewis'. He regularly accompanied her to the theatre, and even lived at Holland House for a while in 1811. But not everyone enjoyed his company. Byron thought Lewis 'a damned bore ... tedious, as well as contradictory, to everything and everybody.' Another Holland House habitué considered him the 'most vapid of all vapid retailers of stale and exploded paradoxes'.[62]

Other men Elizabeth knew through her Jamaican concerns rubbed shoulders even more awkwardly than Lewis with the elevated company at Holland House. The 'vulgar bluntness' of Stephen and Rose Fuller's nephew, John 'Mad Jack' Fuller, 'excited much mirth' but 'he thought the laugh was raised by his waggery, so was delighted'.[63] Thomas William Plummer, son of the Hollands' broker Thomas Plummer, was 'always blundering upon something he had better not'.[64] He delighted in telling Elizabeth his firm had named a ship after her, blithely relating that the *Lady Holland* was their 'bulkiest' vessel, and how, on her maiden voyage, she hit a rock and lost her rudder.[*] Elizabeth's Jamaican connection was also reflected on the menu; in 1801, the Holland House set tucked into a turtle sent from Westmoreland, perhaps using silver plate marked with Florentius Vassall's crest.[65]

Elizabeth strongly believed: 'all women of a certain age and in a situation to achieve it should take to Politicks – to leading and influencing'. She

---

[*] Launched at Rochester in 1811, the *Lady Holland* sailed back and forth to the Caribbean until 1826, when she began sailing to India. She was wrecked on Dassen Island off the Cape of Good Hope in 1830, though all her passengers and a good proportion of her cargo of Madeira wine were saved.

certainly did; writing lengthy analyses in her diary; interrogating and debating her guests; and critiquing Henry's performance in the House of Lords from the Peeresses' Gallery. One can sense an underlying frustration that she herself was not permitted to take the floor in her cool appraisal: 'His power of mind is fully equal to excellence, but he is indolent, and wants method in his arrangement; arguments crowd upon him while speaking, and an overstock of matter makes him confused.'[66]

Future Prime Minister George Canning recognised her soft power. After one dinner, he engaged his hostess in a long conversation 'as to my politics, influence over Lord H., etc.', and 'wanted a confidential opening from me.' On another occasion Elizabeth's close friend Lady Bessborough – the Duchess of Devonshire's sister – observed her opposing 'with all her might (and certainly with might on Lord H.'s mind)' the idea of a Foxite coalition with Prime Minister William Pitt the Younger.[67]

Henry was not the only politician in thrall to Elizabeth's potent mix of brains and beauty. The infatuated Edward Hale Adderley rejected an offer of a seat in Parliament from Canning in 1799 on the strength of her advice.[68] Reverend Sydney Smith, Holland House habitué and *Edinburgh Review* co-founder, was surprised to hear from Lord Chancellor Erskine in 1806 that he had been given a clerical living 'because Lady H. insisted I should do so; and if she had desired me to give it to the *devil*, he must have had it.' Smith was certainly no angel, envying how Henry 'reposes every evening on that beautiful structure of flesh and blood, Lady H.'[69]

Elizabeth's patronage helped project pro-slavery men into positions of power. She eased Thomas William Plummer's way into Parliament in 1806, where he made a last-ditch attempt to argue for a trial suspension rather than abolition of the trafficking of Africans. While 'as much an advocate for liberty as any man', he told the House he thought it 'very dangerous to propagate such an idea ... [and] notions of political right among a people so unintelligent and so easily provoked to revolt as the negroes'.[70]

Elizabeth also aided James Scarlett – an MP from 1819 and later Lord Abinger – brother to one of her Jamaican attorneys, in his stellar political and legal career. Known as 'silver-tongued Scarlett', he advised the 'West India Committee' – a powerful lobbying group representing Caribbean enslavers and merchants – on how to combat the Slave Trade Abolition Bill.[71]

No politician can afford to have embarrassing skeletons in their closet. As Henry's career took off, Elizabeth felt she must come clean about hiding Harriet; the story could ruin her new husband's reputation. In June 1799 she revealed the truth, sending Harriet back to Sir Godfrey, who 'immediately recollected and acknowledged her'. Elizabeth lamented:

> I have renounced a darling child, and my heart aches afresh when I think of the separation. She is so captivating ... with my others I feel gratified to see them healthy and intelligent, but her winning manners convert the duty of maternal attention into a positive enjoyment. I delight in being with her ... Would to God I were allowed to bring her up![72]

Early in the morning on 4 June 1800, Elizabeth and Henry were 'roused by a loud rapping at the bedroom door'. Moments later her mother Mary burst in crying out that Sir Godfrey was dead![73] The day before, he had purchased a new 'brace of pistols', and 'after various devices and stratagems to get his servants out of the way, he but too fatally succeeded and at half past four shot himself in the front drawing room' of his house in Mayfair. It seemed he had 'appeared frequently disordered in his mind' since the previous winter, 'in consequence of ill luck at play'. He had tried twice in recent weeks to kill himself using laudanum, 'but each time his man interposed', once by wrenching the phial from his grasp, the other by forcing him to vomit.

Elizabeth, who had contemplated suicide during their marriage, exclaimed: 'Unhappy man! What must have been the agony of his mind, to rouse him to commit a deed of such horror.' But she could not even express compassion without thinking of her financial interests. Forgiving him all the wrongs he had done her, she swore she would 'willingly ... renounce *all that may accrue to me* from this dreadful event to restore him again to existence' (emphasis added). 'Business compelled' her to go to town that very day. Rather morbidly, she asked her coachman to go via Hanover Square,* where 'the shock of being almost within sight of those mangled remains was too much'.

Thomas Plummer confirmed the Jamaican estates now belonged to the Hollands; they duly added 'Vassall' to their names. 'It appears', Elizabeth noted, 'that the average of the net produced, deducting outfit, annuities, mortgage, jointure, insurance, and in short every expenditure

---

* Sir Godfrey's house was in Tenterden Street, just off Hanover Square; Thomas Plummer was based at 2 Fen Court in the City.

is within a hundred or two of £6,000 p.a., an ample acquisition, but as yet must not be anticipated or enjoyed.' This was because, as Plummer informed her at the funeral, the profligate Sir Godfrey owed his firm £17,000. She bemoaned 'we shall not touch a stiver [a low value Dutch coin] for these eighteen months, and only till then incur trouble and expense'.

On reflection, Elizabeth was glad the 'sad catastrophe' had not occurred at the time of their divorce, when 'the world' and her own fears 'would have assigned me quitting him as the cause'. Instead, later gossips whispered that the shock of Harriet's return from the dead had unbalanced Sir Godfrey's mind, blaming both Elizabeth and Henry. While her 'diabolical deceit' had 'as much murdered – as if she had pulled the trigger which had shot him', Henry 'must have been privy to the deed', and in not stopping her, 'weakly' became 'an accomplice of the crime'.[74]

Elizabeth desperately hoped Sir Godfrey's death would allow her more contact with her three Webster children. She resolved to 'openly seize every occasion of making them know how near an object it is to my heart to be loved by them'. But their minds had already been poisoned against her. Webby, who Elizabeth found 'cold in his disposition, and taught by his father to be a boaster', reminded his younger brother Henry of Sir Godfrey's warning: 'above all things' they must 'remember never to see Lady H. again'. Elizabeth's hopes were dashed when the Court of Chancery appointed Sir Godfrey's brother-in-law Thomas Chaplin guardian.[75]

Soon after this blow, Elizabeth and Henry lost their second son, Stephen. Just twenty-two months old, the toddler was 'just beginning to prattle his little innocent wishes'.* His loss wrought in Elizabeth 'a species of wild despair', impairing her health, and making her anxious for six-year-old Charles Richard who was 'delicate', suffering 'frequent and severe attacks'.[76] Nonetheless, over the next few years, the couple had three more children: Henry Edward, Mary Elizabeth and Georgiana Anne.

Becoming an enslaver through marrying Elizabeth sat extremely awkwardly with Henry's political position. His uncle Charles James Fox was a vocal abolitionist, declaring the traffic 'contrary to the principles of justice, humanity and sound policy'. Henry, so fervent a disciple that

---

* Stephen died on 21 November 1800, Henry's twenty-seventh birthday.

Once harvested, sugar cane needed to be milled within two days. The ruins of the windmills used still scatter the countryside across the Caribbean, even featuring on the Barbados 25-cent coin.

The runoff was then reduced and purified in the boiling house. Many workers suffered life-threatening burns tending the immense cauldrons.

(*Above*) Remnants of a necklace, composed of dog teeth, cowrie shells, fish vertebrae, glass beads and one large carnelian bead found in a grave at Newton Plantation. It is estimated that up to 1,000 people were buried at Newton from the late 17th to early 19th centuries.

(*Left*) An early plan of a Barbados estate, of the kind Sarah's great-grand-uncle Robert Newton established before his death in 1647.

Both Frances Dalzell and Mary Ramsay lived near Kingston Parade in Jamaica as children, depicted here in the mid-nineteenth century by Joseph Bartholomew Kidd.

Wouski by James Gillray, 23 January 1788, depicting Prince William Henry (later King William IV) embracing an attractive Black woman. Caricatures of the period frequently reflect anxieties around relationships between white men and Black or mixed-heritage women, like that between Frances Dalzell's parents.

Dido Elizabeth Belle, the mixed-heritage great-niece of Lord Mansfield – here with her cousin Lady Elizabeth Murray – grew up at Kenwood House. She is sometimes – incorrectly – depicted as a wealthy heiress.

Auchincruive House was built with the riches Mary Ramsay's husband Richard Oswald amassed trafficking tens of thousands of Africans to the Americas from Bance Island – her dowry helped finance his investment in the venture.

Treaty of Paris by Benjamin West, 1783. (*Left to Right*) John Jay, John Adams, Benjamin Franklin, Henry Laurens and William Temple Franklin. Richard Oswald and his secretary refused to pose, though Richard and Mary did host the Americans on their way home.

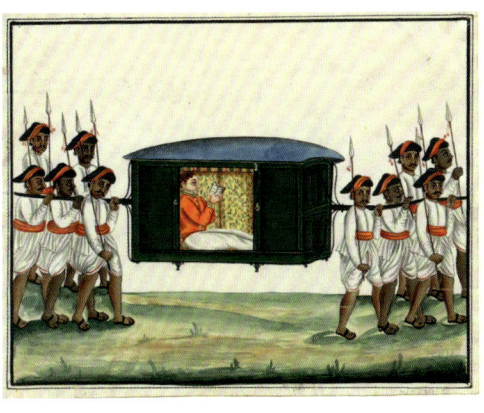

(*Left*) Jane Jarvis's husband Lachlan Macquarie, future Governor of New South Wales, as painted by John Opie, 1805.

(*Right*) 'British Officer in Palanquin with Indian Bearers', anonymous, c. 1830. This image shows six bearers; Lachlan required twelve in 1793.

The ruins of Sweet River Pen Great House, Westmoreland, Jamaica where Elizabeth Vassall was born in 1771.

(*Left*) Elizabeth Vassall's second husband, Henry Richard Fox, Lord Holland, as depicted by François-Xavier Fabre, 1795. At first sight, she found him 'not in the least handsome'.

(*Right*) Lord Holland's statue in Holland Park was painted red in 2020 by activists; would they have done the same to his wife if she had a statue?

The south view of Holland House – where the British Cabinet decided to compensate enslavers to the tune of £20 million after dinner on 29 May 1833 – painted by John Buckler, 1812.

Young Anna Susanna Taylor (*centre*) and her three younger siblings were left behind with their uncle Robert Graham when their parents set out for Jamaica in 1785.

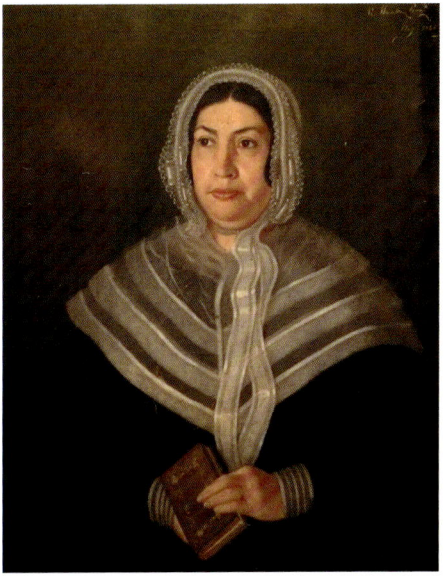

Charlotte Sproule, née Taylor, (1795–1845), one of Anna Susanna's mixed-heritage cousins, received compensation for 53 enslaved people and ended her days in Ireland.

James Hakewill's misleadingly tranquil depiction of the mill yard of the Watson-Taylors' Holland Estate in St Thomas in the East, *c.* 1820–1.

This photograph of sugar cane cutters with a white plantation owner or manager taken in Jamaica *c.* 1880 shows that conditions remained much the same long after emancipation.

Wilberforce called him a 'zealous partisan', echoed his uncle in the Lords, denouncing 'the detestable traffick in human beings on the coast of Africa' as 'inhuman, disgraceful, and degrading to this country'.[77] Elizabeth meanwhile only mentioned her husband speaking 'on the Slave business' in passing in her journal, swiftly moving on to more detailed discussions of metaphysics or taking a bath.[78]

Henry faced a dilemma when their attorney Dr Robert Scarlett urged him to purchase more Africans in 1802. A larger workforce at Friendship and Greenwich (by now amalgamated into one operation, with all crops being stored and processed at Greenwich) would enable cultivation of more sugar cane on extensive, highly fertile, open pastures currently lying fallow.* Less than a third of the people there were currently engaged in producing sugar. The rest were 'superannuated people, invalids, children, domestics, tradesmen and others whose occupations though necessary are too various to be detailed'. Doubling the number of field workers to 200 with an investment of some £7,000 could increase annual output from under 400, to 600 hogsheads of sugar a year.

In general, Scarlett observed, it was risky to buy newly imported Africans, as 'seasoning' them meant 'habituating them indiscriminately to a severe yoke and a more refined system of cruelty, and it is no wonder therefore that thousands should fall sacrifice to it'. But under his care, he flattered himself, they would thrive.

More urgently, Scarlett encouraged Henry to purchase forty-two people previously owned by Sir Godfrey Webster. Sixteen had been purchased relatively recently from Lindo, Lake & Co., major importers of Africans into Kingston. The rest, 'long accustomed to work on the estate', had originally belonged to Richard Gittoes, a well-to-do local carpenter, brother of a former overseer, who had recently purchased the freedom of his three children with a woman named Majorah† from Sir Godfrey.

---

* Sweet River, by contrast, remained profitable; its focus on cattle breeding had allowed it to capitalise on the interruption to food imports occasioned by the war with France.

† Marjorah was recorded as a 'sambo', a now offensive term, used to describe a child of a Black person and a mixed-heritage person. Gittoes replaced Robert, Elizabeth and Mary with three newly arrived Africans: twenty-six-year-old Monimia, 'Congo Mary', aged thirteen, and Robert, ten. Robert ran away in January 1811. Monimia died on 10 October 1817. 'Congo Mary' also later ran away temporarily; she died of 'debility' on 24 May 1822. Gittoes left his son Robert £500, making provision for him to be sent to England for his education. He was to focus on English and Maths, not 'throw away his time on Latin and Greek', and never return to Jamaica.

Scarlett considered the workers rather steeply priced at £3,971. In other circumstances, he would have recommended buying 'new negroes', but these people were 'so connected with the other slaves of the property' that it would be 'difficult and cruel' to separate them in a sale.[79]

Despite his public abolitionism, Henry agreed to purchase the forty-two people Scarlett recommended. His hypocrisy did not go unnoticed. In March 1806 Monk Lewis warned him:

> the Anti-Abolitionists ... have some statement to make respecting large and recent purchases of Negroes for the use of Lady H's Jamaica Estates which (they think) can place in such a light as may be very unfavourable to you.[80]

By this time, the struggle was reaching its crescendo. Charles James Fox finally gained the consent of both Commons and Lords to 'proceed to take effectual measures for abolishing' the trade in June 1806, though he did not live to see the measure passed into law, dying on 13 September.* Henry made a 'pathetic allusion' to his uncle in the Lords calling once more for 'the abolition of this odious traffic' after Prime Minister Grenville introduced the Slave Trade Abolition Bill to that House in early 1807. The future William IV, then Duke of Clarence, meanwhile, spoke forcibly for the other side.[81]

Elizabeth did not even feign support for abolition. She derided Jane Harley, Lady Oxford's, naiveté when she, 'in a whining monotonous, childish tone ... said to Lord H. upon the Slave Trade, "I am always for justice and humanity, ar'n't you?"' On 2 March 1807 – a week after the event – she recorded in her journal: 'The abolition of Slave Trade was carried in the H. of C. by an immense majority, nearly 18 to 1; the opposition only 16.' Rather than adding words of celebration, she recorded the absence of Lord Castlereagh – said to be 'about the last person unconnected with the West Indies who clung to the traffick' – and George Rose, a Dominican enslaver who had resolved never to vote

---

* Elizabeth, who had always had an uneasy relationship with Fox, did not behave 'as one would wish' when he died. Lady Bessborough remarked: 'the cry against her is dreadful. A great deal of this is *manner*, and neither want of feeling or intention, but she really does act foolishly'. It was said that when people outside his 'chamber of death' at Chiswick House asked after Fox's health, she responded by throwing her apron over her head. Keppel, *Sovereign Lady*, p. 138.

on the subject. She also noted William Windham, Secretary of State for War and the Colonies, and 'the Doctor's men' intended to oppose the bill when it came to the Committee stage.*[82]

Their efforts were in vain, and Henry, who had joined the 'Ministry of All the Talents' as Lord Privy Seal in October 1806, was among the lord commissioners who conveyed the royal assent to the Bill on 25 March 1807, Elizabeth's thirty-sixth birthday.

Regardless of Henry's passionate rhetoric, the Hollands continued to buy Africans long after the traffic was abolished. In 1819, eight individuals – two Jamaican-born sisters, Jellico and Beck, with their five children, and an African-born man named George – were imported to Friendship and Greenwich 'by licence' from the Bahamas. They had been purchased to replace a group of recently manumitted people, a mixed-heritage woman named Sally Williams, and another named Hetty with 'her five quadroon children'. Michael Cuff, overseer at Friendship and Greenwich from 1799 until he was sacked by Robert Scarlett in 1809, paid £429 for Hetty and their children's manumission and took them to live with him at his home, Emmaus Pen in St Elizabeth.[83]

Elizabeth had 'taken violently to politics' again, so was dismayed when, on the very same day the Slave Trade Abolition Act passed into law, the Ministry of All the Talents was superseded by a Tory government. She now lost 'the chief pleasure' of Henry and her Whig friends being in office, 'that I knew sooner and better what was going on'.[84] When Henry's name was tipped for Prime Minister in the crisis following the final collapse of George III's mental health in November 1810, Elizabeth was 'in high good humour but *tres affairée* [very busy], and seems already to have all the cares of office on her'. She was devastated when the Prince Regent made it clear Spencer Perceval (now mostly remembered as the only British Prime Minister to be assassinated) would stay in post. Lady Bessborough remarked her 'example proves that, like most other pursuits of mere calcul, all is Vanity and Vexation of Spirit; yet it was hard to be so very near, and all dash'd down in a minute'.[85]

---

* Windham had married Cecilia, daughter of Jamaican enslaver Admiral Arthur Forrest. The 'Doctor's men' were supporters of Tory Henry Addington (Prime Minister 1801–4), known spitefully as 'the Doctor' because his father was one of George III's physicians. Elizabeth was 'a professed Addingtonian' in 1805. 'Admiral Arthur Forrest', LBS: https://www.ucl.ac.uk/lbs/person/view/2146643075; 'Windham, William', HOP: http://www.historyofparliamentonline.org/volume/1790-1820/member/windham-william-1750-1810; Kelly, *Holland House*, p. 43.

Satirists enjoyed making fun of Elizabeth's political aspirations. This was the golden age of British caricature, with no subject too risqué or contentious for the likes of James Gillray, Thomas Rowlandson and George Cruikshank.[86] They ridiculed Elizabeth's supposed dominance over her husband, her dubious past and her worrying penchant for Napoleon. In one print, she appears as a hen pecking Henry's back. In another she is flogging her husband (depicted as a donkey) with a birch-rod, a bottle of 'Godfrey's cordial' – likely a poisonous draught – in her other hand.[87]

In February 1811, 'Sketch for a Prime Minister or how to purchase a peace' literally depicted Elizabeth wearing the breeches while Henry donned her skirts. The couple are knocking on the Treasury door (the Prime Minister's official title is First Lord of the Treasury), which Spencer

'Sketch for a Prime Minister or How to Purchase a Peace'.
Folding plate from the *Satirist*, 1 February 1811.

Perceval defends with a blunderbuss. Elizabeth gloats that with Henry in office 'I shall be Bang Up to everything'. Compounding the horror of a woman ruling the Prime Minister, Elizabeth brandishes a warrant for Wellington's recall while sheltering Napoleon under her cloak. The French Emperor cries *'Et Moi Aussi!'*, holding out an olive branch and a bag of money labelled 'peace offering', but in his other hand he clutches a dagger.[88]

Elizabeth had as many enemies as she had friends. Holland House regular Joseph Jekyll – who, incidentally, wrote the first biography of the extraordinary Black Briton Ignatius Sancho – cast her as the repulsive end of the magnet; Henry the attractive.[89] When Elizabeth's ten-year-old daughter Georgiana died in October 1819, she received:

> an anonymous letter full of triumph at my misfortune denouncing the vengeance of God that my darling being taken was a judgement upon me for being a worthless mother and tyrant wife and a bad mistress and foretelling that my husband will be snatched from me and … I shall be left in contempt and insignificance as I deserve.'[90]

Lady Caroline Lamb targeted Elizabeth in her vitriolic 1816 novel *Glenarvon*. Caroline was the daughter of Elizabeth's friend Lady Bessborough, and wife of future Prime Minister Lord Melbourne. Still smarting from the fallout of her doomed romance with Lord Byron – she was the one who marked him indelibly as 'mad, bad and dangerous to know' – Caroline took aim at everyone she felt had scorned her.

Elizabeth had reproached Caroline for the pain the affair – and her embarrassing attempts to reignite it – had caused. She retaliated by lampooning her as the beautiful but cruel Princess of Madagascar, presiding tyrannically over the 'fawning rabble' who flocked to her court. She calls Holland House 'Barbary House', and its 'reviewers and men of talents' 'that black hord of savages', who 'wear collars and chains around their necks' – a clear, and unflattering, allusion to the source of Elizabeth's wealth. Elizabeth found *Glenarvon* 'a strange farrago', and 'a very wicked one'. It was galling for Elizabeth to have 'every ridicule, folly and infirmity' skewered by a young woman she had known from birth.[91]

*

---

* Elizabeth was at a loss as to who penned this; suspects include Lady Caroline Lamb and Elizabeth Chaplin, Sir Godfrey's sister.

While some of her 'follies' were unfairly exaggerated, Elizabeth *did* have an unhealthy obsession with Napoleon, *and* influenced Henry to support him. It all began in 1798 when she was 'shown under strictest promise of secrecy' private letters intercepted by Nelson after the Battle of the Nile. Discovering Napoleon's 'tender' attachment to his brother, and distress at learning Josephine had taken a lover, placed 'that extraordinary man in a far more amiable point of view'.[92] She had met her hero in Paris in September 1802; his 'gracious smile' could not disguise his 'penetrating, severe and unbending' gaze; his voice was 'so melodious that no heart could resist'. Josephine, herself from Martinique, however, looked 'ghastly, deep furrows on each side of her mouth, fallen-in cheeks, shocking, disgusting, a worn-out hag, prematurely gone, as she is not above 40 years old'.[93]

It was perhaps lucky the meeting was brief. In 1800, Elizabeth had recorded in her journal an encounter between Napoleon and Madame Germaine de Staël, who with her literary and political interests was in many ways Elizabeth's French counterpart. De Staël (later one of Elizabeth's guests at Holland House), 'greeted the hero, and made a political tirade for a full twenty minutes; when she ceased she expected a complimentary eulogism, all he said was "*Madame, a-t-elle nourri ses enfants?*" [Have you fed your children?] A cutting rebuke.'[94]

When Napoleon was exiled to Elba in 1814 Elizabeth planned to visit. She sent him several newspapers, including the 19 October copy of *The Courier* reporting discussions at the Congress of Vienna about sending him to St Helena – a tiny island in the south Atlantic, 1,000 miles from the African coast – intelligence which helped precipitate his escape.[95]

When the 'poor Dear Man' was finally imprisoned on St Helena after Waterloo,* Elizabeth directed the Plummers, whose ships also served her Jamaican plantations, to send him various comforts. These included two French chefs, a microscope, shirts and handkerchiefs, 475 books, and large quantities of wine. One shipment containing claret, Sauternes, Lunelle and Eau de Cologne cost her over £400. According to Henry, 'some preserves which he called "*pruneaux* [prunes] *de Madame Holland*," were nearly the last article of food he ever asked for'.[96]

---

* Elizabeth's second son, Henry Vassall Webster, aide-de-camp to the Prince of Orange, was the messenger who interrupted the Duchess of Richmond's ball with the news the French had crossed the River Sambre.

Henry made enemies of both Wellington and the Prince Regent, first for pleading against the 'foul' and 'dishonourable' execution of Marshal Ney, then for opposing the 'cruel expedient' of exiling Napoleon to St Helena. Napoleon thanked him personally for his advocacy 'in the Senate'. At Henry's own admission, much of his activity was conducted 'chiefly at the request of Lady Holland'.[97]

Elizabeth's attachment to Napoleon was so well-known that she received an anonymous message – '*Le grand homme est mort*' – hours before the news officially broke.[98] In his will, Napoleon left Elizabeth 'the antique Cameo which Pope Pius VI gave me at Tolentino.' This oval image of Bacchus in agate had been set into the lid of a valuable gold snuff box personally used by the Emperor. Inside was a note in Napoleon's own hand, written on a piece of playing card cut from a seven of diamonds: '*L'empereur Napoleon à Lady H. témoignage de satisfaction et d'estime*' ('The Emperor Napoleon to Lady H. A testimony of satisfaction and esteem').[99] She also obtained as souvenirs a lock of his hair, and the key to the bedroom in which he died; she later erected a bust of Napoleon by Canova in her garden.[100]

Despite their love of travel, Elizabeth and Henry never seem to have considered visiting Jamaica. However, they took great interest when they learnt their friend Monk Lewis was, as Byron put it, 'going to Jamaica to suck his sugar canes'. Lewis had decided to inspect the properties he'd inherited from his father. He promised to also visit Friendship and Greenwich, which adjoined his Cornwall estate, and give a 'good account of the property' on his return. Henry sent him a list of questions; Elizabeth's 'commands' were so onerous that he protested she 'mistakes me for one of her runaway negroes'.[101]

Lewis arrived in Black River, St Elizabeth, aboard the Plummers' *Sir Godfrey Webster* on New Year's Day 1816. His first discovery was that all three of them had been sorely deceived in their late attorney, Matthew Parkinson. His letters had:

> expressed the greatest anxiety and attention respecting the welfare and comfort of the slaves; – so much so, indeed, that when I detailed his mode of management to Lord Holland, he observed, 'that if he did all that was mentioned in his letters, he did as much as could possibly be expected or wished from an attorney.'

However, soon after his arrival, Lewis learnt the truth from enslaved brothers Richard and John Fuller (penkeeper and carpenter at Cornwall respectively). Prioritising his own and other far-flung estates, Parkinson had left another man in charge at Cornwall. This 'petty tyrant' had been so cruel that many people had fled into the mountains; 'at length he committed an act of such severity, that the negroes, one and all, fled to Savannah la Mar, and threw themselves upon the protection of the magistrates'. It took this 'public exposure' for Parkinson to dismiss the man. And all the while, Lewis raged, 'my attorney had the insolence and falsehood to write me letters, filled with assurances of his perpetual vigilance for … their perfect good treatment'.[102] And Lewis had recommended Parkinson to the Hollands!

Lewis frequently interacted with people from Friendship and Greenwich during this and the subsequent visit he made to Jamaica from November 1817 to May 1818. It was on his second trip that Lewis gave Mrs Phillis that hearty meal of ham and plantains, a shiny *macaroni* coin and news of her childhood playmate. His other encounters were less jovial. Just as Betsy Newton had sought help from Sir John Gay Alleyne, people enslaved by the Hollands saw Lewis as someone they could appeal to during disputes with their new attorney, Henry Waite Plummer (who had acted for Sir Godfrey Webster in the late 1790s).

On 28 January 1816, a 'large body' of people from Friendship and Greenwich, led by a woman named Nelly,* arrived at Cornwall complaining of 'hard treatment, in various ways, from their overseer and drivers'.[103] The overseer had 'curtailed them of the legal allowance of time for their meals, and the cultivation of their own grounds'. They asked Lewis to raise their complaint with both Plummer and 'their proprietor in England'. He agreed to do so, reluctantly; 'the charges were so strong, that I am certain that they must be fictitious.'

Later that same day Aberdeen, a young African-born cooper from Greenwich, appeared. Though only twenty-five, he was 'in a bad state of health', 'feeble and ill', asthmatic and 'quite heartbroken' with 'tears running down his cheeks'. Afraid he would be 'put to labour beyond his strength', and punished if unable to perform his allotted tasks, he had

---

* This was probably Jamaican-born Big Nelly, aged fifty-six, who had three children – Jose, a twenty-nine-year-old cooper, Betty, aged twenty-three, and Charity, aged twenty-one – and had adopted another, whose name we do not know.

run away repeatedly. Now wishing to return, he asked Lewis to intervene to 'save him from the lash'.

Though Lewis did intercede in both cases, only Aberdeen's situation seems to have improved. Perhaps as a highly skilled man he was harder to replace. Plummer promised to 'take care that he should be only allotted such labour as his strength might be fully equal to', and when Lewis met Aberdeen again two years later, he had fully recovered his health and spirits. The dispute over working hours was referred to the Council of Protection in Savanna la Mar, but, following hostile testimony from white bookkeepers, the complaints were judged 'gross falsehoods and calumnies'. However, the magistrate dismissed Nelly and her friends without punishment, suggesting some doubt remained in his mind.

During Lewis's second visit, several mothers from Friendship and Greenwich protested to him that their overseer was forcing them to stop breastfeeding too soon. Their children were all over eighteen months old, some more than twenty-two months. Caribbean women often retained the West African practice of weaning babies around the age of three.[104] Unable to grasp this, Lewis believed they merely sought to 'retain the leisure and other indulgences annexed to the condition of nursing-mothers' – measures generally introduced after 1807 in the hope of increasing the workforce naturally once importing new Africans became illegal.

From the recorded ages of their children, we can identify the mothers as thirty-three-year-old Hagar, her twenty-seven-year-old sister Candace, Elizabeth, thirty-four, Farina, thirty-two, and Little Whanica, twenty-three. With the exception of Little Whanica, each woman already had between two and four children; they may have hoped continuing to breastfeed would make them less likely to conceive.[105] Constant pregnancies put unbearable strain on women's bodies, already weakened by hard labour and malnutrition; many were reluctant to birth children into enslavement.[106] When their 'demands were rejected ... they went home in high discontent'. One woman declared, 'with a peculiar emphasis and manner', that if her child 'should be put into the weaning-house against her will, the attorney would see it dead in less than a week.'[107]

Lewis was left unsettled by his experiences in Jamaica. In July 1816, he asked Wilberforce how he could ensure 'the happiness of his slaves after his death'. He shunned emancipation, both unwilling to take the financial hit, and fearing the 'dangerous consequences for the white inhabitants of the island'. Instead, he drafted a codicil to his will insisting future owners visit Jamaica at least once every three years on pain of forfeiture. Amongst the witnesses to this unromantic document, signed at the Villa Diodati near Lake Geneva, were poets Byron, Shelley and John William Polidori. Lewis died of scarlet fever on his way back from Jamaica aboard the *Sir Godfrey Webster* in May 1818 – leaving his estates to his two sisters. In the end, he had decided against adding the codicil to his will.[108]

When Elizabeth heard there was, as Henry put it, 'a negress on the estate who calls herself Lady H's foster sister', she doubted 'there being any truth in her appellation'. It was forty years since she had left Jamaica as a young girl; she had probably not given Mrs Phillis much thought since. She now told Henry to ask Plummer whether there was 'any such foundation to … her mother having been about her person when young'. If so, 'she would wish to distinguish the poor woman by some little present or indulgence.'

Henry also asked Plummer to 'mention the most meritorious of the Negroes as well as Negresses', so they could also reward them with gifts. He had heard this sort of attention 'gratifies them extremely and reconciles slaves … very sensibly to their condition.' Many abolitionists had hoped cutting off the supply of fresh labour would force enslavers to treat the people they already exploited 'better'. This approach, focused on improving material conditions rather than the more radical idea of emancipation, became known as 'amelioration'.

Influenced by these ideas, and concerned by what he heard from Lewis, Henry instructed Henry Waite Plummer to give more holidays on Saturdays, and to institute 'irrevocable laws' against beating workers, 'reproaching them with their slavery' or making 'any reflections on their colour'. Plummer should make it clear these prohibitions came directly from the Hollands. It was not until 1831 that Henry admitted he doubted his instructions had been obeyed.[109]

The desire to keep enslaved people happy was always a selfish one. As Henry wrote to Plummer: 'if you think it is *advantageous to the estate* and any sort of comfort to the Negroes that an immediate intercourse should be set up between them and their distant masters, I am sure you will be ready to urge it' (emphasis added).

Certainly, Henry's interventions did not result in improving conditions by the crude measure of whether births outpaced deaths. Following the 1807 abolition, Wilberforce and his allies pushed through legislation requiring enslaved people to be registered every three years, to monitor any unexpected increase and so expose illicit importation. The resulting data shows that, as was typical across the British Caribbean (apart from in Barbados), the number of people at Friendship and Greenwich diminished from an average of 442 between 1801 and 1804 to 367 in 1817, and 262 by 1834.[110] Cause of death was rarely recorded, but in 1817 bones were 'found in the Mill Race', the current of water that turned the water wheel on the mill. The coroner concluded they were the remains of sixteen-year-old Bobby, a Jamaican-born lad who had run away the year before. Two African-born men, Bacchus, and Walcott Holland, both aged thirty-nine, were 'murdered by persons unknown' on 21 October 1821.[111]

Henry suggested one more patronising favour to Plummer:

> I have heard when baptised they are very anxious to have great names and those of princes particularly for their godfathers. If you think this of the slightest consequence I will get the Duke of Sussex's [Prince Augustus Frederick, sixth son of George III] permission to use his name on such occasions, should the Negroes prefer it to that of their master or mistress.[112]

The Hollands had probably heard this spurious information from Monk Lewis. He had a head driver named the Duke of Sully and chose the name Wellington for one boy in the hope 'he would grow up to serve *me* in Jamaica as well as the Duke of Wellington had served his massa, the King of England, in Europe.'[113] A boy born to Little Peggy at Friendship and Greenwich in June 1819 was also named Wellington – perhaps in the same spirit.[114]

Enslaved people were increasingly being baptised, as growing numbers of missionaries from various Protestant sects, notably the Baptists, Methodists and Moravians, poured into the Caribbean. John Samuel Gründer, a Swiss Moravian minister based at Joseph Foster Barham's neighbouring Mesopotamia since 1811, agreed to teach children at Friendship and Greenwich. But he died in 1818; his successor died the following year, and after that the Moravians did not send another minister until 1830.

Monk Lewis was contemptuous of missionaries, considering preaching to Black people 'as nugatory as if a man were to sow a field with horse-hair and expect a crop of colts.'[115] However, the spread of religion, and with it education, would bear fruit. Educated enslaved people could read newspapers and so learn of abolitionist debates in Britain, and churchgoers could share news and plan action. As members of congregations, with new Christian names and surnames, converts gained status; some even became deacons and preachers.

One young man from St James named Archer was christened Samuel Sharpe and became a deacon in Montego Bay. He began to dwell on the story of Exodus and biblical passages about equality in the eyes of God; 'he learnt from his Bible, that the whites had no more right to hold black people in slavery, than the black people had to make the white people slaves'.[116]*

On 31 January 1823, the 'Society for Mitigating and Gradually Abolishing the State of Slavery within the British Dominions' was founded by a mix of veteran campaigners like Wilberforce, Thomas Clarkson and Zachary Macaulay – who Elizabeth called 'the great Saint, Zachariah, & the bitterest foe to all W. India concerns' – alongside a younger cohort, including MP Thomas Fowell Buxton, who would emerge as their leader.[117]

Given Henry had erected a monument to his uncle Charles James Fox in Westminster Abbey the previous summer, proudly highlighting his abolitionism by including the figure of a grateful African, the new society could be forgiven for thinking he would once more cleave to the cause.[118] But in February 1823 Wilberforce and his friends were 'seriously grieved' by Henry's refusal to join them. They had hoped if he could only 'hear all that is to be fairly urged on the subject' he would be convinced enslavement itself must end, despite the poor 'pecuniary prospects'. After Henry rejected his overtures, Wilberforce refused to speak to him for seven years.[119] This was no loss to Elizabeth, with whom he had always had an awkward relationship. Puritanical Wilberforce disapproved of her as a divorced woman, and perhaps also as an enslaver.

---

* Enslavers were well aware of the dangerous messages about freedom in the Bible; in 1807 *Select Parts of the Holy Bible for the Use of the Negro Slaves, in the British West-India Islands*, excising passages about escaping enslavement and emphasising those about obedience, was published on behalf of the Society for the Conversion of Negro Slaves, founded by Beilby Porteus, Bishop of London, who, like Lord Holland, had been vocal in opposing the trafficking of Africans.

He complained guests must 'pay the price of civility to her for their kind reception at Holland House'.[120]

When they first met in Florence some thirty years before, Elizabeth had observed that all young men shared Henry's predilection for radical politics – one acquaintance called him 'a veritable sans culotte' – 'but when they see more of the world they cure of their honesty and love of liberty'.[121] Certainly, when it came to emancipation, 'pecuniary prospects' would outweigh principle in the ageing Henry's mind.

While amelioration could be considered an investment, emancipation would be extremely expensive, if not ruinous. By the 1820s, incomes from Jamaica were dwindling. The diminishing workforce slowed production. Sugar prices fell as the market was flooded with the produce of new colonies such as Trinidad, British Guiana and Mauritius. Preferential tariffs were beginning to be abolished. One estimate suggests profits from Jamaica fell from 9.6 per cent between 1799 and 1819 to 5.3 per cent in the period 1820–34.[122]

In February 1821, Elizabeth wrote to her son Henry Edward: 'our affairs are in a very bad plight'. Though she did not 'buy a single article or give a crown to charity', 'the total failure for two years of Jamaica, not even a shilling from Oxfordshire, & little from Bedfordshire, make even the most rigid economy necessary & hardly equal to the outgoings'.[123]

Elizabeth's idea of 'rigid economy' does not chime with our own. The Hollands continued to spend: entertaining, acquiring more books for their extensive library and adding to their collection of paintings and drawings, including works by Carracci, Van Dyck, Murillo, Reynolds, Goya, Turner, Wilkie and Landseer. Elizabeth heartily resented the expense of launching her daughter Mary Elizabeth Fox into society in 1823. By 1826, their outgoings were over £2,000 more than their yearly income.[124]

Elizabeth wrote to her son again in February 1828, painting a 'frightful' picture of the Jamaican situation, which 'adds much to our embarrassments'. The gross annual profit from Westmoreland, she explained, was £1,660. But, as expenditure was £1,880, her mother's annuity £700, and with interest to pay on two outstanding mortgages inherited from her father, Henry was subsidising the plantations by more than £1,200 from his English assets.[125] Further pressure was put on the Hollands' finances when they took out a £5,000 loan from Coutts to finance a housing development in Lambeth following the opening of Vauxhall

Bridge and the new Camberwell Road. A substantial thoroughfare there is still known as Vassall Road today.[126]

In this context, it is hardly surprising – however unedifying – that Henry switched sides. What did Elizabeth – always a realist – think? She no longer kept a journal; there are few explicit references to the politics of emancipation in her letters. However, her influence over Henry remained unabated. He was still very much in love with her, rhapsodising in one 1813 poem about his 'sweet enchantress', with 'sparkling eyes ... that set my soul on fire', while her 'other charms ... kindle fierce desire'.[127] Given their close emotional and intellectual bond it follows that, especially with her personal link to Jamaica, she helped shape his ideas and actions in this as in other policy areas.

Certainly, men he knew *through her* drew him further into the pro-slavery camp. Elizabeth's childhood friend Charles Rose Ellis had been chairman of the West India Committee since 1810; he now invited Henry to join the group. Other members included the Hollands' agent, John Plummer;* his business partner, Elizabeth's relation Joseph Foster Barham; and her friend John 'Mad Jack' Fuller.[128]

After Wilberforce presented a Quaker petition demanding emancipation to Parliament in March 1823, Henry joined Ellis, Plummer and twelve other men, including Martha Swinburne's relation the younger William Manning, on a Special Committee. They crafted a set of thirteen resolutions denying the need to end enslavement, instead focusing on ameliorative measures such as religious instruction, regulating corporal punishment and improved legal rights. Henry and Ellis's connections allowed them to take these resolutions right to the top. They sought out influential Foreign Secretary George Canning, who had long frequented Holland House. Ellis was such a close friend of his that he had stood as Canning's second when he duelled Lord Castlereagh on Putney Heath in 1809.[129]

Thus primed, when Thomas Fowell Buxton presented a plan 'for ameliorating the Slavery of the West Indies with a View to its gradual Extinction' to Parliament in May, Canning placed the emphasis on amelioration.[130] The House voted unanimously in favour of delaying emancipation to a time when it would be 'compatible with the safety of the colonies and with a fair and equitable consideration of the interests of private property', effectively kicking the idea into the long grass.[131]

---

* John Plummer had taken over the firm after his brother Thomas William's death in 1817.

Enslaved abolitionists rose up in Demerara
(now part of Guyana) in August 1823.

Nonetheless, abolitionists persevered; the brutal suppression of the Demerara uprising of August 1823 produced fresh material for their campaign. By the year's end, 220 abolitionist societies – several led by women – had emerged nationwide and 600 petitions had been presented to Parliament. As in the 1790s, a sugar boycott was organised; 'ethical' consumers signalled their virtue with sugar bowls emblazoned with the words 'East India Sugar Not Made By Slaves'.*[132] Not all agitators advocated a gradual approach. Elizabeth Heyrick, a Leicester Quaker, published a popular pamphlet urging 'Immediate not Gradual Abolition' in 1824. She made the insightful critique:

> The West India planters have occupied too prominent a place in the discussion of this great question. The abolitionists have shown a great deal too much politeness and accommodation towards these gentlemen.[133]

---

* Though vendors, like Mrs B. Henderson of Peckham, told their customers that each family switching to East India sugar would, after twenty-one months, prevent 'the Slavery or Murder of one Fellow-Creature!', working conditions in India were hardly rosy.

The monument to Charles James Fox in Westminster Abbey.

Most Parliamentary abolitionists shared enslavers' fears, stoked by recent uprisings, that immediate action would have violent results. In 1824, George Canning compared emancipation with creating Dr Frankenstein's monster. He warned the House of Commons that, just as in Mary Shelley's 1818 novel, turning 'the negro' loose 'in the manhood of his physical strength, maturity of his physical passions, but in the infancy of his uninstructed reason', would be to unthinkingly 'raise up a creature' with a 'more than mortal power of doing mischief'.[134*] The marble African at Charles James Fox's feet in Westminster Abbey was on his knees, his hands clasped in gratitude; a posture in which many people on both sides of the argument would prefer him to remain.

*

* Sir Robert Peel echoed this sentiment, begging Parliament not to free 'the monster' the year before he became Prime Minister in 1834. Taylor, *Interest*, p. 155.

The belief that Elizabeth had undue influence over her husband continued to limit his political career. When Henry did not form part of Lord Goderich's new government in 1827, future Prime Minister Lord John Russell (a Holland relation who increasingly became a surrogate son) told Elizabeth, 'it is because no man will act in Cabinet with a person whose wife opens his letters'. When he was excluded by the Duke of Wellington the following year, one wit remarked, 'Lady H. is the only dissatisfied Minister out of office'.[135] Elizabeth was delighted when, following the fall of Wellington's government in November 1830, Henry finally became part of Earl Grey's Cabinet, as Chancellor of the Duchy of Lancaster – a position he would hold for the next decade.

Once the Whigs were in power, Elizabeth's political influence was heightened by the fact the Cabinet – so many of whom, including the Prime Minister, were old friends she had hosted for years – often met at Holland House. While Prime Minister in the late 1830s, Lord Melbourne tried to avoid his official papers being sent there because Elizabeth would always say, 'What's that? Let me see what that is', and that though he 'made as good a fight as he could', it was 'often very difficult to prevent her'.

Elizabeth also continued to have a significant, sometimes even physical, influence over her husband. By this time, the Hollands, approaching sixty, were increasingly ill and wheelchair-bound, consulting with seven doctors. In 1829, Elizabeth wrote to her son: 'I cannot walk at all and am even carried up and down stairs ... I am grown immensely large ... from my total inability to take exercise.' When Elizabeth thought Henry was overtiring himself, she would have the servants wheel his chair away from the dinner table in mid-conversation. On one occasion when Earl Grey insisted she let her husband have a slice of melon at dinner (Elizabeth feared it would exacerbate Henry's gout), he remarked, 'Ah, Lord Grey, I wish you were always here. It is a fine thing to be Prime Minister.' A few years later, the young Queen Victoria reported in her diary: 'Lady H, Lord Melbourne says, always thinks first of herself and then of Lord H, who quite obeys her.'[136]

Elizabeth's proximity to power was not lost on the satirists. By this time, satire was less bawdy; in 1820 George Cruikshank had accepted a bribe to avoid portraying George IV 'in any immoral situation'.[137] But it remained biting in the tradition that continues in British media – think of *Private Eye* or *Spitting Image* – to this day. In one print by the prolific John 'H.B.' Doyle, published in November 1830, Elizabeth was depicted as 'Delilah', conspiring with Earl Grey and Lord Durham to make Henry Brougham Lord Chancellor – removing him from his influential role in the Commons. He is Samson, lying in Elizabeth's lap as she cuts his hair, ready for the Chancellor's wig.[138]

New guests in the 1830s included Charles Dickens and Thomas Babington Macaulay, an up-and-coming Whig politician and historian. Before they met, Elizabeth was unsure she would like Macaulay. Though he was 'a clever writer in the *Edinburgh Review*', she had heard he was 'not pleasant nor good to look at'. Much worse, his father was the abolitionist Zachariah Macaulay, derided by Elizabeth as 'the great Saint'.[139]

When he first met Elizabeth in May 1831, Macaulay found her 'a large bold-looking woman, with the remains of a fine person and the air of Queen Elizabeth'. He was surprised – despite all he had heard – at the imperiousness of her manner, issuing orders to a coterie of willing victims like a 'centurion'. Her personal doctor, librarian and social secretary Dr John Allen was 'treated like a negro slave'. He, like Caroline Lamb, could not resist making a jab at the source of her wealth.[140]

The new Whig government proved no more receptive to calls for emancipation than the Tories. Henry was affronted by the 'vehemence' of abolitionists 'reviling our Government as Slave drivers and arraigning some Members of it as apostates from the cause of freedom'; both charges that could be levelled personally at the Hollands. Abolitionists' hopes were shattered when Buxton's speech of 15 April 1831, finally urging *immediate* emancipation, was met only with an offer to impose higher tariffs on colonies perceived to be failing to ameliorate conditions. It transpired 'numerous ... noblemen and gentlemen connected with the West India Interest' had had a private discussion with Earl Grey and Colonial Secretary Lord Goderich earlier that day.[141]

Henry now doubled down on his pro-slavery position. He branded abolitionists' calls for immediate emancipation 'extravagant' and 'impracticable', as they had no 'plan of providing for the subsistence or subordination of the Emancipated'. He insisted Britain should not impose laws on local legislatures such as the Jamaica Assembly, as such behaviour had led to the American Revolution. A few months earlier Elizabeth's childhood friend Charles Rose Ellis, now Lord Seaford, had shown Henry 'some violent and alarming resolutions of parishes in Jamaica, demanding an absolution from allegiance'; there was talk of the island applying to become part of the United States. This was all very well, but, as Wilberforce pointed out when Henry resumed contact with him in October 1830, colonial assemblies were hardly likely to adopt measures that would lead to their 'utter ruin'.[142]

On Sunday 19 February 1832, Henry received 'news of a black insurrection in Jamaica, great loss of life, severe executions and the destruction of fifty-two estates' while he sat in Cabinet.[143] Under the leadership of enslaved Baptist deacon Samuel Sharpe, 60,000 enslaved people had risen up across the island. Able to travel freely as a preacher, he had spread the word that emancipation had been agreed in Westminster, but Jamaican enslavers refused to carry it out, and were planning to kill all the Black men on the island. Women and children would be kept alive to produce the next generation of enslaved workers. The idea was to go on strike after Christmas 1831, refusing to return to work unless offered wages and more free time. However, any notion this would remain a peaceful protest soon went up in smoke. On 27 December, Kensington plantation, in the hills above Montego Bay, was set on fire. As others followed suit, an eyewitness recalled 'the sky became a sheet of flame, as if the whole country had become a vast furnace'. The conflagration spread across St James and into swathes of Hanover and Westmoreland; in the end over a hundred estates burnt to the ground.

Martial law was declared, and local militia rampaged through the countryside, targeting missionaries and their churches with almost as much ire as they did enslaved people. Labourers at Friendship and Greenwich later recalled: 'we could hardly eat our own bread, we were getting so uneasy'.[144] The Baptist War raged for eleven days until the freedom fighters were suppressed by Maroons and several British regiments commanded by Major General Sir Willoughby Cotton – who threatened 'all who hold out will meet with certain death'. Two hundred enslaved people were killed. Conversely, the enslaved abolitionists had expressly avoided killing white people; only fourteen had died in the fighting. This was the biggest uprising ever seen in the British Caribbean, and, as so many times before, the enslavers wreaked terrible retribution, murdering an unknown number of people in the immediate aftermath, and putting 626 'rebels' on trial, executing 312, including Samuel Sharpe – who declared, 'I would rather die upon yonder gallows than live in slavery'.[145]

Henry dismissed the numerous atrocities as 'a few insulated instances of barbarous severity and injustice', which he feared 'orators and preachers' would use to stir up a 'general disgust against the whole government and frame of West Indian society'.[146] In this, he was of one mind with Lord Seaford, who had been a 'great sufferer' in the 'calamity' – one of the key confrontations took place at his Old Montpelier estate in St James. Elizabeth also fed him material from her relation and agent John Foster Barham, who asked her to 'direct Henry's attention' to the fact that, unlike most English labourers, enslaved people on both his and the Hollands' estates owned their own cattle, and could graze them freely, one 'circumstance of benevolent treatment' amongst many.[147]

Henry found the Cabinet discussion about the Baptist War 'long and tiresome', defending enslavers against Lord Chancellor Brougham's assertion they could not be trusted. He and Lord Seaford met with Colonial Secretary Lord Goderich on 21 February. The three men agreed a proclamation should be published immediately 'to undeceive the Negroes and enforce the laws'. A few weeks later, Henry advocated sending a regiment from Bermuda to help restore order in Jamaica.[148]

Elizabeth considered the appointment of Holland House regular Henry Phipps, Lord Mulgrave, as Governor of Jamaica in March 'most advantageous ... for the Govt; & if the "Saints" would allow, may be the means of settling that distracted country into some peaceable state. But *that* is very doubtful'.[149] Henry again took the Jamaican enslavers' part, insisting all efforts to effect change by 'vindictive or rewarding [sugar] duties' should wait until Mulgrave had come to 'some arrangement with the Planters, to which their present distress may induce them to listen.' In May, Henry berated the 'menacing, angry, and scolding' tone of a letter the government proposed sending to Caribbean colonies, ensuring 'we mitigated the harsh expressions and somewhat softened it.'[150]

At this time, the Hollands did not know whether or not their own plantations had been affected by the war. Poet Elizabeth Barrett Browning's diary entry for 3 March 1832 exemplifies the feelings of absentee enslavers: 'It would be agreeable to know that Papa's estates are not burnt up – & still more agreeable to know where we are going! Fear as well as hope deferred maketh the heart sick.'[151] Elizabeth urgently asked John Foster Barham to send her news and in May 1832 he arranged for a 'man from Jamaica', 'fully acquainted with your estates', to give her 'a more intelligent view of the actual state of the slave population'.[152]

It was not until late summer that the Hollands received a definitive account of how their estates had fared. Two men they enslaved had been put on trial for their role in the war. Robert Davis, a twenty-seven-year-old

Jamaican-born man from Sweet River Pen, was 'sentenced by a court martial to transportation for life' – he would be sold off the island. The authorities also sentenced Guy Fawkes, aged thirty, from Friendship and Greenwich, 'to the workhouse for life'.[153]

Their latest attorney, James Lawson, reported several enslaved people had left after a 'gentleman' who 'stated himself to be Lady Holland's relation' – likely Richard Vassall of Hanover – had arrived to speak with them. There is no record of what he said, but according to Lawson, he did not show 'the safest discretion' and certainly did not achieve any 'beneficial results'. This is hardly surprising: a decade earlier he had – notoriously – executed an enslaved man accused of stealing a horse without trial.

Although there had not been much 'actual violence' on the Hollands' estates, the militia still burned the enslaved peoples' houses to the ground on the orders of Sir Willoughby Cotton. When Henry protested this was 'harsh and unnecessary', Lawson insisted 'descendants of savage Africans ... in a state of incomplete civilisation' required military discipline.[154]

Lawson's successor, Thomas McNeil, who took over in August 1832, probably had the same mindset. As a Westmoreland militia officer, McNeil had participated in atrocities committed during the Baptist War. He had personally taken Samuel Sharpe's deputies Robert Gardiner and Thomas Dove into custody in February 1832.* Gardiner's threat that if it had been up to him 'there would neither have been a buckra-man living or buckra-house standing' would be seared in his memory. In this light, McNeil's assurance to Henry that corporal punishment would 'on no account' be 'inflicted beyond a certain slight degree without first having reference to me' is hardly reassuring.

As McNeil was custos – senior magistrate – for Westmoreland, there was not even a slim chance of justice if people complained of ill treatment. This affected hundreds of people across the parish; McNeil himself owned a handful of estates, including his home, Paradise Pen, acting as attorney for several more. His line to Henry that, having lived locally for seventeen years, he had 'the advantage of knowing your people, and being well known to them', sounds an ominous note.[155]

*

---

* Gardiner was executed, his head placed on a spike, while Dove was sentenced to lifetime imprisonment in England.

Although Henry observed the 'alarm created by the insurrection' had to some extent quelled the zeal of the 'Saints', by 1833 the combination of fear of future uprisings, popular agitation in Britain (1.3 million people signed petitions that year for immediate action), and the reformed Parliament* – 212 MPs returned in the 1832 election had pledged their support for emancipation – made ending enslavement inevitable.

The terms of the deal were left undecided. Henry repeatedly pressed the 'West India' lobby's perspective on the Cabinet; for example, suggesting in May 1833 that the new Colonial Secretary, E.G. Stanley, consult Henry Edward Sharpe, Attorney General of Barbados, an enslaver both there and in Grenada.[156] Henry made every effort to ensure the maximum compensation was paid to those who, like himself and Elizabeth, would lose their human 'property', and that newly freed labourers were forced to continue to work for their masters as 'apprentices' to 'train' them for waged labour.

At a Cabinet meeting held on Wednesday 29 May after dinner at Holland House, it was decided to convert a proposed loan of £15 million to enslavers to a £20 million compensation grant they would not have to repay. Henry noted in his journal:

> After discussion was over, Melbourne on one couch and Ch[arles] Grant [Lord Glenelg] on another went fast asleep. Grey said jokingly we should blow out the candles and leave them; and about a week or ten days later a caricature by HB was in all the shops representing our two colleagues asleep at Holland House and the rest of us escaping with our Candles![157]

This was how casually the British government made the decision to spend forty per cent of its annual budget on compensating enslavers. Doing so would require a huge loan, paid off by British taxpayers (including many of Black Caribbean descent) only in 2015. There was no discussion of compensation for enslaved people, even though the issue of 'adequate reparation' and 'restitution for the injuries' had been raised

---

* The 1832 Reform Act expanded the franchise, giving representation to large industrial towns like Birmingham, Manchester and Leeds, and abolishing seats with tiny electorates, the infamous 'rotten boroughs' that had made it so easy for several of the people in this book to buy a seat in Parliament.

as early as 1787 by Ottobah Cugoano in his *Thoughts and Sentiments on the Evil and Wicked Traffic of the Slavery and Commerce of the Human Species*, copies of which he dispatched – in vain – to George III, the Prince of Wales and Edmund Burke.[158]

On 11 June, the 'Act for the Abolition of Slavery throughout the British Colonies; for promoting the Industry of the manumitted Slaves; and for compensating the Persons hitherto entitled to the Services of such Slaves' passed by a large majority in the Commons.[159] I quote the full title as it represents the true nature of the legislation better than the abbreviated 'Slavery Abolition Act'. The £20 million grant and the apprenticeship scheme (representing free labour worth a further £27 million) were crucial conditions for consensus.[160] After passing the Lords, and eventually gaining royal consent from a reluctant William IV on 28 August 1833, the Act became law. It was decreed enslavement would come to an end on 1 August 1834.

The Hollands wasted no time in joining more than 46,000 claimants – forty per cent of whom were women – applying for their share of the £20 million. The Hollands' claim for over £7,000 compensation for 401 people at Friendship and Greenwich and Sweet River Pen was contested by Elizabeth's estranged son, Webby.

Now aged forty-five, married with five sons, and formally known as Sir Godfrey Vassall Webster, Webby was in dire financial circumstances. He had undertaken extensive restoration and renovation of Battle Abbey, left almost in ruins by the time his grand-aunt Lady Martha finally died in 1810. Webby's political ambitions also cost money; he had 'most stupidly squandered between £2,000 and £3,000' to secure his election for Sussex in 1812. Worst of all, Webby had inherited his father's predilection for gambling, leaving him in such bad debt that in 1819 he temporarily fled to France to escape his creditors.[161]

Webby contended he was, as per Florentius Vassall's 1778 will, due to inherit one-third of the Jamaican property on Elizabeth's death, in equal shares with his two surviving legitimate brothers, Henry Vassall Webster* and Henry Edward Fox (neither of whom made a claim). His right to compensation was considered greater than the Hollands' and

---

* Henry Vassall Webster took after his father in a more tragic way, cutting his throat with a penknife in 1847, 'while labouring under temporary insanity', two years after his mother's death. Kiloh, G., 'Henry Webster', Battle and District Historical Society, 2016: https://battlehistorysociety.com/Documents/O17.pdf.

in December 1836 the commission awarded his solicitors £5,000. As he had died that July, the money went to his eldest son.[162]

The Hollands were eventually granted £2,211 13s 9d in compensation, having seen off two further, unsuccessful, counterclaims from John Foster Barham, as mortgagee. Barham's claim was perhaps judged invalid as Elizabeth had lost £1,100 'through the roguery of Plummer', when his firm went bankrupt in December 1830, leaving her servants' salaries unpaid.[163] In a shocking piece of speculation, the Hollands' attorney Thomas McNeil proudly boasted 'he had bought seventeen slaves in 1833 for £9 currency [£6 8s 4d] each, for every one of whom he had received at least £20 sterling compensation.'[164]

And that, you might think, is where the story of enslavement ends. But unpaid apprenticeship was a continuation of enslavement in all but name. News of a six-year term for field workers, and four years for domestics and skilled labourers, was met with outrage in the Caribbean. Some swore 'they will have their heads cut off, or shot, before they will be bound as apprentices'; another asked: 'Who ever hear of free work a field?'[165]

Henry took a keen interest in the implementation of apprenticeship, regularly corresponding on the matter with Lord Seaford; Jamaica's new Governor, Howe Peter Browne, Marquess of Sligo; and several stipendiary magistrates. These were men who had been recruited to implement the new system and mediate between overseers and apprentices. Jamaica received over sixty of these officials during apprenticeship; far more than any other colony. Fifteen were sent to British Guiana, eleven to Trinidad, only eight to Barbados, five to St Kitts and three to St Vincent. Some obtained their positions through Elizabeth and Henry's patronage; Elizabeth herself was particularly active in securing a role for Stephen Bourne in Nassau in 1838.[166]

When Thomas Fowell Buxton moved in Parliament in June 1835 for an inquiry into whether the former enslavers were complying with the Abolition of Slavery Act, Henry was furious. This would 'open the whole question of apprenticeships, alarm the West Indians about the compensation, and thereby discourage those who are bona fide exerting themselves at much trouble and expence to make the new system work well'.[167]

Buxton eventually secured a Parliamentary committee, but their report simply recommended apprenticeship continue as planned until

1840. The radical Quaker abolitionist Joseph Sturge, who would soon found the British and Foreign Anti-Slavery Society – now Anti-Slavery International – denounced it as 'a document which bears strong indications of having emanated from a tribunal in which the accused parties were themselves judges'. Indeed, the committee included several men from enslaving families, such as future premier William Gladstone, whose father had received the largest single compensation payment – £105,000 – for the loss of human 'property' in British Guiana.[168]

Was the new system working at Friendship and Greenwich and Sweet River Pen? Lord Seaford visited the Holland estates in August 1833 and January 1834. He told Elizabeth and Henry he heard few complaints, and observed that McNeil held 'the doctrine that the negroes are to be managed better by a mild than a coercive system'. Apprentices enjoined Seaford 'to convey from them a great many "How d'ees, to massa and mistress"', and to 'member Missis to send a beau gown'.[169]

The Hollands received similarly positive reports from Governor Sligo and Elizabeth's relation Captain Spencer Lambert Hunter Vassall.* Sligo, who himself owned Kelly's and Cocoa Walk in St Dorothy, acquired by his grandfather's marriage to heiress Elizabeth Kelly, visited Sweet River in July 1834. He wrote: 'I have not seen a more respectable set of Negroes since I have been on the island and … Mr MacNeill seems an excellent character for acting and good management.'[170] After Vassall visited both estates in spring 1837, he echoed Sligo: 'your lordship possesses a very fine body of apprentices, happy, and contented.' There was, he believed, 'every reason to suppose they will continue to merit the well-known considerate kindness received from Lady Holland & your lordship'. He found McNeil 'a clever zealous attorney' and 'a humane man'.[171]

However, a different picture emerged when Joseph Sturge and fellow Quaker abolitionist Thomas Harvey visited Sweet River and Friendship and Greenwich that March.[172] At both estates, about fifty or sixty people crowded round to speak with them; they also took more formal statements at Friendship and Greenwich.[173] As these interviews were

---

* Vassall co-owned an estate in Hanover; his naval career was forwarded by Elizabeth, who persuaded the Admiralty to grant him command of HMS *Harrier* in 1831. He was Elizabeth's third cousin once removed. His great-great-grandfather Leonard Vassall (d.1737) was brother to Elizabeth's great-grandfather Florentius Vassall I. 'Spencer Lambert Hunter Vassall', LBS: https://www.ucl.ac.uk/lbs/person/view/42287; Calder, *John Vassall*, p. 31; Keppel, *Sovereign Lady*, pp. 297–8.

conducted in the presence of Thomas McNeil and the overseer, apprentices may not have felt able to talk completely openly. Nevertheless, they made it clear they 'wished they might be free immediately'.

Sturge and Harvey recorded that after apprenticeship ended the labourers 'should be glad to remain on the estate and work for wages, rather than leave … to begin the world again'. This was no doubt what the Quaker abolitionists and their readers wanted to hear. The idea of beginning the world again was frighteningly radical, deployed by Thomas Paine on the eve of the American Revolution.

At Sweet River, apprentices 'expressed great anxiety to know what was to be done respecting their houses and grounds, and said the uncertainty prevented their repairing or improving them'. They did not want to make any long-term agreement with McNeil as he might die or be replaced at any time. Rather, aware he himself was too infirm to make the journey, they 'wished Lord H. would send out "his piccaninny [child] or his cousin" with whom they might talk about the terms upon which they should remain when free.'

An agreement with the family would be more reliable, and professions of love and loyalty should be seen in the context of trying to broker the best terms possible. Just as they had when Sligo and Spencer Vassall visited, apprentices at Sweet River 'enquired very eagerly' after Elizabeth and Henry, 'and desired their best respects to be given to them, saying that they had always been very good to them.' This sentiment was echoed at Friendship and Greenwich, where they singled out Elizabeth, saying, 'Missis has been kind to we', even though she had not set foot on the island for almost fifty years. Subtly critical of this, apprentices pointed out 'a very old negro … intimating he had never seen his owner.'[174]

Though most people enslaved by the Hollands had not seen them in the flesh, they had seen pictures of Henry, and possibly Elizabeth. By October 1838, a young apprentice carpenter at Sweet River Pen had pinned six political caricatures – 'innocent enough' – to his walls, including one depicting Henry. This was John 'H.B.' Doyle's 'Drawing for Twelfth Cakes: A Hint to Cabinet Makers', published in London on 21 December 1830. In this print, etched a month after he depicted Elizabeth as 'Delilah' plotting the same move, Doyle featured Henry enticing Brougham to accept the role of Lord Chancellor with the self-serving words: 'Oh! Never mind them! Take Care of yourself and your friends will like you the better!' The carpenter, who unfortunately is not named, had paid $2 for the set; probably all by Doyle, and perhaps including the one featuring Elizabeth and the one showing Lords Melbourne and Glenelg asleep on the couch having decided on the £20 million compensation scheme. In this, he had something in common with his former enslaver: Elizabeth herself had a full collection of Doyle's prints. On either side of the Atlantic, we can only guess how differently they viewed the same satire.[175]

Sturge and Harvey's report shows the Hollands' paternalistic gestures were not being carried out. Apprentices said they knew Elizabeth thought kindly of them 'whether we get the gifts that she sends or not'. Elizabeth had sent presents to the female apprentices but McNeil withheld them until after the crop was brought in, promising they would be distributed to the best workers, whose names would be sent to Elizabeth so she 'might be sensible who was most deserving of any kindness from her ladyship in future'.[176]

The Hollands had sent £100 to the rector of Westmoreland in November 1836 to help build a new church and a school for Black children at nearby Petersfield.[177] However, the Friendship and Greenwich apprentices told Sturge and Harvey they 'should be grateful to get a lesson ourselves as well as our children'. There was 'at one time talk of a school on the estate, but lately we hear nothing about it.'

Though apprenticeship regulations stated employers were to provide 'food, clothing, lodging, medicine and medical attendance', Sturge and Harvey found the hospital at Friendship and Greenwich 'dirty and out of repair'.[178] Some people had not received any saltfish since 1 August 1834. Only those who worked overtime were rewarded with the weekly ration. Perhaps their only source of protein, this salted cod imported from Newfoundland was a Caribbean staple, still popular today. In Jamaica, it makes up half the national dish of ackee and saltfish. Ackee, a fruit native to West Africa, had grown from seeds enslaved people brought with them to the island, giving the dish a doubly significant historical resonance.

At Friendship and Greenwich, Sturge and Harvey were told there had been no perceptible change in working hours, despite the regulations that apprentices should work 40.5 hours a week. During the sugar harvest, they worked fourteen- or even twenty-four-hour shifts. On the day of Sturge and Harvey's visit, a number of women 'surrounded' McNeil and 'complained that their half Fridays have been taken away in crop [during harvesting], and not repaid them'. He 'reminded them of the numerous indulgences they receive, and said they must not reckon the time due to them with too much nicety'. Sturge and Harvey could not catch much of the ensuing 'noisy discussion', but observed (in language that reveals their own prejudices): 'the deportment of the people was rude and discreditable.'

These disputes stemmed from a difference in opinion on how the mandatory hours should be distributed throughout the week. Apprentices wanted to work four nine-hour days and 4.5 hours on Friday, giving them Friday afternoons to tend to their provision grounds; former enslavers wanted four days of eight hours and one of 8.5 hours, and often extracted more. Furthermore, wages were hardly adequate; the Hollands paid 1s 3d a day, significantly less than the average range of 1s 8d to 2s 6d across the island. Nonetheless, the newly freed were well informed about their rights, and willing to assert them, despite the risk of violent retribution.

Though enslavement was nominally over, vindictive punishments seemed only to increase. The 1833 Act had prohibited former enslavers from whipping, beating or imprisoning labourers; in theory, only the new special magistrates could now authorise such punishments. Apprentice James Williams's *A Narrative of Events, since the First of August 1834*, published by Joseph Sturge in 1837, observed: 'apprentices get a great deal more punishment now than they did when they was slaves; the master take spite and do all he can to hurt them before the free come'. His own master threatened to make workers so weak they would 'be no use to ourselves afterwards.'[179] At Friendship and Greenwich, Sturge and Harvey observed 'a series of substantial, stone, penal cells, which we hope are now chiefly valued as building materials.' The statements they gathered from apprentices said otherwise.

In the first year of apprenticeship, a man named George Blake refused to take on the extra duty of watchman unpaid. He insisted, 'we heard we should never have to do ... extra time without being paid for it.' McNeil's response was to put him in 'the dungeon' for four days and nights to await the Magistrate, who then 'committed him to the workhouse for fourteen days, to work in chains and collars.' He was then forced to pay the lost time back by labouring on Friday and Saturday afternoons for free.

As further punishment, George Blake's wife Catherine, who had been a washerwoman, was sent to work permanently in the field. When she objected, she was put in the bilboes – a long iron bar with sliding ankle constraints – for four weeks, 'without any Magistrate's order'. Forbidden to remove the heavy shackle day and night, she struggled with the hard labour she was unaccustomed to as a former domestic, and found it impossible to find a comfortable sleeping position. Five months later, Catherine remained lame. Adding insult to injury, McNeil also removed her ration of saltfish.

In another case, in 1835, five women: Beatrice Holland, Katie Jones, Dolly Ferguson, Christian Williams and Ruth Allan, refused to work all day on Fridays during harvest without pay or extra time off. They were part of a wider pattern across the island whereby women were at the forefront of resistance to apprenticeship; one stipendiary Magistrate complained, 'the women are on all occasions the more clamorous, the most troublesome and insubordinate, and least respectful of all authority'.[180] The five women were taken before the Magistrate 'for disobedience of orders'. He refused to allow them to speak, and sentenced them immediately to fifteen days on the treadmill. This punishment exacted such a toll that one woman still had pain in her joints two years later, and no one dared to refuse to work again. Apprentices concluded they would get 'no sort of satisfaction' from the special Magistrates.

'An Interior View of a Jamaica House of Correction', c.1837. The treadmill came to exemplify the injustices of the apprenticeship period.

Plantation dungeons were grim. James Williams and Adam Brown, his fellow apprentice at Penshurst, St Ann, suffered ten days' confinement in December 1834 after allegedly failing to turn out the sheep to pasture on time. Cold, damp and dark with an earth floor, the place was barely big enough to lie down in. They were 'never let out of the dungeons for the necessities of nature; nor did anybody ever clean the dungeon out during the ten days; the filth was allowed to remain in it the whole time in a bucket'. Surviving on only a pint of water and two plantains a day, they emerged so weak they 'could scarcely walk', but 'massa and misses said we no punish half enough', and sent them straight back to work.

Such confinement could be fatal. Samuel Smith, who worked at North Sound, Antigua, in the 1890s, witnessed the murder of Harty Mab, a young woman who 'Massa Hinds' locked up for several days for failing to answer when her name was called. When 'he give the order to release her, she was dead. Rats had bitten off her lips and nose'. Samuel, only fifteen at the time, never forgot seeing her body, or that Hinds escaped any punishment. 'Them estate cellars', he said, 'was even specially built to torture slaves ... People that was locked up in the dungeon even for a day and escape death was lucky. Only the planters could say should the two air holes be open or not. If they was close tight, the person couldn't last for long.'

Workhouses were no better. New institutions had been built and existing ones expanded across the island in the wake of emancipation, as the authorities sought new ways to control the Black majority. As James Williams powerfully testified in his *Narrative*, 'dancing tread-mill ... hurt dreadful'; you could hear the inmates 'bawling and crying' a mile away. People were tightly strapped to an overhead bar by the wrists and if they missed a step 'the mill steps keep on batter their legs and knees, and the driver with the cat keep on flog them all the time' until they regained their footing. This was not easy to accomplish as the steps were slippery with so much sweat it was as if water had been thrown on them. Violent flogging 'cut away most of their clothes, and left them in a manner naked'. At the end of a shift, 'all the skin bruise off the shin' and backs and legs were cut up and bloody.[181] Sturge and Harvey remarked McNeil's claim things were going well in Westmoreland was 'not borne out by the crowded state of the workhouse at Savanna la Mar'.

McNeil tried to pre-empt the criticisms the Hollands would hear from Sturge and Harvey. He wrote to Henry claiming they were 'rather satisfied with all they saw and heard'; and had told him the people at

Sweet River were 'the most knowing and clever they had met', and 'it would be well for Jamaica if such mutual good feelings prevailed upon all properties'. These 'gentlemen from Birmingham' had presented themselves as 'particular friends' of Henry, asked 'many extraordinary questions', saying they would be 'glad to convey any complaint or other message' to him. However, McNeil claimed the apprentices had called Sturge a liar; 'their Master would not keep company with the like of him'. A most 'respectable' man at Sweet River accused Sturge of putting words in people's mouths; those who 'did not know better, would commit a sin by answering yes to all his questions'.

McNeil believed Sturge's 'conduct has been base in the extreme'; he had gone to 'very great trouble to make up a tale of misery'. Since apprenticeship began Jamaican workers had been 'very unsettled, and a great deal of angry feelings have been manifest between them and their managers'. Unless his brand of 'humane' management was practised uniformly across the island, 'the Negroes will be kept in a constant state of excitement and do very little useful labour and be the more readily goaded on by designing persons to commit acts of insubordination'.[182] Clearly not entirely sure his management style would have the desired effect, he still kept a small cannon installed outside the Great House at Friendship, and another at his own front door.[183]

Following further campaigning, fuelled by Sturge and Harvey's report and James Williams's damning pamphlet, it was decided in April 1838 that apprenticeship would end two years early on 1 August. As Henry observed when the measure was debated in Parliament:

> The Clamour out of doors for the immediate emancipation of the Negroes has shaken Glenelg and intimidated the members for populous places, who are afraid of the effect on their future elections of any vote they give against it.[184]

For Caribbean apprentices, it would be 1 August 1838, not 1 August 1834, that marked true freedom from enslavement.

Knowing apprenticeship would soon come to an end, Henry wrote to McNeil asking him to ease the path to freedom by 'gratuitously and quietly manumitting every month some of the best behaved of the Negro Apprentices, and offering them ... a lease of the premises they occupy for a small rent, either in money or labour, as they may prefer.'

Governor Sir Lionel Smith reading the proclamation of freedom to large crowds in what is now Emancipation Square, Spanish Town on 1 August 1838.

The chosen few should be told they had been selected personally by Elizabeth and Henry as well as McNeil. Henry wished to know their 'age, sex and habits, whether they know how to read, and whether they have children at school or not, and what religious service they attend'. The Hollands – perhaps prompted by Sturge and Harvey's criticism or more likely by McNeil emphasising that 'offering every care and attention to the rising generation' was a strong inducement for workers to stay – had by now built a school at Friendship and Greenwich large enough for 100 children. The people at Sweet River were 'most anxious' to have one, but McNeil baulked at the cost, given the relatively small number of children.[185] Married people, and those most likely to remain, were to be manumitted first; McNeil should recruit local ministers to help persuade them to stay.

Henry hoped others would also adopt his policy, afraid of 'fearful effects' if full emancipation came 'previous to the appointed time and in defiance of the indignation of all the white inhabitants'. He claimed that if it were up to him, he would have followed the examples of Lord Sligo and Alers Hankey and set all his apprentices free immediately in 1834 but 'such a step would be unfair to my neighbours, disadvantageous to the community, and unjust and cruel to the negroes themselves, especially those who are old & infirm'.[186]

After apprenticeship ended, people felt they had a customary right to continue to live rent free in the homes their families had lived in for generations. In February 1839, they declared to McNeil:

> they will do everything to please and satisfy Lady Holland and your Lordship, but with the same breath declare they will not pay any rents whatever until they see 'the Queen's Law' to say they must do so, that their parents before them had the possession of the lands and had houses where theirs now are, before Lady H. was born and that they cannot think of paying any rent whatever and work for the estate also.[187]

In response, McNeil began evicting any non-labourers who refused to pay rent. Joseph Sturge reproached Henry with this in February 1839, forwarding a report he had received from Baptist missionary William Knibb of a 'shameful' and 'barbarous' case on his estate. Knibb was a long-time antagonist of 'the cursed blast of slavery'. During the Baptist War, he had been arrested and his chapel in Falmouth burnt down. He had theatrically celebrated the end of apprenticeship with his congregation by conducting a mock funeral, burying a coffin filled with whips, chains and collars, marked: 'Colonial Slavery, died July 31 1838, aged 276'.[188]*

Now, he recounted how:

> A woman with an infant about six weeks old because she would not leave her child and work, had her house broken open, her bed and furniture all destroyed, her pigsty taken and the pig ordered to be shot, and she was taken by the police by force, carried with her infant into the Kings highway and forbidden to return to the house where she was born.

'This poor harmless creature' had protested: 'her Liz mistress, meaning Lady H., would not let her be served so, if she knew it.' Henry wrote to

---

* Knibb Anglo-centrically dated the beginning of 'Colonial slavery' to John Hawkins's first slaving voyage of 1562.

McNeil immediately forbidding any further evictions from houses and their surrounding gardens.[189]

However, he did not completely prohibit McNeil from taking back the larger provision grounds. These were not favoured by former enslavers because they gave families a source of sustenance, and a small income from selling produce at market. They preferred wage-dependent workers who devoted all their energies to cultivating sugar.

Sunday markets also provided opportunities to mix with people from other plantations, share news and gossip, and in their employers' nightmares, plan, as McNeil put it, 'acts of insubordination'.[190] Enslaved people had always prized these bustling weekly events. When the Antigua Assembly abolished Sunday markets in 1831 to 'keep the Sabbath holy', there was an armed confrontation in the market square, and arson attacks on twenty-three estates over four nights. In a negotiated victory for the protestors, markets were moved to Saturdays.[191]

Henry reserved the right to evict people in future, exclaiming:

> Nothing can be more false or foolish than their notion that they have any legal possession of their grounds without rent and they had them before Lady Holland was born.[192]

The stark decline in the number of workers provides the most telling verdict on the failure of attempts to retain labour at Friendship and Greenwich. On 1 August 1834, fifty-one men and ninety women laboured in the fields. By 29 October 1838, three months after apprenticeship ended, only forty men and fifteen women remained. These figures, echoed across the Caribbean, record only the numbers in the field.[193] Numbers of female workers dropped dramatically as many retreated from fieldwork to look after young children – all children under six were freed immediately in 1834, and the birth rate began to rise – to grow food, and to sell it at market.

More broadly, labourers left to work for other estates, bought small plots of land themselves, or moved to one of the new free villages bearing names such as Sligoville, Buxton, Sturge Town, Clarksonville and Granville (after Granville Sharp). These were built on land purchased with the help of British Baptists and Quakers, including Joseph Sturge, who sometimes conducted the transactions via intermediaries in England to avoid detection by hostile former enslavers. Others left to reunite with family members sold to other plantations. One mother and her two daughters trekked across Antigua to find their sister, whose whereabouts was uncertain. It was 'only when they find Minty they really believe slavery was all over for sure'.[194]

When Henry died on 22 October 1840, Elizabeth wrote in her dinner book: 'This wretched day closes all the happiness Refinement and hospitality within the walls of Holland House'.[195] The death certificate recorded Henry died of 'obstruction of the bowels'; Elizabeth, Lord Melbourne and his doctors concurred that stress over his opposition to Lord Palmerston's foreign policy hastened his demise. Elizabeth, with him at the end, found that when 'his mind began to wander, Syria, Egypt, Metternich, Palmerston etc. were the words he dropped.'[196]

Henry was buried on 28 October at Millbrook church, near Ampthill estate in Bedfordshire, inherited from his uncle Lord Upper Ossory in 1818. A large monument was erected to him in Westminster Abbey, close to Charles James Fox's. The sculptor, Edward Hodges Baily, would soon go on to produce the statue of Nelson for Nelson's Column in Trafalgar Square.

Thomas Babington Macaulay provided a eulogy at Elizabeth's request, characterising Henry as 'the man whom neither the prejudices nor the interest belonging to his station could seduce from the path of right … the planter, who made manful war on the slave trade'. Macaulay wilfully ignored Henry's pro-slavery stance in the 1820s and 1830s, even though he opposed Macaulay's own father, Zachariah. Macaulay had by now distanced himself from the anti-slavery cause he had espoused in his youth and his tone very much followed that which Henry had adopted in his *Memoirs of the Whig Party*. The book curiously made no mention of the colonies, and very little of enslavement. Henry devoted a mere half paragraph to the 1807 abolition, which 'put to an end one of the greatest evils to which the human race has ever been exposed, or at least *to our share in the guilt of it*'. Ending the book in 1821 had allowed him to avoid discussing his subsequent volte-face.[197]

Continuing to live at Holland House was 'out of the question'; whenever Elizabeth visited her home of over forty years, 'a stillness strikes at the heart and drives me away'. Instead, she moved to Mayfair. 'Society' was 'her greatest support in her unhappiness', and Elizabeth continued to entertain the usual mix of aristocrats, politicians and writers, giving dinner parties four or five times a week. But despite this busy social calendar, she struggled with loneliness as she outlived her oldest friends.

Though she had written to Prime Minister Lord Melbourne after Henry's death: 'you may suppose my interest now in Politicks is extinct', the next moment she admonished him it 'may still be in your power to avert the calamity of war'. Elizabeth continued to exert considerable influence, both cultural and political, through her incomparable network. When Charles Dickens visited New York for the first time in 1842, he bore letters of introduction to Elizabeth's American cousins, one of whom was Clement Clarke Moore, author of ''Twas the Night before Christmas'.[198] Dickens would write *A Christmas Carol* the following year. Queen Victoria complained Lord Melbourne dined more often with Elizabeth than with her. On one occasion, Elizabeth alarmed Melbourne by pressing him to give a friend a peerage before he left office. He exclaimed, 'Why are you in such a damned hurry. How the Devil do you know I am out?'[199]

Elizabeth now became solely responsible for the Jamaican estates. Concerned they were unprofitable, and would bring her only 'plague and worry', Elizabeth considered selling up. But her old friend Lord Seaford persuaded her not to.[200] She decided instead to shore up her financial position by selling the Ampthill estate to the Duke of Bedford.

On 9 November 1845, with twelve guests in the house for dinner, Elizabeth fell into a 'great stupor and general prostration of strength'. She had entertained sixty-two dinner guests that month already. Though she was in great pain, the following day she sipped champagne and demanded to be told what was going on in the world. On the 13th, she was heard to say: 'This is Death'; she died, of heart disease, four days later, 'calm and tranquil to the last'. Elizabeth was buried on 25 November, at Millbrook Church, near Ampthill, Bedfordshire, 'where are deposited those I loved, my dear Lord, John Allen the inestimable friend to us both, and my child Georgiana'.

Despite her claims of poverty, Elizabeth's will left 'goods, chattels and credits' worth £80,000. Her bequests were more generous to friends than to her own children. A major beneficiary was future Prime Minister Lord John Russell. When challenged on this shortly before her death, she exclaimed, 'I hate my sons; I don't like my daughter'. Although Florentius Vassall's 1778 will had decreed the Jamaican estates should be shared equally between her sons, Elizabeth left them solely to her eldest legitimate son with Henry, Henry Edward Fox, and his heirs.[201] Lord Brougham dismissed this legacy as being 'worth exactly nothing'.[202]

Such was Elizabeth's longevity that one descendant described her as 'a woman who started life in a sedan-chair and finished up in a train'. Isambard Kingdom Brunel had personally overseen Elizabeth's first ride, from Paddington to Chippenham, on his Great Western Railway in December 1841.[203]*

Elizabeth is largely remembered today for her scandalous divorce, her reputation as a battle-axe and as a key mover-and-shaker in Whig politics. The source of her wealth, which contributed to over three decades' worth of entertaining some of the most influential figures of her time, and helped propel her husband's political career, is often brushed over. Henry's abolitionism in the run-up to 1807 is trumpeted, his volte-face in the 1820s and 30s ignored. In summer 2020, after protesters tore down Edward Colston's statue in Bristol, a group of activists targeted Henry's statue in Holland Park.† They painted his hands and face red, and placed a sign reading 'I owned 401 Slaves' in his arms.[204] Though her contemporaries – Caroline Lamb, Monk Lewis, Thomas Babington Macaulay – all made unflattering allusions to her as an enslaver, there is no statue of Elizabeth to catch red-handed. Yet, just as the Plummers' *Lady Holland* shipped sugar and rum to London, *she* was the vessel that brought enslavement's riches to the family.

---

* The line initially ran to Bristol; both its director, George Gibbs, and a major investor, Thomas Daniel, were Bristol-based 'West India merchants' and former enslavers, who ploughed compensation money into the project. Railways across the country benefited from similar backers. 'Thomas Daniel', LBS: https://www.ucl.ac.uk/lbs/person/view/92; 'George Gibbs', LBS: https://www.ucl.ac.uk/lbs/person/view/2725; Hall *et al.*, *Legacies*, pp. 91–9; Dennis, 'Slavery and the Railways, Part 1': https://www.londonreconnections.com/2020/slavery-and-the-railways-part-1-acknowledging-the-past.

† Holland House was largely destroyed by bombing in 1940. Holland Park is part of its former garden; Opera Holland Park has staged summer performances in its ruins since 1996.

Thomas Gainsborough's portrait of a young Lady Isabella Bell Cooper, née Franks – an adored only child and grandchild – now in the Birmingham Museum & Art Gallery.

8

Isabella Bell Franks (1768–1855)

The scion of a transatlantic Jewish mercantile and musical dynasty, Isabella must convert to find a husband. In line to inherit from an early age, she waits decades to come into her fortune, by which time enslavement is almost at an end. Would emancipation really change the lives of the people she had inherited?

ONE MAY MORNING IN 1841, two ships, the *Hector* and the *Commissioner Barclay*, arrived in Port Royal, Jamaica, with 267 Africans on board. They had crossed the Atlantic in just thirty-two days and no one had died during the passage. A full thirty-four years had passed since the trafficking of enslaved Africans in British vessels had been abolished; seven since enslavement itself had been outlawed. Yet the scene at the harbour looked not so different to fifty or a hundred years earlier. Like so many generations before, these African men, women and children were destined to labour for life in the sugar fields.

Alexander Barclay, Commissioner General of Immigration for Jamaica, had chartered the two vessels from Sierra Leone himself, despite being refused official backing from Lord John Russell, Secretary of State for the Colonies, who was the surrogate son of Elizabeth, Lady Holland. Barclay had not found a warm reception in Sierra Leone either, where the 'great majority' – many of whom were recent arrivals, 'liberated' from illegal slaving ships by the British navy – were 'evidently strongly opposed to quit the colony'. Those who 'declared themselves willing to make a trial' were assured the right to return.

This was not a promise Barclay would keep. He had spent his entire working life exploiting African labour, from his early days as a book-keeper to his later career as an attorney and enslaver. He had argued against emancipation in the 1820s; and by the 1840s he felt his worst predictions were coming true. He raged:

> No person in England can form the least conception of the present condition of this once flourishing colony in the hands of the manumitted slaves – so absolutely independent of labour that when they condescend to work for extravagant pay they tell us that they do so to 'oblige Massa' giving at the same time the smallest possible modicum of work for the largest sum of money; and if fault is found with them they are instantly off.[1]

His heiress client, Lady Isabella Cooper, was lucky to have him as her attorney, he thought. He had brought the first indentured Africans to her estate, Duckenfield Hall, Jamaica, besides several neighbouring plantations he managed in the Plantain River Valley in St Thomas in the East. With any luck, they would solve the labour problem, so long as they did not pick up Jamaican-born workers' 'bad habits'.

Isabella – who would live to the ripe old age of eighty-seven – was born on 23 May 1768, the daughter of fifty-year-old Jewish merchant Moses Franks and his much younger wife Phila. Moses and Phila were first cousins, both members of a prosperous Ashkenazi[*] transatlantic mercantile dynasty.

Moses arrived in London from America in 1745. Aged twenty-six, he was a tall 'lad of very good sense and very engaging and always merry'. His mother Abigail was glad to see him leave New York – a 'degenerate place', where 'all his company get drunk from Sunday night until Saturday morning'; and where he had been spending too much time with the unhappily married Molly Beckford.[†] Moses had hoped to become the London agent for several New York merchants, but was much 'Out of Temper' to find them loyal to their existing contacts. Instead, he went into army contracting, provisioning British troops in North America.[2]

---

[*] Jews of Central or Eastern European descent, as opposed to the Sephardi of Spanish or Portuguese origin.
[†] Her husband Ballard Beckford was expelled from Jamaica for committing adultery with the wife of Edward Manning (Gibson Dalzell's business partner) in 1739. 'Ballard Beckford I', LBS: https://www.ucl.ac.uk/lbs/person/view/2146649441; Burnard, '"Matron in Rank"'.

Franks Family Tree

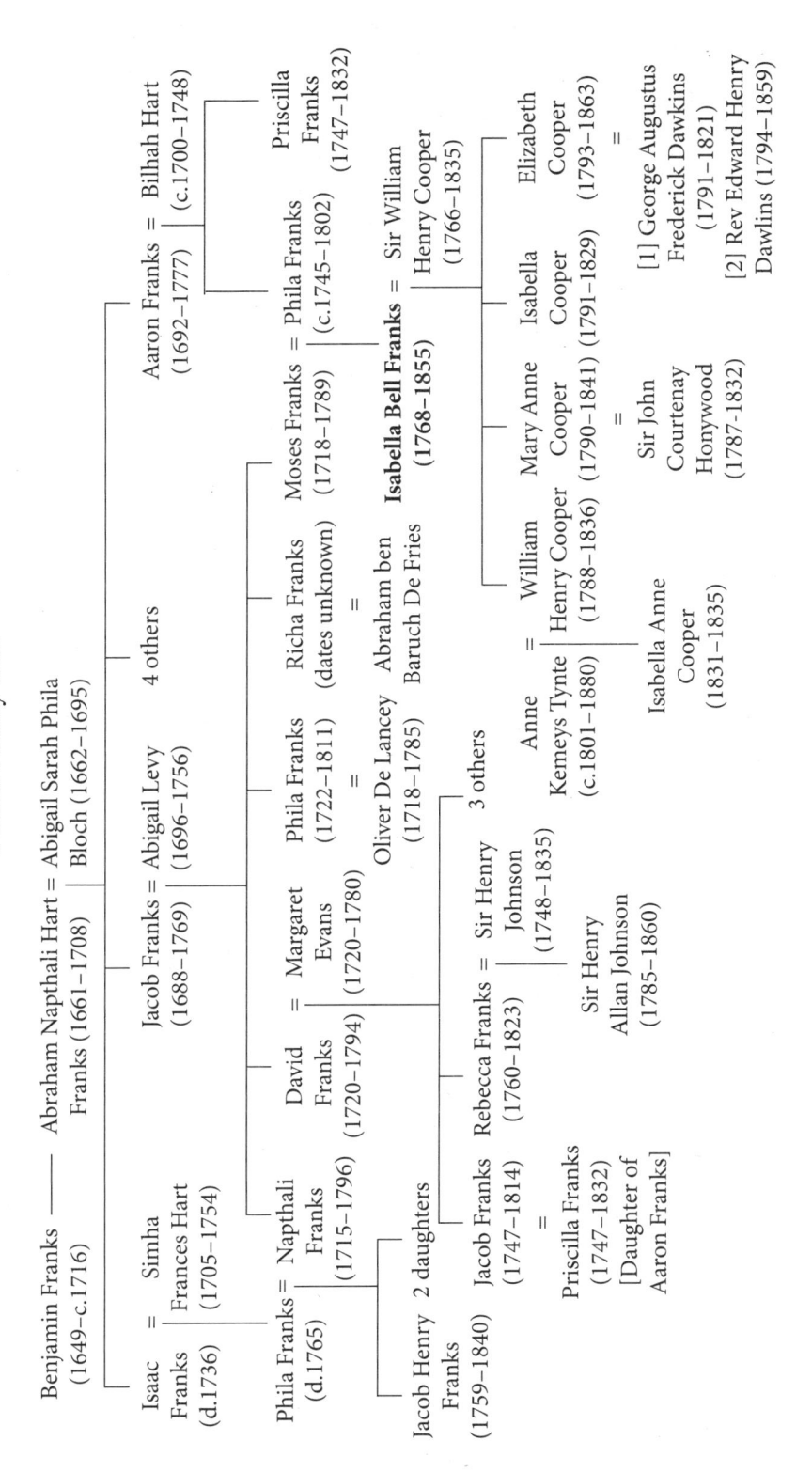

Benjamin Franks (1649–c.1716)

Abraham Napthali Hart Franks (1661–1708) = Abigail Sarah Phila Bloch (1662–1695)

- Isaac Franks (d.1736) = Simha Frances Hart (1705–1754)
- Jacob Franks (1688–1769) = Abigail Levy (1696–1756)
- Aaron Franks (1692–1777) = Bilhah Hart (c.1700–1748)
- 4 others

Children of Isaac Franks and Simha Frances Hart:
- Phila Franks (d.1765) = Napthali Franks (1715–1796)

Children of Jacob Franks and Abigail Levy:
- David Franks (1720–1794) = Margaret Evans (1720–1780)
- Phila Franks (1722–1811) = Oliver De Lancey (1718–1785)
- Richa Franks (dates unknown) = Abraham ben Baruch De Fries

Children of Aaron Franks and Bilhah Hart:
- Moses Franks (1718–1789) = Phila Franks (c.1745–1802)
- Priscilla Franks (1747–1832)

Children of David Franks and Margaret Evans:
- Jacob Henry Franks (1759–1840)
- 2 daughters
- Jacob Franks (1747–1814) = Priscilla Franks (1747–1832) [Daughter of Aaron Franks]
- Rebecca Franks (1760–1823) = Sir Henry Johnson (1748–1835)
- 3 others

Sir Henry Allan Johnson (1785–1860)

Children of Moses Franks and Phila Franks:
- **Isabella Bell Franks (1768–1855)** = Sir William Henry Cooper (1766–1835)

Children of Isabella Bell Franks and Sir William Henry Cooper:
- William Henry Cooper (1788–1836) = Anne Kemeys Tynte (c.1801–1880)
- Mary Anne Cooper (1790–1841) = Sir John Courtenay Honywood (1787–1832)
- Isabella Cooper (1791–1829)
- Elizabeth Cooper (1793–1863) =
  - [1] George Augustus Frederick Dawkins (1791–1821)
  - [2] Rev Edward Henry Dawlins (1794–1859)

Isabella Anne Cooper (1831–1835)

Moses' path in London was smoothed by his uncle Aaron Franks. A diamond merchant, ship owner and East India Company investor, Aaron was so rich that in 1742 he refused payment for lending £40,000 worth of jewels to Augusta, Princess of Wales, to wear to a masquerade. He only desired 'she would tell whose they were'; a form of advertising still deployed by luxury goods companies today.[3] Like so many ambitious protégés, Moses married his patron's daughter, Phila, said to be a great beauty. More unusually, he had to wait twenty years to do so as she was only a 'young babe' when he first arrived in London.[4]

Following their marriage in 1765, Moses and Phila spent some £10,000 building a villa named The Grove in Teddington, close to Aaron's house in Isleworth. Phila's younger sister Priscilla also lived nearby with her husband Jacob Franks, one of Moses' nephews from New York. Isabella's childhood home overlooked the Thames, with lawns cascading down to the riverside. The gardens featured an ornamental temple and greenhouse designed by Sir William Chambers, a founder member of the Royal Academy, who also created Somerset House and the Great Pagoda at Kew.[5]

The Franks cultivated friendships with their Christian neighbours, such as Horace Walpole at Strawberry Hill, whom Moses presented with an 'ancient musket, richly carved'.[6] Walpole also enjoyed attending the regular concerts Aaron held at Isleworth House. Family members were often among the performers. Moses played the violin, harpsichord and flute, and sang well; Phila and Priscilla were accomplished pianists.[7]

Moses and Phila adored their only child, and commissioned Thomas Gainsborough to paint Isabella's portrait. A dark-eyed, rosy-cheeked, serious-looking girl with an unruly fringe, she holds our gaze as she sits in an idyllic rural landscape, a tame lamb on her knee symbolising innocence.[8] Isabella was also Aaron's only grandchild, and he doted on her.

The Franks were among a very small minority of Jewish families wealthy enough to buy a place in the English elite. However, no amount of money or Christian friends could insulate them from antisemitism. Aaron had been amongst the staunchest advocates of the 1753 Jewish Naturalization Act, which allowed Jews civic rights without renouncing their religion. However, opposition to the measure was so strong it was repealed the following year, and not revived for almost a century. Although Catholics and non-conformists faced similar barriers, arguments against the 'Jew Bill' displayed age-old antisemitic slurs. Jews were

Christ-killers, ugly and dirty, greedy, grasping cheats; the 'subtlest and most artful people in the world'.[9]

In 1763, the Dean of Bristol Cathedral recommended Aaron to the Prime Minister, Lord Bute, as 'a very honest man tho' a Jew'. Even displays of charity, such as the £5,000 Aaron donated every year, were dismissed as cynical attempts to buy popularity.[10]

Echoing attitudes to mixed-heritage people from the Caribbean, it was feared that, if allowed to enter Parliament, wealthy Jews would buy political power. Certainly, before the 1832 Reform Act, the electoral system, with its plentiful rotten boroughs, made it easy to buy a place in the legislature. Jews occupied a liminal space between Black and white, later to be starkly delineated in pseudoscientific diagrams of racial hierarchy. In Jamaica, Jews, like free people with mixed ancestry, were forbidden to vote, practise law, hold public office or serve on juries. They were suspected of selling gunpowder to the Maroons in the 1730s and conspiring with enslaved people, especially during Tacky's War.[11]

Isabella's family played a prominent role in the still small community of Ashkenazi Jews in London. Aaron's father, Abraham Naphtali Hart Franks – one of the first twelve Jewish brokers to be admitted to the London Stock Exchange – had helped establish the first Ashkenazi place of worship in London, the Great Synagogue in Duke's Place, near Aldgate in the 1690s. Following his example, Aaron, Moses and Isabella's uncle, Napthali, helped negotiate the purchase of a neighbouring lot in 1765, and between them donated £1,000 towards the construction of a larger building.[12]

Aaron insisted the family keep their Jewish faith, even when it limited their opportunities. He was extremely disappointed when his daughter Priscilla and her husband Jacob (who had a Christian mother and had been baptised in New York) left the Great Synagogue to worship at All Saints Church in Isleworth. When Isabella's Philadelphia-based uncle David Franks considered sending a son to London in 1775 to study law (requiring an oath of allegiance to the Church of England), Moses warned him Aaron 'never would admit a step of that sort in any of his family so avowedly, nor would any of us venture to countenance it, as it would highly incense him.'[13]

As an only child, and only grandchild, Isabella was in line to inherit enslaved people and Caribbean landholdings from both Moses and Aaron. The Franks family had profited from enslavement and colonial trade for generations. The founder of the dynasty, Isabella's great-grand-uncle Benjamin Franks, had arrived in London following a series of quasi-piratical adventures in Barbados, Jamaica (where he lost £12,000 in the Port Royal earthquake of 1692), St Croix, New York and Bombay.[14]

The New York branch of the family – led by Moses' father Jacob and his grandfather Moses Levy – traded regularly with the Caribbean. Though this largely involved exporting foodstuffs and plantation supplies in exchange for sugar, rum, ginger and coffee, the Franks' and Levys' ships also trafficked small groups of Africans to New York; sometimes only one or two, at most no more than twenty-five per voyage. Altogether, they imported seventy-one individuals in this way between 1717 and 1743.[15]* The men and women who worked in the Franks' New York home, including Caesar, Dublin, Lucena, and Samson (young Moses' personal attendant), were probably among them.[16]

Most Africans who arrived in the northern American colonies came via the Caribbean. Transatlantic slavers preferred ports with the greatest demand, such as Kingston, Jamaica (and to a lesser extent Virginia's James River and Charleston, South Carolina), where they could quickly offload their 'cargo'. Intercolonial traders, meanwhile, supplied less significant markets, according to demand. Almost 50,000 Africans were carried from the Caribbean to the North American mainland by smaller-scale slavers like the Franks and Levys before the outbreak of the American Revolution. This 'final passage', following the transatlantic 'middle passage', placed yet more strain on their bodies and minds.[17]

Two years before Isabella was born, Moses acquired a third of the 2,000-acre Duckenfield Hall estate, home to some 350 enslaved labourers. Duckenfield had been established in the early eighteenth century by John Dukinfield, a Bristol slaver and younger son of the Dukinfield family of Dukinfield Hall, some six miles east of Manchester. His son Robert became very wealthy, but when he died in 1756 he left the lion's share to 'Jane Engusson, a free Negro Woman' and their three children. Robert's brother Samuel was forced to sell half the estate – and the people enslaved there – to Samuel Touchet.[18]

However, this prominent MP, cotton merchant and slaver was so financially incontinent – running up debts of over £300,000 – that

---

* Like several men in this book, they named ships after their womenfolk – the *Abigail* and the *Charming Philas*.

Elizabeth Baring warned her banker son to heed 'Mr. Touchet's example of grasping at too much and not being contented with a very handsome profit which he might have had without running such enormous risks'.[19]* Over the next few years, Dukinfield and Touchet were forced to mortgage Duckenfield to Moses Franks, and his two business partners, Sir George Colebrooke (the East India Company merchant we met briefly in Chapter 6) and MP Arnold Nesbitt. By 1767, both Samuels had defaulted. Duckenfield, valued at £66,435 24s 4d, now belonged to Franks, Colebrooke and Nesbitt.[20]

Acquiring Caribbean property by recouping mortgage debts was common. Both Richard Oswald and the Dalzells' bad tenant at Lucky Hill, Hutchison Mure, had obtained estates in this way. John Gladstone, father of Prime Minister William Gladstone, gained much of his property in British Guiana as a mortgagee.[21] They had not set out to establish a plantation, but had become enslavers nonetheless. This trend spread beyond individual lenders to mercantile companies, and right into the heart of the growing banking sector. The Bank of England acquired two plantations in Grenada, Bacolet and Chemin, with almost 600 enslaved people, due to a loan which defaulted in the 1770s, selling them for £100,000 in 1790.[22] When enslavement was abolished in 1834, the commission received over 500 claims for compensation from mortgagees.[23]

Isabella's grandfather Aaron would soon acquire Colebrooke's third of Duckenfield in the same way. Colebrooke's wild speculations in East India trade, hemp and alum helped precipitate the credit crisis and ensuing financial crash of 1772, which led to his downfall. Despite his advantageous marriage to Antiguan heiress Mary Gaynor, Colebrooke's bank failed; he declared bankruptcy in 1777.[24] As his finances spiralled out of control, Colebrooke first mortgaged his share of Duckenfield to Aaron, then relinquished it completely in October 1774.[25]

So, by the time Isabella was six, her father Moses held one-third of the estate, her grandfather Aaron another, and Arnold Nesbitt – 'a shockingly wicked fellow', only 'somewhat singed' by the crisis – had the remaining third.[26] When Aaron died in 1777, he left his share in trust for Isabella's aunt Priscilla, with Moses as trustee. After Priscilla's

---

* Touchet died suddenly of apoplexy in 1773, but rumour had it, according to Martha Swinburne's father John Baker, that 'Touchet had hanged himself – poor man!' *Diary of John Baker*, ed. Yorke, p. 259.

death, the money would go to her children. If she had none, Phila and her heirs stood next in line.

Phila and Priscilla jointly inherited the rest of their father's fortune. However, as with much of the wealth we've seen, it did not exist simply as money in the bank. One of Aaron's major assets was a mortgage debt of £9,325 with considerable arrears of interest owed by speculators Lauchlin Macleane and John Stuart, secured on estates in Grenada.[27] After the Seven Years' War ended in 1763, Macleane and Stuart had formed a syndicate to invest some £200,000 in the newly ceded islands of Grenada and Dominica, hoping to 'take advantage of the madness of people to become purchasers'. Their marks included Sir George Colebrooke, General Robert Monckton (now Governor of New York), and playwright Richard Cumberland, whose 1771 comedy *The West Indian* would later play the 'plight' of the absentee enslaver for laughs. Dramatist David Garrick invested £10,000 in the scheme. However, they overreached themselves and ultimately most of the property and its management was taken over by brokers Peter Simond and John Hankey, who in turn became responsible for paying back Aaron's loan.[28]

As both Phila and Priscilla were nearing forty, it was increasingly likely Isabella wouldn't have any cousins or siblings to rival her claim as eventual heiress to Aaron's fortune. Her only immediate bequest from him, however, was £100 to be invested 'in some public funds on trust'. When she turned fifteen, the money would buy diamonds to be set around a miniature of her grandfather, 'in token of my affection for her'.[29] Not a very practical legacy, but an appropriate way to remember a diamond merchant.

When looking at a Jewish family of enslavers like the Franks, we must contend with antisemitic lies that continue to circulate, claiming Jews financed and dominated both the trafficking of Africans and their subsequent enslavement.[30] This claim is demonstrably false. Not only did Jewish people make up a tiny percentage of the population in Britain and the Americas – the 1,000 or so Jews in Jamaica were the largest community in the entire British Caribbean – they were actually *underrepresented* amongst enslavers. Extremely modest numbers of Jews invested in the Royal Africa or South Sea Companies. Less than a thousand of over 250,000 Africans recorded by the Naval Office as arriving in eighteenth-century Jamaica came on Jewish-owned ships. Less than nine per cent of captives trafficked to New York during Moses Franks's youth arrived on ships owned or part-owned by Jews. Fifty-two of the seventy-two people trafficked by the Franks and Levys came on ships they operated in partnership with non-Jews.[31]

Similarly, apart from in Suriname, a Dutch colony on the north-east coast of South America (though like Guyana politically and culturally part of the Caribbean), Jews held little land and few people. One contemporary remarked: 'very few [Jews] have any notion of planting'. In 1750, out of 1,567 Jamaican plantation owners, only 41 were Jewish. In 1817, Jews (including Priscilla Franks) held less than three per cent of the people enslaved there.[32] None of this makes the Franks any less culpable for their actions, but it is important to keep them in perspective.

Isabella grew up to be 'a most amiable, affectionate, and accomplished woman', 'of youth and beauty'.[33] However, when it came to marriage, her options within the Jewish faith were limited. The Ashkenazi community was very small; marriages with Sephardim frowned upon. When Isabella's New York grand-aunt Rachel Levy married a Sephardi man in 1740, his congregation had erupted 'in a great ferment'. In 1772, the London Sephardi authorities actually forbade a man from marrying an Ashkenazi woman.[34] Finding a Jewish groom from a similarly wealthy family would be even more challenging. It was no accident so many of her relatives had married their cousins.

Otherwise, Isabella would need to find a Christian husband. Her grandparents' generation would have glowered; but the family had become more pragmatic over the years. Her aunt Priscilla and her husband Jacob now lived as Christians at Isleworth House. A New York cousin, Rebecca, married a Gentile, Lieutenant Colonel Henry Johnson; they settled in Bath. In 1785, Moses' sister – another Phila – arrived in London from New York with her Christian husband, Oliver De Lancey, a wealthy Loyalist merchant and politician, and their children. By contrast, Isabella might heed the cautionary tale of her aunt Richa, an old maid after rejecting two proposals from Gentiles in her youth.[35]

To marry a Christian Isabella would have to be baptised. But if she wanted to marry 'well', that might not be enough. In the 1760s, Sir Sampson Gideon found his Jewish birth 'an insurmountable impediment' to finding an aristocratic bride; 'the New Christian was repeatedly rejected for no other reason than because his father was an Old Jew'. Having lowered his sights a little, he married the daughter of Sir John Eardley Wilmot, the judge who would command the Newton family to return Mary Hylas to England from Barbados. His sister Elizabeth fared better, marrying the 2nd Viscount Gage with a dowry of £40,000. This level of wealth *could* open the door to intermarriage between Jews willing to convert and high-ranking Britons.[36]

Isabella's prospects were public knowledge. Her father Moses was 'esteemed by the world as a man of immense fortune'. The *Scots Magazine* reported she would inherit 'above £70,000' on his death, and '£100,000 more' if Phila died without remarrying.[37] This caught the eye of Sir Grey Cooper, who was looking for a bride for his eldest son, William Henry, an Eton-educated ensign in the 3rd Foot Guards (now the Scots Guards).

Moses and Sir Grey had known each other for a long time. As Secretary to the Treasury from 1765 to 1782 – 'a good drudge in business' – Sir Grey had been Moses' main government contact for his army contracting work. He had also interceded at Moses' request when his Philadelphia-based brother David Franks had been accused of treason during the Revolutionary War. Since retiring from Parliament, he had bought an estate at Worlington, in Suffolk. He assumed the Scottish baronetcy of the Coopers of Gogar, though his right to it remained disputed.[38]

Isabella married William Henry at the Coopers' townhouse, 7 Cavendish Square, on 21 May 1787. As they were still legally minors – she eighteen, he twenty – the ceremony was conducted under special licence. The other necessary paperwork was proof of her baptism, performed at St James's, Piccadilly, three weeks before.[39] Speaking of such interfaith unions, one Jewish commentator concluded: 'happiness is not often the result, and I do not doubt but the more prevalent incentive of the other party is the fancied opulence of the Jews'.[40]

The first outward sign Isabella might *not* inherit a great fortune came less than a year after her marriage. In April 1788, her mother Phila suffered a mental collapse. The Commission of Lunacy found her 'a lunatic and of unsound mind'. They did not identify the cause of her breakdown, 'unless by the visitation of God', but it was doubtless exacerbated by the stress of Moses' financial troubles.[41]

Despite appearances, Moses had been in serious difficulties for a long time. Aaron's will forgave his son-in-law a gargantuan £40,000 debt. But even this amnesty was not enough to revive his fortunes. He had no doubt suffered collateral damage from Sir George Colebrooke's collapse. He had made substantial losses as an army contractor during the American Revolution, and was amongst the many Loyalists who lost their American property after the war.[42]

In February 1785, Moses had been forced to mortgage his third of Duckenfield to his brother Naphtali and their nephew Jacob (Priscilla's husband), for £25,000. He promised to pay five per cent annual interest out of his income from the South Sea Company, East India Company and Bank of England stock bequeathed in Aaron's will. Over the next few years, Naphtali and Jacob helped him sell almost enough stock to pay off the entire mortgage. But having received the funds, he refused to hand them over.[43]

So, when Moses died intestate in April 1789, Isabella and William Henry inherited not fabulous wealth, but a very sticky financial situation. Isabella became her father's administratrix, liable for his debts, and embroiled in bankruptcy proceedings. The Commission of Lunacy had ruled Phila incapable of making rational decisions so it was left to the young couple to pick up the pieces alone. Family members who might otherwise have come to their aid were amongst Moses' main creditors.

In January 1790, Napthali and Jacob Franks submitted a bill to Chancery alongside several other plaintiffs demanding Isabella and William Henry pay what was owed. They had few sources of income with which to do so. They sold The Grove, Teddington, at auction in April 1790 for £50,000. However, the purchaser, a Mr Denne, then questioned Moses' title to the property, and refused to pay.[44]* Isabella had £2,000 a year from Moses' third share of Duckenfield. However, after deducting interest payments due to Napthali and Jacob, only £750 remained. She would not benefit from the third Aaron had left in trust for her until after Priscilla's death. Equally, even though the Grenada estates purchased by Macleane and Stuart were proving extremely profitable, Isabella would not see any income from Aaron's interest in them until either her mother or her aunt died.[45]

By June 1790, Isabella and William Henry had agreed their share of Duckenfield profits should be paid to Jacob and Naphtali directly until Moses' mortgage debt was paid off. Given the debt was £25,000, a figure

---

* In 1795, the house was purchased by John Walter, who had founded *The Times* newspaper a decade earlier, after his career as a Lloyds underwriter collapsed under the pressure of ships and Caribbean islands lost to the French, and insurance claims from enslavers after the 1780 hurricane. Walter, *Case of Mr John Walter*, p. 2; Gibb, *Lloyds of London*, pp. 42–5.

that would grow with interest, this would take decades; in 1802 Jacob complained he had *still* not been paid in full.[46]

The Coopers' straitened circumstances were exacerbated by having three children to support: a three-year-old son, named William Henry after his father, and two small two girls, Mary Ann and Isabella. Perhaps in search of a more regular income, William Henry left the army and – in a move that would have Aaron turning in his grave – joined the Church. Through his father's connections, he was appointed rector of Curry Mallet with Curland in Somerset in 1792 by the Prince of Wales; the following year the Lord Chancellor made him a prebend of Rochester Cathedral. Still unable to afford a London lifestyle, the couple 'fell into melancholy' and 'were about to retire, objects of compassion, into the country, on a very small pittance'.[47]

Enter Lord Charles Sloane Cadogan, an old family friend and neighbour of the Coopers in Suffolk, who had served in government with Sir Grey. He had inherited some wealth from his maternal grandparents, Sir Hans Sloane (after whom he named Sloane Square) and Jamaican heiress Elizabeth Langley Rose. He also had an interest in Grenada, having loaned £20,500 to John Stuart, Sir George Colebrooke and two other men to buy estates there in 1774.[48]

Lord Cadogan offered the Coopers the use of apartments in both his London house, 41 Upper Grosvenor Street, and his country home, Downham Hall in Suffolk. The offer was gratefully accepted, and the Coopers were thrown into intimate proximity with the Cadogan family.

They did not land in a nest of connubial bliss. Lord Cadogan was in his sixties; his second wife, Mary Churchill, almost twenty years younger.[49] They had six children, but now 'slept in separate apartments ... not because the one was domestic, while the other was dissipated; not because the hours of one were not suited to the other; not because the one was whoring and gambling, while the other was pursuing her own pleasures', but because of Lady Mary's poor mental health. She had fallen into a deep depression after the death of a daughter six years before, becoming a virtual recluse. She habitually stayed in bed until two or three, and suffered from unexplained stomach cramps and occasionally 'violent convulsion fits'. These 'rendered it necessary to take medicines, which no man could possibly administer, and, therefore, it was necessary that she should be attended by a female in the night.'

Despite all this, while Isabella was pregnant with her fourth child, a liaison began between her twenty-five-year-old husband and the forty-two-year-old Lady Mary. Lady Mary's loyal maid, Farley Murray Bull, was the main aider and abetter, smuggling William Henry in and out of the bedroom, guarding the door, and even hiding him in the adjoining water closet. Lady Mary seemed instantly cured of her depression.

The couple's indiscreet behaviour soon made other servants suspicious. William Henry was observed entering the dressing room adjoining Lady Mary's bedroom in a state of undress at all hours of the day and night. On one occasion, Lady Mary summoned the coachman's wife to make the bed after one of his visits and she found it still warm, with the sheets stained with such marks 'as are made when two persons have been in the act of carnal copulation'.

The other woman – Lady Mary Cadogan, by John Dean, after Joshua Reynolds, 1787.

Gossip spread, and when Lord Cadogan found out he sprang into action. In March 1794, Lady Mary was ejected from Upper Grosvenor Street; she fled to her father's house. Then Cadogan brought a case at King's Bench against William Henry for criminal conversation, demanding damages of £20,000; he had 'violated all the duties of friendship, of hospitality, of gratitude'. With ample evidence, the smutty details echoing around the cavernous Westminster Hall, William Henry was found guilty after just half an hour's deliberation.

The jury awarded Cadogan £2,000 in damages, a tenth of the sum he had demanded. After all, the Cadogans had kept separate beds for years and Lady Mary was 'past the zenith of her youth and beauty'; the extent of her husband's loss could be judged accordingly. The jury might also have taken William Henry's relative poverty into account, though the prosecution lawyer, Thomas Erskine, insisted they disregard his 'disappointed expectations' of a large inheritance from Isabella. After all, he exclaimed, 'if it is once said that a man has no fortune, and therefore he may prey on the happiness and honour of others, life would not be worth the having.' Neither could they make matters worse for Isabella and the children, as he had 'abandoned them already. They have suffered all the bitterness it is possible for them to do.'

William Henry's moral failure, the judge Lord Kenyon declared, 'brought a stigma on that sacred profession to which he belongs'. He had also failed 'as a husband and as a father of innocent children, who have a right to look up to him for protection. He has ruined his own family in undoing the happiness of another.' William Henry was forced to resign from the Church. Sir Grey, who had taken Isabella and her children in at Worlington Hall, was so outraged by his son's conduct that he disinherited him. Instead, he left his estate – worth £9,000 a year – to William Henry's younger brother Frederick.

This was not the end of Isabella's ordeal. Having suffered the pain and embarrassment of watching her husband being found guilty of adultery, she now discovered William Henry and Lady Mary had eloped to Wales. The runaway lovers rented a house near Abergavenny but were soon tracked down by Lord Cadogan's men: principally because Lady Mary made herself conspicuous by insisting on travelling with two bullfinches in a birdcage. Cadogan's solicitor had William Henry thrown into Monmouth Gaol for non-payment of damages. As Erskine had said at his trial, 'he who cannot pay with his purse, must pay with his person'.[50]

*

William Henry languished in gaol for several years until the death of Isabella's mother Phila in January 1801 changed their fortunes. Isabella (and by extension her husband, as no settlement had been made before their marriage) now came into Phila's inheritance from Aaron, including half his interest in Grenada. In May, Jacob Franks, Frederick Cooper and Oliver De Lancey agreed to pay William Henry £2,500 and Isabella £1,500 up front.[51] William Henry used this sum to pay the damages he owed Lord Cadogan and get out of prison. Isabella moved back to London from Worlington. Then, Sir Grey died suddenly at the end of July, aged seventy-five. Although his brother Frederick was the main beneficiary, William Henry inherited the baronetcy, and the deserted Isabella became Lady Isabella.

As soon as he was free, William Henry and Lady Mary eloped to France, a popular destination for British tourists once more following the Peace of Amiens. When war resumed in 1803, Napoleon ordered all British men of fighting age be detained. So, Isabella's errant husband and his lover joined 800 or so men and their dependants – including Martha Swinburne's errant son-in-law 'nabob' Paul Benfield – interned at Verdun. This did not entirely sap their spirits. Lady Mary gained a reputation for throwing lavish parties for internees, who reputedly spent their time 'playing, dancing, singing, and drinking all day long'. The couple were later allowed to move to Nancy, a town Lady Mary knew well as her parents used to have a house nearby.[52]

With William Henry detained in France indefinitely, Isabella was left to bring up their four children alone. Their son William Henry went to Eton, like his father. Isabella then helped him pursue a military career, finding money to fund his various promotions, even petitioning Jacob Franks for help. Not long after becoming Lieutenant in the 3rd Regiment of Dragoons in 1805, the young soldier sprained his ankle while dancing. The ensuing 'dangerous symptoms' left him completely bedridden for ten weeks, his leg wrapped 'with carrot poultices'. Isabella and her youngest daughter Elizabeth rushed to his side. They had trouble finding him lodgings in Nottingham, where his regiment was stationed, but were 'consoled, by kind assurances, of all the officers, that he should never be left alone'. He eventually reached the rank of Major, fighting in the Peninsular Wars under Wellington, suffering 'all the hardships of war ... had a horse shot under him but never wounded'.[53]

Two of Isabella's three daughters made 'good' marriages. In 1808 the eldest, Mary Anne, wed Sir John Courtenay Honywood, a baronet with estates in Kent, who could trace his ancestors back to the Norman Conquest. Mary Anne met Sir John through her uncle Frederick Cooper, whose wife was a Honywood. With William Henry detained in France, it was Frederick who walked Mary Anne down the aisle. Shortly after the wedding, Isabella and her two unmarried daughters moved in with the newlyweds at Evington Place in Kent.

The match, declared William Henry's aunt Lucy Kennedy, was 'a great marriage for her, in Point of Fortune, but above all he is a very amiable young man, she also a charming young woman.' Jane Austen – who met Mary Anne at Chawton House in 1813 – agreed, finding her 'extremely pretty, and her manners have all the recommendations of ease and good humour and unaffectedness ... she is altogether a perfect sort of woman.'[54]

Sir John's widowed mother, by contrast, protested he had been 'drawn in to marry a girl without fortune'. She was:

> by no means ambitious of my son's marrying a daughter of Sir William Cooper's, and still less of his leading one of her Ladyship's daughters to the altar; for, from the very unfavourable impression I had received of her character from the dowager Lady Cooper, I had, independently of her birth, a particular objection to her.

We do not know what William Henry's mother had against Isabella, but Lady Honywood's aversion to her Jewish birth is clear. She 'heartily despised' Isabella, casting her as the villain – a 'woman of consummate art' – in the developing drama with her son. The spendthrift Lady Honywood had racked up enormous debts, which Sir John refused to pay. How could he be so 'dishonourable' towards 'the being to who you owe your existence'? She blamed 'the astonishing power Lady Cooper early obtained over him', going so far as to publish a lengthy 'memorial' repeating all these aspersions in 1812, a copy of which was sent to the Prince Regent. Isabella, appalled, wrote to Mary Anne that Lady Honywood's 'artifice and atrocity to [Sir John] Courtenay must render her character more than ever odious in the sight of all well-judging and respectable people'. Ostracised by English society, Lady Honywood married a Frenchman and moved to Normandy.[55]

In 1818, Isabella's youngest daughter Elizabeth married George Augustus Frederick Dawkins, an officer in the 15th Light Dragoons, and a veteran of Waterloo. He was in line to inherit substantial estates in

Oxfordshire, purchased with profits from Jamaica. The Dawkins family (of whom biologist and atheist Richard Dawkins is a modern descendant) had been on the island since the earliest years of English occupation. At the time of Elizabeth's marriage, they enslaved almost 2,000 people and owned over 20,000 acres in Trelawny, St Catherine, Clarendon and Vere. However, Elizabeth and George had no children, and his father was still alive when he died in 1821, so little Dawkins wealth came Elizabeth's way. After fourteen years of widowhood, Elizabeth married George's cousin, the Reverend Edward Henry Dawkins, a Nottinghamshire vicar, and fellow of All Souls College, Oxford.[56]

William Henry reappeared on the scene after Napoleon's 'British visitors' were liberated by allied forces in January 1814. Lady Mary had died three years earlier, so he returned to England alone. In 'perfect health', he was reunited with 'his wife and children after a separation of twenty years'. William Henry's aunt Lucy Kennedy unconvincingly described the moment as 'a joyful meeting to all party's [sic]'. She alluded to William Henry having been 'long a prisoner' in France, but completely omitted his adultery and elopement.[57]

We cannot know how Isabella truly felt about her husband's betrayal, or why she took him back. Perhaps she could not afford to do otherwise, either socially or financially. Though William Henry's adultery was grounds for 'separation from bed and board' in the ecclesiastical courts, she could not have obtained a full divorce by Act of Parliament. While men could sue for divorce on grounds of adultery, women could do so only if adultery were compounded by something worse, such as incest or bigamy. For this reason, no woman procured a divorce by Act of Parliament until 1801, when a baronet's daughter was able to leave her husband because he had committed adultery with her sister. Only three further divorces were granted to women before 1857.[58]

Isabella's inheritance prospects were now dependent on the longevity, or otherwise, of her aunt Priscilla, who would turn seventy in 1816. Priscilla was now a very wealthy woman, having inherited the bulk of her husband Jacob's £250,000 fortune* when he died in Bath in 1814.[59]

---

* Jacob had inherited £125,000 from Priscilla's aunt Judith Levy, the 'Rich Jewess usually called The Queen of Richmond Green', when she died intestate in 1803. LMA, ACC/0775/790, 791 (Priscilla Franks's letter of administration of Judith Levy's estate, 3 February 1803); Stern, *David Franks*, p. 164; Daiches-Dubens, 'Eighteenth Century Anglo-Jewry', pp. 153–7.

On Priscilla's death, Isabella would be entitled to the profits of the third of the estate Aaron had placed in trust for her. By 1822, Priscilla had purchased the share that originally belonged to the late Arnold Nesbitt.[60] Then, through a series of legal wrangles over the next six years, she gained control of the remaining third the Coopers had inherited from Moses in 1789.[61] This she placed in trust for Isabella, appointing William Henry's brother Frederick and family lawyer Robert Pitches as trustees. Thanks to this last move, in May 1831, Isabella received £5,600 10s from Duckenfield.[62] When her aunt died, she would finally inherit the whole estate.

The other split source of income Isabella was due to inherit in full on Priscilla's death was Aaron's interest in Grenada. She had been entitled to one half of this since her mother Phila's death and would inherit the other half when Priscilla died. The debt was now owed by Thomson Hankey & Co., the firm run by the son and grandson (both named Thomson) of John Hankey, who with his partner Peter Simond had taken over management of the estates back in 1769.[63]

The Hankeys assigned one-eighth of the profits of Grand Bras estate, in St Andrew, about a mile west of the coastal town of Grenville, to paying off the mortgage. However, Grand Bras had taken years to recover from the aftermath of Fédon's Revolution, which began in spring 1795. Some 7,000 people – a quarter of Grenada's Black population – had risen up under the leadership of mixed-heritage enslaver Julien Fédon. Like many other Frenchmen and free people with African ancestry, Fédon felt his rights and privileges had diminished under British rule. As on St Vincent, the volatile atmosphere following the French and Haitian Revolutions and the outbreak of war between Britain and France provided the opportunity. Enslaved people seized their freedom and attacked the hated plantations. Most freedom fighters were killed, 100 executed and 500 sold off the island. An estimated £2.5 million of damage was done to property before Britain regained control in June 1796. At Grand Bras, 'every building was destroyed and every Negro fled'. By the early nineteenth century, the estate had re-established a workforce of some 360 people and produced an average yearly profit of £2,107 or 4.6 per cent, a far cry from the £7,828 or 18.8 per cent achieved with some 430 labourers between 1792 and 1795.[64] In May 1831, Isabella received £228 13s from Grand Bras.[65] She was finally profiting from assets she had been promised more than fifty years before.

*

While Isabella slowly began to profit from owning enslaved people, the emancipation campaign was gaining momentum. One combatant in the pamphlet war was Alexander Barclay, Isabella's future attorney, who deployed examples from Duckenfield to support his case. Barclay had set out from Auchterless in Aberdeenshire in 1805 aged twenty to work as a bookkeeper at neighbouring Holland estate. He would rise to become a partner in a Kingston wharf, Member of the Assembly and custos for St Thomas in the East, attorney for several estates in that parish and owner of Fairfield plantation.[66]

In 1826, he published a pro-slavery pamphlet, *A Practical View of the Present State of Slavery in the West Indies*. The Jamaica Assembly commended him for 'so ably vindicating the conduct of the planters, and stating their views'; his neighbours in St Thomas in the East presented him with 'a splendid piece of silver plate'. Barclay aimed to refute arguments made in a tract published by abolitionist lawyer James Stephen two years before.

Stephen had highlighted how treating human beings as chattel rendered an individual 'liable to be torn at once, and for ever from his home, his friends, his family … all that is dear to him on earth'. Cold transfers of property 'by will, by marriage settlement, by gift, sale, demise' meant 'wife and husband, parent and child, if sold to different masters' were 'effectually divided for life'.[67]

Barclay vehemently denied this, insisting he recalled only two instances of such sales in his twenty years in Jamaica:

> These cases occurred at Hampton Court, and Airy Castle estates, which were thrown up, and from which the slaves, much to their joy, were removed in a body to the more fertile domains of Golden Grove and Duckenfield Hall, in the same neighbourhood; where they may now be considered as permanently attached to the soil, whoever may hold the titles of the estates.[68]

However, the evidence from Duckenfield shows Barclay intentionally misrepresented the frequency and character of such sales. There was no natural increase on the estate from 1817 to 1832, with an average of twenty-nine births and thirty-nine deaths each year.[69] Therefore, like the Hollands, the Franks family augmented the workforce by purchasing more people, long after the transatlantic traffic had been abolished. In the decade before Barclay wrote his pamphlet, a total of 128 men, women and children arrived at Duckenfield.

In 1813 Jacob Franks, along with Arnold Nesbitt's nephew John, had purchased forty-four people from James Forsyth, the deputy marshal of St Thomas in the East. Following Jacob and John's deaths, John's brother Thomas Nesbitt transferred the ownership to Priscilla and Isabella, who both signed and sealed the document in London in May 1818. How long either of them glanced at the neatly printed list of men, women and children is not recorded.[70]

In 1816, Priscilla's attorneys purchased fifty-seven people to work at Duckenfield, formerly belonging to George Girton Saunders. They had come from Pembroke and Hick's Hall, north of Morant Bay, far too far away to be considered 'in the same neighbourhood'. Saunders's will had dictated they were to be sold to provide for Grace Lindsay 'who has lived with me faithfully according to the manner and customs of this country' and their three children.[71]

Following the Airy Castle sale – the one Barclay recalled – fifty-one people arrived at Duckenfield in 1823, two of whom had babies soon after their arrival. Their previous owner, George Grant, had died in 1819. But they had not arrived 'in one body'; there had been 119 people at Airy Castle in 1821, meaning many must have been separated from family and friends.[72]

A further group of twenty people were acquired for Priscilla before 1826. They had passed through several hands in quick succession; an experience very different from the one Barclay evoked. Between 1817 and 1820, they were registered as the property of one Thomas Jones. Their next owners, the Kingston firm of Bogle & Co., who trafficked Africans alongside other mercantile interests, went bankrupt by 1824.* The trustees of Bogle & Co. then sold them on to John McClymont, whose attorney Dominic Loague soon made the deal to transfer them to Duckenfield.[73] So, though Barclay only recalled two sales in the whole parish, there had been four at Duckenfield alone.

The majority of these new arrivals were Jamaican-born, but those born in Africa – at least thirty people – would have been amongst the last generation of people imported before 1807. Twenty-eight-year-old John Mitchell from Airy Castle, born in 1798, would have made the horrific transatlantic crossing as a small boy. Olaudah Equiano

---

* Possibly the same Bogles who had enslaved Cecelia Bogle, mother of freedom fighter and national hero Paul Bogle, born free in St Thomas in the East in 1822 and executed following the Morant Bay War in 1865 – of whom, more later. Renton, *Blood Legacy*, p. 330.

recounted the 'intolerably loathsome ... stench of the hold'; 'the shrieks of the women and the groans of the dying'; the boys and girls who almost suffocated after falling into 'necessary tubs' of excrement. In the last decades of the traffic, more and more children were abducted, as enslavers shifted from primarily wanting strong adults to seeing younger people and women of childbearing age as an investment in an uncertain future.[74]

Barclay also used an example from Duckenfield to excuse the enslavers from James Stephen's condemnation of 'their proud contempt of the African race'. Arguing 'African negroes ... are themselves perfectly sensible of their inferiority, however much at a loss to account for it', Barclay recalled:

> Some years ago, the boiler-men negroes on Duckenfield estate were overheard by the book-keeper discoursing on this subject, (the superiority of the whites,) and various opinions were given, till the question was thus set to rest by an old African: 'When God Almighty make de world, him make two man, a n**ger and a buckra; and him give dem two box, and him tell dem for make dem choice. N**ger (n**ger greedy from time!) when him find one box heavy him take it, and buckra take t'other; when dem open de box, buckra see pen, ink and papers; n**ger box full up with hoe and bill, and hoe and bill for n**ger till this day.'[75]

Who might this 'old African' have been? No one listed at Duckenfield is identified as a boiler-man, though it is not completely clear the parable teller worked as a boiler. The three oldest African-born men living at the time were McKay, who died in 1818 at seventy-four; Ralph, who died aged seventy-one in 1819; and John Gustard, formerly known as James, who was sixty-nine in 1818, an 'infirm' 'invalid' by 1822, and died in 1825. A fourth candidate is Thomas Brown, previously named Hector, who died in 1827, aged sixty-eight. Though he was only fifty-nine in 1818, he was described as 'old and weakly' by 1822, and as a skilled carpenter who might command the respect of others.[76]

It is telling both Barclay and the bookkeeper chose to tell this story at length, rather than laying forth the other, probably less flattering, 'various opinions' expressed. The whole episode shows that far from being 'at a loss to account' for racial inequality, people enslaved at Duckenfield had a range of ideas on the subject. Perhaps the African-born elder realised the bookkeeper was eavesdropping on a conversation where dangerous thoughts were being aired and interjected with a story less alarming to the white man.[77]

One would be inclined to dismiss the strange parable of the two boxes out of hand as Barclay's invention, intended to comfort himself and his readers, were it not for the fact that versions of it appear in a wide range of locations, starting in seventeenth-century West Africa. Ralph Waldo Emerson recalled a similar 'negro tradition' in an abolitionist speech he gave in Concord, Massachusetts, in 1844, finding the story 'very sad'. In Sierra Leone in 1853 the Black man's box contained 'a great variety of fruits, gold, ivory, iron &c.' – the valuable raw materials of Africa; the white man received a book, giving him a 'strong head'. In the version recorded by African American folklorist Zora Neale Hurston in the American South in the 1930s, the tale concludes:

> ever since then de n**ger been out in de hot sun, usin' his tools and de white man been sittin' up figgerin', ought's a ought, figger's a figger; all for de white man, none for de n**ger.

In 1956 a South African journalist recalled hearing the story as a child; here the 'coloured man found a pick and a shovel ... White man found gold in his box.' In the oral tradition of Luba people from the modern-day Democratic Republic of the Congo (recorded in the 1970s), the gifts meant 'White Man got ahead of Black Man' because 'the wisdom of the Black Man dies with him, while the White Man can write down his wisdom and save it for posterity.'[78]

The story does not support Barclay's contention Africans were 'perfectly sensible of their inferiority'. The Black man has the first choice, signifying God's favour. The white man is passive; taking the leftover box hardly displays any greater intellect or foresight. While the Black man is blamed for his greed, cautionary tales of greed proliferate in West African folklore. The white man uses his gifts to enrich himself, proving equally greedy if not more so. As one modern scholar puts it: 'these Jamaican tales are not self-denigrating tales, but rather veiled protests against a racist system in which the Black is destined to lose, fail, and suffer, no matter what he does.'[79]

Isabella was sixty-four when she finally came into her full inheritance. Priscilla died in November 1832, aged eighty-six, leaving £400,000.

Isabella inherited the rest of Duckenfield, the house and estate at Isleworth, and the residue of her aunt's fortune once bequests to family, servants and Jewish charities had been paid. The assets were placed in trust for her under Priscilla's executors: lawyer Robert Pitches and Henry Allan Johnson, the son of Isabella's cousin, Rebecca.[80]

The Coopers moved into Isleworth House, a home she had known from childhood. They engaged architect Edward Blore (best known for completing the work on Buckingham Palace following John Nash's dismissal), who added several embellishments including a campanile or bell tower. The house was refurbished 'in admirable style', featuring a well-stocked library, Boulle furniture (decorated with tortoiseshell pictures inlaid with brass or pewter), and family portraits, including Isabella as a child by Gainsborough, and her parents and aunt Priscilla by Sir Joshua Reynolds.[81]

The main Richmond to Isleworth road was diverted in order to allow the extensive gardens to sweep all the way down to the Thames, just as they had at Isabella's childhood home in nearby Teddington. The family normally arrived at the house by river rather than road; the house was designed to look its best from the riverside. A high brick wall was erected along Richmond Road to enhance their privacy.

The Coopers also acquired and lavishly furnished a fine Robert Adam-designed townhouse, 57 Portland Place. They purchased Victoria House, in Pittville, near Cheltenham, as an investment, leasing it to a series of tenants keen to enjoy the new spa being developed there.[82] In 1834, they acquired the Chilton estate near Hungerford, in Berkshire, for their son William Henry, and his young family.[83]

By this time, despite his less-than-holy past, William Henry had been appointed a Chaplain in Ordinary to George IV (who could hardly take the moral high ground). This made him one of forty-eight clergymen who rotated weekly, preaching in 'the Royal Chapel on Sundays, and other Festivals; and in the Morning before the Household: To read Divine Service before the King … twice a Day in the private Oratory; and to say Grace to the King at Dinner.' The job came with an allowance of £30 a year, but more importantly, 'the Honour of the Employment' put him 'constantly in the King's Eye, for Spiritual Preferment'.[84]

William Henry barely lived long enough to enjoy any of this, as he died on 7 January 1835, leaving Isabella all his 'monies, securities, worldly goods and chattels of any nature'. We do not know how deeply Isabella mourned his loss. Certainly, the inscription on his memorial at

All Saints, Worlington (the Coopers' local church in Suffolk) is sparsely worded: no mention of a 'loving wife', or any list of virtues. More upsetting perhaps was losing her son William Henry the following year. Aged just forty-eight, he left no children; little Isabella Anne – named after her grandmother – had died in February 1835.[85]

The widowed Isabella continued enhancing Isleworth House. In this she was aided by none other than the new King, William IV, whom she had perhaps met through her late husband's court appointment. The King had trees felled in Syon Park so Isabella could see the Kew Gardens pagoda and observatory across the Thames. William IV liked the view so much he purchased the house next door for his illegitimate daughter Lady Augusta Gordon (née FitzClarence), whose sister Mary had married the Hollands' eldest son Charles Richard Fox.[86]

Isabella would officially 'own' all the people at Duckenfield for only one year and eight months after inheriting from Priscilla in November 1832. She was, however, eager to receive compensation for their loss. In October 1835, Isabella pressed her lawyer Robert Pitches: when would the compensation money be paid? She hoped it would come soon, otherwise she might have to sell a significant number of investments. She did not have to wait long. By the end of November, £1,132 3s 10d had arrived from Thomson Hankey & Co. for her eighth of 314 people enslaved at Grand Bras in Grenada, and £6,379 12s 5d in compensation for 336 people enslaved at Duckenfield.[87] The latter figure might have been higher had not forty-three people died there, and one – named Hope – been sentenced to life in the workhouse, since March 1831: many were probably victims of the Baptist War.[88]

Like the Hollands, Isabella now faced the challenge of ensuring a smooth transition to waged labour through apprenticeship and beyond. It would not be an easy task. In December 1834, just four months after emancipation, apprentices at Duckenfield went on strike. The previous week, they had been ordered to start milling at four in the morning but no canes were ready, so they were told to come back at sunrise. After this confusion, they refused to labour in the fields after lunch. Stipendiary magistrate John Daughtrey arrived the next day to hear the case, and ordered them to work that afternoon, which they should have had off, due to the early start. When they acquiesced, 'apparently satisfied at the justice of the decision', Daughtrey cited the victory to Governor Sligo as 'a proof of the improved spirit of the people'. In reality, it shows they were becoming increasingly conscious of their power to withhold labour.[89]

Many fine words were spoken about the need to educate the next generation, but unlike at Friendship and Greenwich, at Duckenfield 'no attention is paid to the free children'. As new births would no longer benefit former enslavers, they stopped trying to incentivise women to reproduce. Now, even women with six children were 'made to work in the field'.

McNeil had put people in the dungeon at Friendship and Greenwich while waiting for the magistrate to arrive. But at Duckenfield, overseer Thomas Scott confined 'people in the dark hole frequently, without sending for the Magistrate.' As nephew to Charles Scott, the principal Duckenfield attorney since 1818, he was able to act with relative impunity. Apprentices on Isabella's estate faced the same long hours, lack of free time, poor nutrition and injustices as those at Sweet River, Friendship and Greenwich, and across the island.

Similarly, once apprenticeship ended on 1 August 1838, many plantation labourers in St Thomas in the East voted with their feet. One stipendiary magistrate in the parish observed: 'the progress of the rural population in establishing themselves as small freeholders has been rapid and unceasing'. Free villages established on abandoned plantations in the parish included Dalvey near Duckenfield, with houses 'erected upon a much more spacious and comfortable scale than those of former days'.[90]

As an absentee, especially in this volatile period, Isabella well knew the importance of having reliable attorneys to manage her estates. However, the long-serving Charles Scott was growing old, and reportedly 'in a very frail state of health'. Not only did she doubt his competence, but in the event of his death, she would be left with just one attorney (James Bell, secondary agent since 1822).[91] Given the high incidence of death or departure amongst the Jamaican elite, this would be a dangerous state of affairs.

In October 1837, Isabella directed Robert Pitches to approach Thomson Hankey junior* about replacing Scott with one Charles Nockells. Nockells

---

* By this time, Thomson Hankey junior had taken over most of the firm's business from his father, who would retire in 1840. He became a prominent figure in the City, a director and later Governor of the Bank of England, and Liberal MP for Peterborough. 'Thomson Hankey junior', LBS: https://www.ucl.ac.uk/lbs/person/view/45726.

acted as attorney for his family's Mount Pleasant estate in St Thomas in the East, and he had already been earmarked to stand in for Charles Scott and James Bell if they were unable to progress Isabella's compensation claim in 1834.[92] His appointment would hardly have improved conditions for apprentices; he was amongst those calling for the United States to annex Jamaica and reinstate enslavement.[93]

Hankey advised: 'it is as well to avoid making substitutions or alterations which might occasion unpleasant feelings'; while Charles Scott was alive, things should continue as before. Pitches disagreed, advising Isabella: 'ever since I have known the name of Duckenfield the estate has always had two attorneys.' Isabella 'must however give the casting vote'.[94]

Isabella seems to have decided against Nockells in the end. But she did insist on having more than one attorney. In January 1841, Charles Scott's nephew, Thomas Scott, was diplomatically chosen as his replacement, alongside Alexander Barclay.[95*] Barclay, who had already begun some 'busy intermeddling' with the estate, was by now Speaker of the House of Assembly and 'confidential friend and adviser of more than one Governor General'. Sturge and Harvey had gone out of their way to call on 'so zealous and celebrated a champion of slavery' during their 1837 tour. They were 'favourably impressed' with his intelligence, but totally at odds with his politics. Tellingly, Barclay complained to them that: 'apprenticeship was so inconsiderably different from slavery, that it furnished no more satisfactory data for judging of the results of entire freedom than slavery itself'.[96]

Barclay was proud 'the days of barbarism and cruelty had long gone by' in Jamaica. However, after apprenticeship ended, he became extremely concerned about 'the difficulty of labour'. He greatly resented having to pay some £200 in wages every month – a bitter pill for a man who was almost fifty when enslavement ended. He grumbled pettily: 'even domestic servants are not to be procured and families are often for

---

* Charles Scott died in 1843, leaving legacies of £6 a year to Eliza Scott of Morant Bay and her two daughters Mary and Ann, with the right to continue living in his house there. This may well have been the same Eliza Scott, originally named Jubena, daughter of Molly Murray and mother to Lewis Wilson and George, who arrived at Duckenfield from Airy Castle (where Charles Scott had been attorney) in 1823, aged thirty-two. 'Charles Scott', LBS: https://www.ucl.ac.uk/lbs/person/view/13114.

weeks without the means of getting their linen washed at any price.' He was worried by 'so few of the young people applying themselves to labour, and a number of the old retiring from the estate to live upon patches of land of their own, which are easily purchased.'[97] Barclay's solution was to turn back the clock. He would import fresh labour from Africa.

Barclay was not the only former enslaver to seek new workers from elsewhere in the Empire. From 1838 to 1917, over 400,000 workers from India and some 18,000 from China, known disparagingly as 'Coolies', were taken to the British Caribbean. The majority went to Guyana and Trinidad; almost 40,000 arrived in Jamaica.[98] It is less well known that over 30,000 West and Central Africans were brought to the British Caribbean from Sierra Leone and St Helena before 1865; some 8,000 of whom were bound for Jamaica.

Despite the disaster faced by Black Loyalists sent to Sierra Leone from London in the 1780s, half a century later it was an established Crown colony, partly peopled by descendants of a second wave of Black Loyalists from Nova Scotia. Britain had also exiled Jamaican Maroons there after the 1796 war, and Barbadians following the uprising led by Bussa in 1816 – the largest Barbados had ever seen.[99] In the wake of 1807, Sierra Leone became the main place the Navy's West Africa Squadron brought illegal transatlantic slaving ships, to be processed by a special Vice Admiralty Court. Around 100,000 'liberated' – more accurately 'recaptured' – Africans arrived between 1808 and 1863. More than 13,000 died before disembarking – they were not allowed to leave the ship and its horrible conditions until after the court had passed judgment. Many survivors became involuntary apprentices either in Sierra Leone or wherever they were needed in the Empire; others were impressed into the army or navy. Few returned home.[100]

St Helena is largely remembered today for being remote enough to contain Napoleon. However, after a Vice Admiralty Court was established there in 1840, it also became a temporary home to over 20,000 recaptured Africans. Britain had occupied the island since 1658; it is still a British overseas territory today. When construction of a new airport began in 2006, 5,000 bodies were discovered buried in Rupert's Valley, a reception depot for recaptured Africans – the majority children and young adults. Like those buried at Newton in Barbados, some were found with filed teeth and jewellery; their remains also testify to the grim conditions recaptured Africans faced.[101]

Alexander Barclay became Jamaica's Commissioner General of Immigration in 1840, and took it upon himself to travel to Sierra Leone in person to obtain fresh labour. Few people wanted to leave. Going to Jamaica, according to one observer, would only appeal to those 'young in years, poor in pocket, unsuccessful in cultivation or adverse from employment in it, and especially those of the liberated Africans settled in Freetown'.[102]

Nevertheless, with false promises of higher wages and better living conditions, Barclay managed to recruit enough 'volunteers' to fill two ships. The *Hector* and the *Commissioner Barclay* sailed into Port Royal in May 1841 carrying 179 recaptured Africans, sixty-four Jamaican Maroons, sixteen Kru men from southern Sierra Leone; and eight village headmen (who would return to encourage further migrants).[103]

After the first few years, all pretence of promoting voluntary migration disappeared. The process became more or less coercive after 1845. In 1850, one group of recaptives was transferred directly into a ship headed for the Caribbean without the case even being referred to the Vice Admiralty Court. By this time, the West Africa Squadron, which had started out with just two ships, had twenty-five. The squadron is often lauded for rescuing people from illegal enslavement. But knowing what became of most of the recaptives places the intervention in a less flattering light. Even squadron officers remarked the Africans' 'freedom is but nominal', and Caribbean emigration would 'perpetuate their slavery'.[104]

Due to Barclay's ties to the parish, many newly arrived Africans settled in St Thomas in the East, where they 'constituted a nucleus for the others to gather into – from their natural desire to be together'. By 1843, fifty Africans had arrived at Duckenfield from Sierra Leone. That year, William Estridge, a descendant of John Estridge of St Kitts, whose estates John Baker managed in the 1770s, visited the plantation. In a long report to Thomson Hankey he observed the new recruits 'have worked admirably and indeed are still doing their duty'.[105]

One former enslaver, who admired Barclay's 'spirited manner' of making the journey to Sierra Leone, considered Africans preferable to 'Coolies' because 'they are at once at home on their arrival in the West Indies, and not infrequently meet many of their old countrymen. Their habits and feelings being alike, they intermingle with each other in a manner convenient for all parties.'[106] At Duckenfield, Estridge observed that due to 'an insufficiency of African women' – twice as many men arrived, as women were particularly reluctant to embark for the Caribbean – 'the men are beginning to court the Creoles'.

However, Estridge feared the formerly enslaved population – stereotyped as lazy with loose morals – would be a bad influence on the new arrivals and warned: 'the incipiencies of Creolism are perceptible'. It was for this reason he regretted Duckenfield 'has not any of the St Helena Africans who are chiefly boys – precisely of that age when they are likely to be steady and serviceable for a long time from being less susceptible of temptation.'

The experience of Africans at Duckenfield demonstrates the promises Barclay and his collaborators had made about what life would be like in Jamaica were false. They were not able to return to Africa after the one-year term of indenture was over. The daily pay at Duckenfield was 1s 6d for the 'first class' of workers, or 2s 'in crop' – meaning an additional three hours' work a day; and 1s for the 'second class'. Pay had not improved since apprenticeship, when average daily wages for ordinary field labour across the island ranged from 1s 8d to 2s 6d.[107] The wages in Jamaica may have been a little higher than in Sierra Leone – where daily rates might range from 3d to 1s – but the working conditions on a sugar plantation were far worse, with far fewer prospects of acquiring land in future.[108] Some workers had their wages docked by Barclay on spurious grounds of 'work badly performed', as well as being 'indolent' and failing to look after cattle. Showing more concern for the treatment of animals than people, he complained the cattle were 'unmercifully beaten and ill-used'.[109]

Accommodation was also inadequate. According to Estridge, Africans were living communally 'in the hospital and another large building', doubtless uncomfortably, though he claimed 'they like to live together'. Thomas Scott's claim new indentured labourers were 'full of noisy merriment and very happy' is not convincing. Estridge was uneasy about their communal living and would 'prefer seeing them in separate houses, as, with their individual comforts about them, they would be less likely to keep one head and be influenced in the mass by any sudden quarrel or disgust, or temptation of any kind to leave the property'. It seems they continued to live communally, however, as in 1865, reference was made to the 'African barracks'.[110]

The newcomers made their mark on St Thomas in the East. The Afro-Jamaican religion Kumina is still practised in the parish today.

Its distinctive songs, dances and drumming style, designed to honour ancestral spirits, echo the beliefs and traditions of people from Central Africa.[111]

Isabella also profited from indentured African labour in Grenada, where a dozen or so of the 2,709 people who arrived from Sierra Leone and St Helena ended up at Grand Bras. Her agent Thomson Hankey, by then also agent for Grenada, was at the forefront of petitioning the government to send more African workers there. He also pressed for indentureship terms to be increased from one to three years. This would, he argued, do more to offset the cost of providing food and lodging and reduce the risk they would be seduced to leave 'by the tampering of small settlers, native labourers and non-agriculturists'. Some workers were even being poached by emissaries from other islands, particularly Martinique. While Henry George, Earl Grey (the son of the former Prime Minister, at this time Secretary of State for War and the Colonies) sanctioned three further shipments to the island, he refused the three-year extension. He reprimanded the proposed daily food allowance of half a pound of saltfish, half a pint of peas or beans, and a pint of corn-meal as 'scarcely adequate in the case of children approaching the age of 14.' Ominously, he also confirmed: 'liberated Africans conveyed to the West Indies at the expense of this country, are not intended to have any claim for return passages'.[112]

The 'difficulty of labour' was only one of several challenges facing Barclay and Scott as they tried to make Duckenfield productive for Isabella after emancipation. In June 1842, Barclay warned: 'Lady Cooper cannot at present I am sure derive much income from it and nor would it be prudent for her to calculate upon a great deal for the future.'

The works were in a bad location, so far west that conveying cane there was extremely arduous. Barclay suggested building a 'good sized canal which may perhaps be rendered fit for punting up some of the canes'.[113]

In 1843, the estate had only one mule and one donkey; labourers had to rely on manpower. Barclay proposed clearing trees to create more pasture to rear livestock. This would be expensive, but Estridge believed an outlay of £1,000 'would soon pay for itself'. When Thomson Hankey asked Isabella for her opinion, she did not reject the idea outright, but was 'very unwilling to lay out any more money in the West Indies and will only consent to the proposed plan under any circumstances in a very clear statement of the prospective advantages to be derived'. Estridge's report would not suffice; Hankey asked Barclay to provide 'the fullest detail of the proposed benefit in a pecuniary view'. The tree clearance never happened, but in winter 1843 Barclay purchased nearby Suffolk Park Pen, without waiting for Isabella's permission.[114]

Another innovation was the purchase of a steam engine from Boulton and Watt's Birmingham factory in 1852.[115] The firm, founded by inventor James Watt and manufacturer Matthew Boulton – heroes of the Industrial Revolution – dominated the market, sending hundreds of engines to the Caribbean in the first half of the nineteenth century.[116] Coincidentally, James Watt's son, who became a partner in the firm, lived at Lady Sarah Holte's old home, Aston Hall, between 1817 and 1848.

Despite Barclay's fears for the future, or perhaps because of its new labour force, Duckenfield rallied and, after a bad year in 1840, when only 160 hogsheads of sugar and seventy-nine puncheons of rum were produced, the workers continued to churn out crops throughout the 1840s and 50s, rivalling and sometimes outdoing those produced during enslavement. An impressive 452 hogsheads of sugar and 240 puncheons of rum were produced in 1850, putting the lie to Barclay's complaints of indolence.[117]

Isabella was invited to attend annual audit meetings held by Thomson Hankey for the proprietors of Grand Bras. Profits were limited in 1842, with Hankey blaming the canes being destroyed by a severe drought, the cost of paying free waged labourers and poor soil. But Grand Bras soon became more productive.[118] One new venture was a blacksmith and coppersmith's shop named Grenville Forge.

Though Isabella received a considerable income from both Jamaica and Grenada throughout the 1840s and 50s, it could not compare with the days of enslavement. Though production remained high, costs were far higher now workers must be paid. In a typical statement from Thomson Hankey in 1849, Isabella received £1,857 13s 6d from Duckenfield and £61 17s 2d from Grand Bras, roughly a third of her income in 1831.[119]

Isabella died at Isleworth House on 27 January 1855, aged eighty-six. She was buried alongside her husband, son and daughter Isabella in the Cooper family vault at All Saints, Worlington. She split her fortune between her surviving daughters Mary Anne Honywood and Elizabeth Dawkins. The Honywoods got the English estates, including Chilton Lodge in Berkshire. The Dawkins inherited the property in Jamaica and Grenada, 57 Portland Place and £30,000.[120] They used the money to buy Moggerhanger estate in Bedfordshire, including its local pub, The Guinea (one of several British taverns named after the coin originally made from West African gold). Elizabeth later built Moggerhanger parish church in her husband's memory.[121]

Isabella also left £200 to the poor of Isleworth, and £25 each to 'Mr Ingram's Almshouses and Mrs Tolson's Almshouses'. While the twelve dwellings erected by Ann Tolson in 1756 have since been replaced by modern buildings, the six endowed by Sir Thomas Ingram in 1664 are now the oldest surviving buildings in Isleworth. Both form part of a charity still providing accommodation for those in need today.[122]

In 1840, a local history, to which Isabella subscribed, had stated: 'The poor of the neighbourhood speak in glowing terms of the innumerable acts of kindness and charity which they experience from the liberal possessor of Isleworth House.'[123] The marble memorial erected 'as a lasting record of her worth' and 'Christian benevolence' by parishioners lauded her as 'Generous and kind, liberal to the poor and ever ready to assist the distressed' – an approach, it almost goes without saying, that did not apply in Jamaica or Grenada.[124]

Although few families in this book were philanthropists, several enslavers did bequeath considerable funds to churches, hospitals, schools and universities, including the Edinburgh Royal Infirmary, Christ's Hospital school in West Sussex and the University of Pennsylvania. Isabella's agent Thomson Hankey senior endowed a charity in his own name with £10,000 in 1854, which would support widows and families of clergymen for the next 140 years. The Foundling Hospital, the RNLI (Royal National Lifeboat Institution) and the RSPCA (Royal Society for the Prevention of Cruelty to Animals) all count enslavers amongst their founders, chairmen and benefactors.[125]

Isabella's death had little impact on the labourers she had profited from. They continued to endure the same terrible working and living conditions, extreme punishments and a lack of access to justice or political representation.* Ten years after Isabella died, tensions over these wrongs boiled over. The people of Duckenfield were amongst those in St Thomas in the East who took a stand.[126]

---

* Fewer than 2,000 Jamaican men out of a population of over 400,000 had the right to vote. Hutton, *Colour for Colour*, p. 26.

On the night of 2 January 1865, the alarm bell and the cry of 'Buckra fire in trash house' rang out at Duckenfield. Two of three trash houses – piled with highly flammable dry canes – were lost, the flames aided by a strong wind from the north-east that had been blowing all day. It was 'only with the greatest difficulty that the works were preserved'.[127] Amongst the first men on the scene was forty-five-year-old night watchman Lewis Wilson. Wilson had been enslaved by the Franks family since he had been purchased from Airy Castle aged three. Deciding to stay on after the end of apprenticeship, by the time he was twenty-six in 1846 he owned over an acre of land.[128] When questioned, he recalled seeing a man ride past a little before the fire broke out, with a chain tied round his horse's neck. No further clues were recovered by the inquiry.

The fire at Duckenfield, one of a series of arson attacks that took place that year in the Plantain Garden River Valley, augured worse to come. On 11 October 1865, Paul Bogle, a Baptist preacher and smallholder from Stony Gut, led a protest march into Morant Bay. People were angry that Bogle and George William Gordon – a mixed-heritage businessman who had recently been elected as a Member of the Assembly for St Thomas in the East – had been expelled from the parish vestry.[129]

This was just the latest flashpoint in an ongoing struggle against a system stacked against Black Jamaicans. White men doubled as estate managers and magistrates, doling out disproportionate and unfair punishments. Duckenfield manager William Moore James had recently sentenced two boys to pay a fine of 18s each, forgo their wages for three weeks and spend twenty days in prison, all because they had accidentally run over some sprout canes with the wheels of a cart. This was not an isolated incident; James passed judgment in forty-one cases, and took labourers to court seventeen times in just two years between 1863 and 1865.

The confrontation in Morant Bay ended with the courthouse burning down and the deaths of eighteen officials and guards besides seven of their assailants. The following day, some 500 men and women led by Prince McLeod of Johns Town marched on a number of estates including Duckenfield. Some were singing:

> Buckras' blood we want
> Buckras' blood we'll have.
> Buckras' blood we are going for
> Till there's no more to have.

Isaac Robinson, who worked at Duckenfield, arrived at Hordley (which had formerly belonged to Monk Lewis) at midnight brandishing a gun, in search of attorney James Harrison. Harrison escaped, and later testified he heard shells being blown, flashes of fire, and indistinct cries from Duckenfield that same night.[130] The Duckenfield Great House was sacked, and one bookkeeper was 'shot on the spot'. The overseer's house and bookkeeper's barracks were left 'quite uninhabitable, everything destroyed, and all stores stolen'.

Three weeks later, matters were more 'settled' at Duckenfield, but attorney William Payne Georges complained of a shortage of 'cane hole diggers, many of these were men from the mountains and were the ringleaders in the late frightful outbreak'. Georges himself had been wounded in the courthouse confrontation. When he sneaked out of his hiding place in the early hours of the next morning, a crowd surrounded him shouting 'white man, chop him down!' He killed their leader, who was brandishing a cutlass, firing his pistol full in his face. Georges hoped 'all will go on quietly in our parish' as 'such an example has been made that can never be forgotten'. Nevertheless, he ordered a case of revolvers to be shipped to him as soon as possible.[131]

George William Gordon and Paul Bogle, both c.1860.

The 'example' he referred to was the heinous retribution perpetrated in St Thomas in the East, for a month after the Governor, Edward John Eyre, declared martial law. In scenes bearing more than a passing resemblance to those during the Baptist War, or any number of other uprisings during enslavement, hundreds were flogged, 1,000 homes destroyed, and almost 500 men, women and children killed, either shot on sight if they 'could not account for themselves' or summarily executed. Leaders Paul Bogle and George William Gordon – now both National Heroes whose images greet you at the airport and grace the walls of primary schools across the island – were amongst the victims, their bodies left hanging outside the Morant Bay courthouse. To eliminate Gordon, Governor Eyre had shipped him from Kingston to St Thomas in the East, where he could be condemned under martial law.[132]

At Duckenfield, soldiers commanded by Lieutenant Herbert Burroughs Adcock of the 2nd Battalion of the 6th Royal Regiment burned nine houses to the ground. Adcock justified this by claiming 'plunder' had been found within; he and his men assumed any items of value must have been stolen.[133]

Lewis Wilson, the Airy Castle-born watchman, took a man named Prince William into Bath for supposedly taking part in the attack on neighbouring Golden Grove. He was tied to a cart and whipped.[134] He probably received the average punishment meted out there of at least fifty lashes, though perhaps as many as a hundred, with a multi-tailed whip threaded with wire for maximum damage. The supervisor of whippings at Bath recalled them lasting from 6 a.m. to 6 p.m., until he 'could not see his way'.[135]

At least six people from Duckenfield were murdered. Three lost their lives merely going about their business, during a military raid on 18 October. One victim was Charles Logan, son of Hannah Grant, a fifty-three-year-old man who lived with his wife Lianta on land they owned themselves. Like Lewis Wilson, he was born at Airy Castle, and so had been enslaved by Isabella in his youth. He was shot by a soldier described as 'red skinned' and 'Sambo'. A second man killed that day was Sydney Tyne, a field worker from a family of African indentured labourers, probably brought to the estate by Alexander Barclay.* Sydney was shot in the cow pasture on his way home from work. His daughter

---

* By 1865, '200 or 300' Africans lived at Duckenfield, representing about half those living in the parish. Parliamentary Papers, *Report of the Jamaica Royal Commission, 1866*, p. 539.

Sarah rushed to his side but had to leave him to die alone for fear the soldiers might return and shoot her too. She came back late that night to bury him, with the help of Tobias Tyne and Patrick Grant. The third victim, a young man named James Davis, was killed in the road, after the soldiers asked him if he had seen a boy run past. His wife Ann heard the gunfire and found her husband dead in her sister's yard, having been shot in the chest and the mouth.[136]

Three days later, on 21 October, another three men from Duckenfield were executed. Their names were Richard (or George) Walton, John McCall (alias George McQuarry) and Tommy Miles (alias Tom Bell).[137] Suspected of stealing oil, nails and rum, they, and a fourth man, Richard Francis, were sent by Duckenfield's headman and constable Peter Phillips to the Post Office at Plantain Garden River to be flogged. Phillips, the oldest man at Duckenfield save 'one ageable man, only able to crawl', had been born on the estate sixty years earlier, so had been enslaved by the Franks and Cooper families until he was twenty-nine.[138]

Richard Francis managed to escape on the way, his hands being tied loosely enough for him to wriggle free. Ensign Francis James Cullen of the 1st West India Regiment ordered the others to be whipped. But, at the suggestion of company surgeon Dr Henry Morris, they were tied to a bamboo fence and shot. The soldiers used the new Enfield rifles that had played such a significant role in the First Indian War of Independence six years before; several men deployed to St Thomas in the East had previously fought in India. Phillips, who saw the corpses later that day, said 'one had an eye knocked out, one had a hole in the skull and the marrow came out, and the third had a wound in his stomach'.

Morris and Cullen were court martialled for this atrocity, but were acquitted after several soldiers, and Duckenfield managers, testified there had not been any shootings that day, while others claimed Morris had been ill in bed so could not have ordered an execution. In fact, Morris claimed he hadn't killed any prisoners during the whole period of martial law, a claim belied by a letter to his father in which he boasted he had 'slain nine people with his sword and revolver'.[139]

Though Morris resigned his commission in 1868, Cullen was promoted to Lieutenant, then Captain. He died fighting in Afghanistan in 1880, his regiment commended for their 'gallantry and devotion to Queen and Country'; his name appears on the Maiwand Lion monument in Reading. The failure to condemn perpetrators – despite John Stuart Mill pressing the Attorney General to put Cullen and Morris on trial in

England – added insult to injury for the people of Duckenfield, and St Thomas in the East more broadly, where the memory of what became known as the 'Killing Time' is still deeply felt.[140]

Though Isabella never set foot in Jamaica or Grenada, her fate and that of those islands were intimately entwined. Leveraging on Caribbean assets had enabled her to marry the son of a baronet and bankroll her children's martial or marital careers. When that income failed, her husband abandoned her for another woman, with scant regard for the family's reputation or Isabella's happiness.

Born almost a century before the Morant Bay War, Isabella lived through the most tumultuous years in Jamaica's colonial history. She saw the impact of the American, French and Haitian Revolutions, the abolitionist struggle, and the transition from enslavement to freedom before her death in 1855. And yet her story and the story of Duckenfield show how many things stayed the same. For the last fourteen years of her ownership, labourers were still being imported from Africa. Ten years after her death, the Morant Bay War, and especially its brutal repression, showed that life on Duckenfield, and in Jamaica, remained plagued by the legacies of enslavement, from remorseless exploitation to untrammelled violence in the face of any assertion of Black power.

Anna Susanna Watson Taylor, née Taylor, a 'star of fashion' and 'amiable hostess' by Sir Martin Archer Shee, *c.*1821.

9

Anna Susanna Taylor (1781–1853)

A true riches-to-rags story. Heiress to one of the richest men in Jamaica – who had no legitimate children – she married a man so profligate that together they squandered her entire fortune…

GEORGE IV needed some furniture. In fact, he needed a lot of furniture. Having created the Indian-inspired Brighton Pavilion during his regency and transformed Buckingham House into Buckingham Palace since coming to the throne, he had now set his sights on refurbishing Windsor Castle. He had commissioned extensive and luxurious new State Apartments, but where was he going to lay his hands on enough high-quality pieces to fill those vast interiors?

The King was delighted, therefore, when in May 1825 he heard that the contents of Anna Susanna and George Watson Taylor's townhouse were up for auction. He had visited the house in Cavendish Square on several occasions, so knew auctioneer James Christie junior was not exaggerating when he advertised the 'truly superb assemblage' of 'sumptuous articles of Parisian and other Furniture, in the first style of magnificence, including several that formerly adorned the Palace of Versailles'.

Christie had initially scheduled the auction for Friday 20 May, but such was the 'disappointment expressed by several of the Nobility' – the date clashed with Epsom Races – that he postponed it to the following weekend. When the day finally came, the King spent almost £5,000 of taxpayers' money on thirty-one lots, including several tables, desks and cabinets, candelabra, a chandelier, and marble and bronze busts of historical figures; many can still be seen at Windsor Castle today.

When attempting to justify the acquisition to his Prime Minister, the

Duke of Wellington, George IV insisted he had acquired these objects, 'worth double', at bargain prices.[1] It had been a fire sale: the couple had been forced to sell after their extravagant expenditure outpaced the income from Anna Susanna's colossal Jamaican inheritance.

The human cost of the auction lots was not recorded in the catalogue.

Anna Susanna was born in London on 20 February 1781, the first surviving child of Sir John Taylor, a newly minted baronet, and his wife Elizabeth Goodin (née Haughton). The couple, both from Jamaican enslaving families, had married three years before, and lived in Hill Street, off Berkeley Square.[2]

Although Sir John had begun his courtship in 1774, it had taken four years to gain Elizabeth's family's consent. The only daughter of Philip Haughton and Mary Brissett, Elizabeth had inherited a substantial fortune. Both the Haughtons and the Brissetts were long-established in Jamaica, major landowners in Hanover, St James and Trelawny. Like many of her peers, Elizabeth had been nursed by an enslaved woman – Abba – then sent to boarding school in England at an early age.[3] By the time she met John she was sixteen and living in Marylebone with her mother and stepfather Neill Malcolm, a Glasgow-born rum merchant, who as Elizabeth's guardian held her Hanover estates for her until she came of age.[4]

By contrast, John was a younger son from a family relatively new to Jamaica, largely financially dependent on his older brother, Simon. Their father Patrick Taylor had arrived from Burrowfield in eastern Scotland in 1728 – the same year as Gibson Dalzell. By the time he died in 1754, he had amassed over £50,000, mostly as a merchant in Kingston, but also through establishing a 900-acre plantation in St Thomas in the East, worked by over 500 people. The place was named Lyssons, after its original proprietor, Nicholas Lycence. One visitor remarked its 'situation is high and the view magnificent', but 'the musquitos tormenting!'[5]

John had attended Eton, then St John's College, Oxford. After enjoying the Grand Tour, he moved to London, joining the Royal Society of Arts (becoming a contemporary of Richard Oswald) and the Society of Dilettanti – 'a club, for which the nominal qualification is having been in Italy, and the real one, being drunk'.[6] An avid art collector, he was amongst the gentlemanly connoisseurs depicted in Zoffany's painting *The Tribuna of the Uffizi*.

Watson-Taylor Family Tree

Patrick Taylor (d.1754) = Martha Taylor née Taylor

John Brissett (d.1740) = Mary Haughton

Richard Haughton (1691–1740) = Elizabeth Goodin (1700–1734)

Simon Taylor (1739–1813) ⌒ Nelly Nugent (fl.1802)

Robert Taylor (d.c.1754)

Ann Taylor (d.1780) = Robert Graham, later Cunninghame Graham (1735–1797)

Richard Brissett (d.1796)

Mary Brissett = Philip Haughton (d.1758)

Mary = Col. John Haughton Reid (1716–1777)

Sarah Blacktree Hunter (fl.1810–1832)

Charlotte Taylor (1795–1849) = James Sproule (d.1840)

Sir John Taylor (1745–1786) = Elizabeth Goodin Haughton (1758–1822)

Richard Haughton Reid (1752–1844)

George Reid (1748–1823)

George Watson (1771–1841) = **Anna Susanna Taylor (1781–1853)**

Simon Richard Brissett Taylor (1783–1815)

Maria Taylor (1784–1829)

Martha Taylor (1786–1817)

Sarah (Sally) Taylor ⌒ William Cathcart (fl.1813–1832)

William Mayne 1776–1843 = Eliza Taylor (1782–1864)

Simon Hunter Taylor Cathcart (1809–?)

Sarah Hunter Taylor Cathcart (1807–1889) = Frederick John Wells (fl.1848)

Elizabeth Mayne (c.1812–1886) = Michael Elijah Impey (1803–1880)

Hannah Charlotte Hay (1818–1887) = Simon Watson Taylor (1811–1902)

Stillborn baby, 1812

John Walter Watson Taylor (1813–1832)

Isabella Watson Taylor (1814–1892)

George Graeme Watson Taylor (1816–1865) = Victorine Joudioux

Emilius Watson Taylor (1819–1879)

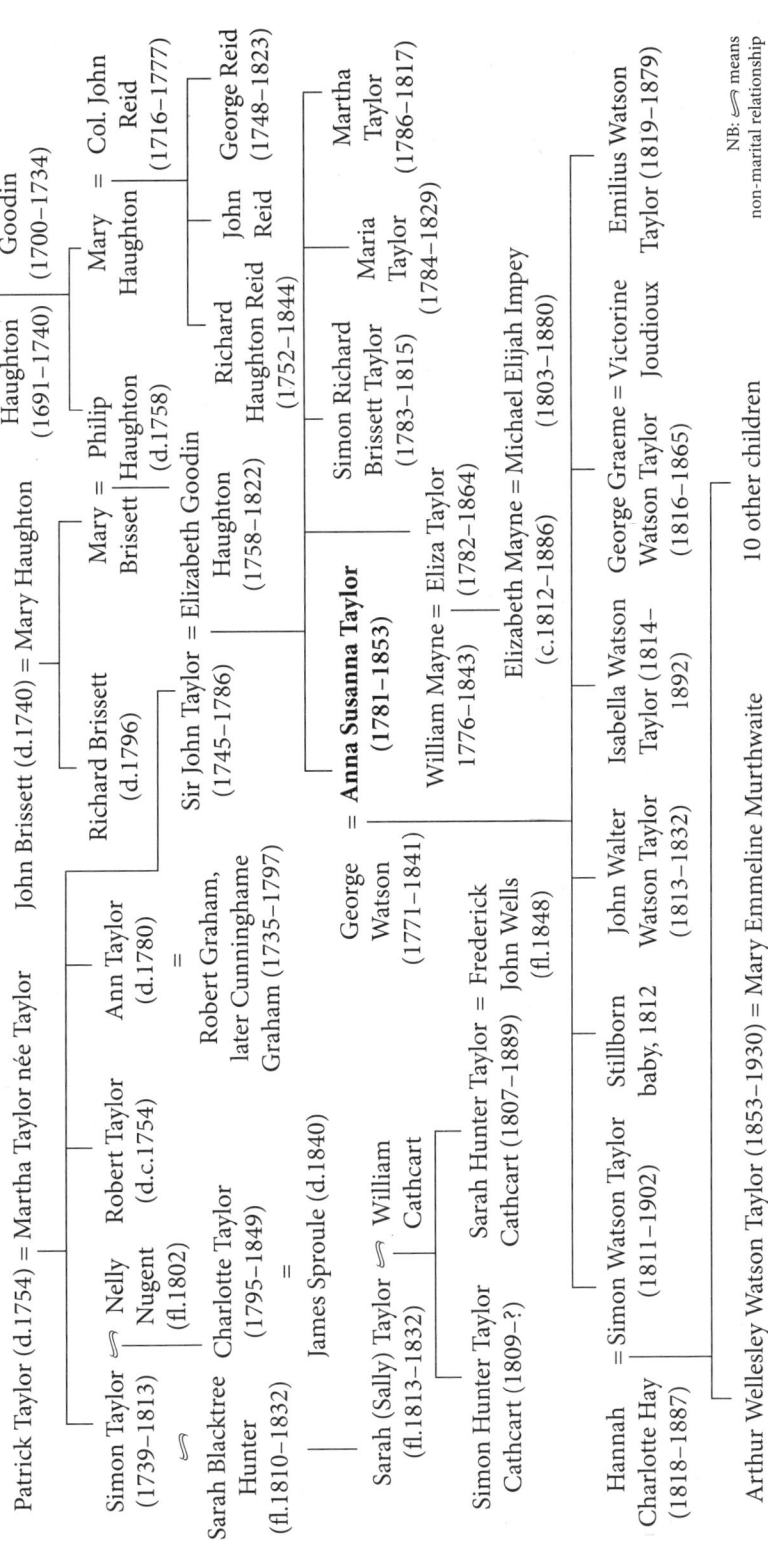

10 other children

Arthur Wellesley Watson Taylor (1853–1930) = Mary Emmeline Murthwaite

NB: ⌒ means non-marital relationship

'The Dilettanti Society', William Say after Joshua
Reynolds. Sir John Taylor stands second from the left,
holding our gaze, clutching a glass to his chest.

While John spent his time 'contriving how to lounge and wear away the day ... enjoying all the sweets of life', his older brother Simon 'had all the toil, fatigue and uneasiness of working up and drinking deep in the bitter drafts of it'.[7] After Eton and a mercantile apprenticeship in Amsterdam, Simon had returned to Jamaica in 1760, where he operated as a merchant in Kingston alongside his sister Ann's husband, Robert Graham.[8*] He also managed Lyssons (of which he owned two-thirds), and acted as attorney for several other estates, most prominently Golden Grove, adjoining Duckenfield.[9]

Around 1765 Simon purchased Llanrumney, the largest estate in St Mary, some five miles south of Port Maria. The plantation had originally

---

* This was the same Robert Graham who had rented Lucky Hill from the Dalzells in the late 1760s.

been established by Welsh privateer turned Lieutenant Governor of Jamaica Sir Henry Morgan (of Captain Morgan rum fame), who named it after his birthplace near Cardiff.[10] In 1771, Simon paid an eye-watering £100,000 for Holland, the largest estate in St Thomas in the East, on the coast to the north-east of Duckenfield. Unable to produce such an 'amazing sum of money' in one go, he paid in instalments, over several 'years of purgatory'.[11]

Simon was a grafter, boasting he had often completed four or five hours of work before nine in the morning. However, he exacted much harder labour from the hundreds of people he enslaved. Though he acknowledged working new arrivals 'immediately hard only breaks their hearts', and 'it is an utter impossibility for negroes to work without a belly full', poor health and high mortality rates were still endemic under his management.[12]

It was only after Simon had given John half of Lyssons, and he had obtained a baronetcy, becoming Sir John Taylor of Lyssons Hall, that Elizabeth's family relented in 1778. By now, Simon was amongst the wealthiest enslavers in Jamaica, having paid what he owed for Holland in full. Nonetheless, Simon – who bankrolled John's existence – worried the couple would live beyond their means, concerned Elizabeth spent

Anna Susanna's wealthy uncle, Jamaican enslaver Simon Taylor.

money as freely as his brother. In a phrase reminiscent of Dickens's Mr Micawber,* he warned John: 'any person who spends the whole of their income must be a beggar if he had the income of the Indias, but every man who lives within his income is rich – therefore be sure you do.'[13]

When Anna Susanna arrived in March 1781, Sir John and Simon were both disappointed she was not a boy. Simon had never married, nor wanted to. Instead, like so many others, he made a habit of sexually exploiting mixed-heritage women. His primary relationship was with Grace Donne, a free woman who had lived with him since 1768. But he also had a daughter, Sally Taylor, with Sarah Blacktree Hunter, who was also free; and another, Charlotte Taylor – a 'sickly delicate child, with straight light-brown hair, and very black eyes' – with Nelly Nugent, the enslaved 'housekeeper' at Golden Grove. When Nelly proudly introduced Charlotte to the Governor's wife Lady Maria Nugent in 1802, she added that Simon had 'a numerous family, some almost on every one of his estates'.[14]

This put the onus on Sir John and Elizabeth to provide legitimate heirs to Simon's fortune. The couple were in love and fulfilled the brief. After Anna Susanna, three more children followed in quick succession: Elizabeth in 1782, Simon Richard Brissett in 1783 and Maria in 1784. More boys would have been preferable, and while it was good to have an heir and a spare, further children were expensive. Simon begged his brother to keep to a budget of £2,000 a year, anxiously reminding him: 'a person who gets children should think to provide for them, whereas if your whole income is spent in dress, show, equipages &c. how will you be able to do it?'

From her earliest years, Anna Susanna was taught to please her distant benefactor. When she was two, her father expressed his hope she would 'soon lisp out her uncle Simon's name'. She was encouraged to write to him as soon as she could scrawl. He thanked his 'dear little girl' for her 'first attempt to make yourself known to me', which he received 'with the greatest pleasure', and promised to send her oranges and cashew nuts on the next ship.[15]

Anna Susanna was four when Simon demanded Sir John come out to manage Elizabeth's Hanover estates. Venture, Unity, Orange Cove and

---

* In Charles Dickens's *David Copperfield*, Wilkins Micawber laments: 'Annual income twenty pounds, annual expenditure nineteen nineteen and six, result happiness. Annual income twenty pounds, annual expenditure twenty pounds ought and six, result misery.'

Mammee Hill Pen were situated on the north coast just west of Lucea, home to some 500 people.[16] While Elizabeth owned all of Venture and Mammee Hill, three-quarters of Unity belonged to her stepfather Neill Malcolm and half of Orange Cove to her father's half-brother, Samuel Williams Haughton – causing several complications. Based between Kingston and St Thomas in the East, with several other estates to attend to, Simon could not visit Hanover regularly. Without closer oversight, he foretold 'certain ruin'. He also warned his brother that Samuel Williams Haughton was 'very absolute and despotic', with a style of management that threatened to 'destroy the negroes'.[17]

Sir John was reluctant, protesting: 'I do not know what use my presence could be of in Jamaica. The Management of a West Indian Estate is not my Forte.' Despite the evident truth of this statement, Simon would not take no for an answer. Sir John initially planned to travel to Jamaica alone, but Elizabeth refused to allow it, bursting into tears whenever he brought up the subject. Eventually they decided to go together, leaving their children behind. They intended to stay on the island for three years, living at Unity, and Sir John promised Simon he would not leave Jamaica 'until the properties are in good order'.[18]

Anna Susanna and her siblings were left in the care of their uncle Robert Graham, now a fifty-year-old widower, who had inherited substantial property in Scotland and just become lord rector of Glasgow University.[*] Robert's close involvement in the children's lives is shown by his inclusion in the intimate family portrait made by Daniel Gardner around this time. At the centre, Anna Susanna looks cherubic with rosy cheeks in her mother's embrace. While Sir John stands beside his wife and children in a proprietorial fashion, Robert has young Simon Richard Brissett and Elizabeth clambering onto his knee.[19]

Sir John did not live long enough to make much impact in Hanover. A year after arriving at Unity, he died of dropsy – or possibly yellow fever – aged just forty-one. His will dictated his children should be maintained 'in a liberal manner', that his son would inherit and his daughters receive generous dowries; but he died so indebted that these provisions were meaningless. What with his flamboyant lifestyle and the difficulties in Hanover, he owed over £46,000.[20]

---

[*] Robert Graham was friends with my fifth great-grandfather, Robert Cooper Lee, inviting him and Priscilla to visit Scotland in 1776. Cunninghame Graham, *Doughty Deeds*, p. 112.

Elizabeth was heavily pregnant when Sir John died. She returned to England in July 1786, almost immediately after giving birth to her last daughter, Martha, with three unnamed 'Jamaican servants' in tow. Sir John's death had left the family not only bereft, but in straitened circumstances. Their London home, and much of Sir John's art collection, had to be sold. With the help of Robert Graham, they downsized to a mansion house named Bolney Court, on the Thames south of Henley, leased from a Kittian family.[21] Five-year-old Anna Susanna and her family were waited on for about a year by the three enslaved Jamaicans, until Simon suggested they would be 'better employed' on the island. Simon, determined 'to make my Brother's Family as happy as I could', 'expended large sums of money in carrying on the plantations' to fund Elizabeth's £2,000 annuity and 'the maintenance and education of her children'.[22]

Anna Susanna continued writing to Simon. He was impressed by her handwriting, and delighted to hear she was also progressing in reading, 'cyphering' (mathematics), French, drawing and music. He sent her a pet macaw and told her 'you are what it is to be a good girl'.[23] She often asked when he would visit, and after promising to do so since 1788, he arrived in summer 1791, when Anna Susanna was ten. He had not set foot on English soil for thirty years.

Simon found his stay most disagreeable 'except when I was among my intimate friends'. He visited Bolney Court for Christmas 1791, gifting money to Anna Susanna, and dolls to her sisters.[24] Simon was generally fond of children. Lady Maria Nugent was surprised when he behaved to hers 'like an affectionate uncle, though in a gruff sort of way', 'for he has the character of loving nothing but money'.[25]

By the time Anna Susanna met Simon, he had become 'by much the richest proprietor in the island, and in the habit of accumulating money, so as to make his nephew and heir one of the most wealthy subjects of His Majesty.'[26] Between attorneyship commissions, sugar and rum sales, investments, and interest payments from debtors, he enjoyed an estimated income of £47,000 a year. He lived in a grand country house, Prospect Pen, just north of Kingston, with beautiful views of the Blue Mountains. Now known as Vale Royal, it is formally designated as the Jamaican Prime Minister's official residence, but is in such a bad state of disrepair that it has not been used as such for several years.[27]

Simon was also politically powerful, 'having great influence in the Assembly', where he was 'violent in his language against the King's

Ministers, for their conduct towards Jamaica'.[28] The 'alarming news' of the Haitian Revolution broke while he was in London. For much of his year-long stay he was preoccupied with finding out 'what the People in this Part of the world mean to do with the West Indies'. He was horrified by the abolitionist views he encountered, decrying the 'malignancy of mind', and 'obstinacy of opinion among men who were entirely ignorant of the matter they spoke on'. He would later blast William Pitt the Younger for having 'encouraged and supported that madman Wilberforce to spread fire and destruction among us'.[29]

In November 1793, when Anna Susanna was twelve, scandalous news arrived from Jamaica, threatening both her mother's reputation and the family's already reduced income. Samuel William Haughton had died and Elizabeth's cousins Richard Haughton Reid and Thomas Reid had seized her Hanover estates.[30] They claimed Elizabeth's father, Philip Haughton, had married one Martha Howard of Eltham while in London as a young man. This made his subsequent marriage to Mary Brissett bigamous, and Elizabeth illegitimate. Simon exerted his best efforts on his sister-in-law's account, but the Reids wanted 'Mountains of Gold', and his attempt to eject them from the property failed. The struggle became 'a millstone round his neck'. In 1797, Simon thought he had 'settled everything' by agreeing to give the Reids £5,000 and half of Orange Cove. However, two years later, after the London authorities confirmed Philip *was* previously married, Simon was forced to give up Orange Cove entirely. A final settlement with the Reids was not reached until 1805.[31] As always, the people enslaved on the disputed estates would suffer the most from the struggle; for who would invest in a place they were uncertain to benefit from?

Though Simon had been able to buy the family a house in fashionable Marylebone before the drama with the Reids, in March 1795, he was forced to halve their annual income to £1,000. Elizabeth economised by sharing a pair of horses and a coachman with a friend, and offered to sell her diamonds; she even considered moving to Italy, where a 'prudent person' could 'live very reasonably' for £150 a year, 'a sum of money which constitutes little more than penury in England'. This was averted when Robert Taylor, a merchant and slaver who was Simon's second cousin and main London agent, agreed to pay off her debts.[32] In 1796, Anna Susanna and her siblings received legacies on the death of their grand-uncle Richard Brissett. Simon, convinced Brissett had known about the bigamous marriage all along, had made him promise to provide for them. However, Elizabeth continued to overspend; Anna Susanna would contribute £150 towards paying off her mother's debts in 1809.[33]

Anna Susanna knew she must secure her uncle's approval of any potential husband. Simon held the family's purse strings; he could easily deny her a dowry. A 'remarkably sensible good young woman, with great ability, and a good disposition', she would not follow her sister Eliza's example. In 1804, Eliza had married William Mayne. His father Robert Mayne, a banker, merchant and army contractor, had killed himself after going bankrupt in 1782. He had no money, no job and no prospects. Furious, Simon cut Eliza off.[34]

Anna Susanna had several suitors. In 1803 General John Ramsay, son of painter Allan Ramsay, and 'an amiable and respectable young man of independent fortune', showed a 'great partiality' for her, but his courtship was interrupted when he was sent to Malta. In May 1805, she received a proposal from George Reid, nephew of her mother's cousin Richard Haughton Reid, but the 'attachment was all on the side of the gentleman'. Simon and her mother objected: 'his fortune is all in the West Indies' – British assets were more reliable. Though it is not mentioned in their letters, they had finally signed the papers concluding the eight-year struggle with the Reid family over the Hanover estates only that January. Why make an alliance with a family who had given them so much trouble? Anna Susanna gave Reid an 'absolute refusal' in July.[35]

Anna Susanna was almost twenty-eight by the time she fell for George Watson in early 1809. Thirty-seven-year-old George was the fourth son of Scottish-born George Watson of Saul's River, St Thomas in the East, Jamaica; his mother Isabella was from the Stevenson family of Barbados.[36] However, George had been born in London and his mother was friends with Anna Susanna's mother, so she had probably known him all her life. George was reputed to be a 'very sensible gentlemanlike man', with a 'most excellent character' and 'much esteemed by all his friends and relations'.[37]

Having studied at St Mary Hall (now part of Oriel College), Oxford, and Lincoln's Inn, George was a well-educated civil servant, writer and aspiring connoisseur, with a sideline in speculative acquisitions of Old Master paintings. Audiences delighted at the anti-French rhetoric deployed in his play *England Preserved*, set during the minority of Henry III, performed at the Theatre Royal, Covent Garden, at George III's request in February 1795. George also wrote political pamphlets and poetry; his poem, 'The Old Hag in a Red Cloak' (1801), poked fun at the Hollands' friend Monk Lewis, and his train of 'ghosts and hobgoblins, and horrible shapes'.[38]

From 'his own merit and abilities' George had secured the position of private secretary to two prominent politicians: first John Pratt, 1st Marquess of Camden, then his nephew (Lord Seaford's best friend) Lord Castlereagh. This took him to Ireland, as Camden acted as Lord Lieutenant there from 1795 to 1798 and Castlereagh was Chief Secretary between 1798 and 1801.[39] It was Castlereagh who presided over the brutal repression of the Irish Rebellion of 1798. Byron condemned the 'cold-blooded, smooth-faced, placid miscreant! / Dabbling … in Erin's gore'; when Shelley met 'Murder', he 'had a mask like Castlereagh'.[40]

The British army certainly used murderous methods to suppress the uprising. In addition to flogging and half-hanging, suspects were subjected to pitchcapping. This involved placing a cap of pitch (boiling tar) and gunpowder on the head, before setting it alight. Those who did not die might be left scalped or blind.[41] The climax came when General

Portrait of George Watson Taylor by Sir Martin Archer Shee, 1820.

Gerard Lake's men, armed with superior weapons, killed over 1,000 Irish at the Battle of Vinegar Hill, whilst sustaining fewer than 100 casualties. Even Lake admitted 'the carnage was dreadful'.

Though not involved in the fighting, George played his part. It was *he* who interviewed United Irishman leader Lord Edward FitzGerald following his violent arrest on 19 May 1798; *he* who personally informed Lady Fitzgerald of her husband's imprisonment. After FitzGerald died in prison from septicaemia, George somehow obtained his uniform as a gruesome souvenir, later presenting it to the Duke of York.*

George also wrote the inflammatory song 'Croppies Lie Down', sung by the troops under General Lake, to which 'more blood has been shed than often falls to the lot of lyrical productions'. 'Croppies' was a derogatory term for the Irishmen who wore their hair cropped short, like French Revolutionaries; George's lyrics characterised them as cowards, killing civilians, and hiding – lying down – in 'ditches and cellars' when the British approached. 'Croppies Lie Down' 'kindled in many a rebel breast a savage, though silent rage'. A blind woman who tried to make a livelihood singing it on the streets of Dublin was murdered in a dark alley. The tune, sung by Protestant Orangemen for years, is still politically potent today.[42]

Anna Susanna accepted George in February 1809, on condition her uncle approved. Elizabeth remarked this was 'the only attachment she has ever shown to any one'; if she could not marry George, she would never marry at all.[43] But it was far from certain Simon would give his blessing. Like the Reids, the Watsons lacked British assets. Furthermore, Simon knew they were not major landholders in Jamaica, and, as a fourth son, George would not inherit much.[44] Alongside his 'very meagre pedigree', George's 'lack of a private income stood in the way of his happiness.' It was not that he was penniless. After returning from Ireland in 1802, George continued working for both Camden and Castlereagh, serving both the Board of Control (which governed India) and the Department for War and the Colonies. In 1806, probably thanks to Camden, he acquired two government posts: Deputy Teller of the Exchequer and Commissioner of Excise, with a combined salary

---

* FitzGerald was Charles James Fox's first cousin. On hearing of his death, Elizabeth, Lady Holland, remarked, 'Death has placed the gallant Ld Edward beyond the reach of his enemies'. *Journal of Elizabeth, Lady Holland*, ed. Ilchester, vol. 1, p. 187.

of £2,200. However, Simon objected these roles were 'only for life and from his station in life it seems impossible for him to leave anything for his children and her'.[45]

Robert Taylor advocated the match. Though not advantageous 'in point of fortune ... happiness is the chief object ... and from Mr Watson's genial character, and his sincere attachment to your niece, I think there is every prospect of his making her a good husband'. In what turned out to be a stupendously inaccurate judgement of character, he observed George was 'by no means expensive, or has any high notions, & says if he can keep a carriage for his wife and give a friend a family dinner, it is all he aspires to'.[46]

Simon eventually acquiesced on condition George invested £10,000 to provide an income for Anna Susanna and any future children, on penalty of £20,000 if he failed to do so.[47] Simon likewise promised to invest £10,000 in Anna Susanna's name within six months of the wedding. A further £10,000 would be invested on her behalf if 'no insurrection of slaves or a general invasion' happened during his lifetime. Careful to protect his niece's position, he stressed in the marriage settlement that all dividends would go directly to Anna Susanna, and if the couple ever inherited his estates, they could sell them only for Anna Susanna's sole benefit.[48]

Simon wrote to Anna Susanna, 'I sincerely wish both you and Mr Watson every happiness that this life can afford'. They wed on 6 March 1810. After a six-week honeymoon, visiting some of George's relations near Bristol, they were 'very happily and comfortably settled' at 23 Hanover Square. A series of back-to-back pregnancies soon followed. Their eldest son, Simon, born in February 1811, was named, like many boys in the family, after Anna Susanna's uncle. She had a difficult and dangerous labour in April 1812; the child was stillborn. Then came John Walter in 1813, Isabella in 1814 and George Graeme in 1816.[49]

Anna Susanna's brother Sir Simon had inherited the baronetcy on their father's death, but his prospects of inheriting their uncle's colossal fortune depended on keeping in his good books. Sir Simon had proved a disappointment from an early age. When he was thirteen, his uncle complained: 'You do write better than you did, but not half so well as your Sister [the seventeen-year-old Anna Susanna] ... and will you let a Lady write better than you?' As he grew to adulthood, Sir Simon preferred travel to gainful employment. His uncle wanted an heir who would be a 'useful Man in Society, not an Empty vain … Gambler or Lounger'.[50] But Sir Simon appeared to be his father all over again.

In January 1806, after the young man protested he was not cut out for a mercantile career, and asked instead to be bought a seat in Parliament, Simon 'resolved firmly to close you for ever from my Affection and Fortune.' Anna Susanna appealed to her uncle on her brother's behalf. Simon snarled that while he would always be very glad to hear from her and her sisters, his nephew's ingratitude was unacceptable.[51] Sir Simon was eventually forgiven after sending several grovelling letters.

In November 1811, worrying news reached Anna Susanna in Brighton. Sir Simon had secretly and suddenly left for Jamaica. Elizabeth feared she might lose her only son in the same way she had lost her husband; Anna Susanna rushed to her side.[52] Sir Simon's hasty departure 'raised a curiosity in all the Jamaica interest'. George tried in vain to get some explanation out of Robert Taylor.[53] His enquiry was not an idle one. For if Sir Simon had displeased his uncle so greatly that he must now appeal to him in person, his whole inheritance must be at stake. And, if he were to be disinherited, Anna Susanna would be next in line.

This time, Sir Simon had angered his uncle by refusing to marry Robert Taylor's eldest daughter. She was only fifteen; Sir Simon protested he did not wish to marry a child.[54] His trip to Jamaica did not go well. Simon was 'nearly superannuated', and in poor health, reliant on a gold-tipped walking stick. Grace Donne had died in 1804, leaving Simon 'like a Fish out of the Water by her loss'. Sir Simon found his uncle being cared for by his daughter Sally Taylor. Sally had recently moved into Prospect Pen, together with her mother and her two children by Scottish enslaver William Cathcart.[55]

Simon found his nephew a nuisance who just lounged about doing nothing. Finding 'no opportunity of conversing with you since my residence in your house', Sir Simon resorted to writing his uncle a letter. Though Sir Simon left Jamaica without a reconciliation, Simon did not cut him off as threatened, perhaps due to the apologetic letters he continued to bombard him with.[56] Or perhaps, despite everything, he still preferred a male heir.

Simon Taylor died of 'debility' on 14 April 1813, aged seventy-three. He had resisted calls from his family to retire to England for years, insisting he would 'only be an incumberance'; he wished 'to lay my bones in my native land'. But towards the end, though bedridden, he changed his mind. He breathed his last at Port Royal, waiting for his ship to sail.

Showing less than his normal foresight, Simon had asked to be buried in the courtyard at Prospect Pen, alongside his brother. However, as he had also dictated the property be sold, both bodies had to be disinterred soon afterwards, and re-buried at Lyssons. The remains were carried on 'a common mule cart' for the forty-mile journey east 'in not a very decent manner'. Perhaps, as with Florentius Vassall's coffin bearers, the cart driver took the opportunity to enact some death rituals of his own.[57]

With total assets worth around £1 million, Simon Taylor was not only the wealthiest Jamaican of his time, but ranked in the top fifteen richest Britons dying in the first half of the nineteenth century. He enslaved significantly more men, women and children than the majority of his contemporaries. His probate inventory listed 2,248 people, 'valued' at £128,550. We can only begin to grasp the enormity of this when we consider it takes over an hour to simply read their names, occupations and assigned 'values' out loud.[58]

Their fates were now in the hands of Sir Simon, who inherited the whole Taylor fortune. This by now comprised the sugar estates of Lyssons, Holland, Llanrumney and Haughton Court (made up of Unity and Venture), and several pens: Prospect, Burrowfield (named for Patrick Taylor's birthplace in Scotland), Montrose, Flint River and Haughton Grove (perhaps formerly Mammee Hill).[59]

Sir Simon did not enjoy his gargantuan inheritance for long. His health had been poor for some time, with an unnamed 'disorder', mentioned as early as 1808. In March 1811, he had developed a dangerous fever 'by overheating himself in hunting a Badger', and was laid low for months, seeking treatment from a top London surgeon. He died on 18 May 1815, aged only thirty-two.[60]

London society thrilled at the 'wonderful wealth' Anna Susanna and George inherited. The windfall's unexpected nature made it even more dramatic. After all, 'Sir Simon was a young man, and likely to marry; so that the Watsons' chance seemed a poor one'. But now, 'the fruits' of a 'long life in accumulation', were 'showered on the Watsons': 'What a wonderful change of fortune for these two persons! – From only having had an income of £2,000 or £3,000 a year, with tastes far beyond such limits, to almost boundless and unequal riches!'[61]

*

George and Anna Susanna knew little about the plantations they had inherited – they didn't even know how many people they enslaved. George admitted to being 'frequently at a loss upon the subject'. By contrast, their attorney assured them, 'on all the estates the name and the situation of Mr Watson Taylor is well known to the people and they regret they have no prospect of seeing their master until your son comes of age'. In August 1819, George expressed a wish to make the journey with eight-year-old Simon. But Anna Susanna was heavily pregnant with Emilius, their last child, and 'suffers much incidentally to her present state'. He decided: 'Mama cannot be left.'[62]

Instead, they relied on Scottish brothers John and William Shand. While John was attorney to several enslavers, William claimed experience of managing 18,000 to 20,000 enslaved people during his thirty-two years in Jamaica, in almost every parish in the island. He boasted he was 'well acquainted with the negro character', this knowledge amounting to a hackneyed distinction between the 'industrious negro' and the 'lazy negro'. The Shands were also both enslavers themselves, with estates in St John, Clarendon and St Catherine, so not best placed to visit the Watson Taylor properties on a regular basis.[63]*

Two of the most inaccessible estates, Llanrumney and Holland, had idiosyncratic and contrasting challenges. John Shand was shocked, when he visited Llanrumney in March 1817, to find the 540 people enslaved there 'in a state totally different from those on the other plantations'.[64] With hardly any white employees, the plantation had a history of resistance. In October 1807, some newly arrived Africans had stabbed their driver; Simon Taylor had believed 'something very ominous' was 'brewing'. He learnt there had been 'some improper communication' with Frontier estate, which had 'always been the foremost in all insurrections from the year 1760, 1765 & 1767'. For Llanrumney was not only close to where Tacky's War began in 1760, but was less than two miles from neighbouring Whitehall, where a group led by head boiler Abruco, an 'old Coromantee', had attempted to 'kill all the white people in the neighbourhood' one night in November 1765 (a smaller uprising

---

* John Shand lived at Clifton Pen in St Catherine with Frances Brown – a free mixed-heritage woman he had formerly enslaved – and their seven children. Their youngest daughter Frances Batty Shand founded the Cardiff Institute for the Blind in 1865. 'A North East Story: African Scottish Families', University of Aberdeen: https://exhibitions.abdn.ac.uk/university-collections/exhibits/show/a-north-east-story/african-scottish-families.

followed in 1767).⁶⁵ Simon had been alarmed that 'All the new negroes know of the insurrection of 40 years ago'. Unless something was going on, why 'would they tell these New Negroes who have not been four months in the island of what happened before any of the negroes sent there were born?' Simon's anxiety on this front endured; '5 stands of arms & accoutrements' remained 'distributed amongst the white people on the estate' at the time of his death.⁶⁶

By contrast, vast Holland had an unusually large population of white bookkeepers, numerous enough to require their own barracks. There was a correspondingly large number of 'domestics', subject to sexual exploitation. Amongst them was fifty-two-year-old African-born 'Old Dolly', considered 'superannuated' and of 'no value' by the time Anna Susanna inherited. In her prime, Dolly had presided over the household. Isabella Cooper's attorney, Alexander Barclay, who had started his career as a bookkeeper for Simon Taylor at Holland, remembered her well.

One day, he recalled, Simon was about to arrive with some friends, 'which always occasioned a considerable bustle in making preparations'. A young white man, Mr Brice, 'who had charge of the stores as key-carrier, was so much annoyed with endless errands' that he cursed Dolly 'for the unnecessary trouble he thought she was giving him.' Barclay believed her response would have greatly surprised abolitionists like his adversary James Stephen, 'who thinks "every negro or mulatto … is far more degraded below the lowest white person in Jamaica."'

Barclay recalled Dolly berating Brice 'with a contempt which, to be conceived, must have been seen and heard':

> *You*, a *poor* good-for-nothing Buckra, take upon yourself to curse *me*! Wharra you? Wharra make *you* come in'o massa plantation for n'yam [to eat]? Wharra! You talk so to *me*! Me have for me *house*, for me *ground*, for me n**ger; where for *you* house, for *you* ground, for *you* n**ger? Curse *me* hey! Me see nough o' buckra, like o' *you*, come in'o massa plantation; but dem *gone*, and *you* will gone, if dem no carry you in o'quahill [the burial ground]. Curse *me*, hey! You take something on yourself, true!

One wonders whether her demeanour and high status as observed by Barclay – not a totally reliable witness – was based on a personal relationship with her enslaver, Simon Taylor, or one of the many white men he employed.

Barclay did not revise his interpretation of the parable of the two boxes at this stage, or after another enslaved person displayed similar confidence. Having 'inadvertently addressed one of the negro boiler-men, "You Sir!" ... he gave me such a pointed and merited rebuke, as I have never forgotten ... "You sir! Who do you call You sir; have I not a name?"' Barclay did *not* bother to record the man's name. He may have been one of five boiler-men living at Holland in 1813: Bauldy, Ben, Punch, Robin and St Matthew.[67]

Barclay claimed people enslaved at Holland were so wealthy that if the property they held in 'slaves, horses, asses, pigs, poultry, furniture and hoarded cash could be realised' it might fetch £10,000. They had a 'coasting vessel, which they employed in carrying plantains, yams, edoes, and corn, from the estate's wharf to market in Kingston, a distance coastwise of sixty to seventy miles.' In return, he said, they received 'Irish salt-pork, butter, mackerel, cod fish, linens, printed cottons, muslins, handkerchiefs, and crockery-ware – articles regularly retailed in the plantation villages.' Artist James Hakewill, who visited and painted all the Taylor properties in 1820–1, found Holland workers 'grumble as much at the low price of yams and plantains as an English farmer at the fall of corn'.[68] However, the people Barclay and Hakewill characterised as rich traders would have belonged to an elite minority.

It's extremely surprising to see Barclay listing 'slaves' amongst enslaved people's assets, and to find Dolly asserting she had 'me n**ger'. William Shand recalled a family with 'negroes of their own' who asked to buy their freedom after Simon Taylor's death, but changed their minds when he told them free people must leave the estate. A later visitor observed 'many of the negroes belonging to this property have slaves'.[69] Such ownership would not have been legally recognised. It may be that, just as the Hylas family claimed others by custom in Barbados, the Holland elite had been bequeathed people in the wills of white men to whom they were related.

In his letters to the Shands, George often invoked Anna Susanna's name, and spoke of 'our sentiments'. As she was the one who had inherited, speaking as one strengthened his authority. George told John Shand they were both glad he believed the 'preservation and comfort of the negroes' should be the 'first object on every well-regulated estate'. George wrote to Shand in December 1815: 'you conceive justly that all severity, beyond the absolute necessity of the case is repugnant to Mrs Watson Taylor's feelings and is equally to mine'. Their wish that 'the negro population of the estates' should be treated with 'pure humanity, benevolence, justice and liberality' was undercut by admitting some cases required 'severity'.

Like the Hollands, the Watson Taylors wished to ingratiate themselves with the people they enslaved. George wrote: 'I should be glad if Mrs Watson Taylor's name and interference could be advantageously introduced to their attention so as to impress them with a favourable sentiment towards our family.'

The Watson Taylors were also 'desirous to have the names of the principal persons upon each of the properties' to whom they might 'send a present of cloth for a suit of clothes'. John Shand advised them in February 1816:

> sending out a few light clothes to be distributed to the children in the name of Mrs Taylor will have the best effect: cotton cloth partly blue and partly white is the best adapted for their use and the mothers will like it better if delivered in cloth than if ready-made up.[70]

Enslaved people preferred cloth to ready-made outfits because clothing was one of the only ways of expressing individuality. Archaeologists have found sewing equipment – needles, thimbles, thread spools – on plantation sites. Enslaved people used a mix of hand-me-downs such as those previously belonging to Jane Macquarie, and cloth such as that gifted to Mary Hylas or purchased at market, to fashion outfits. Given the very limited standard wardrobe allocations, dress was a key way to mark one's status. Elaborate draping and headdresses, aside from echoing West African styles, required more material, so demonstrated a higher position in the social hierarchy.[71]

In October 1816, George sent out some cotton clothing for the 'breeding women and young children' – perhaps some were Anna Susanna's hand-me downs. He emphasised she 'has a family herself and is solicitous for the[ir] comfort'. Mothers were favoured in this way not out of 'benevolence and humanity', but because the Watson Taylors were anxious to promote higher birth rates now they could not buy more captives from Africa. They expressed frustration that, despite 'all that we have done', the hoped-for increase in numbers did not appear to be forthcoming. George was dismayed that out of thirty to forty women at Flint River 'in the prime of life', there had not been a single birth during 1817.[72] Like other enslavers, he seemed unable to understand women's reluctance to birth babies into enslavement, or that hard labour and malnutrition resulted in low fertility.

Poor conditions were exacerbated after a hurricane hit in November 1815; the heavy rains and flooding destroyed ground provisions. John Shand feared it would be a hungry summer, waiting for the next crop of yams to ripen. Some fell ill from eating unripe produce. Shand shipped ten puncheons of rice from Kingston to Lucea for the Hanover estates, but hoped George would send further help. Similar problems arose in May 1819, when another storm resulted in scarcity, and 'great assistance must be requisite' at Haughton Court and Llanrumney, where 'extremes of wet and dry weather have been ungenial to all vegetables'.[73]

Simon Taylor had described his fortune as 'enough to serve any Moderate Man on Earth'.[74] But the ostentatious spending spree Anna Susanna and George embarked upon was anything but moderate. 'Full of projects of splendour and enjoyment', they gave 'sumptuous entertainments' at Syon House, the Duke of Northumberland's palatial home on the Thames, over Christmas 1817, culminating in a Twelfth Night party, featuring a 'very magnificent Twelfth Cake'.[75]

In 1819, the couple spent £20,000 on a townhouse in Cavendish Square (yards from where Isabella Franks married William Henry Cooper thirty-one years before). Built for the 1st Duke of Chandos – a leading investor in the Royal African Company and the South Sea Company – the 'splendour of the house equals ... those belonging to the greatest nobles'. It had even been considered fit for royalty; Princess Amelia, second daughter of George II, had lived there from 1761 to 1780.[76]

George and Anna Susanna could take their pick of England's country estates; but which one should they choose? They considered Houghton Hall in Norfolk, built for Prime Minister Robert Walpole in the 1720s, 'the finest house in England ... altogether a princely domain, surpassing Blenheim'. The Duke of Wellington had rejected it for not being in a 'hunting county'.[77] Anna Susanna 'regarded it with some partiality', perhaps amused by the idea of living at Houghton when her mother had been a Haughton.[78]

Their trustees eventually purchased the Erlestoke estate in Wiltshire for £200,000 in 1819 from the executors of the late MP Joshua Smith (grandfather of Emma Smith, whose marriage to James Edward Austen in 1828 secured his inheritance from Jenny Leigh Perrot). Smith had erected a neoclassical mansion surrounded with the requisite landscaped park and gardens in the 1780s, naming it Stoke Park, 'a very pretty seat'.[79]

Anna Susanna and George furnished their homes lavishly. They spent £48,000 decorating Cavendish Square. The *Morning Post* rhapsodised that the 'matchless magnificence displayed in the architectural ornaments and in the furniture excels description'. The couple visited Paris in 1818, acquiring over 100 pieces of fine French furniture. After the Revolution, Versailles's contents had been auctioned off, with sales held every day for a year from August 1793. Some furniture purchased by the Watson Taylors was by Jean-Henri Riesener, official cabinet maker to Louis XVI; other pieces had previously belonged to Marie Antoinette. They acquired a Sèvres china table, 'painted for Madame du Barri & containing portraits of herself and Louis XV, which is the most beautiful thing that ever was seen', purchasing a room's worth of porcelain direct from the Sèvres factory to complement it.[80]

George enquired of John Shand whether he could send him any of the 'several sorts of fine wood in Jamaica, which can be worked up into handsome furniture', as they would need plenty for their 'future residence in the country', but to no avail. By this time, the majority of the prized Jamaican mahogany trees had been felled, leaving only those in inaccessible interior and mountainous areas. Other Jamaican-grown woods used by pre-eminent furniture makers at this time, such as Gillows of Lancaster, included braziletto, satinwood, manganiel, green ebony and tamarind. Shand explained there was very little mahogany or other 'fine wood' left for sale on the island. Certainly, the Watson Taylor estates had 'long been entirely denuded', and 'hardly afford a stick for fuel'. In a tone of supressed annoyance, Shand pointed out George could see from the accounts that large sums were expended on importing coal and timber, so there could hardly be many trees. It is unsurprising George had not been studying the accounts in detail. But as a man with a love of fine furniture, who owned the two-volume *Indigenous Plants of Jamaica*, one would have thought he would know more about varieties of wood and their availability.[81]

The Watson Taylors were reputedly now 'the richest commoners in England'. Just as Sir Godfrey Webster and Lord Holland had taken the name Vassall as required by Florentius Vassall's will, George now took the additional name of Taylor in line with Simon Taylor's wishes. It was said he had 'refused a baronetcy, and … many higher honours'.[82] Family tradition has it he was holding out for a peerage from Castlereagh.

However, this dream was shattered when, overworked and politically unpopular, George's former mentor cut his own throat in 1822.[83]

Anna Susanna was presented at court by Marchioness Camden (the wife of George's former patron) at a celebration of Queen Charlotte's birthday in February 1817, attended by the future Tsar Nicholas I. Heralded a 'star of fashion', she ranked amongst the most 'peculiarly brilliant and attractive' ladies of the 1819 season. The Watson Taylors intended to give weekly dinners at Cavendish Square from that winter, but the first soirée was delayed until March 1821, due to building works, then an outbreak of dry rot, at Erlestoke.[84]

The parties continued regularly for the next three years. Anna Susanna and George hosted royals including George IV, his cousin the Duke of Gloucester, Prince Leopold of Belgium – whom Napoleon considered the most handsome young man he'd ever seen at the Tuileries – and Prince Esterházy of Hungary. The *Morning Post* reported: 'the apartments were lighted in a style of splendour quite unrivalled in this country'.[85]

Rather like Anna Susanna's father, George fancied himself a connoisseur.[86] He had already become a figure in the art market before their change of fortune; now he could really let rip. Over the next few years, he amassed over 300 paintings by artists including Carracci, Rubens, Van Dyck, Reynolds, Hogarth, Parmigianino, Poussin and Zoffany. The couple possessed enough Hogarths – including *The Graham Children* and *The Shrimp Girl* (now held by the National Gallery) – to create a Hogarth Room at Erlestoke, also featuring a terracotta model of Hogarth's pug dog, Trump.

Anna Susanna may have influenced some purchases. The memory of the 1787 auction of her father's paintings was tied up emotionally with the pain of his loss, and leaving fashionable Mayfair for rural Berkshire with her grieving mother. One painting the family had managed to keep hold of was Parmigianino's *Virgin and Child with Saint John the Baptist and Mary Magdalene* (now at the Getty), the most valuable painting her father had ever bought. Now Anna Susanna had the satisfaction of seeing it joined on the wall by his *Madonna and Child with Saints John the Baptist and Jerome* (now at the National Gallery).[87]

The Watson Taylors also commissioned new works of art. They asked up-and-coming sculptor John Gibson, newly arrived in London from Liverpool, to create marble busts of their whole family. With draped clothing and classical poses, the effect was grandiose, giving an air of Ancient

Anna Susanna Watson Taylor with one of her sons, probably John Walter. John Gibson (Rome, *c*.1817).

Roman senators. Gibson privately complained it was nigh impossible to render a likeness of baby George Graeme. Less than four months old, he was just 'a little thing with no shape at all'. Nevertheless, Gibson dubbed George 'one of the most liberal patrons of art', as well he might; the six family busts and two other commissions cost the Watson Taylors £400. Some of the busts, including Anna Susanna's, were later exhibited at the Royal Academy, before taking pride of place at Cavendish Square.[88]

Gibson found Anna Susanna 'a nice quiet woman, and I did my best to do her justice'. One sketch captures an intimate maternal moment between her and a young son, probably John Walter. She kneels on the floor to embrace him from behind, pressing her cheek to his with a loving kiss or gentle word.[89]

George's library at Erlestoke boasted over 4,000 valuable and 'splendidly bound' books. Highlights included a copy of the first book ever printed in the English language (a popular French anthology of 'Trojan histories' translated by William Caxton, the man who introduced the printing press to England);* Archbishop Thomas Cranmer's signed copy

---

* There are only eighteen known surviving copies; in 2014, the Duke of Northumberland's sold at auction for over £1 million.

of Henry VIII's *Defence of the Seven Sacraments* (the anti-Lutheran tract that won the King the title Defender of the Faith from the Pope less than a decade before he broke with Rome); and a set of Handel's complete works previously owned by Queen Charlotte.[90]

George joined the exclusive Roxburghe Club for bibliophiles, presenting no less than forty-four books, starting in 1827 with his edition of *Poems Written in English by Charles, Duke of Orleans, during his Captivity in England after the Battle of Azincourt* from the original manuscript in the British Museum.[91]

He also printed his own efforts for circulation. His rhyming epistolary novel, *The Cross-Bath Guide; Being the Correspondence of a Respectable Family upon the Subject of a Late Unexpected Dispensation of Honours*, ends with financial ruin of a new baronet obsessed with social advancement – a theme that would come back to haunt him. Rather untactfully, George sent a copy of his play, *The Profligate*, to Lord Byron; its antihero is profligate with love, not money. Having married an heiress, he abandons her to 'pine upon a pittance at Spa', whilst he 'played the devil' with all the ladies of London.[92]

Besides walls lined with books, George ornamented the Erlestoke library with:

> many paintings and busts of poets and scientific, literary, or remarkable persons: – Pope, Dryden, Lord Byron, Sir Walter Scott, Sir Joseph Banks, Dr Johnson, Warren Hastings, Sir Joshua Reynolds, Baretti, etc. ... [and] adorned [it] with splendid mirrors, of great size, and which are so placed as to reflect and apparently multiply, the various objects of Taste, Literature or vertu with which the room abounds.[93]

One astounding object was a cabinet shaped like a trilithon* devoted to ancient monuments. With multiple drawers and cupboards embellished with watercolours and filled with models, books, plans, maps and drawings, its *pièce de résistance* was a model of Stonehenge surrounded by red and orange glass, enabling one, by moving a candle, to see how the stone circle would look at dawn and dusk.[94]

As a local Wiltshire paper later observed:

---

* A trilithon, from the Greek *trilithos*, meaning three stones, is a structure made up of two large vertical stones, with a third balanced on top, as most famously seen at Stonehenge.

Notwithstanding that Mr Watson Taylor was surrounded by a degree of splendour, which it has been well said, might have excited the envy of royalty itself, his mind was scarcely for a moment at ease – he appeared to have an insatiable thirst for something he did not possess. He could not for a moment have thought of the money he was expending.[95]

The colossal change in her sister's fortunes was hard for Maria Taylor to take. She had always had a 'natural violence of temper', and suffered from fits of hysterics. Now, consumed by jealousy, Maria began 'an excessive use of ether and laudanum and occasionally of spirits of wine'. In April 1818, she had a complete mental breakdown. This came while the family were still mourning the death of the youngest Taylor sister, Martha, the previous November. Maria became delusional, and violent towards her mother, believing Elizabeth and George were conspiring with the servants to force her to marry a young glazier she had employed in making alterations to her house in Twickenham. Devastated, Anna Susanna went into labour prematurely and gave birth to a stillborn baby boy.

Maria was formally judged insane by the Commission of Lunacy in June 1821. She spent the rest of her life confined to a house in Alpha Road, near Regent's Park, next door to several well-to-do people in similar circumstances, with 'two women versed in such duties, to relieve each other in perpetual attendance upon her'. She died in July 1829, aged forty-four.[96]

Amongst the beneficiaries of Martha's and Maria Taylor's wills were some of their mixed-heritage relations from Jamaica. Martha bequeathed an annuity of £100 to Simon Taylor's former 'housekeeper', Sarah Blacktree Hunter; Maria assigned £20 to her daughter Sally Taylor.[97]

In October 1820 Sarah Blacktree Hunter contacted Elizabeth to inform her she had arrived in London with her thirteen-year-old granddaughter Sarah Hunter Taylor Cathcart, who had been 'very sickly' in Jamaica and needed 'to finish her education'. The older woman had inherited £357 plus an annuity of £71 for life from Simon, and was by now a pen-owner and enslaver herself. Simon had left £57 a year for the girl's maintenance, and she was to have £1,200 (the maximum inheritance allowable to a person of colour) and an enslaved girl when she turned twenty-one.

Far from being pleased to see his daughter, William Cathcart insisted she return to Jamaica immediately. The 'esteem' she may have held there did 'not extend to England', where the circumstances of her birth would confer 'many disadvantages'. His advice was ignored, but attitudes had hardened since Frances Dalzell's time. Sarah was over forty by the time she married Frederick John Wells, a London chemist, later dentist, in 1848.[98] Nevertheless, the personal correspondence and legacies left to this side of the family suggest the Taylors were more amenable to their mixed-heritage cousins than most.

Cognisant of the political threats to his family's Caribbean income, George Watson Taylor bought himself a seat in Parliament with the explicit intention of taking an active 'part in the discussion, which may there arise, upon West India concerns'. He was first 'elected' in April 1816 for Newport on the Isle of Wight, a rotten borough of twenty-four voters controlled by Tory Sir Leonard Thomas Worsley Holmes. In 1818, George 'purchased Sir John Leach's interest' in the borough of Seaford in East Sussex, becoming 'joint patron of its influence' with Lady Holland's childhood friend, Charles Rose Ellis.

George's career eloquently testified to the need for electoral reform. According to a leading campaigner, in Seaford:

> Mr Ellis owns nearly half the houses, and Mr Taylor has most of the others on lease, so that they can nominate their own tenants, who in return nominate them for Members of Parliament, which makes Seaford, after all the expensive contests that have taken place, as snug a pocket borough as Gatton, or Old Sarum.[99]

If anything, East Looe in Cornwall, George's constituency from 1820 to 1826, was even less democratic, with only thirty-eight eligible voters to Seaford's ninety. In the Parliamentary debates on the 1832 Reform Act, Irish nationalist leader Daniel O' Connell exclaimed: 'there was but one borough more rotten than East Looe, and that was West Looe ... he was glad he had lived to see the day, when ... the two worst of all the nomination boroughs were doomed to destruction.'[100]

When George arrived at Westminster, he was immediately elected to the West India Committee. His 'long habits of friendship with Lord Castlereagh' meant that, in the years prior to Castlereagh's suicide, he had 'ready access to' the Foreign Secretary, bending his ear against emancipation. Here, he was pushing at an open door; as Elizabeth, Lady Holland, had recorded in her journal, Castlereagh was one of the few men who voted against abolition in 1807, despite having no direct involvement in enslavement.

In his very first term, George joined the enslavers in Parliament arguing against Wilberforce's motion for a 'slave register'. He brandished 'the recorded statement of a correspondent' to support his argument that such legislation would provoke repeats of the 'late calamitous events' in Barbados – Bussa's uprising of April 1816. This was probably a letter from his attorney John Shand, who cautioned:

> If the register bill were to be acted upon here, the slave classed, new named, personally inspected, and artificially arranged, nothing would afterwards induce them to believe but that these measures were the prelude to manumission if not the actual deed declaratory of the royal intentions of which they had heard. If they were not immediately afterwards permitted to do what they pleased there can be no doubt that an <u>insurrection and massacre would be attempted.</u>

Shand had made this dire prediction on 13 April, the day before the outbreak of Bussa's uprising. George used this striking coincidence to defend the Jamaica Assembly's reluctance to implement registration.[101]

Though his side lost this battle, George was sure they would win the war, writing in early 1819: 'ministers may from time to time temporise, but they dare not concede ultimately to visionaries', whose calls for emancipation 'all parties know would be the forerunner of the destruction of our colonies'.[102]

Like Lord Holland, George adopted the strategy of focusing on improving conditions – he was 'prepared to support any measures of rational, safe, and just policy, which could be proposed, for the amelioration of the moral, religious, and social condition of the blacks' – and a gradual movement towards freedom, ideally one so slow that it would not happen for many years.

As the tide of public opinion turned against enslavers, George sought to evade responsibility, protesting it was 'not his fault' that he had come to be a 'proprietor of slaves'. Rather, he told the House in 1824, the British nation as a whole, 'for whose benefit and advantage, and under whose laws, the great mass of this property had been called into existence', were 'the responsible authors of the system'. He 'might have as much repugnance to it, in the abstract, as any other gentleman could possibly have'. However, he claimed to have done 'all that he could by possibility contrive' to improve the lives of people he enslaved – he does not appear to have contemplated for a moment that granting them their freedom would be the ultimate 'improvement'.

George emphasised that:

> instead of deriving benefits from his property in slaves, he had incurred considerable loss – instead of looking to them as the means of producing wealth to the sacrifice of their health, their comforts, and their lives, he had looked in common with other proprietors to the good of the Negroes as the primary object of his solicitude.

He claimed to have spent £140,000 'for the care of the young – the infirm – the aged – for their education – in their sickness and old age – in securing for them lodgings and every other comfort of which they stood in need'.

As an example of extraordinary expenditure, he mentioned how at Holland he had:

> removed the houses of a band of negroes from the sea coast to a considerable distance inland, because of some great inconveniences which were to be dreaded from their former situation, not only with regard to their health but their morals.[103]

This situation had come to a head after the November 1815 hurricane caused severe flooding. Artist James Hakewill (whose bucolic Caribbean landscapes bolstered the pro-slavery cause) observed that the enslaved people at Holland:

> are now settled on the sea-shore in a village recently erected at a very great expense. Although the situation of the former settlement was known and felt by the negroes themselves to be unhealthy, so great was their attachment to it, that no persuasion could induce them to abandon it. Fortunately, the elements came in aid of the efforts of the proprietor. A flood, unusual in extent, even where floods are far from uncommon, cleared the village of its inhabitants, who took up with their new and much more commodious habitations, merely as temporary residences, till the effect of the partial deluge should have passed away. A few weeks, however, reconciled them to the new abode. The greater convenience was every day more apparent, and they remained contentedly in a spot to which probably nothing

short of the accidental circumstance above-mentioned could have driven them.

Twenty years before, Lady Maria Nugent had observed 'the situation is low and damp, and ...not healthy', but found the 'negro houses ... neatly built on the borders of Plantain Garden River', under 'innumerable' coconut trees, 'extremely pretty'. However, as John Shand reported, the flood: 'completely opened the eyes of the negroes to the dangerous situation of their houses. The village was completely surrounded by deep and rapid streams, cutting off all communication or means of retreat'. The water level in the houses was four feet high 'and if the river had continued half an hour longer all the children and weakly people must inevitably have been drowned.'[104] So, as he claimed, George *had* spent a significant sum on building new accommodation at Holland, but such expenditure was hardly altruistic; his income depended on the plantation maintaining a healthy and active workforce – even more so since 1807.

Like Lord Holland, George insisted Jamaica's future should be decided by its House of Assembly. He praised its members to Parliament, as 'men of high legal attainments, of sound discrimination, and excellent judgment'. Any 'hastiness, or any warmth of expression' on the Assembly's part should be excused by their being 'surrounded by fearful dangers' to which they were 'tremblingly alive'. Though he was not explicit as to what these dangers were, he was clearly referring to the ever-present fear of uprisings such as in Demerara in 1823, in Barbados in 1816, and – the event that still cast the longest shadow – the Haitian Revolution. George found the speech in which Canning compared enslaved people to Frankenstein's monster 'remarkable for its temperance and for its moderation'.[105]

George could draw on his library for ammunition. He owned a collection of letters published in 1816 by an anonymous 'Colonist', painstakingly critiquing a series of 'disgraceful and dangerous' anti-slavery articles in the *Edinburgh Review*. He received further useful material in May 1826 when Alexander Barclay sent him his pro-slavery tract, *A Practical View of the Present State of Slavery in the West Indies*, 'in acknowledgement of the esteem and gratitude of an old servant', hoping it would meet with his approbation.[106]

No doubt it did, as Barclay cited his former employer Simon Taylor as a model of humanity, who would sack any white employee who raped a married enslaved woman, and paid compensation to people at Holland after cutting down several coconut trees they considered their property.[107] There was it seems no punishment for rape of *unmarried* enslaved women. The limits of Simon's compassion were clear to two Igbo sisters he returned to Kingston as 'faulty goods' in 1790. One had a swollen arm, the other had lost an eye – injuries likely sustained on the traumatic Atlantic crossing. He showed no compunction in separating the girls, though the sister with one eye cried 'most dreadfully'.[108]

Denying such cruelty, George parroted his attorneys and other enslavers, including John Baker and Monk Lewis, in contrasting the dire lot of working-class people in Europe with the 'happiness, cheerfulness, health, and contentment, which he could faithfully aver to be displayed' by enslaved people – despite never having visited the Caribbean.[109]

When Parliament received numerous anti-slavery petitions in March 1824, George objected to the way abolitionists had collected signatures. In Wiltshire, 'itinerant adventurers' had, he felt, taken advantage of the 'poor artisan, mechanic and peasant', appealing to their 'passions' rather than their reason. His account was contradicted by a letter to the Editor of the *Devizes and Wiltshire Gazette* a week after his speech. Rather than representing the overly influenced views of his social 'inferiors', the petition for Devizes had actually been signed by its Mayor, three-quarters of its corporation and 'most of the respectable householders (including our respected curate) of the town and neighbourhood'.[110]

When George first stood for Devizes in 1826, not everyone was in favour of electing an enslaver. A local newspaper suggested 'the Quackery of negro emancipation' might interfere with his election (though in the end it didn't). At a dinner at the town's Bear Inn after the election, a supporter declared George had won because his 'riches are accompanied by liberality, and dispensed with munificence'. He had given the same dining club a 'fine buck' two years before, and a substantial amount of silver plate to Erlestoke village church. After the Swing Riots,* he courted popularity by reducing rents, increasing wages and treating poachers with leniency.[111]

---

* A large uprising of agricultural workers in the south and east of England in 1830, named after the fictional folk character 'Captain Swing', protesting against poor conditions, low wages, and mechanisation, ended in almost 2,000 protestors being put on trial: 19 were hanged, 644 imprisoned and 481 transported to Australia.

George left Parliament in December 1832, having vehemently opposed the Reform Act, which would probably have brought his political career to an end in any case. A letter to the Editor of *The Times* predicted: 'When the householders are possessed of the franchise, some further recommendation than being either a rich army clothier or the accidental possessor of contiguous property, may be requisite to secure a return for a considerable town.'[112]

Though the Taylor fortune was immense, it was not infinite. In August 1819, just four years after inheriting, George wrote to William Shand complaining profits from Jamaica were not enough to 'maintain their establishment'.[113] In May 1821, one friend observed George was 'sadly out of spirits respecting his West India property. I do not believe it produces one third of what it was when he succeeded to the estate.' By the end of the following year, another remarked that George faced financial disaster, 'occasioned by the total failure of his West India remittances.'[114]

The Watson Taylors suffered the same threats to their Caribbean income as other enslavers, but their 'establishment' was ridiculously excessive, even by the standards of the day. Their finances took a further hit when the trustees stopped paying them the dividends from government bonds worth over £30,000 held in Anna Susanna's name. The problem was compounded by the death of all three men in quick succession between 1820 and 1825, leaving no trustees at all until the matter was resolved in Chancery in 1832.[115]

The Shand brothers caused further disruption by retiring to Scotland: John in 1818 and William in 1823. Their successor at Haughton Court and Llanrumney, William Miller, was not well placed to provide detailed oversight. He acted for so many estates – around sixty – that he was known as the 'Attorney General'. His home in Trelawny lay midway between Hanover and St Mary, but was still over sixty miles from either. Thomas McCornock took over in St Thomas in the East. He was at least close by as resident manager at Golden Grove, though he also acted for several other families.[116]

When a later attorney, John W. Cooper, visited in 1835, he concluded the plantations had been 'managed upon an extravagant scale', and 'the managers and agents' were guilty of 'downright roguery', 'getting more pickings that the owners in England are aware of'. The Shand brothers may well have cheated the Watson Taylors. They defrauded the Tharp family so badly that they accumulated debts of £107,000 by 1831.[117]

Unable to rely on an income from Jamaica commensurate with their expensive tastes, Anna Susanna and George were forced to the auction house. Elizabeth, Lady Holland, when writing to her son about their own need to economise in November 1822, remarked 'Watson Taylor's books are upon sale, & his furniture will soon follow'. She joined the throng at Christie's in June 1823, when over 100 paintings were up for grabs. The crowd was 'so great that Mr Christie was obliged to station a person near the door of the Auction room to repeat the biddings from the Nobleman and Gentlemen on the stairs and further end of the room'.[118]

Two years later, George IV purchased a substantial amount of furniture and sculpture from Cavendish Square for Windsor Castle. He also bought a Martin Carlin *bonheur du jour*, or lady's writing desk, made of tulip wood with Sèvres porcelain plaques, for his mistress Lady Conyngham, who adored porcelain mounted furniture.[119] Advising the King on his purchases was Sir Charles Long, a trustee of the National Gallery and the British Museum, whose family had been enslavers in Jamaica ever since the English took the island in 1655.[120]

Despite their worsening financial position, Anna Susanna and George continued to entertain on a grand scale. In August 1827, they hosted no fewer than 700 people at Erlestoke for 'one of the most splendid fetes ever witnessed' in Wiltshire. Their guests enjoyed the 'pleasures of the promenade' in the 'beautiful scenery', feasting on the 'choicest wines and all the delicacies of the season', and dancing quadrilles; 'the hours flew with the wings of birds of paradise'. A huge dinner party followed that October, the table laden with 'everything rare or excellent', served on 'highly embossed silver' and 'beautifully painted china'.

The *Devizes and Wiltshire Gazette* reported obsequiously on these entertainments, extolling the 'taste and opulence of the proprietor', and the 'kind hearted and well-bred courtesy, by which Mr and Mrs Watson Taylor are so eminently distinguished'. Equally, the 'conduct of Mr and Mrs Watson's two sons was distinguished by good sense, candour, and manners greatly beyond their years, and did such honour to those who have the superintendence of their education'. *The Times* praised Anna Susanna in particular as a memorably 'amiable hostess', paying equal and animated attention to her numerous guests, with no trace of the 'haughty condescension' that sometimes marred other ladies' hospitality.

The apogee of the Watson Taylors' social success came when the Duchess of Kent and her daughter, the future Queen Victoria, spent a weekend at Erlestoke in October 1830, playing mother-and-daughter piano duets, attending a large dinner party with local dignitaries and visiting Stonehenge.[121] Unusually, Anna Susanna and George were on friendly terms with both the Duchess of Kent *and* her brother-in-law the Duke of Clarence. Soon after he came to the throne, Clarence – now William IV – disregarding royal etiquette, went for a walk by himself, bumping into George in Pall Mall. As they strolled arm in arm up St James Street, they were mobbed, the crowd pressing upon them 'so much that Watson Taylor's shoes were trodden down at heel'; one woman got close enough to kiss the King. The following day, William IV 'was imprudent enough to make a sort of speech to the West Indian deputation, and pledged himself warmly to support their interests.'[122]

The Watson Taylors tried to economise by selling Cavendish Square and moving to a more modest establishment in Grafton Street. But neither the move nor the over £50,000 achieved at auction proved enough. In May 1832, Grafton Street and most of its contents also had to go.[123] Though Erlestoke could not be sold as it was held in trust, the same did not hold for its contents. Anna Susanna and George had filled the place with so many works of art, furniture, porcelain, plate, books and exotic plants that it took three weeks to auction off the 3,572 lots. They even put the family portraits and the marble busts by Gibson up for sale. Not every item was of high value; the couple resorted to selling off kitchen implements and servants' blankets.

For Anna Susanna, history seemed to be repeating itself; her husband, like her father, forced to sell up after sustaining huge debts. Just two years after George was depicted in a group portrait entitled *Patrons and Lovers of Art*, his collection was torn apart by the vultures who descended on Erlestoke. William Thomas Beckford – another extravagant collector who profited from Jamaican enslavement – attended on four different days; such an avid purchaser that the auctioneer reserved him a special seat. The *Bristol Mirror* reported with glee that some 'cunning commission brokers, half of whom were Jews', were thwarted from making a £300 profit on one painting; sustaining instead a loss of £200.[124]

The press, who had formerly fawned over George's munificence, now criticised his 'vulgar ostentation', citing a 'shovel, tongs, and poker of solid silver, emblazoned with the arms of George Watson Taylor, M.P.' as evidence he sought 'exclamations of wonder': '"How rich be must be. Nobody else but the King can afford it!" And such frequently are the golden calves who are worshipped as patrons of the fine arts and patterns to the people.'[125]

Contemplating the Watson Taylors' fall, Thomas Raikes, a banker, dandy and diarist who married into the Jamaican Bayly family, remarked that, before the inheritance, George had been 'a regular, independent man, with about £1,500 a year, and happy.' But just twelve years later he was 'completely ruined'. The 'state of West Indian property may have contributed to this catastrophe; but his wasteful expenditure was beyond all conception ... Sir Robert Peel said, the other day at dinner, "No man ever bought ridicule at so high a price".'[126]

And George *was* ridiculed. Variations on this pun from the *Chester Chronicle*'s column entitled 'Anecdotes, Points of Humour, &c.' appeared in newspapers across the land: 'CHEAP DEER. – Mr Watson Taylor's deer are announced to be sold cheap. So that they are not dear after all. (To many tradesmen, he himself, or his patronage, has been very dear.)'[127]

By June 1832 the Watson Taylors had decamped to the Continent to evade their creditors. They headed to The Hague, then on to Frankfurt, settling in the Sachsenhausen district on the south bank of the Main.[128] The embarrassment for Anna Susanna, in going from fashionable hostess to exile, was doubtless acute. Her distress was compounded when John Walter died of cholera on 9 October, aged only nineteen. At least one creditor, the lawyer and future South Australian pioneer James Hurtle Fisher, pursued them to Germany. Young Simon Watson Taylor, only just turned twenty-one, was forced to give the man a bill of exchange for £4,000 secured against Anna Susanna's jointure.[129]

In February 1834, the family sought sanctuary at the Abbey of Holyrood House in Edinburgh, which in a quirky remnant of feudalism had shielded debtors from arrest since the sixteenth century. The Bailie, John Dickie, fearing they might flee to Europe once more, interrogated George about his intentions until two in the morning. They moved into Brotherstone's lodgings at 8 Prospect Buildings, within the Abbey precincts, which they could leave only on Sundays (as Scots law prohibited legal proceedings on the Sabbath). Amongst the other lodgers – known as 'Abbey Lairds' – at the time was Thomas De Quincey, author of *Confessions of an English Opium-Eater*. They narrowly missed the exiled and impecunious Charles X of France, who had fled there following the July Revolution of 1830, but moved to Prague just over a year before the

Watson Taylors arrived.[130] It was a far cry from London's glittering high society, or their sumptuous parties at Erlestoke.

By February 1839 George had made arrangements to pay 6s 8d for each pound to creditors whom he owed less than £150. So, if he owed someone £100, he would pay them only £33 6s 8d. Those owed over £150 were to 'sign a deed to take a dividend at seven different instalments'. Despite this, he was still considerably over £60,000 in debt.[131] The largest single sum was £30,000 owed to royal goldsmiths Rundell & Bridge, from whom the Watson Taylors had acquired a silver table set weighing over 18,000 ounces. The Court of King's Bench awarded the goldsmiths Parmigianino's *Virgin and Child with Saint John the Baptist and Mary Magdalene* and three family portraits (two Reynolds portraits of Elizabeth, and one of Sir John by Daniel Gardner) – all withdrawn from the Erlestoke sale. Rundell & Bridge sold these at auction to recover their money.[132]

There seemed no end to the Watson Taylors' creditors. The curate for the parish of Edington near Erlestoke complained to the Court of Rolls in 1838 he had not been paid his £140 a year living for seven years.[133] *Gore's Liverpool General Advertiser* reported that one of the family's lawyers (who earned between £4,000 and 5,000 a year) had most unwisely become George's guarantor for £73,000:

> Immediately upon Mr Watson Taylor's leaving the country he was called upon for the amount; unable to pay it, executions were put into his house – ruin stared him in the face – his brain became disordered, and he is now, we are informed, in St Luke's* leaving a wife and nine or ten amiable children 'to the mercy of a rude world'.[134]

George even owed money to his own tenants and employees in Wiltshire. He was indebted to 'some for malt, others for coal, and one of his gamekeepers ... had actually advanced money to pay the servants' wages'. All these men had been promised the sums loaned would be deducted from their rent, but 'as this promise cannot now be fulfilled, a great deal of dissatisfaction has arisen'. One tenant farmer had lent £200, his entire life's savings. Not only did he not get this back, but he was 'obliged to submit to have his horses, &c., distrained, and sold, for the payment of his rent'.[135]

---

* St Luke's Hospital for Lunatics, Old Street, London, founded 1751, housed the mentally ill until 1916, when the building was acquired by the Bank of England, which used it to print banknotes until the early 1950s.

Ill feeling locally had hardly dissipated by the time the family leased Erlestoke to Sir John Cam Hobhouse, later Lord Broughton – a friend of Lord Byron, and member of the Holland House set – in 1837. One tradesman wrote an angry letter to the *Devizes and Wiltshire Gazette*, remarking the trustees had spent 'A large sum of money … to put the Premises, &c. at Stoke Park, in state of repair, fit for the reception'. Had they 'possessed a single spark of honesty, they would first have selected the tradesmen who were heavy creditors of Mr Watson Taylor, and there are many around us'. Instead, he asserted, men were chosen based on their political persuasions.[136]

The post-emancipation compensation payments came at a welcome moment. George had, like Lord Holland, pushed in Parliament for 'ample indemnification for the sacrifice of property necessarily made by individuals', which surely the 'nation would not think of' ending enslavement without.[137]

The Watson Taylors' claim, for 2,208 people in Hanover, Mary and St Thomas in the East, was amongst the largest made by any family. Their trustees received a total of £40,735 21s 11d compensation in seven instalments between September 1835 and May 1836.[138]* As Anna Susanna's sisters Martha and Maria, and her mother Elizabeth, were all dead by now, the only other claimant was her surviving sister Eliza Mayne and her family.[139] The Watson Taylors paid the Maynes £370 16s 7d to withdraw their application for a one-eighth share of Lyssons and Burrowfield.[140]†

Some of Anna Susanna's Jamaican cousins also received compensation. Charlotte Taylor, now living in Ireland as Mrs James Sproule, received £953 4d for fifty-three people in St Thomas in the East.[141] Sally Taylor received £802 8s for thirty-eight people from Cherry Garden and elsewhere in St David. Her daughter Sarah Hunter Taylor Cathcart received £19 10s 10d for one person, also in St David – presumably the 'negro girl' Simon Taylor had directed be purchased for her.[142]

---

* One trustee was Coutts banker Sir Edmund Antrobus, who owned a neighbouring estate in Wiltshire (including Stonehenge); another Oliver Farrer, of Farrer & Co., 66 Lincoln's Inn, royal solicitors since the 1930s.

† William Mayne, who Simon Taylor had judged so unsuitable, had become a Captain in the Life Guards, known as 'Waterloo Bill' due to his constant retelling of his role in the battle. *Southey Letters*, ed. Pratt and Packer, Letter 3909, n. 24, Romantic Circles: https://www.romantic-circles.org/index.php/editions/southey_letters/3909Southey.

But it was not just Anna Susanna and her family who claimed compensation for people on the Taylor estates. According to a visitor to Holland estate in 1835, one person enslaved there 'sent in a claim for no less than twelve slaves and many for less number – all this appears startling but the facts are on record'.[143] Could this, despite being illegal, be true? We know that several people – Alexander Barclay, William Shand – referred to enslaved slaveholders at Holland. More forensic examination and cross-referencing of compensation records and slave registers would be needed to identify them. One likely candidate is Mary Lindsay, who received £282 5s 6d compensation for *exactly twelve people* in St Thomas in the East in 1835.[144] Could she be the same Mary Lindsay, a field cook at Holland, born 'Amanda' in 1769 to African-born Lydia Brown?[145]

Following emancipation, and George's financial collapse, Anna Susanna needed to reassess her Jamaican assets. Most of her estates were too far from the epicentre to have been badly affected by the Baptist War, except those in Hanover. At Haughton Court, a fifty-seven-year-old man named Quamie was killed by the Maroons and a thirty-year-old woman named Phaba sentenced to the workhouse for life.[146] At Haughton Grove Pen, the 'overseer's house, hospital and stable and every building for a mile in circumference was burned and destroyed'. The overseer 'was shot while storming some negro houses in the vicinity'. The Maroons killed James Stevenson, an enslaved man, aged twenty-three. David Grant Watson, thirty-five, and John Watson Grant, thirty-one, were 'hung for rebellion' and conspiracy. Thirty-nine-year-old George Watson, who had ended up in Westmoreland, was sentenced to 300 lashes and six months' imprisonment, commuted to transportation for life, for 'rebellion and arson', but later received a pardon from Governor Mulgrave. James Grant got 'one hundred stripes'.[147]

Anna Susanna now turned to her friend Benjamin Greene, founder of Greene King brewery, and great-uncle of novelist Graham Greene. He faced similar challenges, as owner of two Kittian plantations, and six on Montserrat. Anna Susanna was hampered not only by being a woman, but by being physically confined to the precincts of Holyrood Abbey. Greene helped her file a case in Chancery against the heirs and executors of the marriage settlement trustees, for failing to account for her investments since 1825.[148] He also appointed John W. Cooper to act as Anna Susanna's attorney. Cooper arrived in Jamaica on 20 December 1834, swiftly visiting all the Watson Taylor estates, and sending detailed reports back to Britain.[149] His assessment was damning; everything had to change. New machinery was required – at Holland he recommended 'a windmill on the beach (similar to those in the fens in Cambridgeshire) for throwing the water into the sea'.

White bookkeepers, agricultural workers and tradesmen must be sent out from England – a common idea at the time that met with little success. Both Thomas McNeil and Alexander Barclay (who became related when Thomas married Alexander's niece Bathia in 1842) were condemned as 'slave-seekers' for their efforts to recruit from Scotland, Ireland, Germany and the United States.[150] Cooper stressed the importance of new recruits bringing out their families, as it would 'keep them from associating with the negroes' while 'the industry and economy of their wives would be an example as well as a stimulus' for apprentices to follow. Almost all the existing white employees must be replaced, otherwise 'the new comers will be contaminated by … the infamous practices of their predecessors.' Cooper condemned men 'addressed as they are white as Mr and Sir' who got 'above their station and become useless'.

But it was sexual relationships between white and Black or mixed-heritage people that Cooper most abhorred. 'There is no one abuse in the management of West India property that requires a more extensive reformation than this.' At Holland, Cooper was appalled to find forty-three domestics, all 'people of colour (mulattoes and mustees˙), the legacies of former overseers and bookkeepers'. There was an equally disproportionate number of craftsmen. Cooper was 'entirely at a loss' to see what the twenty-four carpenters, thirteen coopers, twelve masons and three blacksmiths at Holland did all day, seeing 'but few monuments of their industry.' It is likely that many were also the children and grandchildren of white men. Given her uncle Simon's behaviour, this 'abuse' could not have come as a surprise to Anna Susanna. She and George had manumitted several relatively privileged people of mixed heritage in recent years.[151]

Cooper concluded Thomas McCornock had been too lenient and recommended he be replaced (he later committed suicide).[152] The 'head people' at Holland – Black drivers, constables and cattlemen – he dismissed as 'an indolent and stupid race'. By contrast, at Lyssons, 'they have fortunately had a master who has exacted from them all the work

---

* The now offensive term 'mustee' was used to refer to someone who was one-eighth black (sometimes also called an 'octoroon').

the law will allow; consequently they are happy and contented; this may appear anomalous, but such is the negro character.'

Children under six posed another quandary. Now free, they had, in cold calculation of profit and loss, transformed from future investment to current liability. Cooper looked forward to getting 'rid of the burden of maintaining them' in four years' time. At Llanrumney he found the overseer provided herrings and cloth to free children, but barred them from hospital, no matter how long their parents laboured in the fields. Managers at Lyssons and Holland sustained clothing and food allowances for free children if parents supplied 'an equivalent portion of extra labour'; Cooper found this 'insufficient'.[153]

Abolitionists Sturge and Harvey found similar problems at Holland to those at Friendship and Greenwich, Sweet River and Duckenfield when they visited in 1837. Apprentices worked from dawn to dusk, and had Friday afternoons off only for the first two months, even though they 'never made any agreement to give up their extra time'. Skilled workers, like George Walters, a tradesman, were assigned fieldwork as punishment.

Apprentices told Sturge and Harvey that the special magistrate for St Thomas in the East, George Willis, frequently forced them to work on Saturdays, leaving only Sundays to tend their 'badly off' provision grounds. While former magistrates John Daughtrey and Henry Blake 'used to hear what the people had to say', Willis 'goes by what the overseer says, and will not allow any to speak.'

Examples of Willis's tyrannical approach abound. At Hector's River, he condemned a young housemaid to the treadmill for breaking a glass, even though her mother had purchased two new ones, and she had lost her allowance and days off for a month. At Torrington Pen, acting alongside Alexander Barclay, Willis sentenced seven women to the treadmill and six men to receive fifty lashes. Their crime was to go on strike and appeal to the Governor after their overseer, Robert Jocken, allowed his cattle to destroy their provision grounds, then ordered them to work on a distant plantation. Jocken, 'regarded as a monster in the community', had recently been fined for tying an apprentice to a dead ox, because the animal died in his care.[154] When American abolitionists James Armstrong Thorne and Joseph Horace Kimball met Willis, they concluded he was a 'driver for the master', with no interest in securing justice for apprentices; 'guilty of the grossest violation of his office', he 'proved himself utterly unworthy of it'.[155]

*

George Watson Taylor died in Edinburgh on 6 June 1841. The family had by then moved to a more prestigious address, 10 Carlton Place (now Carlton Terrace), part of the grand Eastern New Town designed by Greek Revival architect William Henry Playfair, but still within the Abbey precincts. Anna Susanna had been deeply in love with her husband when they married. Did she mourn his loss now, after all he had put her through?

George left his whole estate to Anna Susanna – more a burden than a blessing. Their eldest son, Simon, now in his thirties, increasingly took charge of family finances. He later recalled: 'Partly prior to and partly subsequent to my Father's decease, my Mother and I paid off a quarter of a million Pounds of his debts for which we were in no way legally liable'.[156]

In 1844, Anna Susanna entrusted Simon with managing the Jamaican plantations, 'ensuring necessary stock, cattle, cultivation etc. for carrying on the same' and maintaining them, excepting 'losses or destruction by invasion, insurrection, tumult, tempest, fire or other unusual calamity'.[157]* Together, they sold Lyssons in 1849 for £3,000 to James Tuckett, a former manager of Dawkins Caymanas in St Catherine† and investor in the island's first railway.[158] In the same year, Anna Susanna's cousin Charlotte Sproule (née Taylor) died in Ireland. The Watson Taylors reluctantly paid out £500 plus interest to her surviving six children, as dictated in Simon Taylor's will over thirty years before.[159]‡

By this time, Simon had made an advantageous marriage to Lady Hannah Charlotte Hay, one of eight daughters of Field Marshal George Hay, 8th Marquis of Tweeddale. By this union, he became brother-in-law to several influential figures including the Duke of Wellington and Sir Robert Peel, 3rd Baronet (eldest son of Prime Minister Sir Robert Peel). They lived at Urchfont Manor, close to Erlestoke, producing four sons and seven daughters.[160]

---

* Holland, like Duckenfield, benefited from African indentured labour; 'about 100' Africans lived there by 1865, a significant proportion of the 500 to 600 in the parish. *Report of the Jamaica Royal Commission* (1866), p. 539.

† Dawkins Caymanas was owned by the Dawkins family Isabella Cooper's daughter married into; William Shand had been the estate's attorney between 1817 and 1825.

‡ Charlotte's children were unable to provide proof of their parents' marriage or their baptism records. They relied on their father's will, where, the Watson Taylors' adviser commented, 'They are called widow and children but that is no proof of the facts.'

George Graeme graduated from Trinity College, Cambridge, in 1846, and married a Frenchwoman named Victorine Joudioux the following year. Emilius also attended Trinity, then trained as a barrister, but did not practise; both he and Isabella remained unmarried. These two youngest children continued to live with Anna Susanna, who, no longer constrained by her husband's bankruptcy, had moved to a comfortable home in London's Belgravia, where she employed seven servants.[161]

Anna Susanna died in London in January 1853 and was buried in the vault the Watson Taylors had built at Erdington Church alongside her mother, sisters, husband and son John Walter.[162] She left her younger children £20,000 each. Her eldest son Simon inherited the rest, including 'all the cattle, stock, utensils on my plantations or estates in Jamaica and all my personal estate and effects in Jamaica (if any)'.[163]

Despite the family's financial problems, Simon Taylor's foresight in insisting on the purchase of English property, and that Anna Susanna inherited in her own right, ensured George's bankruptcy had not left her or her children destitute. Three left fortunes of between £30,000 and £70,000.[164] The exception was George Graeme, who, taking after his profligate parents, bought the Mediterranean island of Monte Cristo – made famous by Dumas's 1844 novel – in 1852. The price was 52,000 Tuscan lira or £2,000 sterling. He spent a further £30,000 over the next three years building a splendid house, filling it with fine furniture and an extensive library, creating a botanical garden, and even buying two steamboats to make it easier to visit the mainland, requiring further investment to dig a deep enough dock. He lost everything when Garibaldi's troops sacked the island in 1860. His efforts to claim compensation from the new Italian government – which had convicted him and his wife of sedition – failed; he died leaving less than £200.[165]

After Anna Susanna's death, Simon moved into Erlestoke, living off the extensive Wiltshire estates.[166] He sold Llanrumney for £3,500 in 1859 to William Hosack of St George.[167] Briefly following in his father's footsteps, he served as a member of the West India Committee from 1832, and as Liberal MP for Devizes between 1857 and 1859, but otherwise kept out of politics, with one notable exception.[168]

When news of the brutal Morant Bay War reached Britain, a number of public figures, including Charles Buxton (son of abolitionist Thomas Fowell Buxton), John Stuart Mill and Charles Darwin formed a 'Jamaica Committee' calling for Governor Eyre to be prosecuted for his crimes.

Protestors burned Eyre in effigy on Clerkenwell Green. Conversely, Simon Watson Taylor – who still owned Holland in St Thomas in the East – supported the Eyre Defence Fund, designed to cover Eyre's legal costs, alongside Thomas Carlyle, John Ruskin, Charles Kingsley and Alfred, Lord Tennyson. To them, Eyre deserved commendation for preserving 'the lives of 7,000 British men and the honour of 7,000 British women from the murder and lust of black savages'. They prevailed; Eyre was exonerated, the government reimbursed his legal expenses and he lived out his life in Devon on a retired colonial governor's pension.[169]

As at Duckenfield, people formerly enslaved at Lyssons and Holland had been caught up in the fray. Lyssons was close enough to Morant Bay to see the courthouse burning. A witness reported seeing twenty-five Lyssons men running towards the town with cutlasses that night. Both the Great Houses at Lyssons and Holland were destroyed. Detested overseers were targeted by the people they had long exploited. At Lyssons, Mr Wallace faced calls to 'take off his head'. At Holland, a crowd armed with machetes, led by Samuel Walker, chased the overseer Robert James Stewart into the bush for nine or ten miles, beyond Morant Point Lighthouse. He abandoned his horse and ran for it, then resorted to setting out to sea on a raft he made by tying bamboo sticks together with pieces torn from his shirt. He dared not return to land until night fell and his pursuers had left the beach.[170]

During martial law, Stewart had his revenge. He sent Samuel Walker, twelve other men and two women to be flogged at Golden Grove or Bath. Most men got 150 lashes, the women between fourteen and twenty. Richard Rowdon recalled: 'they flogged me until I fainted, the last lick they gave me I don't know, I began to loose my feet'. After his mother 'doctored' his back with 'some boiled bush' and castor oil, he was back at work in a fortnight.

Stewart then had Samuel Walker, whom he saw as the ringleader, shot. Walker had worked at Holland as a wainman (wagon-driver) and cattleman, and lived with his partner Ann Wedderman (who had been born at Holland) and their two children. After his death, Stewart refused to pay Ann the last two weeks' wages he owed her and Walker. She could not afford to pay her rent; without help from her father she 'should not have been able to live, me and my piccaninnies would have died of hunger.'[171]

Simon Watson Taylor died in 1902; Erlestoke was sold in 1919. Much of the house was destroyed by fire in 1950. The site is now a Category

C adult prison – the only one in Wiltshire.[172] Meanwhile, the vast collection of paintings, sculpture, furniture and books the Watson Taylors bought and sold in such a short time is scattered in museums, galleries, libraries and private collections around the world, most prominently of all in Buckingham Palace and Windsor Castle.

At Lyssons, the former Great House is now a private home. Goats graze by the graves of Simon and Sir John Taylor, located down a dirt track in a spot hard to find without local knowledge. One can just about make out the inscription praising 'the honourable' Simon Taylor as 'a loyal subject, a firm friend, and an honest man' who had led 'an active life, during which he faithfully and ably filled the highest offices of civil and military duty in this island'. Sir John's inscription is barely legible; his gravestone was broken into pieces by locals looking for gold in 1987.[173]

The ruined sugar works, overseer's house and hospital at Holland are still recognisable as the same buildings depicted by James Hakewill 200 years before, partly due to their remote location. The site is now home to Jamaica's only crocodile sanctuary. Llanrumney is owned by ACE (American Caribbean Experience), run by an American couple

Sir John and Simon Taylor's smashed graves,
Lyssons, St Thomas in the East, Jamaica.

from Atlanta, Georgia, who also own a local hotel and – inspired by the link to Captain Morgan – have ambitions to develop a tourist attraction.[174]

The Watson Taylor family retained a presence on the island well into the twentieth century. Simon's second son, Arthur Wellesley Watson-Taylor – named for his uncle, the Duke of Wellington – went out to Jamaica, marrying Mary Emmeline, younger daughter of Thomas Murthwaite of Stewart Castle, Trelawny, in 1883. They lived at Haughton Grove, and had five sons.[175]

Reminiscing in 2006, Arthur Dickson, a former High Court judge born in Lucea in 1913, described 'old man Watson-Taylor' – Arthur Wellesley – as 'a lovely, kindly man who looked after his people very well', though he lived at Holland, while the Hanover estate was managed by a relation, George Dewar. Arthur Wellesley's son, Harry Gerald Watson Taylor, later took over, becoming a member of the island's Legislative Council in 1927, and sitting on the Hanover parish council. Dickson recalled that when Harry Gerald bought a new Ford truck, his son:

> Watty was more interested in that and other machines than in any school work. So, Mr McDonald [the headmaster] said to him one day, 'Watson-Taylor, you should take more interest in learning.' 'Watty' replied, 'Mr Mac., you ever hear of a rich man's son learning?'[176]

Education was not required for the family to retain their position in the island's ruling class.

In 1929, the year before he died, Arthur Wellesley donated seven and a half acres at Bayliss Bay, previously used by the Police Cricket Club, to the parish council. This became Watson Taylor Park, Hanover's first public playing field.[177] On 6 August 1962, it was the site of Hanover's ceremony to mark Jamaican Independence. As in every parish across the island, at midnight, the Union Jack was lowered and the Jamaican flag hoisted high. Ivan St George 'Copper Head' Cockburn sang the new Jamaican National Anthem, followed by fireworks and a twenty-one-gun salute from the US Navy.[178] Some of the crowd were probably descendants of people enslaved by Anna Susanna and her family.

Conclusion

When I set out to chronicle the lives of these nine heiresses, I had only an inkling of where the journey would lead. I knew Sarah, Frances, Mary, Jenny, Martha, Jane, Elizabeth, Isabella and Anna Susanna enjoyed substantial wealth and lived dramatic lives. But, as I delved deeper, I found myself constantly encountering not only key figures and well-known parts of British and global history, but also many lesser-known stories that deserve attention. Crucially, I found far more detail about the lives of people the heiresses enslaved than I had imagined possible.

These nine women represent only a fraction of at least 150 heiresses known to have brought the profits of enslavement to Britain. There are many more stories like theirs to uncover, following scattered paper trails of marriage settlements, wills, probate inventories, letters and diaries, which intimately, violently, connect Britain and the Caribbean. When we widen the lens even further to include the full range of ways Britain profited from enslavement – many encountered in this book – a far-reaching, tangled web of connections is revealed.

New research continues to unearth how British families and institutions acquired a stake in the colonial economy. Beyond the obvious routes of setting out to traffic captive Africans or establish a plantation, others made money more indirectly, working as colonial lawyers, doctors or administrators, or by investing in the South Sea Company, Royal African Company or specific slaving voyages. In addition to the merchants who dealt in goods cultivated by enslaved people such as sugar, rum, coffee and tobacco, and who sold plantation supplies, British manufacturers made everything from guns, chains and whips to copper manillas and sheathing for the hulls of ships.

These activities were pursued across the British Isles. While Scottish, Welsh, and Irish national identity is often placed in opposition to the English – invading, colonising or attempting to colonise their neighbours for centuries – in fact all four nations were deeply embedded in the global colonial enterprise. Scots – like the Dalzells, Duffs, Ramsays, Oswalds, Macquaries and Taylors – were disproportionately found on the front line of empire, in part due to a dearth of opportunities at home. Irish people were indentured in Barbados, but also became enslavers, like the Tuites, Ryans and Bodkins of Montserrat, and Governor Sligo of Jamaica. Sir Henry Morgan and Thomas Picton are among the most famous Welsh enslavers. Much clothing worn by enslaved people was made from Welsh wool; Welsh iron made chains and guns; copper for manillas and ships' hulls was mined and manufactured in places like Swansea, Anglesey and Greenfield Valley.[1]

But if we are to fully understand how Britain exploited the Caribbean, we need to recognise the role women played, not only as conduits of human property but as active participants in the business themselves. Many heiresses acquired detailed knowledge of managing 'human resources', the inner workings of sugar cultivation and processing, how plantations were supplied and how to sell their produce. Frances gave Thomas Bontein clear instructions on branding and warned him not to trust Edward Manning; Isabella was reluctant to spend money on clearing new pasture after emancipation rendered the future of sugar production uncertain; Monk Lewis complained that Elizabeth's 'commands' regarding her plantation were better suited for 'one of her runaway negroes'.

Before marriage and as widows, heiresses sometimes took primary responsibility for overseeing their plantations from afar. However, even when their husbands were nominally in charge, their Caribbean assets were often ring-fenced in wills and marriage settlements. The influence and interest of the heiress is clear: see Martha's dogged pursuit of compensation for the damage done to her St Vincent estate, Jenny's anger at not receiving a bigger legacy on her mother's death, or Jane demanding her third share of profits from a crop harvested a decade before. The personal connection endured, even when heiresses had left the Caribbean as children, or never went there at all.

And what of the intimate links forged between heiresses and the people they and their families enslaved? The mother–daughter bonds of women like Frances and Susanna provide the most striking examples;

many more, like Anna Susanna, had enslaved cousins. These women were waited on by enslaved people on both sides of the Atlantic. Elizabeth and Jane both had enslaved nurses. Martha was friendly enough with Jack Beef to buy him theatre tickets. Sarah was served by Mary Revill and John Hylas at Kings Bromley; Mary by Caesar at 17 Philpot Lane; Elizabeth by Robert Loftus in Golden Square; three unnamed Jamaicans waited on Anna Susanna at Bolney Court. More broadly, in a world where the size of a woman's fortune dictated whom she could marry, and the place she would take in the world, these heiresses' happiness depended on the misery of the hundreds of people they enslaved.

Were these women any more compassionate than their menfolk? Mary's 'pious' concern for Bob and his wife, Jane's instruction that people she inherited be taught trades, and Elizabeth and Anna Susanna's presents of clothing pale in comparison to manifold examples of callous inhumanity and self-interest. Mary showed no concern for the thousands of people her husband and his partners trafficked across the Atlantic from Bance Island. A skilled person was more valuable than a field worker. Improving material conditions for a few favoured individuals after it became illegal to import Africans was both an attempt to counter pro-emancipation arguments, and to promote 'natural increase'. Heiresses were well aware of, and condoned – in some cases only by their silence – the abuse of people who laboured for their benefit.

Our nine women knew key historical figures and lived through seismic events. Jenny was Jane Austen's aunt. Mary hosted Benjamin Franklin, John Adams and John Jay on their way home from negotiating peace with her husband in Paris. Martha befriended several European monarchs, including Marie Antoinette; her escape from Revolutionary Paris was as dramatic as any scene from *The Scarlet Pimpernel*. Elizabeth sent comforts to Napoleon in exile, and hosted Lord Byron, Charles Dickens and several British Prime Ministers. Anna Susanna entertained George IV and the future Queen Victoria.

While Elizabeth, as the wife of a Cabinet minister, stood closest to the seat of power, Anna Susanna's money bought her husband a seat in Parliament, and several heiresses counted MPs and politically influential aristocrats and gentlemen amongst their wider family and social circles. This put heiresses in a position to influence policy during the decades of struggle for abolition and emancipation. Their personal knowledge and connections both provided material for these arguments and influenced decisions made by their husbands and trustees. As well as buying political power, heiresses' money and influence – most notably Martha's and Jane's – furthered their brothers', husbands' and sons' careers in the army, navy and colonial administrations, all cogs in the imperial machine.

While several heiresses, like Martha or Isabella, inherited debt from their fathers, and husbands like George spent all their money, the wealth, extracted at great human cost from the Caribbean, was imported into Britain, passed on to the army of lawyers, bankers, architects, builders, art dealers, wine merchants, butchers, seamstresses and domestic servants required to service their every want and need. Or, as Mr Parker put it to Lady Denham in *Sanditon*, 'No people spend more freely, I believe, than West Indians', 'such a diffusion of money among us' bringing prosperity to 'butchers and bakers and traders', speculators and rentiers alike.[2] Heiresses and their husbands, such as the Oswalds in Ayrshire, or the Hollands in Camberwell, invested in improvements to roads, housing and other infrastructure, which still benefit people living in Britain today. Multiple churches, including St Quivox in Ayrshire and Erdington in Wiltshire, continue to use silver or pews they donated. Isabella's daughter built Moggerhanger parish church. The heiresses' former homes – those still standing – are symbols of Britishness, part of how the country is showcased to the world today. Works of art, books and objects they commissioned, inspired or acquired now form part of British – and international – museum collections. These were amassed on the grandest scale by the Watson Taylors, but think also of Zoffany's portrait of Mary in the National Gallery, the young Isabella captured by Gainsborough in the Birmingham Art Gallery, or the series of satirical prints featuring Elizabeth in the British Museum and National Portrait Gallery. This is not just a story of a privileged elite, but one touching the whole of British society. George's words to Parliament in 1824 come to mind: the entire 'British nation' were the 'responsible authors of the system', which had been 'called into existence' for their 'benefit and advantage' and sanctioned by their laws.

Histories of enslavement often deal in large numbers, the big picture. By taking a more personal approach in this book, I have tried to bring these stories home, through the intimate bonds forged between colony and 'motherland'. These connections appear in surprising places.

Visiting the site of the Battle of Hastings; taking a stroll in Holland Park; cheering on Aston Villa from the Holte End stand; or even spending some time at His Majesty's pleasure in Erlestoke prison; one would not imagine these places retain any link to Britain's slaving past. But we are treading in the footsteps of women who also walked across the yard at Sweet River Pen, Westmoreland, Jamaica, past the gibbets in Basseterre, St Kitts, or on the deck of a ship sailing from those islands packed with sugar and rum. Just contemplate these place names for a moment: Kingston, Greenwich, Christ Church, Llanrumney ... where in the world are you? Other Caribbean towns and villages still bear the names of enslavers, like Workmans in Barbados or Duckenfield, Jamaica. Similarly, both in the heiresses' lifetimes and today, people with names like Franks, Vassall, Newton and Jarvis live in both Britain and the Caribbean.

Yet the experience of walking through downtown Kingston, Jamaica, is very different to that of strolling through Kingston-on-Thames. Even during a cost-of-living crisis, the relative comfort and privileges of British life, notably easy access to free education and healthcare, good roads, high speed internet, and cultural institutions such as libraries, museums and research centres, place the challenges faced by former British colonies in sharp relief.

Although many tourists visiting the Caribbean spend their time sealed in all-inclusive beach resort bubbles, those who look out of the window during the airport transfer, or travel outside tourist hotspots, will encounter legacies of British rule and exploitation, not just in place and family names but in buildings, sugar cane fields and communities. The parish churches are still small pieces of Britain imposed on the Caribbean landscape, with identical pews, organs and architecture, the older memorial plaques bearing the names of enslavers. Simon Taylor's former home, Prospect Pen – though crumbling and uninhabited – is still designated the official residence of the Jamaican Prime Minister. The University of the West Indies campus in Jamaica is built on the site of two former sugar plantations, Mona and Papine; students walk past a ruined water mill, aqueduct and bookkeeper's house on their way to class. Barbados is littered with the ruins of so many disused sugar windmills that they have become something of a national symbol, stamped on the twenty-five-cent coin. The island's oldest rum distillery, Mount Gay in St Lucy, still bears the name of Sarah's attorney Sir John Gay Alleyne.

We need to combat the one-dimensional ways Black people often appear in public representations of enslavement. We see abhorrent images of bodies squeezed into a ship's hold as per the diagram of the ship *Brooks* circulated by abolitionists. We see them half-naked at auction or in the fields. In the archives, we find them listed and valued in inventories or enumerated for the purposes of compensation. But the men, women and children enslaved by the heiresses were far from the kneeling supplicants preferred by white abolitionists. They were brave, resilient people striving to make the best possible lives for themselves and their families in a system stacked against them.

Just think of the determination and chutzpah of Betsy Newton and her cousin John Thomas, who escaped the plantation and made it all the way to London to petition for their freedom and that of their kin. Imagine the bravery of the Lucky Hill men who joined Venture's gang in St Mary, or David Grant and John Grant of Haughton Grove Pen, who fought and died for their freedom during the Baptist War. Some, like Mrs Phillis and the young carpenter who collected caricatures of Lord Holland, found other ways to assert their individuality. Without understanding them and their humanity, we cannot hope to grasp the true cost of the wealth heiresses extracted and invested in Britain.

Men and women who enslaved fellow human beings were guilty of injustices that now fall squarely within our definition of 'crimes against humanity'. No amount of self-justification by enslavers and their apologists can diminish the fact that their wealth relied upon repeated violation of human dignity that was intrinsically unjust – no matter what the legal system of the time said. As Quaker Elizabeth Heyrick said in 1824: 'the slave has a *right* to his liberty, a right which it is a crime to withhold'. Enslavement, she argued, 'is opposed to nature, to reason, and to religion. It is also illegal, as far as illegality has any foundation of justice, divine or human, to rest upon.'[3]

In the past, enslavers' physical separation from the Caribbean, and their successful self-fashioning as highly cultured members of the British elite, distanced them from this reality. But now their culpability is clear. In-depth study of their lives is not in any way meant to exonerate them or excuse their actions, or inaction. It is an attempt to unpick the world in which they lived and thought – a world that for years raised little objection to their conduct.

The heiresses we've met lived in a society where racism and the cruel exploitation of Africans were not only commonplace, but a mainstay of the economy. As Daniel Defoe put it in 1713:

> *No African* Trade, *no* Negroes, *no* Negroes, *no* Sugars, Ginger, Indicos, &c.; *no* Sugars &c., *no* Islands; *no* Islands, no Continent; *no* Continent, *no* Trade; that is to say, farewell all your *American* Trade, your *West-India* Trade.[4]

Simon Taylor concurred a century later, complaining abolitionists were taking an 'axe to the root' of the nation's most valuable commerce. It was to Simon Taylor that Nelson wrote from HMS *Victory* four months before Trafalgar:

> I ever have been and shall die a firm friend of our present colonial system. I was bred as you know in the Good old school and taught to appreciate the value of our West India possessions, and neither in the field or the Senate shall their just rights be infringed whilst I have an arm[*] to fight in their defence or a tongue to launch my voice against the damnable cruel doctrine of Wilberforce and his Hipocritical allies.[5]

Heiresses and their families fiercely defended their own financial interests; wilfully disregarding the suffering their fortunes depended on. They oppressed the people they enslaved during their time in the colonies, memorably when Florentius Vassall showed Thomas Thistlewood how to conduct a flogging, or when John Baker oversaw executions in St Kitts, and continued to condone harsh discipline and punishments from afar. When challenged by abolitionists, they insisted stories of cruelty were exaggerated or exceptional, whereas they were 'kind' mistresses and masters, beloved for their benevolent treatment and regular gifts. Elizabeth even insisted on highlighting Henry's youthful abolitionism while drawing a veil over his later fight against emancipation.

When we follow the story beyond 1834, into the years of apprenticeship, indentureship, and 'freedom' under colonial rule, it becomes clear that the more things changed, the more they stayed the same. Whatever the legal position, formerly enslaved people continued to face the same

---

[*] Nelson had lost his right arm at the Battle of Santa Cruz de Tenerife on 27 July 1797.

racism, poor living conditions, harsh punishment and lack of justice, all fuelled by greed, and an intense fear of the Black majority. Witness the dungeons and workhouses endured by apprentices at estates like Friendship and Greenwich for minor or imagined 'offences', African indentured labourers working for a pittance at Duckenfield, and the atrocities perpetrated against people previously enslaved by the Franks and Taylor families during the Morant Bay War.

In the Caribbean, Emancipation Day marks the anniversary of full freedom on 1 August 1838. This makes Britain's tendency to fixate on 1807, conflating the abolition of trafficking Africans with emancipation in 1834 – ignoring 1838 altogether – not only ignorant but offensive. This dangerous confusion enables dismissive statements like 'this happened hundreds of years ago, get over it', and self-congratulatory pride in being 'the first nation to end slavery', a claim that would be untrue even if Britain *had* ended enslavement in 1807.*

After Lord Holland's statue was painted red by activists in 2020, an article appeared in *The Spectator* entitled 'Holland Park Must Not Fall', reproducing almost word for word the spin Henry himself, and later Elizabeth, with the help of Macaulay, put on his career. Fearful Holland Park might be renamed, the author insisted: 'While Henry Vassall-Fox was indeed a plantation owner through marriage' – as if acquiring enslaved people in this way meant that, as George Watson Taylor claimed, 'it was not his fault'– 'he consistently and actively opposed slavery'; though he received compensation he 'had campaigned for abolition in the full knowledge that he would lose income from his plantations.'[6] Besides being apparently unaware of Henry's pro-slavery stance in the 1820s and his efforts to secure the maximum compensation, the author seems blind to the injustice of the perpetrators being compensated, not the victims. Or that Black Caribbean British citizens were amongst the taxpayers who contributed to paying off the required loan, so large that it was redeemed only in 2015. The story didn't end 'hundreds of years ago' in fiscal terms either.

This response exemplifies the resistance and defensiveness that rears its ugly head in certain quarters whenever attempts are made to reckon

---

* Denmark abolished the traffic in 1792 (though this would not take effect until 1803). Revolutionary France abolished enslavement in 1794 (but Napoleon reversed the measure in 1802), as had the northern United States by 1804. But Haiti was the first sovereign nation to unconditionally proclaim emancipation in 1804.

with the more troubling aspects of Britain's past. But while Britain is convulsed in so-called 'culture-wars', Caribbean countries are seriously considering becoming a republic like Barbados, or using royal visits to ask difficult questions about the monarchy's own history of profiting from enslavement. Calls for reparations grow louder by the day on both sides of the Atlantic. The issue is bigger than just Britain and its former Caribbean colonies: the African Union (with fifty-five member states*) has recently joined forces with the Caribbean Community (CARICOM) to form a 'united front' to demand European nations pay for 'historical mass crimes'.[7] And of course there is a concurrent campaign for restitution in the United States, which has its own story, although we should remember Britain's culpability in establishing and maintaining enslavement there from 1619 until the American Revolution.

The need for reparations is often swiftly dismissed by sidestepping any discussion of morality and jumping straight to the – *very real* – problem of practicalities. But this is simply not good enough. Contemplating the sagas in this book, a fraction of the wider story, should make the moral justification for reparations abundantly clear. It is precisely because the moral case is so unassailable that naysayers attempt to avoid it.

So, what should be done to right these wrongs? The first thing required is an apology. As we teach our children, when you have done something bad, you need to own up and say sorry. None of us as individuals is personally guilty of historic crimes, but as nations, those of us who call ourselves British, English, Scottish, Welsh or Irish need to acknowledge what our forebears did, and how we still benefit today.

We can all tell when an apology is heartfelt and when it is not. Expressions of 'regret' or 'sorrow', such as Tony Blair made in 2007, King Charles shared with Commonwealth leaders in 2023 and his son William articulated in Jamaica in 2022, avoid taking responsibility. As a constitutional monarch, the King is restrained by government policy, but he might make a personal apology on the royal family's behalf. Their culpability reaches as far back as Elizabeth I's investment in John Hawkins's slaving voyages in the 1560s, and Charles II and his brother James putting the *Royal* in Royal Africa Company, through to William IV opposing emancipation while Duke of Clarence in the House of Lords.[8]

---

* There are 54 full internationally recognised states in Africa, but the Sahrawi Arab Democratic Republic is a member of the African Union despite its disputed status.

Some fear a formal apology would open the door to legal and financial redress; Rishi Sunak refused to apologise when challenged in Parliament in April 2023. A spokesperson for Keir Starmer stated 'we do not pay reparations' ahead of the Commonwealth Heads of Government summit in Samoa in October 2024, but over the course of the weekend it became clear it was no longer up to him to set the limits of the conversation. It was 'agreed that the time has come for a meaningful, truthful and respectful conversation towards forging a common future based on equity'. It remains to be seen how the Labour government with David Lammy – whose parents came from Guyana, and has been vocal in his support for reparations in the past – as Foreign Secretary, will take this forward. So far, the Green Party is the only British political party explicitly to endorse reparations.

Words are, of course, not enough. However, again in order to dismiss the idea, reparations are often wilfully misunderstood as the idea of handing over a large cheque to Caribbean governments or making some sort of payment to individual descendants of enslaved people. A recent report by economic consulting firm The Brattle Group has calculated that European nations owe £103 trillion worth of damages (the British share being £18.6 trillion). Others have suggested taking the £20 million compensation payment figure – with compound interest, something in the region of £105 to £250 billion today – as a starting point.[9] But though the repair needed will of course cost money, what is required is so much more holistic, personal and wide-ranging than a mere compensation payment.

CARICOM's 2013 ten-point plan for reparatory justice does not ask for a blank cheque. Instead, in addition to an apology, it calls upon European governments to make redress in nine further specific, practical ways.[10] Many connect to the themes of this book. The idea that Caribbean people should have the right to return to Africa, and the call for African knowledge programmes, are clear responses to the millions of people who were forcibly taken in the other direction, ripped from their cultural heritage, including those embarked from Bance Island. The numerous lists of enslaved people identified only by a first name – often one imposed upon them – and a 'value', speaks to the attempted effacement of African identities. An Indigenous development programme would address the consequences of the genocidal approach taken to peoples such as the Garifuna. The argument for investment in public health, both physical and mental, is obvious, especially when we think of the evidence from Newton Burial Ground and the intergenerational trauma caused by enslavement. The negative impacts of sugar monoculture, and the philosophy that 'not a nail' be manufactured in the colonies, make the need for investment in technology plain. When we think of the huge wealth Europeans extracted from their Caribbean colonies, the call for European governments to support debt cancellation measures to help 'clean up the colonial mess in order to prepare for development' makes sense. Perhaps the most egregious example to consider here is that of Haiti, one of the world's poorest and most politically volatile countries. In 1825, France demanded 150 million francs in exchange for recognising its former colony's independence. The loans taken out to meet this huge financial burden were fully repaid only in 1947. There are global precedents: the Jubilee 2000 campaign led to $130 billion of debt cancellation at the dawn of the new millennium; further progress was made at the start of the coronavirus pandemic, but the struggle for debt justice for the Global South continues.[11]

Who could argue that educational goals such as eradicating illiteracy and establishing cultural institutions like museums and research centres would not help combat legacies of enslavement? I'm thinking back to 1796, when Old Doll asked the manager at Newton if two of her grandsons could be taught to read and write. He admitted to the Lane brothers it was a 'cruel thing to withhold instruction when one can bestow it', but 'inclination must give way to policy, and I think it is a bad one, in their situation, to bestow on them the powers of reading and writing', which, as we saw, he thought was 'of little good, and very frequently produces of mischief with them'. It took until 1948 for the British government to establish a higher education institution in a Caribbean colony; degrees at the 'University College of the West Indies' were awarded by the University of London for fourteen years before it gained independent university status in the same year Jamaica gained independence.

CARICOM is planning to add measures focused on women, the diaspora beyond the Caribbean, and environmental reparations – a concept that has its own trajectory – to the list. UK reparations activists, who can trace their history back to the 'Sons of Africa' – a lobbying group including Olaudah Equiano and Ottobah Cugoano – have a more Pan-African and radical vision, but also highlight the need for education, eradicating racism and targeting environmental damage.[12]

As a historian, I have seen the need for educational intervention first hand. The imperatives of tourism have sanitised the Caribbean narrative;

the less palatable elements of Britain's past have been swept under the proverbial carpet. There is no museum in the British Caribbean dedicated to telling the story of enslavement. Even at former plantation sites, like Rose Hall near Montego Bay in Jamaica or Sunbury Plantation Great House in St Philip, Barbados, the narrative somehow manages to elide the experiences of enslaved people. The Barbados government's plan to build a site of memory and exhibition centre at Newton Burial Ground is an important development people in Britain should support. British museums hold many objects that could furnish displays in new or expanded Caribbean cultural institutions. There are 2,471 Taino-related objects in the British Museum collection; Jamaica has called in vain for the return of just two religiously significant wooden carved figures – which are not even on display.[13] I was able to write this book with relatively easy access to sources held in Britain. Travel costs and visa restrictions make it so much harder for Caribbean scholars to read and interpret records of their own countries' history. This is another imbalance that must be redressed, not just because it is unfair, but because a wider range of perspectives will enrich our understanding of our shared histories.

Stories like those you have read in this book do not form part of our common knowledge. Ignorance about the true nature of Britain's colonial past helps propagate injustices today – the Windrush Scandal, disproportionate mortality from Covid-19 and attacks on migrant hotels provide stark recent examples; meanwhile everyday racism – internal, interpersonal, institutional and structural – remains pervasive. Sharing this history widely and collaboratively will be part of my own contribution to the cause. I hope that if British people, with our strong sense of 'fair play', knew what really happened, they would be prepared to acknowledge past wrongs, how we all benefit from them today, and take action to repair the damage.

Some British institutions and individual families *have* recently confronted their histories, made full apologies, and pledged money towards repair, in what the Dean of Trinity College, Cambridge, calls 'Reparations with a small "r"'. Besides his own college, these include the Church of England, Glasgow University, the *Guardian* newspaper, Lloyd's of London, Greene King brewery and members of the Heirs of Slavery group including the Gladstone and Trevelyan families. Many have failed to engage sufficiently with the descendants of enslaved people when formulating their response; why should the beneficiaries of the crime decide the penalty? However, these steps in the right direction are provoking a more serious public discussion of reparations than ever before.[14]

Similarly, I hope the eye-opening stories in this book will further that national and international conversation. If tracing the lives of just nine women and their tainted wealth reveals so much, then the wider-ranging implications for the British history we thought we knew are clear. Correcting the distortions in the telling of our past – reparative history – is an important part of the reparative justice process. We must confront uncomfortable truths head on. Only then will we be able to forge new relationships across divisions of race and class, and take responsibility for working together to place justice and humanity at the heart of our society.

My Family and Enslavement

> History, despite its wrenching pain, cannot be unlived, but if faced with courage, need not be lived again.
>
> MAYA ANGELOU,
> 'On the Pulse of Morning' (1993)[1]

GIVEN THE TANGLED WEB of connections to enslavement in Georgian Britain, it is unsurprising that some of *my* ancestors were involved as perpetrators. Although the Kaufmann side of my family is Viennese Jewish, my mother grew up in North Wales. Due to the same lottery of human reproduction and mortality we have encountered in this book, as an eldest daughter with no brothers or first cousins, I became the heiress to her family's estates and now live in a country house full of historical objects, portraits and documents, with many stories to tell.

North Wales is very close to Liverpool. Two family members were Liverpool slavers in the last few decades of the eighteenth century. John Chambres Jones of Bryn Eisteddfod co-owned five Liverpool slaving ships. The *Chambres*, *Clementine*, *Colonel*, *Doe* and *Rose Hill* made twelve voyages between 1783 and 1791, transporting an estimated 4,697 captive Africans, 386 of whom died during the crossing. Though he is a distant relation – the husband of my fourth great-grand-aunt – he had no grandchildren, so my side of the family eventually inherited his wealth.[2]

One of my fifth great-grandfathers, Edward Wilson, besides importing tobacco, was part-owner (often as part of the Gregson syndicate) of eighteen ships making fifty-three voyages between 1770 and 1793, trafficking an estimated 19,005 enslaved people – 2,683 of whom did not survive the passage.³ One of the Gregson syndicate ships was the *Zong*,* which became infamous after 132 captive African people were thrown overboard, then claimed on the insurance. Outrage that the resulting court case *Gregson v. Gilbert* (1783) was not a murder trial fuelled the abolitionist movement.⁴ Ottobah Cugoano rightly condemned the owners as 'inhuman connivers of robbery, slavery, murder and fraud'.⁵

Edward's daughter Elizabeth Wilson married into our family with a dowry of £5,000 in 1789.⁶ Her sister Martha had died following childbirth the previous year, and Martha's only daughter remained unmarried, so again the Wilson wealth – by the time of Edward's death involving property in Chester and Manchester, and substantial shares in the Lancaster Canal – was left to Elizabeth and her children.⁷

Another of my fifth great-grandfathers was lawyer and enslaver Robert Cooper Lee, Crown Solicitor for Jamaica, then the island's London agent. In 1789, he acquired a quarter of Rose Hall estate, near Linstead, in St Catherine, and the some 200 people who laboured there.⁸ As my family is descended from one of Robert Cooper Lee's daughters, the majority of his wealth did not directly come our way.⁹ However, there is another inheritance to consider, from his wife, Priscilla Kelly. Robert Cooper Lee was one of many men who formed a connection with a mixed-heritage woman while in Jamaica, though he took the relatively unusual step of bringing her back to London with him, along with their four children, marrying her at St George's, Hanover Square, in 1771. We know she had African ancestry because he applied for the 'rights of whites' for their children, as Susanna Augier did in Chapter 2. This means, like many other unsuspecting British people, I have a distant African ancestor.¹⁰

As you may have seen in notes throughout the book, Robert Cooper Lee was personally connected to several of the heiresses and their families. Rose Hall had previously belonged to Charles Price, Frances Dalzell's attorney. The Watson Taylors' attorney William Shand also acted as attorney there for Robert's son Richard Lee. Several legal documents I encountered in my research bore Robert Cooper Lee's name. He witnessed a signature on the lease of Lucky Hill in 1765. He was a trustee of Elizabeth Vassall's 1786 marriage settlement. He was friendly with Anna Susanna's uncle Robert Graham and a good enough friend

---

* The Dutch prize ship, *Zorgue*, was purchased for the Gregson syndicate at Cape Coast Castle, and renamed the *Zong*. It became the *Richard* after arriving in Jamaica.

of her father Sir John Taylor that he left him and his wife Priscilla each a ring worth fifty guineas.

While researching *Heiresses*, I found further, albeit sometimes quite distant, links between my family, the objects in our house, and the stories in this book. I recently realised we have a portrait of Thomas Lane's grandson, Richard Stuart Lane, who inherited Newton plantation, Barbados, in 1870.[11] His wife was my great-grandmother Eleanor Clare Hippisley's aunt and godmother. She died in 1909, leaving Eleanor Clare any of her 'pictures as she may desire to possess'.[12]

Frances Dalzell's half-sister Mary Augier married Gilbert Ford. We have portraits of several Ford family members because my second great-granduncle, John Carstairs Jones, married Anna Maria Bamford-Hesketh, whose grandfather, Dr John Ford, was Gilbert Ford's brother.

Two of Martha Swinburne's daughters, Carolina and Maria Theresa Henrietta, married brothers John Walker and Richard Watt Walker. They were the sons of Liverpool merchant Richard Walker, whose first wife, Martha Wilson, was the other daughter of Edward Wilson, mentioned above.[13]

Those are the bald facts. There is still a lot more research to do, looking at these people in the same way I've approached the families in this book, trying to find out as much as possible about them, their local and global connections and (if possible) their motivation. There is also the task of better estimating exactly how much wealth they amassed from enslavement.

But I know enough to start the process of making amends. I am approaching this in a spirit of humility and collaboration, as a follower not a leader, with respect for a Black-led movement with a very long history, asking what is needed, and listening deeply. It is my duty to do so, however frightening it feels, and whatever opposition I might face.

The first step is to acknowledge this past and apologise.

I am ashamed of and sorry for what my ancestors did.

What am I doing about it? The loudest refrain in all the discussions I have ever heard on the subject is the need for education. I will continue my collaborative work with schools, universities and museums, aiming to ensure this history is fully acknowledged and understood. My house is occasionally open to the public so it can provide a testing-ground for how best to tell these stories in heritage spaces. I've learnt how effective creative responses to painful histories – art, literature, theatre, film, music – can be in cutting through and reaching people's hearts. Working with artists, writers and musicians, I can provide convivial space for creative gatherings, retreats and performances.

As I go forward along this path, there are further things I can give in kind. I will be collating the raw materials from this book, particularly those which give details about the lives of enslaved people, and donating them to the University College London Legacies of British Slavery project – a database that has been foundational to my research. I have shared my findings on my Liverpool slaving ancestors with the forthcoming Register of British Slave Traders database, and aim to make items in my possession, such as John Chambres Jones's business ledger and memorandum book, available for study. I will also be encouraging British archives to do more to make *their* collections widely accessible in both Britain and the Caribbean, with better cataloguing, digitisation and transcription projects. I will continue sharing my platform highlighting the work of Black historians and creatives and co-creating networks and collaborations, both nationally and internationally.

But I also want to *fund* reparative work. I have already taken some small steps in this direction: sponsoring secondary school scholarships in Kingston, Jamaica, and a Black British History Scholarship for a person of Global Majority Heritage at Gladstone's Library near me in North Wales. As part of this ongoing commitment, I intend to donate my proceeds from this book to the cause. I hope, having read this far, you'll understand why, and be glad that in buying a copy, and sharing these stories, you too have contributed to the process of repair.

Intellectual Debts

No historical work is ever truly original, and this book could not have been written without the efforts of generations of scholars who have scoured the archives in order to lay out the scale of, as Sir Hilary Beckles puts it, 'Britain's Black Debt'.

The role of women as enslavers in the Caribbean and the United States has been examined by pioneers including Lucille Mathurin Mair, Cecily Jones, Hilary Beckles, Verene Shepherd, Christine Walker and Stephanie Jones-Rogers.[1] But less attention has been paid to the female enslavers who spent most of their lives in Britain, and their role both as active agents in the 'business' and in bringing the profits of enslavement 'home'.

Eric Williams, historian and former Prime Minister of Trinidad and Tobago, pointed out that 'a West Indian heiress was a desirable plum', in his seminal work *Capitalism and Slavery*, as long ago as 1944.[2] But the scale of the phenomenon has only recently been quantified by the original University College London Legacies of British Slavery team: Catherine Hall, Nick Draper, Keith McClelland, Rachel Lang, Katie Donington, Hannah Young, James Dawkins and Kristy Warren, who found over forty per cent of the individuals awarded compensation in the 1830s for their loss of human property after emancipation were women; half of these resident in Britain.[3] It will be abundantly clear for anyone who has glanced at my endnotes how much my project owes to this game-changing work.

Of these fantastic scholars, Hannah Young has been at the forefront of exploring what it meant, materially, legally, symbolically, for women to own property in the form of other human beings, specifically looking at a mother and daughter pair of heiresses, both named Anna Eliza, who became respectively the Duchess of Chandos and the Duchess of Buckingham and Chandos.[4] Hannah's work on female enslavers, which I first heard her speak so powerfully about at the Little Britain's Memory of Slavery Conference in 2013, has been a touchstone for my own explorations.

I can clearly trace the intellectual origin of this project back to my first meeting with Madge Dresser in Bristol in the autumn of 2006. English Heritage had hired me to conduct a survey of their houses' connections to enslavement and abolition in the run-up to the 2007 bicentenary. Madge, an expert on Bristol's slaving past, told me there were ten types of connection I should look for. One was: 'Heiresses'. Shortly afterwards, I first encountered Elizabeth Vassall; Battle Abbey was close to the top of my alphabetised list of properties to review.

I conducted that survey the same year I inherited my mother's family estates and began to learn about my ancestors' connections to enslavement. This convergence in my own life means that Verene Shepherd's point that the evidence for 'women's involvement in, and profit from, African misery' strengthens 'the rationale for an appeal for women of conscience to become more active in the reparation movement' really hits home.[5] I hope this book will help me answer that call, and I would like to warmly acknowledge the work of all those who have forwarded the cause of reparative justice and continue to do so.

Acknowledgements

My journey in pursuit of *Heiresses* has been a long one (in part due to my inability to avoid the rabbit holes, or leave any stone unturned) and I am indebted to more people than I could possibly name here. Thank you all.

Madge Dresser, you've been such a supportive mentor ever since I started down this road that day in Bristol; this wouldn't have happened without you.

Within the constraints of parenthood and the pandemic it was not possible to make lengthy trips to far-flung archives. This work would not have been possible without the help of my research assistants. My thanks to Paul Clammer for introducing me to the meticulous and hugely knowledgeable Michael Becker. I'm so grateful, Michael, that you were there to scour the Jamaican archives for me, provide contextual reading recommendations, explain some of the more arcane details of Caribbean history and read through chapter drafts. Your invaluable input has made this a far better book. John Shorter, I'm glad you were able to step in after Michael left Jamaica; you've been brilliant in helping me track down some stubborn details and giving me a fresh perspective both while hanging out in Kingston and on our long phone calls. I could never have found what I found in the Barbados archives and countryside without you, Marcia Nurse. I'm lucky to have found someone who knew both the inner workings of the record office and the back roads of St George like the back of her hand.

The indefatigable and remarkable Rhiannon Markless located, photographed and transcribed endless documents in English archives; I am so thankful for that heavy lifting and for your ability to translate eighteenth-century legalese. Others helped with some hard-to-reach places; many thanks to John Cairns and Karen Baston in Edinburgh, Eloise Grey and Alan McInnes in Aberdeen, Celia Mill in Winchester,

Richard Toye in Exeter, and all the dedicated archivists out there who smoothed my path.

Thanks to everyone who hosted me in Barbados and Jamaica. Alissandra Cummins and the Barbados Museum team were hugely generous with their time, helping with preparatory research (thanks Dario Forte), showing me their exhibitions and library and allowing me to present my work on Jane Leigh Perrot at an early stage. Visiting Newton with Kevin Farmer and Kaye Hall brought it all to life. Cheers to Tony Warner for your hospitality and sharing the best beach breakfasts. In Jamaica, thanks to Zach Beier, Verene Shepherd, Moji Anderson, James Robertson, Justine Henzell and others. Special thanks to Ainsley Henriques for driving me out to St Thomas in the East and St Mary. Sorry for getting you stuck in the mud at Llanrumney all because I wanted to find a 200-year-old view! And to Howard Cowell for going in search of Elizabeth Vassall's birthplace with me in Westmoreland.

Thank you to the Institute of Commonwealth Studies, School of Advanced Study, University of London and the University of Liverpool for your institutional support. Much of my research would have been impossible without your magic library cards.

Thanks to my agent Charlie Viney for getting me the gig in the first place, and for your forbearance in the many years since. Thanks to Val Hudson for helping shape the vision and to Tom Bromley for your ability to sort the wheat from the chaff.

Thanks to everyone at Oneworld, I really appreciate the time and energy you have put into making this book the very best version of itself it could be. Thanks to Rida Vaquas and Hannah Haseloff for your invaluable input, and to Kathleen McCully for your judicious final cull. But most of all to Sam Carter who has been patient, kind and encouraging throughout this drawn-out process.

It was always important to me to get a wide range of perspectives on the material I was finding and the way I was interpreting it. I am so grateful to everyone who read drafts of the book. My gratitude to Nick Draper, Kesewa John and Cecily Jones who all read the entire manuscript and improved it with their invaluable feedback. Each chapter took me in wildly different directions and began new academic friendships based on shared niche obsessions. Thank you to Hannah Young, Allan Howard, Katherine Paugh, Tara Inniss, Karl Watson and Jerome Handler on the Newtons and Hylases, and to Anne Powers and Mario Valdes for sharing your detailed genealogical research on the Augiers, Dalzells and

Duffs (and Lees, Anne). Thanks to Victoria Barnett-Woods for introducing me to *The Woman of Colour* (1808) and the fascinating discussions that have ensued. David Hancock, thank you for fielding endless questions about the woman behind the 'great man'. Thank you to Corinne Fowler and Julian North for your advice from an Austenian perspective and David Pugsley for advocating the blackmail plot so convincingly. Thank you Natalie Zacek for sharing your Leewards wisdom, and Désha Osborne for helping me understand St Vincent. Cliff Pereira, thank you for steering me through the uncharted waters of the Indian Ocean and the South China Sea. Robin Walsh, it was an absolute pleasure to pick your brains about Jane Jarvis. Thanks to Padraig Scanlan and Richard Anderson for sharing your knowledge about Sierra Leone. Jean-Pierre Brun's unpublished work on the Dawkins of Moggerhanger was a vital starting point for Isabella Cooper's story. And thanks to Christer Petley, Kate Tammemagi, Hugh Roberts, Elodie Goëssant and Sarah Thomas for your foundational work on the Taylors that made my quest in search of Anna Susanna's story so much easier.

I really appreciate the moral support of my comrades in the fight for reparative history. I'd particularly like to thank Michael Ohajuru and Ebun Culwin, Corinne Fowler, Nathaniel Coleman, Paterson Joseph, James Dawkins, Alex Renton, Thomas Harding, Kesewa John, Malik Al-Nasir and Desirée Baptiste for their comfort and counsel during my ongoing journey towards understanding what role I might play in the struggle.

Thanks to my dear friends who always have been there for me; Ann Berry, Kylie Blackham, Zahler Bryan, Sue Burton, Kathryn De Jesus, Ruth Evans, Ciorsdan Glass, Emily Hacker, Lydia Hickinson, Kate Maltby, John Morgenstern, Jessica Rutberg, Jo Ward and Angus Warrick. Fiona Pearce, Tracey Roberts, Stacey Keen and Alice Jones have lightened my load, bless you.

Dad, you are both my head cheerleader and my most beloved sparring partner, even when we completely disagree. Which has been often on this subject, though I think I've found some chinks in your armour. Thank you for nurturing my love of history, buying me books as rewards for good marks at school, sharpening my wits at the dinner table and your bear hugs. Mum, Augusta and Olivia – the rest of the Kaufmann tight five – thanks for putting up with those heated conversations and for all your love and support. Thanks to my sisters for adding extra players to both the men's and junior teams: Gareth, Mikkel, Jasmine, Dylan, Lily and Wilfred. I love you all immensely. Aunt Loraine, you have probably read more of the manuscript than any other family member; I really appreciate the no-nonsense feedback from your first-class brain.

Olivier, you are still my shelter from the storm, my olive tree whose roots grow by the sea, and I love you more dearly each day. Thank you for building a life with me, weathering the Welsh climate, being the most wonderful Papa to our girls, and holding the fort while I go on research trips, or lock myself in my office. Darling Sophie and Juliette, your infectious joy has helped sustain me throughout. I hope one day you'll understand why Mummy spent so much time on this book, and find it makes interesting reading.

Illustration List

1. Title page of *A master-key to the rich ladies treasury. Or, The widower and batchelor's directory, containing an exact alphabetical list of the duchess dowagers...* by B. M-n (London: J. Roberts, 1742). Digitised by Google Books.
2. Portrait of Lady Sarah Holte, née Newton by Tilly Kettle, *c.*1763.
3. 'A topographicall description and admeasurement of the yland of Barbados in the West Indyaes with the mrs. names of the seuerall plantacons', Richard Ligon, 1657. Courtesy of Library of Congress, Geography and Map Division.
4. An ox-driven sugar mill in Brazil. From Willem Piso, *Historia Naturalis Brasiliae*, 1648. Courtesy of Biodiversity Heritage Library.
5. Portrait of Sir Lister Holte by Tilly Kettle, *c.*1763. Courtesy of Birmingham Museums Trust.
6. Catherine Newton with Isham Baggs from *The Trial of the Hon. Mrs. Catherine Newton... Upon A Libel and Allegations Charging her with the Crime of Adultery...* (London: G. Lister, 1782). Digitised by Google Books.
7. Mary Hylas's descendants, as listed in the 1784 valuation of the Newton plantation. Senate House Library.
8. Portrait of Frances Duff, née Dalzell, *c.*1750. Artist unknown.
9. Freedom fighters captured during Tacky's War gibbeted alive on the outskirts of Kingston, Jamaica. Drawing by Pierre Eugène du Simitière, Kingston, 10 May 1760. Courtesy of Library Company of Philadelphia.
10. Portrait of Mary Oswald, née Ramsay, by Johan Zoffany, *c.*1763–4. Author's photograph.
11. Bance Island, in the Sierra Leone River, *c.*1727. From *Thirty different drafts of Guinea* by William Smith, Surveyor to the Royal African Company of England. Etchings by Gray after William Smith. Courtesy of Yale Center for British Art.
12. Michael Hay's Map of Kingston, *c.*1740. Courtesy of Library of Congress Geography and Map Division.
13. Portraits of Sir Richard Oswald and Margaret Ramsay Oswald by William Denune, *c.*1747 and *c.*1750.
14. Portrait of Jane Leigh Perrot, née Cholmeley, by G.G. and J. Robinson, from *The Lady's Magazine*, 1 May 1800.
15. Portrait of Jane Austen from *A Memoir of Jane Austen* by J. E. Austen-Leigh (London: Richard Bentley, 1870). Engraving by William Home Lizars after watercolour by Cassandra Austen. Wikimedia.

16. 'Plan of Miss Gregory's shop', from *The trial of Jane Leigh Perrot, wife of James Leigh Perrot, esq, charged with stealing a card of lace, in the shop of Elizabeth Gregory, haberdasher and milliner, at Bath* (Taunton: Thomas Norris, 1800). Courtesy of Beinecke Rare Book and Manuscript Library, Yale University.
17. Portrait of Martha Swinburne, née Baker, by Richard Cosway, engraved by Mariano Bovi. V&A.
18. 'Chatoyer the Chief of the Black Charaibes in St. Vincent with his five Wives'. Etching by Charles Grignion after Agostino Brunias (I. Stockdale, Piccadilly, 1796). Courtesy of John Carter Brown Library.
19. Portrait of Henry Swinburne by Pompeo Batoni, 1779. Laing Art Gallery, Newcastle-upon-Tyne, UK, North East Museums / Bridgeman Images.
20. Frontispiece of *The Trial of Governor T. Picton for Inflicting the Torture on Louisa Calderon...* (London: Dewick & Clarke, 1806). Courtesy of Library of Congress.
21. Portrait of Jane Macquarie, née Jarvis, c.1793. Unknown artist. Courtesy of State Library of New South Wales.
22. 'The "*Essex*" East Indiaman, as she appeared when refitted and at anchor in Bombay Harbour', after Thomas Luny's original painting. From E. Keble Chatterton, *The Old East Indiamen* (London: T.W. Laurie, 1914). Courtesy of Cornell University Library.
23. Macao c.1800. Painting by an anonymous Chinese artist. Wikimedia / Erlend Bjørtvedt.
24. Portrait of Lady Elizabeth Webster, née Vassall, with her son by Louis Gauffier, 1794. Wikimedia.
25. Robert Kirkwood's plan of Friendship and Greenwich, 1784.
26. 'Sketch for a Prime Minister or How to Purchase a Peace'. Folding plate from the *Satirist*, 1 February 1811. Bodleian Libraries.
27. 'Retreat of Lieutenant Brady', from Joshua Bryant's *Account of an insurrection of the negro slaves in the colony of Demerara...* (A. Stevenson, Georgetown, 1824). Courtesy of the John Carter Brown Library.
28. The monument to Charles James Fox in Westminster Abbey. Wikimedia / 14GTR.
29. 'Treadwheel', from *Jamaica: its past and present state* by James Mursell Phillippo (London: J. Snow, 1843). Courtesy of Harvard University Library.
30. 'Abolition of Slavery in Jamaica', R. Cartwright, 1838.
31. Portrait of Lady Isabella Bell Cooper, née Franks, by Thomas Gainsborough. Courtesy of Birmingham Museums Trust.
32. Portrait of Lady Mary Cadogan, John Dean after Joshua Reynolds, 1787. Courtesy of Yale Center for British Art.
33. George William Gordon, c.1860. From 'Photography Album Documenting the Morant Bay Rebellion In Jamaica (1865), the Indian Northwest Frontier Hazara Campaign (1867–1870.) Views of Malta, Ireland, Guernsey, Spain, and Elsewhere' by Alexander Dudgeon Gulland, et al. Courtesy of Princeton University Library.
34. Paul Bogle, c.1860. National Gallery of Jamaica.
35. Portrait of Anna Susanna Watson Taylor by Sir Martin Archer Shee, c.1821.
36. 'The Dilettanti Society', William Say after Joshua Reynolds, 1812. Courtesy of Yale Center for British Art.
37. Portrait of Simon Taylor. National Library of Jamaica.
38. Portrait of George Watson Taylor by Sir Martin Archer Shee, 1820. Private Collection. Christie's Images / Bridgeman Images.

39. John Gibson RA, *Kneeling woman with a standing infant*. Pen and brown ink and wash on wove paper. 241 mm x 300 mm. © Photo: Royal Academy of Arts, London. Bequeathed to the RA by John Gibson RA 1866. RA Ref. No. 05/615.
40. Sir John and Simon Taylor's smashed graves, Lyssons, St Thomas in the East, Jamaica. Author's photograph.

PLATE SECTION

1. 'The Mill-Yard.' William Clark, *Ten views in the island of Antigua* (London: Thomas Clay, 1823). Yale Center for British Art.
2. Barbados 25-cent coin. Mark Morgan / Wikimedia.
3. 'The Boiling House.' William Clark, *Ten views in the island of Antigua* (London: Thomas Clay, 1823). Yale Center for British Art.
4. Components of a necklace composed of dog teeth, cowrie shells, fish vertebrae, European manufactured glass beads and a large carnelian bead made in Cambay, India. Courtesy of Jerome Handler. First published in *Plantation Slavery in Barbados: An Archaeological and Historical Investigation* by Jerome S. Handler and Frederick W. Lange (Harvard University Press, 1978).
5. Plan of an estate of 300 acres near Jamestown, or present-day Holetown, Barbados by John Hapcott, 1646. John Carter Brown Library.
6. Joseph Bartholomew Kidd, 'The Parade and Upper Part of Kingston from the Church. Looking towards the Port Royal Mountains', *West Indian Scenery* (London: Smith, Elder, & Co, 1838–40). Yale Center for British Art.
7. *Wouski* by James Gillray, 23 January 1788. British Museum.
8. David Martin's Portrait of Dido Elizabeth Belle and her cousin Lady Elizabeth Murray, c.1788. Wikimedia.
9. Auchincruive House. Author's photograph.
10. *Treaty of Paris* by Benjamin West, 1783. Courtesy of Winterthur Museum, Garden & Library; Gift of Henry Francis du Pont.
11. Lachlan Macquarie by John Opie, c. 1805. Mitchell Library, State Library of New South Wales.
12. British officer in palanquin with Indian bearers, anonymous, c. 1830. The Anne S. K. Brown Military Collection, Brown University Library.
13. The ruins of Sweet River Pen Great House, Westmoreland, Jamaica. Author's photograph.
14. Portrait of Henry Vassall-Fox, 3rd Baron Holland by François-Xavier Fabre, 1795. Wikimedia.
15. Lord Holland's statue in Holland Park painted red in 2020. © Heather Brooke.
16. *South View of Holland House, Middlesex. The Seat of Lord Holland* by John Buckler, 1812. Artvee.
17. The family of Sir John Taylor by Daniel Gardner, 1785. Art Collection 2 / Alamy Stock Photo.
18. Charlotte Sproule by Richard Hooke. Courtesy of Michael Ferriss.
19. 'Mill Yard, Holland Estate, St. Thomas in the East' by James Hakewill in *Views of the Watson Taylor Estates in Jamaica*, c. 1820–1. Yale Center for British Art.
20. 'Sugar-cane cutters in Jamaica, Caribbean', c.1880. National Maritime Museum, Greenwich, London; Michael Graham-Stewart Slavery Collection.

Bibliography

This is a highly selective bibliography of the key sources I consulted for this work. The full bibliography can be downloaded as a PDF from https://oneworld-publications.com/work/heiresses or www.mirandakaufmann.com/heiresses-bibliography.html

ARCHIVES

UK

Aberdeen University Library (AUL)
Edinburgh University Library Manuscripts Collection (EUL)
Hampshire Record Office (HRO)
Institute of Commonwealth Studies, University of London (ICS)
Lincolnshire Archives (LAO)
London Metropolitan Archives (LMA)
National Records of Scotland (NRS)
Senate House Library, University of London (SHL)
Staffordshire Record Office (SRO)
The National Archives, Kew (TNA)
Wiltshire and Swindon History Centre (WSHC)

Caribbean

Barbados Department of Archives, Bridgetown (BDA)
National Library of Jamaica, Kingston, Jamaica (NLJ)
The Jamaica Archives and Records Department, Spanish Town, Jamaica (JARD)
Island Record Office, Spanish Town, Jamaica (IRO)

USA

William L. Clements Library, University of Michigan (CL)

Australia

Mitchell Library, State Library of New South Wales (ML)

PRINTED PRIMARY SOURCES

Anon., *The Trial of the Hon. Mrs. Catherine Newton, Wife of John Newton, Esq; and Daughter of the Right Honourable and Reverend Lord Francis Seymour at the Consistory Court of Doctors Commons* (London: G. Lister, 1782).

Anon., *The Second Part of the Trial of the Hon. Mrs. Catherine Newton, Wife of John Newton, Esq; and Daughter of the Right Honourable and Reverend Lord Francis Seymour at the Consistory Court of Doctors Commons* (London: G. Lister, 1782).

Anon., *The Trial at Large of the Right Honourable Lady Cadogan: For Adultery with the Rev. Mr. Cooper, Before Lord Kenyon and a Special Jury, in Westminster-Hall* (London: J. Ridgway, 1794).

Anon., *The Trial of Mrs. Leigh Perrot* (London: West and Hughes, 1800).

Anon., *Trial of Jane Leigh Perrot* (Gye: Bath, 1800).

Austen, J., and D. Le Faye (ed.), *Jane Austen's Letters* (Oxford: Oxford University Press, 2011).

Austen, J., *Mansfield Park*, ed. I. Littlewood (Ware: Wordsworth Editions, 2007).

Austen-Leigh, R.A., *Austen Papers, 1704–1856* (Priv. print. London: Spottiswoode, Ballantyne & Co., 1942).

Baker, J., and P.C. Yorke (ed.), *The Diary of John Baker, Barrister of the Middle Temple, Solicitor-General of the Leeward Islands* (London: Hutchinson & Co., 1931).

Barclay, A., *A Practical View of the Present State of Slavery in the West Indies: Or, an Examination of Mr. Stephen's 'Slavery of the British West India Colonies'* (London: Smith, Elder & Co., 1826).

Bury, C.S.M., and J. Galt (ed.), *Diary Illustrative of the Times of George the Fourth: Comprising the Secret History of the Court during the Reigns of George III and George IV* (London: Colburn, 1839), 2 vols.

Byres, J., *References to the Plan of the Island of St Vincent, as Surveyed from the Year 1765 to 1773* (London: S. Hooper, 1777).

Clark, L.J., *The Diary of Lucy Kennedy (1793–1816): Memoirs of the Court of George III, Volume 3* (London: Routledge, 2021).

Cunninghame Graham, R.B., *Doughty Deeds: An Account of the Life of Robert Graham of Gartmore, Poet & Politician, 1735–1797* (London: W. Heinemann, 1925).

Franks, A., and E.B. Gelles (ed.), *The Letters of Abigaill Levy Franks, 1733–1748* (New Haven, CT: Yale University Press, 2004).

Hakewill, J., *A Picturesque Tour of the Island of Jamaica* (London: Hurst, Robinson & Co., 1825).

Holland, E.V. Fox, Lady, and the Earl of Ilchester (ed.), *The Journal of Elizabeth Lady Holland (1791–1811)* (London: Longmans, Green, 1909), 2 vols.

Holland, E.V. Fox, Lady, and the Earl of Ilchester (ed.), *Elizabeth, Lady Holland to Her Son: 1821–1845* (John Murray, 1946).

Holland, H.R.V., J. Allen, and A.D. Kriegel (ed.), *The Holland House Diaries, 1831–1840: The Diary of Henry Richard Vassall Fox, Third Lord Holland, with Extracts from the Diary of John Allen* (London: Routledge & Kegan Paul, 1977).
House of Commons, *Parliamentary Papers* (London: H.M. Stationery Office, 1867).
Journals of the Assembly of Jamaica (St Jago, Jamaica: House of Assembly, 1663–1826).
Laurens, H., D.R. Chesnutt, and C.J. Taylor (eds), *The Papers of Henry Laurens* (Columbia, SC: University of South Carolina Press, 2003), 16 vols.
Leslie, C., *A New History of Jamaica* (London: I. Hodges, 1740).
Lewis, M.G., *Journal of a West India Proprietor, Kept during a Residence in the Island of Jamaica* (London: John Murray: 1834).
Ligon, R., with an introduction by K.O. Kupperman (ed.), *A True and Exact History of the Island of Barbados* (Indianapolis, IN: Hackett, 2011).
Long, E., *The History of Jamaica. Or, General Survey of the Antient and Modern State of That Island: With Reflections on Its Situation, Settlements, Inhabitants, Climate, Products, Commerce, Laws, and Government* (London: T. Lowndes, in Fleet-Street, 1774), 3 vols.
Parliamentary Papers, *Report of the Jamaica Royal Commission, 1866* (H.M. Stationery Office, 1866.)
Pinchard, J., *The Trial of Jane Leigh Perrot* (Taunton: Norris, 1800).
Sturge, J., and T. Harvey, *The West Indies in 1837* (London: Hamilton, Adams & Co., 1838).
Swinburne, H., and C. White, *The Courts of Europe at the Close of the Last Century* (London: H.S. Nichols & Co., 1895), 2 vols.
Williams, J., and D. Paton (ed.), *A Narrative of Events since the First of August 1834* (Durham, NC: Duke University Press, 2001).

SECONDARY WORKS

Amussen, S.D., *Caribbean Exchanges: Slavery and the Transformation of English Society, 1640–1700* (Chapel Hill, NC: University of North Carolina Press, 2009).
Anderson, R., and H.B. Lovejoy (eds), *Liberated Africans and the Abolition of the Slave Trade, 1807–1896* (Rochester, NY: University of Rochester Press, 2020).
Araujo, A.L., *Reparations for Slavery and the Slave Trade: A Transnational and Comparative History* (London: Bloomsbury Academic, 2017).
Atkinson, R., *Mr. Atkinson's Rum Contract: The Story of a Tangled Inheritance* (London: HarperCollins, 2020).
Banner, M., *Britain's Slavery Debt: Reparations Now!* (Oxford: Oxford University Press, 2024).
Barczewski, S., *Country Houses and the British Empire, 1700–1930* (Manchester: Manchester University Press, 2017).
Barnett-Woods, V., '"Bequeathed unto My Daughter [...] Slaves": Women, Slavery and Property in the Eighteenth-Century Atlantic', *Journal for Eighteenth-Century Studies*, 44, 2021, pp. 469–86.
Beckles, H. McD., *Britain's Black Debt: Reparations for Caribbean Slavery and Native Genocide* (Kingston: University of the West Indies Press, 2013).
— *Centering Woman: Gender Discourses in Caribbean Slave Society* (Kingston, Princeton, Oxford: Ian Randle, Markus Wieber Publishers, James Currey Publishers, 1999).

Borowitz, A., *Crimes Gone By: Essays by Albert Borowitz* (Cleveland, OH: ATBOSH Media, 2016).
Brown, V., *Reaper's Garden*, reprint ed. (Cambridge, MA: Harvard University Press, 2010).
— *Tacky's Revolt: The Story of an Atlantic Slave War* (Cambridge, MA: Harvard University Press, 2020).
Burnard, T., *Mastery, Tyranny, and Desire: Thomas Thistlewood and His Slaves in the Anglo-Jamaican World* (Chapel Hill, NC: University of North Carolina Press, 2009).
Byrne, P., *The Real Jane Austen: A Life in Small Things*. (London: HarperCollins, 2013).
Calder, C.M., *John Vassall and His Descendants* (Hertford: Stephen Austin and Sons, 1921).
Canny, N. (ed.), *The Oxford History of the British Empire: Volume I: The Origins of Empire* (Oxford: Oxford University Press, 2007).
Chancellor, V.E., 'Slave-owner and Anti-slaver: Henry Richard Vassall Fox, 3rd Lord Holland, 1800–1840', *Slavery & Abolition*, 1:3, Dec. 1980, pp. 263–75.
Chater, K., *Untold Histories: Black People in England and Wales during the Period of the British Slave Trade, c.1660–1807* (Manchester: Manchester University Press, 2011).
Craton, M., *Testing the Chains: Resistance to Slavery in the British West Indies* (Ithaca, NY: Cornell University Press, 2009).
Dadzie, S., *A Kick in the Belly: Women, Slavery and Resistance* (London: Verso Books, 2021).
Daiches-Dubens, R., 'Eighteenth Century Anglo-Jewry in and around Richmond, Surrey', *Transactions of the Jewish Historical Society of England*, 18, 1953, pp. 143–69.
Davidson, A., *A History of the Holtes of Aston, Baronets; with a Description of the Family Mansion, Aston Hall, Warwickshire* (Birmingham: E. Everitt, 1854).
Dominique, L.J., 'African Blood, Colonial Money, and Respectable Mulatto Heiresses Reforming Eighteenth-Century England', in Kimberly Anne Coles *et al.* (eds), *The Cultural Politics of Blood, 1500–1900* (London: Palgrave Macmillan UK, 2015), pp. 84–104.
Dominique, L.J. (ed.), *The Woman of Colour* (Peterborough, ON: Broadview Press, 2007).
Donington, K., *The Bonds of Family: Slavery, Commerce and Culture in the British Atlantic World* (Manchester: Manchester University Press, 2019)
Donington, K., R. Hanley, and J. Moody (eds), *Britain's History and Memory of Transatlantic Slavery: Local Nuances of a 'National Sin'* (Liverpool: Liverpool University Press, 2016).
Draper, N., *The Price of Emancipation. Slave-Ownership, Compensation and British Society at the End of Slavery* (Cambridge: Cambridge University Press, 2009).
Dresser, M., and A. Hann (eds), *Slavery and the British Country House* (Swindon: English Heritage, 2013).
Dunn, R.S., *A Tale of Two Plantations: Slave Life and Labor in Jamaica and Virginia* (Cambridge, MA: Harvard University Press, 2014).
— *Sugar and Slaves: The Rise of the Planter Class in the English West Indies, 1624–1713* (Chapel Hill, NC: University of North Carolina Press, 1972).
Dyde, B., *A History of Antigua: The Unsuspected Isle* (London: Macmillan Caribbean, 2000).
Egerton, D.R., *Death or Liberty: African Americans and Revolutionary America* (New York: Oxford University Press, 2011).
Ellis, M.H., *Lachlan Macquarie, His Life, Adventures, and Times*, 3rd ed. (Sydney, London, Melbourne, Wellington: Angus and Robertson, 1958).
Endelman, T.M., *The Jews of Georgian England, 1714–1830: Tradition and Change in a Liberal Society* (Ann Arbor, MI: University of Michigan Press, 1999).

Evans, C., *Slave Wales: The Welsh and Atlantic Slavery, 1660–1850* (Cardiff: University of Wales Press, 2010).

Ewen, M., 'Capital and Kin: English Women's Intimate Networks and Property in Barbados', *Itinerario*, 46:3, 2022, pp. 325–32.

Faber, E., *Jews, Slaves, and the Slave Trade: Setting the Record Straight* (New York: NYU Press, 1998).

Fairclough, O., *The Grand Old Mansion: The Holtes and Their Successors at Aston Hall 1618–1864* (Birmingham: Birmingham Museums and Art Gallery, 1984).

Flavell, J., *When London Was Capital of America* (New Haven, CT: Yale University Press, 2011).

Fryer, P., *Staying Power: The History of Black People in Britain* (London: Pluto Press, 1984).

Fuentes, M.J., *Dispossessed Lives: Enslaved Women, Violence, and the Archive* (Philadelphia, PA: University of Pennsylvania Press, 2016).

Gaspar, D.B., *Bondmen and Rebels: A Study of Master-Slave Relations in Antigua* (Baltimore: Johns Hopkins University Press, 1985).

Gerzina, G., *Black England: A Forgotten Georgian History*, rev. ed. (London: John Murray, 2022).

Gopal, P., *Insurgent Empire: Anticolonial Resistance and British Dissent* (London and New York: Verso, 2019).

Gragg, L.D., *Englishmen Transplanted: The English Colonization of Barbados, 1627–1660* (Oxford: Oxford University Press, 2003).

Habakkuk, Sir J., *Marriage, Debt, and the Estates System: English Landownership, 1650–1950* (Oxford: Oxford University Press, 1994).

Hall, C., *Civilising Subjects: Metropole and Colony in the English Imagination, 1830–1867* (Cambridge: Polity, 2002).

Hall, C., N. Draper, K. McClelland, *et al.*, *Legacies of British Slave-Ownership: Colonial Slavery and the Formation of Victorian Britain* (Cambridge: Cambridge University Press, 2014).

Hall, D., and T. Thistlewood, *In Miserable Slavery: Thomas Thistlewood in Jamaica, 1750–86* (Kingston: University of the West Indies Press, 1999).

Hamilton, D., *Scotland, the Caribbean and the Atlantic World, 1750–1820* (Manchester: Manchester University Press, 2013).

Hancock, D., *Citizens of the World: London Merchants and the Integration of the British Atlantic Community, 1735–1785* (Cambridge: Cambridge University Press, 1997).

Handler, J.S., 'Custom and Law: The Status of Enslaved Africans in Seventeenth-Century Barbados', *Slavery & Abolition*, 37:2, 2016, pp. 233–55.

— 'Escaping Slavery in a Caribbean Plantation Society: Marronage in Barbados, 1650s–1830s', in *NWIG: New West Indian Guide/Nieuwe West-Indische Gids*, 71:3/4, 1997, pp. 183–225.

Handler, J.S., and F.W. Lange, with R.V. Riordan, *Plantation Slavery in Barbados: An Archaeological and Historical Investigation* (Cambridge, MA: Harvard University Press, 1978).

Hanser, J., *Mr. Smith Goes to China: Three Scots in the Making of Britain's Global Empire* (New Haven, CT: Yale University Press, 2019).

Heuman, G., 'The Apprenticeship System in the Caribbean: The World of the Apprentices', *NWIG: New West Indian Guide/Nieuwe West-Indische Gids*, 97:3/4, 2023, pp. 229–54.

— *The Killing Time: The Morant Bay Rebellion in Jamaica* (Knoxville, TN: University of Tennessee Press, 1994).

Higman, B.W., *Jamaica Surveyed: Plantation Maps and Plans of the Eighteenth and Nineteenth Centuries* (Kingston: University of the West Indies Press, 2001).

— *Plantation Jamaica 1750–1850: Capital and Control in a Colonial Economy* (Kingston: University of the West Indies Press, 2005).

— '"To Begin the World Again": Responses to Emancipation at Friendship and Greenwich Estate, Jamaica', in K.E.A. Monteith and G. Richards (eds), *Jamaica in Slavery and Freedom: History, Heritage and Culture* (Kingston: University of the West Indies Press, 2002), pp. 291–306.

Hochschild, A., *Bury the Chains: The British Struggle to Abolish Slavery* (London: Pan Macmillan, 2005).

Holt, T.C., *The Problem of Freedom: Race, Labor, and Politics in Jamaica and Britain, 1832–1938* (Baltimore: Johns Hopkins University Press, 1992).

Hutton, C., *Colour for Colour, Skin for Skin: Marching with the Ancestral Spirits into War Oh at Morant Bay* (Kingston: Ian Randle Publishers, 2015).

Ide, I., '"A Very Pretty Seat": Erlestoke Park, 1780–1999', *Wiltshire Archaeological and Natural History Magazine*, 93, 2000, pp. 9–19.

Jones, C., *Engendering Whiteness: White Women and Colonialism in Barbados and North Carolina* (Manchester: Manchester University Press, 2007).

Jones-Rogers, S.E., *They Were Her Property: White Women as Slave Owners in the American South* (New Haven, CT: Yale University Press, 2019).

Karras, A.L., *Sojourners in the Sun: Scottish Migrants in Jamaica and the Chesapeake, 1740–1800* (Ithaca, NY: Cornell University Press, 1992)

Kaufmann, M., *Black Tudors* (London: Oneworld, 2017).

Kelly, L., *Holland House: A History of London's Most Celebrated Salon* (London: Bloomsbury, 2013).

Keppel, S., *The Sovereign Lady: A Life of Elizabeth Vassall, Third Lady Holland, with Her Family* (London: Hamish Hamilton, 1974).

Kieza, G., *Macquarie* (Australia: HarperCollins, 2019).

Le Faye, D., *A Chronology of Jane Austen and Her Family, 1600–2000*, 2nd ed. (Cambridge: Cambridge University Press, 2013).

— *Jane Austen: A Family Record* (Cambridge: Cambridge University Press, 2004).

— '"A *Persecuted Relation*": Mrs. Lillingston's Funeral and Jane Austen's Legacy', *Bath History*, 7, 1998, pp. 92–106.

Lightfoot, N., *Troubling Freedom: Antigua and the Aftermath of British Emancipation* (Durham, NC: Duke University Press, 2015).

Livesay, D., *Children of Uncertain Fortune: Mixed-Race Jamaicans in Britain and the Atlantic Family, 1733–1833* (Williamsburg, VA, and Chapel Hill, NC: Omohundro Institute of Early American History and Culture and University of North Carolina Press, 2018).

Macdonald, D.L., *Monk Lewis: A Critical Biography* (Toronto: University of Toronto Press, 2000).

MacKinnon, F.D., *Grand Larceny, Being the Trial of Jane Leigh Perrot: Aunt of Jane Austen* (Oxford: Oxford University Press, 1937).

Mair, L.M., *A Historical Study of Women in Jamaica: 1655–1844* (Kingston: University of the West Indies Press, 2006).

Marshall, P.J. (ed.), *The Oxford History of the British Empire: Volume II: The Eighteenth Century* (Oxford: Oxford University Press, 2001).

McDonald, R.A., 'The Duff House/Montcoffer Papers: A Documentary Source for the History of the British West Indies, with Particular Emphasis on Jamaica', *Journal of Caribbean History*, 26:2, 1992, pp. 210–15.

Menard, R.R., *Sweet Negotiations: Sugar, Slavery, and Plantation Agriculture in Early Barbados* (Charlottesville, VA: University of Virginia Press, 2006).

Mirvis, S., *The Jews of Eighteenth-Century Jamaica* (New Haven, CT: Yale University Press, 2020).

Mulcahy, M., *Hurricanes and Society in the British Greater Caribbean, 1624–1783* (Baltimore: Johns Hopkins University Press, 2008).

Murphy, T., *The Creole Archipelago: Race and Borders in the Colonial Caribbean* (Philadelphia, PA: University of Pennsylvania Press, 2021).

Neely, W., *The Great Hurricane of 1780: The Story of the Greatest and Deadliest Hurricane of the Caribbean and the Americas* (Bloomington, IN: iUniverse, 2012).

Nelson, L.P., *Architecture and Empire in Jamaica* (New Haven, CT: Yale University Press, 2016)

Newman, B.N., *A Dark Inheritance: Blood, Race, and Sex in Colonial Jamaica* (New Haven, CT: Yale University Press, 2018).

Newman, S.P., *A New World of Labor: The Development of Plantation Slavery in the British Atlantic* (Philadelphia, PA: University of Pennsylvania Press, 2013).

Nugent, M., and P. Wright (ed.), *Lady Nugent's Journal of Her Residence in Jamaica from 1801 to 1805* (Kingston: University of the West Indies Press, 2002).

Oliver, V.L., *Caribbeana: Being Miscellaneous Papers Relating to the History, Genealogy, Topography, and Antiquities of the British West Indies* (London: Mitchell, Hughes and Clarke, 1912).

— *The History of the Island of Antigua, One of the Leeward Caribbees in the West Indies, from the First Settlement in 1635 to the Present Time* (London: Mitchell and Hughes, 1899).

Olusoga, D., *Black and British: A Forgotten History* (London: Pan Macmillan, 2016).

O'Malley, G.E., *Final Passages: The Intercolonial Slave Trade of British America, 1619–1807* (Williamsburg, VA, and Chapel Hill, NC: Omohundro Institute of Early American History and Culture and University of North Carolina Press, 2014).

Ono-George, M., '"Washing the Blackamoor White": Interracial Intimacy and Coloured Women's Agency in Jamaica', in Will Jackson and Emily J. Manktelow (eds), *Subverting Empire: Deviance and Disorder in the British Colonial World* (London: Palgrave Macmillan, 2015), pp. 42–60.

O'Shaughnessy, A.J., *An Empire Divided: The American Revolution and the British Caribbean* (Philadelphia, PA: University of Pennsylvania Press, 2000).

Parker, M., *The Sugar Barons: Family, Corruption, Empire and War* (London: Windmill Books, 2012).

Paugh, K., *The Politics of Reproduction: Race, Medicine, and Fertility in the Age of Abolition* (Oxford: Oxford University Press, 2017).

Petley, C., *White Fury: A Jamaican Slaveholder and the Age of Revolution* (Oxford: Oxford University Press, 2018).

Power, O., '"The Quadripartite Concern" of St Croix: An Irish Catholic Experiment in the Danish West Indies', in David T. Gleeson (ed.), *The Irish in the Atlantic World* (Columbia, SC: University of South Carolina Press, 2012), pp. 213–228.

Powers, A.M., *A Parcel of Ribbons: Letters of an 18th Century Family in London and Jamaica* (Lulu: 2012).

Pugsley, D., 'The Trial of Jane Austen's Aunt Jane Leigh Perrot and the Opinion of John Morris, KC', JASNA *Persuasions*, 41:1, 2020: https://jasna.org/publications-2/persuasions-online/vol-41-no-1/pugsley/

— 'Was Aunt Jane a Shoplifter?', *Fundamina* (Pretoria), 24:2, 2018, pp. 82–99.

Reina, G., 'Il Vero Conte di Montecristo. George Graham Watson-Taylor (1816–1865) e la Sua Famiglia', *Atti della Società Italiana di Studi Araldici*, 23, 2014, pp. 269–328.

Renton, A., *Blood Legacy: Reckoning with a Family's Story of Slavery* (Edinburgh: Canongate Books, 2021).

Ritchie, J., *Lachlan Macquarie: A Biography* (Melbourne: Melbourne University Press, 1986).

Roberts, H., '"Quite Appropriate for Windsor Castle": Geo. IV and Watson Taylor', *Furniture History*, 36, 2000, pp. 115–21.

Roberts, J., *Slavery and the Enlightenment in the British Atlantic, 1750–1807* (Cambridge: Cambridge University Press, 2013).

Salih, S., *Representing Mixed Race in Jamaica and England from the Abolition Era to the Present* (London: Routledge, 2010).

Sanghera, S., *Empireland: How Imperialism Has Shaped Modern Britain* (London: Penguin, 2021).

Schafer, D.L., '"A Swamp of an Investment"? Richard Oswald's British East Florida Plantation Experiment', in J.G. Landers (ed.), *Colonial Plantations and Economy in Florida* (Gainesville, FL: University Press of Florida, 2000), pp. 11–38.

Schuler, M., *'Alas, Alas, Kongo': A Social History of Indentured African Immigration into Jamaica, 1841–1865* (Baltimore: Johns Hopkins University Press, 1980).

Scott, J.S., *The Common Wind* (London: Verso Books, 2020).

Shepherd, V.A., 'Women, Slavery and the Reparation Movement in the Caribbean', *Social and Economic Studies*, 68:3/4, 2019, pp. 31–60.

Sheridan, R.B., 'Simon Taylor, Sugar Tycoon of Jamaica, 1740–1813', *Agricultural History*, 45:4, 1971, pp. 285–96.

— *Sugar and Slavery: An Economic History of the British West Indies, 1623–1775* (St Lawrence: Caribbean Universities Press, 1974).

— 'The Rise of a Colonial Gentry: A Case Study of Antigua, 1730–1775', *Economic History Review*, 13:3, 1961, pp. 342–57.

Shuler, K.A., 'Life and Death on a Barbadian Sugar Plantation: Historic and Bioarchaeological Views of Infection and Mortality at Newton Plantation', *International Journal of Osteoarchaeology*, 21:1, 2011, pp. 66–81.

Shyllon, F.O., *Black Slaves in Britain* (London: Oxford University Press for the Institute of Race Relations, 1974).

Smith, K.B., and F.C. Smith, *To Shoot Hard Labour: The Life and Times of Samuel Smith, an Antiguan Workingman, 1877–1982* (London: Karia Press, 1989).

Stanford-Xosei, E., 'The Long Road of Pan African Liberation to Reparatory Justice', in Hakim Adi (ed.), *Black British History: New Perspectives* (London: Bloomsbury Publishing, 2019), pp. 176–98.

Stern, M.A., *David Franks: Colonial Merchant* (Philadelphia, PA: Pennsylvania State University Press, 2010).

Stuart, A., *Sugar in the Blood: A Family's Story of Slavery and Empire* (London: Portobello Books, 2012).

Táíwò, O., *Reconsidering Reparations* (New York: Oxford University Press, 2022).

Tayler, A.N., and H.A.H. Tayler, *The Book of the Duffs* (Edinburgh: W. Brown, 1914).

Taylor, C., *Black Carib Wars: Freedom, Survival, and the Making of the Garifuna* (Jackson, MS: University Press of Mississippi, 2012).

Taylor, M., *The Interest: How the British Establishment Resisted the Abolition of Slavery* (London: Bodley Head, 2020).
Thomas, S., *Chattel: Art, Slavery and the British Art Collector, 1768–1833* (forthcoming).
Tomalin, C., *Jane Austen: A Life* (London: Viking, 1997).
Walker, C., *Jamaica Ladies: Female Slaveholders and the Creation of Britain's Atlantic Empire* (Williamsburg, VA: Omohundro Institute of Early American History and Culture, 2020).
Ward, J.R., 'The Profitability of Sugar Planting in the British West Indies, 1650–1834', *Economic History Review*, 31:2, 1978, pp. 197–213.
Watson, K., *A Kind of Right to Be Idle: Old Doll, Matriarch of Newton Plantation* (Kingston: Dept. of History, University of the West Indies; Barbados Museum and Historical Society, 2000).
Wheeler, R., *The Complexion of Race: Categories of Difference in Eighteenth-Century British Culture* (Philadelphia, PA: University of Pennsylvania Press, 2000).
Williams, E., *Capitalism and Slavery* (Chapel Hill, NC: University of North Carolina Press, 1994).
Williamson, K., *Contrary Voices: Representations of West Indian Slavery, 1657–1834* (Kingston: University of the West Indies Press, 2008).
Wolfram, S., 'Divorce in England 1700–1857', *Oxford Journal of Legal Studies*, 5:2, July 1985, pp. 155–86.
Worsley, L., *Jane Austen at Home: A Biography* (London: Hodder & Stoughton, 2017).
Young, H., 'Negotiating Female Property and Slave-Ownership in the Aristocratic World', *Historical Journal*, 63:3, 2020, pp. 581–602.
Zacek, N.A., *Settler Society in the English Leeward Islands, 1670–1776* (Cambridge: Cambridge University Press, 2010).
Zoellner, T., *Island on Fire: The Revolt that Ended Slavery in the British Empire* (Cambridge, MA: Harvard University Press, 2020).

UNPUBLISHED THESES

Chicenska, C., 'Colonisin' in Reverse! The Creolised Aesthetic of the Empire Windrush Generation' (PhD thesis, Goldsmiths, University of London, 2009).
Goëssant, E., 'George Watson-Taylor, Esq, MP (1771–1841): Collector of Paintings in Regency Britain' (PhD thesis, Sorbonne, Paris, 2016).
Hancock, D., '"Citizen of the World": Commercial Success, Social Development and the Experience of Eighteenth-Century British Merchants who Traded with America' (PhD thesis, University of Michigan, 1990).
Hatton, M., 'The Mark of Cane: A Microeconomic Case Study of Profitability, Accounting and Plantation Management on Three Barbadian Sugar Plantations, 1763–1815' (partial M.A., Dalhousie University, 2014).
Osborne, A.G., 'Power and Persuasion: The London West India Committee, 1783–1833' (PhD thesis, University of Hull, 2014).
Power, O., 'Irish Planters, Atlantic Merchants: The Development of St. Croix, Danish West Indies, 1750 to 1766' (PhD thesis, University of Galway, 2011).
Young, H.L., 'Gender and Absentee Slave-Ownership in Late Eighteenth- and Early Nineteenth-Century Britain' (PhD thesis, University College London, 2017).

UNPUBLISHED SOURCES

Brun, J.P., 'The Dawkins of Moggerhanger' (2013): https://moggerhanger.uk/wp-content/uploads/2021/09/Dawkins-of-Moggerhanger2.pdf.
Cartwright, C., 'The Family of Samuel Newton in Seventeenth Century Derbyshire' (Kings Bromley Historians, 2010).
Howard, A., 'The Anti-Slavery Debate around Lichfield' (Kings Bromley Historians, c.2015).
— 'The Contested Will of Lister Holte' (Kings Bromley Historians, 2018).
— 'The Lane Inheritance: Kings Bromley and Barbados' (Kings Bromley Historians, 2012).
— 'The Scandalous Divorce of John Newton' (Kings Bromley Historians, 2012).
Opala, J., 'Bunce Island, A British Slave Castle in Sierra Leone: Historical Summary', Appendix B, in C. de Corse, *Bunce Island Cultural Resource Assessment and Management Plan* (Harrisonburg, VA: James Madison University, November 2007).

ONLINE SOURCES

Ancestry: www.ancestry.co.uk
British History Online: www.british-history.ac.uk/
British Newspaper Archive: https://www.britishnewspaperarchive.co.uk/
Find My Past: www.findmypast.com
Jamaican Family Search: http://www.jamaicanfamilysearch.com/
Legacies of British Slavery Database, University College London: https://www.ucl.ac.uk/lbs/
Oxford Dictionary of National Biography: www.oxforddnb.com
Scotland's People: www.scotlandspeople.gov.uk
The History of Parliament: https://www.historyofparliamentonline.org/
The Lachlan & Elizabeth Macquarie Archive: www.library.mq.edu.au/digital/lema
Trans-Atlantic and Intra-American Slave Voyages Databases: www.slavevoyages.org

Notes on the Text

INTRODUCTION

1. Latimer, *Annals of Bristol*, p. 493; Stott, *Hannah More*, pp. 133–5, 154–5; Clifford, 'Bristol Elopement': http://www.naomiclifford.com/the-bristol-elopement/; 'Clementina Ogilvie was Perry (née Clarke)', Legacies of British Slavery (LBS): http://wwwdepts-live.ucl.ac.uk/lbs/person/view/2146646531.
2. Thompson, *Heiresses*, pp. 25–48; 'The Duke of Westminster and the Grosvenor Family Net Worth', *Sunday Times* Rich List 2024: https://www.thetimes.co.uk/article/duke-of-westminster-net-worth-sunday-times-rich-list-bqbqpjlqf.
3. Barnard, *Present for an Apprentice*, p. 68.
4. Anon., *Master-key to the Rich Ladies Treasury*.
5. Young, 'Gender', pp. 230, 238; Hall *et al.*, *Legacies*, p. 20.
6. O'Shaunnessy, *Empire Divided*, p. 209.
7. *Lady Nugent's Journal*, ed. Wright, p. 63.
8. Leslie, *New History*, pp. 50–1.
9. Hall *et al.*, *Legacies*, p. 36.
10. Data largely from the UCL Legacies of British Slavery database: www.ucl.ac.uk/lbs. This figure does not capture the whole story, as the database only works backwards from the 1830s compensation records to 1763. See also 'The Peerage &c., in Jamaica', in *Official and Other Personages of Jamaica*, ed. Feurtado, pp. 109–30.
11. Small, 'Montpelier Estate, St John Figtree, Nevis', p. 3: https://seis.bristol.ac.uk/~emceee/montpelierhistory.pdf.
12. 'Tobias Smollett', LBS: https://www.ucl.ac.uk/lbs/person/view/2146664843; Lee, '"Broiling on the Coast of Guinea", pp. 39–40, 51, 54.
13. 'Lady Jane Davy formerly Apreece (née Kerr)', LBS: https://www.ucl.ac.uk/lbs/person/view/2146653133; James, 'Making Money from the Royal Navy', p. 416.
14. Cumberland, *West India*, Act I, scene 3, p. 5.
15. 'Elizabeth Onslow, Lady Onslow (née Knight)', LBS: http://www.ucl.ac.uk/lbs/person/view/2146653249; 'Onslow, Thomas', History of Parliament (HOP): https://www.historyofparliamentonline.org/volume/1690-1715/member/onslow-thomas-1679-1740.
16. By 1801 only 1,020 people in Britain had an annual income over £5,000: Rubinstein, *Men of Property*, p. 62.
17. Clifford, *Disappearance of Maria Glenn*, p. 33.
18. Smollett, *Expedition of Humphry Clinker*, vol. 1, p. 56.

19 Mill, 'Of Property', p. 253. See also Bryant, *Entitled*.
20 Shakespeare, *Timon of Athens*, Act IV, scene 3, ed. Jowett, p. 268.
21 Gikandi, *Slavery and the Culture of Taste*, pp. 97–144.
22 Dresser and Hann (eds), *Slavery*; Barczewski, *Country Houses*; Huxtable *et al.*, *Interim Report*: https://www.nationaltrust.org.uk/who-we-are/research/addressing-our-histories-of-colonialism-and-historic-slavery.
23 Though several enslavers were philanthropic, few of the women studied here were amongst them. Hall *et al.*, *Legacies*, pp. 225–31. Notable exceptions include Elizabeth Knight and Anne, Duchess of Bolton's support of the Foundling Hospital; Mary and Richard Oswald's gifts supporting poor Scots in London; Elizabeth Smyth's 1825 bequest of £2,000 to the Bristol Infirmary; and 'the innumerable acts of kindness and charity' of Lady Isabella Cooper in Isleworth c.1840.
24 Foote, *Cozeners*, p. 75.
25 Wilde, *Importance of Being Earnest*, Act I, scene 1, p. 39.
26 Bronte, *Jane Eyre*, ed. Kriegel, pp. 388–9, 391; Gilbert and Gubar, *Madwoman in the Attic*, xii–xiii, 78, 355–68. A more sympathetic interpretation of Bertha's story appears in Jean Rhys's 1966 novel *Wide Sargasso Sea*.
27 Thomas, 'Tropical Extravagance', pp. 1–17; Meyer, 'Colonialism', pp. 247–68.
28 I am aware of the following heiresses with African ancestry who married in Britain: 1. Frances Dalzell (the subject of Chapter 2); 2. Jane Thresher (née Harry): Donington, K. 'Harry [married name Thresher], Jane', ODNB: https://doi.org/10.1093/ref:odnb/107509; 3. Barbara Ann Durnford (née Shea or Blake) (1771–1851): Herron, K., 'Andrew Durnford m Barbara Blake – Her Father Sir Patrick Blake West Indian Family', 13 December 2014: https://edurnford.blogspot.com/2014/12/4221-andrew-durnford-m-barbara-blake.html; 4. 'Ann Maitland (née Wright)', LBS: https://www.ucl.ac.uk/lbs/person/view/2146638457; 5. 'Rebecca Roberts (née Wright)', LBS: https://www.ucl.ac.uk/lbs/person/view/2146638459; 6. 'Ruth Roberts (née Angell)', LBS: https://www.ucl.ac.uk/lbs/person/view/2146645029; 7. 'Ann Glasgow late Robertson (née Glasgow)', LBS: https://www.ucl.ac.uk/lbs/person/view/44173; 8. 'Elizabeth Mollison (née Fullerton), LBS: https://www.ucl.ac.uk/lbs/person/view/2146662589; 9. 'Elizabeth Young (née Hay)', LBS: https://www.ucl.ac.uk/lbs/person/view/2146644669; 10. 'Helen Praed (née Bogle)', LBS: https://www.ucl.ac.uk/lbs/person/view/2146664869; 11. Rosanna Coates née Middleton: see entry for her father: 'George Bogle', LBS: https://www.ucl.ac.uk/lbs/person/view/2146633005; 12. 'Grace Smellie (née Bogle)', LBS: https://www.ucl.ac.uk/lbs/person/view/2146646311; 13. 'Catherine Ann Smith née Quier', LBS: https://www.ucl.ac.uk/lbs/person/view/43340; 14. Elizabeth Simes (née Wynter) – see entry for her father: 'Nathaniel Phillips of Slebech', LBS: https://www.ucl.ac.uk/lbs/person/view/1330090056; 15–17. Sarah Cator (née Morse), Catherine Green (née Morse), Ann Middleton (née Morse): see entry for their father: 'John Morse', LBS: https://www.ucl.ac.uk/lbs/person/view/2146638283 and extended discussion in Livesay, *Children*; 18. Katharine McLauchlan (née Campbell): Livesay, *Children*, pp. 84, 161.
29 Beckles, 'Property Rights in Pleasure', pp. 169–70.
30 Broad, 'Mary Astell on Marriage', pp. 718–19.
31 Banner, *Britain's Slavery Debt*, pp. 61–2; Woodward, 'From the Archives: "An Unchristian Traffik"', Central England Quakers: https://centralenglandquakers.org.uk/2020/04/23/from-the-archives-an-unchristian-traffik/.
32 Scott, *History of Sir George Ellison*, vol. 1, p. 18.
33 Young, 'Forgotten Women', p. 99.

34 'Dr John Coakley Lettsom', LBS: http://www.ucl.ac.uk/lbs/person/view/2146649667; 'David Barclay', LBS: http://www.ucl.ac.uk/lbs/person/view/2146643749.
35 Such as mixed-heritage heiress Jane Harry: Donington, *Bonds of Family*, p. 169 (see Chapter 2, p. 91), and Gothic novelist Matthew Gregory 'Monk' Lewis (see Chapter 7, p. 251).
36 Shepherd, 'Women', p. 46. Estimates of the relative value of £301,587 in 1834 for 2023 range from £36,610,000 to £1,759,000,000; Measuring Worth: https://measuringworth.com/calculators/ukcompare/.
37 Barnett-Woods, 'Bequeathed unto My Daughter'.

1. SARAH NEWTON (1723–1794)

1 SHL, MS 523/973 (Thomas Lane's report on interview with Betsy Newton, 1796).
2 Cartwright, 'Family of Samuel Newton'.
3 Parker, *Sugar Barons*, pp. 14, 117.
4 TNA, PROB 11/194/411 (Will of Edward Newton, 1 December 1645), PROB 11/202/624 (Will of Robert Newton, 18 December 1647).
5 Menard, *Sweet Negotiations*, p. 25; Taylor, *American Colonies*, p. 206.
6 Gragg, *Englishmen Transplanted*, pp. 74–8; Parker, *Sugar Barons*, pp. 47–8.
7 Ligon, *True and Exact History*, p. 40. It is not clear which side the Newtons took in the Civil Wars, though Robert's father, Edward, left a copy of Foxe's *Book of Martyrs* to their local church, suggestive of the strong Protestant belief usually associated with Parliamentarians: 'Ashover: Memoranda by Titus Wheatcroft, 1722.', p. 29.
8 Parker, *Sugar Barons*, pp. 47–8; Newman, *New World of Labor*, pp. 79–81.
9 Menard, *Sweet Negotiations*, p. 17; Ligon, *True and Exact History*, p. 103; Bennett, 'Cary Helyar', p. 67.
10 Gragg, *Englishmen Transplanted*, p. 100; Newman, *New World of Labor*, p. 58.
11 Ligon, *True and Exact History*, p. 15; *Oxford History of the British Empire*, vol. 1, ed. Canny, p. 224, vol. 2, ed. Marshall, p. 64.
12 Menard, *Sweet Negotiations*, pp. 80–1.
13 Ligon, *True and Exact History*, p. 66; Menard, *Sweet Negotiations*, pp. 82–3.
14 TNA, PROB 11/202/624 (Will of Robert Newton, 18 December 1647). Robert was buried at Christ Church, Barbados, on 10 October 1647. He left Dick and Tim to Major Philip Bishop of Gibbons. As he signed his will on 15 June, he may have sailed on the *Achilles* with Richard Ligon, which departed the Downs on 16 June, arriving in Barbados on 2 September: Ligon, *True and Exact History*, p. 40.
15 Menard, *Sweet Negotiations*, pp. 17, 75.
16 Samuel was in London when he signed a 'financial obligation' to Captain Peter Edney on 11 January 1654, but in Barbados by 2 November 1654, when he purchased the right to use wood from John Clarke's plantation for 2,000lbs of sugar. BDA, Deeds, RB 3/3 ff. 53, 313 (26 March 1657, 13 June 1662); Coldham, *Complete Book of Emigrants*, pp. 372, 399 438; 'Addenda: May 1683', *Calendar of State Papers Colonial* (CSPC), vol. 12, BHO: http://www.british-history.ac.uk/cal-state-papers/colonial/america-west-indies/vol12/p643.
17 Mintz, *Sweetness and Power*, pp. xxi, 48–52.
18 Littleton, *Groans of the Plantations*, pp. 19–20.
19 Menard, *Sweet Negotiations*, pp. 15–17, 76; Gragg, *Englishmen Transplanted*, pp. 100–2; Ligon, *True and Exact History*, pp. 157–64.

20 'assim como com a lembrança do nosso barro, e com as lágrimas se purificam e branqueiam as almas'; Antonil, *Cultura e Opulência do Brasil*, Book 3, chapter 5, p. 171.
21 James, *Beyond a Boundary*, pp. 13–15.
22 SHL, MS 523/1055/1 (John Eston to Samuel Newton, 1 March 1684), MS523/1105 (List of 'Christian servants', 'slaves' and livestock on the estate of Barbara Newton, 11 April 1687).
23 Gragg, '"To Procure Negroes"', pp. 65–84; Newman, *New World of Labor*, pp. 190–3; Ligon, *True and Exact History*, p. 21; Menard, *Sweet Negotiations*, pp. 31, 44, 46, 115.
24 Gragg, *Englishmen Transplanted*, p. 117; Menard, *Sweet Negotiations*, pp. 30–1, 44; Handler, 'Custom and Law', pp. 223–4.
25 Kaufmann, *Black Tudors*, p. 157; Gragg, *Englishmen Transplanted*, pp. 118, 125, 161–2; Ligon, *True and Exact History*, p. 101; Guasco, *Slaves and Englishmen*, pp. 215, 217, 218.
26 Menard, *Sweet Negotiations*, pp. 111–12, 117–18; Amussen, *Caribbean Exchanges*, pp. 129–34; Gragg, *Englishmen Transplanted*, pp. 125, 131.
27 Kaufmann, *Black Tudors*; Habib, *Black Lives in the English Archives*; Nubia, *Blackamoores*; Nubia, *England's Other Countrymen*; Newman, *New World of Labor*, pp. 253–5.
28 BDA, Deeds, RB 3/2, f. 591 (Guye's storehouse on a 80x60 ft plot in Oistins Bay from Edward Oistin, 2 June 1663); RB 3/3 f. 241 (19.5 acres from John Searle for 20,000 lbs sugar, 3 April 1662), f. 294 (51 acres from Robert Marcott, on behalf of Thomas Johnson for 60,000 lbs, 30 May 1662), f. 313 (20 acres from Robert Tudor, 14 acres from Thomas Hill, 13 June 1662); RB 3/5, f. 211 (Thomas Johnson confirms receipt of sugar, 12 December 1662); RB 3/12 f. 24 (6,317-foot plot in Oistins with John Searle from Jeremiah Egginton for £50 current 25 October 1673), f. 42 (title to 400 acres in Christ Church confirmed by Barbados Council, 10 November 1673); *Journal of the Barbados Museum & Historical Society*, vol. 16, (1949), pp. 38–9, citing Minutes of the Council, 12 March 1657 (granted 24 acres of Thomas Johnson, deceased) and Chancery Orders 30 July 1667, 20 August 1667 and 24 September 1667 (gained the late Peter Risley's plantation).
29 BDA, Deeds, RB 3/12 f. 24 (6,317-foot plot in Oistins with John Searle from Jeremiah Egginton for £50 current 25 October 1673); Cartwright, 'Family of Samuel Newton'; *George Sitwell's Letterbook 1662–66*, ed. Riden, pp. xlvii, 109, 194; 'Searles', LBS: https://www.ucl.ac.uk/lbs/estate/view/649; Menard, *Sweet Negotiations*, p. 73; Handler et al., *Plantation Slavery in Barbados*, pp. 58–67, 300–1.
30 Newton was listed amongst 'the most eminent planters in Barbados' in 1673. Only 21 out of 72 owned more land than him. By 1680, the 12 councillors averaged 420 acres and 190 enslaved people, to Samuel's 580/260. 'America and West Indies: May 1673', CSPC, vol. 7, BHO: http://www.british-history.ac.uk/cal-state-papers/colonial/america-west-indies/vol7/pp487-499; 'America and West Indies: April 1680', CSPC, vol. 10, BHO: http://www.british-history.ac.uk/cal-state-papers/colonial/america-west-indies/vol10/pp507-521; Dunn, *Sugar and Slaves*, p. 100; Handler et al., *Plantation Slavery in Barbados*, pp. 62–3; TNA, CO 1/44, no. 45 (1679 Census of Barbados, supplied by Governor Atkins to the Lords of Trade and Plantations).
31 'Anonymous letter from Barbados, 20 March 1767', in *The Register of the Privy Council of Scotland*, ed. Hume Brown, 3rd series, vol. 4, p. 671.
32 'Addenda: May 1683', CSPC, vol. 12, BHO: http://www.british-history.ac.uk/cal-state-papers/colonial/america-west-indies/vol12/p643; Gragg, *Englishmen Transplanted*, p. 153; 'America and West Indies: October 1683, 1–15', CSPC, vol. 11, BHO: https://www.british-history.ac.uk/cal-state-papers/colonial/america-west-indies/vol11/pp511-518.
33 Gragg, *Englishmen Transplanted*, pp. 24–5, 176–7; Dunn, *Sugar and Slaves*, pp. 77–8.

34 Derbyshire Record Office, D518 M/F81 (Sale of Kings Bromley estate by John Agard *et al.* to Samuel Newton, 9 December 1679); William Salt Library, Stafford, SMS 466/22, p. 34 (Dr Richard Wilkes' antiquarian papers for his History of Staffordshire, 1755); Howard, 'Lane Inheritance', p. 3; 'Sarah Bate (née Newton)', LBS: https://www.ucl.ac.uk/lbs/person/view/2146665129.

35 TNA, PROB 11/382/43 (Will of Samuel Newton, 13 January 1686), PROB 11/489/168 (Will of John Newton of Kings Bromley, 3 July 1706).

36 Howard, 'Lane Inheritance', p. 3.

37 Samuel received £850 p.a. from his estates in Staffordshire and Derbyshire: SHL, MS 523/970 (1775 copy of John Newton and Elizabeth Alleyne's marriage settlement, 2 October 1740); Fairclough, *Grand Old Mansion*, p. 47; Hume, 'Value of Money', p. 377.

38 Barbara leased Newton plantation to Alexander Beale and Jeremiah Ward, both of St Philip, for 10 years at £1,800 p.a. in 1685. Within three years, they owed almost £6,000. The two men were so embedded in the Barbados elite that the Newtons were unable to get a judgment against them on the island, even after William III intervened. By 1702, Beale and Ward were dead, the debt still not recovered, and the Newtons had to pursue their descendants. SHL, MS 523/1110 ('The Case of Barbara Newton' drawn up by Mr Allen, 1695). 29 deceased enslaved Africans are listed in MS523/1105 (ii) (Lists of Christian servants, slaves and livestock on the estate of B. Newton, 11 April 1687); 'America and West Indies: December 1700, 11–13', CSPC, vol. 18, BHO: http://www.british-history.ac.uk/cal-state-papers/colonial/america-west-indies/vol18/pp731-744; 'America and West Indies: January 1702, 1–2', CSPC, vol. 20, BHO: http://www.british-history.ac.uk/cal-state-papers/colonial/america-west-indies/vol20/pp1-5; Ewen, 'Capital and Kin', pp. 330–2.

39 Elizabeth Alleyne was baptised at Christ Church, 6 February 1724. Cox and Watson, 'John Alleyne', pp. 109, 113.

40 SHL, MS 523/970 (1775 copy of John Newton and Elizabeth Alleyne's marriage settlement, 2 October 1740, with letter from lawyer Theophilius Levett to James Halsall, 24 December 1739).

41 Parker, *Sugar Barons*, p. 46; Brown, *Reaper's Garden*, pp. 13, 17.

42 Staffordshire Archives, D 4051/1/4 (All Saints King's Bromley parish register); Stone, *Family, Sex and Marriage in England*, p. 46.

43 Fairclough, *Grand Old Mansion*, pp. 13, 44–7; Davidson, *History*, pp. 42–3; 'HOLTE, Sir Lister', HOP: https://www.historyofparliamentonline.org/volume/1715-1754/member/holte-sir-lister-1720-70; Sir Lister stood for election alongside Sarah's second cousin George Venables-Vernon. 'Lichfield', HOP: http://www.historyofparliamentonline.org/volume/1715-1754/constituencies/lichfield.

44 In 1756, John bought an enslaved person for a son, Hazel. The odd name suggests he was possibly illegitimate, the son of a woman enslaved at Newton: SHL MS 523/7 (John Newton, ledger and journal, 1756).

45 *Genealogies of Barbados Families*, ed. Brandow, pp. 19–20; TNA, PROB 11/824/509 (28 September 1756); 'Seawells', LBS: https://www.ucl.ac.uk/lbs/estate/view/599; Howard, 'Scandalous Divorce', p. 3.

46 Hutton, *History of Birmingham*, p. 291; Fairclough, *Grand Old Mansion*, pp. 98–100.

47 SRO, Dioceses of Lichfield & Coventry Marriage Allegations And Bonds (Marriage licence, 29 December 1758), D29/1/4 (St Chad's Lichfield marriage register, 30 December 1758), FindMyPast: https://www.findmypast.co.uk/transcript?id=PRS%2FSTAFFS%2FDIO%2FLICHFIELD%2FMAR%2F002305B and https://www.findmypast.co.uk/transcript?id=GBPRS%2FSTAFF%2FMAR2%2F037984%2F2&tab=this.

Elizabeth Hannay left a man named Hylas to Judith Alleyne in 1755. The marriage licence says he is 21, and she 'over 21'. He is stated to be 33 in his 1766 baptism record (St. James, Piccadilly, 31 January 1766). SHL, MS 523/288 (Sampson Wood's report on 'Negroes' at Newton, 1796) lists Old Doll, Mary's eldest daughter, as '60 odd' in 1796, so Mary must have been in her early teens by c.1736.

48 Howard, 'Anti-Slavery Debate', p. 2.
49 See Hylas family tree, p. 43.
50 Kaufmann, 'English Common Law'; Fryer, *Staying Power*, pp. 113–20.
51 See n. 45 above. The following account is largely taken from: Shyllon, *Black Slaves in Britain*, pp. 40–3; Paugh, *Politics of Reproduction*, pp. 57–68; Hoare, *Memoirs of Granville Sharp*, pp. 47–8; Lyall, *Granville Sharp's Cases on Slavery*, pp. 377–83.
52 To do so, Hylas would have had to skate over the issue of his prior baptism, which would have been required for him to marry Mary in 1758; Figgis, N., 'Hone, Nathaniel', Dictionary of Irish Biography: https://www.dib.ie/biography/hone-nathaniel-a4084.
53 Moore, *How to Create the Perfect Wife*, pp. 158–61; Day and Bicknell, *The Dying Negro*, p. 4.
54 Wise, *Though the Heavens May Fall*, p. 47.
55 City of Westminster Archives Centre, SJSS/PR/5/16 (Baptisms: John Hylas, St George's, Hanover Square, 7 November 1769, Henry Hylas, St James, Piccadilly, 22 February 1771), Ancestry: https://www.ancestry.co.uk/search/collections/61865/records/684340 and https://www.ancestry.co.uk/search/collections/61865/records/2182736.
56 Shyllon, *Black Slaves in Britain*, p. 53.
57 Davidson, *History*, pp. 44–6; Fairclough, *Grand Old Mansion*, pp. 48–50, 91–2; SRO, D564/12/3 (Dr John Ash of Birmingham to 2nd Earl of Dartmouth, 18 April 1770).
58 She was the daughter of Pudsey Jesson of Langley Hall. *A History of the County of Warwick*, ed. L.F. Salzman, vol. 4, BHO: https://www.british-history.ac.uk/vch/warks/vol4/pp230-245.
59 TNA, PROB 11/957/330 (Will of Sir Lister Holte, 18 May 1770); SRO, D564/12/3 (Dr John Ash of Birmingham to 2nd Earl of Dartmouth, 24 April 1770); Davidson, *History*, p. 45.
60 SRO, D564/12/3 (Dr John Ash of Birmingham to 2nd Earl of Dartmouth, 7 and 18 April 1770).
61 Fairclough, *Grand Old Mansion*, p. 50; Davidson, *History*, pp. 45–6.
62 TNA, PROB 11/957/330 (Will of Sir Lister Holte, 18 May 1770); Howard, 'Contested Will', p. 3.
63 There is extensive correspondence on the case in SRO, 7286/4; see also Howard, 'Contested Will'.
64 Hutton, *An History of Birmingham*, pp. 290–2.
65 Fairclough, *Grand Old Mansion*, p. 102; SRO, D564/12/3 (Dr John Ash of Birmingham to 2nd Earl of Dartmouth, 16 April 1770), 7286/4 (Lady Dartmouth to Lady Sarah Holte, 9 December 1773).
66 SRO, 7286/4 (John Lane to Lady Sarah Holte, 8 January 1773, 15 February 1774, William Sadler to Lady Sarah Holte, 25 March 1775).
67 SRO 7286/4 (John Lane to Lady Sarah Holte, 1 February 1774); Bristol Archives, Bristol Cathedral Register, DC/A/10/2 (Burial, 5 February 1774), Ancestry: https://www.ancestry.co.uk/search/collections/61666/records/2163208.
68 There is no further mention of Hazel Newton in the archives. See n. 45 above.
69 Howard, 'Scandalous Divorce', p. 21; Anon., *Trial of the Hon. Mrs. Catherine Newton*, pp. 11, 14, 15.

70 The following account of John Newton's second marriage and subsequent divorce is taken from: Young, 'Gender', pp. 73–4; Howard, 'Scandalous Divorce'; Anon., *Trial of the Hon. Mrs. Catherine Newton* and *Second Part of the Trial of the Hon. Mrs. Catherine Newton*.
71 SRO, K045, 7286/4 (Catherine Newton to Lady Sarah Holte, 21 August and 11 November 1776, 27 January, 8 February and 14 March 1777).
72 'Part 1 Spettisbury House 1735–1800', *The History of St Monica's Priory, Spettisbury, Dorset*: https://sites.google.com/site/stmonicaspriory/Home/part-1spettisbury-house-1735-1800.
73 SRO, K045, 7286/ 4 (Catherine Newton to Lady Sarah Holte, 22 August and 25 December 1776, 12 and 27 January, 8 February and 14 March 1777).
74 Boswell, *Life of Samuel Johnson*, vol. 2, p. 31; Shakespeare, *King John*, Act 1, scene 1, line 72, Folger Shakespeare: https://www.folger.edu/explore/shakespeares-works/king-john/read/1/1/.
75 SRO, K045, 7286/ 4 (Catherine Newton to Lady Sarah Holte, 25 and 27 December 1776, 12 January and 8 February 1777).
76 'Newton's Divorce Bill, 23 April 1782', in *Journal of the House of Lords*, vol. 36, BHO: https://www.british-history.ac.uk/lords-jrnl/vol36/pp439-451. Although butler James Bird does not name which sister wrote the letter, I have deduced it was Sarah, as Elizabeth was resident at Kings Bromley, so could have told her brother in person. Isham may have been a relation of 'Nanny Baggs', a member of the Newton household in 1774: SRO 7286/4 (John Newton to Lady Sarah Holte, 1 and 15 January 1774).
77 Wolfram, 'Divorce', p. 157.
78 In fact, Thomas Cope only joined the family in May 1777, the month after they left Bath, so this unlikely scene could not have taken place. 'New Anecdotes of Mrs N_n of Amorous Memory', *Rambler's Magazine*, January 1783, p. 21 (unpublished transcription by Allan Howard).
79 Elizabeth Fuller was the sister of 'John "Mad Jack" Fuller', LBS: https://www.ucl.ac.uk/lbs/person/view/-1047169191. Their son, Sir Peregrine Palmer Fuller Palmer Acland, inherited the family fortune.
80 SRO, K045, D357/K/5/2 (Heneage Legge to Henry Eyres Landor, 27 April 1813).
81 TNA, PROB 11/1/130 (Will of John Newton, 9 December 1783).
82 Anna Seward to Josiah Wedgwood, 18 February 1788, transcribed in Howard, 'Anti-Slavery Debate', p. 2; Oliver, *Caribbeana*, vol. 3, p. 21.
83 A retired labourer recalled his grandparents identifying the resting place of the 'old people': Handler *et al.*, 'Searching for a Slave Cemetery in Barbados', p. 4.
84 Riley, 'Estimates', p. 539.
85 Handler *et al.*, *Plantation Slavery in Barbados*, p. 99; Shuler, 'Life and Death', p. 75.
86 Ramsay, *Essay*, p. 97.
87 SHL, MS 523/288, 290 (Sampson Wood's report on 'Negroes' and buildings at Newton, 1796).
88 Schiebinger, *Secret Cures of Slaves*, pp. 71–9, 86–106.
89 Shuler, 'Life and Death', p. 77.
90 TNA, HCA 42/7 (Richard Bate to Barbara and John Newton, 31 May 1693).
91 Handler *et al.*, *Plantation Slavery in Barbados*, pp. 67, 300, n.5.
92 SHL, MS 523/276 ('List of negroes on Seawells', 15 April 1791).
93 Higman, *Slave Populations of the British Caribbean*, pp. 295–8; Davies, 'Current Status', https://doi.org/10.3389/fnut.2022.1084589.
94 Shuler *et al.*, 'Health and Life Histories, p. 272.

95 Brown, *Reaper's Garden*, p. 53.
96 Schroeder et al., 'Trans-Atlantic Slavery'; Handler, 'Determining African Birth', pp. 114–15; Handler, 'Prone Burial'; Handler, 'African-Type Healer/Diviner'.
97 Sir John had been the family's Barbados attorney since Samuel Newton's death in 1771. Sarah and Elizabeth probably met him when he visited England in 1756. 'Sir John Gay Alleyne 1st Bart', LBS: https://www.ucl.ac.uk/lbs/person/view/-39601568.
98 Seawells was valued at £15,779, of which enslaved people represented £6,545. The document does not state sterling or current; I have assumed sterling. SHL, MS 523/277, 278 (Valuations of Newton and Seawells made for Sir John Gay Alleyne, 7 June 1784).
99 SHL, 523/290 (Sampson Wood's report on the buildings at Newton, c.1796), f. 9.
100 Hatton, 'Mark of Cane', pp. 82–3.
101 Paton, 'Driveress and the Nurse', pp. 42–5.
102 The following account of the Hylas family is taken from: SHL, MS 523/288 (Sampson Wood's report on 'Negroes' at Newton, 1796); SHL, MS 523/973 (Thomas Lane's report on interview with Betsy Newton, 1796); Watson, *Kind of Right*, pp. 8–22. Paugh, *Politics of Reproduction*, pp. 122, 126–7, 137; Beckles, *Centering Woman*, pp. 130–7; Young, 'Gender', pp. 87–9.
103 William Yard had taken over the role from his father Edward in 1782, having previously managed Seawells since 1776. Hatton, 'Mark of Cane', pp. 100–1, 104.
104 Thorne and Kimball, *Six Months' Tour*, p. 224.
105 Shuler et al., 'Health and Life Histories', pp. 274, 277.
106 Fuentes, *Dispossessed Lives*, p. 83; Burnard, 'Tropical Hospitality'.
107 SHL, MS 523/288, 289, 290 (Sampson Wood's reports on the 'negroes', land, and buildings at Newton, c.1796).
108 Smith and Smith, *To Shoot Hard Labour*, pp. 41–3.
109 SRO, D6584/A/275 (Joint account book of Lady Sarah Holte and Elizabeth Newton, 1784–94); Paugh, *Politics of Reproduction*, p. 136; Hatton, 'Mark of Cane', pp. 82–6; Menard, *Sweet Negotiations*, p. 86; Ward, 'Profitability', p. 210.
110 SHL, MS 523/293 (Sir John Gay Alleyne to John Lane, 21 July 1794, forwarded to Elizabeth Newton); SHL, MS 523/973 (Thomas Lane's report on interview with Betsy Newton, 1796); 'Sir John Gay Alleyne 1st Bart.', LBS: https://www.ucl.ac.uk/lbs/person/view/-39601568.
111 The following account of the crisis of 1794 is taken from: SHL, MS 523/288 (Sampson Wood's report on 'Negroes' at Newton, 1796); SHL, MS 523/973 (Thomas Lane's report on interview with Betsy Newton, 1796); Watson, *Kind of Right*, pp. 12–22: Paugh, *Politics of Reproduction*, pp. 137–8, 146–53.
112 As Sir John's mother was dead, and his sisters married in England, the 'female part' of Alleyne's family at this juncture were his wife Jane (daughter of Abel Alleyne), her mother Jane (née Skeete), and older sister Christian, wife of William White.
113 SRO, K045, D357/K/5/2 (Heneage Legge to Henry Eyres Landor, 27 April 1813); St Peter and St Paul's, Aston, Burials, 9 April 1794, Library of Birmingham, DRO 41, M93, Ancestry: https://www.ancestry.co.uk/search/collections/4961/records/3632485.
114 SHL, MS 523/293 (Sir John Gay Alleyne to John Lane, 21 July 1794, forwarded to Elizabeth Newton).
115 SHL, MS 523/973 (Thomas Lane's report on interview with Betsy Newton, 1796).
116 Taylor, *Black Carib Wars*, p. 8; Murphy, *Creole Archipelago*, p. 41.
117 Handler, 'Escaping Slavery', pp. 201–2.
118 SHL, MS 523/973 (Thomas Lane's report on interview with Betsy Newton, 1796).
119 See entries for these families in LBS database; Osborne, 'Power and Persuasion', pp. 37–8, 73, 265, 267.

120 SHL, MS 523/293 (Sir John Gay Alleyne to John Lane, 21 July 1794, forwarded to Elizabeth Newton).
121 TNA, PROB 11/1254/296 (Will of Elizabeth Newton, 29 January 1795); SRO, K045, D357/K/5/2 (Heneage Legge to Henry Eyres Landor, 27 April 1813); Howard, 'Lane Inheritance', pp. 5-6, 10-11; Young, 'Gender', p. 74.
122 Young, 'Gender', p. 83. They began the process in 1803, and the division was formalized in a deed of partition in 1820. SHL, MS 523/972 (Deed of partition between John and Thomas Lane of estates in Barbados and in Staffordshire, 29 June 1820).
123 Who fathered the child is unknown; Betsy may have been subject to sexual abuse on her sea voyages, or been forced to trade on her sexuality to secure her passage.
124 SHL, MS 523/441 (Elizabeth Ann Miler [Betsy Newton]'s petition, 25 May 1801), MS 523/973 (Thomas Lane's report on interview with Betsy Newton, 1796), MS 523/288 (Sampson Wood's report on 'Negroes' at Newton, 1796), MS 523/967/120 (Thomas Lane to Robert Haynes, 18 January 1819); Watson, *Kind of Right*, pp. 15-16. Her second husband may have been Giles Betts, who married 'Elizabeth Newton, widow', on 13 August 1809: St Giles, Camberwell, LMA, P73/GIS/014, Ancestry: https://www.ancestry.co.uk/discoveryui-content/view/7864999:1623.
125 SHL, MS 523/288 (Sampson Wood's report on 'Negroes' at Newton, 1796); Handler *et al.*, *Plantation Slavery in Barbados*, p. 80; Beckles, *Centering Woman*, p. 135.
126 Paugh, *Politics of Reproduction*, pp. 190-1. Watson, *Kind of Right*, pp. 26-30.
127 SHL, MS 523/974 (Report on an interview with John Thomas, a slave, by Thomas Lane, undated), MS 523/288 (Sampson Wood's report on 'Negroes' at Newton, 1796).
128 BDA, Hughes Queree Index of Plantations, entries for Newton and Seawells, pp. 280-1, 348; Young, 'Gender', pp. 248-50.
129 McLaughlin, A., 'Dear Lady Holte' (2020), commissioned by *We Don't Settle* for Birmingham Museums Trust with support from the National Lottery Heritage Fund.
130 'Passenger & Cargo Statistics', GAIA Inc.: https://gaia.bb/general-information/corporate-info/statistics/. The obliviousness of tourists arriving at the airport was highlighted to me by Hannah Young, in the concluding words of her thesis 'Gender and Absentee Slave-Ownership', pp. 249-50.
131 Zephaniah, *Life and Rhymes*, pp. 15, 22, 23, 34; 'Poet & "Peaky Blinders" Star Zephaniah on His Love for Villa', Aston Villa FC YouTube Channel, 9 March 2015: https://www.youtube.com/watch?v=DnraKuh4FH4; 'Aston Villa Pay Moving Tribute to Poet Benjamin Zephaniah ahead of Arsenal Win', *Independent*, 10 December 2023: https://www.independent.co.uk/tv/sport/aston-villa-benjamin-zephaniah-tribute-arsenal-b2461535.html.

2. FRANCES DALZELL (1729–1778)

1 Tayler and Tayler, *Book of the Duffs*, vol. 1, pp. 131-5; 'General Sir James Duff', LBS: https://www.ucl.ac.uk/lbs/person/view/19162.
2 TNA, CO 137/33, f. 34r (Lovell Stanhope to the Board of Trade, 13 June 1763); *Lady Nugent's Journal*, ed. Wright, p. 87.
3 Odumosu, *Black Jokes*, pp. 106-9, 137-7; Newman, *Dark Inheritance*, pp. 187-9; Fuentes, *Dispossessed Lives*, pp. 58-60.
4 IRO, Wills, vol. 17, f. 159 (Will of Peter Caillard, 27 May 1728). Anne Powers (unpublished genealogical research) has traced Susanna (*c.*1707-57) ∽ Peter Caillard ∽ Gibson Dalzell; Mary (*c.*1709-61) ∽ William Tyndall; Jane (*c.*1710-66) ∽ John Decumming;

Jenny (c.1711–47) ∽ Theophilus Blechyden; Sarah (1712–22); Frances (c.1713–38) ∽ Samuel Spencer; Jacob (c.1717–51) and Elizabeth (c.1719–50) ∽ Richard Asheton. John Augier's 1722 will (see n. 6 below) additionally names William, Peter and Abigail.

5   Livesay, *Children*, p. 25.
6   IRO, Wills, vol. 16, f. 17 (Will of John Augier, 6 December 1722). Several scholars have written that Susanna was manumitted in her father's will. However, there is no mention of her in the document, so she must have been freed earlier.
7   Anne Powers has traced: Mary (28 January 1725–May 1754), Peter (16 March 1726–c.1731), and Susanna (15 May 1728–April 1731). See Powers, A., 'Augier or Hosier – Name Transformations', A Parcel of Ribbons, 7 April 2012: http://aparcelofribbons.co.uk/2012/04/augier-or-hosier-name-transformations/.
8   Sheridan, *Sugar and Slavery*, p. 212.
9   Augier and Caillard were operating together in Kingston by 1693, and were both naturalised in Jamaica on 5 September 1693: *Denizations and Naturalizations in the British Colonies in America, 1607–1775*, pp. 9, 44, Ancestry: https://www.ancestry.co.uk/search/collections/49119/; 'The Frederic de Coninck Letters', Crommelin Family Foundation, 1694: http://www.crommelin.org/history/Biographies/Frederic/Year1694-3.htm, and 1695: http://www.crommelin.org/history/Biographies/Frederic/Year1695.htm; Powers, 'Never Give Up': https://aparcelofribbons.co.uk/2024/09/never-give-up-seeking-john-augier/. John Augier may have had piratical links: Brooks, *Quest for Blackbeard*, p. 111.
10 Powers, *Parcel of Ribbons*, pp. 5–8, 25–7; Burnard and Morgan, 'Dynamics', p. 209; O'Malley, *Final Passages*, pp. 224–42.
11 *Jamaica Courant*, 5 August 1718; 'Peter Caillard', LBS: https://www.ucl.ac.uk/lbs/person/view/2146655513; IRO, Wills, vol. 17, f. 159 (Will of Peter Caillard, 27 May 1728); JARD, 1B/11/3/14, ff. 231–3 (Peter Caillard's Probate Inventory, 12 December 1728); JARD, Crop Accounts, 1B/11/4/1, f. 187 (Crop Accounts for Estate of Peter Caillard, 25 March 1742).
12 Chichester, H.M., rev. J. Spain, 'Dalzell, Robert', ODNB: https://doi.org/10.1093/ref:odnb/7082; 'Anecdote of the late General Dalzell', *Town and Country Magazine*, 12, 1870, p. 594.
13 AUL, Duff Papers, MS 3175, Z/216/1 (i) (Gibson Dalzell Commission as ensign, 4 June 1706), F/50/2/1 (i) (Gibson Dalzell commission as Captain, 24 June 1710).
14 Rutledge, 'Enemies Bound by Trade', p. 41.
15 Nelson, 'Contraband Trade under the Asiento', p. 59.
16 TNA, C 11/2732/20 (Dalzell v. South Sea Company, 1732).
17 'Edward Manning', LBS: https://www.ucl.ac.uk/lbs/person/view/2146635969.
18 JARD, Land Patents, 1B/11/1/18, ff. 254–5 (Gibson Dalzell, 500 acres in Portland, 8 January 1729).
19 Gibson first arrived in Jamaica on 16 April 1728, leaving for London in June. As Susanna gave birth to Caillard's last daughter in mid-May 1728, it seems likely they first met on Gibson's return in the autumn, with Frances being conceived very shortly afterwards.
20 The Lord Justices and the Privy Council – including the Archbishop of Canterbury, the Chancellor of the Exchequer, the Dukes of Montagu and Newcastle, and Earls of Cholmondeley, Abercorn and FitzWalter – ratified the Jamaican Act in Whitehall on 21 May 1741. Livesay, *Children*, pp. 15, 42, 45, 77–8; AUL, MS 3175, Z/198/1 (iii) (Susanna Augier Privilege Act, Privy Council, 21 May 1741); JARD, 1B/5/4/9 (Minutes of Council, 28 June–19 July 1738), 1B/5/3/13 (Minutes of Council, 10 September 1741), 1B/11/1/23, f. 79 (Gibson Dalzell to Alexander Innes, Deputation, 26 April 1744); Fuentes, *Dispossessed Lives*, pp. 67–9.

21 Sheridan, 'Formation of Caribbean Plantation Society', p. 400.
22 Livesay, *Children*, pp. 30, 39, 49, 51, 109; Wheeler, *Complexion of Race*, pp. 289–91; Gwynn, *Huguenot Heritage*, p. 29; Powers, 'Augier or Hosier': http://aparcelofribbons.co.uk/2012/04/augier-or-hosier-name-transformations/.
23 Leslie, *New History*, pp. 26–7; Livesay, *Children*, p. 4; Long, *History of Jamaica*, vol. 2, pp. 278, 274.
24 Musgrave, *Solemn Injunction*, vol. 1, p. 182; Thackeray, *Vanity Fair*, ed. Small, pp. 7–8, 10.
25 Chichester, H.M., rev. J. Spain, 'Dalzell, Robert', ODNB: https://doi.org/10.1093/ref:odnb/7082; AUL, MS 3175 Z/59/2 (Bill for schooling, in the same hand as Z/59/1, letter from Susanna Gibson to Gibson Dalzell, 30 October 1743). Sir John Gibson had slighted Anna Maria Dalzell, and his two sons, leaving Susanna his entire estate: TNA, PROB 11/562/172 (Will of Sir John Gibson, 23 January 1718). I have followed genealogists' use of 'great-' and 'grand-'. See 'Great-Aunt vs Grand-Aunt', Ancestry: https://www.ancestry.com/c/ancestry-blog/great-aunt-vs-grand-aunt-when-to-use-them.
26 AUL, MS 3175, F/46/8/1 (Alexander Hamilton to Gibson Dalzell, 15 June 1743). Hamilton had married Gibson's sister Frances in 1720.
27 AUL, MS 3175, Z/59/1 (Susanna Gibson to Gibson Dalzell, 30 October 1743).
28 JARD, 1B/11/1/23, ff. 92–3 (Gibson Dalzell to Alexander Innes, Deputation, 2 July 1744); Gibson bought three lots (858, 859 and 860), between Stanton Street and Gutter Lane, north of Sutton Street, as marked on Michael Hay's 1745 'Plan of Kingston', Library of Congress: https://www.loc.gov/resource/g4964k.ct001905/, for £310 current. IRO, Deeds, vol. 109, f. 174 (Gibson Dalzell from Charles Dawes et uxor, 9 October 1741).
29 TNA, CO 137/28, ff. 169–75 (List of landowners in St Andrew, 1753), transcribed at Jamaican Family Search: http://www.jamaicanfamilysearch.com/Members/1753Andrew.htm; AUL, MS 3175, Z/214/2, i and ii (John Gascoyne to Gibson Dalzell, 1 December 1739 and 25 March 1740).
30 IRO, Deeds, vol. 110, f. 140 (Edward Trelawny to Susanna Augier, 19 June 1741); ff. 140–1 (Susanna Augier to Gibson Dalzell, 20 June 1741), ff. 141–2 (John Wright to Gibson Dalzell, 26 June 1741).
31 Greene, *Settler Jamaica in the 1750s*, pp. 1, 15; Burnard, 'Prodigious Riches', p. 520.
32 When Peter Caillard died in 1728, one of his executors, Richard Asheton (~ Elizabeth Augier) took possession of his assets and paperwork. After Asheton died in 1731, *his* executor and business partner, William Tyndall (~ Mary Augier), did the same. When Tyndall died in 1735, his executors Edward Manning and John Decumming (~ Jane Augier) took over. Tyndall and Asheton were also traffickers of enslaved Africans: O'Malley, *Final Passages*, pp. 42, 190–1, 243, 245. JARD, 1B/11/25/10, vol. 29, f. 180 (Power of Attorney, Susanna Augier to Gibson Dalzell, 10 March 1739); JARD, 1B/5/3/13 (Minutes of Council, 7 November 1739); JARD, Crop Accounts, 1B/11/4/1, f. 187 (Crop Accounts for Estate of Peter Caillard, 25 March 1742).
33 JARD, Chancery Court Records, 1A/3/13, ff. 242–68 (Manning v. Augier, 4 November 1743).
34 JARD, Land Patents, 1B/11/1/21, f. 71 (Gibson Dalzell, 500 acres in Portland, 8 January 1739); IRO, Deeds, vol. 122, ff. 2–3 (Gibson Dalzell and Edward Manning, 21 May 1744).
35 AUL, MS 3175, Z/259/1(i) (Gibson Dalzell to attorneys in Jamaica, *c.*1744), F/50/2/1(vii) (Dr William Aikenhead to Gibson Dalzell, 15 Sept 1749). Aikenhead doesn't specify whether the bond was sterling or current.
36 AUL, MS 3175, Z/204/1 (Dr William Aikenhead to Gibson Dalzell, 9 April 1746), Z/198/2 (Gibson Dalzell to Richard Boddicott, 22 December 1746).

37 AUL, MS 3175, F/50/2/1(iii) (Gibson Dalzell granted coal meter's place, 29 May 1745), Z/259/1 (ii): Gibson Dalzell to Governor Edward Trelawny Governor of Jamaica, 20 June 1745); LMA, COL/CHD/FR/02/0689-0-696 (City of London Freedoms Admissions, 14 January 1746), Ancestry: https://www.ancestry.co.uk/search/collections/2052/records/749620; 'Gibson Dalzell', LBS: https://www.ucl.ac.uk/lbs/person/view/2146645873.

38 Bob had been at school in Spanish Town in 1747. He likely travelled to London with Alexander Innes in August 1748. 'Robert Dalzell of Wokingham', LBS: https://www.ucl.ac.uk/lbs/person/view/2146644149; Duck, B., 'Robert Dalzell', Westminster School: http://archiveblog.westminster.org.uk/?p=929; AUL, MS 3175, F/50/2/1 (iv) (Alexander Innes to Gibson Dalzell, 25 May 1747), Z/214/2 (v) (William Aikenhead to Gibson Dalzell, 5 July 1747); Z/59/2 (Bill for schooling from R. Pierce, paid 16 September 1749).

39 They lived variously in St James' Place, Burlington Street East and Clifford Street: Westminster Rate Books, 1745–55, FindMyPast: https://www.findmypast.co.uk/transcript?id=GBOR%2FWESTMINSTER_RATEBOO%2F9606035%2F1; AUL, MS 3175, Z/214/1 (Lease of a mansion house from George Hadley, 10 November 1752).

40 AUL, MS 3175, Z 59/2 (Bills for clothing, 1749–53).

41 'A List of the Subscribers', in Fielding, *Lives of Cleopatra and Octavia*.

42 AUL, MS 3175, Z/198/2 (Gibson Dalzell to Richard Boddicott, 22 December 1746).

43 In 1747, Aikenhead promised 100 hogsheads the following year: AUL, MS 3175, Z/214/2 (v) (Dr William Aikenhead to Gibson Dalzell, 5 July 1747). Actually Lucky Hill averaged 56.5 between 1752 and 1756: JARD, Crop Accounts, IB/11/4/2 (1742–55), ff. 151–2, 170–1, IB/11/4/3 (1755–62), f. 178.

44 AUL, MS 3175, F/50/2/1 (vi) (Dr William Aikenhead to Gibson Dalzell, 18 September 1748); AUL, MS 3175, F/50/2/1 (viii) (Dr William Aikenhead to Gibson Dalzell, 6 July 1750).

45 AUL, MS 3175, F/50/2/1 (ix) (Dr William Aikenhead to Gibson Dalzell, 29 November 1751), Z/60/1 (ii) (Dr William Aikenhead to Gibson Dalzell, 11 June 1752).

46 McKee, *Negotiating Freedom*, pp. 22, 94.

47 Mair, *Historical Study*, p. 91; Newman, *Dark Inheritance*, p. 96.

48 'John Morse', LBS: https://www.ucl.ac.uk/lbs/person/view/2146638283.

49 The figure was £2,130 6s: AUL, MS 3175, Z/214/2 (v) (Dr William Aikenhead to Gibson Dalzell, 5 July 1747), F/50/2/1(vii) (Dr William Aikenhead to Gibson Dalzell, 15 September 1749).

50 AUL, MS 3175, F/50/2/1 (viii) (Dr William Aikenhead to Gibson Dalzell, 6 July 1750).

51 AUL, MS 3175, Z/62/1 (Peter Furnell to Gibson Dalzell, 18 July 1747), Z/17 (Gibson Dalzell to Peter Furnall, July 1751).

52 AUL, MS 3175, Z 181/1 (George Duff to Frances Duff, 26 June 1757).

53 These were Bilbo Hall, the lands of Straloch, Dunnideer, Meikle Inverlochty, and Little Inverlochty (Milton): Young, *Annals of the Parish and Burgh of Elgin*, pp. 12–13, 25–6; Tayler and Tayler, *Book of the Duffs*, vol. 1, pp. 144, 149; Forty, 'Financial and Political Study', p. 198.

54 'Rothiemay Castle', Canmore, Historic Environment Scotland: https://canmore.org.uk/site/17821/rothiemay-castle.

55 Tayler and Tayler, *Book of the Duffs*, vol. 1, pp. 110, 118, 171.

56 AUL, MS 3175, Z 59/3 (George Duff to Gibson Dalzell, 2 March 1756).

57 AUL, MS 3175, Z 261/1 (Frances to George Duff, undated, but *c.*1763).

58 AUL, MS 3175, Z/213/2 (George Duff to Frances Duff, 25 July 1757), Z 181/1 (George Duff to Frances Duff, 26 June 1757).

Notes to pages 69–75

59 AUL, MS 3175, Z/14 (Frances Dalzell to Susanna Augier, 22 August 1756).
60 TNA, PROB 11/823/345 (Will of Gibson Dalzell, 2 July 1756); 'Gibson Dalzell', LBS: https://www.ucl.ac.uk/lbs/person/view/2146645873; JARD, Probate Inventories, 1B/11/3/36, f. 208 (Gibson Dalzell, 8 August 1758). See also earlier lists of people enslaved at Lucky Hill: AUL, MS 3175, F/48/2(ii) (List of 125, 21 July 1745) and Z/208 (Lists of 111, January 1754, 31 December 1754).
61 'Sir Charles Price, 1st Bart. of Jamaica', LBS: https://www.ucl.ac.uk/lbs/person/view/2146636974; IRO, Deeds, vol. 163, ff. 144–5 (Sale of 165 acres from Gibson Dalzell to Charles Price, 21 October 1755).
62 AUL, MS 3175, Z/14 (Frances Dalzell to Charles Price, 6 July 1756); Hamilton, *Scotland*, p. 45.
63 TNA, PROB 11/823/345 (Will of Gibson Dalzell, 2 July 1756); TNA, C 11/2529/23 (Duff v. Godfrey, 1757); IRO, Deeds, vol. 501 (1802–3), ff. 135–40 (Conveyance of Land, George Duff jnr. et al. to John Jacques et al., 2 June 1801).
64 AUL, MS 3175, Z/14 (Frances Dalzell to Charles Price, 6 July and 22 August 1756, Frances Dalzell to Samuel Howatt, 7 July 1756).
65 'Thomas Bontein', LBS: https://www.ucl.ac.uk/lbs/person/view/2146662205; Lee, '"Broiling on the Coast of Guinea", p. 51.
66 AUL, MS3175, Z/14 (Frances Dalzell to Charles Price, 6 July 1756, 22 August 1756), Z 259/1 (Frances Dalzell, List of tasks for Thomas Bontein, undated, ?1756).
67 AUL, MS 3175, Z/14 (Frances Dalzell to Samuel Howatt, 7 July 1756), Z/49 (Samuel Howatt to Gibson Dalzell, 10 October 1755), Z/59/1 (iii) (George Paplay to Gibson Dalzell, 27 June 1753); IRO, Deeds, vol. 164, f. 51 (Sale of land from Gibson Dalzell to James Murphy et al., 11 May 1756); 'George Paplay', LBS: https://www.ucl.ac.uk/lbs/person/view/2146640751. Paplay married Manning's niece Sarah Lawrence, who would later inherit a significant proportion of his wealth. 'Edward Manning', LBS: https://www.ucl.ac.uk/lbs/person/view/2146635969.
68 AUL, MS 3175, Z/14 (Frances Dalzell to Samuel Howatt, 7 July 1756 and note beneath Frances Dalzell to Charles Price, 6 July 1756).
69 Atkinson, *Mr Atkinson's Rum Contract*, pp. 48–9; 'Hutchison Mure senior', LBS: https://www.ucl.ac.uk/lbs/person/view/2146639023; 'Duncan Campbell of St Martin in the Fields', LBS: https://www.ucl.ac.uk/lbs/person/view/2146633087.
70 AUL, MS 3175, Z 204/1 (Hutchison Mure to George Duff, 18 December 1758).
71 Young, *Political Essays*, vol. 6, p. 327.
72 AUL, MS 3175, Z 198/1 (Frances Dalzell to Mure and Campbell, October ?1756).
73 AUL, MS 3175, Z 259/1 (Frances Dalzell's list of tasks for Thomas Bontein, undated, ?1756).
74 Keefer, 'Marked by Fire', pp. 659–81; Clarkson, 'Negro Slavery', p. 482.
75 AUL, MS 3175, Z/214/3 (Thomas Bontein's accounts, 1 October 1759); JARD, Probate Inventories, 1B/11/3/36, f. 208 (Gibson Dalzell, 8 August 1758).
76 AUL, MS3175, Z/14 (Frances Dalzell to Charles Price, 22 August 1756, Frances Dalzell to Samuel Howatt, undated, July/August 1756).
77 AUL, MS3175, Z 181/1 (Jean, Lady Braco to George Duff, 1 February 1757); Baird, *Genealogical Memoirs of the Duffs*, pp. 79, 113. William Baird married Lord Braco's sister Anne Duff; their son Charles became comptroller of customs in Antigua in 1764: Tayler and Tayler, *Lord Fife and His Factor*, p. 14.
78 Austen, *Sanditon*, ed. Sutherland, p. 64; Thackeray, *Vanity Fair*, ed. Small, p. 259.
79 AUL, MS 3175, Z 181/1 (Jean, Lady Braco to George Duff, 1 February 1757), Z/49 (fragments of Marriage Settlement between George Duff and Frances Dalzell, 14 March

1757); 'Francis Wilson', British Museum: https://www.britishmuseum.org/collection/term/BIOG209272.
80 Tayler and Tayler, *Book of the Duffs*, vol. 1, pp. 199–200.
81 IRO, Wills, vol. 31, f. 10 (Will of Susanna Augier, 25 February 1757); AUL, MS 3175, Z/53 (Thomas Bontein to Frances Dalzell, 24 March 1757).
82 AUL, MS 3175, Z 181/1 (Jean, Lady Braco to George Duff, 1 February 1757), Z 171/1 (Anne Duff to George Duff, 10 June 1757).
83 AUL, MS 3175, Z 181/1 (George Duff to Frances Duff, 26 June 1757); Tayler and Tayler, *Book of the Duffs*, vol. 1, p. 192.
84 TNA, C 12/2305/23 (Duff v. Dalzell, 1757).
85 MacInnes, 'Political Virtue and Capital Repatriation', p. 53; TNA, C 11/2732/20 (Dalzell v. South Sea Company, 1732).
86 AUL, MS 3175, Z 198/1 (Frances Duff to Thomas Bontein, 23 February ?1759); Livesay, *Children*, p. 256, n. 11.
87 Powers, 'Augier or Hosier'.
88 AUL, MS 3175, Z/53 (Thomas Bontein to Frances Dalzell, 24 March 1757); IRO, Wills, vol. 31, f. 10 (Will of Susanna Augier, 25 February 1757).
89 Mair, *Historical Study*, p. 91; Newman, *Dark Inheritance*, p. 96; JARD, Probate Inventories, 1B/11/3, vol. 39, ff. 99–100. Strangely, only eight enslaved people appear in Susanna's St Andrew probate inventory [Clara (old), Diana and son Ben, Wiltshire (cooper), Leonard, Madam and Onushu (boy)] when she had eighty at Wagwater in 1753. She sold eight to John Roberts [Betty and her children: Jenny, Greta Cicily and Ambrose; Sophia, Castatio, and Bella] in 1754–55 (IRO, Deeds, vol. 165, f. 65) but the majority remain unaccounted for.
90 TNA, C 11/2529/23 (Duff v. Godfrey, 1757), PROB 11/1044/354 (Will of Frances Duff, 29 August 1778).
91 AUL, MS 3175, Z 259/1 (List of tasks connected with Jamaican estate, by Frances Duff, undated).
92 AUL, MS 3175, Z 198/1 (Frances Dalzell to Mure and Campbell, October ?1756), Z/53 (Thomas Bontein to Frances Dalzell, 24 March 1757).
93 JARD, 1B/11/18/15, f. 135 (Estate of Gibson Dalzell, Letters Testamentary given to Thomas Bontein, 13 September, 1757); JARD, Probate Inventories, 1B/11/3/36, f. 208 (Gibson Dalzell, 8 August 1758); AUL, MS 3175, Z 198/1 (Frances Duff to Thomas Bontein, 23 February ?1759).
94 TNA, PROB 11/840/469 (Will of Robert Dalzell, 19 October 1758); An earlier will, dated 29 November 1755 appears in AUL, MS 3175, Z/216/1 (iii).
95 Pirohakul, 'Funeral in England', pp. 62, 64.
96 AUL, MS 3175, Z/53 (James Duff to George Duff, 5 November 1758).
97 AUL, MS 3175, Z 181/1 (Note from Rev. Richard Dixon, 24 January 1758).
98 TNA, PROB 11/840/469 (Will of Robert Dalzell, 19 October 1758).
99 TNA, C 101/457 and C 101/89 (Duff v. Dalzell, rental accounts, 1758–63).
100 Dixon was also the General's sole executor and trustee, and had conducted Frances and George's wedding. AUL, MS 3175, Z 198/1 (Frances Duff to Thomas Bontein, 23 February ?1759).
101 AUL, MS 3175, Z/56/1 (William Beckford to Frances Dalzell 23 December 1758), Z 211/2 (Thomas Goostrey to George Duff, 1 December 1758, Z/53 (Francis Wilson to Frances Duff, 24 November 1758). Harman appears regularly in Gibson's correspondence and business papers: AUL, MS 3175, F/48/2 (i), Z/227/1–3, Z/59/2 (ii), Z/ 214/2–3.
102 MacInnes, 'Political Virtue', p. 53; AUL, MS 3175, Z/198/1(v) (South Sea Company, legal discharge, 27 February 1759).

103 AUL, MS 3175, Z 198/1 (Frances Duff to Thomas Bontein, 23 February ?1759).
104 AUL, MS 3175, Z 204/1 (Hutchison Mure to George Duff, 18 December 1758).
105 Livesay, *Children*, pp. 20, 67, 70; Walker, *Jamaica Ladies*, pp. 300–1; Brown, *Tacky's Revolt*, pp. 162, 133, 137, 314; Newman, *Dark Inheritance*, p. 112; Craton, *Testing the Chains*, pp. 335–40; Winn, *Emancipation*, p. 50; Long, *History of Jamaica*, vol. 2, p. 447.
106 Livesay, *Children*, pp. 70–5, 80–5; *Journal of Assembly of Jamaica*, vol. 5, pp. 1–2 (16 November 1762); TNA, CO 137/33, ff. 34–36 (Lovell Stanhope to John Pownall, Secretary of Board of Trade, 13 June 1763).
107 Livesay, *Children*, pp. 122–6, 136–9, 209–10.
108 'Beckford, Richard', HOP: https://www.historyofparliamentonline.org/volume/1754-1790/member/beckford-richard-1796 and https://www.historyofparliamentonline.org/volume/1790-1820/member/beckford-richard-1796; 'Richard Beckford', LBS: https://www.ucl.ac.uk/lbs/person/view/2146651337; Chater, *Untold Histories*, p. 238.
109 'Townsend, James', HOP: https://www.historyofparliamentonline.org/volume/1754-1790/member/townsend-james-1737-87 ; Latsch, 'Black Lord Mayor', pp. 615–17.
110 'Elizabeth Mollison (née Fullerton)', LBS: https://www.ucl.ac.uk/lbs/person/view/2146661219; 'James Hay of Grenada and Sloane Street', LBS: https://www.ucl.ac.uk/lbs/person/view/2146633165; 'Helen Praed (née Bogle)', LBS: https://www.ucl.ac.uk/lbs/person/view/2146664869. Atkinson, *Mr. Atkinson's Rum Contract*, pp. 253–4, 258–62, 297–300.
111 Livesay, *Children*, pp. 109–11, 144, 153, 173–4.
112 The document shows my fifth great-grandfather, Robert Cooper Lee, witnessing the signature of trustee Francis Wilson. IRO, Deeds, vol. 205, ff. 120-131, vol. 206, ff. 89–95, 95–100 (John Maule *et al.* to Hutchison Mure, lease of Lucky Hill, 26 July 1765).
113 Atkinson, *Mr Atkinson's Rum Contract*, pp. 49, 59, 136, 259–60; 'James Kerr Senior', LBS: https://www.ucl.ac.uk/lbs/person/view/2146638187; Chater, K., 'Jonathan Strong', ODNB: https://doi.org/10.1093/ref:odnb/100415.
114 Bontein was Robert's father's cousin. Frances Davies, Bontein's 'natural daughter' with 'a free negro woman' named Mary Davies, married Reverend William Sibbald, Minister of Johnston, 28 August 1786. 'Robert Cunninghame Graham', LBS: https://www.ucl.ac.uk/lbs/person/view/-719617813; Cunninghame Graham, *Doughty Deeds*, pp. 19, 38–9, 71, 82, 86–7; *Edinburgh Magazine or Literary Miscellany*, vol. 4 (1786), p. 461; Brown, *Tacky's Revolt*, p. 211.
115 AUL, MS 3175, Z/204 (James Charles Sholto Douglas to George Duff, 15 December 1770); National Library of Scotland, Acc. 11335/184 (Robert Graham's Inventory for Lucky Hill, 1784).
116 IRO, Deeds, vol. 250, ff. 83–5 (Sale of land from Robert Dalzell to Edward Manning Paplay, and from George and Frances Duff to Edward Manning Paplay, 10 May 1772).
117 They lived variously at Burlington Street, Clarges Street and Queen Street. Tayler and Tayler, *Book of the Duffs*, vol. 1, p. 144.
118 AUL, MS 3175, Z 56/1 (Jean, Lady Fife, to George Duff, 12 June 1760).
119 Tayler and Tayler, *Book of the Duffs*, vol. 1, pp. 159–60.
120 AUL, MS 3175, Z/213/1 (Deed of prohibition and exemption by William, Lord Fife, 11 June 1760).
121 AUL, MS 3175, Z 181/1 (George Duff to Frances Duff, 9 May 1761), Z/55 (Bond of provision, George Duff to Frances Duff, 9 March 1767).
122 AUL, MS 3175, Z/181/1 (Jean, Lady Braco, to Frances Duff, 30 June 1758).
123 AUL, MS 3175, Z 261/1 (Frances Duff to George Duff, 12 May, no year).
124 AUL, MS 3175, Z/59/3 (Jean, Lady Fife, to Frances Duff, 17 April 1760).

125 Tayler and Tayler, *Book of the Duffs*, vol. 1, p. 145.
126 AUL, MS 3175, Z 259/1 (Robert Dalzell to Frances Duff, undated).
127 'Dodd, John', HOP: http://www.histparl.ac.uk/volume/1754-1790/member/dodd-john-1717-82; *A History of the County of Berkshire*, ed. Ditchfield and Page, BHO: http://www.british-history.ac.uk/vch/berks/vol3/pp433-437: Livesay, *Children*, p. 256.
128 Tayler and Tayler, *Book of the Duffs*, vol. 1, pp. 144–5; AUL, MS 3175/Z/49 (Draft will of George Duff, 15 September 1769); Powers, 'Lunatic in the Family': https://aparcelofribbons.co.uk/2012/08/a-lunatic-in-the-family/.
129 AUL, MS 3175, Z 211/2 (Frances Duff to George Duff jnr., 16 April 1776), Z/50/4 (Frances Duff to George Duff jnr., 10 August 1776).
130 Tayler and Tayler, *Book of the Duffs*, vol. 1, pp. 146, 150.
131 AUL, MS 3175, Z/53 (Jean, Lady Fife, to George Duff, 20 July 1768), Z 59/3 (Jean, Lady Fife, to George Duff, 4 March 1777).
132 City of Westminster Archives Centre, STM/PR/8/17 (St Martin-in-the-Fields, Burials, 30 July 1778), Ancestry: https://www.ancestry.co.uk/discoveryui-content/view/records?recordId=1097261&collectionId=61865.
133 TNA, PROB 11/1044/354 (Will of Frances Duff, 29 August 1778).
134 Elizabeth Herbert, née Sackville, was the wife of MP and major Irish landowner Henry Arthur Herbert of Muckross (1756–1821). Tayler and Tayler, *Book of the Duffs*, vol. 1, pp. 144, 146–8, 149–52; Tayler and Tayler, *Lord Fife and His Factor*, pp. 131–2; Herbert, *Retrospections of Dorothea Herbert*, pp. 113, 129.
135 'John Jacques', LBS: https://www.ucl.ac.uk/lbs/person/view/2146649407.
136 IRO, Deeds, vol. 501, ff. 135–40 (Conveyance of land, George Duff *et al.* to John Jacques *et al.*, 30 March 1802); Livesay, *Children*, p. 256, n. 11, citing *Journal of the Jamaica Assembly*, 13 November 1801, 1–3; 27 November 1801, 3; TNA, PROB 11/1648/2 (Will of Robert Dalzell, 1 September 1821).
137 Tayler and Tayler, *Book of the Duffs*, vol. 1, p. 146. William Maule's assessment was sought by Alexander Francis Taylor, husband to Jane Duff, a cousin, in order to exert his claim to inherit Bilbohall after Major George Duff's death in 1828.
138 See Introduction, n. 30. The poetic old Etonian politician was Winthrop Mackworth Praed, who married Helen Bogle in 1835. 'Helen Praed (nee) Bogle', LBS: https://www.ucl.ac.uk/lbs/person/view/2146664869.
139 Livesay, *Children*, pp. 106–12, 177–82; Donington, K., 'Harry [Married Name Thresher], Jane', ODNB: https://doi.org/10.1093/ref:odnb/107509; Donington, *Bonds of Family*, pp. 162–9.
140 Barnett-Woods, 'Bequeathed unto My Daughter', pp. 469–6.
141 Most recently in the 2013 film *Belle*, directed by Amma Asante.
142 King, R., 'Belle, Dido Elizabeth', ODNB: https://doi.org/10.1093/ref:odnb/73352.
143 Livesay, *Children*, pp. 233–40; Clarkson, *True State of the Case*, , p. 7; Wilberforce, *Debate on a Motion*, p. 11.
144 Dominique, 'African Blood', pp. 88–90.
145 Anon., *Woman of Colour*, ed. Dominique, pp. 73, 77, 102.
146 Thackeray, *Vanity Fair*, ed. Small, pp. 535, 537, 582.
147 Marisa Fuentes critiques such 'success', dependent as it was on 'slave ownership and material accumulation based on white supremacy and the bodily exploitation of people of African descent': *Dispossessed Lives*, pp. 67–9.

3. MARY RAMSAY (1717–1794)

1. *Canongate Burns*, ed. Noble and Scott Hogg, pp. 432–5 (Ode to Mrs. Oswald).
2. NRS, Old Parish Registers, Alloa, Births 465/20, 24 (25 February 1694), 175 (9 September 1717), Marriages 465/ 30, 352 (23 February 1716); Scotland's People: www.scotlandspeople.gov.uk; Hancock, *Citizens of the World*, p. 64, n. 55; Hancock, 'Citizen of the World', p. 121.
3. Defoe, *Tour thro' the Whole Island of Great Britain*, vol. 3, p. 51.
4. Karras, *Sojourners in the Sun*, p. 91.
5. Leslie, *New History*, p. 14; Brown, *Reaper's Garden*, p. 1.
6. Hancock, 'Citizen of the World', p. 121; IRO, Deeds, vol. 72, ff. 182–3 (Giles Deston to William Gordon and Alexander Ramsay, 15 November 1725), ff. 204–5 (John Birch to Alexander Ramsay, 1 January 1726), ff. 246–7 (Samuel Turpin to Alexander Ramsay, 21 November 1726); JARD, 1B/11/3/19, ff. 80–3 (Alexander Ramsay Probate Inventory, 26 April 1738).
7. Hancock, 'Citizen of the World', p. 121; JARD, Land Patents, vol. 18, ff. 128–9 (300 acres in Westmoreland to Alexander Ramsay, 14 April 1726); IRO, Deeds, vol. 81, f. 67 (Alexander Ramsay to Robert Rutherford, 30 September 1729); IRO, Deeds, vol. 146, ff. 64–7 (Richard Oswald to Robert Scott, 30 January 1752).
8. JARD, Chancery Court Records, 1A/3/13, vol. 34, ff. 117–38 (Woollery v. Cunningham, 27 August 1743).
9. Hancock, 'Citizen of the World', p. 122; JARD, 1B/11/3/19, ff. 80–3 (Alexander Ramsay Probate Inventory, 26 April 1738).
10. Nelson, *Architecture*, pp. 126–7.
11. Falconbridge, *Account of the Slave Trade*, pp. 33–5; Edwards, *History of the British Colonies in the West Indies*, vol. 2, pp. 150–1.
12. Burnard, 'Slaves and Slavery in Kingston'.
13. JARD, 1B/11/3/19, ff. 80–3 (Probate inventory of Alexander Ramsay, 26 April 1738).
14. Prince, *History of Mary Prince*, p. 6.
15. Jones-Rogers, *They Were Her Property*, pp. 2–12.
16. JARD, 1B/11/3/19, ff. 80–3 (Probate inventory of Alexander Ramsay, 26 April 1738).
17. 'Alexander Ramsay', LBS: https://www.ucl.ac.uk/lbs/person/view/2146660479; IRO, Wills, vol. 21, f. 109 (Will of Alexander Ramsay, 6 January 1738); JARD, 1B/11/24/10, vol. 29, ff. 203–4 (Power of Attorney, Mary Ramsay to Alexander MacFarlane *et al.*, 25 March 1740); IRO, Deeds, vol. 101, ff. 161–2 (Mary Ramsay to James Graham, 14 July 1738); JARD, 1B/11/4/1, f. 181(Mary Ramsay Crop Account, 25 March 1742).
18. JARD, 1B/11/3/19, ff. 80–3 (Alexander Ramsay Probate Inventory, 26 April 1738); JARD, Chancery Court Records, 1A/3/13, vol. 34, ff. 117–38 (Woollery v. Cunningham *et al.*, 27 August 1743).
19. IRO, Deeds, vol. 146, ff. 64–7 (Richard Oswald to Robert Scott, 30 January 1752).
20. JARD, 1B/11/24/10, v. 29, ff. 7–8 (Power of Attorney, Jean and Mary Ramsay to Matthias Phelp *et al.*, 2 June 1738).
21. NRS, GD 213/52, f. 29v (Mary Oswald to Richard Oswald, 26 January 1761).
22. Ferguson left substantial legacies to widows Susanna Roe, Elizabeth Hall and Rosanna De Wandeller, possibly widows of former business partners or friends. IRO, Wills, vol. 22, ff. 87–8 (Will of James Ferguson, 10 April 1740); JARD, 1B/11/3/22, ff. 178–9 (James Ferguson Probate Inventory, 11 September 1742); JARD, 1B/11/24/10, vol. 29, ff. 203–4 (Power of Attorney, Mary Ramsay to Alexander MacFarlane *et al.*, 25 March 1740).

23 'Intromission n.', Dictionary of the Scots Language: https://www.dsl.ac.uk/entry/snd/intromission.
24 Derbyshire Record Office, D239 M/E 16404 (William Perrin to Stephen Ponytz, 19 March 1750).
25 NRS, GD 213/52, ff. 2v, 14v–15r (Mary Oswald to Richard Oswald, 1 and 14 January 1761).
26 IRO, Deeds, vol. 146, ff. 64–7 (Richard Oswald to Robert Scott, 30 January 1752).
27 Hancock, *Citizens of the World*, p. 90.
28 NRS, GD 213/52, f. 182v (Mary Oswald to Richard Oswald, 28 April 1762).
29 Hancock, *Citizens of the World*, pp. 50–1, 60–9; Hancock, 'Citizen of the World', p. 112; 'Scotstoun', in Annan, Mitchell, and Smith, *The Old Country Houses of the Old Glasgow Gentry*: http://www.glasgowwestaddress.co.uk/Old_Country_Houses/Scotstoun.htm; 'Sir Alexander Grant, 5th Bart.' LBS: https://www.ucl.ac.uk/lbs/person/view/2146632678.
30 Slave Voyages, Intra-American, Voyage ID: 100987: https://www.slavevoyages.org/american/database.
31 *Glasgow Chronicle*, 15 June 1853.
32 Hancock, *Citizens of the World*, pp. 125, 128, 130, 244–5; Slave Voyages, Intra-American, Voyage IDs: 101325, 101335: https://www.slavevoyages.org/american/database.
33 Westminster Archive Centre, STM/PR/6/6 (St Martin-in-the-Fields, Marriages, 17 November 1750), Ancestry: https://www.ancestry.co.uk/discoveryui-content/view/records?recordId=1813831&collectionId=61865; Ayrshire Archives, Hamilton of Rozelle papers, AA/DC17/113 (John Cathcart to Roger Hamilton, 1 December 1750).
34 Hancock, *Citizens of the World*, p. 245; Stone, *Family, Sex and Marriage in England*, p. 46.
35 Richard's portrait is dated 1747, Mary's undated, but before Denune died in June 1750: Potomack Company: https://www.potomackcompany.com/auction-lot/william-de-nune-british-1712-1750-sir-richard_F2D4205BC5.
36 NRS, GD 213/52, f. 270r (Mary Oswald to Richard Oswald, 5 April 1763).
37 Hancock, *Citizens of the World*, pp. 88–94; NRS, GD 213/52, ff. 180v, 176r ((Mary Oswald to Richard Oswald, 31 March and 19 January 1762).
38 Hancock, *Citizens of the World*, p. 65; JARD, 1B/11/3/19, ff. 80–3 (Alexander Ramsay Probate Inventory, 26 April 1738); NRS, Register of Deeds, 2nd series, Mackenzie's Office (Mack), RD 240, ff. 1,054–60 (Copy of the Oswalds' marriage settlement, 21 December 1786).
39 Annual entries 1745–54 in JARD, Kingston Vestry Minutes, 2/6/1B and 2/6/2, Parts 1 and 2.
40 IRO, Deeds, vol. 146, ff. 64–7 (Richard Oswald to Robert Scott, 30 January 1752).
41 Hancock, 'Citizen of the World', p. 123; Hancock, *Citizens of the World*, pp. 65, 139–40, 252, 422; IRO, Deeds, vol. 146, ff. 64–7 (Richard Oswald to Robert Scott, 30 January 1752).
42 Hancock, *Citizens of the World*, pp. 175–7; Opala, 'Bunce Island', pp. 2–7; Coleman, *Henry Smeathman*, pp. 144–51; Hochschild, *Bury the Chains*, p. 158.
43 Hancock, *Citizens of the World*, pp. 188–9, 191; Osborne, 'Research into the Black Country's Links', pp. 9–14, 19–22; Berg and Hudson, *Slavery, Capitalism and the Industrial Revolution*, pp. 131–6.
44 Olusoga, *Black and British*, p. 5.
45 Hancock, *Citizens of the World*, pp. 192–4.
46 Coleman, *Maiden Voyages*, p. 58.
47 Hancock, *Citizens of the World*, pp. 2, 195–8.
48 Hochschild, *Bury the Chains*, pp. 24–5.

49 Slave Voyages, Trans-Atlantic, 30 definite, up to 35 possible voyages, 1752–87: https://slavevoyages.org/voyages/ZoaZgiYE.
50 *Papers of Henry Laurens*, ed. Chesnutt et al., vol. 2, p. 246.
51 Hancock, *Citizens of the World*, pp. 177, 214–5, 244, 389, 419–24. My calculation of Richard's share (£12,755.22 of £30,841) is an average figure, which does not account for fluctuations of profits in different time periods. I have counted the 23 years 1748–71 as the period for which Richard received 3/9ths and the 13 years 1772–84 at 5/9ths, despite the slightly staggered acquisition of the 3rd and 4th shares in 1770 and 1771.
52 NRS, GD 213/52, f. 24v (Mary Oswald to Richard Oswald, 23 January 1761).
53 The last entry mentioning Mary in the Kingston Vestry Minutes is in 1754. Her name does not appear in the next surviving volume, covering 1763–7.
54 *Papers of Henry Laurens*, ed. Chesnutt et al., vol. 2, pp. 169–70, 378–80, 507–8.
55 Hancock, *Citizens of the World*, pp. 227–33; Hancock, 'Citizen of the World', pp. 172–6.
56 NRS, GD 213/52, f. 30r (William Tod to Mary Oswald, 27 January 1761).
57 NRS, GD 213/52, ff. 19r, 42r ((Mary Oswald to Richard Oswald, 17 January and 4 February 1761).
58 NRS, GD 213/52, f. 96r (Mary Oswald to Richard Oswald, 1 July 1761).
59 NRS, GD 213/52, f. 19r (Mary Oswald to Richard Oswald, 17 January 1761); Hancock, *Citizens of the World*, p. 234.
60 NRS, GD 213/52, ff. 22v–23r, 43r (Mary Oswald to Richard Oswald, 22 January and 4 February 1761).
61 NRS, GD 213/52, f. 96v (Mary Oswald to Richard Oswald, 1 July 1761).
62 NRS, GD 213/52, f. 128v (Mary Oswald to Richard Oswald, 7 August 1761).
63 NRS, GD 213/52, ff. 22v, 128v (Mary Oswald to Richard Oswald, 22 January and 7 August 1761).
64 NRS, GD 213/52, ff. 2r, 14v–14r, 270r (Mary Oswald to Richard Oswald, 1 and 14 January 1761, 9 April 1763).
65 NRS, GD 213/52, f. 18r, 43r, 227r (Mary Oswald to Richard Oswald, 17 January and 4 February 1761, 6 December 1762).
66 NRS, GD 213/52, ff. 5r, 28v (Mary Oswald to Richard Oswald, 2 and 26 January 1761)
67 NRS, GD 213/52, f. 89v (Mary Oswald to Richard Oswald, 16 June 1761).
68 NRS, GD 213/52, ff. 220r, 243v. (Mary Oswald to Richard Oswald, October and late 1762).
69 NRS, GD 213/52, ff. 79r, 156r, 157r, 115v, 169r, 171r (Mary Oswald to Richard Oswald, 2 May, 18 July, 15 and 16 November, and late 1761).
70 NRS, GD 213/52, ff. 18v, 211r, 248r (Mary Oswald to Richard Oswald, 17 January 1761, 7 October and late 1762).
71 NRS, GD 213/52, ff. 40r, 48r (Mary Oswald to Richard Oswald, 2 and 8 February 1761).
72 NRS, GD 213/52, ff. 190v, 270r (Mary Oswald to Richard Oswald, 23 May 1762, 9 April 1763).
73 NRS, GD 213/52, ff. 82r, 179r (Mary Oswald to Richard Oswald, 9 May 1761, 19 March 1762).
74 NRS, GD 213/52, ff. 64r, 167r (Mary Oswald to Richard Oswald, 4 April and late 1761).
75 Hancock, *Citizens of the World*, p. 237.
76 NRS, GD 213/52, f. 148v (Mary Oswald to Richard Oswald, 27 August 1761).
77 *Canongate Burns*, ed. Noble and Scott Hogg, pp. 432–5 (Ode to Mrs. Oswald). In reality, it was difficult to get the government, which was left with a debt of £122,603,336 after the war, to cough up. Richard was subjected to extensive bureaucratic wrangling and his family was only paid in full in 1804, twenty years after his death. Egerton, *Death or Liberty*, p. 43; Hancock, *Citizens of the World*, p. 235.

78 Hancock, *Citizens of the World*, pp. 221–39; NRS, GD 213/52, ff. 127v–128r (Mary Oswald to Richard Oswald, 7 August 1761).
79 NRS, GD 213/52, f. 274r (Mary Oswald to Richard Oswald, 9 July 1763).
80 Browning, *Pied Piper of Hamelin*, pp. 14–15; Furnivall, 'Robert Browning's Ancestors'; 'Elizabeth Barrett Browning', LBS: https://www.ucl.ac.uk/lbs/person/view/2146646289.
81 Kirkby and Luckins (eds), *Dining on Turtles*, pp. 1–3; 'A Humourous Account of a Turtle Feast and a Turtle Eater', *The World*, no. 123, 8 May 1755.
82 Hancock, *Citizens of the World*, p. 65; Howes, *Arts and Minds*, pp. 18–19.
83 *Johan Zoffany RA: Society Observed*, ed. Postle, p. 246; *Kingston Gleaner*, 30 May 1939, p. 43; Egerton, *British School*, pp. 350–5.
84 Hancock, *Citizens of the World*, pp. 101–2, 286–7; Hancock, 'Citizen of the World', pp. 162–8; NRS, GD 213/52, f. 274r (Mary Oswald to Richard Oswald, 9 July 1763).
85 NRS, GD 213/53, f.336r (Michael Herries to Richard Oswald, 2 August 1764); 'Introduction', *Runaway Slaves in Britain*: https://runaways.gla.ac.uk/introduction/; Newman, *Freedom Seekers*, pp. 58–9.
86 Flavell, *When London Was Capital*, pp. 32, 55–61; *Papers of Henry Laurens*, ed. Chesnutt et al., vol. 9, pp. 316–17; *Diary of John Baker*, ed. Yorke, 427.
87 Chater, *Untold Histories*, pp. 269–70.
88 Hancock, *Citizens of the World*, pp. 261, 267, 271.
89 Ibid., pp. 144–6, 153–4; Rogers, 'East Florida Society', pp. 481–8; Hamilton, *Scotland*, p. 69.
90 Hancock, 'Citizen of the World', pp. 1005–7; Hancock, *Citizens of the World*, pp. 162, 167, 204; Schafer, 'Swamp', p. 18.
91 *Papers of Henry Laurens*, ed. Chesnutt et al., vol. 7, pp. 217, 317; vol. 8, pp. 176–8, 187–90.
92 Hancock, *Citizens of the World*, p. 289. In 1770, Richard successfully applied for the right to bear the Oswald arms: Martin, *Auchincruive*, p. 178.
93 NRS, GD 213/52, ff. 14v, 48r (Mary Oswald to Richard Oswald, 14 January and 8 February 1761).
94 NRS, GD 213/52, ff. 182r, 190v (Mary Oswald to Richard Oswald, 28 April and 23 May 1762).
95 Hancock, *Citizens of the World*, p. 291; NRS, GD 213/52, f. 274r (Mary Oswald to Richard Oswald, 9 July 1763); EUL, CRC, Dk. 1. 30, f. 73 (John Adam to Richard Oswald, 7 November 1766).
96 TNA, PROB 11/1173/185 (Will of Mary Oswald, 19 December 1788); Hancock, *Citizens of the World*, pp. 334–5, list of paintings, pp. 444–5.
97 Hancock, *Citizens of the World*, pp. 307–8, 377–81.
98 *Letters of Robert Burns*, ed. De Lancey Ferguson and Ross Roy, vol. 1, pp. 385–6 (Robert Burns to John Moore, 23 March 1789).
99 By the 1780s Mary's butler, Thomas Daniel, received £22 5s a year; her housekeeper, Mary Bewes, £21; housemaid, Mary Stewart, £6 6s; and footman, David McGullivray, £4 1s. Between about 1770 and 1820, butlers' wages ranged from £10 to £30; housekeepers' £16 to £25; housemaids' £4 to £10; and footmen's £4 to £14. NRS, GD 213/106, 2 (Mary Oswald's accounts, including servants' wages, 1789); Hecht, *Domestic Servant Class*, pp. 142–8; Horn, *Flunkeys and Scullions*, pp. 190–8.
100 NRS, GD 213/52, f. 117v (Mary Oswald to Richard Oswald, 18 July 1761).
101 EUL, CRC, Dk.1. 30, f. 106 (James Gordon to Richard Oswald, December 1769).
102 Hancock, *Citizens of the World*, pp. 259, 284, 301–7.
103 Ibid., p. 68; NRS, GD 213/52, f. 182v (Mary Oswald to Richard Oswald, 28 April 1762).
104 Hancock, *Citizens of the World*, pp. 144–5, 251, 254; Hancock, 'Citizen of the World', pp.

770, 776–7; 'David Mill of Tobago': https://www.ucl.ac.uk/lbs/person/view/2146632462; NLJ, MS 1206, 1276 (Mortgages, John Bourryau, Robert Turner and Peter John Luard to Richard Oswald, 25 April 1766). The estates were 'Grand Bay', LBS: https://www.ucl.ac.uk/lbs/estate/view/1384, 'Simon', LBS: https://www.ucl.ac.uk/lbs/estate/view/1304, 'Bourryau', LBS: https://www.ucl.ac.uk/lbs/estate/view/3132 and 'Rhine', LBS: https://www.ucl.ac.uk/lbs/estate/view/3252.

105 Hancock, *Citizens of the World*, p. 64; NRS, GD 213/53, ff. 195–6 (Richard Oswald jnr, to Richard Oswald, Kingston, Jamaica, 30 March 1764); McClure, D., 'Our Friend Poor Oswald Is No More', *Ayrshire Notes*, 22, Spring 2002: http://www.ayrshirehistory.org.uk/Oswald/georgeoswald.htm; NRS, GD 213/52, ff. 268r, 273r (Mary Oswald to Richard Oswald, 5 and 10 April 1763).

106 *Papers of Henry Laurens*, ed. Chesnutt et al., vol. 8, pp. 340–1, 439, vol. 10, p. 15; Flavell, *When London Was Capital*, p. 111.

107 *Papers of Henry Laurens*, ed. Chesnutt et al., vol. 8, p. 605; NRS, GD 213/53, f. 69v (John Anderson to Richard Oswald, 26 August 1776).

108 Hancock, *Citizens of the World*, pp. 159–60, 214; Schafer, 'Swamp', p. 24; Anon., *American Husbandry*, vol. 2, pp. 50–1. Davis, 'Richard Oswald', argues convincingly that Oswald authored this anonymous tract.

109 *Papers of Henry Laurens*, ed. Chesnutt et al., vol. 15, pp. 330–404, 617–27, vol. 16, p. 25; University of South Carolina, Kendall Collection, Laurens papers (Henry Laurens to Mary Oswald, 27 October and 30 November 1782).

110 Hancock, *Citizens of the World*, pp. 390–2; Rogers, 'East Florida Society', p. 488, n. 46; Benjamin Franklin to Richard Oswald, 27 June 1782, Founders Online: https://founders.archives.gov/documents/Franklin/01-37-02-0353; 'Preliminary Articles of Peace: Second Draft Treaty', Founders Online: https://founders.archives.gov/documents/Franklin/01-38-02-0205#BNFN-01-38-02-0205-fn-0019

111 *Memoirs of John Quincy Adams*, ed. Adams, vol. 3, p. 559.

112 *Whitefoord Papers*, ed. Hewins, p. 174; University of South Carolina, Kendall Collection, Laurens papers (Henry Laurens to Mary Oswald, 30 November 1782).

113 Hochschild, *Bury the Chains*, pp. 99–101; Robinson, 'Richard Oswald'; Egerton, *Death or Liberty*, p. 199; *Papers of Henry Laurens*, ed. Chesnutt et al., vol. 16, p. 255; Draft Peace Treaty Presented by Richard Oswald to the American Peace Commissioners, 25 November 1782', n. 8, Founders Online: https://founders.archives.gov/documents/Adams/06-14-02-0048.

114 University of South Carolina, Kendall Collection, Laurens papers (Henry Laurens to Mary Oswald, 30 November 1782).

115 Egerton, *Death or Liberty*, p. 204.

116 Olusoga, *Black and British*, pp. 143–97; Coleman, *Henry Smeathman*, pp. 231–7; *Memoirs of the Life and Writings of the Late John Coakley Lettsom*, ed. Pettigrew, vol. 2, p. 272; Starr, D., 'Smeathman, Henry', ODNB: https://doi.org/10.1093/ref:odnb/93969.

117 Matrana, *Lost Plantations of the South*, pp. 135–6; Schafer, 'Swamp', pp. 26–7.

118 *Papers of Henry Laurens*, ed. Chesnutt et al., vol. 5, p. 493, vol. 7, p. 501, vol. 16, pp. 264–8, 661–2; Will of Thomas Ferguson, 24 June 1785, South Carolina Wills and Probate Records, Ancestry: https://www.ancestry.co.uk/discoveryui-content/view/records?recordId=1113017&collectionId=9080.

119 Cox and Watson, 'John Alleyne', p. 111.

120 Lewis, *Journal*, pp. 322–4 (29 January 1817); 'Spring Garden', LBS: https://www.ucl.ac.uk/lbs/person/view/2146643625.

121 *Papers of Henry Laurens*, ed. Chesnutt et al., vol. 16, pp. 661–2.

122 Flavell, *When London was Capital*, pp. 101–2.
123 *Papers of Henry Laurens*, ed. Chesnutt et al., vol. 16, p. 556; *Whitefoord Papers*, ed. Hewins, p. 197; *Morning Chronicle*, 12 November 1784, p. 3.
124 *The Times*, 11 January 1785, p. 3; Hancock, *Citizens of the World*, p. 385; TNA, PROB 11/1125/190 (Will of Richard Oswald, 19 January 1785).
125 NRS, GD 213/106/4, f. 11 (Charlton Palmer's expenses following Mary Oswald's death, 1789, payment to Charles Mason); *Gentleman's Magazine*, December 1812, p. 591; TNA, PROB 11/1538/365 (Will of Charles Mason, 18 November 1812).
126 NRS, GD 213/106/4, f. 16 (Charlton Palmer's expenses following Mary Oswald's death, 1789, including 'cash received from the Treasury on account of losses in Florida'); TNA, T 77/13/8, claim no. 29, ff. 135–51 (East Florida Claims Commission, claimant Mary Oswald).
127 TNA, C 12/1081/6 (Oswald v. Anderson, 1787), C 12/1262/20 (Oswald v. Oswald, 1788); NRS, Register of Deeds, 2nd series, Mackenzie's Office (Mack), RD 240, ff. 1054–60 (Copy of the Oswalds' marriage settlement, 21 December 1786).
128 South Carolina Historical Society, Charleston, Laurens papers (Henry Laurens to Mary Oswald, 19 November 1787).
129 NRS, GD 213/106, f. 11 (Charlton Palmer's expenses following Mary Oswald's death, 1789, payment to Charles Mason). Mason lived in Elstree, Hertfordshire.
130 *Canongate Burns*, ed. Noble and Scott Hogg, pp. 432–5, 438, 704 (Ode to Mrs. Oswald, The Kirk of Scotland's Alarm, Pegasus at Wanlockhead); *Robert Burns and Mrs. Dunlop*, ed. Wallace, vol. 1, pp. 201–5 (Robert Burns to Frances Dunlop, January 1789 and Frances Dunlop to Robert Burns, 22 January 1789); *The Letters of Robert Burns*, ed. De Lancey Ferguson and Ross Roy, vol. 1, pp. 385–6 (Robert Burns to John Moore, 23 March 1789); *Oxford Edition of the Works of Robert Burns*, vol. 1, ed. Leask, p. 80; Morris, 'Robert Burns', pp. 343–59.
131 £200 of the c.£350 bill went on clothes. NRS, GD 213/124 (Mary Oswald's funeral expenses, 1789).
132 Hancock, 'Citizen of the World', pp. 186–9; Opala, 'Bunce Island', p. 17.
133 NRS, GD 213/52, ff. 2v, 148v (Mary Oswald to Richard Oswald, 1 January and 27 August 1761).
134 McLeod, H., 'Float in Inaugural Parade to Highlight Unique Gullah Geechee Culture', *Reuters*, 18 January 2013: https://www.reuters.com/article/us-usa-gullahgechee-idUSBRE90H1DS20130118; Akam, S., 'George W. Bush's Great-Great-Great-Great-Grandfather Was a Slave Trader', *Slate*, 20 June 2013: https://slate.com/human-interest/2013/06/george-w-bush-and-slavery-the-president-and-his-father-are-descendants-of-thomas-walker-a-notorious-slave-trader.html.
135 Hancock, *Citizens of the World*, p. 170; 'The Three Chimneys', Ormond Beach Historical Society: https://www.ormondhistory.org/the-three-chimneys-sugar-works.
136 Yinka Shonibare, *Colonel Tarleton and Mrs Oswald Shooting* (2007); Matovu, R., 'Yinka Shonibare: Poetic, Political Artist', Art UK, 9 October 2017: https://artuk.org/discover/stories/yinka-shonibare-poetic-political-artist.

4. JANE CHOLMELEY (C.1744–1836)

1 Austen, *Mansfield Park*, ed. Littlewood, p. 157.
2 BDA, RL 1/3, pp. 3, 26–7, 245 (St. Michael's parish register, Katherine Cholmeley, bap. 13 October 1739, Robert Cholmeley, bap. 20 June, bur. 24 June 1741, Mary Cholmeley,

bap. 16 September 1749), via 'English Settlers in Barbados, 1637–1800', Ancestry: https://www.ancestry.co.uk/search/collections/61463/. No baptism record has been found for Jenny; other sources give dates from 1744 to 1747. Le Faye, *Chronology*, p. 737; 'Jane Cholmeley Leigh Perrot', Find a Grave: https://www.findagrave.com/memorial/197151669/jane-leigh-perrot; *Gentleman's Magazine*, vol. 160 (1836), p. 665. Even her own recollection is inconsistent: HRO, 23M93/86/3/29, 39 (Jane Leigh-Perrot to James Edward Austen, 19 January and 23 September 1835).

3   *Austen Papers*, ed. Austen-Leigh, pp. 180, 289–90; HRO, 23M93/86/3/29 (Jane Leigh-Perrot to James Edward Austen, 19 January 1835); *Alumni Cantabrigienses*, ed. J.A. Venn, vol. 1, p. 335, Ancestry: tps://www.ancestry.co.uk/search/collections/3997/records/89020; TNA, PROB 11/773/439 (Will of Thomas Baxter, 12 October 1749); 'Records of the Vestry of St Michael', p. 93.

4   *Austen Papers*, ed. Austen-Leigh, p. 186; Anon., *Trial of Mrs. Leigh Perrot* (London: West & Hughes, 1800), p. 27.

5   They were each allotted £2,235. HRO, 23M93/E/B1 (Thomas Workman's 'account of the legacies of Robert Cholmeley who died intestate in 1754, and the state of Miss Cholmeley's fortune', 10 October 1764).

6   The loan was £4,000 Barbados currency, so £2,857 sterling. HRO, 23M93/E/T1, f.1 (Deed between Thomas and Ann Workman, William Maynard and Samuel Bedford, 13 August 1759).

7   'Edward Brace', LBS: https://www.ucl.ac.uk/lbs/person/view/2146652659; 'Rev. Edward Brace', LBS: https://www.ucl.ac.uk/lbs/person/view/2146667065; TNA, PROB 11/732/239 (Will of Edward Brace, 14 March 1744); Cadbury, 'Clergymen Licenced to Barbados', pp. 62–9; BDA, Hughes Queree Index of Plantations, 'Workman's/Brace's', p. 429; BDA, RB 9/3/3 (Population return for St George, 1739), RB 3/40/77 (Deed, Rev. Edward and Ann Brace to Thomas Payne, 7 May 1766).

8   BDA, RL 1/3, pp. 203, 373, 433 (St Michael's parish register, Thomas Workman m. Katherine Maynard, 5 June 1748, Hamlet Workman, bap. 14 September 1753, Katherine Workman, bur. 4 September 1755, Katherine Maynard Workman, bap. 5 September 1755), RL 1/21, p. 127 (Christ Church parish register, Katherine Maynard Workman, bur. 25 December 1756), via 'English Settlers in Barbados, 1637–1800', Ancestry: https://www.ancestry.co.uk/search/collections/61463/, and 'Barbados, Church Records, 1637–1849', Ancestry: https://www.ancestry.co.uk/search/collections/9788/.

9   BDA, RB 8/1 (Powers of Attorney Index), listing RB 7/35/3 and 8 (Thomas Workman Deputation as Casual Receiver and Register in Admiralty, 1759); BL, EAP1086/1/1/9/1, p. 4 (*Barbados Mercury*, 6 December 1783): https://eap.bl.uk/archive-file/EAP1086-1-1-9-1.

10 BDA, RL 1/2, p. 317, RL 1/4, p. 77 (St Michael's parish register, Hamlet Fairchild, bap. 5 December 1728, John Cholmeley Fairchild, son of Hamlet and Katherine Fairchild, bap. 2 October 1758) via 'English Settlers in Barbados, 1637–1800', Ancestry: https://www.ancestry.co.uk/search/collections/61463/; TNA, T 1/411/77-80 (Auditor General's complaint against Thomas Workman, 12 October 1761); Alleyne, *Historic Bridgetown*, p. 41; HRO, 23M93/52/1/3 (William Morris to Jane Leigh Perrot, 10 March 1791), ff. 8–9.

11 HRO, 23M93/52/1/3 (William Morris to Jane Leigh Perrot, 10 March 1791), ff. 1–2, 14, 18; HRO, 23M93/E/T/1, f.1 (Deed between Thomas and Ann Workman, William Maynard and Samuel Bedford, 13 August 1759).

12 HRO, 23 M93/86/3/18 (Jane Leigh Perrot to James Edward Austen, 15 January 1834).

13 Le Faye, *Jane Austen: A Family Record*, pp. 8–9; Austen-Leigh and Austen-Leigh, *Jane*

Austen, *Her Life and Letters*, p. 126; Anon., *The Trial of Mrs. Leigh Perrot* (London: West and Hughes, 1800), p. 28.
14 Austen-Leigh, *Memoir of Jane Austen*, ed. Sutherland, pp. 37, 59, 215–16.
15 'Metal Pattens, Awkward Protection for 18th and 19th Century Shoes', *Jane Austen's World*, 12 February 2011: https://janeaustensworld.com/2011/02/12/metal-pattens-awkward-protection-for-18th-and-19th-century-shoes/.
16 HRO, 23M93/86/3/29 (Jane Leigh-Perrot to James Edward Austen, 19 January 1835).
17 City of Westminster Archives Centre, SMCH/PR/3/10, f. 271 (St Martin-in the Fields, Marriages, 9 October 1764), Ancestry: https://www.ancestry.co.uk/imageviewer/collections/61867/images/61865_314054001181_18036-00276.
18 HRO, 23M93/E/B1 (Thomas Workman's 'account of the legacies of Robert Cholmeley who died intestate in 1754, and the state of Miss Cholmeley's fortune', 10 October 1764). The men were Edward Laming, late owner of Meads, St Andrew and Lammings, St Joseph, and Thomas Pearce of St Michael. BDA, RB6 34/434 (Will of Edward Laming, 10 April 1744); RB6, 21/544 (Will of Thomas Pearce, 1 October 1751).
19 HRO, 23M93/86/3/32, 35, 36 (Jane Leigh-Perrot to James Edward Austen, 8 March, 30 May and 2 June 1835); Le Faye, *Jane Austen: A Family Record*, pp. 8–9, 118; Austen-Leigh and Austen-Leigh, *Jane Austen, Her Life and Letters*, p. 126; 'Barry, Richard, 7th Earl of Barrymore', HOP: https://www.historyofparliamentonline.org/volume/1790-1820/member/barry-richard-1769-93.
20 Pinchard, *Trial*, p. 35; Le Faye, *Jane Austen: A Family Record*, pp. 122–3; *Austen Papers*, ed. Austen-Leigh, p. 241 (James Leigh Perrot to Jane Leigh Perrot, 4 July 1806).
21 HRO, 23M93/86/3/32 (Jane Leigh-Perrot to James Edward Austen, 8 March 1835).
22 *Austen Papers*, ed. Austen-Leigh, p. 209 (Jane Leigh Perrot to cousin Mountague Cholmeley, 1 April 1800).
23 *Gentleman's Magazine*, vol. 37, 1767, p. 610. Following the deaths of Hamlet and John Cholmeley Fairchild, a new deed was drawn up between Thomas and Ann Workman assigning Jenny and Katherine £1,250 current each; the money would still revert to Thomas Workman on their deaths: HRO, 23M93/E/T2 (Deed between Thomas and Ann Workman, William Maynard and Samuel Bedford, 19 December 1767).
24 They married 4 July 1770; Spry died 4 September 1772. Poyer, *History of Barbados*, p. 354; Schomburgk, *History of Barbados*, p. 332.
25 HRO, 23 M93/86/3/21 (Jane Leigh Perrot to James Edward Austen, 1 May 1834).
26 HRO, 23M93/52/1/3 (William Morris to Jane Leigh Perrot, 10 March 1791), ff. 9, 4, 14–15; BDA, RB 3/40/77 (Deed, Reverend Edward and Ann Brace to Thomas Payne, 7 May 1766); Smith, *Slavery, Family, and Gentry Capitalism*, p. 183.
27 BDA, Hughes Queree Index of Plantations, 'Belle', p. 36, 'Burnt House', p. 63, Powers of Attorney Index, RB 8/1, citing RB 7/40/42, 40/43, 40/52, 41/37, 43/102 (various appointments of Thomas and Francis Workman, 1774–81); *Remembrancer*, vol. 13, p. 93; BL, EAP1086/1/1/8/1 (*Barbados Mercury*, 8 November 1783, p. 3): https://eap.bl.uk/archive-file/EAP1086-1-1-8-1; EAP1086/1/1/9/1 (*Barbados Mercury*, 6 December 1783, p. 4): https://eap.bl.uk/archive-file/EAP1086-1-1-9-1; 'Francis Workman', LBS: https://www.ucl.ac.uk/lbs/person/view/2146652727.
28 Paugh, *Politics of Reproduction*, p. 135; HRO, 23M93/52/1/3 (William Morris to Jane Leigh Perrot, 10 March 1791), ff. 11, 15; BDA, RB 9/3/9 (Return of losses, St George's parish, 10 October 1780); Mulcahy, *Hurricanes*, pp. 77, 108–9; Neely, *Great Hurricane*, pp. 116, 145, 190–1, 210.
29 HRO, 23M93/52/1/3 (William Morris to Jane Leigh Perrot, 10 March 1791), ff. 15–17; 'William Morris', LBS: https://www.ucl.ac.uk/lbs/person/view/2146654613.

30 BL, EAP1086/1/1/9/1 (*Barbados Mercury*, 6 December 1783, p. 4): https://eap.bl.uk/archive-file/EAP1086-1-1-9-1.
31 Judy and Rittah had been girls in 1766 when Brace sold them to Thomas Payne. Jubbah Bess may have been related to Old Jubbah and Young Jubbah, also then living at Brace's; Trinculo's Judy and Little Trinculo may have been children of a man named Trinculo. BDA, RB 3/40/77 (Deed, Rev. Edward and Ann Brace to Thomas Payne, 7 May 1766).
32 HRO, 23M93/52/1/3 (William Morris to Jane Leigh Perrot, 10 March 1791), ff. 4, 17; BDA, Hughes Queree Index of Plantations, 'Workmans', p. 429; 'Walkers', LBS: https://www.ucl.ac.uk/lbs/estate/view/534.
33 HRO, 23M93/52/1/1 (Mary Judith Cholmeley to Jane Leigh-Perrot, 10 October 1790), 23M93/52/1/3 (William Morris to Jane Leigh Perrot, 10 March 1791), ff. 1, 7, 11–13, 18; BDA, RB 29, ff. 289–91 (Will of Ann Workman, 15 September 1790). Ann's executors were William Morris, Cholmeley Willoughby and 'Henry Trotman', LBS: https://www.ucl.ac.uk/lbs/person/view/2146643853.
34 BDA, RB 3/40/77 (Deed, Rev. Edward and Ann Brace to Thomas Payne, 7 May 1766), RL 1/6, f. 155 (St Michael's parish register, 'Gusman a free negro', bur. 30 March 1801), via 'Barbados, Church Records, 1637–1849', Ancestry: https://www.ancestry.co.uk/search/collections/9788/; TNA, T 71/520, 527 (Slave Registers, Barbados, 1817, 1820), Ancestry: https://www.ancestry.co.uk/search/collections/1129/; *Parliamentary Papers: 1780–1849*, vol. 28 (1826), p. 59 gives a figure of £4 p.a. which I've assumed is in Barbados currency.
35 HRO, 23M93/86/3/29 (Jane Leigh-Perrot to James Edward Austen, 19 January 1835).
36 BDA, RB 1/198/244 (Executors of Ann Workman, sale of Brace's to Thomas Applethwaite, 1791); Hughes Queree Index of Plantations, 'Workman's/Brace's', p. 429; 'Walkers [previously Willoughby's; incorporating Brace's later Workman's]', LBS: https://www.ucl.ac.uk/lbs/estate/view/534.
37 *Jane Austen's Letters*, ed. Le Faye, pp. 43–4, 49.
38 HRO, 23M93/86/3/32 (Jane Leigh-Perrot to James Edward Austen, 8 March 1835); Fowler et al., 'Interim Report, p. 97: https://www.nationaltrust.org.uk/who-we-are/research/addressing-our-histories-of-colonialism-and-historic-slavery; Le Faye, *Chronology*, pp. 131, 224; *Bath Chronicle*, 16 May 1793, 3 April 1794, 5 November 1795, 19 October 1797; *Passages from the Diaries of Mrs. Philip Lybbe Powys*, ed. Climenson, p. 325.
39 Some have inferred from a letter Jane Austen wrote on 5 May 1801 that the Leigh Perrots had a Black servant in Bath. On arriving at The Paragon, 'Frank, whose black head was in waiting in the Hall window, received us very kindly'. However, this seems inconclusive; 'black head' may merely indicate dark hair. *Jane Austen's Letters*, ed. Le Faye, pp. 41, 85.
40 Le Faye, *Chronology*, pp. 201–2, 224, 226; Austen-Leigh and Austen-Leigh, *Jane Austen, Her Life and Letters*, p.127; Austen, *Northanger Abbey*, ed. Davie, pp. 3–4, 84–5.
41 HRO, 23 M93/85/2 (Fanny Caroline Lefroy's Family History Manuscript), unpaginated; Austen-Leigh, *Memoir of Jane Austen*, ed. Sutherland, p. 58; *Jane Austen's Letters*, ed. Le Faye, pp. 76–7; Le Faye, *Jane Austen: A Family Record*, pp. 128–9; Worsley, *Jane Austen at Home*, p. 187; Tucker, *Jane Austen the Woman*, p. 52.
42 *Jane Austen's Letters*, ed. Le Faye, pp. 70, 80, 92, 110.
43 Ibid., pp. 92, 107–8, 171, 195, 214–15.
44 The Earl had briefly been a pupil of Rev. Austen's at Steventon; he would later be declared insane. Foyster, *Trials of the King of Hampshire*.
45 *Jane Austen's Letters*, ed. Le Faye, pp. 62–5, 94, 536, 553; 'John Hooper Holder', LBS: https://www.ucl.ac.uk/lbs/person/view/2146650127; 'General Edward Mathew', LBS:

https://www.ucl.ac.uk/lbs/person/view/2146645387; 'Richard Maitland', LBS: https://www.ucl.ac.uk/lbs/person/view/2146658769.

46 *Jane Austen's Letters*, ed. Le Faye, pp. 530, 581; Byrne, *Real Jane Austen*, pp. 219–20; 'Sir George Francis Hampson 6th Bart', LBS: https://www.ucl.ac.uk/lbs/person/view/2146650217.

47 'James Langford Nibbs senior', LBS: https://www.ucl.ac.uk/lbs/person/view/2146639585; Le Faye, *Jane Austen: A Family Record*, pp. 18–19, 45; Looser, D., 'Breaking the Silence: Exploring the Austen Family's Complex Entanglements with Slavery', *TLS*, 21 May 2021: https://www.the-tls.co.uk/history/modern-history/jane-austen-family-slavery-essay-devoney-looser.

48 Notman, S., 'Jane Austen and Her Connection to Bermuda', *Bermudian*, 28 April 2024: https://www.thebermudian.com/heritage/heritage-heritage/jane-austen-and-her-connection-to-bermuda/; Perry, 'Austen and Empire': https://jasna.org/publications-2/persuasions/no16/perry/, pp. 95–97.

49 Le Faye, *Chronology*, p. 436; *Jane Austen's Letters*, ed. Le Faye, p. 225; 'James Lewis II', LBS: https://www.ucl.ac.uk/lbs/person/view/2146646275.

50 *Jane Austen's Letters*, ed. Le Faye, pp. 572–3; 'Joshua Smith', LBS: https://www.ucl.ac.uk/lbs/person/view/2146650997.

51 *Jane Austen's Letters*, ed. Le Faye, pp. 87–8, 92, 94; Le Faye, '"Persecuted Relation"', pp. 92–106; 'Abel Dottin I', LBS: https://www.ucl.ac.uk/lbs/person/view/2146650065; TNA, PROB 11/1440/308 (Will of Willielma Lillingston, 27 March 1806); HRO, 23M93/51/1 (Papers concerning James Leigh Perrot's executorship of Mrs Lillingston).

52 The following account of Jane's arrest and imprisonment is largely taken from her correspondence from prison with her Cholmeley relations, published in *Austen Papers*, ed. Austen-Leigh, pp. 179–219; three pamphlets about the trial: Anon., *The Trial of Mrs. Leigh Perrot* (West and Hughes: London, 1800); Pinchard, *Trial*; Anon., *Trial of Jane Leigh Perrot* (Gye: Bath, 1800); MacKinnon, *Grand Larceny*; Borowitz, *Crimes Gone By*, pp. 723–43; Wade, *Jane Austen's Aunt Behind Bars*, pp. 64–75; Pugsley, 'Was Aunt Jane a Shoplifter?'; and Pugsley, 'Trial of Jane Austen's Aunt': https://jasna.org/publications-2/persuasions-online/vol-41-no-1/pugsley/.

53 Though several scholars, notably Borowitz, have argued Jenny was guilty, I am persuaded by David Pugsley's conclusion (shared at the time by John Morris KC) that she was innocent, the evidence against her inconsistent, so she was a blackmail victim.

54 Austen-Leigh and Austen-Leigh, *Jane Austen, Her Life and Letters*, p. 134.

55 John Cam Hobhouse, 'Ilchester Gaol – Treatment of Mr [Henry] Hunt', debated 1 March 1822, Hansard: https://hansard.parliament.uk/Commons/1822-03-01/debates/caf8ed5e-827b-4efd-b8e2-73e7fe76c6d7/IlchesterGaol%E2%80%94TreatmentOfMrHunt.

56 Although Jenny appreciated Scadding's 'respectful behaviour' towards her, she had to bear in mind that he had 'a number of relatives and dependents who are always on the petty jury'.

57 It is unclear which Mr Casamajor. William East's first wife was Hannah Casamajor, daughter of Bristol slaver, Henry Casamajor of Tockington: Jeffares, N., 'The Mystery of the Second Lady East', 12 May 2016: https://neiljeffares.wordpress.com/2016/05/12/the-mystery-of-the-second-lady-east/; See also 'Justinian Casamajor', LBS: https://www.ucl.ac.uk/lbs/person/view/2146631331.

58 'molly, n.1.', *OED Online*: https://doi.org/10.1093/OED/3330173822.

59 Pugsley, D., 'An Enlightening Letter Regarding the Leigh Perrot Shoplifting Case', Jane Austen Centre Blog, 15 March 2022: https://janeausten.co.uk/blogs/authors-artists-vagrants/an-enlightening-letter-regarding-the-leigh-perrot-shoplifting-case.

60 Mary Austen was the granddaughter of Charles Craven (1682–1754), younger brother of William, 2nd Lord Craven: *Jane Austen's Letters*, ed. Le Faye, pp. 511–12.
61 Sir Robert Dallas (heir to William Gemmell of Grenada), Joseph Jekyll, Nathaniel Bond and Albert Pell. 'Dallas, Robert': HOP: http://www.historyofparliamentonline.org/volume/1790-1820/member/dallas-robert-1756-1824; 'Sir Robert Dallas', LBS: https://www.ucl.ac.uk/lbs/person/view/2146658365; 'Jekyll, Joseph', HOP: https://www.historyofparliamentonline.org/volume/1790-1820/member/jekyll-joseph-1754-1837; 'Bond, Nathaniel', HOP: https://www.historyofparliamentonline.org/volume/1790-1820/member/bond-nathaniel-1754-1823; 'Sir Albert Pell', in Woolrych, *Lives of Eminent Serjeants-at-Law*, vol. 2, pp. 753–71.
62 According to Charles James Fox: 'Vansittart, George', HOP: https://www.historyofparliamentonline.org/volume/1754-1790/member/vansittart-george-1745-1825; Thorne, R., 'Griffin, Richard [*formerly* Richard Aldworth Neville], Second Baron Braybrooke', ODNB: https://doi.org/10.1093/ref:odnb/19957.
63 See n. 56. Margie Burns ascribes the anonymous London pamphlet to Pinchard; Pugsley (email correspondence) believes it was authored by Jekyll. Burns, 'Three Pamphlets': https://jasna.org/publications-2/persuasions-online/volume-39-no-1/three-pamphlets-on-the-leigh-perrot-trial-why-austen-sent-susan-to-crosby/.
64 *Lady's Magazine*, vol. 31 (for April 1800), pp. 171–6: https://hdl.handle.net/2027/chi.79263682?urlappend=%3Bseq=209.
65 James, 'Case of Shoplifting', pp. 200–2; Tickell, *Shoplifting in Eighteenth Century England*, p. 189.
66 *Jane Austen's Letters*, ed. Le Faye, p. 225; Austen-Leigh and Austen-Leigh, *Jane Austen, Her Life and Letters*, pp. 155–6, 306; *Austen Papers*, ed. Austen-Leigh, pp. 222–4, 241–5; Le Faye, *Chronology*, pp. 330–1, 360; Byrne, *Real Jane Austen*, pp. 227–30; Worsley, *Jane Austen at Home*, pp. 263–5.
67 *Jane Austen's Letters*, ed. Le Faye, pp. 120–1, 143, 160, 164; Worsley, *Jane Austen at Home*, pp. 252, 263–4, 284–6, 306.
68 HRO, 23M93/86/3/32 (Jane Leigh-Perrot to James Edward Austen, 8 March 1835); Le Faye, *Chronology*, p. 394.
69 *Jane Austen's Letters*, ed. Le Faye, p. 225.
70 Le Faye, *Jane Austen: A Family Record*, p. 201.
71 BL, Add MSS 41253 A, f. 10 (Opinions of Emma, c.1816) in *Jane Austen's Fiction Manuscripts: A Digital Edition*, ed. Sutherland: https://janeausten.ac.uk/search/blopinions/10.html; HRO, 23M93/86/3/4 (Jane Leigh Perrot to James Edward Austen, 29 October 1828).
72 'The Little White Regency Dress', Jane Austen's World, 20 May 2008: https://janeaustensworld.com/2008/05/20/the-little-white-regency-dress/; *Jane Austen's Letters*, ed. Le Faye, pp. 91, 536; 'William Thorpe Holder', LBS: https://www.ucl.ac.uk/lbs/person/view/2146650123.
73 Austen, *Northanger Abbey*, ed. Davie, p.17; Austen, *Mansfield Park*, ed. Littlewood, pp. 84, 154.
74 *Jane Austen's Letters*, ed. Le Faye, p. 207; Perry, 'Austen and Empire': https://jasna.org/publications-2/persuasions/no16/perry/, pp. 96–7; Kelly, *Jane Austen the Secret Radical*, pp. 178–98; Fowler, 'Revisiting Mansfield Park'; Byrne, *Real Jane Austen*, pp. 221–3.
75 Le Faye, *Chronology*, pp. 562–3; *Jane Austen's Letters*, ed. Le Faye, pp. 351, 354.
76 Katherine Spry died at her son-in-law's London house, 10 Wimpole Street, on 8 May 1817, leaving £3,500 to her daughter Wilhelmina. TNA, PROB 11/1592/385 (Will of Katherine Spry, 24 May 1817).

77 *Austen Papers*, ed. Austen-Leigh, p. 262.
78 HRO, 23M93/86/3/4 (Jane Leigh-Perrot to James Edward Austen, 29 October 1828); Le Faye, *Chronology*, p. 663.
79 Worsley, *Jane Austen at Home*, pp. 371–2.
80 TNA, PROB 11/1591/251 (Will of James Leigh Perrot, 17 April 1817); *Jane Austen's Letters*, ed. Le Faye, pp. 354, 356; HRO, 23 M93/85/2 (Fanny Caroline Lefroy's Family History Manuscript), unpaginated.
81 Jenny kept a memorandum book (now in a private collection at Isel Hall, Cumbria), recording all her investments from April 1820 to July 1832: Le Faye, *Chronology*, pp. 607, 645. See also her discussion of her finances in *Austen Papers*, ed. Austen-Leigh, pp. 278, 281, 283.
82 The following account of Jenny's widowhood years is largely taken from her letters to James Edward Austen, HRO, 23M93/86/3/1–45 (1826–35). These are summarised in the HRO catalogue: https://calm.hants.gov.uk/Record.aspx?src=CalmView.Catalog&id=93023%2f1%2f86%2f3, and in Le Faye, *Chronology*, pp. 631–53. Some are printed in *Austen Papers*, ed. Austen-Leigh, pp. 273–92.
83 Le Faye, *Chronology*, pp. 631, 630, 648, citing HRO, 23M93/62/2 (Jane Leigh Perrot to Mary Lloyd Austen, 4 August 1826), 23M93/85/2 (Cassandra Austen to Anna Lefroy, 21 May 1826) and M93/76/1 (Augusta Smith to Augusta Wilder, 15 May 1833).
84 Le Faye, *Chronology*, p. 597; *Austen Papers*, ed. Austen-Leigh, pp. 258–63.
85 HRO, 93023, 23M93/70/3/88 (Emma Austen to Eliza Chute, 4 September 1829).
86 Day, *Sandford and Merton*, vol. 1, p. 2; Moore, *How to Create the Perfect Wife*, pp. 213–14.
87 Critics have made this parallel before, but not to the cows and the watch. Copeland, 'Sanditon and "My Aunt"'; Austen, *Sanditon*, ed. Todd, pp. 94–5, 119, 128, 130, 132.
88 She describes this to James Edward Austen in her letter of 22 December 1828 (HRO, 23M93/86/3/6).
89 TNA, PROB 11/1870/502 (Will of Jane Leigh Perrot, 9 December 1836); Le Faye, *Chronology*, pp. 654–5.
90 Austen-Leigh and Austen-Leigh, *Jane Austen, Her Life and Letters*, p. 127.

5. MARTHA BAKER (1747–1809)

1 'Vous arrivez dans un mauvais moment, chère Madame Swinburne. Vous ne me trouverez point gaie; j'ai beaucoup sur le cœur.'
2 'Je crains que dans ce moment je ne pourrai vous être d'aucune utilité; mais si les temps deviennent meilleurs, vous savez que je n'oublie jamais mes amis.' Swinburne, *Courts of Europe*, ed. White, vol. 2, p. 79; *Diary of John Baker*, ed. Yorke, p. 36.
3 Thomas, b. 1749, Robert b. 1753 and Joseph b. 1754. Three other children did not survive infancy: Robert, d. 1751; Joseph (1751–3) and Mary (b. and d. 1758). See family tree in *Diary of John Baker*, ed. Yorke.
4 *Diary of John Baker*, ed. Yorke, p. 10.
5 Zacek, *Settler Society*, pp. 257–62; *Tryal of John Barbot*, pp. 6, 9; Oliver, *Caribbeana*, vol. 6, p. 38.
6 Assembly Member for Capisterre, 1754–5, and for Nichola Town alongside John Marshall in 1754 and John Ward in 1755. He lost the Nichola Town seat in June 1756: *Diary of John Baker*, ed. Yorke, pp. 82, 88.
7 By 1729, Mary's father Thomas Ryan had a 64-acre estate in St Patrick's parish, worked by 18 enslaved people. Power, 'Irish planters', p. 50; *Diary of John Baker*, ed. Yorke, p. 11.

Notes to pages 173–9

8   Pitman, *Development of the British West Indies*, p. 77, 381; Zacek, *Settler Society*, pp. 29–31.
9   I have assumed Will stole £60 current. *Diary of John Baker*, ed. Yorke, pp. 61, 66, 72, 74, 83, 84, 85. Gerzina, *Black England*, pp. 34–5. Baker also recorded trying 'Wally's Townside and one Toby of Mr Rawlins, and Sabina, (Mr George Taylor's wife) for breaking open Mrs Sam Phillips's [blank]. Condemned Townside, Sabina his wife and Toby acquitted' in August 1767: *Diary of John Baker*, ed. Yorke, p. 188.
10 Zacek, *Settler Society*, pp. 16–19; Sheridan, 'Formation of Caribbean Plantation Society', p. 403.
11 Beckles, *Britain's Black Debt*, p. 29.
12 Dyde, *History of Antigua*, p. 27; Taylor, C., *Black Carib Wars*, pp. 33–5.
13 Beckles, *Britain's Black Debt*, p. 25; 'America and West Indies: November 1683, 16–30', CSPC, vol. 11, BHO: https://www.british-history.ac.uk/cal-state-papers/colonial/america-west-indies/vol11/pp545-557.
14 'Extracts from the Carroll Papers', *Maryland Historical Magazine*, vol. 12, 1917, p. 31; *Diary of John Baker*, ed. Yorke, pp. 24, 71, 73; Power, 'Irish Planters', p. 44.
15 *Diary of John Baker*, ed. Yorke, pp. 62, 65, 85, 86. Likely 'William Warner of Dominica', LBS: https://www.ucl.ac.uk/lbs/person/view/2146645221.
16 *Diary of John Baker*, ed. Yorke, pp. 69–70, 73, 80, 85, 90, 184.
17 *Diary of John Baker*, ed. Yorke, pp. 14, 83, 87–8, 90. Halfway Tree was a 40-acre plantation belonging to Sir Gillies Payne: 'Little Sir Gillies', LBS: https://www.ucl.ac.uk/lbs/estate/view/3437.
18 *Diary of John Baker*, ed. Yorke, p. 75; Gerzina, *Black England*, pp. 35–48.
19 Power, 'Irish Planters', pp. 51, 54, 61, 83; Power, 'Quadripartite Concern', pp. 213–28; Zacek, *Settler Society*, pp. 94–7.
20 Power, 'Irish Planters', pp. 65–6; Power, 'Beyond Kinship': www.irlandeses.org/imsla0711.htm, p. 210. For example, John Baker travelled to St Croix in October 1752, meeting Governor Heylegger and Harry Ryan. En route he saw the guns fire at St Eustacius. *Diary of John Baker*, ed. Yorke, p. 67.
21 Plessens was in Prince's Quarter, Baker owned plots 12, 21 and 20; Concordia was in Queen's Quarter, Baker owned plot 5; Beck, I.M., Map of St. Croix (1754), Library of Congress: www.loc.gov/item/74696186; Power, 'Irish Planters', pp. 68, 162.
22 Power, 'Irish Planters', p. 70.
23 William was the father of Nathaniel Wells, son of an enslaved woman named Juggy, who inherited his father's fortune, becoming a landowner in Britain and High Sheriff of Monmouthshire. 'Nathaniel Wells', LBS: https://www.ucl.ac.uk/lbs/person/view/25474.
24 *Diary of John Baker*, ed. Yorke, pp. 67, 71, 72, 74, 83, 86, 89. Bought 30 June 1755, died 16 March 1756. £50 currency was £35.70. The Liverpool ship, *Fanny*, Captain William Jenkinson: Slave Voyages, Trans-Atlantic, Voyage ID: 90534: https://www.slavevoyages.org/voyage/database.
25 Bodkin re-exported around half of these people to French St Domingue. Power, 'Irish Planters', pp. 81, 134–5; Power, 'Quadripartite Concern', pp. 217–18. Bodkin does not appear in the LBS or Slave Voyages database: www.slavevoyages.org.
26 Westergaard, 'Account of the Negro Rebellion', pp. 50–61. John Baker records 1 Danish rixdollar was worth 1s in 1760: *Diary of John Baker*, ed. Yorke, p. 140.
27 *Diary of John Baker*, ed. Yorke, pp. 63, 142; Power, 'Irish Planters', pp. 105–6.
28 *Diary of John Baker*, ed. Yorke, pp. 12, 48–50, 88, 93.
29 Ibid., pp. 201, 208, 232, 245; Gerzina, *Black England*, 48.

30 Swinburne, *Courts of Europe*, ed. White, vol. 1, p. xii; *Diary of John Baker*, ed. Yorke, pp. 101, 120, 130, 164, 238.
31 *Diary of John Baker*, ed. Yorke, pp. 24–7, 50–1, 172–9; Power, 'Irish Planters', p. 51; *Gentleman's Magazine*, vol. 94, 1824, p. 188; Angelo, *Angelo's Pic Nic*, p. 52.
32 Richard Hussey was attorney general to the Queen 1761– 70: 'Hussey, Richard', HOP: 'https://www.historyofparliamentonline.org/volume/1754-1790/member/hussey-richard-1715-70. Hoffman, *Princes of Ireland*, pp. 175–82; 'Extracts from the Carroll Papers', *Maryland Historical Magazine*, 11, 1916, pp. 344–7; 12, 1917, pp. 27, 34–6.
33 *Diary of John Baker*, ed. Yorke, pp. 27–8, 186; Swinburne, *Courts of Europe*, ed. White, vol. 1, pp. v–vii, x, 373. Thurgood, J.E., 'Swinburne, Henry', ODNB: https://doi.org/10.1093/ref:odnb/26837; French, *Art Treasures in the North*, p. 40; TNA, PROB 11/1061/231 (Will of John Baker, 16 February 1780).
34 In 1766, he visited Grove Place, St Croix (*Diary of John Baker*, ed. Yorke, p. 186) – could this have been named after his home in Southampton? Baker notes two offers to buy Concordia in his diary, from Mr Kirwan in August 1759 (p. 126) and Messrs Craven and Pentheny for £25,000 in March 1762 (p. 157). Baker no longer had a share in Concordia (plot 5) by 1766; he had sold his share of Plessens (plots 12, 21 and 20) to Cornelius Cortright by 1770. Power, 'Irish Planters', pp. 78, 162, 164–5, 174.
35 This most likely occurred during his stay on the island in 1766–7. Baker mentions 'my estate at St Christopher's' on 24 August 1777: *Diary of John Baker*, ed. Yorke, p. 345; John Estridge's will refers to land 'in possession of John Baker', recently purchased from the co-heiress of John Hutchison: TNA, PROB 11/1046/270 (Will of John Estridge, 25 October 1778); 'John Estridge of Brislington, Somerset', LBS: https://www.ucl.ac.uk/lbs/person/view/2146644201. This was 'Bakers', LBS: https://www.ucl.ac.uk/lbs/estate/view/3417.
36 There is some disagreement amongst scholars about which terms should be used to describe the peoples of St Vincent at this time. European sources tend to distinguish between 'Caribs' and 'Black Caribs', the latter being of African as well as indigenous heritage. I have chosen to follow Désha Osborne, Hilary Beckles and Melanie Newton and use the terms 'Kalinago' for the former and 'Garifuna' for the latter, as these are the preferred terms of modern descendants of these groups. Minority Rights Group International, *World Directory of Minorities and Indigenous Peoples – Belize – Garifuna (Garinagu)*, December 2017: https://www.refworld.org/docid/49749d535d.html. See also Murphy, *Creole Archipelago*, pp. 6–7, 41–42; Newton, 'Counterpoints of Conquest'; Beckles, *Britain's Black Debt*, 29–30, 33–5; Osborne, *Hiroona*, p. ix.
37 Taylor, *Black Carib Wars*, pp. 8–11; Murphy, *Creole Archipelago*, pp. 41–2.
38 Murphy, *Creole Archipelago*, pp. 97–9; Taylor, *Black Carib Wars*, pp. 52–5; Sir William Young, 1st Bart.', LBS: https://www.ucl.ac.uk/lbs/person/view/2146632173; Byres, *References to the Plan*, p. vii.
39 'John Collins of Berners Street', LBS: https://www.ucl.ac.uk/lbs/person/view/2146644943. In July 1769, Collins and Baker purchased 172 acres (likely lots 126 (111 acres), 130 (42 acres) and 19 acres of the 62-acre lot 124) from Josias Jackson, whose wife Elizabeth was the daughter of Joseph Gerald, a neighbour of John's in St Kitts. From the commissioners, they purchased twenty-seven acres in June 1771 for £432 and a further twenty-nine acres in May 1773 for £145 (likely lot 145). BL, EAP688/1/1/25 (St Vincent Deed Book 1770–6): https://eap.bl.uk/archive-file/EAP688-1-1-25, ff. 223–4; Byres, J., 'Plan of the Island of St Vincent' (1776), Library of Congress: https://www.loc.gov/item/74691678/; and the entries for St George in Byres, *References to the Plan*, p. 4. The dimensions of Baker's estate, plotted 8 January 1811: BL, EAP688/1/1/59 (St Vincent Deeds Books, 1810–12): EAP688/1/1/59, https://eap.bl.uk/archive-file/EAP688-1-1-59, ff. 143–4.

40 The estate was known as Baker's by 1795, as Dubois c.1817–1822, and as Cane Hall by 1831. Today there is a Cane Hall Road nearby: Shephard, *Historical Account of the Island of St Vincent*, p. 125; 'Cane Hall Estate', LBS: https://www.ucl.ac.uk/lbs/estate/view/3643; TNA, TS 21/90, no. 1 (Certificate of Manning and Collins relative to the Damage and intention of taxing the granted lands, 26 June 1789).

41 Murphy, *Creole Archipelago*, pp. 156–69; Taylor, *Black Carib Wars*, pp. 58–64, 76–81; Craton, *Testing the Chains*, pp. 149–50; *Scots Magazine*, vol. 34, 1772, p. 588.

42 'Chapelry of Medomsley', in Surtees, *The History and Antiquities of the County Palatine of Durham*, vol. 2, BHO: http://www.british-history.ac.uk/antiquities-durham/vol2/pp284-297.

43 Swinburne, *Courts of Europe*, ed. White, p. vii; Vindomora Solutions Heritage Support, 'Hamsterley Hall, Hamsterley, County Durham NZ 14257 55637', pp. 35, 36, 74, 77, 81: https://s3-eu-west-1.amazonaws.com/s3.spanglefish.com/s/37409/documents/hamsterley/vindomor1-158695_1.pdf.

44 *Diary of John Baker*, ed. Yorke, ix.

45 Swinburne, *Courts of Europe*, ed. White, vol. 1, pp. viii–ix.

46 *Diary of John Baker*, ed. Yorke, p. 25, citing MS note of Maria Antonia Jones (née Swinburne) of Fonmon; 'citronelle, n.', OED Online: https://www.oed.com/view/Entry/33548.

47 The paintings' current whereabouts are unknown. *Diary of John Baker*, ed. Yorke, p. 226, 237.

48 *Diary of John Baker*, ed. Yorke, pp. 192, 208; Gerzina, *Black England*, pp. 47–8. Beef was buried at the cemetery just north of the Foundling Hospital, now St George's Gardens. LMA, P82/GEO1/057 (St George's Bloomsbury, Burials, 9 January 1771).

49 *Diary of John Baker*, ed. Yorke, p. 274; Gillow and Trappes-Lomax (eds), *Diary of the 'Blue Nuns'*, pp. 168–9, 419.

50 *Diary of John Baker*, ed. Yorke, p. 216, 275, 278, 280. The busybody was Elizabeth Woodington, née Thicknesse.

51 Swinburne, *Courts of Europe*, ed. White, vol. 1, pp. 144–5.

52 Thurgood, J.E., 'Swinburne, Henry', ODNB: https://doi.org/10.1093/ref:odnb/26837; *Diary of John Baker*, ed. Yorke, pp. 31–3; Eighteenth Century Libraries Online database, *University of Liverpool*: https://c18librariesonline.org/.

53 Swinburne, *Courts of Europe*, ed. White, vol. 1, pp. xii; *Diary of John Baker*, ed. Yorke, p. 450.

54 'Este Ingles … está dotado de tal penetracion, que en dos ó tres dias de mansion en España pudo observar que todos los caminos son malos, detestables todas las posadas y fondas, que el País parece un infierno en donde reyna la estupidez &c.' Swinburne, *Courts of Europe*, ed. White, vol. 1, p. 287; Swinburne, *Travels in the Two Sicilies*, preface to the second edition (1790), p. vii; Pickford, 'Henry Swinburne's *Travels through Spain* (1779) in French and Catalan': https://www.intralinea.org/specials/article/1969.

55 Swinburne, *Courts of Europe*, ed. White, vol. 1, pp. xiii–xiv, 63, 79; Lock, *Catholicism, Identity and Politics*, pp. 59–60.

56 Swinburne, *Courts of Europe*, ed. White, vol. 1, pp. 10, 116, 182, 207, 209, 234–5, 314; *Diary of John Baker*, ed. Yorke, pp. ix, 30, 32, 410.

57 Ibid., vol. 1, 287, 345, 347, 362–4.

58 Swinburne, *Courts of Europe*, ed. White, vol. 1, pp. 213, 253, 255; *Diary of John Baker*, ed. Yorke, p. 33.

59 Murillo, *Saint Anne Teaching the Virgin to Read*, 1655, Museo Del Prado, Madrid; Swinburne, *Courts of Europe*, ed. White, vol. 1, p. 105, 235; *Diary of John Baker*, ed.

Notes to pages 191–7

60 His father Thomas Baker (1682–1748) had died 22 days before turning sixty-six. John reached his sixty-sixth birthday on 6 February 1778. *Diary of John Baker*, ed. Yorke, pp. 345, 413, 437–8.

   Yorke, pp. 29–30; Lock, *Catholicism*, p. 77; Champ, *English Pilgrimage to Rome*, p. 109.

61 Baker bought Collins's half of the estate for £4,000. *Diary of John Baker*, ed. Yorke, pp. 343, 345–7, 356–7, 392, 408, 452, 458, 460, 476; TNA, TS 21/90, no.1 (Certificate of Manning and Collins, 26 June 1789).

62 Yorke has 4,000 lbs in error: *Diary of John Baker*, ed. Yorke, p. 443. By the early 1770s, Manning sold around 20 hogsheads of Baker's sugar from St Vincent each year; some was also sent to Glasgow: pp. 220, 229, 243, 355–6, 413.

63 Slave Voyages, Trans-Atlantic: https://www.slavevoyages.org/voyage/database. While sixty-six slaving ships had transported over 12,000 captive Africans across the Atlantic to St Vincent since 1764, and a further 1,200 had arrived from other Caribbean islands, none arrived at all between 1777 and 1783.

64 His informant was Samuel Esdaile. *Diary of John Baker*, ed. Yorke, pp. 445, 460, 465, 472, 473.

65 Ibid., pp. 19, 204, 211, 214, 236–7, 239, 392; 'Thomas Baker', LBS: https://www.ucl.ac.uk/lbs/person/view/2146633730.

66 *Diary of John Baker*, ed. Yorke, pp. 220–1, 262, 267–9, 339, 343, 347, 478.

67 Ibid., pp. 20–3, 466–7, 470–2.

68 TNA, PROB 11/1061/231 (Will of John Baker, 16 February 1780); 'John Proculus Baker', LBS: https://www.ucl.ac.uk/lbs/person/view/2146645355.

69 Murphy, *Creole Archipelago*, pp. 11, 187–8; Taylor, *Black Carib Wars*, pp. 99–104.

70 TNA, TS 21/90, no. 1 (Certificate of Manning and Collins, 26 June 1789).

71 Swinburne, *Courts of Europe*, ed. White, vol. 1, p. xviii.

72 TNA, TS 21/90, no. 2 (Letters patents Concession of 1000 carreaux, 7 July 1782) and no. 4 (Agent Folliers to Martha Swinburne, undated).

73 'toute les terres incultes vagues et non concédées a l'Isle St Vincent qui n'apartiennent ni aux Caraïbes ni a aucuns particuliers'. TNA, TS 21/90, no. 5 (Grant by Louis XVI to Martha Swinburne of all unconceded land, 9 November 1782).

74 TNA, TS 21/90, no. 7 (Mr Burton's certificate of what the Duke of Manchester said, 30 June 1789).

75 TNA, TS 21/90, no. 13 (John Collins to Henry Swinburne, 29 December 1784).

76 TNA, CO 260/3 (Governor Edmund Lincoln to Lord North, 6 April 1783), TS 21/90, no. 1 (Certificate of Manning and Collins, 26 June 1789), HO 42/64/83, f. 172 (John Collins to Home Secretary Lord Pelham, 30 September 1802); *Diary of John Baker*, ed. Yorke, p. 40.

77 'Pembroke, St Vincent', LBS: https://www.ucl.ac.uk/lbs/estate/view/3651.

78 TNA, TS 21/90, no. 10 (Six valuations in St Vincent's, compiled by Governor Lincoln, undated). The six men were Lowman, Fraser, Kennedy, Ottley, Campbell and Wilkie.

79 TNA, HO 42/64/83, f. 173 (John Collins to Home Secretary Lord Pelham, 30 September 1802), TS 21/90, unnumbered (Case and Petition of Martha Swinburne, 23 October 1806); *Diary of John Baker*, ed. Yorke, p. 40–1.

80 TNA, TS 21/90, unnumbered (Henry Swinburne's 'second letter to the Solicitor General', 29 November 1789); Taylor, *Black Carib Wars*, p. 93.

81 Swinburne, *Courts of Europe*, ed. White, vol. 2, p. 54.

82 Swinburne, *Courts of Europe*, ed. White, vol. 2, pp. 78–81; *Diary of John Baker*, ed. Yorke, pp. 35–6; BL Add MS 33121, ff. 3–10, 13–14, 16 ('Political extracts from Martha

Swinburne's letters from Paris to Henry Swinburne in 1788 and 1789', made for Lord Pelham, 13 February 1809).

83 Swinburne, *Courts of Europe*, ed. White, vol. 2, p. 89; BL Add MS 33121, f. 24 ('Political extracts from Martha Swinburne's letters from Paris to Henry Swinburne in 1788 and 1789', made for Lord Pelham, 13 February 1809).
84 Schmidt, *David Hume*, p. 297; Swinburne, *Courts of Europe*, ed. White, vol. 2, p. 84.
85 TNA, TS 21/90, unnumbered (Martha Swinburne to unknown 'Sir', undated).
86 Swinburne, *Courts of Europe*, ed. White, vol. 2, pp. 89–91.
87 Ibid., vol. 2, pp. 94, 105; *Diary of John Baker*, ed. Yorke, p. 36.
88 BL Add MS 33121, f. 24 ('Political extracts from Martha Swinburne's letters from Paris to Henry Swinburne in 1788 and 1789', made for Lord Pelham, 13 February 1809); Swinburne, *Courts of Europe*, ed. White, vol. 2, pp. 91, 109.
89 CO 260/13, f. 16 (Chief Joseph Chatoyer's Declaration, 12 March 1795); Murphy, *Creole Archipelago*, pp. 217, 294, n. 87. Taylor, *Black Carib Wars*, pp. 129–136; Osborne, 'Facing Our Past: Leith Hall's Tale of Two Duels': https://www.nts.org.uk/stories/facing-our-past-leith-halls-tale-of-two-duels.
90 Shephard, *Historical Account*, p. 125; Taylor, *Black Carib Wars*, pp. 147–8; Murphy, *Creole Archipelago*, pp. 216–21.
91 Northumberland Archives, ZSW/534 (Bond between Henry Swinburne and Sir John Edward Swinburne, 19 April 1791).
92 *Diary of John Baker*, ed. Yorke, p. 47; 'Benfield, Paul', HOP: https://www.historyofparliamentonline.org/volume/1790-1820/member/benfield-paul-1741-1810; Marshall, P.J., 'Benfield, Paul', ODNB: https://doi.org/10.1093/ref:odnb/2092; 'Paul Benfield', LBS: https://www.ucl.ac.uk/lbs/person/view/2146633470; Atkinson, *Mr Atkinson's Rum Contract*, p. 239; Alger, *Napoleon's British Visitors*, pp. 34, 36, 96, 216, 235, 316.
93 Northumberland Archives, ZSW/534 (Henry Swinburne to Sir John Edward Swinburne, 10 September 1802).
94 Swinburne, *Courts of Europe*, ed. White, vol. 2, pp. 114–15, 145, 147, 152, 203.
95 Ibid., vol. 2, pp. 194, 229; Psalm 37: 35–6.
96 *Diary of John Baker*, ed. Yorke, pp. 43–4; Swinburne, *Courts of Europe*, ed. White, vol. 2, pp. 229, 300, 309, 320; Winfield, *British Warships in the Age of Sail*, p. 214.
97 Swinburne, *Courts of Europe*, ed. White, vol. 2, pp. 327, 342.
98 Ibid., vol. 2, p. 343.
99 Northumberland Archives, ZSW/534 (Henry Swinburne to Sir John Edward Swinburne, 28 June and 10 September 1802); Swinburne, *Courts of Europe*, ed. White, vol. 2, pp. 326, 353–8, 361; Candlin and Pybus, *Enterprising Women*, pp. 50–6.
100 Evans, *Slave Wales*, pp. 97, 104; BL, Add MS 33110, ff. 224r–225r (Henry Swinburne to Lord Pelham, 2nd Earl of Chichester, 8 December 1802).
101 Paton, *Cultural Politics of Obeah*, pp. 79–80.
102 Candlin, K., 'Calderon, Louisa', ODNB: https://doi.org/10.1093/odnb/9780198614128.013.90000380692.
103 Swinburne, *Courts of Europe*, ed. White, vol. 2, p. 356. See M'Callum, *Travels in Trinidad*, p. 209, for a list of punishments carried out at St Joseph.
104 Swinburne, *Courts of Europe*, ed. White, vol. 2, p. 376.
105 Ibid., vol. 2, pp. 357, 361–2, 377.
106 Ibid., vol. 2, pp. 366–7.
107 Though the convoy did stop at Bequia on the way to Roatan: Gonzales, *Sojourners of the Caribbean*, p. 39.

108 Murphy, *Creole Archipelago*, p. 226; Beckles, *Britain's Black Debt*, p. 25.
109 TNA, CO 260/17 (President Drewry Ottley to the 3rd Duke of Portland, 3 August 1801, 26 August 1801). 'Drewry Ottley of St Vincent', LBS: https://www.ucl.ac.uk/lbs/person/view/2146632338; *Diary of John Baker*, ed. Yorke, pp. 61, 86, 124, 145, 312.
110 TNA, CO 260/19 (*St Vincent Gazette and General Advertiser*, 13 July 1805, Report on Legislative Council's address to Governor George Beckwith, 10 July 1805).
111 Forte, *Arima Born*, p. 307.
112 Swinburne, *Courts of Europe*, ed. White, vol. 2, pp. 366–7; LAO, JARVIS/5/A/1/8 (Christiana Scott to George Ralph Payne Jarvis, 30 February 1798); 'Archibald Gloster', LBS: https://www.ucl.ac.uk/lbs/person/view/2146635462.
113 BL, Add MS 33110, f. 225v (Henry Swinburne to Lord Pelham, 8 December 1802), f. 230 (William John Struth to John Collins, Bristol, 9 December 1802), f. 240 (William Manning to Lord Pelham, 19 December 1802), f. 284 (Martha Swinburne to Lord Pelham, December 1802); *Diary of John Baker*, ed. Yorke, pp. 40–1; 'Sir William John Struth', LBS: https://www.ucl.ac.uk/lbs/person/view/2146636892; 'William Manning', LBS: https://www.ucl.ac.uk/lbs/person/view/-430637747.
114 *A Catalogue of the Extensive and Very Valuable Library of Henry Swinburne ... Sold by Leigh, Sotheby & Son* (1803). He had considered selling these himself before he left for Trinidad: Northumberland Archives, ZSW/534 (Henry Swinburne to Sir John Edward Swinburne, 10 September 1802).
115 BL, EAP 688/1/1/17 (St Vincent Deed Books, 1803a): https://eap.bl.uk/archive-file/EAP688-1-1-17, ff. 289–308; EAP 688/1/1/21 (St Vincent Deed Books, 1810): https://eap.bl.uk/archive-file/EAP688-1-1-21, ff. 387–90; EAP 688/1/1/59 (St Vincent Deed Books, 1810–12): EAP688/1/1/59, https://eap.bl.uk/archive-file/EAP688-1-1-59, ff. 141–50; 'George Maitland', Find a Grave: https://www.findagrave.com/memorial/262573335/george-maitland; John Wilson Carmichael took on the estate in 1810: 'John Wilson Carmichael', LBS: https://www.ucl.ac.uk/lbs/person/view/29088.
116 Swinburne, *Courts of Europe*, ed. White, vol. 2, pp. 377–9.
117 Brown, *Reaper's Garden*, pp. 132–5.
118 Swinburne, *Courts of Europe*, ed. White, vol. 2, pp. 377–8; Northumberland Archives, ZSW/534 (Henry Swinburne to Sir John Edward Swinburne, 10 September 1802).
119 *Diary of John Baker*, ed. Yorke, pp. 44–5; Swinburne, *Courts of Europe*, ed. White, vol. 2, pp. 374–5 (Swinburne mentions 'H', likely Hayes). Maria Antonia described Hayes as 'nephew to the late Sir Isaac Heard'; Charles Augustus Hayes was the nephew of Issac Heard's (1730–1822) second wife Alicia Felton, née Hayes.
120 Havard, R., 'Picton, Sir Thomas', ODNB: https://doi.org/10.1093/ref:odnb/22219; Epstein, *Scandal of Colonial Rule*, pp. 15–30; Taylor, '"Most Holy Virgin Assist Me"', pp. 75–96; Draper, *Address to the British Public*, pp. 54–5.
121 Fullarton, *Statement, Letters, and Documents*, p. 136; TNA, CO 295/17 ff. 283–4 (Martha Swinburne to Governor of Trinidad, c.1807); University of Manchester Library, GB 133 DDWF/14/23 (Sarah Wesley to Mrs Dickenson, 24 February 1809); London *Evening Standard*, 15 June 1843.
122 TNA, TS 21/90 (Various correspondence of Martha Swinburne, August 1806, decision on her Petition, 23 October 1806).
123 Courtney, W.P., 'Swinburne, Henry', *Dictionary of National Biography* (1885–1900), vol. 55, pp. 229–31; Swinburne, *Courts of Europe*, ed. White, vol. 2, p. 339.
124 *Diary of John Baker*, ed. Yorke, p. 45; TNA, PROB/11/1480/69 (Will of Thomas Swinburne, 13 May 1808). The estate was sold to the Surtees family, who had loaned Sir John Edward Swinburne the money he in turn loaned to Henry Swinburne in 1791: Northumberland

Archives, ZSW/534 (Bond between Henry Swinburne and Sir John Edward Swinburne, 19 April 1791).
125 *Diary of John Baker*, ed. Yorke, pp. 45–6; Swinburne, *Courts of Europe*, ed. White, vol. 2, pp. 306, 318; Baugh, C., 'Loutherbourg, Phillipe Jacques', ODNB: https://doi.org/10.1093/ref:odnb/17037; University of Manchester Library, GB 133 DDWF/14/23 (Sarah Wesley to Mrs Dickinson, 24 February 1809).
126 TNA, HO, 42/64/3, f. 174 (Note by Martha Swinburne, 26 September 1802).
127 *Diary of John Baker*, ed. Yorke, pp. 25, 37.

6. JANE JARVIS (1772–1796)

1 Sheridan, 'Rise', p. 345; 'Thomas Jarvis, senior', LBS: https://www.ucl.ac.uk/lbs/person/view/2146630389; 'Thibou's Estate', LBS: https://www.ucl.ac.uk/lbs/estate/view/383; Oliver, *History of the Island of Antigua*, vol. 2, pp. 96–101, vol. 3, pp. 123–8, 320–1; 'Thibou Plantation', Antigua Sugar Mills: https://sugarmills.blogs.bucknell.edu/thibou-plantation/.
2 Other neighbours included the Nibbs family, for whom George Austen had served as trustee. 'Ralph Payne, 1st Baron Lavington', LBS: https://www.ucl.ac.uk/lbs/person/view/2146631769.
3 ML, A789, f. 62 (Lachlan Macquarie to James Morley, 24 October 1796); LAO, 057, JARVIS/5/A/1/2 (Jane Macquarie to George Ralph Payne Jarvis, 4 November 1794).
4 Oliver, *History of the Island of Antigua*, vol. 2, p. 105; LAO, 057, JARVIS/5/A/1/8 (Christiana Scott to George Ralph Payne Jarvis, 30 February 1798).
5 'Archibald Gloster', LBS: https://www.ucl.ac.uk/lbs/person/view/2146635462; Parisis and Parisis, 'Le siècle du sucre', pp. 54–6; Oliver, *History of the Island of Antigua*, vol. 2, pp. 99, 104.
6 Dyde, *History of Antigua*, pp. 5–10, 21, 29, 96–7; Smollett, *Present State of All Nations*, pp. 484–5; Zacek, *Settler Society*, p. 16.
7 'John Richardson Herbert', LBS: https://www.ucl.ac.uk/lbs/person/view/2146643581; Small, 'Montpelier Estate, St John Figtree, Nevis', pp. 17–18, 27; Laughton, J.K., 'Nelson, Frances Herbert, Viscountess Nelson', rev. T. Pocock, ODNB: http://www.oxforddnb.com/view/article/19876.
8 Dyde, *History of Antigua*, p. 96; Lightfoot, *Troubling Freedom*, pp. 23, 26, 28; Dator, 'Frank Travels', pp. 342–3.
9 Gaspar, *Bondmen and Rebels*, pp. 3–64; Brown, *Tacky's Revolt*, p. 105.
10 Flannigan, *Antigua and the Antiguans*, vol. 2, p. 80.
11 Smith and Smith, *To Shoot Hard Labour*, p. 101.
12 CL, Jarvis Family Papers, Box 2, Thomas Jarvis Letterbook, f. 46 (Thomas Jarvis to Benjamin and Nathaniel Heywood, 27 May 1791).
13 Oliver, *History of the Island of Antigua*, p. 96 (Summary of Will of Thomas Jarvis, 24 March 1786); 'Thomas Oliver of Friar's Hill, Antigua', LBS: https://www.ucl.ac.uk/lbs/person/view/2146640411; Oliver's first wife was Elizabeth Vassall of Massachusetts, a relative of the family we will meet in Chapter 7. Byam Freeman chose Thomas Jarvis senior as Harriet's trustee and guardian: 'Byam Freeman', LBS: https://www.ucl.ac.uk/lbs/person/view/2146655449; TNA, PROB 11/968/280 (Will of Byam Freeman of Antigua, 21 June 1771).
14 CL, Jarvis Family Papers, Box 2, Thomas Jarvis Letterbook, f. 84 (Thomas Jarvis to Christiana Scott, 17 October 1791).

15 Ellis, *Lachlan Macquarie*, pp. 41–2; Ritchie, *Lachlan Macquarie*, p. 33; Kieza, *Macquarie*, p. 97; Digital Library of the Middle East, 'Letter from James Morley at Bushire [Bushehr], to Henry Moore at Bussora [Basra], 1768': https://dlmenetwork.org/library/catalog/81055%2Fvdc_100024189854.0x000112_dlme; LAO, 057 JARVIS/5/A/1/8 (Christiana Scott to George Ralph Payne Jarvis, 30 February 1798).
16 Thomas Jarvis wrote: 'My sister Jane gone to the East Indies': CL, Jarvis Family Papers, Box 2, Thomas Jarvis Letterbook, f. 23 (Thomas Jarvis to Benjamin and Nathaniel Heywood, 5 February 1791); *Bombay Gazette*, 22 September 1790.
17 Bulley, *Bombay Country Ships*, p. 18; Nightingale, *Trade and Empire in Western India*, p. 14; Kieza, *Macquarie*, p. 66; *Report on the Population Estimates of India (1820–1830)*, ed. D. and B. Bhattacharya, pp. 12, 130, 241.
18 Forbes, *Oriental Memoirs*, vol. 1, pp. 96, 99: CL, Jarvis Family Papers, Box 2, Thomas Jarvis Letterbook, f. 84 (Thomas Jarvis to Christiana Scott, 17 October 1791); Mackintosh, *Memoirs*, vol. 1, p. 212.
19 National Library of Australia, MS 772, ff. 1–20 (Lachlan Macquarie to Murdoch Maclaine, 1 January 1794).
20 Ellis, *Lachlan Macquarie*, pp. 43, 49; 'Monument to Lt-Col John Nugent in St Thomas's Cathedral, Bombay', Victorian Web: https://victorianweb.org/sculpture/baconsenior/7.html; Spray, 'Surveys of John McCluer', p. 247; CL, Jarvis Family Papers, Box 2, Thomas Jarvis Letterbook (1790–2), f. 100 (Thomas Jarvis to George Ralph Payne Jarvis, 16 February 1792).
21 'John Forbes of Bombay', Clan Forbes Society: https://www.clan-forbes.org/people/John-Forbes-of-Bombay; LAO, 057 JARVIS/5/A/1/8 (Christiana Scott to George Ralph Payne Jarvis, 30 February 1798), JARVIS/5/A/1/2 (Jane Macquarie to George Ralph Payne Jarvis, 4 November 1794).
22 Transcriptions of Lachlan Macquarie's Journals, nos. 1–6 (1787–1807), kept at the Mitchell Library, Sydney, (refs: A768, A769, A700) are available online through the Lachlan and Elizabeth Macquarie Archive (LEMA) Project: https://www.mq.edu.au/macquarie-archive/lema/documents.html; LEMA, Macquarie's Journal no. 2, 7 November 1792: https://www.mq.edu.au/macquarie-archive/lema/1792/1792nov.html.
23 Lachlan and a friend, Lieutenant Robert McDonald, stayed with Donald McDonald at Banks estate, St Ann, then Dr Hector McClean in St Mary. NRS, GD174/1373/1 (Lachlan Macquarie to Murdoch Maclaine, 5 March 1784), f. 2v; NLA, MS 772/1, ff.1–4 (Lachlan Macquarie to Murdoch Maclaine, 2 August 1783).
24 McLachlan, N.D., 'Lachlan Macquarie', Australian Dictionary of Biography: https://adb.anu.edu.au/biography/macquarie-lachlan-2419; Ritchie, J., Macquarie, Lachlan', ODNB: https://doi.org/10.1093/ref:odnb/17735.
25 '"The Good Old Days" I. Recollections of Macquarie', p. 6.
26 Ellis, *Lachlan Macquarie*, pp. 41–2, 544; LEMA, Macquarie's Journal no. 2, 20, 24 November 1792: https://www.mq.edu.au/macquarie-archive/lema/1792/1792nov.html, 25 and 31 December 1792: https://www.mq.edu.au/macquarie-archive/lema/1792/1792dec.html, 9 and 14 May 1793: https://www.mq.edu.au/macquarie-archive/lema/1793/1793may.html, 4 June 1793: https://www.mq.edu.au/macquarie-archive/lema/1793/1793june.html.
27 LEMA, Macquarie's Journal no. 2, 15–16 July 1793: https://www.mq.edu.au/macquarie-archive/lema/1793/1793july.html.
28 Ellis, *Lachlan Macquarie*, p. 43; Kieza, *Macquarie*, p. 101; LEMA, Macquarie's Journal no. 2, 23 April 1793: https://www.mq.edu.au/macquarie-archive/lema/1793/1793april.html, 2 August 1793: https://www.mq.edu.au/macquarie-archive/lema/1793/1793aug.html.

29 In February 1791, Thomas was unsure whether Jane had left any instructions as to whom the interest on her fortune should be paid after she left London. By May he wrote: 'my sister Jane being out of the Kingdom and under age her money cannot be paid into the hands of any other person but must remain in those of her Guardian': CL, Jarvis Family Papers, Box 2, Thomas Jarvis Letterbook (1790–2), ff. 23, 46 (Thomas Jarvis to Benjamin and Nathaniel Heywood, 5 February 1791, 27 May 1791).

30 LEMA, Macquarie's Journal no. 2–5, 7, 12, 14 August 1793: https://www.mq.edu.au/macquarie-archive/lema/1793/1793aug.html; Boswell, *Journal of a Tour to the Hebrides*, pp. 399–403.

31 LEMA, Macquarie's Journal no. 2, 2 September 1793: https://www.mq.edu.au/macquarie-archive/lema/1793/1793sept.html. In 1786, David Scott and Alexander Adamson chose to reap 9% (£540) interest in Indian investments on Charlotte Smith's £6,000 dowry, as opposed to £223 they would obtain in England: Hanser, *Mr Smith Goes to China*, p. 154.

32 LEMA, Macquarie's Journal no. 2, 8 September 1793: https://www.mq.edu.au/macquarie-archive/lema/1793/1793sept.html; James Morley's first wife (married 13 July 1775 at Surat, Gujarat) was Sarah Richardson (1756–84). She is buried in Gloucester Cathedral.

33 LEMA, Macquarie's Journal no. 1, 30 August 1788: https://www.mq.edu.au/macquarie-archive/lema/1788/1788aug.html#30.

34 TNA, PROB 11/1304/178 (Will of James Morley, 27 March 1798); Nightingale, *Trade and Empire in Western India*, p. 28; Hyam, *Empire and Sexuality*, p. 115; Hanser, *Mr Smith Goes to China*, p. 165.

35 Barczewski, *Country Houses*, p. 146.

36 ML, Z A787, f. 36 (Lachlan Macquarie to Murdoch Maclaine, 1 January 1794); LEMA, Macquarie's Journal no. 2, 8, 9, 17 September 1793: https://www.mq.edu.au/macquarie-archive/lema/1793/1793sept.html.

37 LAO, 057 JARVIS/5/A/1/8 (Christiana Scott to George Ralph Payne Jarvis, 30 February 1798); NRS, GD174/1486 (Jane Macquarie to Margaret Macquarie, 7 January 1794); Byrne, *Real Jane Austen*, pp. 29–30.

38 ML, Z A787, f. 6 (Lachlan Macquarie to Rachel Jarvis, 28 September 1793), ff. 36–7 (Lachlan Macquarie to Murdoch Maclaine, 1 January 1794), f. 83 (Lachlan Macquarie to John Abercromby, 12 January 1794); 'sonsie', *Dictionary of the Scots Language*: https://www.dsl.ac.uk/entry/snd/sonsie.

39 LEMA, Macquarie's Journal no. 2, 24 October 1793: https://www.mq.edu.au/macquarie-archive/lema/1793/1793oct.html.

40 5,200 Bombay rupees – £1 was worth 10 rupees. Hanser, *Mr Smith Goes to China*, p. 169.

41 Ellis, *Lachlan Macquarie*, p. 62.

42 LEMA, Macquarie's Journal no. 2, 6 November 1793: https://www.mq.edu.au/macquarie-archive/lema/1793/1793nov.html, 31 January 1794: https://www.mq.edu.au/macquarie-archive/lema/1794/1794jan.html.

43 LEMA, Macquarie's Journal no. 2, 22 November 1793: https://www.mq.edu.au/macquarie-archive/lema/1793/1793nov.html, 23 April 1794: https://www.mq.edu.au/macquarie-archive/lema/1794/1794april.html.

44 Ellis, *Lachlan Macquarie*, p. 57; ML, Z A787, f. 39 (Lachlan Macquarie to Murdoch Maclaine, 1 January 1794), f. 129 (Lachlan Macquarie to Dorothea Morley, 18 March 1794), Z A789, f. 94 (Lachlan Macquarie to Dorothea Morley, 24 October 1796).

45 LEMA, Macquarie's Journal no. 2, 16 March 1794: https://www.mq.edu.au/macquarie-archive/lema/1794/1794march.html#mar16.

46 LAO, JARVIS/5/A/1/8 (Christiana Scott to George Ralph Payne Jarvis, 30 February 1798).
47 LEMA, Macquarie's Journal no. 2, 16 January 1794: https://www.mq.edu.au/macquarie-archive/lema/1794/1794jan.html.
48 ML, A787, ff. 129, 156 (Lachlan Macquarie to Dorothea Morley, 18 March and 12 August 1794).
49 ML, A788, f. 119 (Lachlan Macquarie to John Tasker, 6 May 1795). Morley sailed for China on 26 June 1794, on his ship the *Sarah*, and sailed for England the following year.
50 LAO, 057, JARVIS/5/A/1/2, 3 (Jane Macquarie to George Ralph Payne Jarvis, 4 November 1794, 17 March 1795).
51 ML, A788, f. 120 (Lachlan Macquarie to John Tasker, 6 May 1795), f. 78 (Lachlan Macquarie to Murdoch Maclaine, 20 March 1795).
52 CL, Jarvis Family Papers, Box 2, Thomas Jarvis Letterbook, f. 54 (Thomas Jarvis to Jacob Jarvis of Trinidad, 30 June 1791).
53 TNA, CO 152/59 (Governor Burt to Lord Germain, 3 May 1779); Bowen, E., *Map of Antigua* (1752), Library of Congress: https://www.loc.gov/resource/g5050.ar199901/?r=0.087,0.223,0.891,0.533,0; Berland and Endfield, 'Drought and Disaster'.
54 He had given up 'Sir William Pepperill's works, Mrs. Vassall's land and Negroes and Mrs Trant's Negroes': CL, Jarvis Family Papers, Box 2, Thomas Jarvis Letterbook (1790–2), f. 46 (Thomas Jarvis to Benjamin and Nathaniel Heywood, 27 May 1791); 'Heywood Brothers and Co.', NatWest Group: https://www.natwestgroup.com/heritage/companies/heywood-brothers-and-co.html.
55 CL, Jarvis Family Papers, Box 2, Thomas Jarvis Letterbook, f. 82 (Thomas Jarvis to Rachel Jarvis, 9 October 1791).
56 Thomas had to take out a loan to pay Arthur Jarvis £1,000 in 1791 to aid his endeavours in Trinidad, but this was only a fraction of the £6,000 owed: CL, Jarvis Family Papers, Box 2, Thomas Jarvis Letterbook, ff. 57–8 (Thomas Jarvis to Arthur Jarvis, 19 and 24 July 1791). Arthur, Jacob (1752–91) and William (1756–91) had all moved to Trinidad. George Ralph Payne Jarvis was frustrated not to have funds to buy himself an army promotion: LAO, 057, JARVIS/5/A/1/5–7 (James Morley to George Ralph Payne Jarvis, 16 May 1796 and 4 October 1797, Dorothea Morley to George Ralph Payne Jarvis, 16 May 1796). He only received what was due to him after Thomas's death: CL, FP 7479 (George Ralph Payne Jarvis's receipt for legacy of his brother, 18 December 1813).
57 LAO, 057, JARVIS/5/A/1/41 (Christiana Scott to George Ralph Payne Jarvis, 18 November 1799).
58 LAO, 057, JARVIS/5/A/1/2 (Jane Macquarie to George Ralph Payne Jarvis, 4 November 1794).
59 Ellen (née Freeman) was wife of Major Marlborough Parsons Stirling (c.1755–95); Dorothea (née Bowles) was wife of Major Henry Oakes (1756–1827).
60 LEMA, Macquarie's Journal no. 2, 15–18 June 1794: https://www.mq.edu.au/macquarie-archive/lema/1794/1794june.html.
61 LAO, 057, JARVIS/5/A/1/2 (Jane Macquarie to George Ralph Payne Jarvis, 4 November 1794).
62 TNA, PROB 11/1241/157 (Will of Rachel Jarvis, 12 February 1794).
63 ML, A787, ff. 131–2 (Lachlan Macquarie to General Allan Maclean, 13 March 1794); LEMA, Macquarie's Journal no. 2, 14 August 1793: https://www.mq.edu.au/macquarie-archive/lema/1793/1793aug.html, 22 February 1794: https://www.mq.edu.au/macquarie-archive/lema/1794/1794feb.html.

64 LAO, 057, JARVIS/5/A/1/2, 3 (Jane Macquarie to George Ralph Payne Jarvis, 4 November 1794, 17 March 1795). Samuel Martin had witnessed at Dorothea's wedding: ML, A789, f. 102 (Lachlan Macquarie to James Morley, 24 October 1796); 'Samuel Martin', LBS: https://www.ucl.ac.uk/lbs/person/view/1316001327.

65 CL, Jarvis Family Papers, Box 2, Thomas Jarvis Letterbook, ff. 81–2 (Thomas Jarvis to Rachel Jarvis, 9 October 1791).

66 Dalrymple, *Anarchy*, pp. 327, 330–1.

67 LEMA, Macquarie's Journal no. 2, 17 June 1793: https://www.mq.edu.au/macquarie-archive/lema/1793/1793jun.html.

68 Oliver, *History of the Island of Antigua*, vol. 2, p. 96.

69 Carlebach *et al.* (eds), *Posen Library of Jewish Culture and Civilization*, vol. 6, p. 40.

70 LEMA, Macquarie's Journal no. 2, 24 September 1794: https://www.mq.edu.au/macquarie-archive/lema/1794/1794sept.html.

71 ML, A788, f. 26 (Lachlan Macquarie to Charles Ker, 25 January 1795).

72 ML, Z A789, f. 94 (Lachlan Macquarie to Dorothea Morley, 24 October 1796).

73 Ellis, *Lachlan Macquarie*, pp. 62–4, 70–1, 88; Kieza, *Macquarie*, p. 121; Ritchie, *Lachlan Macquarie*, p. 141; Sanghera, *Empireland*, p. 5.

74 LEMA, Macquarie's Journal no. 3, 25 January 1795: https://www.mq.edu.au/macquarie-archive/lema/1795/1795jan.html.

75 ML, A788, f. 228 (Lachlan Macquarie to Colin Anderson, 16 May 1796).

76 LAO, JARVIS/5/A/1/2, 3 (Jane Macquarie to George Ralph Payne Jarvis, 4 November 1794, 17 March 1795).

77 Adam, *Law and Custom of Slavery*, p. 128.

78 In 1781 the East India Company settlement of Bencoolen (Bengkulu today) in Sumatra held 914 slaves, of which 639 were African, 12 Malabari and the remainder from Southeast Asia: Allen, *Slavery in a Remote but Global Place*; Major, *Slavery, Abolitionism and Empire in India*, pp. 49–84.

79 The Peche family, from Guildford in Surrey, supplied three sons to the East India Company army: John, James and Onslow. Their sister Charlotte Peche married George Smith of Canton: Hanser, *Mr Smith Goes to China*, p. 58.

80 Ellis, *Lachlan Macquarie*, pp. 71–2; LEMA, Macquarie's Journal no. 3, 21, 23 July 1795: https://www.mq.edu.au/macquarie-archive/lema/1795/1795july.html, 19 August 1795: https://www.mq.edu.au/macquarie-archive/lema/1795/1795aug.html, 8, 18 September 1795: https://www.mq.edu.au/macquarie-archive/lema/1795/1795sept.html, 10, 14 November 1795: https://www.mq.edu.au/macquarie-archive/lema/1795/1795nov.html.

81 LEMA, Macquarie's Journal no. 3, 27 September 1795: https://www.mq.edu.au/macquarie-archive/lema/1795/1795sept.html, 4 October 1795: https://www.mq.edu.au/macquarie-archive/lema/1795/1795oct.html, 23, 31 December 1795: https://www.mq.edu.au/macquarie-archive/lema/1795/1795dec.html, 1, 3 January 1796: https://www.mq.edu.au/macquarie-archive/lema/1796/1796jan.html.

82 ML, Z A789, f. 103 (Lachlan Macquarie to Dorothea Morley, 24 October 1796).

83 ML, Z A789, ff. 111–12 (Lachlan Macquarie to Dorothea Morley, 24 October 1796). James Kerr had married Anne Dick on New Year's Eve 1793: LEMA, Macquarie's Journal no. 2, 6 January 1794: https://www.mq.edu.au/macquarie-archive/lema/1794/1794jan.html.

84 ML, Z A789, ff. 154–9 (Lachlan Macquarie to Marianne Clephane (née Maclean), 24 October 1796).

85 Lamas, *Everything in Style*, pp. 29–30.

86 ML, A788, ff. 217–22 (Lachlan Macquarie to Colin Anderson, 7 May 1796); LEMA, 'Tomb Inscription: Jane Macquarie (née Jarvis)': https://www.mq.edu.au/macquarie-archive/lema/1797/1797inscription.html.
87 'Captain Lestock Wilson formerly Cockburn', LBS: https://www.ucl.ac.uk/lbs/person/view/2146641001.
88 The following account of Jane's last days in Macao are largely taken from ML, Z A789, ff. 66–114 (Lachlan Macquarie to Dorothea Morley, 24 October 1796).
89 Hanser, *Mr Smith Goes to China*, pp. 60–2.
90 They had been recommended to Reid by Bombay cotton merchant Alexander Adamson. Nightingale, *Trade and Empire in Western India*, p. 25; Bulley, *Bombay Country Ships*, p. 197.
91 Coates, *Macao and the British*, pp. 71–3.
92 Greenberg, *British Trade and the Opening of China*, pp. 26–9, 115–16.
93 LEMA, 'Tomb Inscription: Jane Macquarie (née Jarvis)': https://www.mq.edu.au/macquarie-archive/lema/1797/1797inscription.html.
94 ML, A789, ff. 35–43 (Lachlan Macquarie to George Ralph Payne Jarvis, 24 August 1796), f. 118 (Lachlan Macquarie to Thomas Jarvis, 24 October 1796).
95 Marx, K., 'Revolution in China and in Europe', *New York Daily Tribune*, 14 June 1853; Amare, V., 'Blood in Her Veins: 2,000-Year-Old Mummy Looks Like She Recently Died', *Medium*, 5 November 2021: https://medium.com/lessons-from-history/blood-in-her-veins-2-000-year-old-mummy-looks-like-she-recently-died-51b92b0dff21; Scharping, N., 'The Eternal Mummy Princesses', *Discover*, 6 February 2017: https://www.discovermagazine.com/planet-earth/the-eternal-mummy-princesses.
96 Ellis, *Lachlan Macquarie*, pp. 85, 115, 139.
97 ML, A790, f. 60 (Lachlan Macquarie to Mrs Coggan, 11 February 1798), ff. 66–7 (Lachlan Macquarie to Dorothea Morley, 13 February 1798).
98 ML, A790, f. 53 (Lachlan Macquarie to George Ralph Payne Jarvis, 10 December 1797).
99 ML, A789, ff. 133–43 (Lachlan Macquarie to Charles Macquarie, 24 October 1796), ff. 164–5 (Lachlan Macquarie to James Drummond, 6 November 1796), f. 165 (Lachlan Macquarie to Alexander Duncan, 6 November 1796).
100 Hanser, *Mr Smith Goes to China*, pp. 108–19, 133.
101 'Emperor Qian Long, Letter to George III, 1793', Internet Modern History Sourcebook, Fordham University: https://origin-rh.web.fordham.edu/Halsall/mod/1793qianlong.asp.
102 Ellis, *Lachlan Macquarie*, p. 86.
103 LEMA, 'Tomb Inscription: Jane Macquarie (née Jarvis)': https://www.mq.edu.au/macquarie-archive/lema/1797/1797inscription.html.
104 At first he wanted to get the marble tombstone inscribed by the Chinese but it was not possible to get a big enough slab of marble in Macao.
105 Ellis, *Lachlan Macquarie*, p. 115.
106 LAO, 057, JARVIS/5/A/1/2 (Jane Macquarie to George Ralph Payne Jarvis, 4 November 1794); 'Oswald Wilkins and Antigua', *Woodbury Local History Society Newsletter*, 5, December 2005, pp. 1–2: http://www.woodburyhistorysociety.co.uk/uploads/5/6/3/8/56381833/newsletter_2005.pdf.
107 Ellis, *Lachlan Macquarie*, p. 88; BL, IOR, L/AG/34/29/342, f. 77 (Will of Jane Macquarie, 5 May 1795); Find My Past: https://search.findmypast.co.uk/record?id=bl%2fbind%2fl-ag-24-29%2fwill%2f58431.
108 ML, A790, f. 93 (Lachlan Macquarie to Murdoch Maclaine, 15 December 1798).
109 The legacy still hadn't reached her by 1799: ML, A790, f. 135 (Lachlan Macquarie to Dorothea Morley, 25 June 1799).
110 Ellis, *Lachlan Macquarie*, pp. 114, 139.

111 ML, A790, f. 11 (Lachlan Macquarie to Dorothea Morley, 18 September 1797).
112 Ellis, *Lachlan Macquarie*, pp. 89, 91; ML, A790, ff. 11–12, 64, 134 (Lachlan Macquarie to Dorothea Morley, 18 September 1797, 13 February 1798, 25 June 1799), f. 151 (Lachlan Macquarie to John Swinton Jarvis, 16 December 1799); Chicenska, 'Colonisin' in Reverse!', pp. 106, 126–32, 137, 139, 148, 245, 359.
113 Ritchie, *Lachlan Macquarie*, p. 43; ML, A789, ff. 105–6 (Lachlan Macquarie to Dorothea Morley, 24 October 1796); ML, A790, f. 60 (Lachlan Macquarie to Mrs Coggan, 11 February 1798); ff. 66–7 (Lachlan Macquarie to Dorothea Morley, 13 February 1798).
114 ML, A790, ff. 50–3 (Lachlan Macquarie to George Jarvis?, 18 December 1797).
115 LAO, JARVIS/A/9/30 (Papers belonging to John Swinton Jarvis of Antigua); ML, Z A790, f. 135 (Lachlan Macquarie to Dorothea Morley, 25 June 1799), f. 152 (Lachlan Macquarie to John Swinton Jarvis, 16 December 1799).
116 Hall *et al.*, *Legacies*, p. 62.
117 'George Colebrooke', LBS: https://www.ucl.ac.uk/lbs/person/view/2146640519; 'Colebrooke, George', HOP: http://www.historyofparliamentonline.org/volume/1754-1790/member/colebrooke-george-1729-1809; Harris, C.A., and L. Milne, 'Colebrooke, Sir William Macbean George', ODNB: https://doi.org/10.1093/ref:odnb/32601.
118 'Eliza Kearton Cox (née Horne)', LBS: https://www.ucl.ac.uk/lbs/person/view/2146664847.
119 Jeppesen, 'East Meets West', p. 104.
120 The total cost was £10,060. The Jarvisfield estate extended northwards from Loch Squabain along the west bank of the River Forsa to Salen and westwards to the Sound of Ulva in Kilninian and Kilmore parish. NRS, 'Plan of the Estate of Jarvisfield in the Island of Mull, the Property of Lachlan Macquarrie' (1826), Site ID: RHP3273: https://scotlandsplaces.gov.uk/record/nrs/RHP3273/plan-estate-jarvisfield-island-mull-property-lachlan-macquarrie-argyll/nrs.
121 Ellis, *Lachlan Macquarie*, p. 90.
122 LEMA, Macquarie's Journal no. 4, 7 January 1801: https://www.mq.edu.au/macquarie-archive/lema/1801/1801jan.html, no. 6, 16 July 1804: https://www.mq.edu.au/macquarie-archive/lema/1804/1804july.html.
123 LAO, 057, JARVIS/5/A/2/51 (Lachlan Macquarie to George Ralph Payne Jarvis, 17 February 1809).
124 LEMA, Elizabeth Macquarie to William and Ann Cowper, 3 November 1825 (ML C254): https://www.mq.edu.au/macquarie-archive/lema/1825/1825nov.html.
125 LEMA, Macquarie's Diary and Memorandum Book, 10 April 1816: https://www.mq.edu.au/macquarie-archive/lema/1816/1816april.html.
126 'Sydney Man Says Gluing Massacre Poster to Macquarie Statue Was Freedom of Speech', *Guardian*, 15 December 2020: https://www.theguardian.com/australia-news/2020/dec/15/sydney-man-says-gluing-massacre-poster-to-macquarie-statue-was-freedom-of-speech; Kieza, *Macquarie*, pp. 386–92; LEMA, Macquarie's Diary and Memorandum Book, 4 May 1816: https://www.mq.edu.au/macquarie-archive/lema/1816/1816may.html.
127 Bell, *Short History of Thuringowa*, p. 20.
128 LEMA, 'Mary Jarvis': https://www.mq.edu.au/macquarie-archive/lema/biographies/profiles/jarvismary.html; Walsh, R., 'Jarvis, George (1790–1825)', *Australian Dictionary of Biography*: https://adb.anu.edu.au/biography/jarvis-george-13005; Elizabeth Henrietta Macquarie Trust: https://findthatcharity.uk/orgid/GB-SC-SC015034.
129 Hall *et al.*, *Legacies*, pp. 60–4; 'Colonial Australia's Foundation is Stained with the Profits of British Slavery', *Guardian*, 21 September 2018: https://www.theguardian.com/

world/2018/sep/21/colonial-australias-foundation-is-stained-with-the-profits-of-british-slavery; Fernandes, *Island Off the Coast of Asia*, pp. 12–16.

7. ELIZABETH VASSALL (1771–1845)

1. Mrs Phillis had two surviving children, Philip, aged 16, and Richmond, aged 12 in June 1817. Might she have considered Philip, going on 17, to be old enough to fend for himself? Or had one of the boys died in the intervening eight months? TNA, 71/178 (Slave Registers, Jamaica, Westmoreland, 1817), Ancestry: https://www.ancestry.co.uk/search/collections/1129/.
2. Lewis, *Journal*, pp. 357–9 (1 March 1818).
3. No baptism record has been found, but she records her birthday in her journals. Sonia Keppel says she was born at her parents' house in Golden Square: Keppel, *Sovereign Lady*, p. 5. But the family did not move to London until she was seven years old. Other sources state birth in Jamaica, i.e. Wright, C.J., 'Fox, Elizabeth Vassall', ODNB: https://doi.org/10.1093/ref:odnb/10028; Higman, '"To Begin the World Again"', p. 291; and Higman, *Jamaica Surveyed*, p. 106. The definitive proof of her Jamaican birth is the fact that she was nursed there by Mrs Phillis's mother.
4. Keppel, *Sovereign Lady*, p. 359. Thomas Clarke died in 1777, leaving Mary £1,000. On her mother's death she would inherit a quarter of his estate. Will of Thomas Clarke, of New York City, 6 November 1776: *New Jersey Abstract of Wills*, vol. 35, p. 81, Ancestry: https://www.ancestry.co.uk/search/collections/2793/.
5. Much of the following comes from BL, Add MS 62898 (Florentius Vassall's Notes on Family History, undated) and Calder, *John Vassall*. Samuel Vassall (1586–1667) co-owned at least three slaving ships, conducting five voyages in 1648 and 1652, transporting over 500 enslaved people to Hispaniola and Barbados: Slave Voyages, Trans-Atlantic, Voyage IDs: 26255, 26256, 21879, 99023, 99024 : https://www.slavevoyages.org/voyage/database. Elizabeth was descended from Samuel's brother, William Vassall (1592–1655). Appleby, J.C., 'Vassall, Samuel', ODNB: https://doi.org/10.1093/ref:odnb/28120, and 'Vassall, John, including 'Vassall, William', ODNB: https://doi.org/10.1093/ref:odnb/28119.
6. Calder, *John Vassall*, pp. 8–9, 20–1. The Vassalls' acquisition of land 1672–1731 can be traced in JARD, St Elizabeth Land Patents, 1B/11/2/16, vol. 3, ff. 494–5, 498–502, 504–5, 507–8, 510.
7. 'Florentius Vassall', LBS: https://www.ucl.ac.uk/lbs/person/view/2146651009; 'Colonel Julines Herring', LBS: https://www.ucl.ac.uk/lbs/person/view/2146660705.
8. Phillis was forty-five years old in 1817, so born in 1772, and listed as 'Creole', meaning she was born in Jamaica: TNA, T 71/178, ff. 189–93 (Slave Registers, Jamaica, Westmoreland, 1817), Ancestry: https://www.ancestry.co.uk/search/collections/1129/. She does not appear on the return for 1820.
9. *Journal of Elizabeth Lady Holland*, ed. Ilchester, vol. 1, p. 131.
10. Burnard, *Mastery*, p. 87.
11. Ibid., pp. 3, 62, 104, 124, 156, 260–1; Hall and Thistlewood, *In Miserable Slavery*, pp. 12–14, 51, 72, 122.
12. Zoellner, *Island on Fire*, p. 23.
13. Yale University, Beinecke Library, Diaries of Thomas Thistlewood, Box 5, Folder 29 (1778), ff. 105–6: https://collections.library.yale.edu/catalog/11873957; Brown, *Reaper's Garden*, pp. 66–7, 89–91; Hall and Thistlewood, *In Miserable Slavery*, pp. 256–7; Burnard,

Mastery, p. 62 (the footnote misdates the funeral to 29 July). Florentius's body returned to England with Captain Ayton aboard the *Fort William*.

He was buried in Marylebone alongside his second wife Elizabeth. Jamaican Family Search: http://www.jamaicanfamilysearch.com/Members/bcarib49.htm.

14 TNA, PROB 11/1046/9 (Will of Florentius Vassall, 14 September 1778). Florentius's first wife Mary, daughter of 'Col. John Foster', LBS: https://www.ucl.ac.uk/lbs/person/view/2146638203, died in childbirth in Yorkshire in 1736: BL, Add MS 62898 (Florentius Vassall's Notes on Family History, undated), f. 2v; Sutton on the Forest, Burials, 30 May 1736, Borthwick Institute for Archives, Ancestry: https://www.ancestry.co.uk/search/collections/62230/records/569669. Vassall left his estates in St Elizabeth to his brother-in-law, 'Joseph Foster Barham', LBS: https://www.ucl.ac.uk/lbs/person/view/2146635192, and his Foster nephews. Dunn, *Tale*, p. 30.

15 Richard Vassall's will included a legacy to 'my mulatto servant boy Robert Loftus an annuity of 12 guineas p.a. If he should attempt to sell the annuity then I direct the sum shall cease.' TNA, PROB 11/1347/13 (Will of Richard Vassall, 19 March 1795). He may have been the son of Robert Loftus, salaried carpenter at Friendship in 1775: BL, Add MS 62898, (Florentius Vassall's Notes on Family History, undated), f. 5v. The Loftus name also appears on slave registers in the 1800s.

16 Hall and Thistlewood, *In Miserable Slavery*, p. 265; JARD, 1B/11/24/41, vol. 93, ff. 220–1 (Power of Attorney, Richard Vassall to Clement Cooke Clarke, 18 June 1785).

17 'Stephen Fuller', LBS: http://wwwdepts-live.ucl.ac.uk/lbs/person/view/2146645307; 'Rose Fuller, MP of Jamaica and Rose Hill Sussex', LBS: http://wwwdepts-live.ucl.ac.uk/lbs/person/view/2146649557. Florentius Vassall's mother Anne (née Herring) re-married Richard Mill when Florentius was still a young boy. Mill's daughter Ithamar married Rose Fuller in 1737, so was technically Florentius's adopted or stepbrother-in-law.

18 Wright, C.J., 'Fox, Elizabeth Vassall', ODNB: https://doi.org/10.1093/ref:odnb/10028. says they were living in Golden Square by 1781, but in fact Richard Vassall first appears in the Westminster Rate Books in 1779, at Golden Square East, St James, Piccadilly. Higman, '"To Begin the World Again"', p. 291, says they left Jamaica in 1786 with no references; he must have been confusing this with the date of her marriage.

19 Keppel, *Sovereign Lady*, pp. 5, 38; *Journal of Elizabeth Lady Holland*, ed. Ilchester, vol. 1, pp. 86, 158–9.

20 'Anthony Morris Storer', LBS: https://www.ucl.ac.uk/lbs/person/view/2146645281. Anthony's father Thomas Storer offered Thistlewood a job which he turned down in favour of Florentius Vassall's offer. Burnard, *Mastery*, pp. 43–4.

21 *Journal of Elizabeth Lady Holland*, ed. Ilchester, vol. 1, pp. 5–6; 'Charles Rose Ellis, Lord Seaford', LBS: https://www.ucl.ac.uk/lbs/person/view/13399; Powers, A., 'Lost at Sea', A Parcel of Ribbons, 18 February 2012: https://aparcelofribbons.co.uk/2012/02/lost-at-sea/.

22 Keppel, *Sovereign Lady*, p. 3.

23 *Journal of Elizabeth Lady Holland*, ed. Ilchester, vol. 2, p. 70.

24 Whittick, C., 'Webster family', *ODNB*: https://doi.org/10.1093/ref:odnb/74132; 'Archives of the Webster Family of Battle Abbey', TNA: https://discovery.nationalarchives.gov.uk/details/r/5c5915bf-6608-4adf-9241-b92ef59911e7; Pettigrew, *Freedom's Debt*, p. 77; 'Sir Godfrey Webster, 4th Bart.', LBS: https://www.ucl.ac.uk/lbs/person/view/2146644171; 'Seaford', HOP: http://www.historyofparliamentonline.org/volume/1754-1790/constituencies/seaford; Keppel, *Sovereign Lady*, pp. 4, 8–9.

25 It was only after her second marriage that Elizabeth's mother wrote: 'I am proud in saying I now have a Son to love and admire which is more than I could ever say, my child': Keppel, *Sovereign Lady*, p. 74.

26 My fifth great-grandfather, Robert Cooper Lee, served as a trustee to their marriage settlement.
27 Wright, C.J., 'Fox, Elizabeth Vassall', ODNB: https://doi.org/10.1093/ref:odnb/10028; Keppel, *Sovereign Lady*, p. 42; *Journal of Elizabeth Lady Holland*, ed. Ilchester, vol. 1, pp. xi–xii, 38, 107, 159; Powlett, *History of Battle Abbey*, p. 210.
28 Keppel, *Sovereign Lady*, p. 11. In order to service the debt, Richard tried to auction off 3,000 acres of land near Seven Rivers estate in St James: JARD, 1B/11/24/51 (Powers of Attorney), vol. 105, ff. 1–4 (Richard Vassall et al. to Francis Grant, 5 May 1788); 'Seven Rivers Estate', LBS: https://www.ucl.ac.uk/lbs/estate/view/2053; Somerset Heritage Centre, DD/DN/8/1/25, nos. 44, 45, 50, 51, 52, 54 (Correspondence of Rose and Stephen Fuller with Richard Vassall and Sir Godfrey Webster, 20 September to 30 October 1789).
29 They met at Masino Castle, on the road between Milan and Turin in July 1793. Swinburne, *Courts of Europe*, ed. White, vol. 2, p. 261; Keppel, *Sovereign Lady*, pp. 31, 33; *Journal of Elizabeth Lady Holland*, ed. Ilchester, vol. 1, pp. 60–2; 'Heytesbury', HOP: https://www.historyofparliamentonline.org/volume/1790-1820/constituencies/heytesbury.
30 *Journal of Elizabeth Lady Holland*, ed. Ilchester, vol. 1, p. 14; *Private Letters of Edward Gibbon*, ed. Prothero, vol. 2, p. 257.
31 Keppel, *Sovereign Lady*, p. 17; *Journal of Elizabeth Lady Holland*, ed. Ilchester, vol. 1, p. 7.
32 *Journal of Elizabeth Lady Holland*, ed. Ilchester, vol. 1, pp. 19–20, 36, 47.
33 Keppel, *Sovereign Lady*, pp. 37–40; *Journal of Elizabeth Lady Holland*, ed. Ilchester, vol. 1, pp. 59, 82, 92–5, 97.
34 Keppel, *Sovereign Lady*, pp. 42–5; *Journal of Elizabeth Lady Holland*, ed. Ilchester, vol. 1, pp. 95–100, 113–14.
35 Keppel, *Sovereign Lady*, pp. 29, 35, 38, 49, 65–6; *Journal of Elizabeth Lady Holland*, ed. Ilchester, vol. 1, pp. 53–4, 68, 72, 138, 142, 219.
36 Keppel, *Sovereign Lady*, pp. 49, 65–6. See also 'Frederick Augustus Hervey, 4th Earl of Bristol and Bishop of Derry', National Trust Collections: https://www.nationaltrustcollections.org.uk/object/851764; *Journal of Elizabeth Lady Holland*, ed. Ilchester, vol. 1, pp. 68, 72. 138, 142, 219.
37 Fisher, D., 'Pelham, Thomas, Second Earl of Chichester', ODNB: https://doi.org/10.1093/ref:odnb/21799.
38 Keppel, *Sovereign Lady*, pp. 16, 51–2, 56, 64–5; *Elizabeth, Lady Holland to Her Son*, ed. Ilchester, p. 43; BL, Add MS 51809, f. 64 (Elizabeth Holland to Thomas Chaplin, ? October 1797); Hanley-Smith, 'Gossip and Sexual Transgression', p. 69.
39 *Journal of Elizabeth Lady Holland*, ed. Ilchester, vol. 1, pp. 13–14, 35, 40, 61, 86, 97.
40 Suggested by Whittick, C., 'Webster Family', ODNB: https://doi.org/10.1093/ref:odnb/74132. Elizabeth first met Spencer on 21 July 1792; Henry was born 29 weeks later, on 10 February 1793.
41 *Journal of Elizabeth Lady Holland*, ed. Ilchester, vol. 1, pp. 116–17, 121, 125; 'Fox, Hon. Charles James', HOP: https://www.historyofparliamentonline.org/volume/1754-1790/member/fox-hon-charles-james-1749-1806.
42 *Journal of Elizabeth Lady Holland*, ed. Ilchester, vol. 1, pp. 208, 226.
43 Williams, *Capitalism and Slavery*, p. 91; *Memorials and Correspondence of Charles James Fox*, ed. Lord John Russell, vol. 1, pp. 93–4; Lockhart, *Life of Sir Walter Scott*, vol. 7, p. 105 (Diary entry, 9 May 1828); *Female Artifice; or, Charles F-x Outwitted*; 'An Heroic and Elegiac Epistle from Mrs. Grieve, in Newgate, to Mr. C- F-', *Westminster Magazine*, March 1774; Life, P., 'Grieve, Elizabeth Harriet', ODNB : https://doi.org/10.1093/ref:odnb/65504; Cohen, 'Foote, Fox, and the Mysterious Mrs Grieve, pp. 41–63.

44 *Journal of Elizabeth Lady Holland*, ed. Ilchester, vol. 1, pp. 116–17, 121.
45 Ibid., pp. 14–15, 53, 69, 85, 114.
46 Ibid., pp. 144, 131; Keppel, *Sovereign Lady*, p. 63.
47 JARD, 1B/11/24/69 (Powers of Attorney), vol. 123, ff. 138–9 (Godfrey Webster to Robert Peart et al., 4 July 1795); 'Henry Waite Plummer', LBS: https://www.ucl.ac.uk/lbs/person/view/24366; 'Thomas Plummer', LBS: https://www.ucl.ac.uk/lbs/person/view/2146637244.
48 TNA, PROB 11/1258/183 (Will of Richard Vassall, 19 March 1795); JARD, 1B/11/3/87 (Probate Inventories), vol. 87, ff. 200–1 (Richard Vassall Probate Inventory, 14 November 1797).
49 Barczewski, *Country Houses*, p. 106; 'Up and down the Kennebec Valley: Augusta & Vassalboro', *Town Line*, 25 March 2020: https://townline.org/up-and-down-the-kennebec-valley-augusta-vassalboro/; New York Public Library, 'Kennebeck Purchase Company Records, 1754–1756', Plymouth Company (1749–1816), MSS Col 22731: https://archives.nypl.org/mss/22731.
50 *Journal of Elizabeth Lady Holland*, ed. Ilchester, vol. 1, pp. 263–4; Keppel, *Sovereign Lady*, p. 67; BL, Add MS 51809, ff. 106–7 (Lady Holland's account of the story, undated, ?1801) – transcribed in *Spanish Journal of Elizabeth Lady Holland*, ed. Ilchester, pp. viii–x; Bury, *Diary*, vol. 1, pp. 179–80; *Leaves from the Note-Books of Lady Dorothy Nevill*, ed. Nevill, p. 61.
51 Rubenhold, *Lady Worsley's Whim*, p. 248.
52 Austen, *Pride and Prejudice*, ed. Kinsley, p. 219.
53 Much of the following account is draw from Keppel, *Sovereign Lady*, pp. 69–74.
54 BL, Add MS 51809, ff. 15, 18 (Lord Holland's notes on Sir Godfrey's conduct, sometime after November 1796).
55 Keppel, *Sovereign Lady*, p. 313.
56 Divorce Act: Vassall 1797 37 Geo 3 c 132; *Journals of the House of Commons*, vol. 52 (1803), pp. 648, 651, 670–1, 698; *Journal of Elizabeth Lady Holland*, ed. Ilchester, vol. 1, p. 147.
57 BL, Add MS 51809, f. 64 (Elizabeth Holland to Thomas Chaplin, October 1797).
58 Sir Godfrey was granted a 99-year lease for a token 10 shillings; he should pay £800 annual rent directly into Henry's account at Coutts. IRO, Deeds, vol. 445, ff. 214–215 (Elizabeth Vassall to Sir Godfrey Webster, 5 July 1797); BL, MS 51819 f. 1 (Lady Holland to Messrs Plummer and Barham, 20 December 1797).
59 Wolfram, 'Divorce', p. 169; *Journal of Elizabeth Lady Holland*, ed. Ilchester, vol. 1, pp. 147–8, 159, 183; Keppel, *Sovereign Lady*, pp. 73–4.
60 *Gentleman's Magazine*, vol. 14 (July to December 1840), p. 653; Anon., 'Winterslow House Burned', pp. 347–8; Keppel, *Sovereign Lady*, p. 72; Wright, C.J., 'Fox [afterwards Vassall], Henry Richard, Third Baron Holland', ODNB: https://doi.org/10.1093/ref:odnb/10035.
61 *Journal of Elizabeth Lady Holland*, ed. Ilchester, vol. 1, pp. 227, 257; BL, Add MS 51950 (Lady Holland's Dinner Books, 1799–1845); 'Dined: A Dinner Book Database', QMUL: https://dined.qmul.ac.uk/pages/index.html; Kelly, *Holland House*, p. 71; Keppel, *Sovereign Lady*, p. 99.
62 Elizabeth's great-great-grandmother Anna had been a Lewis. *Letters of Lord Granville Leveson Gower*, ed. Granville, vol. 2, p. 397; *Journal of Elizabeth Lady Holland*, ed. Ilchester, vol. 1, pp. 167, 216, 230; vol. 2, pp. 39, 54, 87–8.
63 *Journal of Elizabeth Lady Holland*, ed. Ilchester, vol. 1, pp. 232. Fuller owned two Jamaican estates, which along with the family's Sussex gun foundry made him hugely wealthy.

Elizabeth may have got to know him in Sussex; his home, Rose Hill, Brightling, was some six miles to the north-west of Battle Abbey. 'John Fuller "Mad Jack"', LBS: https://www.ucl.ac.uk/lbs/person/view/-1047169191.

64 'Plummer, Thomas William', HOP: https://www.historyofparliamentonline.org/volume/1790-1820/member/plummer-thomas-william-1817.

65 BL, Add MS, 51813, f. 3 (James Scarlett to Lord Holland, 2 October 1801).

66 *Letters of Lord Granville Leveson Gower*, ed. Granville, vol. 2, p. 381; *Journal of Elizabeth Lady Holland*, ed. Ilchester, vol. 1, pp. 170, 183, 248, 265.

67 *Journal of Elizabeth Lady Holland*, ed. Ilchester, vol. 1, pp. 250, 253, 259; Kelly, *Holland House*, p. 43.

68 *Journal of Elizabeth Lady Holland*, ed. Ilchester, vol. 1, pp. 273–4.

69 Kelly, *Holland House*, pp. 51–2.

70 Contribution of Mr. T.W. Plummer, 'Slave Trade Abolition Bill' debated Commons 16 March 1807, Hansard, vol. 9, column 135: https://hansard.parliament.uk/commons/1807-03-16/debates/88131361-39f2-4d9f-9f44-d24c84b2c927/SlaveTradeAbolitionBill#contribution-e7059c57-7b80-403e-a689-5897924796ab.

71 *Journal of Elizabeth Lady Holland*, ed. Ilchester, vol. 2, p. 38: 'James Scarlett, 1st Baron Abinger', LBS: https://www.ucl.ac.uk/lbs/person/view/14399; 'Scarlett, James', HOP: https://www.historyofparliamentonline.org/volume/1790-1820/member/scarlett-james-1769-1844.

72 *Journal of Elizabeth Lady Holland*, ed. Ilchester, vol. 1, pp. 262–4, 266.

73 Most of the following section is taken from *Journal of Elizabeth Lady Holland*, ed. Ilchester, vol. 2, pp. 90–93, 97–8. See also Sussex Record Office, BAT/6/4/6/4880 for a newspaper clipping reporting the suicide.

74 Bury, *Diary*, vol. 1, 179–80.

75 *Journal of Elizabeth Lady Holland*, ed. Ilchester, vol. 1, p. 237; Keppel, *Sovereign Lady*, p. 110.

76 *Journal of Elizabeth Lady Holland*, ed. Ilchester, vol. 2, pp. 125, 134–5.

77 Chancellor, 'Slave-Owner and Anti-Slaver', p. 263; 'Lords Chamber', 24 June 1806, Hansard: https://hansard.parliament.uk/Lords/1806-06-24/debates/3848fd54-27cc-402e-b856-f10cddeb621a/AbolitionOfTheSlaveTradehighlight=slave#contribution-64cf831f-c702-415c-8f1a-454a95498b20; 'Slave Trade Abolition Bill', 5 February 1807, Hansard: https://hansard.parliament.uk/Lords/1807-02-05/debates/33ed0d6f-cf5f-4908-b76c-4168215006b8/SlaveTradeAbolitionBill.

78 *Journal of Elizabeth Lady Holland*, ed. Ilchester, vol. 1, pp. 259, 271, 275.

79 TNA, 71/178, ff. 189–93 (Slave Registers, Jamaica, Westmoreland, 1817), Ancestry: https://www.ancestry.co.uk/search/collections/1129/; TNA, PROB 11/1360/336 (Will of Richard Gittoes, 30 July 1801). The Gittoes family appear in Florentius Vassall's notes on family history (BL, Add MS 62898, f. 2v) and received legacies in Richard Vassall's will. Scarlett's letter has the figures in currency: investment of £10,000 (£7,142 sterling) and price of £5,560 (£3,971 sterling): BL, Add MSS 51819, ff. 2–5 (Robert Scarlett to Lord Holland, 6 April 1802; Higman, *Jamaica Surveyed*, p. 105; 'Robert Scarlett', LBS: https://www.ucl.ac.uk/lbs/person/view/2146644321; 'Lindo and Lake', LBS: https://www.ucl.ac.uk/lbs/firm/view/2144929155; JARD, 1B/11/3/98, ff. 51–5 (Sir Godfrey Webster Probate Inventory, 12 June 1801); TNA, 71/178, ff. 189–93, 180, ff. 8, 11–13 (Slave Registers, Jamaica, Westmoreland, 1817 and 1823), Ancestry: https://www.ancestry.co.uk/search/collections/1129/.

80 Macdonald, *Monk Lewis*, p. 52; BL, Add MS 51641, f. 98 (Monk Lewis to Lord Holland, undated 'Saturday', ?1 March 1806 or later).

81 'Slave Trade Abolition Bill', 5 February 1807, Hansard: https://hansard.parliament. uk/Lords/1807-02-05/debates/33edod6f-cf5f-4908-b76c-4168215006b8/SlaveTrade AbolitionBill; Schwarz, 'Royal Attitudes', pp. 497–527.
82 *Journal of Elizabeth Lady Holland*, ed. Ilchester, vol. 2, pp. 9, 205; Bew, *Castlereagh*, p. 220; 'George Rose', LBS: https://www.ucl.ac.uk/lbs/person/view/2146631262.
83 Twenty-seven-year-old Jellico had four children: Jack (10), Elsey (8), Bella (7) and Hall (4). Beck (25) had a four-year-old, John. TNA, 71/179, ff. 1–5 (Slave Registers, Jamaica, Westmoreland, 1820), Ancestry: https://www.ancestry.co.uk/search/collections/1129/; BL, Add MS 51819, f. 11 (Michael Cuff to Lord Holland, 5 June 1818); 'Michael Cuff', LBS: https://www.ucl.ac.uk/lbs/person/view/2146630743. I have assumed the £600 Cuff's letter mentions was currency and converted to sterling.
84 Kelly, *Holland House*, p. 43; *Spanish Journal of Elizabeth Lady Holland*, ed. Ilchester, p. 317.
85 Keppel, *Sovereign Lady*, p. 183; *Letters of Lord Granville Leveson Gower*, ed. Granville, vol. 2, p. 381.
86 Bury, S.J., and A.W. Mellon, 'British Visual Satire, 18th–20th Centuries', *Oxford Art Online*: https://www.oxfordartonline.com/page/1632.
87 Samuel De Wilde, *Miller's Asses*, 1 September 1808, British Museum: https://www.britishmuseum.org/collection/object/P_1867-0112-10; William Henry Brooke, *The Anti Royal-Menagerie*, 1 December 1812, British Museum: https://www.britishmuseum.org/collection/object/P_1868-0808-12683.
88 Samuel De Wilde, *Sketch for a Prime Minister or How to Purchase a Peace*, 1 February 1811, British Museum: https://www.britishmuseum.org/collection/object/P_1868-0822-7176.
89 Schmid, *British Literary Salons*, p. 77.
90 Keppel, *Sovereign Lady*, p. 238.
91 Lamb, *Glenarvon*, vol. 1, pp. 250–2; Keppel, *Sovereign Lady*, pp. 198–200; *Creevey Papers*, ed. Maxwell, vol. 1, p. 255.
92 *Journal of Elizabeth Lady Holland*, ed. Ilchester, vol. 1, p. 200.
93 Keppel, *Sovereign Lady*, p. 120.
94 *Journal of Elizabeth Lady Holland*, ed. Ilchester, vol. 2, p. 101.
95 MacDonogh, K., 'A Sympathetic Ear: Napoleon, Elba and the British', *History Today*, 44:2, 1994, pp. 29–35.
96 Keppel, *Sovereign Lady*, pp. 224–6; *Foreign Reminiscences, by Henry Richard Lord Holland*, ed. Holland, pp. 196–7. The firm was now headed by John Plummer, following his brother Thomas William's death in 1817. 'John Plummer', LBS: https://www.ucl.ac.uk/lbs/person/view/23815.
97 Keppel, *Sovereign Lady*, pp. 216–19.
98 Kelly, *Holland House*, p. 115.
99 'Gold snuff-box; cameo', made in Paris by Adrien Jean Maximilien Vachette, c.1797–1809, British Museum: https://www.britishmuseum.org/collection/object/H_1846-0124-1.
100 'Case inset with a lock of hair, purportedly Napoleon's', Lot 207, Christie's Napoleonica auction, 19 May 1998: https://www.christies.com/lot/a-presentation-case-inset-with-a-lock-917099/?intObjectID=917099&lid=1; Semmel, 'Reading the Tangible Past', p. 25, n. 88; 'Key to Room where Napoleon Died Found in Scotland', BBC News, 11 January 2021: https://www.bbc.co.uk/news/uk-scotland-edinburgh-east-fife-55618318 Keppel, *Sovereign Lady*, pp. 210, 214.
101 BL, Add MS 51641, ff. 149–54 (Monk Lewis to Lord Holland, 21 October 1815, 3 November 1815, and undated).
102 Lewis, *Journal*, pp. 115–18 (19 January 1816); 'Matthew Parkinson', LBS: https://www.ucl.ac.uk/lbs/person/view/2146634974.

103 There were two women named Nelly at Friendship in 1817. Due to her seniority, Big Nelly is more likely to have been the one who visited Lewis than Little Nelly, aged forty-three, with two daughters. For more on adoption, see Vasconcellos, *Slavery, Childhood and Abolition*, p. 27; and Turner, *Contested Bodies*, pp. 103–5.
104 Bush, 'African Caribbean Slave Mothers and Children'.
105 On the register of enslaved people dated 20 June 1817, seven months and three weeks before Lewis met the mothers on 3 February 1818, the babies listed on the estate who were between ten and fourteen months were: Boys: Sandy, eleven months, son of Candace (daughter of Fidelia), aged twenty-seven, with two children). Toby, one, son of Little Whanica, aged twenty-three. Girls: Eliza, aged one, daughter of Hagar (daughter of Fidelia), aged thirty-three, with four children, Sally, aged one, daughter of Farina, aged thirty-two, with four children, Pussey, aged eleven months, daughter of African-born Elizabeth, aged thirty-four, with two children. TNA, 71/178, ff. 189–193 (Slave Registers, Jamaica, Westmoreland, 1817), Ancestry: https://www.ancestry.co.uk/search/collections/1129/.
106 Dadzie, *Kick in the Belly*, pp. 141–2, 150–2; Turner, *Contested Bodies*, pp. 189–201.
107 Lewis, *Journal*, p. 144 (28 January 1816), p. 156 (31 January 1816), pp. 180–1 (21 February 1816), pp. 328–9 (1 February 1818), pp. 331–2 (3 February 1818).
108 Leask, N., 'Lewis, Matthew Gregory [Called Monk Lewis]', ODNB: https://doi.org/10.1093/ref:odnb/16597; Peck, *Life of Matthew G. Lewis*, p. 158; Macdonald, *Monk Lewis*, p. 58.
109 BL, Add MS 51820, ff. 65–6 (Lord Holland to Henry Waite Plummer, 28 October 1817); Chancellor, 'Slave-Owner and Anti-Slaver', p. 266.
110 JARD, 2/7/1/1 (Friendship and Greenwich in Westmoreland Tax Rolls, 1801–4); 'Friendship and Greenwich', LBS: https://www.ucl.ac.uk/lbs/estate/view/8352; Dunn, *Tale*, p. 424.
111 TNA, T 71/178, ff. 189–93, T 71/180, ff. 8, 11–13 (Slave Registers, Jamaica, Westmoreland, 1817 and 1823), Ancestry: https://www.ancestry.co.uk/search/collections/1129/. A Bacchus was amongst the men Sir Godfrey Webster bought from Lindo and Lake – valued at £140 currency (£100 sterling).
112 BL, Add MS 51820, ff. 65–6 (Lord Holland to Henry Waite Plummer, 28 October 1817).
113 Lewis, *Journal*, p. 82 (8 January 1816), p. 123 (21 January 1816).
114 By 1823, the pair had become John Wellington and Peggy Gittoes: TNA, 71/179, ff. 1–5, 180, ff. 8, 11–13 (Slave Registers, Jamaica, Westmoreland, 1820 and 1823), Ancestry: https://www.ancestry.co.uk/search/collections/1129/.
115 Dunn, *Tale*, pp. 257–60. Dunn (ibid., p. 256), mistakenly cites Lewis's visit to Grunder as occurring in 1806, when the minister was Joseph Jackson; Lewis, *Journal*, pp. 183–5 (22 February 1816).
116 Bleby, *Death Struggles of Slavery*, p. 116; Zoellner, *Island on Fire*, pp. 26–7, 80–2.
117 *Elizabeth, Lady Holland to Her Son*, ed. Ilchester, p. 108. Other prominent group members included the Hollands' friends Henry Brougham (an MP and lawyer who had recently represented Queen Caroline in her divorce from George IV), and Dr Stephen Lushington, whose brother Henry had married Monk Lewis's sister in 1799, later inheriting part of Hordley estate in St Thomas in the East. 'Frances Maria Lushington (née Lewis)', LBS: https://www.ucl.ac.uk/lbs/person/view/14328.
118 Dresser, 'Set in Stone?', p. 196 n. 51.
119 *Correspondence of William Wilberforce*, ed. Wilberforce and Wilberforce, vol. 1, pp. 326–7 (25 February 1823); Chancellor, 'Slave-Owner and Anti-Slaver', p. 266.
120 *Life of William Wilberforce*, ed. Wilberforce and Wilberforce, vol. 5, p. 26 (Diary, 17 May 1819).

121 *Journal of Elizabeth Lady Holland*, ed. Ilchester, vol. 1, p. 121; Keppel, *Sovereign Lady*, p. 48.
122 By contrast, newer endeavours in Trinidad and British Guiana had returns of 13.3%: Ward, 'Profitability', p. 207.
123 *Elizabeth, Lady Holland to Her Son*, ed. Ilchester, p. 2.
124 Kelly, *Holland House*, p. 149; Wright, C.J., 'Fox [*afterwards* Vassall], Henry Richard, third Baron Holland', ODNB: https://doi.org/10.1093/ref:odnb/10035.
125 BL, Add MS 51767, ff. 119–20 (Lady Holland to Henry Fox, 5 February 1828). The Plummer and Barham 'Vassall mortgage' was £4,000; another due to 'Lady Affleck (Elizabeth's mother) as claimant upon my father' was £2,000.
126 'Brixton: Lambeth Wick estate', in *Survey of London: Volume 26, Lambeth: Southern Area*, ed. Sheppard: British History Online: http://www.british-history.ac.uk/survey-london/vol26/pp108-122.
127 Keppel, *Sovereign Lady*, p. 189.
128 Lord Holland attended two WIC meetings between 1807 and 1815: Ryden, 'Sugar, Spirits, and Fodder', p. 60, n. 16.
129 They also showed them to Lord Liverpool and Colonial Secretary Earl Bathurst. Taylor, *Interest*, p. 164; Osborne, 'Power and Persuasion', pp. 220–3; Chancellor, 'Slave-Owner and Anti-Slaver', p. 266.
130 Like Lord Holland, he had performed a volte-face: Elizabeth recorded his 'great satisfaction at acting in concert with Ld H. about the Slave Trade' back in 1799. *Journal of Elizabeth Lady Holland*, ed. Ilchester, vol. 1, p. 259.
131 Taylor, *Interest*, pp. 61–5.
132 Weaver-Paul, A., 'An Anti-Slavery Sugar Bowl', V&A, 28 June 2024: https://www.vam.ac.uk/blog/museum-life/an-anti-slavery-sugar-bowl; Everill, *Not Made by Slaves*; Bosma, 'East Indian Sugar'.
133 Heyrick, *Immediate not Gradual Abolition*, p. 20; Taylor, *Interest*, p. 48. On the division between Sturge and Buxton, see Coleman, N.A.T., 'Britain's #BLM Statue, Episode 2: Back to Plaque?' (September 2021–January 2022): https://henry-moore.org/discover-and-research/sculpture-research-programme/research-seasons/monuments/#britain-s-blm-statue.
134 Taylor, *Interest*, p. 98.
135 Kelly, *Holland House*, pp. 156–7.
136 Keppel, *Sovereign Lady*, pp. 12–313, 279; T.B. Macaulay to Hannah and Margaret Macaulay, 14 August 1832 in *Life and Letters of Lord Macaulay*, ed. Trevelyan, vol. 1, p. 241.
137 Bury and Mellon, 'British Visual Satire'.
138 John 'H.B.' Doyle, 'Sampson and Dalilah', 27 November 1830, British Museum: https://www.britishmuseum.org/collection/object/P_1857-1222-32.
139 *Elizabeth, Lady Holland to Her Son*, ed. Ilchester, p. 108.
140 Kelly, *Holland House*, pp. 186–7.
141 Taylor, *Interest*, p. 187.
142 *Holland House Diaries*, ed. Kriegel, pp. 55–6, 60, 91; BL, Add MS 51820 (William Wilberforce to Lord Holland, 12 October 1830), f. 40v.
143 *Holland House Diaries*, ed. Kriegel, p. 136.
144 Sturge and Harvey, *West Indies in 1837*, Appendix, Section IV Statements of Apprentices, lix.
145 Zoellner, *Island on Fire*, pp. 85, 112, Taylor, *Interest*, pp. 198–214; Holt, *Problem*, pp. 13–16.

146 *Holland House Diaries*, ed. Kriegel, pp. 137, 142.
147 BL, Add MS 51820, f. 96 (John Foster Barham to Lady Holland, 31 May ?1832); 'John Foster Barham', LBS: https://www.ucl.ac.uk/lbs/person/view/17690.
148 Taylor, *Interest*, p. 217; *Holland House Diaries*, ed. Kriegel, pp. 136–7, 150–1.
149 *Elizabeth, Lady Holland to Her Son*, ed. Ilchester, p. 129. Mulgrave was known as Viscount Normanby until his father's death in 1831; that is the name he mostly appears under in the Holland papers.
150 *Holland House Diaries*, ed. Kriegel, pp. 140, 175–6.
151 Zoellner, *Island on Fire*, p. 207.
152 BL, Add MS 51820, f. 96 (John Foster Barham to Lady Holland, 31 May ?1832).
153 Seventeen adults died at Sweet River and Friendship & Greenwich between 1829 and 1832; doubtless some were killed during the conflict. TNA, 71/189, ff. 246–8 (Slave Registers, Jamaica, Westmoreland, 1832), Ancestry: https://www.ancestry.co.uk/search/collections/1129/; TNA, CO 137/185, f. 583 ('Slave Rebellion Trials', 1832).
154 BL, Add MS 51820, ff. 97–8 (James Lawson to Lord Holland, 5 August 1832). James Lawson had replaced Henry Waite Plummer by 1829. 'James Lawson', LBS: https://www.ucl.ac.uk/lbs/person/view/2146634986. Richard Vassall had written to Lord Holland in 1822 re: execution of Duncan alias William Dehany: BL, Add MS 51819, ff. 13–14 (Richard Vassall to Lord Holland, 14 May 1822).
155 BL, Add MS 51816 (Thomas McNeil to Lord Holland, 17 August 1832); Sturge and Harvey, *West Indies in 1837*, p. 241; Zoellner, *Island on Fire*, pp. 179–85; 'Thomas McNeel', LBS: https://www.ucl.ac.uk/lbs/person/view/24180.
156 *Holland House Diaries*, ed. Kriegel, pp. 140, 212–13; Chancellor, 'Slave-Owner and Anti-Slaver', p. 269; 'Henry Edward Sharpe', LBS: https://www.ucl.ac.uk/lbs/person/view/10994.
157 The 'caricature' was John 'H.B.' Doyle's 'Sleeping Partners in a Doubtful Concern', National Portrait Gallery: https://www.npg.org.uk/collections/search/portrait/mw211185/Sleeping-Partners-in-a-Doubtful-Concern. Though Elizabeth had dined with her sister-in-law Caroline Fox that night, Earl Grey, Lord Melbourne and Lord John Russell slept at Holland House, so could regale her in the morning with their escapades. *Holland House Diaries*, ed. Kriegel, p. 213. The dinner appears in BL, Add MS 51955, f. 45v (Lady Holland's Dinner Party Books, 1831–9).
158 Stanford-Xosei, 'Long Road', p. 184.
159 *Holland House Diaries*, ed. Kriegel, pp. 218–19; Taylor, *Interest*, p. 266.
160 Extract from Sir Hilary Beckles' speech to House of Commons, 16 July 2014; 'Reparations for Native Genocide and Slavery', CARICOM, 13 October 2015: https://caricom.org/reparations-for-native-genocide-and-slavery/.
161 Whittick, C., 'Webster Family', ODNB: https://doi.org/10.1093/ref:odnb/74132; 'Archives of the Webster Family of Battle Abbey', TNA: https://discovery.nationalarchives.gov.uk/details/r/5c5915bf-6608-4adf-9241-b92ef59911e7; 'Webster, Sir Godfrey, 5th Bt.', HOP: http://www.histparl.ac.uk/volume/1790-1820/member/webster-sir-godfrey-1789-1836; Barczewski, *Country Houses*, p. 106–7.
162 This Sir Godfrey Vassall Webster, 6th Baronet, married Jamaican heiress Sarah Joanna Ashburnam – who had a fortune of over £30,000 – in 1851; my third great-granduncle, Robert Cooper Lee Bevan, was one of the trustees of their marriage settlement. 'Sarah Joanna Ashburnham later Webster (née Murray)', LBS: https://www.ucl.ac.uk/lbs/person/view/2146653877.
163 'Jamaica Westmoreland 27' (Sweet River Pen [includes Friendship]), LBS: https://www.ucl.ac.uk/lbs/claim/view/22693; Keppel, *Sovereign Lady*, p. 299.

164 Sturge and Harvey, *West Indies in 1837*, p. 244.
165 Heuman, 'Apprenticeship System', pp. 233, 246.
166 Lord Holland secured positions in Jamaica for stipendiary magistrates Edward Baynes and Stephen Bourne (Elizabeth helped his son). Their extended correspondence from 1834–8 is in BL, Add MS 51817. He also set up George Ross in Guyana (see BL, Add MS 51819, ff. 50, 63, 67–8, 74–86). Chancellor, 'Slave-Owner and Anti-Slaver', p. 272; Griffith-Hughes, 'Mighty Experiment', pp. 72, 103–4; BL, Add MS 51817 (Stephen Bourne Jnr. to Lady Holland, 7 October 1838).
167 *Holland House Diaries*, ed. Kriegel, pp. 307, 310.
168 Taylor, *Interest*, p. 289; Sturge and Harvey, *West Indies in 1837*, p. vi.
169 BL, Add MS, 51818, ff. 48–9 (Lord Seaford to Lord Holland, 2 September 1833); Higman, '"To Begin the World Again"', p. 296.
170 Elizabeth was the daughter of Chief Justice Dennis Kelly, also the 'natural' father of my fifth-great-grandmother Priscilla Kelly, a woman of colour who married Robert Cooper Lee. Chambers, *Great Leviathan*, p. 306.
171 Vassall arrived in February 1837, and visited Sweet River before 8 March, and Friendship and Greenwich sometime between 8 March and his departure in June. BL, Add MS 51819, ff. 40–3 (Spencer Lambert Hunter Vassall to Lord Holland, 8 March and 11 August 1837).
172 Sturge and Harvey visited both estates on 10 March 1837. Higman, '"To Begin the World Again"', p. 304.
173 The Holland estates are described in Sturge and Harvey, *West Indies in 1837*, pp. 242–4, and Appendix Section IV, Statements of Apprentices, lviii–lix.
174 The following year, stipendiary magistrate Stephen Bourne met an old woman in the head ploughman's house who could remember Elizabeth's mother, Mary Vassall, 'and spoke very kindly about her'. BL, Add MS 51817, f. 144v (Stephen Bourne to Lord Holland, 13 October 1838).
175 BL, Add MS 51817, f. 145v (Stephen Bourne to Lord Holland, 13 October 1838); John 'H.B.' Doyle, 'Drawing for the Twelfth Cake: A Hint to Cabinet Makers', 21 December 1830, National Portrait Gallery: https://www.npg.org.uk/collections/search/portrait/mw205890/Drawing-for-the-Twelfth-Cake-A-Hint-to-Cabinet-Makers. A full set of caricatures by H.B. is mentioned in Elizabeth's will: TNA, PROB 11/2032/308 (Will of Elizabeth Vassall Baroness Holland, 16 March 1846).
176 BL Add MS 51816, f. 188 (Thomas McNeil to Lord Holland, undated, 1839?).
177 BL, Add MS 51819, ff. 33–5 (Thomas Stewart to Lord Holland, 14 November 1836), Add MS 51816, f. 117 (?Thomas McNeil to Lord Holland, 3 September 1836).
178 Sturge and Harvey, *West Indies in 1837*, p. 241. Large amounts of medicine were ordered for 1838, however. See BL, Add MS 51819, f. 69 (List of supplies required for Friendship & Greenwich estate, 1838).
179 Williams, *Narrative of Events*, ed. Paton, pp. 32, 5; Hall, 'Apprenticeship Period', p. 155.
180 Heuman, 'Apprenticeship System', p. 242.
181 Williams, *Narrative of Events*, ed. Paton, pp. 7, 10–12, 55; Smith and Smith, *To Shoot Hard Labour*, pp. 73–75.
182 BL, Add MS 51816, f. 127 (Thomas McNeil to Lord Holland, 20 May 1837), ff. 139–43 (Thomas Mc Neil to Lord Holland, 16 July 1838).
183 Sturge and Harvey, *West Indies in 1837*, p. 244.
184 *Holland House Diaries*, ed. Kriegel, p. 385.
185 BL, Add MS 51817, f. 144v (Stephen Bourne to Lord Holland, 13 October 1838), Add MS 51816, f. 142 (Thomas McNeil to Lord Holland, 16 July 1838).

186 BL, Add MS 51816, ff. 146–9 (Lord Holland to Thomas McNeil, 1 April 1838), Add MS 51819, ff. 61–2 (William Lascelles to Lord Holland 5 April 1838).
187 BL Add MS 51816, f. 174v (Thomas McNeil to Lord Holland, 15 February 1839).
188 Zoellner, *Island on Fire*, pp. 250–1.
189 BL, Add MS 51819, f. 72 (Joseph Sturge to Lord Holland, enclosing report from William Knibb, 28 February 1839); Add MS 51816, f. 182 (Lord Holland to Thomas McNeil, 15 July 1839).
190 Higman '"To Begin the World Again"', p. 300.
191 Lightfoot, *Troubling Freedom*, pp. 57–83.
192 BL, Add MS 51816 f. 183v–184r, (Lord Holland to Thomas McNeil, 15 July 1839).
193 Dunn, *Tale*, 462; Chancellor, 'Slave-Owner and Anti-Slaver', p. 271.
194 Smith and Smith, *To Shoot Hard Labour*, p. 32.
195 BL, Add MS 51957, f. 68 (Lady Holland's Dinner Book, 22 October 1840).
196 Keppel, *Sovereign Lady*, p. 346.
197 Hall, 'Troubling Memories', p. 157; Hall et al., *Legacies*, pp. 171–2.
198 Keppel, *Sovereign Lady*, pp. 346, 354–60, 371.
199 *Holland House Diaries*, ed. Kriegel, p. 399.
200 For details about the estate workforce and produce by this time, see Higman '"To Begin the World Again"', p. 299; Chancellor, 'Slave-Owner and Anti-Slaver', p. 273; BL, Add MSS 51819, f. 115 (Inventory, 1840); BL, Add MS 51818, f. 151 (Lord Seaford to Lady Holland, 1841) and f. 172 (Lord Seaford to Lady Holland, 16 November 1844).
201 'Parishes: Millbrook', in *A History of the County of Bedford*, ed. Page, vol. 3, BHO: https://www.british-history.ac.uk/vch/beds/vol3/pp316-320; TNA, PROB 11/2032/308 (Will of Elizabeth Vassall Baroness Holland, 16 March 1846); BL, Add MS 51957, f. 186v (Lady Holland's Dinner Book, 17 November 1845); Keppel, *Sovereign Lady*, pp. 375–7.
202 This was not quite true. See Higman, *Jamaica Surveyed*, pp. 105–10; Sales Particulars of Friendship and Greenwich Estate, 1875, Library of Congress: https://www.loc.gov/item/2016586780/.
203 She visited the Lansdownes at Bowood. Keppel, *Sovereign Lady*, pp. 356–7; *Journal of Thomas Moore*, ed. Dowden, vol. 5, p. 2211.
204 Middleton, J., 'Statue to 19th Century Politician Lord Holland Who Owned 401 Slaves on His Jamaican Estate is Targeted by Vandals and Left Covered in Red Paint', *Daily Mail*, 24 June 2020: https://www.dailymail.co.uk/news/article-8454399/Statue-19th-century-politician-Lord-Holland-targeted-vandals-left-covered-red-paint.html.

8. ISABELLA BELL FRANKS (1769–1855)

1 LMA, ACC/0775/ 929/4 (Alexander Barclay to Thomson Hankey, 23 June 1842).
2 *Letters of Abigaill Levy Franks*, ed. Gelles, Moses's personality and career: pp. 42, 144, 151, 154, 156; Molly Beckford: pp. 43, 64, 75, 99, 103.
3 Stern, *David Franks*, p. 6; Woolf, 'Eighteenth-century London Jewish Shipowners', pp. 199–200.
4 *Letters of Abigaill Levy Franks*, ed. Gelles, p. 154; Daiches-Dubens, 'Eighteenth Century Anglo-Jewry', p. 152.
5 'Teddington: Introduction', in *A History of the County of Middlesex*, ed. Reynolds, vol. 3, pp. 66–9, BHO: http://www.british-history.ac.uk/vch/middx/vol3/pp66-69.
6 *Letters of Horace Walpole to Sir Horace Mann*, vol. 4, p. 400.

7   *Letters of Abigaill Levy Franks*, ed. Gelles, pp. 12, 41–2, 49–50, 56–7; Letter 79; Daiches-Dubens, 'Eighteenth Century Anglo-Jewry', p. 152.
8   Gainsborough, 'Isabelle Franks', *c.*1775–8, Birmingham Museums Trust.
9   Endelman, *Jews of Georgian England*, pp. 98–102.
10 Woolf, 'Eighteenth-Century London Jewish Shipowners', p. 200; Stern, *David Franks*, p. 6; Endelman, *Jews of Georgian England*, p. 252.
11 Mirvis, *Jews*, pp. 61, 75, 90.
12 Roth, C., *History of the Great Synagogue*, chapters 3 and 10, Susser Archive: https://www.jewishgen.org/jcr-uk/susser/roth/index.htm; *Palgrave Dictionary of Anglo-Jewish History*, ed. Rubinstein *et al.*, p. 296.
13 Stern, *David Franks*, p. 92; Endelman, *Jews of Georgian England*, pp. 265–6.
14 Oppenheim, 'Benjamin Franks', pp. 229–34; Mirvis, *Jews*, pp. 50–1; Deposition of Benjamin Franks, 20 October 1697, in *Privateering and Piracy in the Colonial Period*, ed. Jameson, pp. 190–4: https://www.gutenberg.org/cache/epub/24882/pg24882-images.html.
15 Slave Voyages, Intra-American, Voyage IDs: 107317, 107325, 107534, 107694, 107719, 102499, 107948: https://www.slavevoyages.org/american/database; Faber, *Jews, Slaves, and the Slave Trade*, p. 134.
16 *Letters of Abigaill Levy Franks*, ed. Gelles, pp. 92, 150.
17 O'Malley, *Final Passages*, p. 171.
18 'Robert Duckinfield', LBS: https://www.ucl.ac.uk/lbs/person/view/2146656893; 'Samuel Touchet', LBS: https://www.ucl.ac.uk/lbs/person/view/2146665101; LMA, ACC/0775/805 (Heads of Agreement, 6 December 1756); ACC/0775/812 (Conveyance of one half of Duckenfield Hall, May 1761).
19 Atkinson, *Mr. Atkinson's Rum Contract*, p. 48.
20 Various mortgage and conveyances: LMA, ACC/0775/817–19 (1763), 823–8 (1766), 830–5 (1767).
21 'John Gladstone', LBS: https://www.ucl.ac.uk/lbs/person/view/8961.
22 Bennett, M., 'A Story of Archival Discovery: The Bank of England and the Grenada Plantations', 30 September 2022: https://www.bankofengland.co.uk/museum/online-collections/blog/a-story-of-archival-discovery.
23 Claimant category 'Mortgagee', LBS: https://www.ucl.ac.uk/lbs/search/.
24 'Sir George Colebrooke 2nd Bart.', LBS: https://www.ucl.ac.uk/lbs/person/view/2146640519; Sheridan, 'Rise of a Colonial Gentry', p. 356.
25 LMA, ACC/0775/843–6, 848–50 (Sir George Colebrooke's mortgages with Aaron Franks, 1772–4).
26 'Nesbitt, Arnold', HOP: http://www.histparl.ac.uk/volume/1754-1790/member/nesbitt-arnold-1721-79.
27 Macleane was MP for Arundel 1768–71, and Lieutenant Governor of St Vincent in 1766. He died in a shipwreck returning to England from India in 1778. LMA, ACC 775/025 (Abstract of Mrs Isabella Cooper's Settlement, 22 May 1801).
28 LMA 0775/953/1, Summary of ownership of Grenada estates (Upper La Tante, Lower La Tante, St Cloud, Le Grand Bras, Chantilly, ?Tron Bombac, and one unnamed); JARD, 7/14 BRA 1118, nos. 93–9 (Leases of one-eighth of La Tante, Grenada, Lauchlin Macleane and John Stuart to Robert Monckton, 1766–70, Robert Monckton to Moses Franks, 1769–70); Maclean, *Reward is Secondary*, pp. 82–4, 147, 251; 'Lachlin Macleane', LBS: https://www.ucl.ac.uk/lbs/person/view/2146645275; 'Richard Cumberland', LBS: https://www.ucl.ac.uk/lbs/person/view/2146665051.
29 TNA, PROB 11/1035/126 (Will of Aaron Franks of Isleworth, 1 October 1777).

30. This slur appeared at length in *The Secret Relationship Between Blacks and Jews*, vol. 1 (Nation of Islam, 1991), a book championed by former Klansman David Duke, and has proliferated ever since. Labour activist Jackie Walker wrote on Facebook in 2016 that 'many Jews (my ancestors too) were the chief financiers of the sugar and slave trade'. She was subsequently suspended from the party: 'Labour Suspends Activist over Alleged Anti-Semitic Comments', BBC News, 5 May 2016: https://www.bbc.co.uk/news/uk-england-kent-36203911.

31. Faber, *Jews, Slaves, and the Slave Trade*, pp. 22–34, 132, 134, 176. Faber, writing in 1998, used Naval Office shipping returns for Jamaica in TNA, CO 142, 1719–1806. However, the online Slave Voyages database (2008) gives almost one million Africans imported to Jamaica: https://www.slavevoyages.org/. Nevertheless, the 0.36% proportion (960 out of 260,124) is probably broadly accurate. The forthcoming Register of British Slave Traders database will throw further light on the subject.

32. In 1754, only 1.5% of land in Jamaica was owned by Jewish people. Faber, *Jews, Slaves, and the Slave Trade*, pp. 64–5, 125; Mirvis, *Jews*, p. 66.

33. Anon., *Trial at Large of the Right Honourable Lady Cadogan*, p. 5.

34. *Letters of Abigaill Levy Franks*, ed. Gelles, pp. 68, 78; Mirvis, *Jews*, pp. 161–2.

35. Richa did eventually marry in 1789, aged over sixty, a younger Jewish widower, Abraham ben Baruch De Fries: Stern, *David Franks*, p. 170.

36. Endelman, *Jews of Georgian England*, pp. 254, 266. The Gideon (formerly Abundiente)'s wealth stemmed in part from 'West India' trade, enslavement in Barbados, Antigua and Nevis, and ownership of South Sea Company shares. Samuel, E., 'Gideon, Samson', ODNB: https://doi.org/10.1093/ref:odnb/10645.

37. Anon., *Trial at Large of the Right Honourable Lady Cadogan*, p. 6; *Scots Magazine* (1789), p. 206. Her inheritance would include two-thirds of Duckenfield, recently valued at £157,380: LMA, ACC/0775/942 (Valuation of Duckenfield Hall, 19 June 1784).

38. Stern, *David Franks*, p. 147; 'Cooper, Grey', HOP: https://www.historyofparliamentonline.org/volume/1754-1790/member/cooper-grey-1726-1801.

39. City of Westminster Archives Centre, STJ/PR/1/6 (St James, Piccadilly, baptism 1 May 1787), Ancestry: https://www.ancestry.co.uk/search/collections/61865/records/1968769; LMA, P89/MRY1/172 (St Marylebone Marriages, 21 May 1787), Ancestry: https://www.ancestry.co.uk/discoveryui-content/view/records?recordId=5646581&collectionId=1623.

40. Endelman, *Jews of Georgian England*, p. 266.

41. TNA, C 211/9/F56 (Phila Franks, of Teddington, Commission of Lunacy, 7 May 1789).

42. Stern, *David Franks*, pp. 100, 134, 170.

43. LMA, ACC/0775/859–862 (Bond of Moses Franks to Jacob and Napthali Franks, 26 February 1785); IRO, Deeds, vol. 717, ff. 216–23 (Transfer of mortgage, Jacob Henry Franks to Priscilla Franks, 31 August 1822).

44. *The Times*, 26 March 1790; *London Gazette*, issue 13195, 24 April 1790, p. 252; Cooper vs Denne (1792) in *Reports of Cases, High Court of Chancery*, ed. Brown, vol. 4, pp. 59–64; TNA, C 13/478/63 (Franks v Cooper, 1802).

45. During the 1790s, Duckenfield Hall regularly produced revenues of £6,000 to £7000 a year with a high watermark of £16,000 in 1797: JARD, 4/31/1, Frederick George Tansley Collection: Duckenfield Hall Shipments (1797). Between 1783 and 1791, Grand Bras in St Andrew was making £5,036 a year, a return of 15.5%. Ward, 'Profitability', p. 212.

46. LMA, ACC/0775/863 (Deeds between Coopers and Jacob and Napthali Franks; George and John Scott appointed attorneys in Jamaica, 8 June 1790); TNA, C 13/478/63 (Franks v Cooper, 1802).

47 *Diary of Lucy Kennedy*, ed. Clark, p. 24; Anon., *Trial at Large of the Right Honourable Lady Cadogan*, p. 6.
48 'Charles Sloane Cadogan, 1st Earl Cadogan', LBS: https://www.ucl.ac.uk/lbs/person/view/2146648147.
49 Mary was related to the Duke of Marlborough on her father's side, and a granddaughter of Robert Walpole on her mother's.
50 Anon., *Trial at Large of the Right Honourable Lady Cadogan*, pp. 13, 24–5, 28–9, 36, 44, 51; Stone, *Broken Lives*, pp. 536–45; Stone, *Road to Divorce*, pp. 262–7, 274; *Diary of Lucy Kennedy*, ed. Clark, pp. 24, 94; TNA, PROB 11/1362/307 (Will of Sir Grey Cooper, 30 September 1801).
51 LMA, ACC 775/025 (Abstract of Mrs Isabella Cooper's Settlement, 22 May 1801).
52 Alger, *Napoleon's British Visitors*, pp. 196, 198; Duche, 'Prisoners of War', p. 8; Brun, 'Dawkins'.
53 LMA, ACC/ 0775/029/5 (Isabella Cooper requests £200 from the estate of Moses Franks to buy William Henry Cooper Jnr. an army commission, 27 June 1805); *London Gazette*, issue 15839, 31 August 1805, p. 1105; *Diary of Lucy Kennedy*, ed. Clark, p. 245; TNA, PROB 11/1557/237 (Will of Jacob Franks, 7 August 1814).
54 *Diary of Lucy Kennedy*, ed. Clark, p. 137; *Jane Austen's Letters*, ed. Le Faye, p. 263.
55 Centre for Kentish Studies, U951 Z49/19 (*The Memorial of the Hon. Lady Honywood*, 1812), transcr. Whitfield: https://william1768courtenay.com/lady-honywoods-memorial-1812/; Kaplan, *Jane Austen among Women*, pp. 54–6.
56 Dawkins, J., 'Dawkins, Henry', ODNB: https://doi.org/10.1093/ref:odnb/107418; Dawkins, 'Dawkins Family'.
57 *Diary of Lucy Kennedy*, ed. Clark, pp. 137, 245.
58 Wolfram, 'Divorce', p. 157.
59 TNA, PROB 11/1557/237 (Will of Jacob Franks, 7 August 1814).
60 Arnold Nesbitt had died insolvent in 1779; his residuary heir was his nephew: 'John Nesbitt', LBS: https://www.ucl.ac.uk/lbs/person/view/2146631946; LMA, ACC/0775/901–910 (Papers concerning Priscilla Franks' purchase of the Nesbitt third of Duckenfield, 1817–28); IRO, Deeds, vol. 719, ff. 102–5 (Conveyance from Edward Goldsmid to Priscilla Franks, 2 October 1822); *Reports of Cases Argued and Determined in the High Court of Chancery between 1789 and 1817*, ed. Vesey, vol. 14 p. 443 ('Scott v. Nesbitt', 1808).
61 TNA, C 13/794/10 (Franks v. Cooper, 1823), C 101/390 (Franks v. Cooper, 1826–36), C 79/315, no. 6 (Franks v Cooper, 1823–8), accessed at Anglo American Legal Tradition: http://aalt.law.uh.edu/AALT7/C78/C79no315/IMG_0103.htm); IRO, Deeds, vol. 717, ff. 216–23 (Transfer of mortgage, Jacob Henry Franks to Priscilla Franks, 1 May 1823); LMA, ACC/0775/868 (Transfer of mortgage, Jacob Henry Franks to Priscilla Franks, 31 August 1822), 869 (Copy Chancery Bill, Franks v. Cooper, 12 December 1827).
62 LMA, ACC/0775/870 (Conveyance of 1/3 of Duckenfield into trust, August 1828), ACC/0775/929/1 (Robert Pitches to Isabella Cooper, 19 May 1831); 'Robert Pitches', LBS: https://www.ucl.ac.uk/lbs/person/view/43491.
63 'Thomson Hankey', LBS: https://www.ucl.ac.uk/lbs/person/view/45720 ; 'Thomson Hankey junior', LBS: https://www.ucl.ac.uk/lbs/person/view/45726.
64 LMA, ACC/0775/953, no. 18 (Grenada accounts); Murphy, *Creole Archipelago*, pp. 202–16, 224; Martin, 'Citizens and Comrades-in-Arms'; Ward, 'Profitability', pp. 205, 212.
65 LMA, ACC/0775/929/1 (Robert Pitches to Isabella Cooper, 19 May 1831).
66 Schuler, 'Alas, Alas, Kongo', p. 2; 'Alexander Barclay', LBS: https://www.ucl.ac.uk/lbs/person/view/15549; Higman, *Plantation Jamaica*, pp. 89–90; Sturge and Harvey, *West Indies in 1837*, pp. 300–1.

67 Stephen, *Slavery of the British West India Colonies Delineated*, p. 72.
68 Barclay, *Practical View*, pp. 60–1. Hampton Court was amalgamated with nearby Stoakes Hall around 1815, after owner Alexander Donaldson died in debt on a passage to England in 1807. Seventy-one 'Hampton Court negroes' appear on the 1817 register for Golden Grove, including a Jane Donaldson. 'Alexander Donaldson', LBS: https://www.ucl.ac.uk/lbs/person/view/2146631898; 'Stoakes Hall', LBS: https://www.ucl.ac.uk/lbs/estate/view/1788; 'Hampton Court', LBS: https://www.ucl.ac.uk/lbs/estate/view/17323; TNA, 71/ 145, f. 89 (Slave Registers, Jamaica, St Thomas in the East, 1817), Ancestry: https://www.ancestry.co.uk/search/collections/1129.
69 Several groups of mothers with their children, and sometimes grandchildren, *were* kept together as they arrived at Duckenfield. For example, Jamaican-born Molly Murray, aged seventy-one, arrived from Airy Castle with her four sons: forty-six-year-old William Geoghegan (known before baptism as Punch), Richard Dick (formerly Johnston), aged forty-three, George West (formerly Jeffrey), thirty-three, David Smith (formerly Thomas), aged thirty-one; and two daughters: forty-one-year-old Cecelia Steel (Fanny) and thirty-two-year-old Eliza Scott (Jubena). Eliza arrived with her two small children: Lewis Wilson, who was three and a half, and George, just one. It is much harder to trace paternal connections as these were rarely recorded by enslavers, because enslaved status was inherited from the mother. TNA, 71/145, ff. 270–9, 146, ff. 138–40, 147, ff. 123–7, 148, ff. 118–20, 149 (unpaginated), 150, ff. 191–2 (Slave Registers, Jamaica, St Thomas in the East, 1817, 1820, 1823, 1826, 1829, 1832), Ancestry: https://www.ancestry.co.uk/search/collections/1129.
70 LMA, 0775/ 920–3 (Conveyance of forty-four enslaved people, Thomas Nesbitt to Priscilla and Isabella Franks, 8 May 1818).
71 LMA, ACC 775/919 (Conveyance of fifty-seven enslaved people to Priscilla Franks, 12 August 1816); 'George Girton Saunders', LBS: https://www.ucl.ac.uk/lbs/person/view/2146651035.
72 Charles Scott being attorney to both Airy Castle and Duckenfield facilitated the sale. LMA, ACC/0775/924, (Conveyance of fifty-one enslaved people from William Fraser Tytler and Margaret Cussans Tytler (née Grant) to Priscilla Franks, 11 August 1823); 'Airy Castle', LBS: https://www.ucl.ac.uk/lbs/estate/view/192; 'George Grant of Burdyards', LBS: https://www.ucl.ac.uk/lbs/person/view/2146648705; 'William Fraser Tytler', LBS: https://www.ucl.ac.uk/lbs/person/view/16655; 'Charles Scott', LBS: https://www.ucl.ac.uk/lbs/person/view/13114.
73 TNA, 71/147, ff. 237–8 (Slave Registers, Jamaica, St Thomas in the East, 1823), Ancestry: https://www.ancestry.co.uk/search/collections/1129; 'Unknown, St Thomas in the East', LBS: https://www.ucl.ac.uk/lbs/estate/view/19635.
74 Equiano, *Interesting Narrative*, ed. Carey, p. 41; Vasconcellos, *Slavery*, pp. 21, 38.
75 Barclay, *Practical View*, pp. 236, 239.
76 TNA, 71/145, ff. 270–9, 146, ff. 138–40, 147, ff. 123–7, 148, ff. 118–20, 149 (unpaginated), 150, ff. 191–2 (Slave Registers, Jamaica, St. Thomas in the East, 1817, 1820, 1823, 1826, 1829, 1832), Ancestry: https://www.ancestry.co.uk/search/collections/1129.
77 Barclay continued to argue against Emancipation using examples from Duckenfield: Barclay, *Effects of the Late Colonial Policy*, p. 20.
78 Emerson, *Address Delivered at Concord*, p. 6; *Anti-Slavery Reporter and Aborigines' Friend*, ser. 3, vol. 1, 1853, p. 57; Hurston, *Mules and Men*, pp. 74–5; Pointer, *Passion to Liberate*, p. xxi; Vecsey, 'Facing Death', p. 32; Burton, *Magic Drum*, p. 72.
79 Piersen, *Black Legacy*, pp. 12–35; Dance, *Folklore from Contemporary Jamaicans*, p. 3.
80 TNA, PROB 11/1809/28 (Will of Priscilla Franks, 1 December 1832); 'Priscilla Franks',

LBS: https://www.ucl.ac.uk/lbs/person/view/-535810822; 'Sir Henry Allen Johnson 2nd Bart', LBS: https://www.ucl.ac.uk/lbs/person/view/24495.
81 Brun, 'Dawkins'; TNA, PROB 11/2206/379 (Will of Isabella Cooper, 27 February 1855).
82 'Pittville Estate History', Pittville History Works: https://pittvillehistory.org.uk/estate/estate.php; LMA, ACC/0775/690-760 charts the Pittville ownership, leases and mortgages, 1830-1865; Barczewski, *Country Houses*, p. 242.
83 William Henry junior married Anne Kemeys Tynte, daughter of Charles Keymes Tynte, MP, in 1827. LMA, ACC/0775/626-89 (Chilton Lodge Estate Papers 1809-55); 'Chilton Foliat', in *A History of the County of Wiltshire*, ed. Crowley, vol. 16, BHO: https://www.british-history.ac.uk/vch/wilts/vol16/pp88-109 https://www.british-history.ac.uk/vch/wilts/vol16/pp88-109#anchorn216.
84 William Henry was appointed Chaplain on 7 April 1830. 'The Chapel Royal: Chaplains, 1660-1837', in *Office-Holders in Modern Britain:* vol. 11, ed. Bucholz, pp. 251-78, BHO: http://www.british-history.ac.uk/office-holders/vol11/pp251-278.
85 TNA, PROB 11/1841/122 (Will of Reverend Sir William Henry Cooper, 31 January 1835), PROB 11/1857/210 (Will of Sir William Henry Cooper of Chilton Lodge, 9 February 1836); 'Sir William Henry Cooper', Find a Grave: https://www.findagrave.com/memorial/102019005/william-henry-cooper.
86 Gordon House had once belonged to Isabella's great-grandfather Moses Hart (Aaron's father-in-law). Brun, 'Dawkins'; Daiches-Dubens, 'Eighteenth Century Anglo-Jewry', p. 153.
87 LMA, ACC/0775/079-081 (Robert Pitches to Isabella Cooper, 28 and 30 October, 25 November 1835); Young, 'Gender', pp. 208-9; 'Grenada, claim 769 (Grand Bras Estate)', LBS: https://www.ucl.ac.uk/lbs/claim/view/10510; 'Jamaica St Thomas-in-the-East, Surrey, claim 114 (Duckenfield Hall)', LBS: https://www.ucl.ac.uk/lbs/claim/view/24495.
88 TNA, 71/150, ff. 191-2 (Slave Registers, Jamaica, St Thomas in the East, 1832), Ancestry: https://www.ancestry.co.uk/search/collections/1129.
89 'Papers Relative to the Abolition of Slavery in the British Colonies', House of Lords, *Accounts and Papers*, vol. 34 (1835), pp. 69-70 (John Daughtrey to Governor Sligo, 17 December 1834).
90 The Duckenfield population had already dwindled to 267 by 1837. Besides demographic decline, some apprentices were manumitted, and others may have run away. Higman, *Jamaica Surveyed*, p. 257; Sturge and Harvey, *West Indies in 1837*, p. lxviii; Paget, 'Free Village System in Jamaica', pp. 43, 49.
91 IRO, Deeds, vol. 719, ff. 102-5 (Conveyance from Edward Goldsmid to Priscilla Franks, 2 October 1822); LMA, ACC/0775/912 (Power of Attorney, 28 May 1832).
92 LMA, ACC/0775/929/2 (Robert Pitches to Bell, Scott and Nockells, 30 June 1834).
93 Thomas, 'Between Skin and Heart', p. 40 n. 50, citing Charles Nockells to Sir Henry Fitzherbert, 22 November 1847.
94 LMA, ACC/0775/ 86 (Thomson Hankey to Robert Pitches, 30 October 1837), ACC/0775/89 (Robert Pitches to Lady Cooper, 3 January 1838).
95 Charles died in 1843, leaving legacies of £6 a year to Eliza Scott of Morant Bay and her two daughters Mary and Ann, with the right to continue living in his house there. This may well have been the same Eliza Scott, originally named Jubena, daughter of Molly Murray and mother to Lewis Wilson and George, who arrived at Duckenfield from Airy Castle (where Charles Scott had been attorney) in 1823, aged thirty-two. 'Charles Scott', LBS: https://www.ucl.ac.uk/lbs/person/view/13114.
96 LMA, ACC/0775/929/4 (Alexander Barclay to Thomson Hankey, 23 June 1842); 'Alexander Barclay', LBS: https://www.ucl.ac.uk/lbs/person/view/15549; Sturge and Harvey, *West Indies in 1837*, pp. 300-1.

97 Schuler, 'Alas, Alas, Kongo', p. 2; LMA, ACC/0775/929/4 (Alexander Barclay to Thomson Hankey, 23 June 1842).
98 Dowlah, *Cross-Border Labor Mobility*, p. 126; Beckles and Shepherd, *Freedoms Won*, pp. 59, 75.
99 Schuler, 'Alas, Alas, Kongo', pp. 1, 5–6.
100 Costello, *Black Salt*, p. 36; Sherwood, *After Abolition*, pp. 119–20; Anderson and Lovejoy (eds), *Liberated Africans*, pp. 13, 45; Anderson, *Abolition in Sierra Leone*, p. 81; Schwarz, 'Reconstructing the Life Histories', pp. 175–207; Lester, *Ruling the World*, p. 54.
101 'Archaeologists Find Graves Containing Bodies of 5,000 Slaves on Remote Island', *Guardian*, 8 March 2012: https://www.theguardian.com/world/2012/mar/08/slave-mass-graves-st-helena-island; Pearson, *Distant Freedom*; Anderson and Lovejoy (eds), *Liberated Africans*, p. 11.
102 Schuler, 'Alas, Alas, Kongo!', p. 6.
103 The headmen were sent back to Sierra Leone in the *Commissioner Barclay*, but the ship was wrecked near the Bahamas. They survived and returned home on the *Herald*. UK Parliament, House of Commons Select Committee on the West Coast of Africa, *Report: Together with Minutes of Evidence, Appendix and Index* (1842), vol. 2, pp. 282, 467; TNA, CO140/133 (Return of immigrants to Jamaica 1840–1), transcr. Jamaica Family Search: http://www.jamaicanfamilysearch.com/Members/mimmigranto3.htm; Immigration Report, 1841, from the 1842 Jamaica Almanac, transcr. Jamaican Family Search: http://www.jamaicanfamilysearch.com/Samples/immig.htm.
104 Schuler, 'Alas, Alas, Kongo', pp. 7–8; Wills, 'Royal Navy', pp. 194–5.
105 Much of the following is from JARD, 7/14 BRA 1118, no. 67 (William Estridge to Thomson Hankey, 1843).
106 McGeachy, *Irrigation in the West Indies*, p. 20.
107 Hall, 'Apprenticeship Period', p. 155.
108 Personal correspondence with Padraig Scanlan and Richard Anderson. TNA, CO 267/91, p. 77 (Sierra Leone Commissioners of Enquiry: Report and Appendix, A, 1827); TNA, CO 267/172 (R.R. Madden's 1841 report on Sierra Leone); TNA, CO 267/200 (Colonial Office to H.U. Addington: Compulsory Emigration, 11 November 1847).
109 JARD, 7/4/BRA/1118, no. 35 (Alexander Barclay's accounts for Duckenfield); LMA, ACC/0775/929/4 (Alexander Barclay to Thomson Hankey, 23 June 1842).
110 LMA, ACC/0775/ 929/37 (Duckenfield arson attack investigation, 4 January 1865).
111 'Kumina', in *The Encyclopaedia of Caribbean Religions*, ed. Taylor and Case, vol. 1, pp. 481–94; Hutton, *Colour for Colour*, pp. 150–6, 164–9.
112 *Accounts and Papers of the House of Commons*, vol. 40 (1850), pp. 287, 292, 347–52; Georger, 'Diaspora Consciousness'; Pearson, *Distant Freedom*, pp. 284–7.
113 An undated plan of Duckenfield shows 'the canal from the works' and 'the proposed canal from Cocorocoe gully to Cox's pond': NLJ, St Thomas 937.
114 It's unclear whether the £1,000 was sterling or currency. LMA, ACC/0775/929/8 (Thomson Hankey to Alexander Barclay, 31 March 1843); 929/10 (Thomson Hankey to John Wilkinson, 23 November 1843); 929/21 (Thomas McCulloch to Thomson Hankey, 6 January 1863).
115 Library of Birmingham, Boulton & Watt Co., Henry Hazelton, Catalogue of Old Engines, List of Engines of the Independent Type Supplied to the Sugar Plantations in Jamaica, Watt Room, Soho Foundry, Birmingham: 1 engine ordered by Thomson Hankey for Duckenfield in 1852 (thanks to Tracey Thorn for this reference).
116 Berg and Hudson, *Slavery, Capitalism and the Industrial Revolution*, p. 81.
117 JARD, Crop Accounts, 1B/11/4/84, f. 43 (Duckenfield, 6 March 1841), 1B/11/4/93, ff.

96–7, 126, 210–11 (Duckenfield, 8 March 1850, 19 March 1850, 10 February 1851). Before 1834, the estate had regularly produced 300–350 hogsheads of sugar a year and roughly around 200 puncheons of rum. Higman, *Jamaica Surveyed*, p. 256.
118 LMA, 0775/954/2 (Thomson Hankey to Isabella Cooper, 24 May 1842).
119 National Archives of Jamaica, 7/14 BRA 1118, no. 33, item 5 (Isabella Cooper's account with Thomson Hankey, 1849–50).
120 TNA, PROB 11/2206/379 (Will of Lady Isabella Cooper, 27 February 1855); Young, 'Gender', p. 225.
121 Brun, 'Dawkins'; Bedfordshire Archives, WL1000/1/Mog/1/1 (Abstract of title to the Guinea and adjoining land, 1858–85): https://bedsarchivescat.bedford.gov.uk/Details/archive/110169620.
122 'Our Almshouses', Isleworth & Hounslow Charity: https://www.iahcharity.org.uk/.
123 Aungier, *History and Antiquities of Syon Monastery*, p. 231.
124 The memorial was lost when the church was subject of an arson attack in 1943. 'Isabel Bell Cooper (1769–1855, Isleworth', in 'Middlesex Monumental Inscriptions', Find My Past: https://www.findmypast.co.uk/transcript?id=PRS%2FMIDD%2FMONUINSC%2F27325.
125 Hall *et al.*, *Legacies*, pp. 51–3, 59, 232, 264; Institutions in 'Cultural Legacies': LBS: https://www.ucl.ac.uk/lbs/cultural/; Adams, R., 'Elite UK Schools' Financial Links to Slavery Revealed', *Guardian*, 3 May 2023: https://www.theguardian.com/world/2023/may/03/elite-uk-schools-financial-links-to-slavery-revealed.
126 In 1865, Duckenfield belonged to the Dawkins family; it was sold, debt-ridden, at auction in 1877: TNA, CO 441/12/1 (Papers, Correspondence and Plans: Dawkins: Duckenfield Hall: Jamaica: No. 121, 1868–77).
127 Heuman, *Killing Time*, pp. 74–5.
128 Higman, *Jamaica Surveyed*, p. 258.
129 Higman, *Plantation Jamaica*, p. 90.
130 Parliamentary Papers, *Report of the Jamaica Royal Commission, 1866*, pp. 531–2; Hutton, *Colour for Colour*, p. 67; Gopal, *Insurgent Empire*, p. 104.
131 LMA, ACC/0775/ 929/40A (William Payne Georges to Thomson Hankey, 7 November 1865, 24 November 1865); Heuman, *Killing Time*, p. 12; Parliamentary Papers, *Report of the Jamaica Royal Commission, 1866*, p. 4.
132 Gopal, *Insurgent Empire*, p. 91, Hutton, *Colour for Colour*, pp. 174–6.
133 Adcock was aide-de-camp to Brigadier-General Alexander Abercromby Nelson, who oversaw George William Gordon's court martial and was later tried (but acquitted) for his murder at the Old Bailey. Stearn, R.T., 'Nelson, Sir Alexander Abercromby', ODNB: https://doi.org/10.1093/ref:odnb/19875.
134 Adcock said he burned four or five houses; the official tally records nine: Parliamentary Papers, *Report of the Jamaica Royal Commission, 1866*, pp. 700, 963–4.
135 Heuman, *Killing Time*, pp. 135–6.
136 Ibid., pp. 574, 954–5, 962; Jemmott, *Ties that Bind*, p. 149. Tobias Tyne's small plot of land appears on an 1846 plan of the estate: Higman, *Jamaica Surveyed*, p. 259.
137 Tommy Miles was born a 'Creole Negro' to Eliza Wilson at Duckenfield in 1825, so was forty at the time of his death: TNA, 71/148, ff. 118–20 (Slave Registers, Jamaica, St Thomas in the East, 1826), Ancestry: https://www.ancestry.co.uk/search/collections/1129. McCaul could have been related to James and Sophia Mccall, who arrived from Sierra Leone in 1841: TNA, CO140/133 (Return of immigrants to Jamaica 1840–1), transcr. Jamaica Family Search: http://www.jamaicanfamilysearch.com/Members/mimmigranto3.htm.
138 Testimony of Peter Phillips in 'Proceedings of the Courts Martial Recently Held in Jamaica upon Ensign Cullen and Assistant Surgeon Morris of Her Majesty's Service',

p. 147. Phillips was possibly the eleven-year-old boy named Peter, son of Oriana, listed in 1817.
139 'Proceedings of the Courts Martial Recently Held in Jamaica upon Ensign Cullen and Assistant Surgeon Morris of Her Majesty's Service', pp. 1–298; Bennett, 'Picturing the West India Regiment', pp. 142–3, 153–7.
140 *London Gazette*, 26 June 1868, p. 3584; 'Captain Francis James Cullen', Find a Grave: https://www.findagrave.com/memorial/253027921/francis-james-cullen; '66th Regiment Girishk Maiwand and Kandahar', Ref: WMO/187164, War Memorials Online: https://www.warmemorialsonline.org.uk/memorial/187164/; 'The Recent Court Martial in Jamaica – Question', 1 August 1867: https://api.parliament.uk/historic-hansard/commons/1867/aug/01/the-recent-court-martial-in-jamaica.

9. ANNA SUSANNA TAYLOR (1781–1853)

1 Roberts, '"Quite Appropriate"'. The May 1825 sale comprised eighty-eight lots: forty-five lots of furniture, thirty-one of sculpture and twelve of furnishing objects, lights, etc. *Morning Herald* (London), Thursday 17 February 1825, Saturday 21 May 1825.
2 Westminster Archives Centre, STG/PR/2/4 (St George, Hanover Square, Baptisms, 12 April 1781), Ancestry: https://www.ancestry.co.uk/search/collections/61865/records/694782; 'Sir John Taylor 1st Bart', LBS: https://www.ucl.ac.uk/lbs/person/view/2146634176; ICS, 120 13/A/4 (Robert Taylor to Simon Taylor, 31 July 1792).
3 'Elizabeth Goodin Taylor (née Haughton)', LBS: https://www.ucl.ac.uk/lbs/person/view/2146650689; NLJ, MS 300, vol. 7, no. 6 (Hazel Hall's notes on the Haughton and Watson Taylor families).
4 'Neill Malcolm 11th of Poltalloch', LBS: https://www.ucl.ac.uk/lbs/person/view/2146637316; 'Neill (i) Malcolm', in Kilburn, M., 'Malcolm Family of Poltalloch', ODNB: https://doi.org/10.1093/ref:odnb/107421.
5 Petley, *White Fury*, pp. 27–8; *Lady Nugent's Journal*, ed. Wright, p. 66.
6 Horace Walpole, cited in Thomas, *Chattel*.
7 ICS, 120 1/A/52 (Simon Taylor to Robert Graham, 15 July 1785).
8 'Robert Cunninghame Graham', LBS: https://www.ucl.ac.uk/lbs/person/view/-719617813.
9 Simon and John had a brother, Robert. Patrick left Lyssons in equal shares to the three brothers. Robert died intestate *c.*1754, leaving Simon heir-at-law. Petley, *White Fury*, p. 229, n. 27. Simon's client at Golden Grove was 'Chaloner Arcedeckne', LBS: https://www.ucl.ac.uk/lbs/person/view/2146640845.
10 Petley, *White Fury*, p. 230 n. 28; Zahedieh, N., 'Morgan, Sir Henry', ODNB: https://doi.org/10.1093/ref:odnb/19224; Evans, *Slave Wales*, p. 12.
11 He committed to pay £10,000 interest-free annually for six years, then £5,000 a year for the next eight years at five per cent interest. Petley, *White Fury*, p. 74; Sheridan, 'Simon Taylor', p. 295.
12 Petley, *White Fury*, pp. 27–8, 48–9, 55–7.
13 Ibid., p. 84.
14 Donne was described as 'quadroon', Hunter as 'mulatto', and Nelly Nugent's father was 'a Mr. Nugent from Ireland'. *Lady Nugent's Journal*, ed. Wright, p. 68; Ono-George, '"Washing the Blackamoor White"', p. 46; 'Charlotte Tayler', LBS: https://www.ucl.ac.uk/lbs/person/view/43524; Tammemagi, K., 'Charlotte Taylor – Quadroon', Sproule Genealogy, 28 March 2014: https://sproulegenealogy.blogspot.com/2014/03/charlotte-

taylor-quadroon.html; 'Sarah Taylor', LBS: https://www.ucl.ac.uk/lbs/person/view/12951; ICS, 120 20/A/ 6 (Sarah Taylor to Simon Taylor, undated). ICS, 120 2/B/36 (Simon Taylor to Sir John Taylor, 27 January 1783) also mentions a son, John or Jack Taylor. See ICS, 120 1/J/48 (Simon Taylor to Robert Taylor, 19 September 1811), and 20/A/2, 3 (John 'Jack' Taylor to Simon Taylor, 22 January 1785, 4 March 1796). In 1783, Simon Taylor manumitted 'a certain Negro Woman named Daphney together with her offspring and increase', who might have been his: JARD, Manumissions, 1B/11/6/17, f. 65 (Simon Taylor to Daphne, 17 October 1783).

15 ICS, 120 2/B/30 (Sir John Taylor to Simon Taylor, 26 August 1783), 7/A/1 (Simon Taylor to Anna Susanna Taylor, no date, probably late 1786 or early 1787).

16 Sheridan, 'Jamaican Slave Insurrection Scare of 1776', Table 1, p. 308.

17 NLJ, MS 300, vol. 7, no. 6. (Hazel Hall's notes on Haughton and Watson Taylor families); ICS, 120, 2/A/37 (Simon Taylor to Sir John Taylor 19 May 1779).

18 ICS, 120 2/B/29, 31, 34, 35 (Sir John Taylor to Simon Taylor, 1 May 1783, 16 October 1783, 16 August 1784, 27 October 1784).

19 Ann Graham died in 1780. Robert Graham appears in 'Sir John Taylor and his Family', by Daniel Gardner (c.1784), LBS: https://www.ucl.ac.uk/lbs/cultural/view/2135896549. The figure had previously been identified as Simon Taylor (private correspondence with Christer Petley).

20 Amongst the recipients of mourning rings in Sir John Taylor's will appear my fifth great-grandparents, Robert Cooper Lee and his wife Priscilla. TNA, PROB 11/1153/27 (Will of Sir John Taylor, 3 May 1787); 'Sir John Taylor 1st Bart.', LBS: https://www.ucl.ac.uk/lbs/person/view/2146634176. Simon forgave his brother's £46,000 debts in his will: TNA, PROB 11/1548/177 (Will of Simon Taylor, 24 September 1813), despite his property on the island, including over 500 people in Hanover and St Thomas, being valued at around £39,000: JARD, Probate Inventories, 1B/11/3/71, ff. 192–4 (Sir John Taylor: Kingston, 27 October 1786), ff. 194–9 (Sir John Taylor: St Thomas in the East, 24 February 1787), 1B/11/3/73, ff. 16–21 (Sir John Taylor: Hanover, 26 January 1787).

21 Bolney belonged at this time to Kittian enslaver Anthony Hodges, LBS: https://www.ucl.ac.uk/lbs/person/view/2146645319; 'Rural Parishes: Harpsden', in *A History of the County of Oxford*, ed. Townley, vol. 16, BHO: http://www.british-history.ac.uk/vch/oxon/vol16/pp231-265; Cunninghame Graham, *Doughty Deeds*, pp. 133–40.

22 ICS, 120 3/B/1, 4, 6, 11, 13 (Simon Taylor to Lady Taylor, 17 July and 6 December 1786, 6 February, 3 July and 7 September 1787); 10/A/73 (Robert Graham to Simon Taylor, 25 May 1787); 1/J/13 (Simon Taylor to Anna Susanna Watson Taylor, 17 August 1810); Cunninghame Graham, *Doughty Deeds*, p. 137; TNA, PROB 11/1548/177 (Will of Simon Taylor, 24 September 1813).

23 ICS, 120 7/A/2, 3, 5 (Simon Taylor to Anna Susanna Taylor, 29 April and 3 November 1787, 29 March 1789).

24 ICS, 120 13/A/1 (Robert Taylor to Simon Taylor, 28 December 1791), 7/A/8 (Simon Taylor to Anna Susanna Taylor, 6 December 1792).

25 *Lady Nugent's Journal*, ed. Wright, pp. 126, 241–2.

26 Sir George Nugent, 'Sketch of the Characters of the Principal Persons in Office in Jamaica', 1806, quoted in *Lady Nugent's Journal*, ed. Wright, p. 318.

27 Petley, *White Fury*, pp. 31–3, 74; Sheridan, 'Simon Taylor', p. 295; Higman, *Jamaica Surveyed*, pp. 228–30.

28 Sir George Nugent, 'Sketch of the Characters of the Principal Persons in Office in Jamaica', 1806, quoted in *Lady Nugent's Journal*, ed. Wright, p. 318.

29 Petley, *White Fury*, pp. 141, 165; University of Michigan, William Clements Library, Tailyour Papers (Simon Taylor to John Tailyour, 4 January 1792); ICS, 120, 1/B/27 (Simon Taylor to Robert Taylor, October 1798).

30 Elizabeth's aunts Mary and Rebecca Haughton had married brothers Colonel John Reid (1710–77) and Colonel Thomas Reid. It was Mary's son, Richard Haughton Reid (1752–1844), and Rebecca's son, Thomas Reid junior (1744–98), who now claimed ownership. 'Hawtayne/Haughton' in Oliver, *Caribbeana*, vol. 6, part 1, transcr, Jamaican Family Search: http://www.jamaicanfamilysearch.com/Members/bcarib53.htm; TNA, PROB 11/884/416 (Will of Richard Haughton, 23 February 1763); ICS, 120 3/A/3 (Elizabeth Taylor to Simon Taylor, 6 March 1793); 'Richard Haughton Reid', LBS: https://www.ucl.ac.uk/lbs/person/view/2146634288.

31 ICS, 120 4/A 1–10, 4/B/4/ 1–9 (Correspondence between Simon Taylor and Neil Malcolm, February 1788 to September 1794), 16/B/11 (Simon Taylor to Robert Graham, 14 September 1794), 13/A/65, 207 (Robert Taylor to Simon Taylor, 29 September 1796 and 3 January 1805).

32 ICS, 120 3/A/3, 14 (Lady Taylor to Simon Taylor, 6 March 1793, 1 June 1796), 13/A/38, 44, 45, 47 (Robert Taylor to Simon Taylor, 5 November 1794, 4 March 1795, 1 April 1795, 6 May 1795); Coxe, *Picture of Italy*, p. xv.

33 ICS, 120 3/B/28 (Simon Taylor to Lady Taylor, 15 September 1794), 16/B/10 (Simon Taylor to Robert Graham, 8 August 1794), 13/A/263 (Robert Taylor to Simon Taylor, 2 February 1809); 'Richard Brissett', LBS: https://www.ucl.ac.uk/lbs/person/view/2146634150.

34 ICS, 120 13/A/206, (Robert Taylor to Simon Taylor, 5 December 1804), 1/G/21 (Simon Taylor to Lady Taylor, 14 April 1805), 1/G/26 (Simon Taylor to Anna Susanna Taylor, 1 May 1805), 1/H/25 (Simon Taylor to Eliza Mayne, 24 August 1805); 'William Mayne', LBS: https://www.ucl.ac.uk/lbs/person/view/2146630695; 'Mayne, Robert', HOP: http://www.historyofparliamentonline.org/volume/1754-1790/member/mayne-robert-1724-82.

35 ICS, 120 13/A/206, 212, 215 (Robert Taylor to Simon Taylor, 5 December 1804, 2 May 1805, 7 August 1805); ICS, 1/G/28, 35 (Simon Taylor to Robert Taylor, 28 June and October 1805), 34 (Simon Taylor to Lady Taylor, 7 October 1805); *A Political Index* (1806), p. 272; 'George Reid junior', LBS: https://www.ucl.ac.uk/lbs/person/view/1304262911.

36 NLJ, MS 300, vol. 7, no. 6 (Hazel Hall's notes on Haughton and Watson Taylor families); 'George Watson-Taylor', LBS: https://www.ucl.ac.uk/lbs/person/view/-1221895888.

37 One relation the Taylors considered worthy of note was an uncle by marriage, Sir Walter Farquhar, physician to the Prince of Wales and William Pitt the Younger. Payne, J.F., and K. Bagshaw. 'Farquhar, Sir Walter', ODNB: https://doi.org/10.1093/ref:odnb/9181.

38 George was baptised at St Marylebone, 12 May 1771: LMA, P89/MRY1/005, Ancestry: https://www.ancestry.co.uk/search/collections/1624/records/297557; 'Watson-Taylor, George', 1790–1820, HOP: http://www.historyofparliamentonline.org/volume/1790-1820/member/watson-taylor-george-1770-1841, and 1820–32, HOP: http://www.historyofparliamentonline.org/volume/1820-1832/member/watson-taylor-george-1771-1841; Beaumont, D., 'Taylor, George Watson', *Dictionary of Irish Biography*: https://www.dib.ie/biography/taylor-george-watson-a8474; Thomas, *Chattel*.

39 ICS, 120 13/A/263 (Robert Taylor to Simon Taylor, 2 February 1809).

40 Byron, *Don Juan*, Dedication, stanza 12; Shelley, *Masque of Anarchy*, vol. 2, pp. 5–6.

41 'Irish Legal Heritage: Pitchcapping', *Irish Legal News*, 2 November 2018: https://www.irishlegal.com/articles/irish-legal-heritage-pitchcapping.

42 Beaumont, D., 'Taylor, George Watson', *Dictionary of Irish Biography*: https://www.dib.ie/biography/taylor-george-watson-a8474; 'Croppies Lie Down: A Favourite Irish Song',

printed G. Kauntz (1797); Lecky, *History of Ireland in the Eighteenth Century*, vol. 5, p. 88.
43   ICS, 120 13/A/274 (Robert Taylor to Simon Taylor, 5 October 1809).
44   'Saul's River', LBS: https://www.ucl.ac.uk/lbs/estate/view/20659; ICS, 120 13/A/263 (Robert Taylor to Simon Taylor, 2 February 1809).
45   Ide, '"Very Pretty Seat"', pp. 10–12; ICS, 120, 6/A/84 (Simon Richard Brissett Taylor to Simon Taylor, 1 March 1809), 13/A/263 (Robert Taylor to Simon Taylor, 2 February 1809), 1/J/17 (Simon Taylor to George Hibbert, 27 August 1810).
46   ICS, 120 13/A/269, 271 (Robert Taylor to Simon Taylor, 8 June 1809, 6 July 1809).
47   It's not entirely clear where he got the money. Perhaps from savings of his salary, or loans from family such as Sir Walter Farquhar or his patron Lord Camden.
48   The 2 March 1810 settlement is rehearsed in: IRO, Deeds, vol. 791, ff. 171–81 (Anna Susanna and George Watson marriage settlement, 1834), and TNA, C 13/1192/24 [C1838 T9] (Taylor v Hibbert, 5 April 1838).
49   ICS, 120 7/A/23 (Simon Taylor to Anna Susanna Taylor, 3 February 1810), 1/J/2 (Simon Taylor to Simon Richard Brissett Taylor, 18 April 1810), 1/J/17 (Simon Taylor to George Hibbert, 27 August 1810), 13/A/305 (Robert Taylor to Simon Taylor, 4 April 1812).
50   ICS, 120 1/B/15 (Simon Taylor to Simon Richard Brissett Taylor, 27 March 1798), 1/D/34 (Simon Taylor to Lady Taylor, 6 October 1800); Petley, *White Fury*, p. 190.
51   ICS, 120 6/A/50 (Simon Richard Brissett Taylor to Simon Taylor, 6 November 1805), 13/A/229 (Robert Taylor to Simon Taylor, 4 September 1806), 1/G/41 (Simon Taylor to Simon Richard Brissett Taylor, 15 January 1806), 7/A/20 (Simon Taylor to Anna Susanna Taylor, 24 August 1806).
52   ICS, 120 6/C/7 (George Watson Taylor to Simon Richard Brissett Taylor, 8 February 1812).
53   ICS, 120 13/A/302 (Robert Taylor to Simon Taylor, 5 March 1812).
54   ICS, 120 6/A/99 (Simon Richard Brissett Taylor to Simon Taylor, 5 June 1811).
55   Ono-George, '"Washing the Blackamoor White"', pp. 42, 55–6; 'Sarah Blacktree Hunter', LBS: https://www.ucl.ac.uk/lbs/person/view/2146647377; 'Sarah Hunter Taylor Cathcart', LBS: https://www.ucl.ac.uk/lbs/person/view/12954; 'William Cathcart', LBS: https://www.ucl.ac.uk/lbs/person/view/12007.
56   ICS, 120 1/J/49 (Simon Taylor to Robert Taylor, 23 December 1811), 6/A/107 (Simon Richard Brissett Taylor to Simon Taylor, 28 March 1812); Pearsall, *Atlantic Families*, pp. 137–41.
57   TNA, PROB 11/1548/177 (Will of Simon Taylor, 24 September 1813); Petley, *White Fury*, pp. 199–201, 221–2; Brown, *Reaper's Garden*, pp. 90–1.
58   'Simon Taylor of Jamaica', LBS: https://www.ucl.ac.uk/lbs/person/view/2146634174; Sheridan, 'Simon Taylor', pp. 289–96; Petley, *White Fury*, p. 212; JARD, IB/11/3, vol. 123, ff. 216–58 (Simon Taylor Probate Inventory, 1813).
59   Unity and Venture had been managed together since at least 1784, the last year they appear in the Accounts Produce records: 'Unity', LBS: https://www.ucl.ac.uk/lbs/estate/view/17441; 'Venture', LBS: https://www.ucl.ac.uk/lbs/estate/view/17435. Haughton Court is first mentioned in these in 1787; Haughton Grove Pen first appears in a letter from Governor Balcarres in 1799: 'Haughton Court', LBS: https://www.ucl.ac.uk/lbs/estate/view/3156; 'Haughton Grove Pen', LBS: https://www.ucl.ac.uk/lbs/estate/view/1885. Unity was renamed Haughton Court: Lawrence-Archer, *Monumental Inscriptions*, p. 332; WSHC, 3605/1 (Conveyance, Watson Taylors to Robert Taylor and John Shand, 25 June 1834) refers to an 1810 conveyance of Haughton Court 'formerly cultivated as two plantations called Venture and Unity'.

60 ICS. 120 13/A/256 (Robert Taylor to Simon Taylor, 4 August 1808), 1/J/29 (Simon Taylor to Robert Taylor, 29 March 1811), 1/J/39 (Simon Taylor to Simon Richard Brissett Taylor, 18 June 1811). The surgeon was Henry Cline: Bevan, M., 'Cline, Henry', ODNB: https://doi.org/10.1093/ref:odnb/5673; 'Sir Simon Richard Brissett Taylor', LBS: https://www.ucl.ac.uk/lbs/person/view/2146634178.
61 Bury, *Diary Illustrative of the Times of George the Fourth*, vol. 3, pp. 295–7.
62 ICS, 120 8/B/8 (John Shand to George Watson Taylor, 24 February 1816), 8/D/22 (George Watson Taylor to William Shand, 5 August 1819).
63 'John Shand', LBS: https://www.ucl.ac.uk/lbs/person/view/2146635763; 'William Shand of Fettercain', LBS: https://www.ucl.ac.uk/lbs/person/view/2146632949; House of Commons, *Report from Select Committee on the Extinction of Slavery Throughout the British Dominions*, pp. 407–10.
64 ICS, 120 8/B/25 (John Shand to George Watson Taylor, 5 March 1817).
65 Petley, *White Fury*, p. 50; Brown, *Tacky's Revolt*, pp. 221–4, 242; Leigh and Sorrell, 'How to Control the History', pp. 19–56. There is a brief mention of an unnamed rebellion, probably in Trelawny, in early January 1767 in *Roger Hope Elletson's Letter Book 1766–1768*, ed. Jacobs, pp. 80, 83–4.
66 ICS, 120 1/I/43 (Simon Taylor to George Hibbert, 31 October 1807); Brown, *Tacky's Revolt*, p. 242; Petley, *White Fury*, p. 50.
67 Barclay, *Practical View*, pp. 24, 265, 273–4; ICS, 120 7/B/1 (John Cooper's report on Holland to Anna Susanna Watson Taylor, 1 January 1835); JARD, 1B/11/3, vol. 123, ff. 216–58 (Simon Taylor's Probate Inventory, 1813). In 1817 Dolly had a twenty-year-old son, Primus, and a twenty-five-year-old daughter, Frankey or Elizabeth Jamieson, but both were described as 'Negro': TNA, T 71/145, ff. 782–95 (Slave Registers, Jamaica, St Thomas in the East, 1817), Ancestry: https://www.ancestry.co.uk/search/collections/1129.
68 Barclay, *Practical View*, p. 272; Hakewill, *Picturesque Tour*, Introduction (unpaginated).
69 The family had applied again to Shand's successor, McPherson, but he gave the same answer: House of Commons, *Report from Select Committee on the Extinction of Slavery Throughout the British Dominions*, p. 410; ICS, 120 7/B/1 (John Cooper's report on Holland to Anna Susanna Watson Taylor, 1 January 1835).
70 ICS, 120 8/B/5, 8 (John Shand to George Watson Taylor, 18 November 1815 and 24 February 1816), 8/A/6 (George Watson Taylor to John Shand, 7 December 1815), 8/D/7 (George Watson Taylor to William Shand, 4 October 1816).
71 Chicenska, 'Colonisin' in Reverse!', pp. 106, 126–32, 137, 139, 148, 245, 359.
72 ICS, 120 8/D/7, 14, 22 (George Watson Taylor to William Shand, 4 October 1816, 5 March 1818, 5 August 1819).
73 ICS, 120 8/B/4, 9 (John Shand to George Watson Taylor, 6 November 1815, 31 March 1816); 8/E/8 (William Shand to George Watson Taylor, 9 May 1819).
74 ICS, 120 2/B/36 (Simon Taylor to Sir John Taylor, 27 January 1783).
75 Bury, *Diary Illustrative of the Times of George the Fourth*, vol. 3, pp. 295–7; 'Christmas Festivities', *Morning Post*, 7 January 1818.
76 They bought the house which is now 15–17 Cavendish Square, with 2–14 Harley Street. Sir Grey Cooper lived at no. 7. Roberts, '"Quite Appropriate"', pp. 116, 123, n. 15; 'Watson Taylor, George', HOP (1820–32): https://www.historyofparliamentonline.org/volume/1820-1832/member/watson-taylor-george-1771-1841. On the Duke of Chandos, see Mitchell, '"Legitimate Commerce"', pp. 544–78.
77 Bury, *Diary Illustrative of the Times of George the Fourth*, vol. 3, p. 296.
78 ICS, 120 8/B/25 (John Shand to George Watson Taylor, 5 March 1817).

79 The estate encompassed much surrounding land, including the manors of East Coulston, Great Cheverell, Potterne, Edington and Urchfont. Ide, '"Very Pretty Seat"', pp. 9–10, 18.

80 Roberts, '"Quite Appropriate"', pp. 117–18, 124 n. 28; Freyberger, 'In the Presence of Marie-Antoinette', p. 22.

81 ICS, 120 8/A/6 (George Watson Taylor to John Shand, 7 December 1815), 8/B/8 (John Shand to George Watson Taylor, 24 February 1816); Bowett, 'Specimen Wood Workbox', pp. 71–96; Anderson, *Mahogany*, pp. 85–8. My thanks to Hannah Cusworth for her advice on this question.

82 Bury, *Diary Illustrative of the Times of George the Fourth*, vol. 3, pp. 295–7.

83 Roberts, '"Quite Appropriate"', p. 123 n. 19.

84 'Court Circular', *The Times*, 21 February 1817, p. 3; 'The Fashionable Season', *Morning Post*, 8 February 1819.

85 Ide, '"Very Pretty Seat"', p. 12.

86 My understanding of George as a collector is informed by the work of Goëssant, 'George Watson-Taylor', and Thomas, *Chattel*.

87 Cultural Legacies listed at 'George Watson Taylor', LBS: https://www.ucl.ac.uk/lbs/person/view/-1221895888; 'George Watson Taylor', National Gallery: https://www.nationalgallery.org.uk/people/george-watson-taylor; Christie's catalogue of the sale of Sir John Taylor's collection, 26–27 April 1787: https://n10318uk.eos-intl.eu/N10318UK/Details/Record.aspx?BibCode=14989762.

88 After their fifth child, Emilius, arrived in September 1819, his bust was commissioned from up-and-coming sculptor Edward Hodges Baily, who would later create the monument to Lord Holland in Westminster Abbey, and Nelson's statue for Trafalgar Square. Gibson, *John Walter Watson Taylor*, 1816, Victoria and Albert Museum, London: http://collections.vam.ac.uk/item/O312897/john-watson-walter-taylor-bust-gibson-john/john-watson-walter-taylor-bust-john-gibson/; Ferrari and Sullivan, 'Men Thinking': https://www.tate.org.uk/research/tate-papers/29/john-gibson-portraiture-practice; Ferrari, 'Gibson and the Watson Taylor Family', 11 February 2017: http://bklynbiblio.blogspot.com/2017/02/gibson-and-watson-taylor-family.html; Ferrari, 'Before Rome', pp. 137, 144.

89 Eastlake, *Life of John Gibson*, pp. 40–3; Gibson, *Kneeling Woman with a Standing Infant*, Rome, c.1817, Royal Academy of Arts, London.

90 Nichol, *Catalogue*.

91 'George Watson Taylor Esq.', Roxburghe Club: https://www.roxburgheclub.org.uk/membership/index.php?MemberID=34; Husbands, 'Literary and Cultural Significance', pp. 111–13, 177–9, 228–30; Husbands, *Early Roxburghe Club*, pp. 56–7. He also edited the letters of Henrietta Hobart, Countess of Suffolk and her second husband George Berkeley.

92 Watson Taylor, *Profligate*, p. 152.

93 Ide, '"Very Pretty Seat"', p. 14.

94 'Britton cabinet', Wiltshire Museum: https://www.wiltshiremuseum.org.uk/artworks/britton-cabinet/; 'Celtic Cabinet Stonehenge', Clonehenge: https://clonehenge.com/2009/06/11/celtic-cabinet-stonehenge-wiltshire-heritage-museum/.

95 Ide, '"Very Pretty Seat"', p. 15.

96 ICS, 13/A/156, 173 (Robert Taylor to Simon Taylor, 3 March 1801, 4 August 1802), 8/D/13 (George Watson Taylor to William Shand, 4 November 1817), 8/A/11 (George Watson Taylor to John Shand, 5 May 1818), 8/D/15 (George Watson Taylor to William Shand, 6 May 1818); TNA, C 211/25/T79 (Commission of Lunacy, 2 June 1821); 'Lunatics',

St John's Wood Memories: https://www.stjohnswoodmemories.org.uk/content/arts/literature-writers/lunacy_-_how_facts_and_fiction_intermingle_in_st_johns_wood.
97 TNA, PROB 11/1599/246 (Will of Martha Taylor, 17 December 1817); TNA PROB 11/1763/174 (Will of Maria Taylor, 11 November 1829).
98 'Sarah Blacktree Hunter', LBS: https://www.ucl.ac.uk/lbs/person/view/2146647377; 'Sarah Hunter Taylor Cathcart (later Wells)', LBS: https://www.ucl.ac.uk/lbs/person/view/12954; Ono-George, '"Washing the Blackamoor White"', p. 56; Petley, *White Fury*, p. 215; ICS, 120 3/C/4, 5 (Sarah Blacktree Hunter to Lady Taylor, 20 October 1820, copy of William Cathcart to Sarah Blacktree Hunter, 16 October 1820). All figures converted to sterling.
99 'Watson Taylor, George', HOP (1820–30): https://www.historyofparliamentonline.org/volume/1820-1832/member/watson-taylor-george-1771-1841; 'Seaford', HOP: http://www.historyofparliamentonline.org/volume/1790-1820/constituencies/seaford.
100 House of Commons, 22 July 1831, Hansard: https://api.parliament.uk/historic-hansard/commons/1831/jul/22/parliamentary-reform-bill-for-england#S3V0005P0_18310722_HOC_78.
101 'Watson Taylor, George', HOP (1790–1820): https://www.historyofparliamentonline.org/volume/1790-1820/member/watson-taylor-george-1770-1841; *Colonial Journal*, vol. 1 (January–July 1816), pp. 562–3; ICS, 8/B/10 (John Shand to George Watson Taylor, 13 April 1816).
102 'Watson Taylor, George', HOP (1820–30): https://www.historyofparliamentonline.org/volume/1820-1832/member/watson-taylor-george-1771-1841.
103 House of Commons, 16 March 1824, Hansard: https://hansard.parliament.uk/Commons/1824-03-16/debates/4a657d28-435c-430f-82dc-103125e88076/AmeliorationOfTheConditionOfTheSlavePopulationInTheWestIndies; *Devizes and Wiltshire Gazette*, 18 March 1824. When Hakewill visited in 1820–1, a large hospital or 'change-of-air house' was available 'for the use of convalescents on the estate', though, as we know, such places were less than salubrious: Hakewill, *Picturesque Tour* (unpaginated). It's not entirely clear how long it had been there.
104 ICS, 120 8/B/4, 6 (John Shand to George Watson Taylor, 6 November 1815, 30 December 1815); Hakewill, *Picturesque Tour* (unpaginated); *Lady Nugent's Journal*, ed. Wright, pp. 66, 69. Their position is clear in the 1780 plan of the estate by Smellie and Sherriff: Higman, *Jamaica Surveyed*, pp. 238, 240.
105 House of Commons, 16 March 1824, Hansard: https://hansard.parliament.uk/Commons/1824-03-16/debates/4a657d28-435c-430f-82dc-103125e88076/AmeliorationOfTheConditionOfTheSlavePopulationInTheWestIndies. He made a similar point at the 10 February 1824 West India Committee meeting, voting in favour of submitting a petition to the King laying out their grievances. 'West India Proprietors', *The Times*, 11 February 1824, p. 3; Osborne, 'Power and Persuasion', pp. 236–7; Taylor, *Interest*, 98.
106 *The Edinburgh Review and the West Indies* (1816) appears in the sale catalogue of his library. A signed first edition of *A Practical View of the Present State of Slavery in the West Indies*, with letter from Barclay enclosed, was sold on Ebay: WorthPoint: https://www.worthpoint.com/worthopedia/1826-african-slavery-caribbean-413719492.
107 Barclay, *Practical View*, pp. 53, 100.
108 Petley, *White Fury*, pp. 145–6; Slave Voyages, Trans-Atlantic, Voyage ID 18052: https://www.slavevoyages.org/voyage/database.
109 House of Commons, 16 March 1824, Hansard: https://api.parliament.uk/historic-hansard/commons/1824/mar/16/amelioration-of-the-condition-of-the#S2V0010P0_18240316_

HOC_92; House of Commons, *Report from Select Committee on the Extinction of Slavery Throughout the British Dominions*, p. 410.
110 House of Commons, 15 March 1824, Hansard: https://api.parliament.uk/historic-hansard/commons/1824/mar/15/abolition-of-slavery#S2V0010P0_18240315_HOC_10; *Devizes and Wiltshire Gazette*, 25 March 1824.
111 *John Bull*, 27 February 1826, p. 68; *Devizes and Wiltshire Gazette*, 2 March 1826, 2 September 1824; Hampton, R., 'A History of Erlestoke': https://www.erlestoke.org/information/village-history-by-roger-hampton/; 'Watson Taylor, George', HOP: https://www.historyofparliamentonline.org/volume/1820-1832/member/watson-taylor-george-1771-1841.
112 'To the Editor of *The Times*', *The Times*, 16 August 1831, p. 3.
113 ICS, 120 8/D/22 (George Watson Taylor to William Shand, 5 August 1819).
114 John Macarthur and Hudson Gurney, quoted in 'Watson Taylor, George', HOP: https://www.historyofparliamentonline.org/volume/1820-1832/member/watson-taylor-george-1771-1841.
115 The trustees had control of £16,528 18s 6d in consols, or 3% bank annuities placed in Anna Susanna's name by Simon Taylor at the time of her marriage in 1810, and purchased a further £15,830 1s consols after his death as there had not been an uprising or invasion. Richard Grant died in 1820, Robert Taylor senior died in 1823 and John Shand died in 1825. IRO, Deeds, vol. 791, ff. 171–81 (Anna Susanna and George Watson marriage settlement, 1834); TNA, C 13/1192/24 [C1838 T9] (Taylor v Hibbert, 5 April 1838).
116 'Hon. William Miller (Attorney)', LBS: https://www.ucl.ac.uk/lbs/person/view/2146637296; 'Thomas McCornock', LBS: https://www.ucl.ac.uk/lbs/person/view/24516.
117 ICS, 7/B/1 (John Cooper to Benjamin Greene, 2 January 1835); Higman, *Plantation Jamaica*, p. 101; Donington, *Bonds of Family*, pp. 88–9.
118 *Elizabeth, Lady Holland to Her Son*, ed. Ilchester, p. 15; Roberts, '"Quite Appropriate"', p. 116; *Devizes and Wiltshire Gazette*, 19 June 1823.
119 Roberts, '"Quite Appropriate"', p. 119; French writing table, c.1766, https://api.waddesdon.org.uk/docs/Furniture/2336.pdf?_ga=2.29831551.1730036134.1647432555-850647265.1647432555.
120 Roberts, '"Quite Appropriate"', pp. 115–21; The writing desk was later purchased by the Rothschilds and is now at Waddesdon Manor, near Aylesbury: https://waddesdon.org.uk/the-collection/item/?id=167; 'Sir Charles Long, 1st Baron Farnborough', LBS: https://www.ucl.ac.uk/lbs/person/view/2146638829; Hall, *Lucky Valley*, pp. 241–2.
121 *Devizes and Wiltshire Gazette*, 16 August 1827, 4 October 1827; Ide, '"Very Pretty Seat"', p. 15; *The Times*, 16 August 1831.
122 Lord Ellenborough, *Political Diary*, ed. Lord Colchester, vol. 2, p. 319.
123 Roberts, '"Quite Appropriate"', p. 123 nn. 10, 18; *Globe*, Thursday 10 May 1832; *Public Ledger and Daily Advertiser*, 1 June 1832.
124 Ide, '"Very Pretty Seat"', p. 16; Roberts, '"Quite Appropriate"', pp. 116, 122, nn. 8, 10; *Bristol Mirror*, 11 August 1832.
125 *Freeman's Journal*, 15 August 1832.
126 *A Portion of the Journal Kept by Thomas Raikes*, p. 26.
127 *Chester Chronicle*, 31 August 1832.
128 *Morning Chronicle*, 8 October 1832.
129 'Sir James Hurtle Fisher', Australian Dictionary of Biography: https://adb.anu.edu.au/biography/fisher-sir-james-hurtle-2045; *Public Ledger and Daily Advertiser*, 27 November 1837, reporting Watson Taylor v Bailie. See also TNA, C 13/331/17, C 13/332/34, C 13/1057/49, C 13/336/20 (Taylor v Fisher, 1833–4).

130 Cadell, *Abbey Court & High Constables*, p. 35; NRS, RH2/8/20 (Copy of Register of Protections of the Sanctuary of Holyroodhouse, 4 February 1834, 5 May 1834, De Quincey: 27 November 1833); Mackenzie-Stuart, *French King at Holyrood*. Interestingly, John Cooper's report on the Jamaican estates, made in early January 1835, were addressed to Anna Susanna at Campagne Ducloux, close to Geneva in Switzerland.
131 *The Times*, 25 February 1839, p. 3.
132 Roberts, '"Quite Appropriate"', p. 122, nn. 7, 10; information from Elodie Goëssant: Daniel Gardner, *Sir John Taylor*, c.1780, Ackland Art Museum, Chapel Hill, North Carolina: https://www.artres.com/archive/-2UNTWARUYF82.html; Reynolds, *Lady Elizabeth Taylor*, c.1780, Frick Collection, New York, and at Petworth House, West Sussex.
133 *London Evening Standard*, 13 January 1838.
134 *Gore's Liverpool General Advertiser*, 2 August 1832. It's possible this was James Hurtle Fisher – he had ten children, and emigrated to Australia in 1836. However, his name does not appear in the St Luke's Hospital curable patients books, August 1831– August 1832, nor does anyone else with the profession 'lawyer'. Wellcome Collection, H64/B/01/12–13: https://wellcomecollection.org/works/gra2edbw.
135 *Salisbury and Winchester Journal*, 1 April 1833.
136 *Devizes and Wiltshire Gazette*, 27 April 1837.
137 House of Commons, 16 March 1824, Hansard: https://api.parliament.uk/historic-hansard/commons/1824/mar/16/amelioration-of-the-condition-of-the#S2V0010P0_18240316_HOC_92.
138 Hall et al., *Legacies*, p. 109; 'Sir Edmund Antrobus', LBS: https://www.ucl.ac.uk/lbs/person/view/23866; 'Oliver Farrer', LBS: https://www.ucl.ac.uk/lbs/person/view/43487; 'William Matthew Coulthurst', LBS: https://www.ucl.ac.uk/lbs/person/view/46462.
139 Eliza and 'William Mayne', LBS: https://www.ucl.ac.uk/lbs/person/view/2146630695; and their son-in-law 'Michael Elijah Impey', LBS: https://www.ucl.ac.uk/lbs/person/view/-2092309274.
140 WSHC, 3605/2 (Agreement between Simon Watson Taylor, William Mayne and others, 11 April 1836).
141 The couple were never legally married, but Charlotte lived as James's wife at Mellmount, Strabane, Country Tyrone, Ireland, where they moved in 1835. Charlotte held eighteen people as joint executor with none other than Alexander Barclay. Estate of Eleanor Madden, LBS: https://www.ucl.ac.uk/lbs/estate/view/19641; 'Charlotte Taylor', LBS: https://www.ucl.ac.uk/lbs/person/view/43524; Tammemagi, K., 'The End of the BIG Story', Sproule Genealogy, 14 April 2014: https://sproulegenealogy.blogspot.com/2014/04/the-end-of-big-story.html.
142 'Sarah Blacktree Hunter', LBS: https://www.ucl.ac.uk/lbs/person/view/2146647377; 'Sarah Taylor', LBS: https://www.ucl.ac.uk/lbs/person/view/12951; 'Sarah Hunter Taylor Cathcart (later Wells)', LBS: https://www.ucl.ac.uk/lbs/person/view/12954.
143 ICS, 120, 7/B/1, f. 2 (John Cooper's report on Holland to Anna Susanna Watson Taylor, 1 January 1835).
144 Only eight claims were made for exactly twelve people in St Thomas in the East. Half can be ruled out as UCL has identified the claimants. There remain four women: Eleanor Minot, Mary Phillips, Grace Dun Walker and Mary Lindsay: 'Mary Lindsay', LBS: https://www.ucl.ac.uk/lbs/person/view/17846. There was also *a* Mary Lindsay listed amongst the enslaved people at Holland in 1817: TNA, T 71/145, ff. 782–95 (Slave Registers, Jamaica, St. Thomas in the East, 1817), Ancestry: https://www.ancestry.co.uk/search/collections/1129. That same year *a* Mary Lindsay reported owning nine people in St

Thomas in the East. The figure had grown to thirteen by 1826. In the 1820 record, her name is first written as Taylor, then this surname is crossed out in favour of Lindsay, which tends to support the idea that this was the same woman. TNA, T 71/145, ff. 455–65, T 71/146, f. 264, T 71/147, f. 208, T 71/148, f. 190 (Slave Registers, Jamaica, St Thomas in the East, 1817, 1820, 1823, 1826), Ancestry: https://www.ancestry.co.uk/search/collections/1129.

145 JARD, 1B/11/3, vol. 123, ff. 216–58 (Simon Taylor's Probate Inventory, 1813).
146 TNA, T 71/199, ff. 256–7 (Slave Registers, Jamaica, Hanover, 1832), Ancestry: https://www.ancestry.co.uk/search/collections/1129.
147 ICS, 120, 7/B/3 (John Cooper's report on Haughton Court to Anna Susanna Watson Taylor, 20 January 1835); TNA, T 71/199, f. 254 (Slave Registers, Jamaica, Hanover, 1832), Ancestry: https://www.ancestry.co.uk/search/collections/1129; TNA, CO 137/185, Part 2, ff. 459, 583 (Slave Rebellion Trials, 1832).
148 'Benjamin Greene', LBS: https://www.ucl.ac.uk/lbs/person/view/25002; TNA, C 13/1090/24 (Taylor v Hibbert, October 1835), C 13/1124/15, (Taylor v Miles, February 1836), C 13/1158/15 (Taylor v Taylor, April 1837), C 13/1192/24 (Taylor v Hibbert, April 1838). WSHC, 3605/1 (Conveyance of Jamaican estates to new trustees, by order of Chancery, 12 February 1844).
149 Most of the following is from ICS, 120 7/B/1–4 (John Cooper's reports to Anna Susanna Watson Taylor on her estates, January to February 1835).
150 Senior, 'Limerick "Slaves" for Jamaica', pp. 33–40; 'Register Excerpts – Lamby to Wisdom', Jamaican Family Search: http://www.jamaicanfamilysearch.com/Members/Rw_l-w.htm.
151 JARD, Manumissions, 1B/11/6/65, f. 96 (Mary Brown of Trelawny, 'a free person of colour', pays Watson Taylors £100 current to manumit James Allaidice, 'quadroon', 3 October 1829). Perhaps an alias of Mary Lindsay, daughter of Lydia Brown?; 1B/11/6/68, f. 130 (Peter McKie, 'planter' of St Catherine, pays Watson Taylors £120 current to manumit Jane Creighton 'mulatto' and her (presumably their) daughter Sally McKie, 'quadroon', of Montrose Pen, St Mary, 2 August 1833). Might these have been relations to Becky McKay of Prospect Pen, daughter of 'a mulatto slave named Sally, now dead', who appeared in Simon's will?

At Haughton Court, William Benson, twenty-two, and Iowa Mary, twenty-eight, were exchanged for Mary Macintosh (thirty-six-year-old Creole 'quadroon') and her three 'mustee' boys: William Thomas, George and John Holbrook, aged twelve, eleven and eight, manumitted at Haughton Court between 1829 and 1832. But Iowa Mary died soon afterwards: TNA, T 71/199, ff. 256–7 (Slave Registers, Jamaica, Hanover, 1832), Ancestry: https://www.ancestry.co.uk/search/collections/1129.
152 'Thomas McCornock', LBS: https://www.ucl.ac.uk/lbs/person/view/24516.
153 Vasconcellos, *Slavery*, pp. 86–7.
154 Sturge and Harvey, *West Indies in 1837*, pp. lxviii, 307–8, 425.
155 Thorne and Kimball, *Six Months' Tour*, pp. 379–83.
156 Roberts, '"Quite Appropriate"', p. 122, n. 7; 'Carlton Terrace', Historic Environment Scotland: https://portal.historicenvironment.scot/designation/LB49752; TNA, PROB 11/1992/138 (Will of George Watson Taylor, 15 January 1844); *Notes and Queries*, 4th series, vol. 9, 16 March 1872, p. 227.
157 TNA, PROB 11/2169/269 (Will of Anna Susanna Watson Taylor, 19 March 1853).
158 IRO, Deeds, vol. 898, ff. 230–3 (Sale of Lyssons by Anna Susanna Watson Taylor, Simon Watson Taylor and other siblings to James Tuckett, 7 December 1849); Green, 'Planter Class', p. 457 n. 3; *Acts of Jamaica passed in the year 1845*, Railway Act, pp. 342–3.

159 Simon Taylor left £700 Jamaica currency to Charlotte in his will. WSHC, 3605/2 (Correspondence regarding the Sproull claim, 1850; Assignments: 1851 – William Taylor and Robert Samuel Sproule; 1851 – William and Matilda Ann Smyth (née Sproule) and 'the late Ellen Madden Sproule'; 1856 – Sarah Charlotte Sproule; 1861 – Jane Nugent Sproule, perhaps named after Nelly Nugent, her probable grandmother).
160 'Parishes: Urchfont', in *History of the County of Wiltshire*, ed. Crittall, vol. 10, BHO: http://www.british-history.ac.uk/vch/wilts/vol10/pp173-190.
161 Their address was 5 Upper Eccleston Street. 1851 England Census, Ancestry: https://www.ancestry.co.uk/search/collections/8860/records/2251972; Venn, *Alumni Cantabrigienses*, Ancestry: https://www.ancestry.co.uk/search/collections/3997/records/89020.
162 George's body was moved from Holyrood to Edington in 1844, suggesting the family stayed in Edinburgh for a few years after his death. Information from Elodie Goëssant.
163 TNA, PROB 11/2169/269 (Will of Anna Susanna Watson Taylor, 19 March 1853).
164 *England & Wales, National Probate Calendar (Index of Wills and Administrations), 1858–1995*, John Walter (1879), p. 365; Isabella (1893), p. 237; Simon (1903), p. 278, Ancestry: https://www.ancestry.co.uk/search/collections/1904/. Emilius was able to buy Headington Manor House, Oxford (now part of the John Radcliffe Hospital site) in 1858, where he and Isabella lived until their deaths. https://www.headington.org.uk/history/listed_buildings/manorhouse.htm.
165 Reina, 'Il vero conte di Montecristo'; 'The Alleged Outrage on Mr Taylor', House of Commons, 13 June 1862, Hansard: https://api.parliament.uk/historic-hansard/commons/1862/jun/13/the-alleged-outrage-on-mr-taylor-papers ; *England & Wales, National Probate Calendar (Index of Wills and Administrations), 1858–1995*, George Graeme Watson Taylor (1865), p. 23, Ancestry: https://www.ancestry.co.uk/search/collections/1904/.
166 Hampton, R., 'A History of Erlestoke': https://www.erlestoke.org/information/village-history-by-roger-hampton/.
167 IRO, Deeds, vol. 930, ff. 21–4 (Sale of Llanrumney, Simon Watson Taylor to William Hosack, 7 December 1859).
168 'Watson Taylor, George', HOP: https://www.historyofparliamentonline.org/volume/1820-1832/member/watson-taylor-george-1771-1841 n.48. He was also a member of the Roxburghe Club: 'Simon Watson Taylor Esq.', Roxburghe Club: https://www.roxburgheclub.org.uk/membership/index.php?MemberID=88.
169 Simon donated £100, the same amount as the Duke of Portland, the Earl of Powis, and John Ruskin. Isabella Cooper's agent Thomson Hankey gave £50. Gopal, *Insurgent Empire*, p. 88; Draper, *Price of Emancipation*, Appendix 13; Petley, *White Fury*, p. 215; Hall, *Civilising Subjects*, pp. 24–5, 64–5; Finlason, *History of the Jamaica Case*, 368pp, 368tt.
170 Though Simon Watson Taylor still owned Holland, it was by this stage leased to unpopular magistrate Samuel Shortridge, owner of Plantain Garden River estate, and attorney for Holland, Hordley and several other estates in the area. *Report of the Jamaica Royal Commission, 1866*, pp. 21–3, 36, 105, 229, 337, 377, 538–9.
171 Those whipped were Robert Johnson, Richard Rowdon, Theodore, Morris Brooks, Samuel Walker, Gordon, Allen, Rowe, James Anderson, James Francis, Tommy Russell, Philip Aleck Baugh, Mary Williams and Lydia Francis. Ibid., pp. 228, 248, 251, 391, 392, 405–6; Jemmott, *Ties that Bind*, p. 151.
172 Ide, '"Very Pretty Seat"', pp. 18–19.
173 Petley, *White Fury*, pp. 1, 218.
174 'American Caribbean Experience (ACE)': https://www.acexperience.org/.

175 They married on 1 October 1883: 'Extracts from *The Times*, London, England, concerning Jamaicans', Jamaican Family Search: http://www.jamaicanfamilysearch.com/Members/0TimesExtracts.htm; Montgomery Seaver, *Taylor Family Records*, p. 13.
176 'Arthur Dickson, 1913–2011', Jamaican Family Search: http://www.jamaicanfamilysearch.com/images2/DicksonArthur.htm; 'A Snapshot of People and Life in Lucea & Hanover, circa 1913–1933: Some Recollections of Arthur Richard Dickson, Born Lucea 1913' (unpublished paper); *Blue Book for the Island of Jamaica* (1928), p. 104; *Jamaica Gleaner*, 29 April 1927. George Dewar of Harmony Hall was Harry Gerald Watson Taylor's father-in-law. A.W. Watson-Taylor is listed as owner of Holland in 1907: NLJ, 727.45qdb (*The Plan of the Parish of St Thomas, Jamaica – Compiled from Actual Surveys in 1881* by Thomas Harrison, Government Surveyor, rev. May 1907 by Colin Liddell, Surveyor General). By the 1955 revision of the map, Holland had been granted to the West India Import Company.
177 *Jamaica Gleaner*, 12 November 1928, 18 April 1929; Earle, 'Watson Taylor Park Beach Facility': https://jis.gov.jm/watson-taylor-park-beach-facility-to-be-renovated/.
178 Curtin, *Story of Hanover*, chapter 18 (unpaginated ebook).

CONCLUSION

1 In 1823, Sir Humphrey Davy, inventor of the Davy mining lamp and husband to Antiguan heiress Jane Apreece, née Kerr, was granted the Navy contract to devise a way to stop this copper eroding. See Introduction, n. 13; James, 'Davy in the Dockyard', pp. 205–25.
2 Austen, *Sanditon*, ed. Todd, p. 118.
3 Heyrick, *Immediate, not Gradual Abolition*, pp. 8, 30.
4 Defoe, D., *Review*, 10 January 1713, I, no. 44, p. 89. See also Berg and Hudson, *Slavery*, pp. 35–7, for many similar statements.
5 BL, Bridport Papers, Add MS 34959 (Horatio Nelson to Simon Taylor, 10 June 1805, from the *Victory* off the coast of Martinique), transcribed here: https://nelson-society.com/nelson-letter-a-forgery/. A similar version was printed in: *Cobbett's Political Register*, vol. 11, no. 8 (21 February 1807), pp. 295–6. See Petley, 'Lord Nelson and Slavery', *BBC History Magazine*, Christmas 2018.
6 West, P., 'Holland Park Must Fall', *Spectator*, 25 June 2020: https://www.spectator.co.uk/article/it-would-be-a-mistake-to-rename-holland-park/.
7 Gentleman, A., 'African and Caribbean Nations Agree Move to Seek Reparations for Slavery', *Guardian*, 17 November 2023: https://www.theguardian.com/world/2023/nov/17/african-and-caribbean-nations-agree-move-to-seek-reparations-for-slavery.
8 Fleary, S., 'William's "Profound Sorrow" is the New "Statement of Regret" – but Where is the Apology for Slavery?', *The Voice*, 24 March 2022: https://www.voice-online.co.uk/news/uk-news/2022/03/24/williams-profound-sorrow-is-the-new-statement-of-regret-but-where-is-the-apology-for-slavery/.
9 'Brattle Consultants Quantify Reparations for Transatlantic Chattel Slavery in Pro Bono Paper', Brattle, 29 June 2023: https://www.brattle.com/insights-events/publications/brattle-consultants-quantify-reparations-for-transatlantic-chattel-slavery-in-pro-bono-paper/; Banner, *Britain's Slavery Debt*, pp. 5, 113–17.
10 'Ten Point Plan for Reparatory Justice', CARICOM: https://caricom.org/caricom-ten-point-plan-for-reparatory-justice/. See also CARICOM Reparations Commission (https://caricomreparations.org/), the Decolonizing Wealth Project (https://decolonizingwealth.com/), the National African American Reparations Commission (https://

Notes to pages 402–8

       reparationscomm.org/) and the Reparations Finance Lab (https://reparationsfinancelab.org/).
11   Chow, H., 'Our New Name: Debt Justice', 16 May 2022: https://debtjustice.org.uk/news/our-new-name-debt-justice
12   Stanford-Xosei, 'Long Road', pp. 176–95.
13   Harris, G.,'Growing Pressure on the British Museum as Jamaica is Latest Government Seeking Return of Objects', *Art Newspaper*, 8 August 2019: https://www.theartnewspaper.com/2019/08/08/growing-pressure-on-the-british-museum-as-jamaica-is-latest-government-seeking-return-of-objects.
14   Key texts on reparations include: Beckles, *Britain's Black Debt*; Beckles, *How Britain Underdeveloped the Caribbean*; Banner, *Britain's Slavery Debt*; Araujo, *Reparations*; Taiwo, *Reconsidering Reparations*.

MY FAMILY AND ENSLAVEMENT

1   Angelou, M., 'On the Pulse of Morning' (1993): https://poets.org/poem/pulse-morning. First read at the inauguration of President Bill Clinton in 1993.
2   Again, I have followed genealogists' use of 'great-' and 'grand-'.
3   The syndicate usually comprised William Gregson, his sons John and James Gregson, his son-in-law George Case and James Aspinall. Slave Voyages, Trans-Atlantic: https://www.slavevoyages.org/voyage/database; Craig and Jarvis, *Liverpool Registry of Merchant Ships*, pp. 9, 33, 34, 41, 42, 60, 73, 78, 96, 104, 130, 138; Pope, 'Wealth and Social Aspirations', pp. 164–226.
4   Walvin, *Zong*. Walvin is quiet on the biographies of the owners, with Edward Wilson only mentioned by name once.
5   Cugoano, *Thoughts and Sentiments*, p. 112. See also Moody, *Persistence of Memory*, pp. 261–6.
6   Hartsheath MSS, private collection, North Wales, no. 889 (Marriage settlement, John Jones and Elizabeth Wilson, 10 December 1789).
7   TNA, PROB 11/1406/220 (Will of Edward Wilson of Chester, 19 March 1804).
8   'Robert Cooper Lee', LBS: https://www.ucl.ac.uk/lbs/person/view/2146645287.
9   The line of descent is: Robert Cooper Lee (1735–94) → Favell Bourke Lee (1780–1841) → Richard Lee Bevan (1811–1900) → Favell Isabella Gertrude Bevan (1841–1906) → Wilson Cuthbert Bevan Jones-Mortimer (1872–1965) → Hugh Maurice Carstairs Jones-Mortimer (1908–80) → Johanna Favell Jones-Mortimer (b. 1949) → Miranda Kaufmann (b. 1982).
10   Powers, *Parcel of Ribbons*, p. 151; 'One in Five Britons Has Black Ancestor', *BioNews*, 4 October 1999: https://www.progress.org.uk/one-in-five-britons-has-black-ancestor/. Examples include the Barber family of Litchfield, descended from Dr Johnson's heir (Bundock, *Fortunes of Francis Barber*, pp. 211–13) and Peter Bluck, descended from Black Tudor, Henry Jetto (Kaufmann, *Black Tudors*, pp. 110, 239).
11   'Richard Lane', LBS: https://www.ucl.ac.uk/lbs/person/view/2964.
12   Will of Emily Eliza Lane, 9 October 1909, obtained from https://www.gov.uk/search-will-probate.
13   'Richard Walker', LBS: https://www.ucl.ac.uk/lbs/person/view/2146635635; 'Richard Watt Walker', LBS: https://www.ucl.ac.uk/lbs/person/view/43237; 'John Walker', LBS: https://www.ucl.ac.uk/lbs/person/view/45948.

INTELLECTUAL DEBTS

1. Mair, *Historical Study*; Shepherd, *Engendering History*; Beckles, *Centring Woman*; Jones, *Engendering Whiteness*; Walker, *Jamaica Ladies*; Jones-Rogers, *They Were Her Property*.
2. Williams, *Capitalism and Slavery*, p. 91.
3. Hall *et al.*, *Legacies*; LBS: https://www.ucl.ac.uk/lbs/.
4. Young, 'Gender'; Young, 'Forgotten Women'; Young, 'Negotiating Female Property'.
5. Shepherd, 'Women', p. 31.

Index

Page numbers in *italics* refer to artworks and illustrations. Place names are indexed by country, with the exception of those in the UK.

Those people enslaved for at least part of their lifetimes are denoted with the suffix '*', often to distinguish them from others with similar names. Where enslaved people have no clear surname, they can be found indexed by the first letter of the first part of their name.

Abba * 350
Abercromby, Sir Ralph 200, 222
Abercromby, Sir Robert 222, 223–4
Aberdeen * 280–1
Aberdeen Whaling Company 120
Abinger, James Scarlett, Baron 270
abolition of enslavement 10, 133, 202, 283, 284, 290, 378
    consequences of 338–9
    early opposition to slavery 9, 37, 230, 309
    opposition to 257, 281–2, 286, 329, 357
    Slavery Abolition Act (1833) 295, 300
    Slave Trade Abolition Act (1807) 270, 274–5, 281, 283, 307
    see also emancipation; Wilberforce, William
Acland, John 36
Adam, William 69, 119
Adams, John 123, 125
Adams, John Quincy 123
Adcock, Herbert Burroughs 345
Adderley, Edward Hale 270
Adjaye, David 51
Affleck, Lady Mary née Clarke (Vassall) 252, 254, 258, 267, 271
Affleck, Sir Gilbert 268
African Union 401
Agard, Charles 23
Aikenhead, William 68
Akan people 80, 87, 103
Albany, Charlotte Stuart, Countess of 190
Allen, John 290, 308
Alleyne, Elizabeth *later* Newton 23, 26, 27, 32, 42, 127
Alleyne, Lady Jane 46–7, 48
Alleyne, Sir John Gay 40, 46–7, 48, 49
Alleyne, Judith 26, 27, 32
Alleyne family, other 23, 24, 127
Alvimart, Octavien d' 201
American Revolution 92, 122–5, 180, 194, 223, 233, 290
    effect on plantation economy 41, 46, 65, 192, 316, 321

Anderson, Alexander 128, 129, 131
Anderson, James 126
Anderson, John 122, 128, 129, 131
Angelou, Maya 407
Angola 58
Anthony, Prince of Saxony 263
Antigua 3, 106, 111, 144, 172, 217, 228, 230
   Antigua Assembly 216, 306
   conflict in 175, 219, 233
   Jarvis estates (Bird Island, Long Island, and Thibou's) 215, 216, 219, 230, 232
   other plantations in 152
Antill family 249
antisemitism 314–15, 318
Anti-Slavery International 297
Apongo * 81
apprenticeship 294, 295, 296–305, *301*, 334–6, 337, 387
Apreece, Jane *see* Jane Kerr
Archer (Samuel Sharpe) * 284, 291, 293
Arden, John 49
Asante people 40, 219
Ash, John 30
Ashkenazi community 312, 315, 319
Ashwell, Charles 37
Astell, Mary 8
Aston Hall, Warwickshire 24, 25–6, 31–2, 33, 35, 48, 51–2, 341
Aston Villa Football Club 26, 51–2
Atlantic slave economy, *see* Transatlantic slave economy
Auchincruive, Ayrshire 119–20, 128, 132–3
Augier, John 56–8, *57*, 59, 62
Augier, Susanna * 55, 58, 59–60, 61–2, 64–6, 67–8, 69, 75–6, 77, 82
Augier family 56–8, 65, 68, 72, 77, 84, 409
Augusta of Saxe-Gotha, Princess of Wales 314
Austen, Cassandra née Leigh (Mrs) 140, 150, 156, 157, 158, 161, 163

Austen, Cassandra (junior) 150, 151, 152, 156, 160, 164, 165, 167
Austen, Frank 161, 164, 166, 167
Austen, George 140, 150, 152, 158, 160
Austen, Henry 161, 164
Austen, James 150, 151, 152, 157, 160, 164, 165, 166, 173
Austen, Jane 135, 140, *149*, 150–1, 159, 160–3, 164, 168–9, 326
   Emma 162, 163
   Mansfield Park 135, 152, 162–3, 227
   Northanger Abbey 150, 160, 162
   Persuasion 139, 153
   Pride and Prejudice 160, 161, 162, 228, 266
   Sanditon 7, 74, 167, 396
   Sense and Sensibility 161, 162
   Susan 150, 160
Austen, Mary 151, 157, 165, 167
Austen family, other *142*, 150–2, 160, 166–7
Austen-Leigh, Emma née Smith 166, 368
Austen-Leigh, James Edward 161–2, 165, 166, 167–8
Australia 6, 72, 154, 247–9

Bacchus * 283
Baggs, Isham 35, *35*
Bagot, Lewis 30, 31, 32
Bahamas, The 125, 247, 274, 296
Baker, John 172–3, 175–83, 186–7, 188, 191–3, 338, 378
Baker, Martha *later* Swinburne *170*, 171–212, *174*
Baker, Mary née Ryan 172, 176, 179, 182, 186
Baker, Tom 192–3, 197
Baker family, other 172, *174*, 193
Balfour, James 222, 237, 244
Bance Island, Sierra Leone 97, *98*, 108–12, 118, 122–3, 124, 126, 129, 131, 132
Bank of England 3, 105, 108, 207, 317, 321

Banks, Sir Joseph 188, 234, 372
baptism 19, 27, 283
Baptist Church 283, 306
Baptist War 291–4, 292, 305, 334, 385
Barbados 3, *14*, 15, 41, 51–2, 144, 296, 401, 404
   Barbados Council 19, 20–1
   Bridgetown 56, 136, 137–8
   Newton estates (Mount Alleyne, and Newton and Seawells) 14–17, 20–1, 25–6, 32, 37–51
      enslaved people at 41–2
      see also Hylas, Mary née Revill
   Cholmeley/Workman estate (Brace's estate) 136–8, 143–8
      enslaved people at 145, 147
   other plantations in 73, 136–7
   plantation economy in 14–16, 18–20, 65, 173, 217, 394
   uprisings in 337, 375, 377
Barbados Mercury 145
Barbados Slave Code (1661) 20, 62
Barbot, John 172
Barclay, Alexander 311–12, 329–332, 336–41, 345, 365–6, 377, 386, 387
Barclay's Bank 226
Barham, Joseph Foster 265, 283, 286, 292, 296
Baring, Elizabeth 317
Barr, Agnes 105, 121
Barrett Browning, Elizabeth 115, 292
Barrymore, Richard Barry, Earl of 140–1
Bath, Somerset 30, 149–51, 153–4, 159, 162, 164
Battle Abbey, East Sussex 258, 259, 261, 295
Bayley, Mary 217
Bayly family 382
beads 40
Beale, Daniel 240
Beale, Elizabeth 241
Beckford, Molly 312
Beckford, Richard 84
Beckford, William Thomas 80, 83, 84, 381

Beckford family 252
Bedward, George 127–8
Beef, Jack * 176, 179, 186, 187
Belize 206, 212
Bell, James 335, 336
Belle, Dido Elizabeth 92
Benfield, Paul 200–1, 246, 325
Benin 108
Bentley, Sir Martin 21
Berbice 200
Bermuda 292
Bessborough, Henrietta Ponsonby, Countess of 270, 274, 275, 277
Birmingham 24, 31, 109, 294, 303, 310, 341, 396
Bicknell, John, *The Dying Negro* 27–8
Blackall, Samuel 152
Black Loyalists 124–5, 337
Blackman family 49
Blake, Catherine * 300–1
Blake, George * 300
Blake, Henry 387
Blizard, Geoffry * 219
Blizard family 216, 219
Blore, Edward 333
Board of Trade 56, 82–3
Bob * 127, 128
Bobby * 283
Bodkin, Laurence 177, 178, 192
Bogle, Helen 84
Bogle, Paul * 343, *344*, 345
Bogle & Co. 330
Bontein, Thomas 71–3, 76–7, 78, 79, 80, 86
Boswell, James 116, 225
Bouillé, François Claude Amour, marquis de 194
Boulton, Matthew 341
Bouverie, Edward 49
Bowen, Emmanuel 230–1
Boyd, John 108, 121, 131
Brace, Ann 136–7, 138
Brace, Edward 136–7, 138, 143
Braco, Lord, William Duff 55, 69, 74, 75, 76, 87

Brathwaite, John 49
Brattle Group, The 402
Braybrooke, Richard Griffin, Baron 157
Brazil 16, 18, *18*
Brissett, Mary *later* Haughton 354
Brissett, Richard 265, 357
Brissett family 350
Bristol 1, 77, 163, 207, 309, 315, 316, 361, 412
Bristol, Frederick Hervey, Earl of 262
Bristol Mirror 381
Britain, *see* Great Britain
British and Foreign Anti-Slavery Society 297
British Civil War 15
British Guiana 285, 296, 297
British Museum, London 5, 380
Brome family 49
Bronte, Charlotte, *Jane Eyre* 7
Brougham, Henry Brougham, Baron 290, 292, 298, 309
Broughton, John Cam Hobhouse, Baron 384
Brown, Adam * 302
Brown, Thomas * 331
Browning, Robert 115
Buckingham Palace, London 333, 391
Bull, Farley Murray 323
Burke, Edmund 116, 200, 295
Burns, Robert 98, 115, 120, 130–1
Bush, George W. 132
Bussa * 337, 375
Buxton, Thomas Fowell 236, 284, 286, 290, 296–7, 389
Byron, George Byron, Baron 266, 269, 277, 279, 282, 359, 372

Cabenus * 173
Cadogan, Charles Sloane Cadogan, Earl 322, 324–5
Cadogan, Mary Cadogan née Churchill, Countess 322–5, *323*, 327
Cadogan family 322
Caesar * 117

Caillard, Mary *later* Ford 58, 61, 65, 68, 77
Caillard, Peter 58, 59–60, 61, 62, 65, 77, 82
Calderon, Louisa 203, *204*, 209
Camden, Frances Pratt, Marchioness 370
Camden, John Pratt, Marquess of 359, 360
Cameron, David 75, 90
Cameroon 109
Campbell, Duncan 72
Campbell, Elizabeth *later* Macquarie 247, 249
Canning, George 270, 286, 288, 377
Capheaton, Sir John Swinburne, Baronet of 182
Caribbean Community (CARICOM) 401, 402–3
Carleton, Sir Guy 125
Carlyle, Thomas 390
Carnwath, Earldom of 55
Carriacou 121
Carroll, Charles 180–2
Cassius * 245, 246
Castlereagh, Robert Stewart, Viscount 274, 286, 359, 360, 369–70, 374
Cathcart, Sarah Hunter Taylor 262, 373–4, 384
Cathcart, William 362, 373
Catherine of Braganza, Queen 220
Catholicism 98–9, 172, 177, 179–80, 206, 221, 314
Cavendish Square, London 349, 368, 369, 370–1, 380, 381
Cavens House, Dumfrieshire 119, 132
Chandos, Anna Eliza Brydges, Duchess of 7, 9
Chandos, James Brydges, Duke of 368
Chaplin, Elizabeth 277
Chaplin, Thomas 272
Charles I, King 198, 255
Charles II, King 175, 220, 401
Charles III, King 401

Charlotte of Mecklenburg-Strelitz, Queen 199, 262, 370, 372
Chatoyer, Joseph, Garifuna Chief 183, *184*, 185, 193, 199–200
chattel enslavement 4, 19, 329
Chelsea Physic Garden, London 5
Chichester, Thomas Pelham, Earl of 207–8, 262–3, 267
Chilton Lodge, Berkshire 333, 341
China 238–44, *239*, 337
Chocolate * 173
Cholmeley, Ann née Willoughby *later* Workman 135–8, 139, 140, 144–8
Cholmeley, Jane 'Jenny' *later* Leigh Perrot *134*, 135–69, *142*
Cholmeley, Katherine 135, 137, 138, 141–3, 145–7, 148, 156, 163
Cholmeley, Mary Judith 144, 145, 146, 147, 148
Cholmeley, Montague 147
Cholmeley, Mountague 156, 158
Cholmeley, Penelope 136, 158
Cholmeley family, other 135–6, 138–9, *142*, 156
Christian VII, King of Denmark 210
Christie, James 349, 380
Christ Church, Oxford 60, 88, 264, 269
Christ's Hospital, West Sussex 342
Church of England 73, 404
Chute, William 152
Clarke, Clement Cooke 257
Clarke, Clementina *later* Perry 1–2
Clarke, Thomas 252
Clarkson, Thomas 73, 93, 163, 284
Clinton, Henry 3
Colebrooke, Sir George 247, 317, 318, 320, 322
Colebrooke family 247
Collins, John 183, 191, 194, 195, 207
Columbia (Cartagena) 59, 60
Columbus, Christopher 58
Commission of Lunacy 320, 321, 373
Committee for the Relief of the Black Poor 125

compensation, after emancipation 4, 10, 294–7, 317, 334, 384–5, 398
Cooper, Elizabeth *later* Dawkins 325, 326–7, 341–2
Cooper, Frederick 324, 325, 326, 328
Cooper, Sir Grey 320, 322, 324, 325
Cooper, Isabella Anne 334
Cooper, Lady Isabella Bell née Franks *310*, 312–47, *313*
Cooper, Isabella (junior) 322, 341
Cooper, John W. 379, 385–6
Cooper, Mary Ann *later* Honywood 322, 325–6, 341
Cooper, William Henry 320–8
Cooper, William Henry (junior) 322, 325, 333–4
Cooper family (Austen family relations) 160
Cope, Thomas 35, 36
Cotton, Sir Willoughby 291, 293
Courier, The 278
Coutts bank 285, 384
Cox family 247
Critical Review 188
Cromwell, Oliver 15, 58
Crookshanks, Alexander 181
Cruikshank, George 276, 289
Cuba 60
Cubina * 252
Cudjo * 178
Cudjo, Captain 67
Cugoano, Ottobah * 295, 403, 408
Cullen Francis James 346
Cumberland, Richard 318
Currie, George 67

Dalzell, Anna Maria née Gibson 60
Dalzell, Frances *later* Duff 54, 55–94, *57*
Dalzell, Gibson 55, 60–71, 76–80, 82, 83, 84, 86, 88
Dalzell, Jane née Dodd 88
Dalzell, Robert 60, 63–4, 66. 78–9
Dalzell, Robert 'Bob' 64, 65–6, 70–1, 76–7, 79, 85, 86, 88, 91

Dalzell, Susanna, *see* Augier, Susanna
Daniel * 231
Daniel family 49
Danish West India Company 177
Darwin, Charles 389
Daughtrey, John 334, 387
Davies, Mary *later* Grosvenor 2
Davinier, Dido Elizabeth née Belle 92
Davis, Ann 346
Davis, James 346
Davis, Robert * 292–3
Davis, William 178
Davy, Sir Humphrey 5
Dawkins, Elizabeth née Cooper 325, 326–7, 341–2
Dawkins, George Augustus Frederick 326–7
Dawkins, Richard 327
Dawkins family 326–7, 341–2, 388
Day, Thomas 27–8, 167
Decumming, John 65, 67
Defoe, Daniel 99, 399
De Lancey, Oliver 319, 325
Demerara 47, 287, 287, 377
Democratic Republic of the Congo 332
Denmark 177, 178–9 182, 202, 210, 400
Derby * 256
Devizes and Wiltshire Gazette 378, 380, 384
Devonshire * 173
Devonshire, Georgiana Cavendish, Duchess of 188, 261, 270
Diamond * 219
Dick * (enslaved by Newton family) 15, 16, 19, 20
Dick * (enslaved by Vassall family) 255
Dick, George 226
Dickens, Charles 269, 290, 308, 354
Dickson, Arthur 392
Digby, Wriothesley 30, 31, 32
Digweed, William 150
Dinah * 216, 219, 245–6
Directory of Heiresses 2–3, 5
divorce 266, 327

Dodd, John 88
Doll * 26, 42–4, 47, 50
Dolly ('Old Dolly') * 365, 366
Dominica 121, 151, 175, 182, 183, 192, 202, 274, 318
Dominican Republic 58
Donne, Grace 354, 362
Dottin, Abel 152
Dove, Thomas * 293
Downing, George 19
Doyle, John 'H.B.' 289–90, 298–9
Drax family 14–15
Duff, Frances née Dalzell 54, 55–94, 57
Duff, Frances 'Fanny' (junior) 88, 89, 90
Duff, George 55, 68–9, 74–6, 77–80, 86–90
Duff, George (junior) 88, 89, 90–1
Duff, Sir James (General) 90
Duff, James, Lord Fife 79, 87, 90
Duff, James 'Jem' (Thompson) 88–9, 90, 91
Duff, Jane Dorothea 88, 89, 90
Duff, Lady Jean née Grant 69, 74, 75, 76, 87–8, 89–90
Duff family, other 75, 76, 87–9, 90
Duff House, Aberdeenshire 69
Dukinfield family 316–17
Duncan, Alexander 240–1
Dunlop, Frances 131, 233
Dunlop, James 233

East Florida Society 118, 123
East India Company 236, 240, 243, 287
 investors in 3, 108, 118, 314, 321
 personnel 193, 200, 214, 220, 225, 247, 317
Easton Hall, Lincolnshire 136
Edinburgh 69, 76, 99, 216, 248, 382, 388
Edinburgh Courant 131
Edinburgh Review 270, 290, 377
Edinburgh Royal Infirmary 342
Elizabeth I, Queen 16, 25, 401
Elizabeth Henrietta Macquarie Trust 249

Elgin, Moray 76, 87, 90
Ellis (coachman) 179, 186
Ellis, Charles Rose 257, 260, 267, 286, 290, 374
  as Lord Seaford 290, 292, 296, 297, 308, 359
emancipation 10, 19, 58, 70, 245–6, 304
  attempts by MP towards 286–90, 294–5
  compensation following 4, 10, 294–7, 317, 334, 384–5, 398
  opposition to 70, 124, 257, 281, 282, 285, 311–12, 374–5
  supposed consequences of 247, 291, 302, 304, 312, 334, 378
  see also abolition
Emancipation Day 400
Emerson, Ralph Waldo 332
English College, Rome 190
Engusson, Jane 316
enslaved people:
  baptism of 19, 27, 283
  branding of 73
  education of children 283–4, 299, 304
  health of 38–40, 42, 45, 111, 299, 353
  in India 235–6
  murder of 37, 101, 283, 302
  privileged minority 42, 44, 51, 65–366, 385, 501
    see also Betsy Newton, Dolly Newton, Hylas family, Jack Beef, Jenny Newton
  punishment of 256, 300–2, *301*, 335, 343, 400
  retirement 127–8
  suicide of 208
  women, treatment of 45, 47, 109–10, 281, 335, 367–8
  rape 7, 56, 109–10, 255–6, 377–8
  uprisings of 178, 219, 287, *287*, 328, 337, 364–5, 375, 377
    see also Baptist War; Morant Bay War; Tacky's War

see also plantations
Equiano, Olaudah * 126, 330, 403
Erlestoke Park, Wiltshire 368–72, 378, 380–1, 383, 384, 389, 390–1
Erskine, Thomas Erskine, Baron 270, 324
Esther * 44
Estridge, John 182, 338
Estridge, William 338–9, 340–1
Estwick family 49
Ethiopia 124
Eton College 25, 91, 179, 197, 257, 264, 268, 320, 325, 350, 352
Eudosia (cook) 179
Ewing, Humphrey 91
Eyre, Edward John 345, 389–90

Fairchild, Hamlet 137
Fairchild, John Cholmeley 138
Falconbridge, Anna Maria 110
Fanny * 219, 245
Fanny (junior) * 245
Fatima * 176
Fawkes, Guy * 293
Fédon, Julien 328
Ferguson, James 99, 103, 104
Ferguson, Thomas 127, 128
Fielding, Sarah, *The Lives of Cleopatra and Octavia* 67
Fife, James Duff, Earl 79, 87, 90
Fife, William Duff, Earl, Lord Braco 55, 69, 74, 75, 76, 87
Filby, Charles 153, 154, 156, 157, 158
First Opium War 239, 240, 242–4
Fisher, James Hurtle 382
FitzGerald, Lord Edward 360
Fitzpatrick, Richard 267
Fleming, Gilbert 179
Florence 190, 250, 260, 262, 263, 265, 266, 285
Foote, Samuel 141, 264
Forbes, John 222, 228, 244
Ford, Gilbert 68, 77, 409
Ford, Mary née Caillard 58, 61, 65, 68, 77

Ford family 409
Forsyth, James 330
Forth-Clyde Canal 120
Fortune * *81*
Foundling Hospital, London 342
Fowle, Thomas 152
Fox, Caroline 265, 267
Fox, Charles James 263–4, 267, 268, 272–3, 274, 284, 288, *288*, 360
Fox, Charles Richard (Vassall) 267, 272
Fox, Georgiana Anne 272, 277, 308
Fox, Henry Edward 272, 285, 295, 308
Fox, Henry Richard, Lord Holland 263–5, 266–8, 270–9, *276*, 282–94, 296–8, 302–9, 375–6, 400
Fox, Sir Stephen 263, 264
Fox family, other 272, 285
France 180, 199, 325, 327, 400
　colonies in Caribbean 3, 173, 175, 182, 183
　Revolution 171, 196–9, 230, 236
　wars 49, 122, 193, 200–1
　Revolutionary Wars 49, 201, 232–3, 260–1, 400
　see also Napoleon I, Emperor
　see also Paris
Francis, Richard 346
Franklin, Benjamin 116, 123, 125, 126, 128–9
Franks, Aaron 314–15, 317–18, 320–1, 325, 328
Franks, David 315, 320
Franks, Lady Isabella Bell *later* Cooper *310*, 312–47, *313*
Franks, Jacob 314, 315, 316, 319, 321–2, 325, 327, 330
Franks, Moses 312–14, 315–17, 318, 320–1, 328
Franks, Phila 312, 314, 318, 320, 321, 325
Franks, Priscilla 314, 315, 317–18, 319, 321, 327–8, 330, 332–3
Franks family, other 312, *313*, 315–16, 319, 321

Frederick V, King of Denmark 177, 178
freedom, *see* emancipation
freedom fighters, *see* enslaved people, uprisings of
French * 178
French Revolution 171, 196–9, 230, 236
Fryer, George 108, 109
Fullarton, William 204, 205
Fuller, John 'Mad Jack' 269, 286
Fuller, Richard & John * 280
Fuller, Rose & Stephen 257, 259, 265, 269
Fullerton, Elizabeth 84
Furnell, Peter 78

Gallwey family 173
Gambia, the 40
Gardiner, Robert * 293
Garifuna people 183–5, *184*, 193, 194, 199–200, 205–7, 212
Garrick, David 176, 179, 186, 211, 318
Gaynor, Mary 247, 317
geophagy 39
George (George Jarvis) * 232, 235, 246, 247, 248, 249
George (William Wells) * 117
George II, King 219
George III, King 87, 122, 123, 183, 207, 244, 261, 275, 295, 358
George IV, King 289, 333, 349–50, 370, 380
　as Prince Regent 261, 275, 279, 295, 326
Georges, William Payne 344
Germany 98, 112–13, 114, 260, 382, 386
　see also Prussia
Ghana 40, 80, 84, 108, 121
Gibbon, Edward 188, 260
Gibson, John 370–1, *371*, 381
Gibson, Susanna 64, 79
Gideon, Sampson 319
Gilbert, Nathaniel 152

Gittoes, Richard 273
Gladstone, William 297, 317
Gladstone family 404
Gladstone's Library, Flintshire 410
Glascott, Caroline Augusta 167
Glascott, Cholmeley 168
Glasgow 104, 105, 106, 116, 119, 129, 216, 350, 355, 404
Glasgow University 404
Glenelg, Charles Grant, Baron 294, 299, 303
Glenn, Maria 5
Gloster, Archibald 207, 216–17
Goderich, F.J. Robinson, Viscount 289, 290, 292
Goostrey, Thomas 77, 80
Gordon, George William * 343, *344*, 345
Gordon, Lady Augusta née FitzClarence 333
Gore's Liverpool General Advertiser 383
Gosling, Francis and William 225, 230
Graham, James 104
Graham, Robert 86, 352, 355, 356, 408
Grand Tour 121, 259–60, 262, 350
Grant, Alexander 105, 108, 118, 121, 131
Grant, David * 385, 398
Grant, James * 385
Grant, James (East Florida Governor) 118
Grant, John Watson * 385, 398
Grant, Hannah * 345
Grant, Patrick 346
Grant, Sir Ludovick 75
Great Britain 16, 80, 393–4, 400–4
  colonies, see American Revolution; Antigua; Bahamas, The; British Guiana; Dominica; Grenada; India; Jamaica; St Kitts; St Lucia; St Vincent; Trinidad
  government, see abolition; emancipation
  and indigenous peoples 175, 183–5, 206

  wars 100, 205, 236, 239, 240, 242–4
  see also France, wars; Seven Years War
Greene, Benjamin 385
Greene, Graham 385
Greene King (brewing company) 385, 404
Gregory, Elizabeth 153, *153*, 154, 156, 157, 158
Grenada 111, 175, 182, 192
  plantations in 37, 121, 317, 318, 328, 334, 340, 341
Grenadines, the 192, 205–6
Grenville, George 274
Grenville, Henry 136
Grey, Charles Grey, Earl 261, 289, 290, 294
Grey, Henry George Grey, Earl 340
Grieve, Elizabeth Harriet 264
Grosvenor, Mary née Davies 2
Grove Place, Nursling, Hampshire 179, 182, 210
Grove, The, Teddington, Surrey 314, 321
Gründer, John Samuel 283
Guadeloupe 179, 202, 230
Guardian 404
Guatemala 206, 212
Gullah Geechee people 132
Gusman * 148
Gustard, John * 331
Guyana 200, *287*, 319, 337
  see also Demerara
Gye, William 156, 159

Habeas Corpus Act 28
Haiti 58, 123, 202, 400
  revolution in 92–3, 152, 199, 230, 328, 357, 377
Hakewill, James 366, 376–7, 391
Hamilton, Alexander 64, 70, 77
Hamilton, Sir William 188
Hamilton! The Musical 122
Hampson family 151
Hamsterley Hall, County Durham 182, 185, 195, 200, 202, 210

Hankey, Alers 304
Hankey, John 318, 328
Hankey, Thomson (senior) 328, 335, 342
Hankey, Thomson (junior) 328, 335, 336, 338, 340, 341
Hannay, Elizabeth 25, 32, 49
Hardwicke, Philip Yorke, Earl of 27, 28
Harman, Nicholas 80
Harpur family 24, 25, 32
Harrison, James 344
Harry, Charity 92
Harry, Jane *later* Thresher 91–2
Harvey, Thomas 297–300, 302–3, 304, 336, 387
Hatheway, Isaac 35, 36
Haughton, Elizabeth Goodin *later* Taylor 350, 353–8, 360, 362, 373
Haughton, Samuel Williams 355, 357
Haughton family 350, 357
Hawkins, Sir John 163, 305, 401
Hay, Lady Hannah Charlotte 388
Hay, James 84
Hayes, Charles Augustus 209
Hector * 235, 246, 247, 249
Heirs of Slavery 404
Henry, Patrick 124
Herbert, John Richardson 4, 217
Herries, Michael 116, 117, 119, 129
Herring family 252
Hesselberg, Engelbrecht 178
Hewie, Samuel 118
Heyrick, Elizabeth 287, 398
Hibbert, George 91
Higginbotham, John 19
Hippisley family 409
Hispaniola (St Domingue) 58, 92, 123 *see also* Haiti
Hogarth, William 179, 370
Holder, John Hooper 151
Holland, Lady Elizabeth née Vassall 250, 251–309, 253, 276, 360, 374, 380
Holland, Henry Richard Vassall Fox, Baron 263–5, 266–8, 270–9, *276*, 282–94, 296–8, 302–9, 375–6, 400

Holland, Stephen Fox, Baron 263, 264
Holland, Walcott * 283
Holland House, Kensington 268, 269, 277, 285, 294, 307, 309
Holte, Lady Anne 29–32
Holte, Sir Charles 29–32
Holte, Sir Lister 24–5, *24*, 29–32, 38, 48, 50
Holte, Mary Elizabeth 30, 31
Holte, Sarah née Newton *12*, 13–14, 22, 23–42, 46–52
Holte family, other 24, 25
Holyrood Abbey, Edinburgh 382, 385, 388
Honduras 206, 212
Hone, Nathaniel 27, 186
Honywood, Sir John Courtenay 325–6
Honywood, Mary Anne née Cooper 322, 325–6, 341
Honywood family 341
Hood, Samuel 204
Hope * 334
Hopton, John 118–19
Horne, Eliza Kearton 247
Horsham Park, West Sussex 186, 187
Houghton Hall, Norfolk 368
Howard, Charles, Duke of Norfolk 180, 211
Howard, Martha 357
Howatt, Samuel 71, 74, 75, 78
Howe, Richard Howe, Earl 136
Huguenots 62, 252
Hunter, Sarah Blacktree 354, 373
hurricanes 41, 144–5, 148, 368, 376
Hurston, Zora Neale 332
Hutton, William, *History of Birmingham* 31
Hylas, (Thomas) John * 26–9, *43*
Hylas, Mary née Revill * 13, 14, 26–9, 42, *43*, 44, 48, 51
Hylas family * 29, 42–4, *43*, 44, 45, 48, 50–1, 56

Iland, Anthony 19
Ilchester Gaol, Somerset 155–6

India 40, 226, 232, 236, 247
  Bombay (Mumbai) 220–35, *221*, 237–8, 242–6, 248–9
  Calicut (Kozhikode) 233–5, 236–7
  enslavement in 222, 235–6, 249, 337
indentured servants (Barbados) 15, 20, 21
indentured African labourers 312, 339, 340, 345, 388
indigenous Australians 248, 249
indigenous peoples 3, 183, 206, 402–4
  see also Garifuna people; indigenous Australians; Kalinago people; Taíno people
Ingram, Sir Thomas 342
inheritance cap law in Jamaica 82–3, 84, 91
Ireland 15, 172, 359–60, 384, 386, 388
Irish people 172, 359, 360, 374, 394, 401
  see also Montserrat, St Croix
Isleworth House, Middlesex 319, 333, 334, 341, 342
Italy 188–9, 262, 265, 350, 357
  see also Florence, Naples, Rome

Jack * 245
Jacobite Rebellion 98–9, 189
Jacques, John 91
Jamaica 58–9, 125, 285, 296, *304*, 337, 392
  conflict in 3, 100, 291
    see also Tacky's War
  Dalzell estates (Lucky Hill and Friendship) 64, 65–6, 67, 70–4, 78, 80, 85–7, 91, 94
    enslaved people at 66, 70, 73, 86–7
  Franks estate (Duckenfield) 312, 316–17, 321, 328–31, 334–6, 338–47
    African indentured labourers at 330–1, 345–6
    compensation, after abolition 334, 336
    under apprenticeship scheme 334–41, 342–47
  Jamaica Assembly 61, 62, 82, 290, 329, 356, 375, 377
  Kingston *81*
    Dalzell's residence in 59, 60–1, 64, 66, 68, 76, 77
    Ramsay family in 98, 99, 100–2, *101*, 103–4, 108
    other plantations in 1, 121, 152, 255–6, 354–5, 357, 408
  Ramsay estates (Spring Garden, Westmoreland) 100, 103, 108, 111–12, 127
    enslaved people at 102
  Taylor estates (Burrowfield Pen, Flint River Pen, Haughton Court, Haughton Grove Pen, Holland, Llanrumney Lyssons, Mammee Hill Pen, Orange Cove, Prospect Pen, Unity, and Venture) 350, 352–5, 357, 363–8, 379, 384–92, *392*
    compensation, after abolition 384
    enslaved people at 363, 364, 366, 367–8, 376–7, 385, 386
  Vassall estates (Friendship and Greenwich, Sweet River Pen, and Vineyard Pen) 251, 252–7, *254*, 255–6, 265, 268, 269, 271–2, 273–5
    compensation, after abolition 295–6
    during Baptist War 291, 292–3
    enslaved people at 275, 280–1, 283, 300–1
    following emancipation 304, 306, 308
    under apprenticeship scheme 297–300
  Wagwater estate 59–60, 77
    enslaved people at 59
Jamaica Committee 389
James I, King 24
James II, King 73, 122, 190
James, C.L.R., *Beyond a Boundary* 18
James, William Moore 343
Jardine Matheson 240

Jarvis, Dorothea *later* Morley 216, 220, 222, 223, 224, 227, 229, 231, 234, 245
Jarvis, George * 232, 235, 246, 247, 248, 249
Jarvis, George Ralph Payne 216, 220, 222, 231–2, 235, 237, 246, 249
Jarvis, Hector * 235, 246, 247, 249
Jarvis, Jane *later* Macquarie 214, 215–49, *218*
Jarvis, John Swinton 217, 233, 245, 246
Jarvis, Marianne * 222, 229, 240, 242, 246, 249
Jarvis, Rachel née Thibou 216, 220, 227, 229, 231–2
Jarvis, Rachel *later* Wilkins (junior) 217, 231, 245
Jarvis, Thomas (junior) 216, 219, 221, 222, 228, 230–1, 245
Jarvis, Thomas (senior) 215–16, 219
Jarvis family, other 215–16, *218*, 219, 231, 233, 247
Jay, John 123
Jefferson, Thomas 124
Jekyll, Joseph 158, 277
Jelly, Mary 248
Jenny * 219, 245
Jewish Naturalization Act (1753) 314–15
Jewish people 312, 314–15, 318–19, 326
Jimmy, King of Koya 126
Jocken, Robert 387
Jodrell, Richard Paul 258
Johnny Newcome in Love in the West Indies 56
Johnson, Henry Allen 333
Johnson, Samuel 9, 34, 91, 116, 225, 258
Jones, John Chambres 407, 410
Jones, Thomas 330
Joseph II, Holy Roman Emperor 189
Josephine, Empress 278
Jupiter * 178

Kalinago people 173–5, 183, 217
Kaufmann family 407
Kelly, Priscilla 66, 408
Kelway, Joseph 179
Kennedy, Lucy 326, 327
Kent, Victoria of Saxe-Coburg-Saalfeld, Duchess of 380–1
Kenyon, Lloyd Kenyon, Baron 324
Kerr, James of India 238
Kerr, James of Jamaica 85
Kerr, Jane *later* Apreece *then* Davy 5
Kerr, Patrick 104
Kimball, Joseph Horace 387
Kings Bromley Hall, Staffordshire 23, 26, 31, 33, 35
Kingsley, Charles 390
Kingston * *81*
Kirkham, John 15, 16–17
Knatchbull, Mary Dorothea 165
Knibb, William 305
Knight, Elizabeth *later* Baroness Onslow 5
Knox, John 201
Kongo, Kingdom of 58
Kumina 339–40

Lady's Magazine, The 134, 159
Laing, James 91
Lake, Gerard 360
Lamb, Lady Caroline 277, 290
Lamoinary, Adelaide 84
Lane, John 32, 35, 49–50
Lane, Richard Stuart 409
Lane, Thomas 35, 49–50
Langley Rose, Elizabeth *later* Lady Sloane 4–5, 322
Lascelles, Ann *later* Smollett 5, 71
Lascelles family, Earls of Harewood 49
Laurens, Henry 83, 111, 112, 117, 118–19, 121, 122–5, 127–8, 129
Laurens, John 121–2, 124, 128, 191
Laurens, Robert Scipio * 117
Lawes, Sir Nicholas 100
Lawrence, James 265
Lawson, James 293

Leachy, William 19
Leclerc, Charles 202
Lee, Robert Cooper 66, 355, 408
Leeward Islands 172, 173, 179, 206, 217
Lefroy, Benjamin 165
Lefroy, Fanny Caroline 150, 164
Legge, Heneage 30, 31, 32
Leigh family 138, 160, 161
Leigh Perrot, James 138–62, *142*, 164–5
Leigh Perrot, Jane 'Jenny' née Cholmeley *134*, 135–69, *142*
Lesser Antilles 144, 173
Levy family 316, 319, 327
Lewis, Matthew Gregory 'Monk' 251–2, 269, 274, 279–82, 283, 344, 359, 378
Lewis, Susannah 152
'liberated' Africans, *see* recaptured Africans
Lichfield, Staffordshire 23, 25, 26, 27, 37
Ligon, Richard *14*, 15, 209
Lillingston, Willielma Johanna née Dottin 152
Lincoln, Edmund 195
Lincoln's Inn 27, 32, 136, 358, 384
Lindo, Lake & Co. 273
Lindsay, Grace 330
Lindsay, Mary* 385
Lindsay, Sir John 92
Lindsay, William 104
Lisle, David 28, 85
Liverpool 133, 163, 177, 211, 370, 407, 409, 410
Lloyd's of London 404
Loague, Dominic 330
Loftus, Robert* 257
Logan, Charles* 345
Logan, Lianta 345
London
  City of London 66, 70, 98, 105
  Philpot Lane 106, 107, 110, 116–17, 125, 131, 132
  Marylebone 220, 350, 357
  Mayfair 2, 66, 105, 271, 307, 370
  Westminster 66, 69, 76, 78, 117, 129, 130, 284, 288, 307, 324

London Magazine 172
London Star 131
London Stock Exchange 315
Long, Edward 63, 83–4
Long, Sir Charles 380
Lopez da Moura, José 109
Loughborough, Alexander Wedderburn, Baron 196
Louis XVI, King of France 171, 194, 197–8, 199, 369
Louis XV, King of France 189, 369
Louis Philipe I, King of the of French 268
Louis Philipe II, Duke of Orléans 198
Loutherbourg, Philip de 211
L'Ouverture, Toussaint 202
Luba people 332
Lycence, Nicholas 350

Mab, Harty 302
McCall, John (George McQuarry) 346
Macao 239, 240, 241, 243, 244
Macaulay, Thomas Babington 290, 307
Macaulay, Zachary 284, 290, 307
McClymont, John 330
McCornock, Thomas 379, 386
MacFarlane, Alexander *101*, 104
McKay* 331
Maclaine, Murdoch 223, 227, 247
Macleane, Lauchlin 318, 321
McNeil, Thomas 293, 296, 297, 298–9, 300–6, 386
Macquarie, Charles 247
Macquarie, Elizabeth née Campbell 247, 249
Macquarie, Jane née Jarvis *214*, 215–49, *218*
Macquarie, Lachlan 215, 222–49
MacQuarie, Lachlan (cousin) 245
MacQuarrie of Ulva, Lauchlin (clan chief) 225
Madagascar 193, 236
Madison, James 124
Maitland, George 208
Majorah* 273

Malcolm, Neill 350, 355
Manchester 231, 294, 316, 408
Manchester, George Montagu, Duke of 194
Manning, Edward 61, 65, 67, 70, 71, 75, 78, 86–7
Manning, William (senior) 117, 191, 192, 193
Manning, William (junior) 207, 286
Mansfield, William Murray, Earl of 29, 92, 163
'manumit' term 19
Maria Carolina of Austria, Queen of Naples 189, 190–1
Marianne * 222, 229, 240, 242, 246, 249
Maria Theresa of Austria, Empress 115, *170*, 189
Marie Antoinette, Queen of France 171, 189, 191, 194, 196–7, 198, 199, 261
Marina * 255, 256
Marlborough, duchy of 63, 140
Marlborough, Charles Spencer, 3rd Duke of 63
Marlborough, George Spencer, 4th Duke of 140, 263
Maroon communities 58, 217, 337, 338
  involved in conflicts 67, 80, 100, 291, 315, 385
Martin, Samuel 83, 232
Martinique 115, 179, 194, 200, 202, 278, 340
Mary * 19
Maryburgh Salt Works, Prestwick 120
Mason, Charles 129, 130
Mathew, Anne, *later* Austen 165, 173
Mathew, Brownlow 151
Mathew, Daniel 173
Mathias * 231, 245
Maule, John 75, 78, 79, 89, 91
Maule, William 91
Mauritania 108
Mayne, Eliza née Taylor 358, 384

Mayne, William 358, 384
Melbourne, William Lamb, Viscount 267, 277, 289, 294, 299, 307, 308
Melville, Thomas 108, 121
Methodism 9, 211, 283
Middleton, Nathaniel 84–5
Miles, Tommy (Tom Bell) 346
Mill, David 121
Mill, John 107–8, 111, 116, 121
Mill, John Stuart 6, 346, 389
Miller, William 379
Mills, John 173
Mills, Matthew 172, 173
Mingo (of St Kitts) * 173
Mingo (of Barbados) * 41
Minty * 307
Mitchell, John * 330
mixed-heritage, people of 7, 58, 61, 62–3, 80–4, 91–4, 226
  and relationships with white people 56–7, 62, 354, 373–4, 386
  see also enslaved people, women, treatment of
Moggerhanger, Bedfordshire 342
Moll * 173
Moll, Jane 216
Monckton, Robert 194, 318
Montserrat 172, 173, 176, 177, 202, 230, 385
Moore, Clement Clarke 308
Morant Bay War 343–5, 347, 389, 390
Morgan, Sir Henry 58, 353, 392
Morley, Charles 225
Morley, Dorothea née Jarvis 216, 220, 222, 223, 224, 227, 229, 231, 234, 245
Morley, James 215, 220, 222, 222–5, 226, 227, 228, 229–30
Morley, Maria 220
Morning Chronicle 128, 193
Morning Post 193, 369, 370
Morris, Henry 346
Morris, Valentine 192, 196
Morris, William 145, 146, 147, 148, 167–8

Morse, John 68, 84–5
Mozambique 236
'mulatto' term 56
Mulgrave, Henry Phipps, Earl of 292, 385
Mull, Isle of 223, 247, 248–9
Mungo * 236
Mure, Hutchison 72, 80, 84, 85–6
Myers, Sir William 200

Naples 188, 189, 191, 259, 260, 262
Napoleon I, Emperor 202, 276–7, *276*, 278–9, 325, 327, 337, 370
National Gallery, London 133, 370, 380
Natural History Museum, London 5
NatWest 231
Naval Office 318
Necker, Jacques 196, 197, 198
Nelly * 280, 281
Nelson, Frances "Fanny" née Nisbet, Viscountess 4, 217
Nelson, Horatio Nelson, Viscount 4, 217, 278, 307, 399
Nerode * 176
Nesbitt, Arnold 317, 328, 330
Nesbitt family 330
Netherlands, the 123, 232, 236, 260
  colonies 3, 47, 200, 217, 235, 237, 246, 319
Nevis 3, 4, 172, 176, 217
'new money' 5–6, 21, 74
Newton, Betsy * 13–14, 42, 46, 47–9, 50
Newton, Catherine née Seymour 32–7, 35, 49
Newton, Dolly * 44, 45, 47
Newton, Elizabeth née Alleyne 23, 26, 27, 32, 42, 127
Newton, Elizabeth 13, 23, 30, 31, 32, 33, 37, 40–50
Newton, Hylas * 47
Newton, Jenny * 50
Newton, John 23–4, 25, 26–37
Newton, Rev. John (slaver turned abolitionist) 111

Newton, Robert 14, 15, 16, 19, 20
Newton, Samuel 14, 16–17, 18, 20–4
Newton, Sarah *later* Holte 12, 13–14, 22, 23–42, 46–52
Newton family, other 16, 23, 32
Newton, Sir Isaac 79
Nibbs family 152, 168
Nicaragua 206, 212
Nigeria 177
Nisbet, Frances 'Fanny' *later* Viscountess Nelson 4, 217
Nockells, Charles 335–6
Norfolk, Charles Howard, Duke of 180, 211
Norris, Robert 163
Northedge Hall, Derbyshire 14, 21
Northleigh, Oxfordshire 138, 140
Norton, Sir Fletcher 28
Nugent, John 222, 228
Nugent, Lady Maria née Skinner 3, 8, 18, 56, 354, 356, 377
Nugent, Nelly * 354
Nugent, Sir George 3

Oakes, Dorothea 231, 235, 237, 238
Obama, Michelle 132
O' Connell, Daniel 374
Ogé, Vincent 92–3
'old money' 5–6, 21, 74
Oliver, Thomas 219, 232
Onslow, Elizabeth Onslow née Knight, Baroness 5
Oswald, Alexander 105–6
Oswald, George 105, 121
Oswald, George (of Scotstoun) 129, 131
Oswald, Mary née Ramsay 96, 97–133, *107*
Oswald, Richard 97, 106–32, *107*
Oswald, Richard (junior) 105, 121
Othello * 176
Oxford, Jane Harley, Countess of 274

Paine, Patrick 47
Paplay, George 71–2, 75, 78, 87

Paplay family 86–7
'Pappah' people 177–8
Paris 75, 92, 93, 115, 123, 124, 125, 180, 182, 186, 187, 189, 194, 196, 197, 198, 199, 259, 278
Parkinson, Matthew 279–80
Payne, Ralph 173
Payne, Sir Ralph (junior) 216
Payne, Thomas 143, 148
Peche, John 236
Peel, Sir Robert 288, 382, 388
Pelham, Sir Thomas, Earl of Chichester 207–8, 262–3, 267
Pepper, James 192
Perceval, Spencer 275, 276–7, 276
Perrot, James Leigh, *see* Leigh Perrot, James
Perrot, Thomas 138–9
Perry, Clementina née Clarke 1–2
Perry, Richard Vining 1–2, 4, 8
Phelp, Mathias 103, 104–5
Phibba * 231, 245
philanthropy 6, 342
Phillips, Peter * 346
Phillis, Mrs * 251–2, 254, 280, 282
Philpot Lane, London 106, 107, 110, 116–17, 125, 131, 132
Phipps, James 84
Phipps family 176, 264
Pickstock, Ralph 29
Picton, Thomas 203–5, 209–10, 249
Pitches, Robert 328, 333, 334, 335, 336
Pitt the Younger, Sir William 195–6, 198, 270, 357
Pius VI, Pope 189, 279
plantations:
  burial sites 14, 21, 37–40, 45
  dungeons 300, 302, 335, 400
  hospitals 38, 299, 339
  workhouses 302, 334, 385
  see also Antigua; Barbados; Grenada; Jamaica; South Carolina; St Croix; St Kitts; St Vincent
Plummer, Henry Waite 265, 280–1, 282, 283

Plummer, John 286
Plummer, Thomas 265, 269, 271, 272, 278, 279, 296
Plummer, Thomas William 269, 270, 278, 279, 286, 296
Polgreen, Rachel Pringle 56
Portland, Henry Bentinck, Duke of 100, 195
Portsmouth, John Wallop, Earl of 151
Portugal 56, 115, 221, 239, 242, 260
  enslavement by 16, 20, 27
Price, Charles 70–1, 74, 78, 80
Prince, Mary 103
Prince Klass (Kwaku) * 219
Prince McLeod * 343
Prince Quakoe (Kwaku) * 178
Prince William * 345
privilege petitions 61, 62, 64
Prussia 112, 115, 240, 260
Publick 193

Qianlong, Emperor 244
'quadroon' term 93
Quakerism 9, 10, 15, 92, 286, 287, 297–8, 306
Quamina * 178
Quasheba * 231, 245

Raikes, Thomas 382
Raines, Sarah 157
Ralegh, Sir Walter 203
Ralph * 331
Rambler's Magazine 36
Ramsay, Alexander 98–103
Ramsay, Jean née Ferguson 98, 103–4
Ramsay, Mary *later* Oswald 96, 97–133, *107*
Ramsay family, other 358
rape 7, 56, 109–10, 255, 256, 377–8
recaptured Africans 311, 337, 338, 340
Reform Act (1832) 294, 315, 374, 379
Reid, David 240, 241
Reid family 351, 357–8
reparations 294–5, 401–2, 403, 404–5

Revill, Mary *later* Hylas * 13, 14, 26–9, 42, *43*, *44*, 48, 51
'Rice Coast' 111
Richards, Gordon and Kennion 73
Richmond * 251
RNLI (Royal National Lifeboat Institution) 342
Robinson, Isaac * 344
Robinson, Sir Thomas 138
Rodney, George 115, 144
Rome 188, 189, 190, 371
Rose, Elizabeth Langley *later* Lady Sloane 4, 322
Rose, George 274
Rossington, Francis Warren 173
Rothiemay Castle, Banffshire 69, 89
Rowdon, Richard 390
Roxburghe Club 372
Royal African Company 73, 108, 318, 368, 393, 401
Royal Society of Arts 116, 350
RSPCA (Royal Society for the Prevention of Cruelty to Animals) 342
Rundell & Bridge 383
Runnells, Mr 173
Ruskin, John 390
Russell, Lord John 289, 308, 311
Rutherford, Robert 100, 103, 108
Rutherford, Susannah 127
Ryan, Henry 176–7, 192, 193

Saer, George * *43*, 44, 45
Saer, John * *43*, 44
Saer, Mary Ann * *43*, 44, 51, 52
Saer, Nat 26, 44
St Croix 177–8, 181, 182, 192, 202, 316
  Baker estates (Concordia and Plessens) 177, 181, 182
St Helena 278–9, 337, 339, 340
St John 80, 202, 215, 219, 364
St Kitts 3, 111, 121, 129, 217, 296, 385
  Baker family in 172–5, 179, 182, 202
St Lucia 125, 184, 193, 194
St Martin 217, 246

St Martin in the Fields, Westminster 69, 75, 90, 106
St Paul's Cathedral 209, 255
St Thomas 176, 202, 312
St Vincent 49, 175, 182–3, 184, 192–5, 205–7, 296, 328
  Baker plantations in 183, 191, 193, 200, 208
  plantations in 5, 171, 191, 200, 208
  St Vincent Assembly 195, 206
Sally * 232
Sargent, John 108, 111
Saunders, George Girton 330
Scadding, Edward 155
Scadding, Martha 155, 159
Scarlets, Berkshire 140, 149, 163, 164, 165, 166, 168
Scarlett, James *see* Abinger, James Scarlett, Baron
Scarlett, Robert 273–4, 275
Scotch Mine Company 70, 77
Scots Corporation 121
Scots Magazine 185, 320
Scott, Charles 335, 336
Scott, David 231
Scott, Eliza (Jubena) * 336
Scott, John * 47, 50
Scott, Robert 108
Scott, Sarah 9
Scott, Sir Walter 264, 269
Scott, Thomas 335, 336, 339, 340
Seaford, Charles Rose Ellis, Baron, *see* Ellis, Charles Rose
Seaford, East Sussex 258, 374
Searle, Daniel 20
Searle, John 20, 21
Second Carib War 205
Senegal 40, 111
Sephardim community 312, 319
Sercey, Pierre César Charles Guillaume, marquis de 243
Seven Years War 69, 98, 112–15, 123, 178, 179, 182, 318
Seward, Anna 26
Seymour, Lord Francis 32, 34

Shakespeare, William 6, 34
Shand, John 364, 366, 367, 368, 369, 375, 377, 379
Shand, William 364, 366, 379, 408
Sharp, Granville 28, 29, 85, 126, 306
Sharpe, Henry Edward 294
Sharpe, Samuel * 284, 291, 293
Shaw, Anna 234, 235
Sheffield, John Baker Holroyd, Earl of 260
Shelburne, William Fitzmaurice, Earl of 125
Shelley, Mary 5, 288
Shelley, Percy Bysshe 282, 359
Sheridan, Richard Brinsley 269
Shonibare, Yinka 133
Sierra Leone 125–6, 311, 332, 337, 338, 340
   Bance Island 97, 98, 108–12, 118, 122–3, 124, 126, 129, 131, 132
Simond, Peter 318, 328
Skerrett, Bridget 180
Slavery Abolition Act (1833) 295, 300
Slave Trade Act (1807) 270, 274–5, 281, 283, 307
Sligo, Howe Peter Browne, Marquess of 296, 297, 298, 304, 334
Sloane, Lady Elizabeth née Langley 4–5, 322
Sloane, Sir Hans 5, 322
smallpox 25
Smeathman, Henry 125–6
Smith, Adam 116, 188
Smith, Joshua 368–9
Smith, Rosetta 203
Smith, Samuel 45
Smith, Sir Lionel 304
Smollett, Ann née Lascelles 5, 71
Smollett, Tobias 5, 71, 217
Society for the Encouragement of Arts, Manufactures and Commerce 116
Society of Dilettanti 350, 352
South Sea Company 55, 60–1, 76, 80
   investors in 3, 258, 318, 321, 368, 393

Spain 25, 55, 113, 115, 155, 173, 206, 260
   colonies in Caribbean 3, 58–60, 118, 127, 203
   enslavement by 20, 27
Spall, Jan van 236
Spectator, The 400
Spencer, Lord Henry 263
Spettisbury House, Dorset 33–4
Sproule, Charlotte née Taylor * 354, 384, 388
Spry, Wilhelmina 141–3, 147, 167
Spry, William 141, *142*
Sri Lanka 237
Staël, Madame Germaine de 278
Stamp Act (1765) 122
Stanhope, Lovell 83, 84
Stanley, E.G. 294
Steele, Joshua 84
Stephen, James 329, 331, 365
Sterne, Lawrence 121
Stevens, George Alexander, *The Dramatic History of Mrs Llwhuddwhydd* 93
Stevenson, James * 385
Stevenson, Mr 222, 225
Stevenson family of Barbados 358
Steventon parsonage, Hampshire 140, 150, 152, 158, 168
Stewart, Robert James 390
stipendiary magistrates 296, 301, 334, 335
Stoneleigh, Warwickshire 160–1, 168
Storer, Anthony Morris 257
Strong, Jonathan * 28, 85
Struth, William John 207
Stuart, Charles Edward 'Bonnie Prince Charlie' 189, 190
Stuart, John 318, 321, 322
Stuart royal family 98–9, 189, 190
Sturge, Joseph 297–300, 302–3, 304, 305, 306, 336, 387
Sue * 39
sugar trade 3, 14, 16–18, *18*, 20, 64–5, 100

Sunday * 176
Sun Fire (insurance company) 63–4, 66, 70, 77, 78, 90
Suriname 200, 319
Swinburne, Henry 182, 185–90, *187*, 192, 193, 194, 195, 196–8, 200–11
Swinburne, Henry 'Harry' (junior) 185, 186, 196–8, 199, 201–2, 260
Swinburne, Sir John, Baronet of Capheaton 182
Swinburne, Joseph Anthony 202, 210
Swinburne, Maria Antonia 189, 209, 211, 212
Swinburne, Martha née Baker *170*, 171–212, *174*
Swinburne, Martha 'Patty' (junior) 185, 186, 190
Swinburne, Mary Frances 'Fanny' 185, 186–7, 196, 200–1
Swinburne family, other 189, 200, 210, 409

Tacky's War 80–2, *81*, 92, 315, 364
Taíno people 26, 58, 67, 217, 404
Talbot, Charles 27, 28
Tarleton, Sir Banastre 133
Tasker, John 225–6, 228, 230
Tasker, John William 226
Taunton Courier 5
Taylor, Anna Susanna *later* Watson Taylor 348, 349–50, *351*, 354–92, *371*
Taylor, Charlotte *later* Sproule * 354, 384, 388
Taylor, Elizabeth Goodin née Haughton 350, 353–8, 360, 362, 373
Taylor, Sir John 350–2, *352*, 353–6, 391, *391*, 409
Taylor, Robert 357, 361, 362
Taylor, Sally 354, 362, 373, 384
Taylor, Simon 350, 352–8, *353*, 360–5, 368, 373, 377–8, 284, 388–91, *391*, 399
Taylor, Sir Simon Richard Brissett 354, 355, 361–2, 363

Taylor family, other 86, 350, *351*, 354, 356, 373, 388
Temne people 126
Tennyson, Alfred Tennyson, Lord 390
Thackeray, William Makepeace, *Vanity Fair* 7, 63, 74–5, 93–4
Tharp family 379
Thibou, Jacob 216
Thistleton, John 222, 244
Thistlewood, Thomas 45, 255–6
Thomas, Billy * 44, 47
Thomas, John * 51
Thompson, Archibald 177
Thomson Hankey & Co. 328, 334
Thorne, James Armstrong 387
Thresher, Jane née Harry 91–2
Thresher, Joseph 91–2
Thurlow, Edward Thurlow, Baron 37
Tim * 15, 16, 19, 20
Times, The 1, 129, 234, 321, 379, 380
Tipu Sultan 220, 223, 232, 233, 247
Tobago 192
Togo 177
Tolson, Ann 342
Tom * 173
Tomboy * 219
Tommy * 44
Tortola 202
Tory Party 275, 290, 374
Touchet, Samuel 316–17
Townsend, James 84
Transatlantic slave economy 3, 4, 15, 59, 132, 311, 316, 378
   after abolition 329, 337–8
   Bance Island, Sierra Leone 97, *98*, 108–12, 118, 122–3, 124, 126, 129, 131, 132
Treaty of Paris (1763) 182
Treaty of Utrecht (1713) 59, 60
Treaty of Versailles (1783) 194
Trelawny, Edward 62
Trevelyan family 404
Trial of the Hon. Mrs Catherine Newton, The 35, 36

Trinidad 202, 203–9, 285, 296, 337
Tuckett, James 388
Tuite, Nicholas 177, 178–9, 180, 181
Tyndall, William 61, 77
Tyne, Sarah 345–346
Tyne, Sydney 345–6
Tyne, Tobias 346

United States of America (USA) 3, 111, 123, 212, 336, 400
　Florida 118, 120, 121, 123, 126–7, 129, 132, 195, 196
　Georgia 111, 122, 124, 126–7, 392
　Maine 265
　New York 59, 125, 252, 315–16, 318–19
　South Carolina 83, 98, 112, 118, 122, 124, 127, 129, 316
　Virginia 3, 15, 59, 105, 106, 122, 264, 316
　see also American Revolution
University College London (UCL) 410
University of Cambridge 136, 389, 404
University of Oxford 25, 35, 88, 138, 264, 268, 269, 327, 350, 358
University of Pennsylvania 342
Urquhart, James 90

Vansittart, George 157
Vassall, Charles Richard, *later* Fox 267, 272
Vassall, Elizabeth *later* Lady Webster, *then* Lady Holland 250, 251–309, 253, 276, 360, 374, 380
Vassall, Florentius 83, 252–7, 265, 269, 295, 308
Vassall, Mary née Clarke 252, 254, 258, 267, 271
Vassall, Richard 252, 254, 256, 257, 259, 260, 265
Vassall family, other 252, 253, 255, 293, 197
Venter or Venture, Quaco * 67
Versailles, Palace of, Paris 171, 180, 197–8, 349, 369

Victoria House, Pittville near Cheltenham 333
Victoria, Queen 267, 289, 308, 380–1
Vienna 189, 259, 278

Wales 65, 324, 353, 394, 407, 410
Walker, Samuel 390
Walker, Thomas 'Beau' 132
Walker family 211, 409
Wallis, James 248
Walpole, Horace 116, 156, 264, 314
Walter, George 151
Walter, John 321
Walter, William 151
Walters, George * 387
Walton, Richard (or George) 346
Warner, Sir Thomas 173, 175, 217
Warner, Captain Edward 217
Warner, Philip 175
Warner, Thomas 'Indian' 175
Washington, George 122, 124, 125
Watson family 358
Watson Taylor, Anna Susanna née Taylor 348, 349–50, *351*, 354–92, *371*
Watson Taylor, Emilius 364, 389
Watson Taylor, George 358–64, *359*, 366–89
Watson Taylor, George Graeme 361, 371, 389
Watson Taylor, John Walter 361, 371, *371*, 382, 389
Watson Taylor, Simon 361, 364, 382, 388, 389–91
Watson Taylor family, other 361, 392
Watt, James 341
Webbe, Lady Helen 180, 182, 189
Webbe, Sir John 180
Webster, Lady Elizabeth née Vassall *later* Lady Holland 250, 251–309, 253, 276, 360, 374, 380
Webster, Sir Godfrey, 4th Baronet 258–68, 271–3
Webster, Sir Godfrey, 5th Baronet 'Webby' 250, 259, 260, 263, 267, 272, 295

Webster, Harriet *later* Lady Pellew 263, 266, 271, 272
Webster, Henry Vassall 278, 295
Webster family, other 258, 259, 260, 263, 295
Wedderman Ann 390
Welby, Sir William 167
Wellington, Arthur Wellesley, Duke of 203, 277, 279, 283, 289, 350, 368, 388
Welsh people 5, 40, 93, 203, 209, 353, 394, 407
Wells, William 117, 177
Wells, William (George) * 117
Wentworth, Mrs 139
Wesley, John 9, 211
Wesley, Sarah 211
West Africa, traditions in 4, 21, 40, 281, 332, 367
West Africa Squadron 337, 338
West India Committee 286, 294, 374, 389
Westminster Abbey 78, 284, 288, 307
Westminster, Duchy of 2
Westminster School 66, 76
Whigham, Edward 130
Whig Party 268, 275, 289, 290, 309
'white,' legal definition of 61–2, 64, 65, 82
Whitehead, Jane 216
Wilberforce, William 92–3, 273, 281, 283, 284–5, 286, 291, 357, 375, 399
Wilde, Oscar, *The Importance of Being Earnest* 6–7
Wilkins, John 216, 231, 245
Wilkins, Louisa 245
Wilkins, Rachel née Jarvis 217, 231, 245
Will * 173
William III, King (Prince of Orange) 122, 236
William IV, King 56, 217, 274, 295, 334, 381
Williams, James * 300, 302, 303

Willis, George 387
Willoughby, Lady Ann 21
Willoughby, Ann *later* Cholmeley *then* Workman 135–8, 139, 140, 144–8
Willoughby family 136, 146
Wilmot, Sir John Eardley 28, 319
Wilson, Francis 75, 78, 80
Wilson, Lestock 239
Wilson, Lewis * 343, 345
Wilson family 407–9
Windham, William 275
Windsor Castle, Berkshire 349, 380, 391
Windward Isles 151
Winterslow, Wiltshire 268
Woman of Colour, The 93
Wood, Sampson 50–1
Woodford, Sir Ralph 209
Woolf, Virginia 168
workhouses in the Caribbean 302, 334, 385
Workman, Francis 137, 143, 145–6
Workman, Gusman 148
Workman, Hamlet 137, 143, 145–6
Workman, Thomas 137–8, 139–40, 141, 143–5, 147–8
Worlington Hall, Suffolk 320, 324, 325, 341
Worsley, Seymour Fleming, Lady 266
Wouski, 1788 print by James Gillray 56
Wynne, Robert 195

Yard, William 44–5, 46–8, 50
York, Henry Benedict Stuart, Cardinal Duke of 190
York, Frederick, Duke of 261, 360
York, James, Duke of, *later* James II 73
Yorke-Talbot slavery opinion (1729) 27, 28
Young, Sir William 183–4, 185, 195

Zephaniah, Benjamin 52
Zoffany, Johan 96, 116, 132–3, 350